Tax and Government in the Twenty-First Century

With an accessible style and clear structure, Miranda Stewart explains how taxation finances government in the 21st century, exploring tax law in its historical, economic and social context. Today, democratic tax states face an array of challenges, including the changing nature of work, the digitalisation and globalisation of the economy, and rebuilding after the fiscal crisis of the COVID-19 pandemic. Stewart demonstrates the centrality of taxation for government budgets and explains key tax principles of equity, efficiency and administration. Presenting examples from a wide range of jurisdictions and international developments, Stewart shows how tax policy and law operate in our everyday lives, ranging from family and working life to taxing multinational enterprises in the global digital economy. Employing an interdisciplinary approach to the history and future of taxation law and policy, this is a valuable resource for legal scholars, practitioners and policymakers.

MIRANDA STEWART is a professor at Melbourne Law School, The University of Melbourne, Honorary Professor at The Australian National University, International Research Fellow of the Centre for Business Taxation at the Said Business School, Oxford University and Vice-Chair of the Permanent Scientific Committee of the International Fiscal Association. Her other books include *Income Taxation Commentary and Materials* (2022), *Death and Taxes* (2021), *Tax, Social Policy and Gender* (2017) and *Tax, Law and Development* (2013).

Law in Context

Series editors
Professor Kenneth Armstrong
University of Cambridge
Professor Maksymilian Del Mar
Queen Mary, University of London
Professor Sally Sheldon
University of Kent

Editorial advisory board
Professor Bronwen Morgan
University of New South Wales
Emeritus Professor William Twining
University College London

Since 1970, the Law in Context series has been at the forefront of a movement to broaden the study of law. The series is a vehicle for the publication of innovative monographs and texts that treat law and legal phenomena critically in their cultural, social, political, technological, environmental and economic contexts. A contextual approach involves treating legal subjects broadly, using materials from other humanities and social sciences, and from any other discipline that helps to explain the operation in practice of the particular legal field or legal phenomena under investigation. It is intended that this orientation is at once more stimulating and more revealing than the bare exposition of legal rules. The series includes original research monographs, coursebooks and textbooks that foreground contextual approaches and methods. The series includes and welcomes books on the study of law in all its contexts, including domestic legal systems, European and international law, transnational and global legal processes and comparative law.

Books in the Series
Acosta: *The National versus the Foreigner in South America: 200 Years of Migration and Citizenship Law*
Ali: *Modern Challenges to Islamic Law*
Alyagon Darr: *Plausible Crime Stories: The Legal History of Sexual Offences in Mandate Palestine*
Anderson, Schum & Twining: *Analysis of Evidence, 2nd Edition*
Ashworth: *Sentencing and Criminal Justice, 6th Edition*
Barton & Douglas: *Law and Parenthood*
Baxi, McCrudden & Paliwala: *Law's Ethical, Global and Theoretical Contexts: Essays in Honour of William Twining*
Beecher-Monas: *Evaluating Scientific Evidence: An Interdisciplinary Framework for Intellectual Due Process*
Bell: *French Legal Cultures*

Bercusson: *European Labour Law, 2nd Edition*
Birkinshaw: *European Public Law*
Birkinshaw: *Freedom of Information: The Law, the Practice and the Ideal, 4th Edition*
Blick: *Electrified Democracy: The Internet and the United Kingdom Parliament in History*
Broderick & Ferri: *International and European Disability Law and Policy: Text, Cases and Materials*
Brownsword & Goodwin: *Law and the Technologies of the Twenty-First Century: Text and Materials*
Cane & Goudkamp: *Atiyah's Accidents, Compensation and the Law, 9th Edition*
Clarke: *Principles of Property Law*
Clarke & Kohler: *Property Law: Commentary and Materials*
Collins: *The Law of Contract, 4th Edition*
Collins, Ewing & McColgan: *Labour Law, 2nd Edition*
Cowan: *Housing Law and Policy*
Cranston: *Legal Foundations of the Welfare State*
Cranston: *Making Commercial Law Through Practice 1830–1970*
Darian-Smith: *Laws and Societies in Global Contexts: Contemporary Approaches*
Dauvergne: *Making People Illegal: What Globalisation Means for Immigration and Law*
David: *Kinship, Law and Politics: An Anatomy of Belonging*
Davies: *Perspectives on Labour Law, 2nd Edition*
Dembour: *Who Believes in Human Rights?: Reflections on the European Convention*
de Sousa Santos: *Toward a New Legal Common Sense: Law, Globalization, and Emancipation*
Diduck: *Law's Families*
Dowdle: *Transnational Law: A Framework for Analysis*
Dupret: *Positive Law from the Muslim World: Jurisprudence, History, Practices*
Emon: *Jurisdictional Exceptionalisms: Islamic Law, International Law, and Parental Child Abduction*
Estella: *Legal Foundations of EU Economic Governance*
Fortin: *Children's Rights and the Developing Law, 3rd Edition*
Garnsey: *The Justice of Visual Art: Creative State-Building in Times of Political Transition*
Garton, Probert & Bean: *Moffat's Trusts Law: Text and Materials, 7th Edition*
Ghai & Woodman: *Practising Self-Government: A Comparative Study of Autonomous Regions*
Glover-Thomas: *Reconstructing Mental Health Law and Policy*
Gobert & Punch: *Rethinking Corporate Crime*
Goldman: *Globalization and the Western Legal Tradition: Recurring Patterns of Law and Authority*
Haack: *Evidence Matters: Science, Proof, and Truth in the Law*
Harlow & Rawlings: *Law and Administration, 4th Edition*
Harris: *An Introduction to Law, 8th Edition*
Harris, Campbell & Halson: *Remedies in Contract and Tort, 2nd Edition*
Harvey: *Seeking Asylum in the UK: Problems and Prospects*
Herring: *Law and the Relational Self*
Hervey & McHale: *European Union Health Law: Themes and Implications*

Hervey & McHale: *Health Law and the European Union*
Holder & Lee: *Environmental Protection, Law and Policy: Text and Materials, 2nd Edition*
Jackson & Summers: *The Internationalisation of Criminal Evidence: Beyond the Common Law and Civil Law Traditions*
Kostakopoulou: *The Future Governance of Citizenship*
Kreiczer-Levy: *Destabilized Property: Property Law in the Sharing Economy*
Kubal: *Immigration and Refugee Law in Russia: Socio-Legal Perspectives*
Lewis: *Choice and the Legal Order: Rising above Politics*
Likosky: *Law, Infrastructure and Human Rights*
Likosky: *Transnational Legal Processes: Globalisation and Power Disparities*
Lixinski: *Legalized Identities: Cultural Heritage Law and the Shaping of Transitional Justice*
Loughnan: *Self, Others and the State: Relations of Criminal Responsibility*
Lunney: *A History of Australian Tort Law 1901–1945: England's Obedient Servant?*
Maughan & Webb: *Lawyering Skills and the Legal Process, 2nd Edition*
McGaughey: *Principles of Enterprise Law*
McGlynn: *Families and the European Union: Law, Politics and Pluralism*
Mertens: *A Philosophical Introduction to Human Rights*
Moffat: *Trusts Law: Text and Materials*
Monti: *EC Competition Law*
Morgan: *Contract Law Minimalism: A Formalist Restatement of Commercial Contract Law*
Morgan & Yeung: *An Introduction to Law and Regulation: Text and Materials*
Nash: *British Islam and English Law: A Classical Pluralist Perspective*
Ng: *Political Censorship in British Hong Kong: Freedom of Expression and the Law (1842–1997)*
Nicola & Davies: *EU Law Stories: Contextual and Critical Histories of European Jurisprudence*
Norrie: *Crime, Reason and History: A Critical Introduction to Criminal Law, 3rd Edition*
O'Dair: *Legal Ethics: Text and Materials*
Oliver: *Common Values and the Public–Private Divide*
Oliver & Drewry: *The Law and Parliament*
Palmer & Roberts : *Dispute Processes: ADR and the Primary Forms of Decision-Making, 1st Edition*
Palmer & Roberts: *Dispute Processes: ADR and the Primary Forms of Decision-Making, 3rd Edition*
Picciotto: *International Business Taxation*
Probert: *The Changing Legal Regulation of Cohabitation: From Fornicators to Family, 1600–2010*
Radi: *Rules and Practices of International Investment Law and Arbitration*
Reed: *Internet Law: Text and Materials*
Richardson: *Law, Process and Custody*
Roberts & Palmer: *Dispute Processes: ADR and the Primary Forms of Decision-Making, 2nd Edition*
Rowbottom: *Democracy Distorted: Wealth, Influence and Democratic Politics*
Sauter: *Public Services in EU Law*

Scott & Black: *Cranston's Consumers and the Law*
Seneviratne: *Ombudsmen: Public Services and Administrative Justice*
Seppänen: *Ideological Conflict and the Rule of Law in Contemporary China: Useful Paradoxes*
Siems: *Comparative Law, 3rd Edition*
Stapleton: *Product Liability*
Stewart: *Gender, Law and Justice in a Global Market*
Tamanaha: *Law as a Means to an End: Threat to the Rule of Law*
Tuori: *Properties of Law: Modern Law and After*
Turpin & Tomkins: *British Government and the Constitution: Text and Materials, 7th Edition*
Twining: *General Jurisprudence: Understanding Law from a Global Perspective*
Twining: *Globalisation and Legal Theory*
Twining: *Human Rights, Southern Voices: Francis Deng, Abdullahi An-Na'im, Yash Ghai and Upendra Baxi*
Twining: *Jurist in Context: A Memoir*
Twining: *Karl Llewellyn and the Realist Movement, 2nd Edition*
Twining: *Rethinking Evidence: Exploratory Essays, 2nd Edition*
Twining & Miers: *How to Do Things with Rules, 5th Edition*
Wan: *Film and Constitutional Controversy: Visualizing Hong Kong Identity in the Age of 'One Country, Two Systems'*
Ward: *A Critical Introduction to European Law, 3rd Edition*
Ward: *Law, Text, Terror*
Ward: *Shakespeare and Legal Imagination*
Wells & Quick: *Lacey, Wells and Quick: Reconstructing Criminal Law: Text and Materials, 4th Edition*
Young: *Turpin and Tomkins' British Government and the Constitution: Text and Materials, 8th Edition*
Zander: *Cases and Materials on the English Legal System, 10th Edition*
Zander: *The Law-Making Process, 6th Edition*

International Journal of Law in Context: A Global Forum for Interdisciplinary Legal Studies

The *International Journal of Law in Context* is the companion journal to the Law in Context book series and provides a forum for interdisciplinary legal studies and offers intellectual space for ground-breaking critical research. It publishes contextual work about law and its relationship with other disciplines including but not limited to science, literature, humanities, philosophy, sociology, psychology, ethics, history and geography. More information about the journal and how to submit an article can be found at http://journals.cambridge.org/ijc

Tax and Government in the Twenty-First Century

MIRANDA STEWART
University of Melbourne

CAMBRIDGE
UNIVERSITY PRESS

CAMBRIDGE
UNIVERSITY PRESS

University Printing House, Cambridge CB2 8BS, United Kingdom

One Liberty Plaza, 20th Floor, New York, NY 10006, USA

477 Williamstown Road, Port Melbourne, VIC 3207, Australia

314–321, 3rd Floor, Plot 3, Splendor Forum, Jasola District Centre, New Delhi – 110025, India

103 Penang Road, #05-06/07, Visioncrest Commercial, Singapore 238467

Cambridge University Press is part of the University of Cambridge.

It furthers the University's mission by disseminating knowledge in the pursuit of education, learning, and research at the highest international levels of excellence.

www.cambridge.org
Information on this title: www.cambridge.org/9781107097469
DOI: 10.1017/9781316160701

© Miranda Stewart 2022

This publication is in copyright. Subject to statutory exception and to the provisions of relevant collective licensing agreements, no reproduction of any part may take place without the written permission of Cambridge University Press.

First published 2022

A catalogue record for this publication is available from the British Library.

Library of Congress Cataloging-in-Publication Data
Names: Stewart, Miranda, 1968– author.
Title: Tax and government in the 21st century / Miranda Stewart, University of Melbourne.
Description: First edition. | Cambridge, United Kingdom ; New York, NY : Cambridge University Press, 2022. | Series: Law in context | Includes bibliographical references and index.
Identifiers: LCCN 2022007082 (print) | LCCN 2022007083 (ebook) | ISBN 9781107097469 (hardback) | ISBN 9781107483507 (paperback) | ISBN 9781316160701 (epub)
Subjects: LCSH: Taxation–Law and legislation. | Fiscal policy.
Classification: LCC K4460 .S74 2022 (print) | LCC K4460 (ebook) | DDC 343.04–dc23/eng/
    20220526
LC record available at https://lccn.loc.gov/2022007082
LC ebook record available at https://lccn.loc.gov/2022007083

ISBN 978-1-107-09746-9 Hardback
ISBN 978-1-107-48350-7 Paperback

Cambridge University Press has no responsibility for the persistence or accuracy of URLs for external or third-party internet websites referred to in this publication and does not guarantee that any content on such websites is, or will remain, accurate or appropriate.

It was Alistair who said, on national television, that being a Tax Officer was the most pleasant work imaginable, like turning on a tap to bring water to parched country. It felt wonderful to bring money flowing out of multinational reservoirs into child-care centres and hospitals and social services. . . . He sold taxation as a public good.

Peter Carey, *The Tax Inspector*

Contents

List of Figures	*page* xvii
List of Tables	xix
List of Boxes	xx
Acknowledgements	xxi
List of Acronyms	xxiii

PART I PRINCIPLES AND CONCEPTS	1
1 Introduction	3
Overview	3
The Tax State	3
Challenges for the Tax State	4
Structure of This Book	6
Disciplinary Approaches to Tax Law	7
Comparative and Sociological Approaches	7
Public Finance and Economics	9
Law and Accounting	10
Tax Statistics	12
Tax Structure	13
Definition of a Tax	13
Tax Level	14
Tax Mix	16
Tax Concepts	18
Elements of a Tax System	18
Tax Incidence	19
Types of Taxation	21
Income Tax	21
Social Security Tax	22
Consumption Tax	24
Wealth, Property and Land Taxes	26
Tax Rates	26

2	**Tax and Government**	28
	History of Tax and Government	28
	Origins and Theory of the Tax State	28
	Debt, Taxes and the Rise of the Citizen-Taxpayer	30
	The Tax and Welfare State	33
	Taxes to Finance Welfare in the *Socialstaat*	33
	Social Welfare versus Liberal Approaches to Fair Taxation	35
	Expansion of the Tax State in the Twentieth Century	36
	A Crisis of the Tax State?	39
	The Limits of Taxation	39
	Economic Globalisation and Tax Reform	40
	The Benefit Theory of Taxation	43
	Taxes for a Civilised Society	43
	Public Goods	45
	The Taxpayer-Voter	48
	Taxation for the Public Good	49
3	**The Budget**	51
	The Budget Constraint	51
	The Traditional Budget	51
	The Level of Government Debt	53
	Fiscal Institutions	54
	A New Era of Fiscal Discipline	54
	Fiscal Rules	55
	Fiscal Transparency	57
	Independent Fiscal Institutions	59
	Fiscal Policy in the COVID-19 Pandemic	63
	Linking Taxes to Spending	65
	Budget Earmarking and Mandatory Spending	65
	Tax Expenditure Budgeting	67
	Benchmarking Tax Expenditures	69
	Gender, Distributional and Other Values in Budgets	70
	The Budget as an Ethical Document	70
	Gender Budgeting	71
	Distributional Impact of Budgets	72
	Green Budgeting	73
4	**Tax Principles**	75
	Origins of Tax Principles	75
	The Maxims of Adam Smith	75
	Equity	78
	Tax Equity and Distributive Justice	78
	Ability to Pay and Progressive Tax Rates	79
	Ability to Pay and the Concept of Income	81
	Ability to Pay and the Myth of Ownership	84

	The Tax-Transfer System	86
	Substantive Equity, Rights and Discrimination in Tax Law	88
	Life Course and Intergenerational Equity	90
	Efficiency	91
	Optimal Tax Theory and Incentives	91
	The Principle of Neutrality	96
	Taxes, Externalities and Market Failure	97
	Challenges and Limits of Efficiency Analysis	98
	Opening the Borders of the Tax State	100
	Tax Policy in a Global Economy	100
	Supply-side Tax Policy	102
	A Tax Mix Switch from Income to Consumption?	103
	Resilience of the Tax State	106

PART II TAX LAW IN CONTEXT   111

5 Tax, Work and Family   113

	The Income Tax on Wages	113
	The Importance of Taxing Labour	113
	From the Poll Tax to the Progressive Income Tax	114
	The Genius of Pay-as-you-go Withholding	117
	Tax Rates and Work Incentives	118
	The Design of Progressive Tax Rates	120
	The Tax Burden on Labour Income	121
	The Tax Unit	123
	History of the Tax Unit and Women's Economic Independence	123
	The Tax Unit, Equity and Efficiency	126
	The Tax-transfer Unit and Childcare Costs	127
	Taxing the Top 1 Per Cent	130
	Challenges for the Progressive Tax on Labour Income	133
	Income Splitting	133
	Capitalisation of Labour Income	135
	Taxing the Gig Economy	135
	Automation and Taxing Robots	138
	Basic Income	139
	Concept and Justification of a Basic Income	139
	Designing a Basic Income	141

6 Taxation of Saving and Wealth   144

	Taxing Capital	144
	The Complex Role of Capital	144
	Inequality of Income and Wealth	146
	Theory of Taxing Savings	146
	The Hybrid Income-Consumption Tax	152
	Economic Rent	154

	Capital Gains Tax	155
	Taxation of Capital Gains Compared to Income	155
	Accrual Taxation of Capital Gains	157
	Dual Income Tax	158
	Taxing Retirement Saving	161
	Retirement Incomes Policy	161
	Income or Consumption Approach	161
	Hybrid Tax Systems for Retirement	162
	Taxing the Home	163
	The Role of Home Ownership	163
	Imputed Rent and Capital Gains on the Home	165
	Taxation of Wealth	166
	Wealth Inequality	166
	Justification for Taxation of Wealth	168
	Net Wealth Tax	171
	Inheritance Tax	172
	Land and Property Taxation	174
7	**Corporate and Business Taxation**	**177**
	Why Tax Corporations?	177
	Corporations Are Important	177
	Complexity of the Corporate Tax	180
	Corporate Tax Revenues and Rates	182
	Incidence of the Corporate Tax	184
	Integrating Corporate and Shareholder Tax	187
	The Corporate Tax on Economic Rents	190
	Taxation of Business Investment	191
	Tangible and Intangible Business Assets	191
	Tax Policy for Innovation and Entrepreneurship	192
	Small Business	194
	Start-ups and Venture Capital	195
	Research and Development	196
	Directions for Corporate Tax Reform	199
	The Business Cash Flow Tax	199
	Allowance for Corporate Equity	200
	Comprehensive Business Income Tax	201
	A Hybrid, Messy but Essential Tax	202
8	**Tax, Charity and Philanthropy**	**204**
	Charity and Government	204
	The Boundaries of Tax and Charity	204
	The Size of the Not-for-profit Sector	205
	The Tax Privilege of Charity	207
	Origins and Justification of the Charitable Exemption	207
	Commercial Activities of Not-for-profits	209
	Social Enterprise	212

	Tax and Philanthropy	213
	The Deduction for Charitable Giving	213
	Private Foundations and 'Big Philanthropy'	214
	Charities, Tax Avoidance and Evasion	216
	The Globalisation of Charity	217
	Tax and Charity across National Borders	217
	Dissolving the Borders of Charity in the European Union	218
	Tax, Charity and Global Public Benefit	220
9	**Administration, Compliance and Avoidance**	**222**
	Tax Administration	222
	Certainty and Convenience in Taxation	222
	Administrative Elements for Effective Taxation	223
	The Rise of the Tax Authority	225
	Tax Compliance and Evasion	230
	Quasi-voluntary Compliance	230
	Self-assessment and Responsive Tax Regulation	233
	Tax Data and Automation	237
	Tax Planning and Avoidance	239
	The Ubiquity of Tax Planning	239
	Tax Shelters	243
	Anti-avoidance Approaches	244
	Legal Definitions of Tax Avoidance	244
	Judicial Anti-avoidance Doctrines	246
	Statutory General Anti-avoidance Rules	247
	The Tax Gap	249
	PART III THE TAX STATE IN THE GLOBAL DIGITAL ERA	251
10	**Tax Jurisdiction**	**253**
	Tax Jurisdiction	253
	The Borders of the Tax State	253
	Residence and Source	254
	Tax Treaties	257
	Residence of Individuals	259
	Defining Tax Residence	259
	Justification for Residence Taxation	260
	New Residents, Departing Residents	261
	The Citizen-Taxpayer	262
	Jurisdiction over Labour Income	263
	Source of Labour Income	263
	Transnational Workers	264
	Taxing the 'Brain Drain'	267
	Tax Jurisdiction in a Global Remittance Economy	270
	Mobility of the Working Elite	271
	Cross-border Retirement Saving	273

Jurisdiction over Capital Income 274
   Mobility of Capital 274
   The Terrain of 'Offshore' 277
   From Eurobonds to Offshore Bank Accounts 279
Bringing 'Offshore' into the Tax Jurisdiction 280
   Extending Legal Jurisdiction to Offshore Holdings 280
   A History of Non-cooperative Sovereigns 284
   The Era of Bank Secrecy Is Over 285
   Collecting Tax across Borders 287
   Taxpayer Rights in a Global Context 289
   VAT on E-commerce and the One-stop Shop 290
   Towards Transnational Tax Administration 292

11 States and Corporations in the Global Digital Economy — 295

Competition and Cooperation of Tax States 295
   Tax Sovereignty 295
   Harmful Tax Competition 298
Corporate Tax Policy in a Global Economy 300
   Corporate Tax Jurisdiction 300
   The Legal Fiction of Corporate Residence 304
   Source and Permanent Establishment 307
   Stateless Income 308
Base Erosion and Profit Shifting 311
   The BEPS Project 311
   Multilateralism in Corporate Tax 315
   Transnational Corporate Tax Administration 317
   Anti-abuse Approaches 319
   Harmful Tax Practices 320
The Global Digital Economy 322
   The Tax Consequences of Digitalisation 322
   Digital Services Taxes 324
   Destination-based Cash Flow Tax 325
   The Inclusive Framework Consensus 326

12 The Future Tax State — 330

The Tax State's 'Good Twentieth Century' 330
Reassembling the Tax State for the Twenty-first Century 332
   The Community of the Tax State 332
   The Interdependence of Tax Sovereignty 334
   Transnational Tax Law and Administration 335
   Justice and Legitimacy of the Future Tax State 337

References 340
Index 388

Figures

1.1	Tax and expenditure as a share of GDP, OECD countries, 2019	page 15
1.2	Tax mix of selected OECD countries, share of GDP, 2018	17
1.3	Tax mix of selected OECD countries, share of total taxation, 2018	17
1.4	Progressive, proportional and regressive tax rates	27
2.1	Tax as share of GDP, Australia, 1902–2019	38
2.2	Tax as share of GDP, selected OECD countries, 1965–2018	38
2.3	Structure of government expenditure by function, OECD countries, 2016	47
3.1	Gross debt of OECD countries, share of GDP, 2019	53
3.2	UK fiscal targets and rules, 1997–2020	57
3.3	Open Budget Index ranking, selected OECD countries, 2019	60
4.1	Effect of taxes and transfers on Gini coefficient of OECD countries, 2018 or latest data	87
4.2	(a, b) Basic model – economics of a tax	93
4.3	System resilience	107
5.1	Personal income tax rates for single taxpayers in Germany and Australia	122
5.2	Income tax and social security contributions (SSC) as share of wage cost, selected OECD countries, 2019	123
5.3	Marginal effective tax rate on second earner, cameo example, Australia, 2018	130
5.4	Share of income of the top 1 per cent, selected OECD countries, 1920–2019	131
6.1	Share of household income and wealth of the top 10 per cent, selected OECD countries, 2015	147
6.2	Per capita public, private and net time transfers by age, selected European countries, 2016	150
6.3	Distribution of household wealth by quintiles, Australia, 2017	150
6.4	Distribution of wealth over the life course, Germany, France, 2015	151
6.5	Marginal effective tax rates on different asset classes, Australia, 2020	153

6.6	Ultra-high-net worth individuals, 2020	167
7.1	Corporate income tax, share of total taxation and of GDP, selected OECD countries, 2017	182
7.2	Average statutory corporate income tax rates by region, 2000–2021	183
8.1	Sources of revenue of the not-for-profit sector in Europe, 2014	206
9.1	Tax administrative functions	227
9.2	Example of regulatory practice with ATO compliance model	234
9.3	Compliance and policy gaps	250
11.1	Double Irish-Dutch Sandwich tax planning structure	309

Tables

3.1	Examples of fiscal rules	*page* 58
5.1	Basic income with 50 per cent flat tax	142
6.1	Benchmarks for taxation of retirement saving	162
7.1	Corporate-shareholder tax systems	188
7.2	Tax concessions for research and development	198
9.1	Oversight of tax authorities	229

Boxes

1.1	Comprehensive income compared to the 'real' income tax	*page* 22
2.1	Example of a public good	46
3.1	Evolution of fiscal policy in the eurozone	62
3.2	The fiscal response to COVID-19	64
4.1	Threats to tax system resilience	108
5.1	Progressive tax rates, inflation and bracket creep	121
5.2	Example of high effective tax rates on women's work	129
6.1	The Netherlands 'box' system – back to the future	159
6.2	Taxing the return to wealth	170
7.1	Income shifting between the corporate and personal income tax systems	186
7.2	Hedge funds and the carried interest controversy	197
8.1	Taxing the business income of charities	211
9.1	Taxpayer rights	236
9.2	Passive investment losses as a tax shelter	241
10.1	The mobile professor	265
10.2	A brain drain tax for higher education	269
10.3	The digitalised professor	273
10.4	Retiring from cold countries to warm countries	274
10.5	Exit taxes	276
10.6	The United States goes it alone: FATCA	286
10.7	Collecting tax across borders	288
11.1	Corporate tax neutrality	302
11.2	Untethering the MNE from the nation state	306
11.3	Base erosion and profit shifting by MNEs	313
11.4	The BEPS Action Plan	314

Acknowledgements

I owe thanks to a great many people for this book, which has been years in the gestation. It is an honour to be included in the *CUP Law in Context* series, which has only one previous volume on taxation, Sol Picciotto's groundbreaking *International Business Taxation: A Study in the Internationalisation of Business Regulation* (1992). I am grateful to the editorial advisory board, Bronwen Morgan, who invited me to propose this book, and William Twining. These two eminent scholars of regulation and international law influenced my approach to the book. Three anonymous referees provided insightful comments that greatly improved the proposal and encouraging words that I could achieve it. My gratitude to the editorial team at CUP, especially to commissioning editors Caitlin Lisle and Marianne Nield for their extraordinary patience and encouragement as the years rolled by and the shape of the project changed, Sandra Kerka and Vinithan Sedumadhavan for copy-editing, and to the production and marketing team at CUP. All errors, omissions and inadequacies are my own.

Thanks to Richard Vann and Patricia Apps of the University of Sydney Law School, and Daniel Shaviro of NYU School of Law. Their deep and wide expertise and teaching in taxation law and policy helped to establish my intellectual framework and their mentoring has helped to shape my career. I honour the memory of Paul McDaniel, director of the International Tax Program at NYU School of Law, where I was a student and then an assistant professor, who encouraged my interest in comparative and international tax scholarship and set me firmly on an academic pathway.

Many of the authors cited in this book are esteemed colleagues and friends in the world of tax scholarship. I value this community highly, and I hope this book goes some way to showing how much I have learnt from them. This book builds on many previous writings and I am grateful for the exchange and development of ideas with co-authors including Sarah Blakelock, Yariv Brauner, Graeme Cooper, Meredith Edwards, Daniel Halliday, David Ingles, Holly Jager, Sunita Jogarajan, Emily Millane, Lisa Philipps, Ben Phillips, Marian Sawer, Edwin Simpson, Sarah Voitchovsky, Peter Whiteford and Roger Wilkins. Thanks to Lisa Philipps for her critical insights and positivity early in this project; Graeme Cooper for supporting and challenging me at different points in my career; Marian Sawer for her generosity in sharing her knowledge; and Peter Whiteford for enjoyable collaborations in teaching and writing that taught me a great deal about the tax and transfer system. Thanks to Marie Coleman for excellent Canberra dinners and conversation; to Geoffrey Brennan for rigorous analysis delivered with a smile; and Greg Smith for his friendship and support. I also thank my students for their enthusiasm and fresh perspectives as I shared my ideas in various tax subjects over many years

I was assisted with charts and data by Peter Martin, Ben Phillips, Mathias Sinning and Paul Tilley at the Australian National University, David Plunkett (whose charts are "off the charts!"), Brian Walker of the CSIRO and Isabelle Stockton of the Institute of Fiscal Studies. The book was supported by research assistance by excellent young scholars including Maria Sandoval Guzman, Daniel Minutillo, Richard Reid, Steve Thomas and Teck Chi Wong. My gratitude to Christopher Hood for sending me his book chapter on the tax state's 'good twentieth century' when all was closed during the pandemic lockdown in 2021. Various aspects of the research were supported by funding from the Australian Research Council, the International Budget Project, and the Academy of Social Sciences of Australia. Thanks to the Melbourne Law School, University of Melbourne and the Tax and Transfer Policy Institute of the Australian National University for research support.

Finally, I thank my family who supported me through the long journey. My love and gratitude to my partner Kristen and my son Alfred, for everything but especially their willingness – up to a point – to engage in regular dinner conversation about tax law and its impact on everything. Thank you to our New Zealand whanau, Graeme and Bryan who professed to be deeply interested in tax law on more than one occasion; to my parents, Mary and David, for their unfailing encouragement to 'do the book!' and for space to think and delicious food during periods of writing and editing; and to my sister Jessica, whose professional skills in editing and pithy sentences are unsurpassed. Finally, this book is for my brother Thomas, the musician, who is always in my heart.

Acronyms

ACE	allowance for corporate equity
ATO	Australian Taxation Office
BEPS	Base Erosion and Profit Shifting
CbC	country-by-country
CBIT	comprehensive business income tax
CCCTB	common consolidated corporate tax base
CEN	capital export neutrality
CFC	controlled foreign corporation
CIN	capital import neutrality
CJEU	Court of Justice of the European Union
CRS	Common Reporting Standard
DBCFT	destination-based cash flow tax
DST	digital services tax
EC	European Commission
EEC	European Economic Community
EET	exempt-exempt-tax
EFTA	European Free Trade Association
EU	European Union
FATCA	Foreign Account Tax Compliance Act
GAAR	general anti-avoidance rule
GDP	gross domestic product
GLoBE	Global anti-Base Erosion Rule
GST	goods and services tax
HMRC	Her Majesty's Revenue and Customs
IMF	International Monetary Fund
IRS	Internal Revenue Service
MAP	mutual agreement procedure
METR	marginal effective tax rate
MLI	multilateral instrument
MNE	multinational enterprise
OBI	Open Budget Index
OECD	Organisation for Economic Co-operation and Development
PAYG	pay-as-you-go
PFIC	personal foreign investment company
PPT	Principal purpose test
R&D	research and development
SME	small or medium-sized enterprise
TEE	tax-tax-exempt

UBI	universal basic income
UBIT	unrelated business income tax
UN	United Nations
VAT	value added tax

Part I
Principles and Concepts

1

Introduction

> The human ends of government are individual and collective at the same time.
> Gerhard Colm, 'Theory of Public Expenditures'

Overview

The Tax State

People in wealthy countries live in a state that is defined by the power to tax and dependent on taxation to fund government, which we call a 'tax state'.[1] Most of the member states in the Organisation for Economic Co-operation and Development (OECD) are tax states. This book discusses taxation law and policy in the economic, social, legal and political context of tax states and explores the many challenges faced by these tax states in the twenty-first century.

A tax state is a particular form of fiscal governmental organisation that relies on tax revenues extracted in a sustainable fiscal bargain with taxpayers, who may be citizens, investors, workers or multinational enterprises, depending on the context.[2] Tax states evolved over the last three centuries but they are fundamentally a product of the twentieth century. Many successful tax states are democratic; the slogan 'no taxation without representation', with historical origins in Magna Carta, made famous in the American revolution of the eighteenth century, was repeated as far afield as the Australian colonies in the nineteenth century.[3] During the twentieth century, successful tax states combined economic growth to lift incomes and well-being, with effective taxation that harnessed the returns for public expenditure and redistribution across their populations.

---

[1] Joseph A Schumpeter, 'The Crisis of the Tax State' [1918] (1954) 4 *International Economic Papers* 5–38, trans. Wolfgang Stolper and Richard A Musgrave. The term 'tax state' was coined and its 'crisis' was first proclaimed by Rudolf Goldscheid, *State Socialism or State Capitalism* (1917): Richard A Musgrave, 'Schumpeter's Crisis of the Tax State: An Essay in Fiscal Sociology' (1992) 2(2) *Journal of Evolutionary Economics* 89–113.

[2] Margaret Levi, *Of Rule and Revenue* (Berkeley, CA: University of California Press, 1988), 49.

[3] Ballarat Reform League, 'Taxation without Representation Is Tyranny', Eureka Stockade, Colony of Victoria, Australia, 11 November 1854.

This book examines the evolution of tax law in a fiscal bargain for a 'good democracy'.[4] The fiscal bargain established through taxation, like government itself, has a dual character, forming both the collective organisation and individual choices and outcomes. Taxation has quasi-constitutional status and is a lever for governmental management of the macroeconomy through fiscal policy. At the same time, taxation law (with property and other laws) demarcates what individuals own and consume privately and what is shared in the state.[5] Taxation affects the preferences and behaviours of individuals across all economic and social spheres. For example, taxation influences an individual's decision to work for a wage in the market or unpaid in the home; as a sole contractor or an employee; to invest in a house or in shares; to set up a business in a company or a partnership; to reduce or increase the use of polluting energy; to donate to a charity; to shop online; to stay in one's country of origin or move abroad. Tax laws also produce new behaviours specific to the tax system including decisions to seek advice in tax planning, to work for cash or in the informal or barter economy, or to carry out schemes for tax avoidance or tax evasion activities.

Challenges for the Tax State

In the twenty-first century, mature tax states face an array of economic and social challenges. This book explores the evolution of tax law in response to challenges to the fiscal bargain between citizens and the state, the distribution of taxation on workers and capital and the boundaries of the territorial tax state. These challenges for the tax state include:

- slowing economic growth;
- globalisation and digitalisation of the economy;
- aging and longer lived populations, forcing governments to rely on a smaller working age population to pay taxes;
- the changing nature of family and care, including fewer children and more elderly, combined with a dramatic increase in women's market work;
- inequality of wealth and income within and across generations;
- the gig economy, which increases risk, insecurity and fragmentation of work while wages stagnate;

---

[4] Following John G Head, who sought to develop a 'normative theory of public economy, based upon the premise of individual preference in a democratic society', *Public Goods and Public Welfare* (Durham, NC: Duke University Press, 1969), 223.
[5] Liam Murphy and Thomas Nagel, *The Myth of Ownership: Taxes and Justice* (Oxford: Oxford University Press, 2002).

- technological change that is accelerating a shift of economic value into digital or intangible assets and causing increasing returns to capital relative to labour; and
- health, environmental and resource challenges of global scope.

Globalisation and digitalisation have changed how we imagine community, citizenship and social obligations. Yet tax laws, social security and public goods remain, on the whole, territorially bounded in nation states. On the one hand, individuals are increasingly direct participants as consumers in global markets. Engaging in international social and political issues, we come to see ourselves as global 'citizens'.[6] On the other hand, individuals support states to vigorously renew and reinforce national territorial and juridical borders, including the borders of the tax and welfare state. This raises questions about who is responsible for, or entitled to, redistribution and how to achieve the effective financing of public goods in a global and digital era.

The coronavirus (COVID-19) pandemic has added to these challenges. Governments applied their fiscal systems to dramatically increase social and health expenditure, relying on debt while generating lower tax revenues. The ability of developed country governments to respond quickly with fiscal measures is a sign of the resilience of the tax state and the effectiveness of its systems of tax collection and social security. However, the contraction in economic activity produced by the pandemic caused disruption to government budgets that will be felt for years to come. The pandemic has also accelerated economic and social trends, including demographic changes, the growth of the digital economy and the insecurity and instability of work.

Governments are likely to need increased fiscal resources to address these challenges, yet few governments are leading on a platform of higher taxes to rebuild or transition out of crisis. The COVID-19 fiscal crisis has arisen after decades of attempts to shrink the state, even taking an approach of 'fiscal austerity'.[7] Governments are concerned about slowing economic growth and are inclined to deliver 'stimulus' by lowering taxes and enacting short-term expansions in public expenditure in response to the pandemic.

Many of the issues discussed in this book are relevant to tax systems of all countries, not only the wealthy member states of the OECD. However, the book is not comprehensive in coverage and it omits some issues of importance for developing country tax systems.[8] The book does not address

---

[6] William Twining, *Globalisation and Legal Theory* (Cambridge, UK: Cambridge University Press, 2000), 7–8; Saskia Sassen, *Globalization and Its Discontents* (New York: New Press, 1998).
[7] Florian Schui, *Austerity: The Great Failure* (New Haven, CT: Yale University Press, 2014).
[8] There is a wide literature on tax and development. An overview on the developing tax state in Africa is Attiya Waris, *Financing Africa* (Bamenda, Cameroon: Langaa Rpcig, 2019). See also Yariv Brauner and Miranda Stewart (eds.), *Tax, Law and Development* (Cheltenham: Edward Elgar, 2013).

environmental and resource taxation in any depth, including the policy or legal design of a carbon tax or emissions trading scheme. These issues are important for all countries and must be part of the global policy response to address climate change.[9] Nor does it explore in any detail the topics of trade, excise or consumption taxes, or the role of taxes in federal systems. Inevitably, because of limitations of language and scope, this book focuses on the Anglosphere although it also draws on examples and literature from European and other countries.

Structure of This Book

Part I (**Chapters 1 to 4**) presents concepts, principles and processes of taxation. The remainder of **Chapter 1** outlines approaches to studying tax law in context and explains core tax concepts and statistics to support the analysis of the tax law and policy issues discussed in the book. **Chapter 2** explains the history of the 'tax state'. It then discusses the benefit theory of taxation as a justification for paying taxes to fund the public good, in a fiscal bargain that constrains governmental power to tax based on consent and the rule of law. **Chapter 3** explains the process of government budgeting, the relationship of tax and debt and approaches to fiscal discipline and budget accountability. **Chapter 4** introduces and explains the main principles of taxation, including critical approaches to tax principles, with a focus on equity, efficiency and resilience of tax systems.

Part II (**Chapters 5 to 9**) discusses selected topics of tax law in context. **Chapter 5** examines tax, work and the family, focusing on the relationship between taxes and transfers, or the welfare state. It considers the definition of the tax unit, the impact of taxes on incentives to work, especially for women with care responsibilities, and challenges for taxation such as the gig economy and automation. The chapter consider possible responses to these challenges including a robot tax or a basic income. **Chapter 6** discusses the taxation of personal saving including capital income and gains, with a focus on retirement saving and home ownership. It discusses inequality in capital income and wealth and explores wealth and inheritance taxation and specific taxes on land and property. **Chapter 7** examines the corporate tax, including its incidence, complexity and the taxation of corporations and shareholders. It then examines the tax rules applicable to business investment. It focuses on taxation of innovation, small business, entrepreneurship and research and development.

---

[9] Useful resources include Hope Ashiabor, Janet E Milne and Mikael Skou Andersen (eds.), *Environmental Taxation in the Pandemic Era. Vol 23: Critical Issues in Environmental Taxation Series* (Cheltenham: Edward Elgar, 2021); International Monetary Fund/OECD, *Tax Policy for Climate Change, IMF-OECD Report for the G20 Finance Ministers and Governors* (April 2021), www.oecd.org/tax/tax-policy/tax-policy-and-climate-change-imf-oecd-g20-report-april-2021.pdf.

Chapter 8 examines the intersection of tax with charities and philanthropy, including the large size of the not-for-profit sector, the history and role of charitable tax concessions and taxing charity in the international context. Chapter 9 examines selected issues in tax administration, compliance and avoidance. The discussion in each chapter is illustrated with examples and case studies from various countries.

Part III (Chapters 10 to 12) turns to the global and digital challenges to the tax state. Chapter 10 discusses the concept of tax jurisdiction and the territorial limits of the tax state. It explains the core principles of residence and source for establishing jurisdictional nexus of individuals and applies these principles to labour and capital income. Chapter 10 then introduces the terrain of 'offshore' tax havens and governmental responses to these, finishing with a discussion of the trend towards transnational tax administration between tax states. Chapter 11 considers tax competition and cooperation between states in the global digital economy, with a focus on corporate taxation. It discusses tax jurisdictional rules for corporations, and the inadequacies of these rules. It then examines how tax states, through international forums, are seeking to address the taxation of multinational enterprises in the global economy. Chapter 11 discusses the Base Erosion and Profit Shifting (BEPS) project and the recent developments in the Inclusive Framework Consensus on digital taxation and explores their potential to transform international tax. Chapter 12 considers the future tax state and the challenge of taxation for a good democracy in the twenty-first century.

Disciplinary Approaches to Tax Law

Comparative and Sociological Approaches

Taxation can be approached from disciplines of law and legal theory, economics, political science, history, psychology, sociology, accounting and philosophy. Approaching tax law through the lens of these different disciplines helps to understand the design, operation and effects of tax law. This book refers to sources from these various disciplines at different points and draws on the rich tradition of comparative literature on the law, politics, economics and administration of different country tax systems.[10]

A discussion of challenges to tax states is meaningful despite the many differences between tax systems of different countries. This is because tax laws

---

[10] See, e.g. Cedric Sandford, *Why Tax Systems Differ: A Comparative Study of the Political Economy of Taxation* (Bath: Fiscal Publications, 2000); Chris Evans, John Hasseldine, Andrew Lymer, Robert Ricketts and Cedric Sandford, *Comparative Taxation: Why Tax Systems Differ* (Bath: Fiscal Publications, 2017); Victor Thuronyi, Kim Brooks and Borbála Kolozs, *Comparative Tax Law*, 2nd ed (Alphen aan den Rijn, Netherlands: Kluwer, 2016); Hugh J Ault, Brian J Arnold and Graeme Cooper, *Comparative Income Taxation*, 4th ed (Alphen aan den Rijn, Netherlands: Wolters Kluwer, 2020).

in different countries evolved to address the same issues of legitimate and stable finance for government in the context of capitalism. From the earliest times in the evolution of the tax state, information was shared about the design and administration of tax laws. Today, the epistemic community of tax policy, law and administration is increasingly international. Tax ideas, norms and experts travel across borders. Comparing tax issues of mature tax states is often how tax policy and reform is done today. The OECD plays a large role in sharing experiences, knowledge, statistics and new developments in taxation between member states.

Taxation is fundamentally a social and political process. Early theorists of taxation were political philosophers who saw taxes primarily as an exercise of coercive state power.[11] Historical analysis can give us the origins of detailed tax statutory provisions and help explain the broad sweep of political compromises required for stable tax systems. Historians demonstrate the growth and changes over time of the 'tax state' in the context of economic development, drawing on long time series of data about tax and expenditure systems.[12] Joseph Schumpeter said a century ago that we can use a tax lens to present a 'view of the state, of its nature, its forms, its fate, as seen from the fiscal side'.[13] Rudolf Goldscheid invented the study of fiscal sociology, which overlaps with political economy and political and economic history, and explained that it helps to understand the role of tax in society and the evolution of the tax state.[14]

Most successful tax states have developed democratic systems of government that harness the returns from economic growth to deliver public goods and redistribution.[15] Governments that seek to raise substantial and stable revenues without democratic governance must still respond to popular

---

[11] For example, Thomas Hobbes, *Leviathan* (London: Pelican Classics [1651], 1968), Project Gutenberg eBook www.gutenberg.org/files/3207/3207-h/3207-h.htm.

[12] José Luis Cardoso and Pedro Lains (eds.), *Paying for the Liberal State: The Rise of Public Finance in Nineteenth-Century Europe* (Cambridge, UK: Cambridge University Press, 2010); Martin Daunton, *Trusting Leviathan: The Politics of Taxation in Britain, 1799–1914* (New York: Cambridge University Press, 2001); Martin Daunton, *Just Taxes: The Politics of Taxation in Britain, 1914–1979* (New York: Cambridge University Press, 2002); Sven Steinmo, *Taxation and Democracy: Swedish, British and American Approaches to Financing the Modern State* (New Haven, CT Yale University Press, 1993).

[13] Schumpeter, 'The Crisis of the Tax State', 101 (see n 1).

[14] Rudolf Goldscheid, 'A Sociological Approach to Problems in Public Finance' in Richard A Musgrave and Alan T Peacock (eds.), *Classics in the Theory of Public Finance* (New York: Palgrave Macmillan, 1918, trans. Elizabeth Henderson; 1958), 202–13; Marc Leroy, *Taxation, the State and Society: The Fiscal Sociology of Interventionist Democracy. Public Action Vol 7* (Brussels: PIE Peter Lang, 2011; trans. from the French edition, 2010); Isaac W Martin, Ajay Mehrotra and Monica Prasad, *The New Fiscal Sociology: Taxation in Comparative and Historical Perspective* (New York: Cambridge University Press).

[15] John L Campbell 'The State and Fiscal Sociology' (1993) 19 *Annual Review of Sociology* 163–85; Andrew C Gould and Peter J Baker, 'Democracy and Taxation' (2002) 5 *Annual Review of Political Science* 87–110.

demands for social provision and the rule of law in taxation. For example, China is working to strengthen its welfare state, to reform its personal income tax to make it more progressive and its business income taxes to more accurately tax net business profits.[16]

Political science and public policy scholarship on expertise, policy change, international relations and global governance help us understand tax policy and reform processes and tax system adaptation in the global and digital economy.[17] Tax systems are dependent on administrative capacity of states and the agency charged with responsibility for tax collection is usually one of the largest and most efficient government agencies. Theories of public administration can inform us about the development and organisation of tax bureaucracies and technologies and methods of administration that are of central importance for the tax state. Theories of system adaptability and resilience can help us to understand the many components of the tax and transfer system, and how it may adapt so as to maintain its identity and equilibrium in the face of external and internal shocks and changes.

Public Finance and Economics

The study of public finance (and public economics in general) examines the relationship between government and the market, with the aim of designing policy and regulation to achieve collective economic welfare. There is a wide public economics literature from a range of different perspectives.[18] This book, as have so many in the field, takes inspiration from Richard and Peggy Musgrave, leading public finance economists of the twentieth century, whose careers spanned the most important decades of development of the tax state and whose work addressed all aspects of the topic.[19]

---

[16] Global Legal Monitor, 'China: Individual Income Tax Law Revised', Library of Congress (24 September 2018), www.loc.gov/law/foreign-news/article/china-individual-income-tax-law-revised-2/. However, note that the Chinese approach to tax administration tends to maintain bureaucratic control of tax assessment, rather than shifting to self-assessment, which may lead to calls for improved transparency and due process in tax administration: Wei Cui, *The Administrative Foundations of the Chinese Fiscal State* (Cambridge, UK: Cambridge University Press, 2022).

[17] Thomas Rixen, *The Political Economy of International Tax Governance* (New York: Palgrave Macmillan, 2008).

[18] Accessible discussions that are relied on in this book include Joel Slemrod and Jon Bakija, *Taxing Ourselves: A Citizen's Guide to the Debate over Taxes*, 5th ed (Cambridge, MA: MIT Press, 2017); Alan J Auerbach and Kent Smetters (eds.), *The Economics of Tax Policy* (New York: Oxford University Press, 2017); Peter Abelson, *Public Economics* (Sydney: Applied Economics, 2018, https://appliedeconomics.com.au/wp-content/uploads/2021/10/public-economics-principles-and-practice-book-by-peter-abelson.pdf). For an accessible critical approach, see June Sekerka, *The Public Economy in Crisis: A Call for a New Public Economics* (Cham: Springer, 2016).

[19] Richard A Musgrave, *The Theory of Public Finance: A Study in Public Economy* (New York: McGraw-Hill, 1959); Richard A Musgrave and Peggy B Musgrave, *Public Finance in Theory and Practice*, 5th ed (New York: McGraw-Hill, 1989); Richard Musgrave, *Public Finance in a*

The economic analysis of taxes explores how to raise revenue with minimal economic or welfare loss produced by distorting economic incentives in the market. The classic welfare economics approach assumes that a certain level of revenue is required by government and seeks to optimise taxes to raise that revenue in the most efficient and equitable manner. Tax policy also aims to respond to market failure. For example, tax laws may be devised to discourage environmentally damaging activities, or to support innovation that is insufficiently provided in the market. Tax laws create a multiplicity of planning margins that shape the behaviour of individuals and firms in tax systems; the effects may be examined through theoretical and empirical economic analysis.

Law and Accounting

Law is central to taxation in three main ways. First, taxation must be imposed by legislation and not by executive fiat. The rule of law constrains the ability of the sovereign to impose taxation by coercion. This constitutional principle of the tax state ensures the legitimacy of tax rules and protects the legitimacy of the state itself.

It is no mere metaphor to call the law and institutions of taxation and spending the 'fiscal constitution'.[20] The revenue raised by taxation finances the benefit of government through a negotiated political and legal framework. This approach, which incorporates the level of taxes into the framing of the political constitution, contrasts with the framing of the 'problem' of taxation to achieve a given revenue level for a pre-existing state in welfare economics. The taxation law itself – for example, the income tax – even though only a statute, is so fundamental to the state that it may itself be considered quasi-constitutional.

Second, we apply normative theories of law and justice to taxation.[21] These range from a simple matrix of horizontal equity (like should be treated alike) and vertical equity (those with more should pay more), to nuanced theories of distributive justice based on endowment or ability to pay. Scholars of law and society examine how tax law enables or limits individual rights in form and substance, for example by identifying the explicit and implicit

---

Democratic Society. The Foundations of Taxation and Expenditure: Vol III (Northampton MA: Edward Elgar, 2000); Peggy Musgrave, 'Comments on Two Musgravian Concepts' (2008) 32 *Journal of Economics and Finance* 340–7.

[20] Geoffrey Brennan and James M Buchanan, *The Power to Tax: Analytical Foundations of a Fiscal Constitution* (Cambridge, UK: Cambridge University Press, 1980).

[21] There is a wide literature on justice and taxation; for example, Murphy and Nagel, *The Myth of Ownership: Taxes and Justice* (see n 5); Martin O'Neill and Shepley Orr (eds.), *Taxation: Philosophical Perspectives* (Oxford: Oxford University Press, 2018).

sexist or racist discriminatory effects of tax law. The rule of law in taxation seeks to ensure certainty in taxation, procedural fairness, the right to appeal and taxpayer rights.

Third, the tax law of any country is embedded in the wider matrix of the legal system of that country. Tax laws often depend for their meaning on other laws, for example, the laws of corporations, partnerships or trusts; property, contract or family law. The relationship between tax laws and other laws presents one of the largest difficulties in comparing tax systems of different countries, as it requires analysis of the legal framework, culture and relations in those countries.

However, tax law is distinct from the legal system in which it operates. In most mature tax states, whether civil or common law, the tax law is a body of statutory law, combined with judicial decision-making in cases at all levels of the court system and administrative regulations and guidance, which together are voluminous and often highly complex. Increasingly, tax law requires knowledge of international tax treaties, cases and commentaries layered on top of domestic rules and guidance. The interpretation and application of tax rules have become a specialist area of legal practice.[22] Different approaches, for example, purposive or literalist in nature, may produce different results in application of the tax law. One significant challenge for tax law in all countries is how to approach abusive transactions and the application of anti-avoidance rules. Tax avoidance is difficult to define and to distinguish from acceptable tax planning. Courts, administrators, advisors and taxpayers must interpret and apply specific and general anti-avoidance rules, which are on the rise in tax laws around the world.

Tax practice also engages the discipline of accounting, both private and public, and in this it differs from other areas of legal practice. Taxation requires a metric of income, expenditure, profit and loss of the taxpayer. Public accounting of revenues and expenditures, assets and liabilities is necessary for government. Accounting principles may play an important role in the tax law. In some civil law systems, such as Germany, financial accounting is the foundation for determination of taxable profit. In contrast, in common law systems, tax law concepts of income and expenses sit alongside accounting concepts and do not always have a direct relationship with them.[23] Financial accounting principles are likely to dominate the new global approach to taxation of multinational enterprises, which we discuss in Part III of the book.

---

[22] Robert F van Brederode and Richard Krever (eds.), *Legal Interpretation of Tax Law*, 2nd ed (Alphen aan den Rijn, Netherlands: Wolters Kluwer, 2017).

[23] A comparative discussion of tax accounting is in Ault et al, *Comparative Income Taxation* (see n 10).

Disciplines of law and accounting have played significant, and sometimes competing, roles in the practice of tax law.[24] The role of tax accounting grew during the twentieth century; today, the accounting profession dominates the global professional field of tax advising. The well-known global advisory firms have developed a specialist practice of taxation advice and planning with national and international dimensions, which is separate from other forms of accounting practice. They are major players in providing tax advice for businesses around the world. This has led to changes in the tax law profession, as it too establishes global networks to keep up with changes in tax planning. Domestically in many countries, individuals and small businesses rely predominantly on tax accountants and tax agents to manage their tax affairs.

Tax Statistics

The governments of most successful tax states compile and publish aggregate tax data in budget and general statistical publications. Tax statistics are a measure of knowledge of the state about its people, and can tell us a great deal about government itself. Over thousands of years, the great skill of writing was applied 'to record payments of taxes and tributes to kings and rulers, and to keep track of the numbers of tax-payers in censuses'.[25] Piketty observed that:

> Taxation is ... a way of requiring all citizens to contribute to the financing of public expenditures and projects and to distribute the tax burden as fairly as possible; it is also useful for establishing classifications and promoting knowledge.[26]

Tax records of the last two centuries are among the best sources of information about the income, assets and wealth of governments and of people. They provide information about income and wealth distribution and inequality. The World Inequality Project relies on administrative tax statistics with national income statistics and household surveys to map the income of the top 1 per cent in countries around the world.[27]

---

[24] See, e.g. Charles Rembar, 'The Practice of Taxes' (1954) 54 *Columbia Law Review* 333–58 (discussing the role of law and accounting professions in the United States); Albert Lee and Martin Rabenort, 'The Changing Role of the Tax Professional' (2009) 20(8) *International Tax Review* 32–4.

[25] British Museum, 'Support Notes for Tutors. ESOL Workshop: Origins of Writing', www.britishmuseum.org/sites/default/files/2019-11/Origins-of-writing-support-notes-for-teachers_final.pdf, 1, accessed 18 March 2022, observing that some of the earliest surviving written texts from Mesopotamia and Egypt were tax records.

[26] Thomas Piketty, *Capital in the Twenty-First Century*, trans. Arthur Goldhammer (Cambridge, MA: Harvard University Press, 2014), 16.

[27] World Inequality Database, https://wid.world, accessed 16 March 2022.

The OECD collates national tax statistics from its member states and from a growing number of other countries in online statistical databases.[28] Other international institutions including the International Monetary Fund (IMF) collect revenue statistics; however, the OECD has made strenuous efforts to occupy the field of tax statistics and it is pre-eminent in this regard.

The publication of tax statistics enables cross-country comparisons and contributes to the transfer of concepts, ideas and metrics about taxation across countries. Increasingly, governments are compiling and releasing administrative tax data, including confidentialised unit record files about taxpayers to researchers (an example is Denmark) or longitudinal tax data to support research (an example is the Australian Taxation Office longitudinal database of personal tax statistics).[29] These data enable innovative economic research into tax systems, incomes and economic behaviour of individuals and businesses.

The quality of tax statistics has greatly improved in recent decades, but caution is required in doing cross-national, and historical, comparisons. These depend on standardised categories and definitions and on the continued delivery of high-quality data by governments. Even applying standardised definitions, countries or institutions sometimes take different approaches and there are always gaps in tax data. With these cautions in mind, this book draws on tax statistics from the OECD to illustrate and compare some aspects of tax systems between countries and over time.

Tax Structure

Definition of a Tax

This part presents key concepts necessary for understanding tax statistics and debates. These are the definition of a **tax**, the **tax level** of a country and its **tax mix** or **tax structure**.

A commonly accepted definition of a **tax** is a 'compulsory and unrequited payment to general government'.[30] This definition is used for statistical purposes and includes payments to all levels of government (including central, provincial and local government). A tax is 'unrequited' in the sense of not being paid directly for a specific good or service of similar value. A fee or charge, even if paid to a public agency, is not included in this definition of tax.

---

[28] OECD, OECD.Stat, https://stats.oecd.org/, accessed 16 March 2022. Open access charts and data on a wide range of historical and contemporary tax issues are available from Esteban Ortiz-Ospina and Max Roser, 'Taxation', OurWorldInData.org/taxation.

[29] Australian Taxation Office, 'A-Life (ATO Longitudinal Information Files)' (2020), https://alife-research.app/info/overview, accessed 16 March 2022.

[30] OECD, 'Revenue Statistics – Tax Structures', www.oecd.org/ctp/tax-policy/revenue-statistics-tax-structures.htm, box 1.1, accessed 16 March 2022.

A tax is not a fine or penalty that, although compulsory, is levied as punishment for a specific act. This statistical definition of a 'tax' therefore implicitly incorporates the central element of legality of taxation: its imposition by a valid taxation law and its enforceability by the government under that law.

Tax Level

The **tax level** of a government is total tax revenue as a share of gross domestic product (GDP). Total tax revenue includes taxes paid to all levels of government. This annual statistical measure is sometimes called a measure of the 'tax burden' in a country.[31] The tax level is measured on a nominal basis, in respect of both revenue and GDP. A country's GDP measures the market value of goods and services produced using prices determined from standardised national accounts and income surveys. This measure has many limitations that are well documented.[32] Most importantly, it ignores the 'non-market' or household economy and the environmental impact of economic activity. Bearing in mind its limitations, the tax level provides information about the size of the state in the economy and enables comparisons over time and with other countries. The full size of the state is indicated by its expenditures as a share of GDP, financed by a combination of taxes, debt and other revenue sources.

The tax and expenditures levels of OECD member countries are shown in Figure 1.1. Expenditures range from 24 per cent of GDP in Ireland to 55 per cent of GDP in France. Taxes range from 16 per cent of GDP in Mexico to 45 per cent of GDP in France. While taxes provide most government finance in successful tax states, the difference is made up by other revenues (in most OECD countries, non-tax revenues raise from 5 to 10 per cent of GDP) and by government debt. Norway is exceptional in raising nearly one fifth of GDP from non-tax revenues: this is the return to the budget from the Government Pension Fund, established in the 1990s with revenues from North Sea oil and now the largest sovereign wealth fund in the world.[33]

---

[31] Evans et al, *Comparative Taxation* (see n 10), 9.
[32] The indicator and measurement of GDP ignores non-market household production such as infant breastfeeding, childcare, or food preparation; misses many activities in the digital economy, such as social media; and fails to measure economic costs arising from destruction of infrastructure, environmental degradation and depletion of natural resources. See, e.g. Joseph E Stiglitz, Amartya Sen and Jean-Paul Fitoussi, *The Measurement of Economic Performance and Social Progress Revisited: Reflections and Overview* (Paris: French Observatory of Economic Conditions, Economics Research Center, 2009), http://spire.sciencespo.fr/hdl:/2441/5l6uh8ogmqildh●9h4687h53k/resources/wp2009-33.pdf.
[33] Norges Bank Investment Management, http://nbim.no/en/, accessed 16 March 2022.

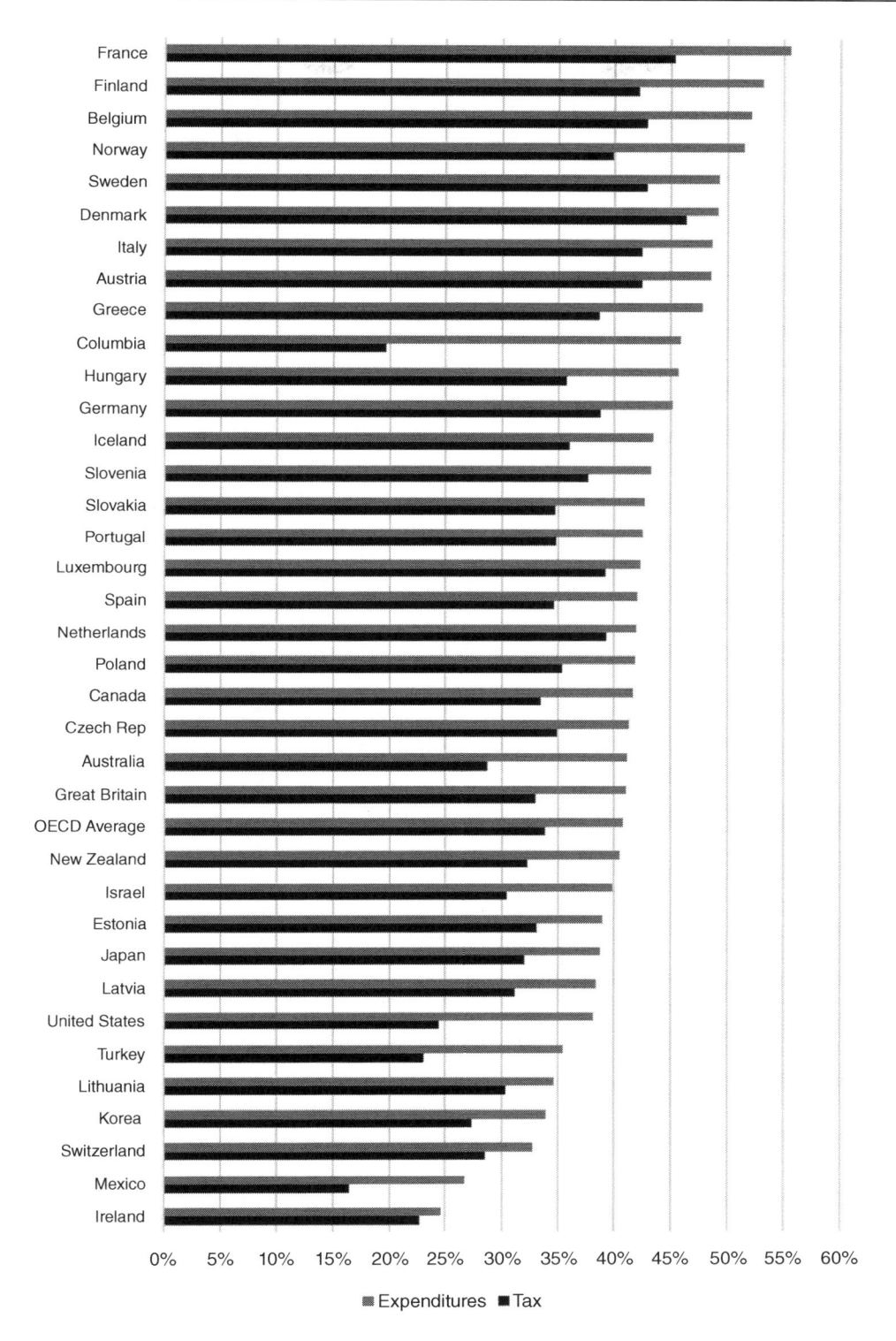

Figure 1.1 Tax and expenditure as a share of GDP, OECD countries, 2019
Sources: OECD Data, Tax Revenue, https://data.oecd.org/tax/tax-revenue.htm; OECD, 'Government at a Glance' (2019) StatLink https://doi.org/10.1787/888934257033.

A government's tax level will fluctuate with the business cycle, policy changes and economic factors such as commodity prices or unemployment. It will change more slowly in response to long-term economic growth and demographic trends. If GDP grows strongly but tax revenues do not grow as fast, the tax level will decline, even though tax revenues may have increased.

A tax that grows with, or faster than, the economy is called a growth or buoyant tax, which is understandably attractive to governments seeking a stable revenue stream.[34] For example, a tax on the sale of goods and services may grow rapidly if consumption is rising; or a tax on wages will grow if wages are increasing faster than economic growth. This is sometimes described as improved 'tax effort'. If tax revenues grow more rapidly than the economy, the tax level will rise. Because tax laws are applied to nominal income or consumption, tax revenues also increase with inflation.

The COVID-19 pandemic had a significant negative effect on tax revenues in 2020 and 2021, due to the sharp contraction in economic activity. Business losses and the consequential tax impact are likely to be felt for some years after economic responses to the pandemic are lifted.

Tax Mix

The **tax mix** or **tax structure** of a government is the combination of different taxes and their relative importance as a share of tax revenue. The OECD measures a country's tax structure by the share of major taxes in GDP and in total taxes.[35] This reveals the main types of taxation in successful tax states to be personal and corporate income tax, social security tax, a broad-based consumption tax and excises on fuel, alcohol, tobacco and some other specific goods, and property taxes. Some tax states also levy inheritance or wealth taxes. The tax mix of successful tax states has been relatively stable over the past few decades. There are also significant, and stable, differences between country tax structures.

To illustrate, the tax mix of selected OECD countries is shown in Figure 1.2, presenting the major taxes as a share of GDP, and Figure 1.3, presenting the major taxes as a share of total tax revenues. The income tax and social security tax together comprise more than half of the tax revenues of most OECD countries, with the next largest category being consumption taxes on goods

---

[34] Vincent Belinga, Dora Benedek, Ruud A de Mooij and John Norregaard, *Tax Buoyancy in OECD Countries* IMF Working Paper No 14/110 (Washington, DC: International Monetary Fund, 2014).

[35] OECD, 'Revenue Statistics – Tax Structures' (see n 30).

Tax Structure

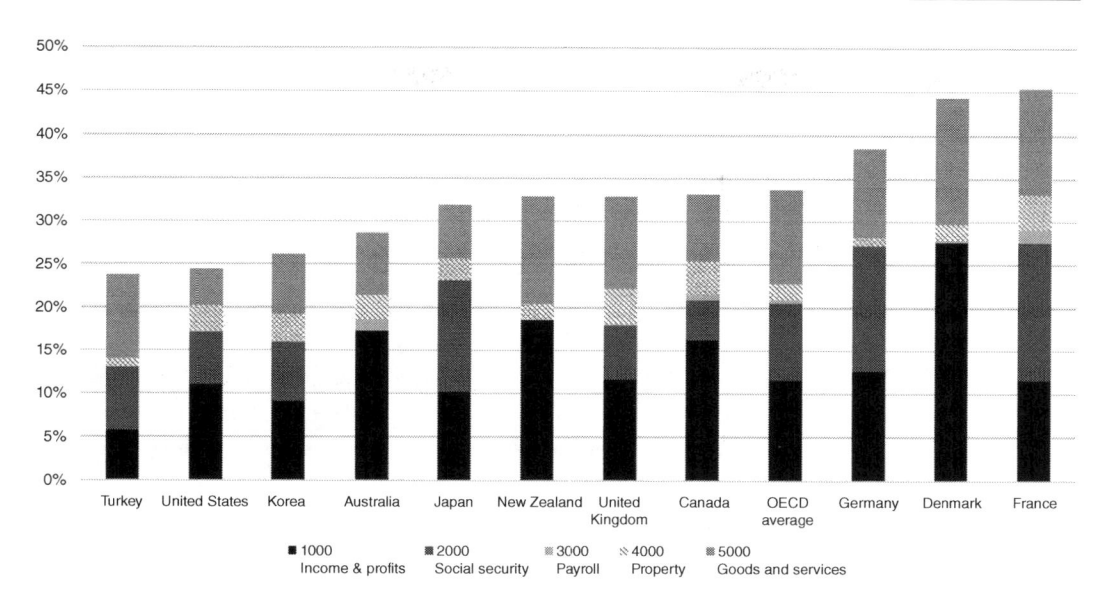

Figure 1.2 Tax mix of selected OECD countries, share of GDP, 2018
Source: OECD, Revenue Statistics 2020, Table 3.3, www.oecd-ilibrary.org/taxation/revenue-statistics-2020_8625f8e5-en.

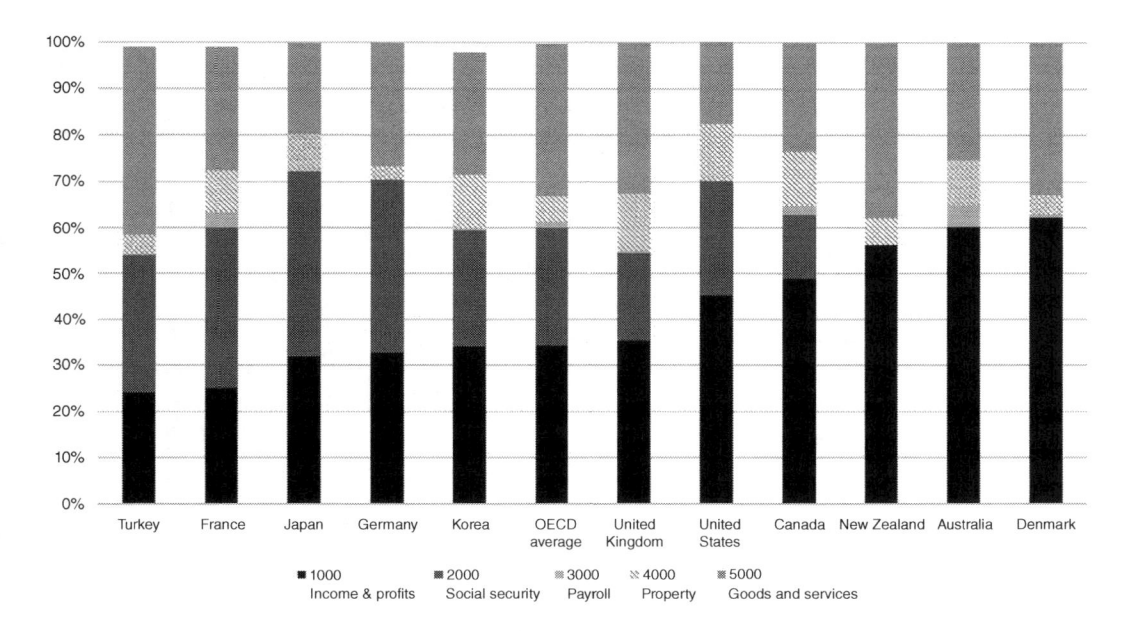

Figure 1.3 Tax mix of selected OECD countries, share of total taxation, 2018
Source: Author Chart from OECD, Revenue Statistics 2020, Table 3.4, www.oecd-ilibrary.org/taxation/revenue-statistics-2020_8625f8e5-en.

and services. Property taxes make up a much smaller proportion of tax collected, although they are important in the United States, UK, France and Canada.

Tax Concepts

Elements of a Tax System

This section introduces the concept of the **tax base** and **tax incidence**, **direct and indirect taxes**, the **tax unit** and **tax rates**.

The **tax base** refers to the underlying economic factors or uses that are subject to taxation. Economists define the tax base by reference to **factors** of production in the economy: labour, capital and land, or by **uses** of income or consumption. The tax base may also refer to the population of taxpayers who are registered or identified in the system. The classification of types of taxation refers to concepts of income, consumption and wealth or specific transactions or activities that are subject to tax. The statistics presented here show that successful tax states do not rely only on one kind of taxation but on a mix of taxes. This likely increases the complexity of tax systems, but it also enables improved enforcement and better coverage of the economic transactions that make up the tax base.

There is a wide literature on tax policy and reform that advocates an ideal tax system and suggests that there is a 'right' answer to the question of the tax base that may be arrived at scientifically. For example, there may be a view that the ideal tax base comprises income, consumption or land. Contemporary tax theory accepts that no system is ideal and instead aims to optimise tax systems in a 'second-best' world for efficiency and equity (as explained in Chapter 4). Yet even this theoretical 'optimising' exercise may be insufficiently pragmatic as an approach to tax reform, which is fundamentally political and legal in nature.

From a legal perspective, Paul McDaniel observed that the designer of a tax must have the answers to six fundamental questions in order to establish the elements of the tax system enacted in law:[36]

1. *Tax base:* What is the tax base that the statute is to embody and how is it defined?
2. *Tax rate:* What rates of tax are to be applied to that base?
3. *Timing:* How often is the tax to be imposed (what is the tax period)?
4. *Tax unit:* What is the taxable unit (e.g. individual, family)?

---

[36] Paul McDaniel, 'Comments' in Joseph Pechman (ed.), *What Should Be Taxed: Income or Expenditure?* (Washington, DC: Brookings Institution, 1980), 282–3.

5. *Intermediaries:* How are firms, or legal intermediary entities such as corporations, trusts, pension funds, mutual associations or partnerships, to be treated?
6. *Jurisdiction:* What are the rules of jurisdiction? How is the tax to be applied to taxpayers who engage in activities across national borders?

In relation to these fundamental elements, McDaniel explained:

> There is little or nothing in tax law theory as such – nor, I should add, in tax economics or accounting – that provides the correct answers to these questions. They must be answered by political leaders drawing upon the broad social, philosophical, economic, jurisprudential, and historical perspectives of the society. What the tax expert can do is supply the policymaker with a variety of possible solutions to each problem and an analysis for the equity, economic, and administrative implications of each solution. Although it is sometimes implied to the contrary, the selection of a particular tax base (question 1) does not dictate the answers to the remaining questions; in fact, that selection may make it more difficult to solve some of them.[37]

Tax reform is an outcome of negotiation of political interests, layered with the development and transfer of tax policy ideas between tax experts and bureaucrats in a dynamic and iterative process of law making.[38] Modern tax reform processes usually engage in substantial public consultation, in contrast to earlier decades when 'the making of tax policy was often shrouded in secrecy'.[39] For a mass tax, such as the personal income tax, value added tax (VAT) or goods and services tax (GST), the politics of tax reform are manifest in widespread and heated public debate. For more specialised tax reforms, tax consultation takes place through relatively closed networks of tax professionals, corporate or niche taxpayers and administrative experts.

Tax Incidence

A fundamental question for tax policy is who bears the economic **incidence** or burden of taxation. Ultimately, individuals – real people – must bear the burden of taxation.

The **legal incidence** of a tax is on the defined **tax unit** or legal taxpayer who is liable to pay the tax to the government. The legal taxpayer may differ from

---

[37] Ibid., 283.
[38] Sven Steinmo, 'The Evolution of Policy Ideas: Tax Policy in the 20th Century' (2003) 5(2) *British Journal of Politics and International Relations* 206–36; Holger Nehring and Florian Schui (eds.), *Global Debates about Taxation* (London: Palgrave Macmillan, 2007). For analysis of pathways of influence beyond developed tax states, see Miranda Stewart, 'Global Trajectories of Tax Reform: The Discourse of Tax Reform in Developing and Transition Countries' (2003) *Harvard International Law Journal* 44(1) 139.
[39] Brian J Arnold, 'The Process of Tax Policy Formulation in Australia, Canada and New Zealand' (1990) 7 *Australian Tax Forum* 379–94, 393.

the person who bears the **economic incidence** of the tax paid. The incidence of a tax may be **shifted** from one person to another, or by changing market behaviour, the burden may be shifted more broadly in the market. The extent of shifting of tax incidence depends on the **elasticity** of economic response to the tax; we return to this concept in Chapter 4.

A **direct tax** is assumed to levy both the legal and economic burden directly on the ultimate taxpayer, the most obvious example being the personal income tax. Even direct taxes are very often collected and remitted by an intermediary, such as by wage withholding from an employer. Nonetheless, it is generally accepted that the economic burden is borne by the individual. A land tax is usually considered to be borne by the landowner. A tax on the transfer of property is paid by one party, usually the buyer, but may have quite unclear incidence as between the seller and buyer of property.

A direct tax imposed on a **tax unit** that is a legal construct cannot be borne directly by that tax unit. For example, income tax levied on a **joint unit** defined as a married 'couple' must be borne, in some ratio, by each individual member of the couple. It may commonly be the case that the individuals in a 'couple' bear the tax levied on the joint unit equally; but this is unlikely to be true in all, or even most, cases. This is because the tax burden on a couple unit is shifted between the individuals in the couple through intra-household bargaining. We discuss the equity and efficiency implications of a joint unit in Chapter 5.

The legal incidence of the **corporate income tax** falls on the taxpayer defined as the corporation, but a corporation is a legal fiction, not a real person. Ultimately, the burden of corporate tax must be shifted to individuals by reducing the return to the owners of capital, or through wages or prices in the economy. Who bears the corporate tax is one of the most debated issues in tax policy; we return to this question in Chapter 7.

An **indirect tax**, such as a tariff, excise or broad-based VAT, is always paid by an intermediary (the vendor, or supplier in a business supply chain). The economic burden of this indirect tax is assumed to be shifted in the price to the ultimate consumer of the goods or services. For example, VAT on a restaurant meal is paid to the tax authority by the restaurant owner but it is assumed to be borne by the customer in the price they pay for the meal. Whether the shifting occurs will depend on the price charged by the restaurant owner to the customer. The behaviour of both restaurant owner and customer may also be responsive to other factors, such as local competition or the opportunity for fraud.

Public economists seek to analyse the incidence of taxation and expenditure to understand where the burdens and benefits are distributed in society.[40] An even broader way to conceive of the tax burden might require us to

---

[40] See, e.g. Musgrave and Musgrave, *Public Finance* (1989), chapter 14 (see n 19).

examine who benefits from government as a whole. Successful tax states embed governments with markets, so that an individual's pre-tax income is a function of the entire complex of regulatory processes and institutions of the state. Viewed in this way, the tax law performs a fundamental role in demarcating what may be privately owned or consumed by an individual (net of taxation) and what is shared in the collective, through the state (by taxation and expenditure).[41] We return to the implications of this approach for tax justice in Chapter 4.

Types of Taxation

Income Tax

The modern income tax levied on individuals and corporations was instituted in successful tax states in the early twentieth century, although it is based on antecedents dating back centuries. Today the income tax remains of central importance, albeit with wide variation as shown in Figures 1.2 and 1.3. For example, in 2018 the income tax raised about 6 per cent of GDP (24 per cent of total taxes) in Turkey, 18 per cent of GDP (56 per cent of total taxes) in New Zealand and 27 per cent of GDP (62 per cent of total taxes) in Denmark. Many governments with a lower reliance on income tax are newer OECD member states. France is an exception, being a state with a high tax level that relies more heavily on social security tax and consumption taxes, primarily the VAT, than on the income tax.

There is debate about whether reliance on income tax by tax states is growing or declining. In the 50 years from 1965 to 2017, 13 OECD member states increased the share of personal income tax in total taxation, while 10 decreased the share of personal income tax.[42] Each of Sweden, Norway and the Netherlands saw a dramatic change in share of the income tax in total taxes during this period. In Sweden, personal income tax revenue declined from 48.7 per cent of total taxes in 1965 to 28 per cent of total taxes in 2017. However, these trends need to be interpreted with caution. A closer look at the data shows that the Swedish tax system expanded dramatically during this period and in fact, income tax revenues remained steady. Revenues from other taxes, especially VAT, grew significantly and this funded the growth in government from 1965 onwards.

The **economic concept of income** as a tax base is usually called **comprehensive income**.[43] Comprehensive income is equal to all consumption plus

---

[41] Murphy and Nagel, *The Myth of Ownership* (see n 5).
[42] OECD, 'OECD Tax Statistics – Comparative Tables 1965–2018', https://doi.org/10.1787/data-00262-en.
[43] Henry C Simons, *Personal Income Taxation: The Definition of Income as a Problem of Fiscal Policy* (Chicago: University of Chicago Press, 1938). Sometimes known as the Schanz-Haig-Simons concept of income.

(or minus) the change in net wealth of the taxpayer, so the comprehensive income tax applies to net economic gain that accrues to a taxpayer in a period (such as one year), regardless of source or cause. This **uses** concept of income reflects what an individual can buy through consumption or additions to wealth.[44]

The economic concept of income is commonly expressed in the following relation:

$$Y = C + \Delta W$$

where: Y = income, C = consumption and ΔW = the change in net wealth (positive or negative).

The income tax in the real world has many differences from the ideal comprehensive income tax.[45] Some of the differences are summarised in Box 1.1 and we return to these issues later in the book.

Box 1.1 Comprehensive income compared to the 'real' income tax

1. Comprehensive income includes economic income adjusted for inflation. In contrast, real income taxes apply to nominal income and are rarely, and only partially, adjusted for inflation. If inflation is low, this is not of major policy importance, but even a small 'fiscal drag' or 'bracket creep' produced by inflation enables automatic buoyancy of tax revenues and increases the tax take (see further Chapter 5). If inflation is high, nominal income may be much higher than real income. This can lead to significant unfairness and instability in the income tax system.

2. A comprehensive income tax applies to net economic gain whether or not it is converted to monetary form. This is sometimes called an 'accrual' tax system. Real income taxes generally operate on a 'realisation' basis, taxing a gain or recognising a loss only when it is derived in a transaction such as the sale of the asset.

3. A comprehensive income tax applies to imputed or in-kind benefits, such as the benefit derived from living in a home you own, or from household-provided or non-market services such as childcare, housework or home-grown food. Real income taxes usually do not tax these 'imputed' benefits, although historically, imputed rent from home ownership was included in the tax base.

4. A comprehensive income tax applies the same marginal tax rate structure to income of all sources and kinds. Real income taxes often tax different kinds of income or gain at different rates. It is common for real

---

[44] David Bradford, *Untangling the Income Tax* (Cambridge, MA: Harvard University Press, 1986), 15.
[45] The same applies, of course, to all taxes, as eloquently demonstrated for the VAT by Kathryn A James, *The Rise of the Value-Added Tax* (New York: Oxford University Press, 2015).

income taxes to apply a lower tax rate to capital income than to labour income. This has the effect of shifting the income tax base towards a consumption tax by reducing taxation on the change in net wealth.

5. In a comprehensive income tax, expenses in gaining assessable income are deductible but expenses for personal consumption are not deductible. This important distinction also applies in real income taxes but the line between a personal expense and an expense incurred for deriving income may be difficult to draw. For example, is the cost of childcare or commuting a work or a personal expense? Real income tax laws often respond to this challenge by drawing somewhat arbitrary lines or placing limits on deductible expenses.

6. A comprehensive income tax requires a deduction for the decline in value of capital assets such as plant and equipment over their economic life. This also applies in real income taxes; however, identifying a depreciable asset, measuring its economic life and calculating how rapidly its cost should be depreciated is difficult. The depreciation deduction in real income taxes is often modified to make it more generous, permitting write-off faster than the life of the asset, or 'expensing' or immediate deduction of the cost of business assets. This shifts the base towards a consumption tax by lowering the tax on investment.

Social Security Tax

Social security tax or social insurance contributions fund large portions of the welfare state in some countries, especially unemployment benefits and old age pensions. Social security taxes are usually contributed by both the employer and the employee based on a fraction of the employee wage, collected from the employer by withholding from wages. In many countries, social security taxes are paid into a fund that is directly hypothecated to social security benefits. This may help 'to make the programs (and the taxes) more palatable to citizens who might object to receiving (or paying for) welfare'.[46]

The economic incidence of social security taxes is usually assumed to be on the employee, although this may not always be the case. From the employee's perspective, social security taxes are similar to income tax on wages, but are usually levied on a 'gross' not a 'net' basis, with no deductions allowed and at a flat rate. In some countries, social security taxes are applied on wages up to a ceiling.

Figure 1.3 shows that social security taxes in many OECD member states comprise as much as 40 per cent of tax revenues. In Germany, France and Japan, social security taxes raise more revenue than the income tax. In contrast, Australia, Denmark and New Zealand do not levy social security

---

[46] B Guy Peters, *The Politics of Taxation: A Comparative Perspective* (Cambridge, MA: Blackwell, 1991), 32.

taxes. These countries rely more heavily on the income tax and also provide a regulated system of private saving for retirement.

Social security contributions to government funds are included as a tax in OECD statistics. However, contributions to private funds, which occur in many countries, are excluded. For example, Australia has a policy of compulsory private superannuation instead of a social security tax. As superannuation contributions do not go into a government fund, they are not treated as a tax in OECD statistics.[47]

Consumption Tax

A **consumption tax** is an indirect tax that is levied on the sale, or supply, of goods or services but is intended to be borne by the ultimate consumer of the good or service. Specific taxes on consumption, such as excises on specific goods like salt, or trade taxes such as import and export duties or tariffs, have existed for thousands of years. Historic sumptuary taxes on luxury goods are a form of consumption tax.

Schumpeter suggested in 1917 that the era of income tax was over; he argued that it had been suited to the 'liberal' nineteenth century but that it should be replaced in the twentieth century by a consumption tax that would support growing industrialised economies based on mass consumption.[48] During the twentieth century, governments did indeed begin to levy broad-based consumption taxes. With hindsight, Schumpeter was wrong about the demise of the income tax but he was right in predicting the rise of consumption taxes in successful tax states. However, Figure 1.3 reveals significant diversity between countries. Consumption tax revenues range from a low of 17 per cent of taxes in the United States to a high of 40 per cent of taxes in Turkey.

The most striking policy development since the mid-twentieth century has been the widespread adoption of a specific type of broad-based consumption tax, the VAT (or GST). These broad-based consumption taxes supported the expansion of the tax state (and its revenues). The VAT is applied in all member countries of the European Union and has spread to most countries worldwide. The United States remains the only OECD member that does not impose a VAT at the national or state level.

The VAT is a multistage tax applied to the supply of goods and services by business enterprises at each stage of the chain from original producer to ultimate consumer. The consumers themselves have no obligation to pay the tax, which is remitted by the enterprises through the supply chain. For each

---

[47] OECD, 'Revenue Statistics' (see n 30), box 1.1. The International Monetary Fund excludes social security contributions from its statistical definition of a 'tax', producing significantly lower measures of total taxation: see data.imf.org.
[48] Schumpeter, 'The Crisis of the Tax State' (see n 1).

registered supplier, a tax credit is allowed for VAT paid on business inputs. This means that the net value added is taxable for enterprises that are in the business of supplying the goods or services. The final consumer is not an enterprise and is not eligible for an input credit. Assuming the tax is passed on in the price of the good or service, the final consumer bears the tax. The VAT is applied to a wide range of goods and services at a single flat rate, although variable rates and exemptions also apply in most countries. There is substantial variation in base, rates and revenues of VATs in different countries.[49]

The ideal consumption tax base has a close relationship to the comprehensive income tax. It can be expressed by modifying the definition of comprehensive income as follows:

$$C = Y - \Delta W$$

where: C = consumption, Y = income and ΔW = the change in net wealth (positive or negative).

The VAT is equivalent to an ideal consumption tax only if rather strict conditions are satisfied: it must tax all goods and services consumed and the incidence of this indirect tax must be ultimately borne by the consumer through price shifting through the supply chain.[50] The first condition is not satisfied in any tax state, although New Zealand comes close. The second may often be true but depends on the elasticity of demand for the good or service that is supplied.

The equation defining comprehensive income shows that in theory, a consumption tax could be achieved by deducting savings and investment from the comprehensive income tax base. If a single flat tax rate is imposed, the ideal consumption tax is economically equivalent to an income tax levied on wages where the wages are consumed (not saved). Imagine an individual who earns a wage and spends it all immediately on rent, food and living costs. For this individual, a 20 per cent income tax levied on their wage is equivalent to a 20 per cent consumption tax levied on their consumption. On the other hand, if an individual earns a wage and then saves all of it, the wage and the return to saving would be subject to income taxation but not to consumption taxation (until consumed in future). A reduced tax rate on the return to saving and expensing of the cost of business assets also shifts the income tax towards a consumption tax, as explained in Box 1.1. We return to these issues concerning the tax base in Chapters 6 and 7.

---

[49] OECD, *Consumption Tax Trends 2020* (Paris: OECD, 2020), www.oecd-ilibrary.org/taxation/consumption-tax-trends-2020_152def2d-en; Rita de la Feria (ed.), *VAT Exemptions: Consequences and Design Alternatives* (Alphen aan den Rijn, Netherlands: Wolters Kluwer, 2013).

[50] Similarly to the income tax, numerous differences exist between the 'real world' VAT or GST and the ideal consumption tax: James, *The Rise of the Value-Added Tax* (see n 45).

Wealth, Property and Land Taxes

Wealth, property and land taxes apply to the stock of wealth or assets, defined and valued at a point in time, in contrast to income or consumption, which are flows. Taxes on wealth or assets have a long history in tax systems but today they comprise a relatively small share of·tax collected in successful tax states. The most important component by share of tax is property taxation, as shown in Figure 1.3. A wealth transfer tax such as estate, inheritance or gift tax may be levied at the time of a transfer of assets – for example, a bequest on death or the transfer of land. There is renewed interest today in wealth as a tax base, in the context of increasing wealth and income inequality in many countries. We return to this in Chapter 6.

Tax Rates

The **tax rate** is the proportion of the measured tax base that must be remitted as taxation (for example, 10 per cent of the purchase price of a good or service). A tax could be designed as a lump-sum tax, which requires each taxpayer to pay an identical amount (for example, $100 per head). This is known as a poll or head tax. Fees or charges for some services, such as vehicle registration or garbage collection, may be designed in this way. Usually, a tax will have a single rate or multiple rates based on thresholds or levels of income or consumption.

Tax rates may be **proportional**, **progressive** or **regressive**. In general, we describe a tax as **progressive** or **regressive** by comparing the tax paid by an individual with the income of the individual. Alternatively, we could compare the tax paid to the consumption or wealth of the individual.[51]

Figure 1.4 shows a stylised representation of progressive, proportional and regressive tax rates. A **proportional** or **flat tax** collects a constant percentage of income in tax for all taxpayers. As income rises, the quantum of tax paid rises, but the proportion of income paid in tax does not.

A **progressive tax** is a tax where the **average tax rate** increases as the taxpayer's income increases. The average tax rate measures the total amount of tax paid as a percentage of income. A tax may be progressive if people with higher incomes pay a higher tax rate (e.g. the personal income tax).

A **regressive tax** is the opposite, where the average tax rate, or amount of tax paid as a percentage of income, decreases as income increases. While a lump-sum tax is equal in the sense that each taxpayer pays exactly the same amount, it is regressive because the amount of tax paid as a percentage of income decreases as income increases.

---

[51] See further Peter Varela, *What Are Progressive and Regressive Taxes?* TTPI Policy Brief 2/2016 (Canberra: Tax and Transfer Policy Institute, Australian National University, 2016).

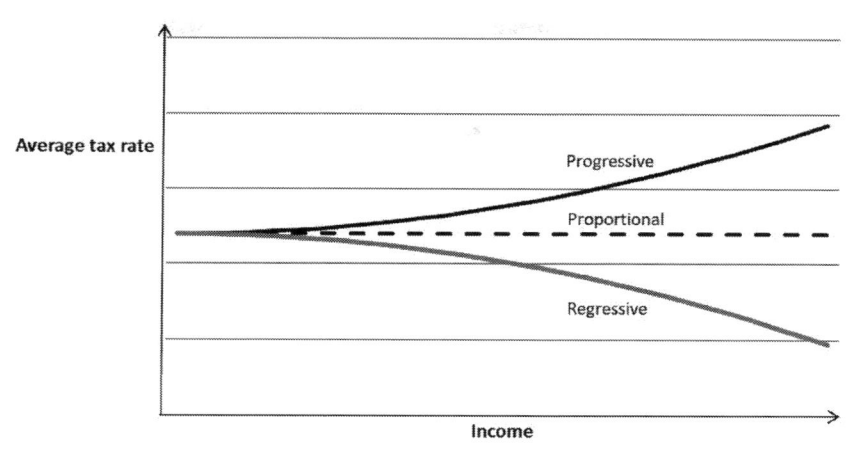

Figure 1.4 Progressive, proportional and regressive tax rates
Source: Peter Varela, 'What Are Progressive and Regressive Taxes?' TTPI Policy Brief 3/2016 (Canberra: Tax and Transfer Policy Institute, Australian National University, 2016), Figure 1.

The **marginal tax rate** in a **progressive income tax** is the rate on the 'next' dollar of income. In most income tax laws, progressivity is achieved by stepped increases in the tax rate structure, where the marginal tax rate increases as income reaches each threshold. An example of progressive income tax rate structures is in Chapter 5, Figure 5.1.

A tax may be progressive where it is levied on a base that is unequally distributed between rich and poor, even if it applies a flat (proportional) rate. This is because the tax by its nature falls on those who have income or assets, compared to those who do not. For example, a land tax falls on the owner of land.

A broad-based consumption tax such as a VAT, levied at a proportional rate on all consumption, is regressive with respect to income. The reason is that higher income individuals save more, and consume less, of their income and savings are not taxed in a consumption tax.

2

Tax and Government

That sure, steady, and permanent revenue which can alone give security and dignity to government.

Adam Smith, *Wealth of Nations*

History of Tax and Government

Origins and Theory of the Tax State

The long history of taxation in empires, kingdoms and nations has been studied by legal, economic and political historians.[1] The history of the 'tax state', or a government that is dependent on the power and capacity to tax, is much shorter – at most, about 250 years. A 'tax state' is established when a sovereign is able to raise sufficient tax revenues to consolidate, stabilise and centralise government based on this source of finance.[2]

Economic historians generally agree that Great Britain was the first 'tax state', identified as reaching this status by the mid-eighteenth century, based

---

[1] Joel Slemrod and Michael Keen, *Rebellion, Rascals and Revenue: Tax Follies and Wisdom through the Ages* (Princeton, NJ: Princeton University Press, 2021); Denis P O'Brien (ed.), *The History of Taxation*, 8 vols. (Brookfield, VT: Pickering & Chatto, 1999); David F Burg, *A World History of Tax Rebellions: An Encyclopedia of Tax Rebels, Revolts, and Riots from Antiquity to the Present* (New York: Routledge, 2004); Andrew Monson and Walter Scheidel (eds.), *Fiscal Regimes and the Political Economy of Premodern States* (New York: Cambridge University Press, 2015); Steven A Bank, Kirk J Stark and Joseph J Thorndike, *War and Taxes* (Washington, DC: Urban Institute Press, 2008); and the Cambridge series, Studies in the History of Tax Law (Hart Publishing) including Miranda Stewart, 'The Tax State, Benefit and Legitimacy' in Paul Harris and Dominic de Cogan (eds.), *Studies in the History of Tax Law: Vol 7* (London: Hart Publishing, 2015) 483–515.

[2] Wenkai He, *Path toward the Modern Fiscal State* (Cambridge, MA: Harvard University Press, 2013); Bartolome Yun-Casalilla, Patrick O'Brien and Francisco Comín (eds.), *The Rise of Fiscal States: A Global History* (Cambridge, UK: Cambridge University Press, 2012); Ajay K Mehrotra, *Making the Modern American Fiscal State: Law, Politics, and the Rise of Progressive Taxation, 1877–1929* (New York: Cambridge University Press, 2013); Isaac William Martin, Ajay Mehrotra and Martin Prasad, *The New Fiscal Sociology: Taxation in Comparative and Historical Perspective* (New York: Cambridge University Press, 2009); Marc Leroy, *Taxation, the State and Society: The Fiscal Sociology of Interventionist Democracy. Public Action: Vol 7* (Brussels: PIE Peter Lang, 2011; trans. from the French edition, 2010).

on evidence that the British crown had by then established a reasonably reliable revenue stream through direct and indirect taxes on land, trade and goods. This development may have occurred in Japan a century later, between 1868 and 1880,[3] while in other countries, including Germany, Sweden and France, it has been suggested that the state financed by taxation was consolidated towards the end of the nineteenth century. By 1918, as explained in Chapter 1, Schumpeter identified the political and economic formation of the 'tax state' as a more general phenomenon.

As governments gradually came to depend on taxation for financing the state, the theory of taxation also evolved. Adam Smith, who lived and worked during the period when the 'tax state' of Great Britain was being established, was the first political economist to pay attention to the detailed policy and design of taxation. Adam Smith is most famous for the idea of the 'invisible hand' of the market, so it may surprise some that he was a strong advocate of taxes to finance government.

Smith analysed taxation in the context of his theory of political economy, described in *The Wealth of Nations* as a legislator's or statesman's science that aimed 'first, to provide a plentiful revenue or subsistence for the people, or more properly to enable them to provide such a revenue or subsistence for themselves; and secondly, to supply the state or commonwealth with a revenue sufficient for the public services'.[4] Observing that the state had long been financed from various sources, Smith concluded that only taxes could provide the 'sure, steady and permanent' revenue that the state required. None of the other sources of revenue, including tribute from conquered lands and colonies; revenues from the 'king's domain' of land or assets; seigniorage from the currency;[5] and debt, were suitable to finance modern government in the market economy. Debt was too risky, seigniorage was inadequate and the 'king's domain' would be better off in private hands – consistent with Smith's view of the importance of the market.[6]

As taxation must fund government, Smith gave the principles and practice of taxation close attention. His lengthy discussion in the *Wealth of Nations* reveals a sophisticated understanding of tax law, policy and administration, derived partly from theories of government, justice and the economy and partly from empirical observation of how taxes operated in practice. Smith paid attention to the impact of taxation on the choices of taxpayers about

---

[3] He, *Paths toward the Modern Fiscal State* (see n 2).
[4] Adam Smith, *An Inquiry into the Nature and Causes of Wealth of Nations* (London: Methuan, first published 1776, compilation by Edward Cannan, 1904, of 5th ed, 1789), www.econlib.org/library/Smith/smWN.html, Book IV, 'Of Systems of Political Economy', Introduction.
[5] The revenue obtained from the issue of money: Martin Klein and Manfred JM Neumann, 'Seigniorage: What Is It and Who Gets It?' (1990) 126(2) *Weltwirtschaftliches Archiv* 205–21 https://doi.org/10.1007/BF02706356.
[6] Smith, *Wealth of Nations* (see n 4), Book V, Chapter II, Part I, 'Of the Funds or Sources of Revenue Which May Peculiarly Belong to the Sovereign or Commonwealth'.

work, entrepreneurship and savings and to the need for effective tax laws and administration. He discussed the unpopularity of tax collectors and the goal of minimising inconvenience in tax compliance. Smith developed four fundamental Maxims of equality, certainty, simplicity and efficiency of taxation that remain influential to this day. We return to discuss these Maxims in Chapter 4.

Debt, Taxes and the Rise of the Citizen-Taxpayer

The development of the 'tax state' laid the foundation for a new identity – that of a 'taxpayer'. The taxpayer had an explicit and legitimate monetary investment in the state and sought and obtained a voice in its governance. To understand the rise of the 'taxpayer' as the tax state evolved, we need first to consider the relationship between taxes and debt, and the privileged status of the creditor who lends money to the state, historically and today.

Sovereigns have relied on debt to finance government for thousands of years.[7] Even in ancient times, sovereign debt was often linked to taxation. Margaret Levi discusses the example of tax farming in the Roman Empire, in which tax collection was contracted or 'farmed out' to subsidiary rulers or private agents. Tax farming was 'as much a banking as a taxing system'; the tax farmers gave rulers 'a loan secured by the revenues they then are authorized to collect from taxpayers', keeping an interest charge as well as a commission on tax collected.[8]

Medieval Italian city states issued bonds that merchant citizens were required to purchase. This compulsory loan to the state was made in exchange for a promise of regular annual interest. This enabled these government 'bonds' to become negotiable, facilitating a market in government debt.[9] This innovation spread across Europe and government bonds were increasingly dispersed among the merchant classes. One result was that 'the commercial classes in those mercantile republics that pioneered these new forms of financing did end up seeing themselves as owning the government'.[10] Not surprisingly, governments often acted in their interest, producing in the words of John Kenneth Galbraith a 'close, even intimate, association between the state authority and the merchant interest'.[11]

The governors of the European city states themselves negotiated a fiscal bargain with the kings and emperors who lorded over them. They offered wealth and a certain tax return while in exchange seeking to protect their mercantile citizens from arbitrary and burdensome taxation. The

---

[7] David Graeber, *Debt: The First 5,000 Years* (Brooklyn, NY: Melville House Printing, 2011).
[8] Margaret Levi, *Cf Rule and Revenue* (Berkeley, CA: University of California Press, 1989), 77.
[9] Graeber, *Debt* (see n 7), 338.
[10] Ibid., 339.
[11] John Kenneth Galbraith, *A History of Economics: The Past as Present* (London: Penguin, 1987), 36.

establishment of clearly defined and certain taxes became increasingly important in the financial relations between cities and their sovereigns. For example, in medieval France:

> Towns were granted specific protections, including better taxation arrangements – they were more institutionalised and regular, fitting the interests of burghers [who] ... formed communes, which were sworn associations of equals; taxes were increasingly paid by the town as a whole, and burghers began to negotiate for the right to self-assessment.[12]

The taxpaying burghers voted in assemblies in their cities concerning the election of officials and the introduction of new laws. They sought to enshrine their rights and liberties with respect to the sovereign on 'the principle that citizens' obligations were to be set in advance and that citizens could not be taxed on whatever else they might have gained beyond those specific obligations'.[13]

These 'citizen-lenders' and 'citizen-taxpayers' in the newly powerful cities presaged the citizens of the nation state. At the same time, a symbiotic relationship evolved between debt and taxes that remains today. While Great Britain was a nascent 'tax state' in the eighteenth century, fiscal security was lacking and the sovereign lurched from one debt crisis to another. During much of this period, debt interest absorbed about half of the revenues collected by the British crown.[14] It is hardly surprising that Smith concluded that 'the unstable and perishable nature of stock and credit ... render them unfit to be trusted' for generating the steady revenue needed by government.[15]

At the end of the eighteenth century, government debt in Britain exceeded 200 per cent of national income, after the costly American War of Independence and the Napoleonic wars. The nation had regressive, inadequate and unpopular taxes including specific commodity taxes on items such as salt that were widely evaded through smuggling. The resulting fiscal crisis led to the introduction of the first annual income tax in 1799. The concept of a tax on income was known earlier; in the *Wealth of Nations*, Smith discusses taxes on 'the private revenue of individuals' arising from 'rent, profit, and wages' derived from land, stock (movable property) and labour, a taxonomy familiar

---

[12] Saskia Sassen, *Territory, Authority, Rights: From Medieval to Global Assemblages* (Princeton, NJ: Princeton University Press, 2006), 53.

[13] Ibid., 65.

[14] Garry Young, Carl Emmerson, Jagjit Chadha and Paul Johnson, 'Debt Interest as a Share of Revenues at a 320 Year Low', in *COVID-19: Deficits, Debt and Fiscal Strategy* (London: National Institute of Economic and Social Research and Institute of Fiscal Studies, 2020), https://ifs.org.uk/uploads/Presentations/Covid-19-Deficits-debt-and-fiscal-strategy.pdf, slide 22.

[15] Smith, *Wealth of Nations* (see n 4), Book V, Chapter II, Part I, 'Of the Funds or Sources of Revenue Which May Peculiarly Belong to the Sovereign or Commonwealth'.

to modern-day economists and lawyers.[16] The income tax was re-enacted for a few years and then repealed, before being reintroduced in 1842.

During the nineteenth century, the government of Great Britain established its finances on a more secure footing. Regular taxes, most importantly the income tax, financed most current expenditures and secured long-term debt. This fiscal transformation was achieved at a political price: the extension of the property franchise for the vote in parliament.[17] Martin Daunton explains that political acceptance of the income tax:

> rested on creating a belief that it would help to constrain the state rather than provide it with additional resources ... The principle was no representation without taxation: there was a close correlation between paying income tax and possessing a vote in parliamentary elections under the terms of the Reform Act of 1832.[18]

The success of the nineteenth-century British tax state, which accompanied the massive growth of the British economy through the industrial revolution, demonstrated 'the ultimate complementarity of the modern tax system and the modern method of issuing government debt'.[19] Another country that achieved a similar fiscal consolidation at this time was Sweden, where 'on the one hand there were income taxes and indirect taxes on monetary streams and on the other hand state borrowing was long term with a large funded debt'.[20] The successful combination of tax and debt appears to have been an important factor in the rise of the nation states of Europe, although these nations were also enriched through many other channels including imperial acquisition.

Tax systems incrementally evolved during the nineteenth century. Direct taxes on income, land and inheritance raised increasing revenues and were established as politically acceptable. These taxes gradually took over the dominant role in the tax system from tariffs and specific taxes on goods, as well as tithes of produce or property. Each country's tax system developed in a unique way but overall a pattern emerged, 'defined by the execution of forms

---

[16] Ibid., Book V, Chapter II, Part II, 'Of Taxes'; Peter Harris, *Income Tax in Common Law Jurisdictions* (Cambridge, UK: Cambridge University Press, 2006), 389.

[17] Larry Neal, 'Conclusion: The Monetary, Fiscal, and Political Architecture of Europe, 1815–1914' in José Luis Cardoso and Pedro Lains (eds.), *Paying for the Liberal State: The Rise of Public Finance in Nineteenth-Century Europe* (New York: Cambridge University Press, 2010), 279–302; Mark Dincecco, 'Fiscal Centralization, Limited Government, and Public Revenues in Europe, 1650–1913' (2006) 69(1) *The Journal of Economic History* 48–103.

[18] Martin Daunton 'Creating Legitimacy: Administering Taxation in Britain, 1815–1914' in José Luis Cardoso and Pedro Lains (eds.), *Paying for the Liberal State: The Rise of Public Finance in Nineteenth-Century Europe* (New York: Cambridge University Press, 2010), 27–56, 39.

[19] Neal, 'Conclusion: Monetary, Fiscal, and Political Architecture of Europe' (see n 17), 299.

[20] Lennart Schön, 'The Rise of the Fiscal State in Sweden, 1800–1914' in José Luis Cardoso and Pedro Lains (eds.), *Paying for the Liberal State: The Rise of Public Finance in Nineteenth-Century Europe* (New York: Cambridge University Press, 2010), 162–85.

of financing government activity by taxing the economy efficiently and by servicing political and social consensus'.[21] The modern state 'was able to survive and flourish because it made fiscal sense: it was a form of political organisation that was particularly well-suited to taxing wealth and commerce'.[22]

The Tax and Welfare State
Taxes to Finance Welfare in the *Socialstaat*

A new source of governmental instability arose out of the industrial capitalism of the nineteenth century, accompanied by the development of the competitive labour market described by Karl Polanyi as the 'great transformation'.[23] The commodification of waged labour in this unregulated and exploitative market economy presented an increasing political and social challenge, as workers began to rebel against their inadequate livelihoods, economic security, education, health protection and quality of life. Ultimately, the great transformation led towards regulation of capitalism and waged labour, which was the basis for a massive transformation of the tax state.

Nineteenth-century European governments provided little in the way of direct welfare or redistribution to their people, but historically, countries had various systems of provision for the poor. Great Britain had established a basic form of welfare in the Elizabethan Poor Law of 1601. This had a universal need-based structure in local communities, financed by local taxes and complemented by charitable contributions that helped support hospitals and other basic institutions (we return to the history of charity and tax in Chapter 8). The Elizabethan Poor Law contributed to Britain's success in eliminating famine, in contrast to much of the continent; this supported a growing and healthier population, which contributed to economic growth.[24] However, it was inadequate for a much larger, urbanised and mobile working population more than two centuries later. The conditions of moral deservedness in the Elizabethan poor laws were significantly expanded in the notorious Poor Law

---

[21] José Luis Cardoso and Pedro Lains, 'Introduction' in *Paying for the Liberal State: The Rise of Public Finance in Nineteenth-Century Europe* (New York: Cambridge University Press, 2010), 1–26, 21.

[22] Roland Paris, 'The Globalization of Taxation? Electronic Commerce and the Transformation of the State' (2003) 47(2) *International Studies Quarterly* 153–82, 154.

[23] Karl Polanyi, *The Great Transformation: The Political and Economic Origins of Our Time*, 2nd ed (Boston, MA: Beacon Press, 2001), especially see 80–7.

[24] Simon Szreter, Ann Louise Kinouth, Natasha M. Kriznik, and Michael P. Kelly, 'Health, Welfare, and the State – The Dangers of Forgetting History' (3 December 2016) 388 *The Lancet* 2734–5; Lone Charlesworth, *Welfare's Forgotten Past: A Socio-Legal History of the Poor Law* (Abingdon: Routledge, 2010).

of 1834, an extremely harsh form of welfare, which essentially forced people to work, punishing those who could not with life in the workhouse in appalling conditions.[25]

Polanyi identified a social reaction to address the hardship of workers, a 'double movement' seeking the 'self-protection of society'.[26] Gradually, government intervened to moderate the effects of labour commodification, through a great variety of legal and policy changes across Europe. These ranged from factory laws to local welfare organisations, and ultimately resulted in increased governmental spending on education, administration, utilities, transport and social security. By the end of the nineteenth century, a 'social welfare' approach to the public budget began to develop in some European states.

The social welfare approach was most developed in the German states where it began in Prussia and was expanded in the unified German nation under Chancellor Otto von Bismarck.[27] The *Socialstaat* ('social state') delivered welfare support as an entitlement in social security legislation for health insurance (1883), accident insurance (1894) and old age insurance (1889). A central aim of the social state was 'to take the wind out of the socialists' sails' – Bismarck's goal 'was to make the labourer a dependant of the state, someone who feared that he risked his pension should the socialist overthrow the bourgeois order'.[28] The German social state was financed by a combination of taxes; revenues from public ownership of utilities such as railways, mines and postal services; and government debt.[29]

Observing the growth of government expenditures and activities, German economist Adolphe Wagner in 1863 pronounced his theory that 'the wealthier a country becomes, the more the share of public activity (and thus expenditure) will increase'.[30] The growth of the state is a logical consequence of levying taxes on a growing economic base, with a growing population.[31] At the same time, revenue-raising is a coercive political process, requiring negotiation

---

[25] Polanyi, *The Great Transformation* (see n 23).
[26] Ibid.
[27] Mark Spoerer, 'The Evolution of Public Finances in Nineteenth-Century Germany' in José Luis Cardoso and Pedro Lains (eds.), *Paying for the Liberal State: The Rise of Public Finance in Nineteenth-Century Europe* (New York: Cambridge University Press, 2010), 103–31, https://doi.org/10.1017/CBO9780511845109.006.
[28] Ibid., 103.
[29] Ibid., 127.
[30] Adolph Wagner, 'Three Extracts on Public Finance' in Richard A Musgrave and Alan T Peacock (eds.) *Classics in the Theory of Public Finance* (New York: Palgrave Macmillan, 1958), 2–5.
[31] Spoerer concludes, based on local, provincial and federal taxation data, that Wagner made 'a valid empirical description of the development of the public-sector share during his time'; 'The Evolution of Public Finances' (see n 27), 112.

by interests and elites outside and within the state as a locus of power, social organization and redistribution.[32]

German economists, including Wagner, developed the concept of *Finanzwissenschaft*, the 'financial science' of the state. This approach supported the expansion of taxes to fund social provision and to intervene in the economy. This in turn depended on growth of market activities and monetisation of the economy, effective tax administration, and political legitimacy and consent to the government's activities among taxpayers.

Social Welfare versus Liberal Approaches to Fair Taxation

A division of views about the role of taxation to finance public goods and social provision became increasingly apparent during the nineteenth century. By the end of the century, Wagner had moved from identifying the growth of government to expressing a new and radical idea about the role of taxation in redistribution. Wagner observed that:[33]

> Taxation can become a regulating factor in the distribution of national income and wealth, generally by modifying the distribution brought about by free competition. I stand firmly by this conception against all polemics. I should even go further now and say that this second, regulatory purpose of interference with the uses of individual incomes and wealth ... leads to an extended, or if preferred, a second conception of taxation. This is a 'social welfare' concept beside the 'purely financial' one.

The Anglo liberal political economists, in particular John Stuart Mill, accepted that government must be funded by taxes and that this burden must be allocated on a fair basis. They were less interested in the expansion of government to deliver social provision and more concerned to protect property rights and limit coercive intrusion from the sovereign. Social welfare, or the greatest good of the greatest number (in the classic utilitarian formulation) is a laudable goal, but government should be limited and should supplement the market, delivering public goods or essential services only if the market failed to do so.

The liberal economists accepted that there is a role for public expenditure on education and other public goods that would facilitate economic activity. They also supported governmental intervention to remedy the historic unequal distribution of land and wealth, including through taxes on land and inheritance (see Chapter 6). Otherwise, the liberal view was that taxes should be as low as possible, and should be designed on the basis of 'equal sacrifice' or ability to pay to fund limited government activities.

---

[32] Sven Steinmo, *Taxation and Democracy: Swedish, British and American Approaches to Financing the Modern State* (New Haven, CT: Yale University Press, 1993).
[33] Wagner, 'Three Extracts' (see n 30), 8–9.

The various theories of tax and government that developed in the nineteenth century were a rich source for the development of tax ideas in Europe and increasingly, around the world.[34] The idea of progressive income taxation to deliver redistribution and to fund the welfare state, and the use of taxes and expenditure to intervene in the economy, gained traction across Europe and in the 'New World' of Canada, Australia, New Zealand and the United States (though earlier and on a different pathway). These ideas about tax and redistribution were increasingly intertwined with ideas about consent in representative democratic government.

Expansion of the Tax State in the Twentieth Century

In 1908, Edwin Seligman, a leading American scholar of taxation, summarised the arguments and trend towards progressive taxation to finance growth and development of the modern state:[35]

> The need is felt for better roads, for more canals, for improved methods of communication through the postal service. Then the less material ends of government are recognized. Education must be provided, hospitals and asylums must be erected, and the sanitary conditions must be looked after. Finally comes the immense growth of the modern state, with its new functions due partly to the industrial revolution, partly to the growth of democracy, partly to the recognition in legislation of the preventive as against the repressive principle. These new functions mean fresh expenditures; and these expenditures mean increased taxes.

This progressive narrative was not accepted by all. Schumpeter expressed concern that the public demand for social expenditures would exceed the ability or willingness to pay of taxpayers and said that this 'may generate a crisis which the tax state cannot survive'.[36] Yet the tax state did survive and grow in the ensuing decades, through a twentieth century punctuated by war, disaster, economic depressions and class conflict. By the second half of the twentieth century, many governments succeeded in increasing tax collections to finance the growth of interventionist and social welfare states.

---

[34] Hans Gribnau and Henk Vording, 'The Birth of Tax as a Legal Discipline' in Paul Harris and Dominic de Cogan (eds.), *Studies in the History of Tax Law: Vol 8* (London, Hart Publishing, 2017), 37–66, trace how Anglo and German political economists and tax lawyers influenced the study and discipline of taxation in the Netherlands; while the Irish economist Charles F Bastable, *Public Finance*, 3rd ed (London: Macmillan, 1903, www.econlib.org/library/Bastable/bastbPF.html) explained the approach of *Finanzwissenschaft* in a text that was widely read in the English-speaking world.
[35] Edwin RA Seligman, *Essays in Taxation*, 7th ed (London: Macmillan, 1915), 7, www.google.com/books/edition/Essays_in_Taxation/JGAtAAAAIAAJ?hl=en&gbpv=1.
[36] Joseph A Schumpeter, 'The Crisis of the Tax State' [1918] (1954) 4 *International Economic Papers* 5–38, trans. Wolfgang Stolper and Richard A Musgrave.

The most notable development of the early twentieth century was the spread of income taxes with progressive rates. Ajay Mehrotra explains how the enactment of the US federal progressive income tax represented a new fiscal bargain that laid the foundation for the twentieth-century American welfare state.[37] The United States first enacted an income tax in 1895 and subsequently, after a constitutional amendment, in 1913.[38] Britain, Sweden and India (under a colonial influence) had older income taxes, but the early decades of the twentieth century led to significant expansion. Japan enacted a modern income tax in 1887; New Zealand in 1895; Australia enacted a national income tax in 1915 (after some of the Australian colonies, which became states in the federation, had earlier introduced an income tax); Canada enacted a national income tax in 1917 (and earlier in some provinces); France in 1914; the Netherlands in 1893; and Germany enacted a national income tax in 1920 (the Prussian income tax had started in 1891).

We can present the history of the tax state through long-run statistics that reveal the changing level of taxes as a share of gross domestic product (GDP). Australia provides an interesting example, as its tax history can be presented from the birth of the unified nation in 1901 to the present day. Figure 2.1 shows the history of the Australian tax state. It reveals the fluctuations in tax collections with the business cycle and the overall steady increase until the end of the century.

During and after World War II, the size and role of the tax state in many countries increased dramatically, as illustrated by the example of Australia in Figure 2.1.[39] By the 1960s, when the Organisation for Economic Co-operation and Development (OECD) was established, many governments had reached tax levels of between 20 to 35 per cent of GDP. Ken Messere observed that 'between 1955 and around 1975 there was economic growth and increased standards of living in most industrialised countries and a corresponding readiness of taxpayers to accept more tax burdens to contribute to a better welfare state'.[40] The trend to the present day is shown for selected OECD countries for the period 1965 to 2017 in Figure 2.2.

The welfare state of the twentieth century, financed by taxation, developed in tandem with the market economy. Governmental policy aimed at full

---

[37] Mehrotra, *Making the Modern American Fiscal State* (see n 2).
[38] Hugh J Ault, Brian J Arnold and Graeme Cooper, *Comparative Income Taxation*, 4th ed (Alphen aan den Rijn, Netherlands: Wolters Kluwer, 2020).
[39] Stein Kuhnle and Anne Sander, 'The Emergence of the Western Welfare State', 73–92, and Herbert Obinger and Uwe Wagschal, 'Social Expenditure and Revenues', 333–52 in Francis G Castles, Stephan Leibfried, Jane Lewis, Herbert Obinger and Christopher Pierson (eds.), *The Oxford Handbook of the Welfare State* (Oxford: Oxford University Press, 2010), https://doi.org10.1093/oxfordhb/9780199579396.003.0005; Vito Tanzi and Ludger Schuknecht, *Public Spending in the Twentieth Century* (Cambridge, UK: Cambridge University Press, 2000).
[40] Ken Messere, *Tax Policy in OECD Countries: Choices and Conflicts* (Amsterdam: IBFD, 1993), 119.

Figure 2.1 Tax as share of GDP, Australia, 1902–2019
Source: Paul Tilley, Data Compiled from Australian Bureau of Statistics Revenue Statistics of Commonwealth and State Governments, www.abs.gov.au/statistics/economy/government/taxation-revenue-australia.

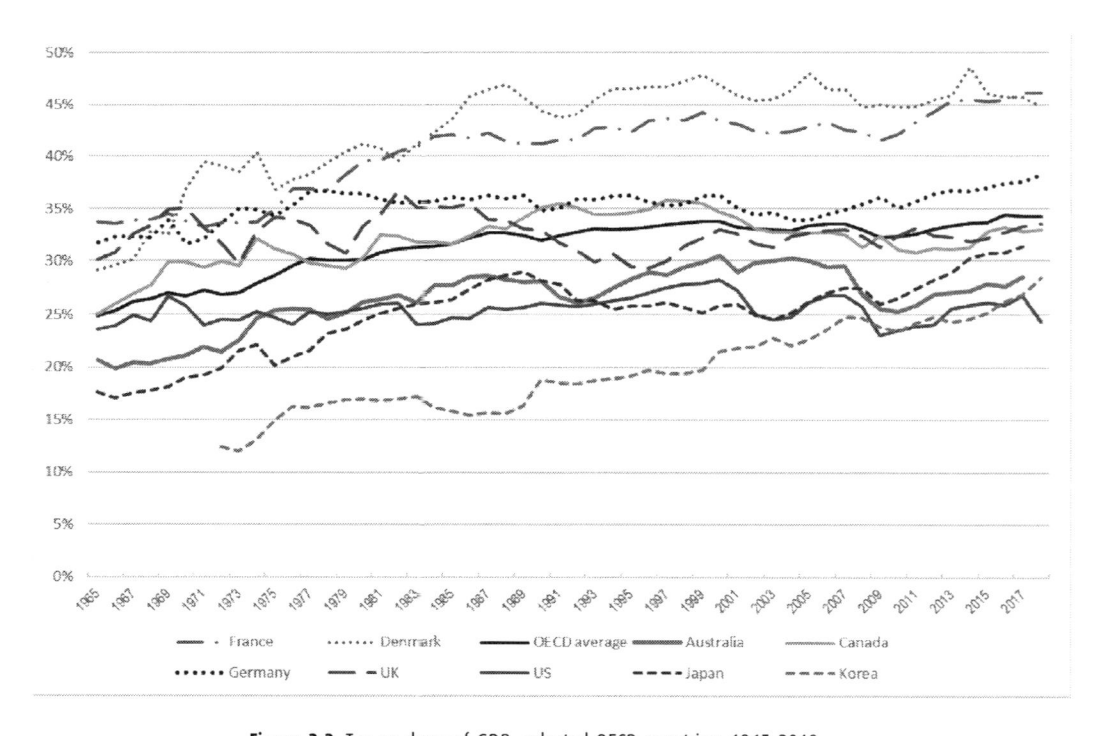

Figure 2.2 Tax as share of GDP, selected OECD countries, 1965–2018
Sources: OECD, Revenue Statistics 2020, Comparative Tables 2019, www.oecd-ilibrary.org/taxation/revenue-statistics-2019_0bbc27da-en; Government at a Glance 2019, Figure 1.1.

employment and taxes that financed vastly increased expenditures on health, education and a social safety net, were crucial in sharing the benefits of economic growth widely across a growing and relatively young population. These policies produced relatively equal societies in terms of income, wealth and opportunity, while leading to dramatic increases in longevity of the population, all of which supported increased prosperity.

The success of the tax state was premised on healthy economic growth – including wage growth – relative to the cost of living. By the end of the twentieth century, Richard Musgrave summarised the trajectory of tax and government as follows:[41]

> [T]he western world saw the typical state share in GNP rise from 20 to over 40 per cent. In part this reflected rising military budgets, but more importantly the growth of social programs to serve the interests of lower and middle-income groups. The propertied class did not dominate voting rights and, in strategic areas, even sponsored the infusion of social concern into the market system. By and large, the rise in expenditures was matched by rising tax revenue; and where instances of over-indebtedness led to fiscal collapse (typically as the product of war finance), that crisis was soon liquidated by bankruptcy and inflation. Thereafter, the capitalist system with its tax state reemerged none the worse.

A Crisis of the Tax State?

The Limits of Taxation

The growth in the tax state was accompanied by a growing debate about the role of government, with John Keynes[42] at one end of the spectrum and Friedrich Hayek[43] at the other. The debate reflected some of the themes of the nineteenth-century debate between liberal and socialist economists and it came to a head during the 1970s. In this era of widespread economic stagnation, high inflation, unemployment and rising expenditures, governments faced increased deficits and debt despite levying taxes at high rates on nominal income. For example, the US government 'lost significant financial and military power, in both material and symbolic terms. The average US household had lost buying power, and firms in many different sectors were not posting profits'.[44] A point was reached that was described by some as a fiscal crisis of the state.[45] In many other countries, the political and economic compact supporting the tax state appeared

---

[41] Richard A Musgrave, *Public Finance in a Democratic Society, Vol III: The Foundations of Taxation and Expenditure* (Northampton, MA: Edward Elgar, 2000), 101.
[42] John Maynard Keynes, *The General Theory of Employment, Interest and Money* (London: Macmillan, 1936).
[43] Friedrich Hayek, *The Road to Serfdom* (London: Routledge & Kegan Paul, 1944).
[44] Sassen, *Territory, Authority, Rights* (see n 12), 157.
[45] James O'Connor, *The Fiscal Crisis of the State* (New York: St Martin's Press, 1973); Sam Peltzman, 'The Growth of Government' (1980) 23(2) *Journal of Law & Economics* 209–87.

to falter. Concerns were raised about the political sustainability of government when debt was large, expenditure seemed to be ever expanding and tax rates were high. There was growing scepticism about the ability of governments to respond to the economic and fiscal crises of the 1970s.

It was in this context that public choice theorists raised concerns about government failure and called for limits on government size and taxes.[46] They developed a critique of the 'welfare economics' approach to tax policy which assumes that government seeks to raise a certain amount of revenue and then aims to design the tax system to achieve that level of revenue as efficiently and equitably as possible (see further Chapter 4). Instead, Geoffrey Brennan and James Buchanan argued that the level and even type of taxation is part of the bargain that establishes the fiscal constitution of the state. This also implied that some forms of taxation may be more amenable to a legitimate fiscal bargain than others. In particular, the income tax has been suggested by some theorists to be more transparent, direct and legitimate than consumption taxation and therefore better suited to establish democratic consent.[47]

Economic Globalisation and Tax Reform

The collapse of capital and currency controls in the 1970s and early 1980s, that had maintained the economic borders of nation states, led to a new era of economic globalisation. This had a dramatic effect on taxation. Tax policy had 'traditionally been thought of as an entirely domestic matter' but 'in an increasingly global world economy, nations can no longer afford to design their tax system without accounting for the effects on international trade and investment'.[48]

By the end of the 1970s, tax experts and politicians agreed that 'one truth is unquestionable: it is difficult to further increase the tax burden'.[49] Instead, one policy lever at the disposal of governments desperate to stimulate economic growth was a reduction in taxation. Governments turned to neoliberal 'supply-side' economic theory and sought to encourage the 'supply' of capital investment and entrepreneurship by significantly lowering tax rates on individuals and firms. This was also a response to rampantly growing tax avoidance and political dissent. On the expenditure side, governments sought to

---

[46] Geoffrey Brennan and James M Buchanan, *The Power to Tax: Analytical Foundations of a Fiscal Constitution* (Cambridge, UK: Cambridge University Press, 1980).

[47] Patrick Emerton and Kathryn James, 'The Justice of the Tax Base and the Case for Income Tax' in Monica Bhandari (ed.), *The Philosophical Foundations of Tax Law* (Oxford: Oxford University Press, 2017), 125–66, https://doi.org/10.1093/acprof:oso/9780198798439.003.0007.

[48] Joel Slemrod, 'Tax Principles in an International Economy' in Michael J Boskin and Charles E McLure Jr (eds.), *World Tax Reform: Case Studies of Developed and Developing Countries* (San Francisco, CA: ICS Press, 1990), 11–24.

[49] Francesco Forte and Emilio Giardina, 'The Crisis of the Fiscal State' in Karl W Roskamp and Francesco Forte (eds.), *Reforms of Tax Systems* (Detroit, MI: Wayne State University Press, 1981), 1–9.

tighten fiscal discipline and to target welfare and other expenditures, as well as privatisation of many governmental functions.

The US tax cuts of 1981 kickstarted the global 'decade of tax reform'.[50] These tax cuts and the subsequent US base broadening and rate lowering reform of 1986, under President Ronald Reagan, were influential around the world. In the United Kingdom, Prime Minister Margaret Thatcher led a transition to the 'enterprise' state, with a focus on lower taxes to provide incentives to business investment, savings and work; privatisation of government assets; and acceptance of greater economic inequality.[51]

The 1980s reforms were not all led by conservative governments. Under Prime Minister Roger Douglas, New Zealand implemented what came to be known as 'Rogernomics', becoming a model of a 'stripped back' state.[52] In the space of a few years, the New Zealand government removed trade and investment barriers, floated the currency, cut government expenditures, reduced and flattened income tax rates and introduced a broad-based consumption tax. The moderate overall level of taxation of New Zealand enabled it to deliver a parsimonious welfare state and drew the attention of other governments. In Australia, a Labor government carried out supply-side tax reform and increased targeting of the welfare system in the mid-1980s based on an 'accord' between business and labour.[53]

Sven Steinmo has observed the contradiction of governments reducing tax rates in response to economic crisis, which seemed to go against a public desire for more progressivity in taxation:

> The public resented their tax systems but generally on the grounds that they were not progressive enough. ... Why did tax reform in these democratic nations get defined as policies that patently flew in the face of the voting majority's policy preference? When most people felt that what was wrong with their system was that the wealthy and the corporations paid too little in taxes, why did policy makers cut tax rates on the wealthy and on corporations? ... By the 1980s, the argument for social justice was overwhelmed by the argument for economic growth. Growth, moreover, was increasingly an issue of international competitiveness.[54]

---

[50] See, e.g. Michael J Boskin and Charles E McLure Jr (eds.), *World Tax Reform: Case Studies of Developed and Developing Countries* (San Francisco, CA: ICS Press, 1990); Cedric Sandford, *Successful Tax Reform: Lessons from an Analysis of Tax Reform in Six Countries* (Bath: Fiscal Publications, 1993).

[51] Martin Daunton, *Just Taxes: The Politics of Taxation in Britain, 1914–1979* (New York: Cambridge University Press, 2002).

[52] Robert Stephens, 'Radical Tax Reform in New Zealand' (1993) 14(3) *Fiscal Studies* 45–63; Johan Christensen, 'Bringing the Bureaucrats Back in: Neo-liberal Tax Reform in New Zealand' (2012) 32(2) *Journal of Public Policy* 141–68.

[53] Julie P Smith, *Taxing Popularity: The Story of Taxation in Australia*, 2nd ed (Sydney: Australian Tax Research Foundation, 2004).

[54] Steinmo, *Taxation and Democracy* (see n 32), 157–8.

The Nordic states of Denmark, Sweden, Norway and Finland, which had gone far in establishing communitarian social welfare states funded by high taxes, reduced personal and corporate tax rates in sometimes painful tax reform processes. These changes shifted their tax systems to accommodate increased mobility of capital while maintaining a welfare state that had widespread popular support.[55] Perhaps it was this combination that led the Nordic states to invent the 'dual income tax' with progressive tax rates on labour and lower flat rates on capital income, which we discuss in Chapter 6. They also, with other European countries, increased the value added tax (VAT).[56] Overall, these tax states maintained relatively high levels of taxation while reorienting their systems towards the global economy.

Successful tax states survived the fiscal crisis of the 1970s and 1980s. Tax rates came down, but tax as a share of GDP was stable or even increased in many countries. In the 50 years from 1965 to 2017, the average tax level in OECD member states increased by one third, from about 25 per cent to 34 per cent of GDP. It appears to have stabilised at that level today as shown in Figure 2.2.

The overall trend masks substantial variation between countries, even those with similar levels of economic development and growth during this period. Tax levels in the United Kingdom and Canada are close to the OECD average over time but the US tax level is lower; in 1965, it was 23.6 per cent of GDP, increasingly slightly to 24.3 per cent of GDP in 2017. Germany and France have tax levels significantly above the OECD average and have trended up over time, while the tax levels of the Nordic states, including Denmark, have declined slightly in the last decade. The Republic of Korea commenced collecting statistics in 1971 and its tax level shows a steady trend up; while still below the OECD average, Korea's tax level now exceeds the US tax level. Australia is below the OECD average at 28.5 per cent in 2017 but tax revenues reached their highest level ever during the 2000s, a result of a resources boom in a growing global economy.

Economic growth accelerated in many countries after the 1980s, in part due to the tax reforms. Taxation continued to be buoyant and grew with the economy. Some governments relied heavily on debt to finance public expenditures, but other governments sought to constrain their expenditure to taxes. Tax states did not shrink, but Figure 2.2 reveals that the upward trend in the size of the tax state halted by the end of the twentieth century. Vito Tanzi and Ludger Schuknecht identified this change and argued for smaller and more efficient governments, which they suggested would 'provide an appropriate framework for market forces to stimulate both growth and social welfare'.[57] Developed country governments could redefine the role of the state 'so as to

---

[55] Ibid.; Boskin and McLure, *World Tax Reform* (see n 50).
[56] Junko Kato, *Regressive Taxation and the Welfare State: Path Dependence and Policy Diffusion* (Cambridge, UK: Cambridge University Press, 2010).
[57] Tanzi and Schuknecht, *Public Spending in the Twentieth Century* (see n 39), 132.

decrease public spending without sacrificing much in terms of social and economic objectives'.[58] However, Tanzi and Schuknecht warned, 'the regulatory role of the state will need to become more important, better directed, and more efficient' for these benefits of privatisation and reliance on market forces to be realised.[59] It is far from clear that the suggested benefits have been realised in many countries.

In Chapter 3, we examine the turn to fiscal discipline during the 1990s, which remains influential 30 years later. In Chapter 4, we discuss tax policy in a global economy. Despite the emphasis on constraining expenditure in most tax states, the share of government in the economy remained stable even through significant shocks, including the Global Financial Crisis of 2008–9 and the COVID-19 pandemic.

The Benefit Theory of Taxation

Taxes for a Civilised Society

Justice Oliver Wendell Holmes famously said in 1927 that 'taxes are what we pay for civilised society'.[60] This approach, premised on the **benefit theory** of taxation, has a long history. Thomas Hobbes, concluding that government is necessary to prevent our lives being 'nasty, brutish and short', proposed that people should pay taxes to government in proportion to their benefit from society.[61] A century later, Smith said that we should all pay tax as partners in the 'great estate' of government and argued that governments needed to spend more, financed by taxes, if they were to advance beyond a mere 'shepherd' state.[62] In particular, Smith advocated increased public expenditure on education and infrastructure.

A central assumption of economics is that markets are the most efficient and effective way to provide for the wants of people. Governments should provide goods only where they cannot be provided by the market or where there is market failure; acknowledging some weaknesses of markets, economists accept that there is a role for government. Despite this, many economists only grudgingly accepted the benefit theory of taxation, and it lost favour among tax theorists in the nineteenth and twentieth centuries, as the theory of taxation based on **ability to pay** became dominant (we return to ability to pay in Chapter 4).

---

[58] Ibid., 131.
[59] Ibid., 134.
[60] Justice Holmes in *Compañia General de Tabacos de Filipinas v Collector of Internal Revenue* (1927) 275 US 87, 100 (Supreme Court) (US).
[61] Thomas Hobbes, *Leviathan* (London: Pelican Classics, [1651], 1968), Project Gutenberg eBook, www.gutenberg.org/files/3207/3207-h/3207-h.htm.
[62] Smith, *Wealth of Nations* (see n 4), Book V, Chapter II, Part I, 'Of the Funds or Sources of Revenue Which May Peculiarly Belong to the Sovereign or Commonwealth'.

In the twentieth century, US economists Gerhard Colm and Richard Musgrave, revived the benefit theory. Colm described taxpayers as 'partners' in the joint endeavour of state and society,[63] while Musgrave described the state as 'an association of individuals engaged in a cooperative venture, formed to resolve problems of coexistence and to do so in a democratic and fair manner'.[64] This justified taxes to deliver public goods and social welfare.

Musgrave combined the tradition of the European social sciences with liberal economic theory and public finance in the United States to develop a fiscal model of government with three branches: Allocation, Distribution and Stabilisation.[65] In the Musgravian model, the Allocation branch of government collects taxes to pay for public goods – the 'benefit' theory in modern terms. Musgrave suggested that we could analyse this role of government separately from the role of taxes and welfare payments made by the Distribution branch to achieve the desired (re)distribution of income or wealth between people in society. This separation (though metaphorical only) is preferable to the other extreme, 'of considering the placement of the entire tax bill as a distributional problem'.[66] The Stabilisation branch would address the goals of balance of payments, employment, inflation and monetary stabilisation. This framework remains influential. One public economics text puts it this way:

> **Three weaknesses of markets.** Despite the invisible hand, markets have three main sets of weaknesses: (1) market failures: under certain conditions markets allocate resources inefficiently and fail to supply goods that consumers want; (2) income inequality: markets often result in inequitable distribution of income; (3) macroeconomic instability: markets may not produce full employment and price stability. . .
>
> **Three potential government functions.** These three forms of market weakness provide three potential economic functions for government: allocation, redistribution and stabilisation functions. The allocation function requires government to respond to market inefficiencies: to provide public goods, regulate externalities, promote competitive markets or regulate market power and protect individuals from information failures. The redistribution function requires government to alleviate poverty and reduce income inequality. The stabilisation function involves management of aggregate demand to achieve price stability

---

[63] Gerhard Colm, *Essays in Public Finance and Fiscal Policy* (New York: Oxford University Press, 1955).

[64] Richard A Musgrave, 'The Nature of the Fiscal State: The Roots of My Thinking' in James M Buchanan and Richard Musgrave, *Public Finance and Public Choice: Two Contrasting Visions of the State* (Cambridge, MA: MIT Press, 1999), 29–49, 31.

[65] Richard A Musgrave, *The Theory of Public Finance: A Study in Public Economy* (New York: McGraw-Hill, 1959); Peggy Musgrave, 'Comments on Two Musgravian Concepts' (2008) 32 *Journal of Economics and Finance* 340-7, 340.

[66] Richard A Musgrave and Alan T Peacock (eds.), *Classics in the Theory of Public Finance* (New York: Palgrave Macmillan, 1958), 21–2.

and high levels of employment and to reduce fluctuations in output over the business cycle.[67]

Governments may also fail. John Head observed that 'the extent to which government should carry out any economic role depends not only on the weaknesses of markets but also on the ability of government to deliver improved outcomes. Government actions may be costly or unfair. Government has limited information, is not always efficient and has limited control over private responses to its actions'.[68]

Public Goods

The challenge of public economics is to identify in what circumstances government provision, or intervention in the market, will increase social welfare. To support a normative theory of public finance that explains what government *should do* and what it *should not do* (what should be left to the market), economists have sought to define a 'public good'. A 'public good' should in economic theory be provided by government only in the event of the failure of the market to deliver the good, or enough of it, to maximise welfare.

Smith produced an early definition of 'those public institutions and those public works' that 'though they may be in the highest degree advantageous to a great society are, however, of such a nature that the profits could never repay the expenses to any individual or small number of individuals and which it therefore cannot be expected that any individual or small number of individuals should erect'.[69] This definition reflects a widely understood concept of public goods today – they deliver a benefit that outweighs the benefit to any one individual, frequently at a cost that exceeds the capacity of any individual; hence, the state must step in.

A more precise definition of a 'pure' public good was developed in the 1950s by Paul Samuelson to mean a good that is both 'nonexcludable' and 'nonrival'.[70] An example is provided in Box 2.1. A public good is 'nonexcludable' because it must be consumed in equal amounts by all and each person benefits from it equally.[71] The non-excludability of public goods distinguishes them from private goods that are excludable and so can be priced in the market.

---

[67] Peter Abelson, *Public Economics* (Sydney: Applied Economics, 2018, https://appliedeconomics.com.au/wp-content/uploads/2021/10/public-economics-principles-and-practice-book-by-peter-abelson.pdf).
[68] John G Head, *Public Good and Public Welfare* (Durham, NC: Duke University Press, 1969), 86.
[69] Smith, *Wealth of Nations* (see n 4), Book V, Chapter II, Part II, 'Of Taxes'.
[70] Paul A Samuelson, 'The Pure Theory of Public Expenditure' (1954) 36(4) *The Review of Economics and Statistics* 387–9; Paul A Samuelson, 'Diagrammatic Exposition of a Theory of Public Expenditure' (1955) 37(4) *The Review of Economics and Statistics* 350–6.
[71] Head, *Public Goods and Public Welfare* (see n 68).

> **Box 2.1 Example of a public good**
>
> Consider a country at risk of hurricanes, where the government provides a hurricane warning system that consists of a text message automatically sent to every individual with a mobile phone in the country. Once the benefit of the warning system is made available to individual A, it must also be made available to individual B. Each individual's benefit from the warning system is identical to the good itself: each receives the same text warning. The cost of the system should be financed through taxation.
>
> Government-provided goods and services may be partly excludable – whether this is so may depend on technology. In the example of the hurricane warning system, if only one part of a country is susceptible to hurricanes, the warning system benefits only those in the region affected. Other people cannot opt out of the 'benefit' of the warning system, which is delivered uniformly to all. If the government could accurately identify those in the vulnerable region and target the text message to them, should it do so, and further, should it make only those who live in the vulnerable region pay for the warning system? This would render the financing of this public good more like a service, to be paid for by a fee, than a public good that should be financed by a tax. A middle ground may be that the local government of the vulnerable region delivers the warning system, financed by taxes levied on people in that region. However, this may be regressive; it may be fairer to finance the warning system by everyone in the country, so as to share at least partly the burden of hurricanes across the whole population.

A public good is 'non-rival' meaning that if it is provided to person A, it can also be provided to person B at no additional cost (indeed, arguably must be provided to person B).[72] This theory of 'pure' public goods applies where there are large numbers of people, such as a nation state; it may not apply to small or local communities. A large-number scenario is one in which each individual or consumer's contribution is insignificant relative to the whole.[73]

There are several difficulties with the narrow concept of a 'pure' public good. The majority of goods and services provided by contemporary governments do not satisfy the strict conditions of the definition in economic theory; thus, a question arises about its explanatory power in understanding what governments do. Most government expenditures today are on social protection, education and health, which together comprise two thirds of expenditure in OECD countries as shown in Figure 2.3. All of these deliver a combination

---

[72] Ibid., 80.
[73] Ibid., 86.

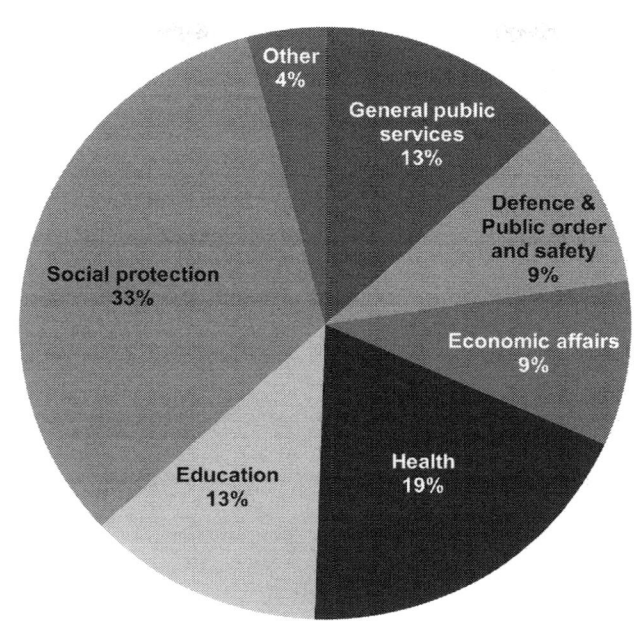

Figure 2.3 Structure of government expenditure by function, OECD countries, 2016.
Source: OECD, *Budgeting and Public Expenditures in OECD Countries 2019* (Paris: OECD Publishing, Paris, 2019), https://doi.org/10.1787/9789264307957-en, figure 2.6.

of public and private benefit – they are both 'individual' and 'collective' at the same time.[74]

A better term for core government goods and services might be 'social goods'. Government expenditures on education and health are primarily financed by taxes but governments do, to some extent, levy fees or require private contribution to such benefits, reflecting their partly 'private' characteristics. The imposition of fees may lead to less of the good being purchased by some people, undermining the collective benefit of health and education for the population as a whole. Social goods may have a redistributive effect, although they do not always redistribute consistently from rich to poor.

Another difficulty with the concept of a 'pure' public good is that governments seek to influence what people want, changing preferences in the market through expenditures and regulation. Governments provide goods and services that it has been decided (through collective decision-making processes) that people *should have* even if they do not want them. Musgrave referred to these as 'merit goods', the delivery of which is an important, though contested, activity

---

[74] Gerhard Colm, 'Theory of Public Expenditures' (1936) 183(1) *The Annals of the American Academy of Political and Social Science* 1–11, 5.

of governments.[75] Related to this concept, government regulation plays a central role in constituting the market economy and channelling consumer preferences within it. It is nearly impossible to imagine a completely 'free' market transaction without government intervention. Examples range from expenditure on speed humps, seat belt laws and traffic police to mandatory schooling, tobacco controls, occupational health and safety, licensing, labelling and registration of professionals (such as doctors, lawyers and financial advisors).

The Taxpayer-Voter

A system of political choice – in a democracy, the system of voting – is needed to enable collective decision-making about public goods and how to finance them.[76] The market cannot determine a price for public goods. Nonetheless, public economics has generally sought to understand the provision of public goods by analogy to the exchange relationship in the market.

The main approach is to identify the 'tax-price' chosen by the voter for public goods. This hypothetical exercise was explained by Musgrave:

> The real-world setting is one in which there exists a given distribution of money income and in which taxes must be imposed to transfer resources to public use. Most important, consumer preferences are unknown. The crucial role of assigning tax prices in this setting (a term more appropriate than that of distributing tax 'burdens') is to induce preference revelation by voting on tax-expenditure issues. This is essentially the spirit of benefit taxation. Ideally, the voting process would be one where all conceivable cost distributions (tax-prices payable by various individuals) would be matched with all conceivable public service programs, but this is hardly feasible. Selected expenditure and tax programs must be considered and tax programs must be expressed in terms of generally applicable tax formulae, rather than as a set of individual tax-prices.[77]

As observed by Graeme Cooper, the taxpayer-voter theory suggests that government, in providing various goods and services, essentially 'tries to emulate the activity of a market and so the choice and extent of government-provided services as well as their tax "price" is tied to the expression of a desire for that service through the consumer's willingness to pay for it'.[78]

---

[75] E.g. John G Head, 'On Merit Goods' (1966) 25(1) *FinanzArchiv* 1–29; Geoffrey Brennan and Loren Lomasky, Institutional Aspects of "Merit Goods" Analysis' (1983) 41(2) *FinanzArchiv* 183–206.

[76] Robert Scherf and Matthew Weinzierl, *Understanding Different Approaches to Benefit-Based Taxation*, NBER Working Paper 26276 (Cambridge, MA: National Bureau of Economic Research, 2019).

[77] Musgrave (see n 65), 58; see Frans AAM van Winden, 'The Economic Theory of Political Decision-Making: A Survey and Perspective' in Julien Van Den Broeck (ed.), *Public Choice* (Dordrecht: Springer, 1988), 9–42.

[78] Graeme Cooper, 'The Benefit Theory of Taxation' (1994) 11 *Australian Tax Forum* 397–509, 414.

Taxation for the Public Good

The definition and theory of public goods also has implications for how they should be financed. In ideal theory, public goods should be paid for by a lump-sum tax paid by each taxpayer-voter. In the example of the hurricane warning system, we may decide that each individual in the community should contribute $100 to support the system. This lump-sum tax would be perfectly efficient. To the extent that some people may not be able to pay the tax, this distributional issue should be dealt with separately by providing transfers to those individuals.

However, in the real world, lump-sum taxes are even more unusual than pure public goods. They are most often found in the guise of flat fees for services, such as annual car registration fees, although even these may be based on ability to pay. Lump-sum taxes are impossible to levy at scale. Therefore, taxes that distort market decisions and that have both behavioural and distributional effects must be used to fund most government activity.[79] Musgrave's conceptual solution to this dilemma was that taxes funding the Allocation branch (public goods) should be proportional and designed to have the broadest possible base, whereas those in the Distribution branch, combined with welfare payments, would be progressive, based on ability to pay.

It has often been argued that the benefit theory is of limited use in debates about how best to design a tax system, because it cannot tell us how much tax is owed by each individual for the benefit they receive from government. This was an important problem for John Stuart Mill in the nineteenth century, who rejected the benefit theory and focused on a concept of equal sacrifice to answer the question of how to allocate the tax burden fairly. As taxation levels grew in the twentieth century and the income tax became more dominant, the benefit theory was associated with those who rejected progressivity in taxation or sought to reduce the level of taxation overall. Seligman called the idea that taxes should vary according to the benefits that persons receive from government 'a principle based on "a false political philosophy" from which follows "a false political economy"'.[80] Henry Simons argued that the benefit theory was 'a significant element in a reactionary social philosophy, constructed from the gratuitous implications of laissez-faire economics'.[81] David Duff suggests that the benefit theory can be most useful in designing taxation to provide specific goods, analogous to a fee or charge, where the benefit funded

---

[79] Raymond I Batina and Toshihiro Ihori, *Public Goods: Theory and Evidence* (New York: Springer, 2005), 10.
[80] David G Duff, 'Benefit Taxes and User Fees in Theory and Practice' (2004) 54 *University of Toronto Law Journal* 391–447, 391.
[81] Henry C Simons, *Personal Income Taxation: The Definition of Income as a Problem of Fiscal Policy* (Chicago: University of Chicago Press, 1938), 34.

by the tax can be clearly defined but is not so helpful in analysing broad-based, mass taxation.[82]

The concern that it is impossible to quantify each individual's benefit derived from the state seems overstated. Government financed by taxes is more than the sum of its separately delivered goods and services. With this broader view in mind, a plausible approach to determining benefit for purposes of allocating the tax burden is to conclude that a person with higher income or wealth (or ability to consume) has benefited more under the state than a person with less. We can find support for this in Smith's original formulation of tax equity (see further in Chapter 4), in which he identifies the individual's income or wealth as an indicator of the benefit of government. As Beverly Moran has observed, 'Smith believed that the primary government benefit was the protection of each individual's wealth'; she identifies his connection of tax to benefit 'because of his theory of the relationship of private property to government'.[83]

We can accept that in considering the distribution of the tax burden, the principle of ability to pay must play a central role – we return to this in Chapter 4. At this point, we need only observe that the critique of the benefit theory concerning *distribution* of the tax burden does not undermine the theory as a *justification* for taxes to finance the necessary collective endeavour of the state. A 'well-defined comprehensive benefit notion' sits alongside the theory of ability to pay and is 'capable of sustaining a coherent tax policy framework *both* for taxes based on marginal benefits (such as fees and charges) *and* for taxes based on notions of total benefits (such as broad-based income and consumption taxes)'.[84]

Ultimately, it may be more useful to define what government delivers, and normatively what it *should* deliver, as *the* public good, rather than relying on the narrow concept of a 'public good' developed in economic theory. In so doing, we can reclaim the idea of a government acting for public benefit which evolved in the context of a different, but closely related sphere of human activity: charity law (see Chapter 8). Taking this approach, we may also be able to address the problem of tax and redistribution in a different way. The choice of the level of redistribution in a state is itself a choice (by taxpayer-voters) about the public good. This approach helps us to decide collectively on the overall level of taxation as the 'price' of civilisation.[85]

---

[82] Duff, 'Benefit Taxes and User Fees' (see n 80), 391.
[83] Beverly Moran, 'Adam Smith and the Search for an Ideal Tax System' in Isaac W Martin, Ajay Mehrotra and Monica Prasad (eds.), *The New Fiscal Sociology: Taxation in Comparative and Historical Perspective* (Cambridge, UK: Cambridge University Press, 2009), 201–15, 206.
[84] Cooper, 'Benefit Theory of Taxation' (see n 78), 407 (emphasis added).
[85] Richard A Musgrave, *The Future of Fiscal Policy: A Reassessment* (Leuven: Leuven University Press, 1978).

3

The Budget

> The single most important policy document of governments, where policy objectives are reconciled and implemented in concrete terms.
>
> Organisation for Economic Co-operation and Development, 'OECD Best Practices for Budget Transparency'

The Budget Constraint

The Traditional Budget

Budgeting is a political process constrained by rules and institutions for legislating and financing policy, combined with an annual accounting and allocation of resources to expenditures, functions and agencies in government. Aaron Wildavsky explained in 1974 that the 'traditional', annual line-item cash budget 'is a product of history, not logic. It was not so much created as evolved. Its procedures and its purposes represent accretions over time rather than propositions postulated at a moment in time'.[1]

When Wildavsky made this observation nearly 50 years ago, the annual cash budget was already perceived to be out of date. Since then, budgeting has become more sophisticated. Public financial management in many governments today includes 'program' and 'medium-term' budgeting that aims to constrain government departmental allocations linked to outputs, over a time period that extends beyond one year. Many governments now adopt accrual budgeting, which seeks to account for the value of government assets net of liabilities. These are useful innovations in budgeting, yet the annual cash budget survives. This is because it performs a critical role connecting executive decisions on taxes and expenditures to legislative appropriation and oversight, supporting accountability of the executive to the legislature and the public.

A balanced budget is one in which expenditures are financed through revenues each year, so there is neither deficit nor surplus. Balancing the budget

---

[1] Aaron Wildavsky, 'A Budget for All Seasons? Why the Traditional Budget Lasts' (1978) 38(6) *Public Administration Review* 501–09, 502; Aaron Wildavsky, *The Politics of the Budgetary Process*, 4th ed (New York: Little, Brown, 1984).

has a common sense appeal. It is usually considered to be a prudent way for governments to carry out their taxation and expenditure functions, by an analogy with household budgeting. Concepts of fiscal balance and discipline of governments have a long history, with political origins about accountability and constraining power. In the nineteenth century, political philosophers such as John Stuart Mill sought to constrain taxing and spending to limit the power of government.

Before the middle of the twentieth century, 'virtually all democratic countries embraced the balanced budget rule, including some that often breached the rule or did not have any legal constraint on unbalanced budgets'.[2] The balanced budget approach was consistent with expectations of responsible government, before the advent of Keynesian economics. After World War II, a new approach that supported expansionary government expenditures to grow the economy developed. Specific budget rules and institutions were further developed in many countries reflecting a political contest between the executive and legislature in the context of a broader goal of achieving stability in tax and expenditure systems.

There are two crucial differences between governmental and household budgeting. First, sovereign governments have the option to raise taxes, limited only by political consent, unlike households limited by a credit constraint. Second, sovereign governments control the currency, or money supply. Advocates of 'modern monetary theory' argue that the fundamental constraint on governments is not fiscal but monetary, being the ability of a government to purchase goods and services in its own issued currency.[3] This implies that the limiting factor for government finances is inflation, not taxes. The classic exercise of balancing the budget, in this analysis, is irrelevant and may even be harmful to social and economic well-being.

Without entering into this sometimes heated monetary-fiscal policy debate, it seems to be true that balancing the budget, or keeping debt very low, is not essential for successful government in many contexts. We can see this empirically by observing governments around the world, which have operated on a stable basis despite relying heavily on deficits and debt for decades (examples include Japan, France and the United States). One reason these governments can do this is that they have effective tax systems, which enable the symbiotic relationship between taxes and debt explained in Chapter 2. In any event, we

---

[2] Allen Schick, 'The Role of Fiscal Rules in Budgeting' (2003) 3(3) *OECD Journal on Budgeting* 7–34, 15.

[3] See, e.g. Stephanie Kelton, *The Deficit Myth: Modern Monetary Theory and the Birth of the People's Economy* (New York: Public Affairs, 2020).

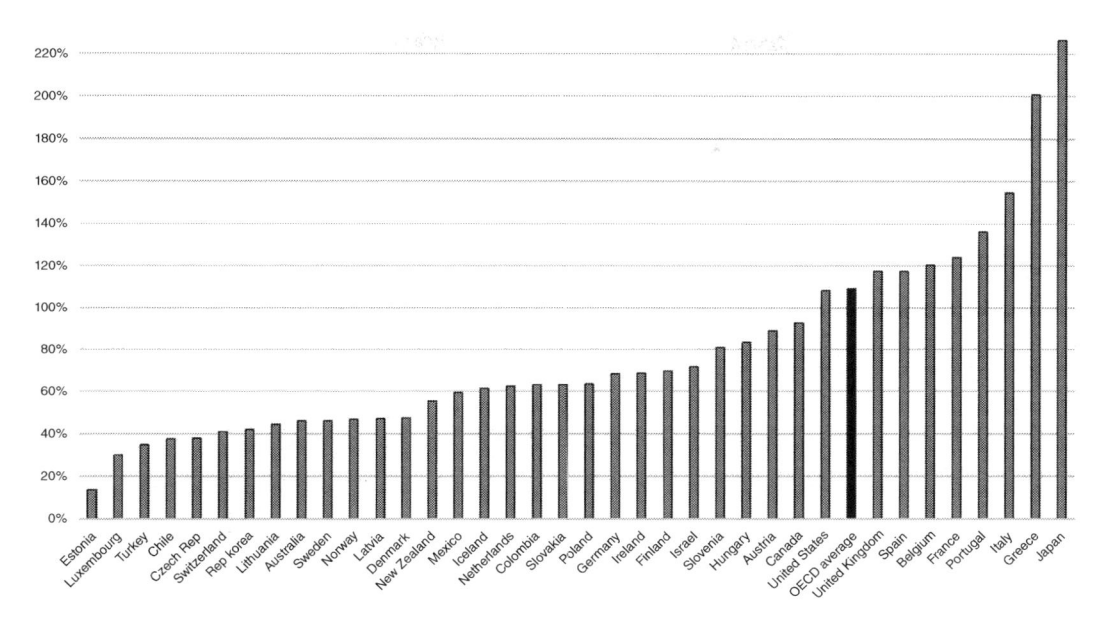

Figure 3.1 Gross debt of OECD countries, share of GDP, 2019
Source: OECD, National Accounts Statistics Database, Eurostat Government Finance Statistics Database.

can be clear that modern monetary theory does not imply that governments should abolish taxes.[4] Taxation remains central to the fiscal compact even when deficit financing has become widespread, because taxation is the most transparent, politically contestable process for negotiating the allocation and distribution of resources in society and the economy.

The Level of Government Debt

Countries vary widely in the level of public debt, as they do in the level of taxes. Figure 3.1 presents debt levels of selected Organisation for Economic Co-operation and Development (OECD) countries as a share of gross domestic product (GDP), before the COVID-19 pandemic. Government debt has increased dramatically as a result of the pandemic; we return to discuss this later.

---

[4] If it is true that for 'money' to be recognised as currency requires the state to accept it as 'that which is necessary to pay taxes', and this authority is lost only when the state is in crisis or loses legitimacy, then the tax system is also a necessary foundation for the monetary system: see William Mitchell, L Randall Wray and Martin Watts, *Macroeconomics* (London: Macmillan International, 2019), Kindle Book, Loc 10877.

Japan has had the highest level of government debt in the world for decades, much of which is borrowed domestically; it continues to govern on a sustainable basis, albeit facing slow growth and a serious challenge of population ageing. The United States has had a high level of government debt and deficit for many years, and the COVID-19 fiscal response pushed the United States to its highest deficit ever, close to 10 per cent of GDP. The United States has the highest external debt of any country. Other countries seem to have a political aversion to public debt, including Germany, the Netherlands, Spain and Australia. Even after COVID-19, these differences in levels of government debt remain, and each country will bring its unique approach to debt and taxes as governments seek to move out of the crisis.

Fiscal Institutions

A New Era of Fiscal Discipline

After the tax reforms of the 1980s, the 1990s ushered in a new era of fiscal discipline[5] Having reduced tax rates, governments now sought to constrain expenditure and control debt. This led to numerous innovations in fiscal institutions; most of these innovations aim to strengthen fiscal discipline by putting a brake on debt, taxes or spending, but some aim to improve political transparency and accountability of fiscal decision-making.

At the end of the twentieth century, although public budgets stabilised and economies grew, global financial capitalism became increasingly unstable. The Asian Financial Crisis of 1997 was a harbinger for the Global Financial Crisis of 2008, which affected most countries around the world. In response to that crisis, some governments applied an expansionary or stimulus fiscal approach through higher spending (and lower taxes), but other governments, including the United Kingdom, sought to control the budget so tightly that this spurred a new concept of governing under 'austerity'.[6]

---

[5] Alasdair Roberts, *The Logic of Discipline: Global Capitalism and the Architecture of Government* (Oxford: Oxford University Press, 2010); Alberto Alesina and Roberto Perotti, 'Fiscal Discipline and the Budget Process' (1996) 86 *American Economic Review* 401–7, 403. A critical view is provided by Lisa Philipps, 'Discursive Deficits: A Feminist Perspective on the Power of Technical Knowledge in Fiscal Law and Policy' (1996) 11(1) *Canadian Journal of Law and Society* 141–76; Lisa Philipps and Miranda Stewart, 'Fiscal Transparency: Global Norms, Domestic Laws, and the Politics of Budgets' (2009) 34(3) *Brooklyn Journal of International Law* 797–860; Ann Mumford, *Fiscal Sociology at the Centenary : UK Perspectives on Budgeting, Taxation and Austerity* (London: Palgrave Macmillan UK, 2019).

[6] Some now suggest austerity was a failure of public policy; see, e.g. Florian Schui, *Austerity: The Great Failure* (New Haven, CT: Yale University Press, 2014); and that fiscal stimulus does not cause negative long-term consequences: Alan J Auerbach and Yuriy Gorodnichenko, *Fiscal Stimulus and Fiscal Sustainability*, NBER Working Paper 23789 (Cambridge, MA: National Bureau for Economic Research, 2017), www.nber.org/papers/w23789.

One goal of fiscal discipline seemed to be removing fiscal decision-making as much as possible out of the hands of elected politicians. This followed the apparently successful removal of monetary policy from politicians into independent central banks in the late 1980s.[7] New Zealand was a pioneer. The Reserve Bank of New Zealand Act 1989 established an independent bank and a 'transparent' process of implementing interest rates 'without interference from Government, Treasury, or anybody else', which was claimed to have 'no exact parallels anywhere else in the world'.[8] Other countries quickly followed. Governments sought to depoliticize monetary policy and credibly influence market expectations, largely by delegating the determination of interest rates to an independent central bank, thereby creating conditions to achieve low inflation.

Some have suggested that an independent authority could be established to set tax rates but no government has ever delegated their powers to set tax or fiscal policy.[9] To do so could undermine the 'fiscal constitution'. An alternative approach could be an automatic income support system that would trigger government payments to individuals when certain economic indicators about unemployment or recession were met.[10] This would be equivalent to a cut in the tax rate for the relevant period, adding an automatic stabilizer to the system to provide income support and help manage consumption in a recession. Evidence from various countries in the COVID-19 pandemic indicates that such payments can work to achieve both goals.

Fiscal Rules

Numerical fiscal rules aim to restrict the open-ended nature of traditional budgeting 'by compelling budget-makers to tax and spend within fixed constraints that do not waver with shifts in political sentiment or economic conditions'.[11] It is an interesting question why democratically elected governments agree to constrain their freedom to tax and spend in this way. One reason is the need to establish legitimacy and consent to the fiscal bargain of

---

[7] Carl Emmerson and Isabel Stockton, 'Rewriting the Fiscal Rules: IFS Green Budget' in Carl Emmerson, Paul Johnson and Ben Zaranko (eds.), *The IFS Green Budget* (London: Institute for Fiscal Studies, 2021), 147–82, https://ifs.org.uk/publications/15693.

[8] Donald T Brash, 'New Zealand's Remarkable Reforms' (Speech, Annual Hayek Memorial Lecture, Institute of Economic Affairs, 4 June 1996).

[9] E.g. Nicholas Gruen, 'Greater Independence for Fiscal Institutions' (2001) 1(1) *OECD Journal on Budgeting* 89–115, 89.

[10] Claudia Sahm, *Direct Stimulus Payments to Individuals* (Washington, DC: Brookings Institution and Hamilton Project, 2019), www.hamiltonproject.org/papers/direct_stimulus_payments_to_individuals.

[11] Schick, 'The Role of Fiscal Rules in Budgeting' (see n 2), 10; Isabelle Joumard, Per Mathis Kongsrud, Young-Sook Nam and Robert Price, 'Enhancing the Cost Effectiveness of Public Spending: Experience in OECD Countries' (2004) (37) *OECD Economic Studies* 109–61, 120.

the state.[12] Fiscal rules are legislative or constitutional expressions of political commitment. They are rarely binding in the sense that they can be judicially enforced and are often explicitly excluded from judicial review.

Numerical fiscal rules may be thought to be necessary to convince global markets to invest or lend. Such rules took on additional importance following the flotation of currencies and removal of capital controls during the 1980s. Governments of the newly opened economies of this era were subjected to intense and powerful forms of market scrutiny, including by global credit-rating agencies.[13] Maintaining the 'triple A' credit rating directly impacted the cost of debt and became a crucial indicator of good economic governance.

Fiscal rules are frequently honoured in the breach. Their rigidity creates incentives for the government to do 'creative accounting', leading to a decrease in budget transparency, contrary to the purpose of the rules.[14] The 2008 Global Financial Crisis caused many governments to breach fiscal rules as they were forced to borrow to finance activities leading to a dramatic increase in deficits and debt. This triggered a new wave of reform of such rules. The United Kingdom presents an interesting example of sequential changes in fiscal rules and targets, some met but many missed, as shown in Figure 3.2.

Fiscal rules continue to proliferate around the world; in 2021, more than 100 countries had at least one fiscal rule compared to fewer than 10 countries in 1990.[15] Examples of fiscal rules are presented in Table 3.1, which reveals that fiscal rules may seek to limit government expenditure, require a balanced budget, limit deficit or debt, establish 'pay for' budgeting processes in which new expenditure must be financed by cuts to the budget elsewhere, cap taxes, or limit new taxes or new expenditures.

---

[12] Schick, 'The Role of Fiscal Rules in Budgeting' (see n 2).

[13] See, e.g. Peter A Hall, 'Policy Paradigms, Social Learning, and the State: The Case of Economic Policymaking in Britain' (1993) 25 *Comparative Politics* 275–96, 285; Paul Posner and Chung-Keun Park, 'Role of the Legislature in the Budget Process: Recent Trends and Innovations' (2007) 7(3) *OECD Journal on Budgeting* 83 www.oecd.org/gov/budgeting/43411793.pdf.

[14] Lars Calmfors, *The Role of Independent Fiscal Policy Institutions*, CESifo Working Paper No 3367 (Munich: CESifo Group, February 2011), 13; Lisa Philipps, 'The Rise of Balanced Budget Laws in Canada: Legislating Fiscal (Ir)responsibility' (1996) 34 *Osgoode Hall Law Journal* 681–740, 681.

[15] Hamid R Davoodi, Paul Elger, Alexandra Fotiou, Daniel Garcia-Macia, Xuehui Han, Andresa Lagerborg, W Raphael Lam and Paulo Medas, *Fiscal Rules and Fiscal Councils: Recent Trends and Performance during the COVID-19 Pandemic*, IMF Working Paper WP/22/11 (Washington, DC: International Monetary Fund, 2022); James L Chan, 'Major Federal Budget Laws of the United States' in Siamack Shojai (ed.), *Budget Deficits and Debt: A Global Perspective* (Westport, CT: Praeger, 1999), 17–25; Miguel Braun and Nicolás Gadano, 'What Are Fiscal Rules for? A Critical Analysis of the Argentine Experience' (2007) 91 *CEPAL Review* 53–66.

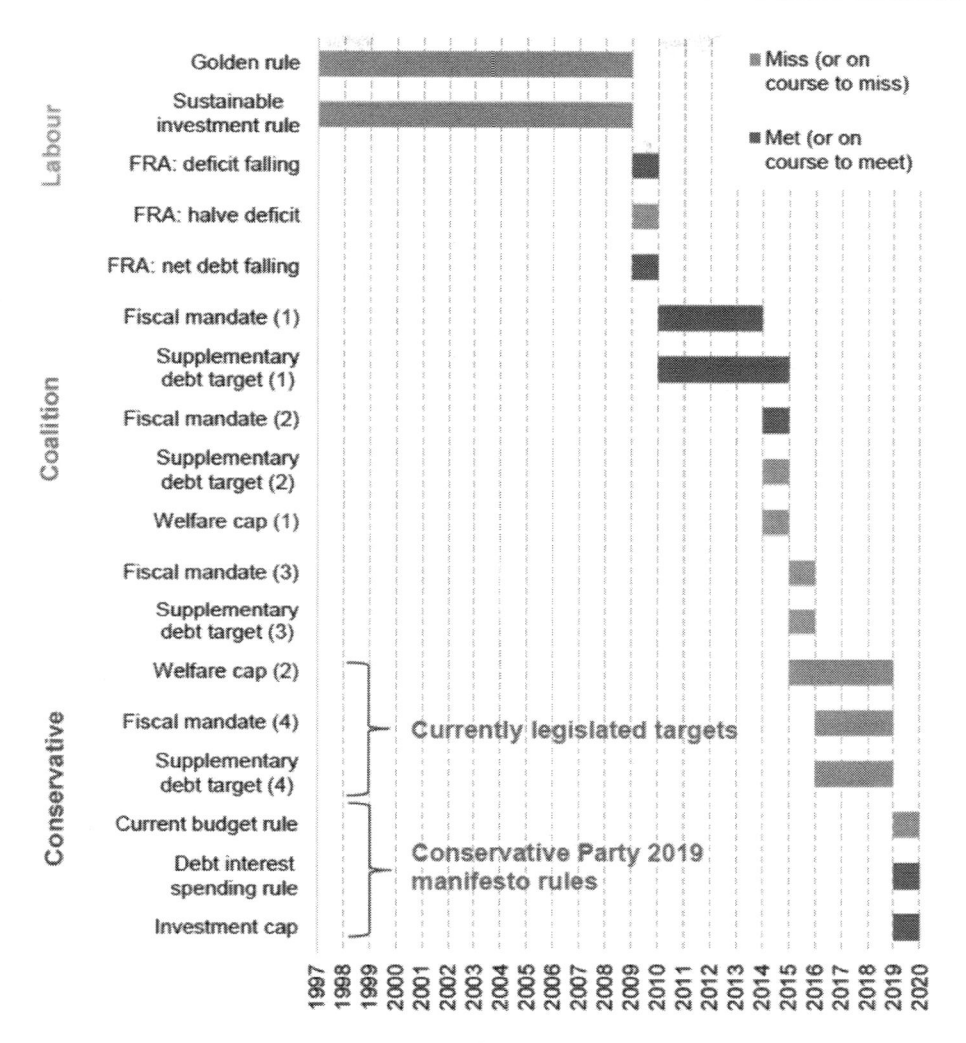

Figure 3.2 UK fiscal targets and rules, 1997–2020.
Source: Carl Emmerson and Isabel Stockton, 'Rewriting the Fiscal Rules: IFS Green Budget' Figure 4.6, in Carl Emmerson, Paul Johnson and Ben Zaranko (eds.), *The IFS Green Budget* (London: Institute for Fiscal Studies, 2021), 147–82, https://ifs.org.uk/publications/15693.
Note: FRA indicates Fiscal Responsibility Act 2010.

Fiscal Transparency

A different approach is to enact a principle of fiscal prudence and put in place rules for regular forecasting, credible budget projections and reporting obligations to the legislature and the public. This approach has been advocated to improve fiscal decision making and enhance democratic

Table 3.1. Examples of fiscal rules

Country	Type of rule
Austria	Balanced budget rule: The structural deficit of the central government shall not exceed 0.35 per cent of GDP.
Denmark	Expenditure rule: Sets legally binding limits for expenditures in central government, municipalities and regions, to be adopted in the legislature and covering a continuous period of four years.
France	Revenue rule: Central government and social security funds must define ex ante the allocation of higher than expected tax revenues.
India	Deficit rule: Target of deficit reduction to 3 per cent of GDP, subject to exclusions for exceptional circumstances as specified by the central government.
Japan	PAYG (pay-as-you-go) rule: Any measure that involves increases in expenditure or decreases in revenue must be offset by permanent reductions in expenditures or permanent revenue-raising measures.
Netherlands	Revenue rule: Within the electoral period and framework for tax base and rates, any additional tax relief must be compensated through tax increases and vice versa and 50 per cent of any windfall revenue must be used to reduce debt.
New Zealand	Balanced budget rule: Government must run operating surpluses annually until 'prudent' debt levels are achieved; on average total operating balances should not exceed total operating revenues.

Note: Examples are illustrative only and may no longer be current, as they change frequently with political and economic circumstances.
Source: Victor Lledó, Sungwook Yoon, Xiangying Fang, Samba Mbaye and Young Kim, Fiscal Rules at a Glance: The IMF Fiscal Rules Dataset 1985–2015 (Washington, DC: International Monetary Fund, 2017).

deliberation.[16] New Zealand was again an early mover with its Fiscal Responsibility Act 1994.[17] The Minister of Finance stated:

> [T]he key is transparency – indeed, chronologically it was the transparency in the Reserve Bank Act which inspired the idea of attempting something similar for fiscal policy. Government's hands are tied only by the need to make policy intentions absolutely unambiguous to the public – surely a fundamentally sound principle.[18]

---

[16] Charles Wyplosz, 'Fiscal Policy: Institutions versus Rules' (2005) 191 *National Institute Economic Review* 64–78, 74–6; Philipps and Stewart, 'Fiscal Transparency' (see n 5); Mark Burton, 'Citizens as Partners: Foundations for an Effective Tax System in the New Democratic Era' (2006) 24(2) *Law in Context* 169–93.

[17] John Janssen, *New Zealand's Fiscal Policy Framework: Experience and Evolution*, Treasury Working Paper No. 1/25 (Wellington: New Zealand Treasury Department, 2001). The New Zealand legislation was highlighted in OECD, *Budgeting for the Future*, OECD Working Paper No 95 (Paris: OECD, 1997), 19–23.

[18] Brash, 'New Zealand's Remarkable Reforms' (see n 8).

The 1990s saw the migration of ideas about transparency to the international arena leading to their adoption in many countries around the world.[19] The International Monetary Fund sought to encourage budget transparency in developing countries, largely for the benefit of external donors and creditors. The OECD produced Best Practices for Budget Transparency in which it expressed the main goal of fiscal prudence to be achieved by revealing the 'true cost of government activities'.[20] An example is Australia's *Charter of Budget Honesty*, which states that the budget is to be managed in accordance with 'prudent' fiscal practice and requires the government to publish fiscal strategies, outlook and performance reports and a long-term intergenerational report.[21] A related development, which sought to constrain government expenditures over a longer time frame, was the implementation of a medium-term expenditure framework. Now widely adopted, this applies three- to five-year forward estimates as the starting point for departmental and program finance bids in each annual budget.

Public reporting of the annual budget, taxes and expenditures and government assets and liabilities is important, although not sufficient, for democratic accountability, and the call for budget transparency has been taken up by citizen groups and non-governmental organisations. Today, the most important cross-country analysis is conducted by the International Budget Partnership, which surveys countries in its Open Budget Survey and produces a budget transparency ranking every two years.[22] The index assesses public access to timely and accurate publication of eight key budget documents, budget participation opportunities audit and oversight of the budget of central governments. Figure 3.3 presents the index ranking for selected OECD countries. A score below 60 indicates only limited budget information is available. New Zealand is, again, at the top of the list.

Independent Fiscal Institutions

Another approach, which has been widely adopted in the early twenty-first century, is for governments to establish independent fiscal institutions, sometimes called fiscal councils. These institutions are tasked with various functions including economic or fiscal forecasting, costing of policies, supporting the legislature with research and advice about fiscal matters and publishing

---

[19] Francisco Bastida and Bernardino Benito, 'Central Government Budget Practices and Transparency: An International Comparison' (2007) 85 *Public Administration* 667–716, 684–5.
[20] OECD, 'Fiscal Sustainability: The Contribution of Fiscal Rules' (2002) 72 *OECD Economic Outlook* 117–36, 117.
[21] Charter of Budget Honesty Act 1998 (Cth) (Austl) s 5.
[22] International Budget Partnership, *Open Budget Survey 2019*, 8th ed (Washington, DC: IBP, 2020), www.internationalbudget.org/sites/default/files/2020-04/2019_Report_EN.pdf.

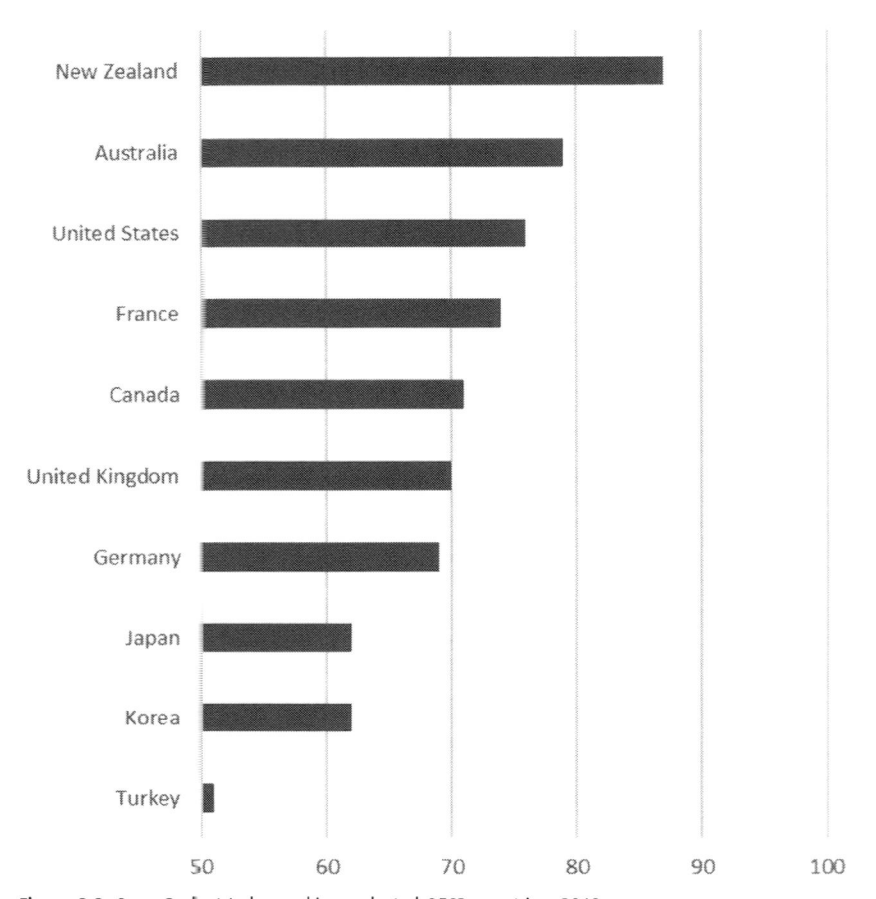

Figure 3.3 Open Budget Index ranking, selected OECD countries, 2019
Source: International Budget Partnership, Open Budget Survey 2019, Rankings, www.internationalbudget.org/open-budget-survey/rankings.

short- and long-term budget analyses.[23] Some countries have 'veteran' institutions such as the Netherlands Central Planning Bureau[24] and the Congressional Budget Office (CBO) in the United States.[25]

---

[23] OECD Working Party of Senior Budget Officials, 'Draft Principles for Independent Fiscal Institutions: Background Document No 3' (presented at the Parliamentary Budget Officials and Independent Fiscal Institutions 4th Annual Meeting, Paris, 23–24 February 2012); Barry Anderson, 'The Changing Role of Parliament in the Budget Process' (2009) 9(1) *OECD Journal on Budgeting* 1–11, 4; Xavier Debrun and Keiko Takahashi, *Independent Fiscal Councils on Continental Europe: Old Wine in New Bottles?*, CESifo DICE Report 9(3) (Munich: ifo Institut – Leibniz-Institut für Wirtschaftsforschung an der Universität München, 2011), 44.

[24] Debrun and Takahashi, *Independent Fiscal Councils on Continental Europe* (see n 23), 3; Frits Bos, *The Dutch Fiscal Framework: History, Current Practice and the Role of the Central Planning Bureau* (The Hague: Central Planning Bureau, July 2007), 22.

[25] James V Saturno, *A Brief Overview of the Congressional Budget Process*, Report No R46468 (Washington, DC: Congressional Research Service, 29 July 2020).

The CBO was established by the Congressional Budget and Impoundment Control Act 1974 to give Congress greater power over the budget process. This legislation was a result of the struggle for budgetary control between the US Congress and the executive branch between 1966 to 1974 that came to a head when President Nixon attempted to use the executive power of impoundment to refuse to disburse appropriations. It is, therefore, a 'consequence of the strict separation of powers that characterises the American constitutional system and of a long historical development in which new layers of institutional innovation were successively added to existing ones'.[26]

Today, the CBO is a large and well-funded agency with eight divisions and over 250 staff. It performs a valuable function in analysing all aspects of US fiscal policy, taxing and spending. It is more difficult to identify the impact of the CBO on US government tax and expenditure policy. One analysis has suggested that the CBO assisted in enactment of the 'Obamacare' Medicaid program through provision of detailed analysis of costs and benefits.[27] The existence of the CBO does not appear to have constrained the growth of US deficits and debt, a topic on which it reports regularly to the Congress and the public.

The Canadian Parliamentary Budget Office (PBO) was established in 2006 by the Harper government when it came to office after criticising the previous government's fiscal forecasting.[28] Almost from the beginning of its operation, the Canadian PBO attracted controversy, perhaps because of the forthright independence of the first officer, Kevin Page and controversial reports including politically damaging costings regarding the Afghanistan war.[29] Despite disputes about bureaucratic control of the PBO, it has survived these skirmishes to date and carries out research and policy costings for the Canadian Parliament.

The Global Financial Crisis provided impetus for creation of new fiscal institutions in many countries. In 2012 the United Kingdom established the Office of Budget Responsibility and gave it the task of economic forecasting, removing that from the Treasury. Australia established a Parliamentary Budget Office in the same year, with policy costing and research responsibilities to support the legislature but no forecasting function. In 2013, the European Commission required each country in the eurozone to establish an independent fiscal council. Box 3.1 illustrates how fiscal policy evolved in the eurozone.

Independent fiscal institutions have diverse powers and responsibilities, but they all represent an attempt to remove some level of fiscal control from the executive ministries either into independent agencies or the legislative arm of

---

[26] Jon R Blondal, Dirk-Jan Kraan and Michael Ruffner, 'Budgeting in the United States' (2003) 3 (2) *OECD Journal on Budgeting* 7–53, 8.
[27] Usman Chohan, 'Independent Budget Offices and the Politics-Administration Dichotomy' (2018) 41(12) *International Journal of Public Administration* 1009–17.
[28] Established under the Federal Accountability Act and Parliament of Canada Act (Canada).
[29] Lars Calmfors and Simon Wren-Lewis, 'What Should Fiscal Councils Do?' (2011) 26 *Economic Policy* 649, 651–95, 676.

Box 3.1 Evolution of fiscal policy in the eurozone

Member states in the eurozone were required to join the Maastricht Stability and Growth Pact established in 1992 to stabilise and support the currency union.[30] The Pact established fiscal rules requiring member states to 'avoid excessive government deficits' (above 3 per cent of GDP) and government debt (above 60 per cent of GDP).[31] Article 104 of the Pact set out the consequences for member states that breach this requirement, escalating in severity from completion of a confidential Commission report, a Council recommendation, publicity requirements, constraints on borrowing from the European Investment Bank, a required deposit with the Community and fines.[32]

The experience with the Maastricht fiscal caps has often been negative. The numerical restraints were too rigid and were ignored or encouraged gaming, as governments tried to hide non-compliance through accounting changes or off-budget spending. After the Global Financial Crisis, the rules and processes for review and enforcement were modified.[33] The constraints of monetary union proved disastrous for some member states, most prominently for Greece, which required a major bailout package and underwent extreme fiscal austerity measures. In 2011 the European Commission mandated that each member state of the eurozone should establish an independent fiscal council in its national budgetary processes.[34] This was a significant intervention in domestic fiscal institutions and required constitutional reform in some countries.

Even before the COVID-19 pandemic, there were calls for abandonment of the Maastricht fiscal rules and a new approach to fiscal stability in the eurozone. One analysis called for it to be replaced with a much softer 'eyeballing' approach to make sure debt is 'not too big', stating bluntly, 'after twenty years, the conclusion is unescapable: the Stability and Growth Pact has failed'.[35]

The challenge in the eurozone is that budgets were always the responsibility of national governments, and explicitly left that way by the European Treaty, yet monetary policy was shifted to the level of the Union. Centralised fiscal discipline may be possible only if there is greater sharing of fiscal and economic risk, which implies a European Union budget or fiscal policy.

---

[30] European Union Maastricht Treaty art. 103, 7 February 1992, O.J. 1992 C191/6; *Resolution of the European Council on the Stability and Growth Pact*, 1997 O.J. (C 236).

[31] Ibid. art 104(c); Protocol annexed to the Pact, art. 1

[32] Ibid. art 104(c).

[33] European Commission, *Six-Pack? Two-Pack? Fiscal Compact? A Short Guide to the New EU Fiscal Governance* (Brussels: Directorate-General for Economic and Financial Affairs, 14 March 2012), http://ec.europa.eu/economy_finance/articles/governance/2012-03-14_six_pack_en.htm; European Commission, *Public Finances in EMU-2010* (Brussels: Directorate-General for Economic and Financial Affairs, 2010), 103.

[34] Cristina Fasone and Elena Griglio, 'The Setting Up of the Fiscal Councils and the Perspectives for the National Parliaments: Comparing Belgium, Germany and the UK' in Bruno De Witte, Adrienne Heritier and Alexander H Trechsel (eds.), *The Euro Crisis and the State of European Democracy: Contributions from the 2012 EUDO Dissemination Conference* (Florence: European University Institute, 2013).

[35] Charles Wyplosz, 'Fiscal Discipline in the Eurozone: Don't Fix It, Change It' in *Forum: Fiscal Rules for Europe. CESifoDICE Report* (Munich: ifo Institute–Leibniz-Institut für Wirtschaftsforschung an der Universität München, 2019).

government.[36] They have potential to enhance democratic fiscal decision-making through independent analysis to educate the legislature and the public. In no country do these bodies have power to generate, or even recommend, tax reform to address fiscal challenges.

Fiscal Policy in the COVID-19 Pandemic

The COVID-19 pandemic and the ensuing global economic crisis presented a new challenge to budgets. The pandemic has led to the highest global public debt in recorded history.[37] Deficits and debt in many countries increased to levels not seen since World War II. The OECD average general government debt – driven largely by very highly indebted countries – now exceeds 100 per cent of GDP.

The unprecedented scale of the COVID-19 fiscal response caused many governments to breach or suspend balanced budget rules or deficit limits in 2020. This is leading to significant rethinking of fiscal discipline in many countries. The cost of government borrowing remains low, in an era of historically low interest rates. Relatively large debt and deficits are fiscally sustainable, at least for a time. A summary of the main fiscal responses to the pandemic and the 'Great Lockdown' is in Box 3.2. Governments have dramatically increased expenditures and reduced taxes in response to the pandemic, while also facing a shortfall in revenue collections because of the economic contraction.

The economic and fiscal impact of the COVID-19 crisis may cause governments to rethink their approach to taxes and expenditure for the longer term, but the direction for change is not clear. Many argue that taxes may need to be increased, but there is also significant concern about how to stimulate the economy with the potential to 'grow' out of debt.

There are also longer term challenges that may lead to increasing needs for government expenditure and increasing contestation about the taxation required to finance it. The most significant is demographic ageing, which leads automatically to rising costs of health care, disability and age pensions.[38] An important policy response is to encourage women's workforce participation, especially in a context of declining fertility. Economic stagnation and slow growth, combined with increasing environmental costs and risks have led some governments, such as Germany, to a goal of negotiating a new fiscal compact permitting more debt or higher taxes.[39] Other governments may continue on paths of fiscal austerity and shrinking the tax state.

---

[36] Miranda Stewart and Holly Jager, 'The Australian Parliamentary Budget Office: Shedding Light on the Dark Arts of Budgeting' (2013) 24(4) *Public Law Review* 267–88.

[37] Vitor Gaspar and Gita Gopinath, 'Fiscal Policies for a Transformed World', IMFblog, 10 July 2020, https://blogs.imf.org/2020/07/10/fiscal-policies-for-a-transformed-world/, referring to global public debt exceeding 100 per cent of global GDP.

[38] OECD, 'Fiscal Sustainability' (see n 20).

[39] For example, Michael Nienaber, 'Germany Eyes Fiscal U-turn with New Debt to Finance Climate Plan', Reuters, 8 August 2019, www.reuters.com/article/us-germany-debt-exclusive/exclusive-germany-eyes-fiscal-u-turn-with-new-debt-to-finance-climate-plan-idUSKCN1UY1NS.

> **Box 3.2 The fiscal response to COVID-19**
>
> During 2020, governments implemented a wide range of tax and fiscal responses to the crisis, as the 'lockdown' to contain the health impact of the virus led to an extraordinary drop in economic activity by firms and households. Most immediate fiscal measures were temporary and many were administrative; they have been frequently altered or extended as the crisis evolved. Key types of short-term fiscal response are summarised here.[40]
>
> 1. Tax measures
>   - Deferral of tax payments for corporate and personal income tax, value added tax (VAT) and social security taxes
>   - Waiving of penalties, more flexible debt payments and debt amnesties
>   - Extension of tax filing deadlines
>   - Faster tax refunds in the VAT or other taxes
>   - Extending tax loss deductions and offsets, for example by permitting carryback of losses or extended carryforward periods
>   - Temporary holidays or exemptions from social security, payroll and property taxes
>   - Temporary or permanent lowering of tax rates
> 2. Cash transfers
>   - Cash transfers for individuals and families in case of loss of work or self-employed business, including emergency payments and payments for those in the informal sector
>   - Relaxation of conditions, income tests and work requirements for cash transfers
>   - Extending sick leave paid for by governments or assisting employers
>   - Subsidies to businesses to maintain employees or pay wages
>   - Rules enabling release of retirement savings
> 3. Government support for health care
>   - Payments to individuals and households
>   - Funding for tests and personal protective equipment
>   - Lowering or removal of import tariffs on relevant health equipment and products
>   - Significant expansion in hospital funding
>   - Support for scientific research into treatment and a vaccine
> 4. Business bailouts and support
>   - Government loan guarantees, direct lending and insolvency relief
>   - Public acquisition or nationalisation of businesses such as airlines
>   - Direct grants and subsidies for business and industrial sectors
> 5. Development of tax and expenditure policy reforms
>   - Stimulating economic activity including credits or deductions for business investment
>   - Raising taxes to repair the budget, or return tax revenues to normal, such as wealth taxes
>   - Redirecting tax administration to raise revenues from sectors that recover more quickly from the crisis

[40] OECD, 'Tax and Fiscal Policy in Response to the Coronavirus Crisis: Strengthening Confidence and Resilience' (updated 19 May 2020), www.oecd.org/coronavirus/policy-responses/tax-and-fiscal-policy-in-response-to-the-coronavirus-crisis-strengthening-confidence-and-resilience-

Linking Taxes to Spending

Budget Earmarking and Mandatory Spending

The expenditure appropriated in a government's annual budget may be only a fraction of total government revenues and expenditures in each year. The remaining government expenditure, while still appropriated according to law, may be subject to longer term legislative arrangements or enacted in separate budgetary funds. It would likely be unacceptable to the public if the government found itself without funds to pay for age pensions or public hospitals. These significant components of government spending therefore become quasi-constitutional elements of the state that must be financed by taxes. In ageing populations, pension and health expenditures are increasing relative to other expenditures and taxes, creating a growing challenge for the tax state. Although the annual budget may not cover the full range of government expenditure, it remains important from a political perspective because it presents the marginal revenues and expenditures that are contestable and able to be redirected or allocated in the short term to different policy goals.

The United States is an interesting example. Discretionary expenditure in the US federal budget was estimated in 2018 to be about 34 per cent of total expenditure (US$1.3 trillion); it is this proportion of the budget that is subject to Congressional appropriation every year, encompassing defence spending and most other federal government functions.[41] The remaining 66 per cent of total expenditure (US$2.5 trillion in 2018) is 'mandatory' or 'entitlement' spending. This comprises mostly social security and Medicare, which is controlled by legislation that sets the terms, conditions and formulas for payments that are made to large proportions of the population and on which they rely.

On the tax side of the budget, an approach of hypothecation or 'earmarking' directly links taxation revenues to specific expenditures. This is most common for social security taxes that are managed in funds separate from the annual budget and used to finance pensions and other welfare payments. This is the case in the United States, although social security taxes do not cover the full extent of US mandatory expenditure.

Earmarking of taxes may be done in other contexts. Vehicle and fuel taxes are often formally or informally earmarked to the repair and maintenance of

---

60f640a8/; Susan Betts, Patrick De Mets, Rene Louis Ossa and Enrique Rojas, *Postcrisis Revenue Generation for Tax Administrations*, Special Series on COVID-19 (Washington, DC: International Monetary Fund, 28 July 2021), www.imf.org/-/media/Files/Publications/covid19-special-notes/en-special-series-on-covid-19-postcrisis-revenue-generation-for-tax-administrations.ashx.

[41] Leigh Angres and Jorge Salazar, *Discretionary Spending in 2018: An Infographic* (Washington, DC: Congressional Budget Office, 2019), www.cbo.gov/publication/55344; Leigh Angres and Jorge Salazar, *Mandatory Spending in 2018: An Infographic* (Washington, DC: Congressional Budget Office, 2019), www.cbo.gov/publication/55343.

roads.[42] The issue of earmarking has received attention in recent years in the context of proposals to enact specific environmental or health-related taxes, such as a carbon tax or sugar tax, with revenue earmarked for compensation for low-income people, or to fund environmental or health benefits.[43]

Some see earmarking as a means of limiting government expenditures, others as a means to obtain political approval to raise taxation for a specific purpose.[44] The earmarking of taxes to spending may also be thought of as an expression of the benefit theory of taxation, discussed in Chapter 2. It makes visible the use of tax revenues and it may enhance political accountability for the taxes raised. A 'soft' earmarking through political commitments may be better than rigid funds-based earmarking for this purpose.

Recalling discussion of the 'taxpayer-voter' in Chapter 2, an earmarking approach to taxes and expenditure could permit selective decision-making by voters about what to pay for with taxes. Earmarking is often popular with taxpayers who may, however, be misled as to the level of control of government spending that earmarking is able to deliver. Earmarking may also contribute to public misunderstanding of the cost of government and what taxes pay for.

However, while it might be fair for the 'taxpayer-voter' to decide that only some proportion of taxes should finance 'pure' public goods, the issue is different for social goods such as education or health. For these goods, some can privately provide for themselves and others cannot. Earmarking would simply permit the better off to opt out of publicly financing those goods, undermining their universality and public benefit, as was explained by Margaret Wilkinson:

> Though tax hypothecation might have an expedient role to play in getting a specific project or part of a programme undertaken, it is not a solution to the large-scale and very difficult problems that governments face in making decisions on taxes and public spending. The problems that arise in providing services within resource constraints and in meeting the expectations of voters cannot be solved by earmarking, with or without referendums. Governments must weigh the alternatives, and determine priorities with full knowledge of the complexities that are involved, and then be accountable to the electorate for them.[45]

Most public finance experts consider that earmarking adds too much rigidity to the system, causing difficulties if earmarked revenues are too large or too

---

[42] Margaret Wilkinson, 'Paying for Public Spending: Is There a Role for Earmarked Taxes?' (1994) 15(4) *Fiscal Studies* 119–35.
[43] Cheryl Cashin, Susan Sparkes and Danielle Bloom, *Earmarking for Health: From Theory to Practice*, Health Financing Working Paper No 5 (Geneva: World Health Organisation, 2017).
[44] Wilkinson, 'Paying for Public Spending' (see n 42), 125.
[45] Ibid., 134.

small for the specified purpose, and leading to a loss of flexibility of the budget. Ultimately, earmarking cannot solve the challenges of government decision-making about taxes and expenditure.

Tax Expenditure Budgeting

Tax laws are not only the means by which governments raise revenue; they are also an essential part of the government 'toolkit' for regulation of the market and a vehicle for government expenditure. Tax laws are frequently used to deliver subsidies or concessions supporting particular activities or taxpayers. These are called 'tax expenditures'. The comprehensive and regular reporting of 'tax expenditures' can help the legislature and public to understand the fiscal cost and beneficiaries of tax concessions.

Tax expenditure reporting began in the late 1960s on opposite sides of the Atlantic. In Germany, since 1967, the Treasury has published an annual 'Federal Subsidy Report' (*Subventionsbericht des Bundes*). In the United States, the first tax expenditure report was published in 1968 on the initiative of Secretary of the Treasury Stanley Surrey. The US 1974 Budget Law that established the CBO required the US Treasury to report tax expenditures annually in the budget.

Subsequently, tax expenditure reporting began to be adopted in other countries, including Canada, France and Spain in 1979 and Australia in 1982. International comparative analysis of tax expenditures around the world during the 1980s helped to systematise the analysis of tax expenditures and to identify and measure tax concessions that could be removed or wound back to support base-broadening and rate-lowering reform.[46]

A tax expenditure is defined as the estimated revenue foregone from a tax concession or preference for a class of taxpayer or activity. The existence of a tax expenditure is established by comparing the actual tax system with a benchmark system that identifies what tax structure should apply to taxpayers. Consider two scenarios:

- A government collects $100 in tax from a taxpayer and then pays a subsidy of $100 to that taxpayer (a direct expenditure); or
- A government does not tax the same taxpayer to the extent of $100 in circumstances where the government otherwise would collect that tax (a tax expenditure).

---

[46] Stanley Surrey and Paul McDaniel *Tax Expenditures* (Cambridge, MA: Harvard University Press, 1985); Paul McDaniel and Stanley Surrey (eds.), *International Aspects of Tax Expenditures: A Comparative Study* (Cambridge, MA: Harvard University Press, 1985); Yariv Brauner and Michael McMahon (eds.), *The Proper Tax Base: Structural Fairness from an International and Comparative Perspective* (Alphen aan den Rijn, Netherlands: Wolters Kluwer, 2012); Lisa Philipps, Neil Brooks and Jinyan Li (eds.), *Tax Expenditures: State of the Art* (Toronto: Canadian Tax Foundation, 2011).

In both scenarios, the economic effect on the taxpayer is the same. If the analogy between a direct subsidy and a tax expenditure is accepted, it follows that the consideration of each form of government spending ought be subject to the same level of scrutiny in the budgetary process.[47] However, direct expenditures usually receive closer political scrutiny than tax expenditures because they require formal budget appropriations. In contrast, once enacted, tax expenditures do not receive annual approval by the legislature and will remain in effect until the tax law is changed. One way that tax expenditures may be limited is through a legislated review or sunset clause that operates after a period of years.

Tax expenditure reports of OECD countries reveal a wide range of exemptions, concessions or deductions for diverse purposes.[48] One of the oldest tax expenditures in many countries is the exemption from taxation of home ownership. The tax concession for philanthropy is another example. Many tax expenditures mirror direct expenditure by governments on core functions, including:

- Tax credits to provide support for low-income individuals or households including 'make work pay' credits for earned income;
- Tax concessions to subsidise retirement savings and lower taxes for capital income and gains;
- Concessions targeted at health expenditure including subsidies for the cost of private health insurance;
- Tax credits or deductions for education expenses; and
- Business and investment concessions and targeted industry support, such as lower tax rates for defined investments, entities or regions, and the research and development tax concession.

The use of tax expenditures to deliver social policy is well established in the United States, especially through the Earned Income Tax Credit, which is a major federal cash transfer program. Even in the welfare states in Europe, the use of tax expenditures has been identified as delivering significant 'fiscal welfare'.[49] Social benefits provided through the tax system have become more prevalent in Europe in the context of the 'discreet privatisation of social insurance schemes' and strict fiscal rules and expenditure controls. Tax expenditures have been estimated to comprise more than 10 per cent of gross

---

[47] Mark Burton and Kerrie Sadiq, *Tax Expenditure Management: A Critical Assessment* (Cambridge, UK Cambridge University Press, 2013).
[48] OECD, *Tax Expenditures in OECD Countries* (Paris: OECD, 2020) https://doi.org/10.1787/9789264076907-en, a comparative study of Canada, France, Germany, Japan, Korea, the Netherlands, Spain, Sweden, the United Kingdom and the United States.
[49] Nathalie Morel, Chloé Touzet and Michael Zemmour, 'Fiscal Welfare in Europe: Why Should We Care and What Do We Know So Far?' (2018) 28(5) *Journal of European Social Policy* 549–60.

social spending in Germany, the Netherlands, the United Kingdom and the United States.[50]

Benchmarking Tax Expenditures

The identification and measurement of tax expenditures require comparison with a defined, benchmark tax system. Applying an ideal benchmark helps to identify where the existing tax law departs from a policy ideal. This recalls our discussion of the ideal comprehensive income tax in Chapter 1 and its main differences from a 'real' income tax. The main benchmarks for tax expenditures are:

- Comprehensive income tax benchmark, defined to be all economic gains in the control of a taxpayer in the tax year, with limited modifications to take account of policy trade-offs or practical tax administration. This benchmark could include imputed rent from living in your own home and all accrued capital gains (adjusted for inflation) and may require that all income be taxed at the basic defined rate structure, ignoring aspects such as concessions for family members or low income taxpayers.
- Broad-based consumption tax benchmark, defined to cover consumption of all goods and services by consumers in the jurisdiction. The benchmark may require that all consumption be taxed at the same flat rate.
- Neutral land tax benchmark, defined to include all land, whether privately owned, developed or vacant, urban or rural, agricultural or industrial and may require that all land be taxed at the same rate without any concessions for small holdings, homes, or low income landowners.

In practice, governments report tax expenditures against a pragmatic benchmark based on the 'normal' policy expressed in the tax law. Usually, imputed income is ignored and some structural modifications, such as the realisation of income, are included in the benchmark. Consumption tax benchmarks may include, or exclude, government-provided goods and services.

The most common method of measuring tax expenditures estimates the revenue foregone by comparing the revenue raised under the existing tax law including the tax expenditure with an estimate of the revenue that would have been raised excluding the tax expenditure. This method assumes that all other tax provisions, and other laws remain the same and that taxpayer behaviour is unchanged in response to the hypothetical abolition of the tax expenditure.

However, the abolition of a tax expenditure is unlikely to generate as much additional revenue as implied by an estimate of revenue foregone. For example, assume that a government decided to abolish all tax expenditures for retirement saving by individual taxpayers. Taxpayers may choose, instead,

---

[50] Ibid., figure 1 based on 2011 data.

to put some of their savings into another concessionally taxed, or exempt, savings vehicle. For example, taxpayers might invest in a more expensive home, which is frequently exempt from tax. Consequently, the savings in tax revenue would be lower than expected. The revenue forgone method ignores such behavioural effects. This can cause substantial inaccuracy as taxpayers do modify their behaviour, with varying elasticity of response, depending on the tax framework and opportunities available to them.

An alternative approach is to estimate revenue gain, which aims to measure the anticipated revenue that would be gained from abolition of a tax expenditure. This aims to take into account likely taxpayer responses to that hypothetical abolition of the tax expenditure and other 'second order' effects such as the interaction of tax laws with other laws. It requires high-quality data to estimate the elasticity of behavioural response of taxpayers to the abolition of a tax expenditure.

A third approach measures how much it would cost to deliver the same after-tax benefit to the beneficiaries of the tax expenditure by way of a cash grant. It assumes that the cash grant would be subject to the normal application of the existing tax law without the tax expenditure. This method offers the opportunity of assessing the merits of alternative means of delivering the government benefit. However, measuring the actual benefit in the hands of the beneficiaries requires high-quality data about the taxpayer.

In sum, there are many difficulties in measuring the cost of tax expenditures accurately, so tax expenditure reports provide estimates rather than precise budget allocations and cannot be directly compared with direct budget spending. Nonetheless, scrutiny of tax expenditures through this method ensures that governments can be held accountable for 'spending' through the tax system. This may provide evidence to support tax reform through eliminating concessions and broadening the tax base.

Gender, Distributional and Other Values in Budgets

The Budget as an Ethical Document

The budget is a political and ethical as well as a technical document. Budgeting has a necessary technocratic focus on metrics such as the fiscal balance, detailed program budgeting and appropriation, the accurate accounting of assets, liabilities, income and outgoings and the correct legal appropriation of funds. Yet it is also a vehicle for the social and ethical values of the government and community. Increasingly, there have been moves for governments to be explicit about their values in the budget. The budget process can be a forum for government to present its values and goals beyond the achievement of economic growth and to show how its objectives will be prioritised and achieved.

Three areas in which budget practices and approaches have shifted towards more explicit engagement with ethical goals are gender budgeting, the distributional analysis of budgets and 'green' budgeting for long-term environmental sustainability. The increased focus on targets and outcomes in each of these areas is supported by the shift towards medium-term and program budgeting, which provide a policy framework of more than one year, while enabling tracking of criteria and outcomes on a year by year basis.

Gender Budgeting

In all countries, including most wealthy countries in the OECD, gender inequality remains entrenched despite significant progress in the last few decades.[51] Budgeting, and tax policy, usually appears gender-neutral but like all government policy, it has a differential impact on men and women who are differently situated in the economy and society. Since the 1980s, feminist activists and experts have advocated for governments to carry out gender impact analysis of tax and expenditure measures, to inform budgets, monitor their effects and assess and evaluate outcomes for the promotion of gender equality.[52] Civil society organisations have also monitored budgets and tax reform for gender impact, for example, the long-standing Women's Budget Group of the United Kingdom.[53]

Gender budgeting starts from the proposition that the budget is a central political document that activates government policy by raising revenues and allocating expenditures legislated by the parliament. In this context, a widely used definition of gender budgeting is 'a gender-based assessment of budgets, incorporating a gender perspective at all levels of the budgetary process and restructuring revenues and expenditures to promote gender equality'.[54] Gender budgeting may be partial, focused on specific policies or programs, or government-wide. In recent years, more countries have adopted gender budgeting approaches, in response to domestic and international political pressure. Today, about half of OECD member states officially do some form of gender budgeting.[55] Some governments, such as Korea or Spain, have laws to mandate gender analysis of the budget. Other governments rely on bureaucratic or political processes, informal strategies and indicators at various levels of policy formulation, costing, financing and delivery through government agencies, departments and at cabinet level.

---

[51] OECD, *The Pursuit of Gender Equality: An Uphill Battle* (Paris: OECD, 2017), https://doi.org/10.1787/9789264281318-en.

[52] Marian Sawer and Miranda Stewart, 'Gender Budgeting' in Marian Sawer, Fiona Jenkins and Karen Downing (eds.), *How Gender Can Transform the Social Sciences: Innovation and Impact* (Cham: Palgrave Macmillan, 2021), 117–26.

[53] See https://wbg.org.uk/.

[54] Council of Europe, *Gender Budgeting: Practical Implementation. Handbook* (Strasbourg: Council of Europe, Directorate General of Human Rights and Legal Affairs, 2009).

[55] Ronnie Downes and Sherie Nichol, *Designing and Implementing Gender Budgeting* (Paris: Public Governance Directorate, OECD, 2019), 5. www.oecd.org/gov/budgeting/designing-and-implementing-gender-budgeting-a-path-to-action.pdf.

Gender budgeting challenges gender-blindness in core technocratic agencies of government. As was observed in a recent OECD report, the central budget authority of governments, usually the ministry of finance, is 'not necessarily attuned to complex gender equality issues; and these ministries often have an inherent culture of conservatism ... in tension with the requirements of deep-seated social change'.[56]

Increasingly, the 'economic' as well as 'equity' case for gender budgeting is being recognised, as it can help to deliver economic growth, especially increased market work participation of women, and better and more effective policy delivery across all fields. Gender budgeting can be implemented as a process of tracking policy by applying targets, indicators and measures of achievement. Gender impact analysis is an important input to gender budgeting and it is directly relevant to income taxation and social policies. As explored further in Chapter 5, women and men are differently situated in the labour market and in the household, especially in relation to caregiving roles. This unequal economic and social environment is often exacerbated by facially neutral tax and transfer policy, with long-term effects for women's lifetime income and economic security and well-being.

A key requirement for gender impact analysis is data disaggregated by sex or gender, and the establishment of goals aimed at gender equality. For example, gender budgeting may be applied to identify the differential impact of health expenditures, analyse the best use of policing expenditures in a rural area, or improve gender equality in industrial policy aimed at growing sectors in the economy such as technology, science manufacturing or services.

Distributional Impact of Budgets

The budget may present the distributional impact of tax and spending policy to help illuminate the benefits received by different social groups and firms. Therefore, budgets may include discussion of effects of government policy, sometimes measured by indicators such as income or wealth inequality, gender inequality, rural compared to urban citizens, or people of different ethnic, racial or religious backgrounds.

For example, the budgets of Finland, Germany, the Netherlands, Sweden and the United Kingdom each present a distributional impact analysis of the budget on households at different levels of income.[57] However, only a few countries, including Germany, present the impact of the budget on income inequality, poverty and social deprivation, regions and minority groups.

---

[56] Ibid., 6.
[57] OECD, *Budgeting and Public Expenditures in OECD Countries* (Paris: OECD Publishing, 2019), https://doi.org/10.1787/9789264307957-en, 103.

Some governments are broadening the focus of their budgets to focus on social and personal well-being, not just economic or financial indicators. The New Zealand government established a 'well-being' budget in 2019, which set five priorities for improving the quality of life of the people of New Zealand. These include environmental transition to a low carbon economy; digital access for all; lifting Maori and Pacific incomes, skills and opportunities; reducing child poverty; and supporting mental health.[58] The challenge for governments seeking to connect the budget to 'well-being' is that tax and expenditure systems depend on economic activities in the market. Budgets must therefore link the social and distributional impact of government policy with underlying economic and fiscal metrics and indicators.

Green Budgeting

Budgeting for the environment, in particular climate change, is the least well advanced of ethical or values-based approaches to the budget. Despite the urgency of this issue, budgets rarely account for environmental damage or depreciation, or address long-term economic and fiscal risks of environmental change. One possible forum for environmental and gender budget analysis is the intergenerational equity reports produced by some governments. However, in the United Kingdom, the House of Lords produced a special report on intergenerational fairness in 2019, which focused on housing, work, education and taxation, not on the environment.[59] The most recent *Intergenerational Report* released by the Australian Treasury discusses demographic and work trends and refers to the impact of climate change, but does not present a detailed analysis or estimated costing of these issues.[60]

In 2017, the OECD initiated the Paris Collaboration on Green Budgeting, which was joined by the United Kingdom in 2021.[61] This initiative aims to evaluate the environmental impacts of budgetary and fiscal policies, assess their coherence towards delivery of national and international commitments and contribute to policy and debate on sustainable growth. The goal is to pilot green budget methodologies with a particular focus on low-carbon and energy initiatives, but also including work on biodiversity and pollution.

---

[58] Government of New Zealand Treasury Department, *The Wellbeing Budget 2019* (30 May 2019), https://treasury.govt.nz/sites/default/files/2019-05/b19-wellbeing-budget.pdf.

[59] House of Lords (UK), Select Committee on Intergenerational Fairness and Provision, *Tackling Intergenerational Unfairness*, Report of Session 2017-19 (London: Parliament of the United Kingdom, 2019), https://publications.parliament.uk/pa/ld201719/ldselect/ldintfair/329/329.pdf.

[60] Australian Treasury, *2021 Intergenerational Report: Australia over the Next 40 Years* (Parkes, ACT: Commonwealth of Australia, June 2021), https://treasury.gov.au/sites/default/files/2021-06/p2021_182464.pdf.

[61] OECD, *Green Budgeting in OECD Countries* (Paris: OECD Publishing, 2021), https://doi.org/10.1787/acf5d047-en.

Budgeting for the environment raises global issues, as global public goods – and harms – of the environment affect all governments. This requires engagement beyond the national budget. Together with gender analysis that takes the distribution of market and care work seriously across generations, environmental budgeting has the potential to support governments in a long-term reorientation of taxation and expenditure approaches for fiscal sustainability.

4

Tax Principles

All nations have endeavoured, to the best of their judgment, to render their taxes as equal as they could contrive; as certain, as convenient to the contributor, both in the time and in the mode of payment, and, in proportion to the revenue which they brought to the prince, as little burdensome to the people.

Adam Smith, *Wealth of Nations*

Origins of Tax Principles

The Maxims of Adam Smith

Tax policy refers almost universally to principles of equity, efficiency and simplicity, with modifications in definition and emphasis in different contexts.[1] These three principles originate in four Maxims of taxation developed by Adam Smith early in the era of the tax state: equity, certainty, convenience and efficiency.

Fifty years after the *Wealth of Nations* was published, John Stuart Mill in his treatise on political economy observed that 'the qualities desirable, economically speaking, in a system of taxation, have been embodied by Adam Smith in four maxims or principles, which, having been generally concurred in by subsequent writers, may be said to have become classical'.[2] The Maxims also had a significant effect in many other nations, for example, influencing taxation law and theory in the Netherlands.[3] It is therefore worth extracting the Maxims in full here, while recognising that some aspects relate specifically to their time.

***

---

[1] To take just three examples: US Treasury, *Blueprints for Tax Reform* (Washington, DC: US Government Printing Office, 1977), 1; Australian Treasury, *Australia's Future Tax System: Final Report* (Canberra: Commonwealth of Australia, 2010), 17; James Mirrlees, Stuart Adam, Tim Besley, Richard Blundell, Stephen Bond, Robert Chote, Malcolm Gammie, Paul Johnson, Gareth Myles and James M Poterba, *Tax by Design. Mirrlees Review: Vol 2* (Oxford: Oxford University Press, 2011), https://ifs.org.uk/publications/5353, 22.

[2] John Stuart Mill, *Principles of Political Economy* (London: Longmans, 1848), www.econlib.org/library/Mill/mlP.html?chapter_num=1#book-reader, Book V. Ch 1 Sec 1, 538.

[3] Hans Gribnau and Henk Vording, 'The Birth of Tax as a Legal Discipline' in Peter Harris and Dominic de Cogan (eds.), *Studies in the History of Tax Law: Vol 8* (London: Hart Publishing, 2017), 37–66.

Maxims of Taxation[4]

I. The subjects of every state ought to contribute towards the support of the government, as nearly as possible, in proportion to their respective abilities; that is, in proportion to the revenue which they respectively enjoy under the protection of the state. The expence of government to the individuals of a great nation is like the expence of management to the joint tenants of a great estate, who are all obliged to contribute in proportion to their respective interests in the estate. In the observation or neglect of this maxim consists what is called the equality or inequality of taxation. . . .

II. The tax which each individual is bound to pay ought to be certain, and not arbitrary. The time of payment, the manner of payment, the quantity to be paid, ought all to be clear and plain to the contributor, and to every other person. Where it is otherwise, every person subject to the tax is put more or less in the power of the tax-gatherer, who can either aggravate the tax upon any obnoxious contributor, or extort, by the terror of such aggravation, some present or perquisite to himself. The uncertainty of taxation encourages the insolence and favours the corruption of an order of men who are naturally unpopular, even where they are neither insolent nor corrupt. The certainty of what each individual ought to pay is, in taxation, a matter of so great importance that a very considerable degree of inequality, it appears, I believe, from the experience of all nations, is not near so great an evil as a very small degree of uncertainty.

III. Every tax ought to be levied at the time, or in the manner, in which it is most likely to be convenient for the contributor to pay it. A tax upon the rent of land or of houses, payable at the same term at which such rents are usually paid, is levied at the time when it is most likely to be convenient for the contributor to pay; or, when he is most likely to have wherewithal to pay. Taxes upon such consumable goods as are articles of luxury are all finally paid by the consumer, and generally in a manner that is very convenient for him. He pays them by little and little, as he has occasion to buy the goods. As he is at liberty, too, either to buy, or not to buy, as he pleases, it must be his own fault if he ever suffers any considerable inconveniency from such taxes.

IV. Every tax ought to be so contrived as both to take out and to keep out of the pockets of the people as little as possible over and above what it brings into the public treasury of the state. A tax may either take out or keep out of the pockets of the people a great deal more than it brings into the public treasury, in the four following ways.

First, the levying of it may require a great number of officers, whose salaries may eat up the greater part of the produce of the tax, and whose perquisites may impose another additional tax upon the people.

---

[4] Adam Smith, *An Inquiry into the Nature and Causes of Wealth of Nations* (London: Methuan, first published 1776, compilation by Edward Cannan, 1904, of 5th ed, 1789), www.econlib.org/library/Smith/smWN.html, Book V, Chapter II, Part II, 'Of Taxes'.

Secondly, it may obstruct the industry of the people, and discourage them from applying to certain branches of business which might give maintenance and employment to great multitudes. While it obliges the people to pay, it may thus diminish, or perhaps destroy, some of the funds which might enable them more easily to do so.

Thirdly, by the forfeitures and other penalties which those unfortunate individuals incur who attempt unsuccessfully to evade the tax, it may frequently ruin them, and thereby put an end to the benefit which the community might have received from the employment of their capitals. An injudicious tax offers a great temptation to smuggling. But the penalties of smuggling must rise in proportion to the temptation. The law, contrary to all the ordinary principles of justice, first creates the temptation, and then punishes those who yield to it; and it commonly enhances the punishment, too, in proportion to the very circumstance which ought certainly to alleviate it, the temptation to commit the crime.

Fourthly, by subjecting the people to the frequent visits and the odious examination of the tax-gatherers, it may expose them to much unnecessary trouble, vexation, and oppression; and though vexation is not, strictly speaking, expence, it is certainly equivalent to the expence at which every man would be willing to redeem himself from it.

It is in some one or other of these four different ways that taxes are frequently so much more burdensome to the people than they are beneficial to the sovereign.

***

Adam Smith's first Maxim concerns **equity** in taxation, which Smith called 'equality'. This Maxim is expressed rather broadly, encompassing benefit (discussed in Chapter 2) and ability to pay (to which we return later). The second Maxim concerns **certainty** of taxation, in the sense of taxation that is *not arbitrary*, which has become a foundational principle in the fiscal constitution of successful tax states. Smith's third Maxim of **convenience** maps onto contemporary tax policy goals of simplicity and ease of administration and compliance with tax law. We return to certainty, simplicity and convenience in taxation in Chapter 9.

Smith's fourth Maxim concerns the economic costs of taxation. He explains that taxation has a cost for taxpayers and the economy in general, *over and above what taxes bring into the treasury of the state*. Today, we call this **efficiency**, which refers mainly to the impact of taxes on decisions to work, save or invest in the market economy. While not using the term 'efficiency', Smith observed that tax may 'obstruct the industry of the people' and provide a great 'temptation to smuggling' – both economic responses to taxation.

Equity

Tax Equity and Distributive Justice

The dominant philosophical theories of distributive justice of the twentieth century, propounded by John Rawls and Ronald Dworkin, as explained by David Duff, indicate that justice is logically prior to other goals of government, 'the first virtue' and therefore the first principle of the 'virtuous sovereign', including in taxation.[5] This book contests that position, to some extent, as it was argued in Chapter 2 that the first purpose of government is to provide for the public benefit of all of its people. Accepting this, a central element of the project of the tax state is distributive justice. Taxation based on ability to pay, combined with the use of tax revenues to deliver redistribution of incomes through welfare expenditures, is essential to achieve this goal.

Richard Musgrave identified the goal of tax equity or justice as the function of the Distribution branch of government, as discussed in Chapter 2. The Distribution branch includes both progressive taxation and the provision of welfare payments in the transfer system. Social experiments in deliberative decision-making about distributive justice suggest that many people agree on the combined goals of a minimum floor below which no person should fall, while maximising the 'size of the pie' for society as a whole.[6] This suggests that distributive justice in the perception of many requires a combination of economic prosperity and the distribution of the benefit or increment from economic growth in a way that is just.

A simple and widely repeated statement of the principle of tax equity has two elements:

- **Horizontal equity** requires that individuals who are similarly situated should be taxed equally, or should receive equal benefits, measured with respect to income or some other measure. It requires a level playing field in the tax system. The challenge is to identify who is similarly situated for this purpose and what factors should be taken into account for that determination.
- **Vertical equity** requires distribution of the tax burden based on **ability to pay**, according to an individual's income, consumption or another measure of capacity. The challenge is to identify the appropriate metric of ability to pay, and the level of redistribution to be achieved by the tax system.

Equity in taxation does not require either that we all contribute the same amount of tax (a poll tax does not satisfy either horizontal or vertical equity),

---

[5] David G Duff, 'Tax Policy and the Virtuous Sovereign: Dworkinian Equality and Redistributive Taxation' in Monica Bhandari (ed.), *Philosophical Foundations of Tax Law* (Oxford: Oxford University Press, 2017), 161–91, https://doi.org/10.1093/acprof:oso/9780198798439.003.0008.
[6] Gillian Brock, 'Egalitarianism, Ideals, and Cosmopolitan Justice' (2005) 36 *Philosophical Forum* 1–30.

or that we all have equal income or wealth after tax. However, tax equity may deliver reduced inequality in income or wealth, especially through the application of progressive tax rates.

Ability to Pay and Progressive Tax Rates

Different types of tax rate (progressive, proportional and regressive) were introduced in Chapter 1, Figure 1.4. Most attention has been paid to the use of progressive tax rates in achieving tax equity on the basis of ability to pay. The concept of 'ability' predates Adam Smith. In his history of income tax in common law jurisdictions, Peter Harris traces the concept of 'ability' to the Saladin Tithe of 1188.[7] In the British poll tax of 1380, the concept of 'ability' was defined as the value of the estate of each person, so that:

> each lay person shall be charged equally according to his ability, and in the following manner: that is to say, that for the total sum to be accounted for in each township the well-to-do shall according to their ability help the less...[8]

Early taxes such as that levied in colonial New England (in the United States) were levied at a flat (or proportional) rate. However, these taxes were progressive in the design of the base, in the sense that those who owned property contributed more than those who did not, so that 'the amount of the contribution was determined by the ability of the inhabitant to pay, and his ability, by the amount of land and property he possessed'.[9]

During the nineteenth century, ability to pay began to be emphasised as the central principle of tax justice in place of the benefit theory (as explained in Chapter 2). However, tax justice was still not aimed at *redistribution,* or *changing* the pre-existing or market distribution of income. Instead, the obligation to pay tax must be defined in a way that is fair. John Stuart Mill sought to confine the obligations of individuals to the state to those that are strictly necessary, and to ensure a fair distribution of those obligations. His theory of ability focused on 'equal sacrifice' in taxation. Discussing the Maxims of Adam Smith, Mill observed:

> For what reason ought equality to be the rule in matters of taxation? For the reason that it ought to be so in all affairs of government. As a government ought to make no distinction of persons or classes in the strength of their claims on it, whatever sacrifices it requires from them should be made to bear as nearly as possible with the same pressure upon all, which, it must be observed, is the mode by which least sacrifice is occasioned on the whole. If any one bears less than his fair share of the burthen, some other person must suffer more than his

---

[7] Peter Harris, *Income Tax in Common Law Jurisdictions: From the Origins to 1820* (Cambridge, UK: Cambridge University Press, 2006), 45–46.
[8] Ibid., 103.
[9] Ibid., 176.

share, and the alleviation to the one is not, cæteris paribus, so great a good to him, as the increased pressure upon the other is an evil. Equality of taxation, therefore, as a maxim of politics, means equality of sacrifice. It means apportioning the contribution of each person towards the expenses of government so that he shall feel neither more nor less inconvenience from his share of the payment than every other person experiences from his.[10]

To achieve this, Mill advocated a proportional rate of taxation on income. Following Jeremy Bentham, Mill would leave untaxed 'a certain minimum of income, sufficient to provide the necessaries of life', so that the tax would be progressive in effect. However, Mill was parsimonious with his tax minimum and was concerned to ensure that the basic exemption should not 'be stretched further than to the amount of income needful for life, health, and immunity from bodily pain'.[11] Above the tax threshold, Mill's proportional income tax would leave the existing distribution of income unchanged: it was not designed to interfere in the market allocation of income or wealth. Mill argued against a graduated rate on higher incomes, observing:

> I am as desirous as any one that means should be taken to diminish those inequalities, but not so as to relieve the prodigal at the expense of the prudent. To tax the larger incomes at a higher percentage than the smaller is to lay a tax on industry and economy; to impose a penalty upon people for having worked harder and saved more than their neighbours.[12]

The only exception that Mill makes to proportionality in taxation concerns the inequality of inherited wealth; we return to the taxation of wealth and inheritance in Chapter 6.

Contrary to Mill's position, by the end of the nineteenth century it was increasingly accepted that taxation should play a role in directly modifying the distribution of income and wealth, as advocated by Adolph Wagner (see Chapter 2). Progressive income taxation came to be seen as the best way to achieve this outcome, although this did not happen without a significant struggle. In his exhaustive study of the history and application of progressive taxes, Edwin Seligman observed that 'practice seems to be tending more and more to the partial or complete adoption of the progressive principle', especially in the relatively new income taxes in various countries.[13]

One widely adopted justification for progressive tax rates, which is often assumed without discussion, is the **declining marginal utility of income**.[14] The theoretical idea is, simply, that everyone experiences income subjectively

---

[10] Mill, *Principles of Political Economy* (see n 2), Book V.2 [2].
[11] Ibid.
[12] Ibid.
[13] Edwin RA Seligman, 'Progressive Taxation in Theory and Practice' (1908) 9(4) *American Economic Association Quarterly*, 3rd Series, 564.
[14] See, e.g. Reuven S Avi-Yonah, 'Globalization, Tax Competition and the Fiscal Crisis of the Welfare State' (2000) 113(7) *Harvard Law Review* 1573–676, 1649.

as having declining utility, or generating less happiness, as income rises; that is, the next dollar is 'worth more' to a poorer person than to a richer person.[15] If everyone is assumed to have the same utility function *and* utility is assumed to decline with income, then this theory supports redistribution from richer people to poorer people, to generate a greater utility overall in society. The theory of declining marginal utility has intuitive appeal; it is obvious that a $100 note found on the street will matter more for a poor person than a rich person. However, observation also suggests that it matters to the rich that they are rich! If this were not the case, tax planning and evasion by taxpayers at the top of the distribution would be less of a concern for tax systems.

Hans Gribnau and Henk Vording note the important contribution by Mill in making tax equity concrete, rather than a vague and open principle. From this time onward, equity became 'the primary aim of any tax system, and an object of calculation and measurement'.[16] A great advantage of the income tax is that it provides a measurable, objective measure of ability to pay. Ultimately, the choice about redistribution must be made in the political arena of the tax state. As Henry Simons argued in 1938, progressive income taxation rests on the case against inequality of outcome: 'on the ethical or aesthetic judgment that the prevailing distribution of wealth and income reveals a degree (and/or kind) of inequality which is distinctly evil or unlovely'.[17] We return to the issue of progressive tax rates on labour income in Chapter 5.

Ability to Pay and the Concept of Income

The concept of ability and the concept of income both originated from concepts of tax 'faculty' or 'endowment' that were well established by the time of Adam Smith. Tax 'faculty' was an objective measure that was identified by applying a proxy that identified a certain level of tax owed based on their trade, guild membership, land holding or other status attributes.[18] This status measure was ultimately replaced by the more general proxy of 'income', legally defined.

During the twentieth century, tax theorists dissatisfied with the proxy of 'income' again became interested in taxing 'endowment', in the sense of an individual's attributes, or earning potential, rather than their actual earnings.[19] The idea of taxing endowment appears logical in theory; we each differ in our

---

[15] Sarah B Lawsky, 'On the Edge: Declining Marginal Utility and Tax Policy' (2011) 95 *Minnesota Law Review* 904–52, 905.
[16] Gribnau and Vording, 'The Birth of Tax as a Legal Discipline' (see n 3), 48.
[17] Henry C Simons, *Personal Income Taxation: The Definition of Income as a Problem of Fiscal Policy* (Chicago: University of Chicago Press, 1938), 18–19.
[18] Harris, *Income Tax in Common Law Jurisdictions* (see n 8), 389–90.
[19] Henk Vording, 'Talents, Types, and Tags: What Is the Relevance of the Endowment Tax Debate?' in Monica Bhandari (ed.), *Philosophical Foundations of Tax Law* (Oxford: Oxford University Press, 2017), https://doi.org/10.1093/acprof:oso/9780198798439.003.0011.

endowments, and a fair tax will appropriately differentiate in its application to each of us. A tax on 'endowments' will tax those with greater potential to earn income at a higher rate. The example is often given of the beach bum who earns just enough to go to the beach and surf, and pays very little tax; but who could have been a surgeon, so should be treated as having a high taxable income, even if the beach bum has only a fraction of the income of the surgeon in reality.

However, we cannot rely on taxing endowment in a real income system. The theory of taxing endowment would require us to identify 'a man's [sic] income-earning potential from his apparent IQ, the number of his degrees, his address, age or colour: but the natural, and one would suppose the most reliable, indicator of his income-earning potential is his income'.[20] An investigation of an individual's 'endowments' would interfere unduly with individual freedom and may bring taxation dangerously close to conscription.

In contrast, a tax on income has two great advantages: it is practical, as we can identify and measure the tax base; and it is objective, based on the income earned in the market. The income tax has the further merit of automatically taking account of market inequalities, such as discrimination in market returns to labour. Assume a man and woman have equal talents and do equivalent work, but the woman earns less than the man as a result of a gender pay gap (as widely evidenced across countries). An endowment tax would result in taxation at the same level, but that would be unfair, because it would fail to recognise the effect of discrimination in the labour market. Under an individual income tax, even levied at a flat rate, the woman (who earns less income) will pay less tax than the man (who earns more income for equivalent work). A progressive income tax goes further in redressing the market inequality, as the higher earning man will face a higher tax burden. The income tax alone cannot remedy the pay gap, but nor does it compound the discrimination evident in the labour market.

It could be relevant in thinking about taxation to ask *how* an individual achieved their level of 'endowment'. While the example of talent implicitly refers to an individual having attained endowment by a natural, genetic or birth process, this is far from the most important way in which individuals achieve endowments. If individual endowment is produced through benefit from public or social goods financed by taxes, this may justify an individual obligation to pay taxes under the benefit theory (as discussed in Chapter 2). However, in reality the question of how much tax the individual is required to pay must still depend on the objective income of the individual.

The Carter Commission into tax reform in Canada that reported in 1966 presented a strong case for operationalising a comprehensive definition of income

---

[20] James A Mirrlees, 'An Exploration in the Theory of Optimum Income Taxation' (1971) 38(2) *The Review of Economic Studies* 175–208, 175.

to achieve progressive taxation based on ability to pay.[21] A key focus of the Commission was 'discretionary economic power', as measured by income from work, capital gains, saving, gifts and bequests. The Commission stated:[22]

> [W]e favour very strongly the ability-to-pay approach.... Taxation according to ability to pay, is inherently as arbitrary as the benefit approach, in the sense that the fundamental propositions on which it is based cannot be proved or disproved. There is, however, an important difference. We do not believe there is an equitable method of allocating taxes according to the benefits of government expenditures. There are, however, principles that we believe provide a fair basis for the allocation of taxes according to ability to pay.
>
> We can do no more in designing a tax system than found it upon these principles. In a democracy, equity questions ultimately must be resolved in terms of the shared values of the people. There is no higher authority. It is our earnest hope that the ability-to-pay principles in which we believe, and from which we have derived our major recommendations, commend themselves to most Canadians.
>
> In our judgment taxes should be allocated among tax units in proportion to their ability to pay. We believe this would be achieved when taxes were allocated in proportion to the discretionary economic power of tax units. This statement is only meaningful if the term 'discretionary economic power' is defined. For this purpose we have found it useful to think of discretionary economic power as the product of the tax unit's total economic power and the fraction of the total economic power available for the discretionary use of the unit.
>
> By 'tax units' we mean families and unattached individuals. By 'total economic power' we mean the power of a tax unit to command goods and services for personal use, whether the power is exercised or not. By the 'fraction of the total economic power available for discretionary use', we mean the proportion of the unit's total economic power that does not have to be exercised to maintain the members of the unit. Maintenance is not synonymous with bare, physical subsistence. Rather, it denotes the provision of the services necessary to maintain the appropriate standard of living of the family or unattached individual relative to others. ...

The Carter Commission recommendations generated substantial political and popular opposition, even though the Commission advocated reducing top post-World War II marginal rates from as high as 80 per cent to levels below 50 per cent, close to top marginal income tax rates today. The opposition was largely due to its advocacy of a uniform tax base and the removal of many special tax concessions from the system; the result, even with lower marginal rates, would have been higher taxation of many well-off Canadians. One

---

[21] Canada Privy Council Office, *Report of the Royal Commission on Taxation. Vol 3: Taxation of Income: Part A, Taxation of Individuals and Families/Kenneth LeM Carter, Chairman* (Ottawa: Privy Council Office, 1966).

[22] Ibid., chapter 7, 3. See Kim Brooks (ed.), *The Quest for Tax Reform Continues: The Royal Commission on Taxation Fifty Years Later* (Toronto: Thomson Carswell, 2013).

author described the fallout as follows: 'How a Nice Bay Street Accountant End Up Hated by His Neighbours: The Tale of Kenneth Carter'.[23]

Ability to Pay and the Myth of Ownership

Taxation is just one of the complex of government policies that aim to produce what Colin Farrelly has called 'the fair distribution of the benefits and burdens of social cooperation' – 'distributive justice'.[24] How wide should we cast the net to identify distributive justice in taxation, given the importance of other elements of government provision of services, social welfare and market intervention in determining outcomes for individuals?

Liam Murphy and Thomas Nagel argued in *The Myth of Ownership* that in contemporary tax states, the property of individuals is fundamentally constituted by the tax law as well as by property law and other regulations. Their starting point is taxation in a capitalist economy and they suggest that tax justice can be considered only in the context of a comprehensive economic picture 'including expenditures for public goods and redistribution either in money or by public provision, together with the effects of all this on employment, economic growth, and the distribution of wealth and income'.[25]

This approach implies that the traditional criterion of equity in taxation is unduly limited. If private property is a legal convention, defined by all of the laws and regulatory mechanisms of the state *including* taxation, then 'taxes must be evaluated as part of the overall system of property rights that they help to create'.[26] Therefore, the idea that you own your 'pre-tax' or 'market income' is a myth, or a fallacy. It is not possible to determine the fairness of tax rates or base solely by applying the notions of 'vertical equity, horizontal equity, the benefit principle, equal sacrifice, ability to pay, and so forth', which are staples of tax theory.[27]

The approach of Murphy and Nagel in considering the overall benefits and burdens of government financed by taxes is consistent with the fundamental approach of welfare economics to the distribution of market income and the tax burden. Despite the obvious logic of this approach, the concept of 'market' or 'pre-tax' income resonates with many people, who hold strongly to the idea of private property, and that they 'own' their income earned through work or investment. Taxpayers, and tax lawyers, habitually reason in terms of 'income' or 'gains' of a taxpayer, whether wages of an individual or the profit of a corporation. There are some good reasons for this, not least that this is

---

[23] Linda McQuaig, *Behind Closed Doors: How the Rich Won Control of Canada's Tax System ... and Ended Up Richer* (Toronto: Viking, 1989), 154–5.
[24] Colin Farrelly, 'Taxation and Distributive Justice' (2004) 2 *Political Studies Review* 185–97, 185.
[25] Liam Murphy and Thomas Nagel, *The Myth of Ownership: Taxes and Justice* (Oxford: Oxford University Press, 2002), 162.
[26] Ibid., 8.
[27] Ibid., 7.

what the tax law requires. The taxpayer, as defined in law, must identify their 'income' and 'deductions' and through this process ascertain their 'taxable income' subject to tax rates. Once modified by tax credits or other adjustments, this process will identify the tax paid and therefore the 'after-tax' income remaining to the taxpayer.

Once we move away from the theoretical inquiry into tax fairness and acknowledge the existence of tax planning and economic decision-making by taxpayers, we can see that the tax paid by individuals is a product of economic activity in the market (working, saving or investing) *combined* with the choices available to them in the tax system. Therefore, in a real and not just illusory sense, taxpayers do have control over and make choices about pre-tax and taxable income. More generally, taxes create incentives that may generate behavioural responses, in economic and other decisions of taxpayers. To understand how and why taxpayers behave the way they do in a tax system, we need to understand how taxpayers perceive their 'income', 'gains', or transactions subject to tax law, and what they do in the tax system.

It is also important to acknowledge that tax law, especially tax rates on high incomes, are crucial policy levers to achieve equity in situations where transfers or other elements of the tax-transfer system do not reach. It is impossible to address inequality at the top of the income or wealth distribution without applying tax rates, as few other government policy measures are relevant. The justification of tax payable by top income earners must be because of the benefit of government, but the design of the tax rates that affect them must be justified more specifically by a principle of ability to pay in respect of the 'pre-tax' income of those taxpayers.

However, Murphy and Nagel are right to observe that some individuals are acutely conscious of the 'burden' of taxation, and this concept may play a significant role in political discourse. This is the problem of 'everyday libertarianism', which focuses popular anger and misguided attention on tax rates, ignoring all other benefits and burdens of government. Some politicians and media have actively contributed to 'inventing' and harnessing 'tax rage', obsessively focused on tax rate reduction and making it increasingly difficult for public debates to encompass both taxing and spending in the collective bargain about the public good.[28]

The COVID-19 pandemic may have led to a shift in public perceptions about the value and role of government and generated support for greater government expenditure, especially on health and income support. However, it is less clear that it will lead to greater public support for taxation. Most additional government spending, so far, has been financed by debt, not taxes, in countries around the world.

---

[28] Andre Broome, 'Setting the Fiscal Policy Agenda: Economic News and Election Year Tax Debates in New Zealand' (2006) 24(2) *Law in Context* 60–77; Larry Patriquin, *Inventing Tax Rage: Misinformation in the National Post* (Halifax: Fernwood Publishing, 2004).

The Tax-Transfer System

In the contemporary tax and welfare state, which evolved in the second half of the twentieth century, cash payments or 'transfers' became a central role of government and it is accepted that both taxes and transfers are necessary to achieve a just distribution of income. The 'transfer' system encompasses most elements of welfare states including social security payments, the age pension, family and child benefits, unemployment benefits, housing allowances, student and youth allowances and disability pensions.

For example, a review of Australia's tax system published in 2010 stated:

> The tax and transfer system should treat individuals with similar economic capacity in the same way, while those with greater capacity should bear a greater net burden, or benefit less in the case of net transfers. This burden should change more than in proportion to the change in capacity. That is, the overall system should be progressive.[29]

Optimal tax theory (which we discuss later) analyses the tax-transfer system as a coherent whole by modelling the system as a single 'net tax function'. In this approach, 'people with high incomes pay some of that income in positive taxes to the government, and people with a low income receive money from the government (by paying negative taxes); no conceptual distinction is made between net recipients from and net contributors to the state's finances'.[30]

Consistently with this approach, most statistical measures of poverty or inequality focus on private income net of taxes and transfers, which is called **disposable income**. The most common measure of income inequality is the **Gini coefficient** of disposable income. The Gini coefficient is zero if everyone in the society has the same disposable income and one in a fully unequal society where one person has all of the disposable income and others have none.

In most OECD member states, the tax-transfer system contributes significantly to equalising disposable income across society, although there is significant variation across countries. Figure 4.1 shows, for example, that the Gini coefficient of market income in Ireland in 2017 was about 0.53, whereas the Gini coefficient of disposable income was below 0.3. This indicates that the tax-transfer system of Ireland is quite progressive and significantly lowers inequality in disposable income. Figure 4.1 also shows that in some countries, including Chile and Mexico, the tax-transfer system has little equalising effect.

---

[29] Australian Treasury, *Australia's Future Tax System* (see n 1), part 1 box 2.1, 17.
[30] Mike Brewer, Emmanuel Saez and Andrew Shephard, 'Means Testing and Tax Rates on Earnings' in Stuart Adam, Tim Besley, Richard Blundell, Stephen Bond, Robert Chote, Malcolm Gammie, Paul Johnson, Gareth Myles and James M Poterba, *Dimensions of Tax Design. Mirrlees Review: Vol 1* (Oxford: Oxford University Press, 2010), 90–201, www.ifs.org.uk/publications/7184

Equity

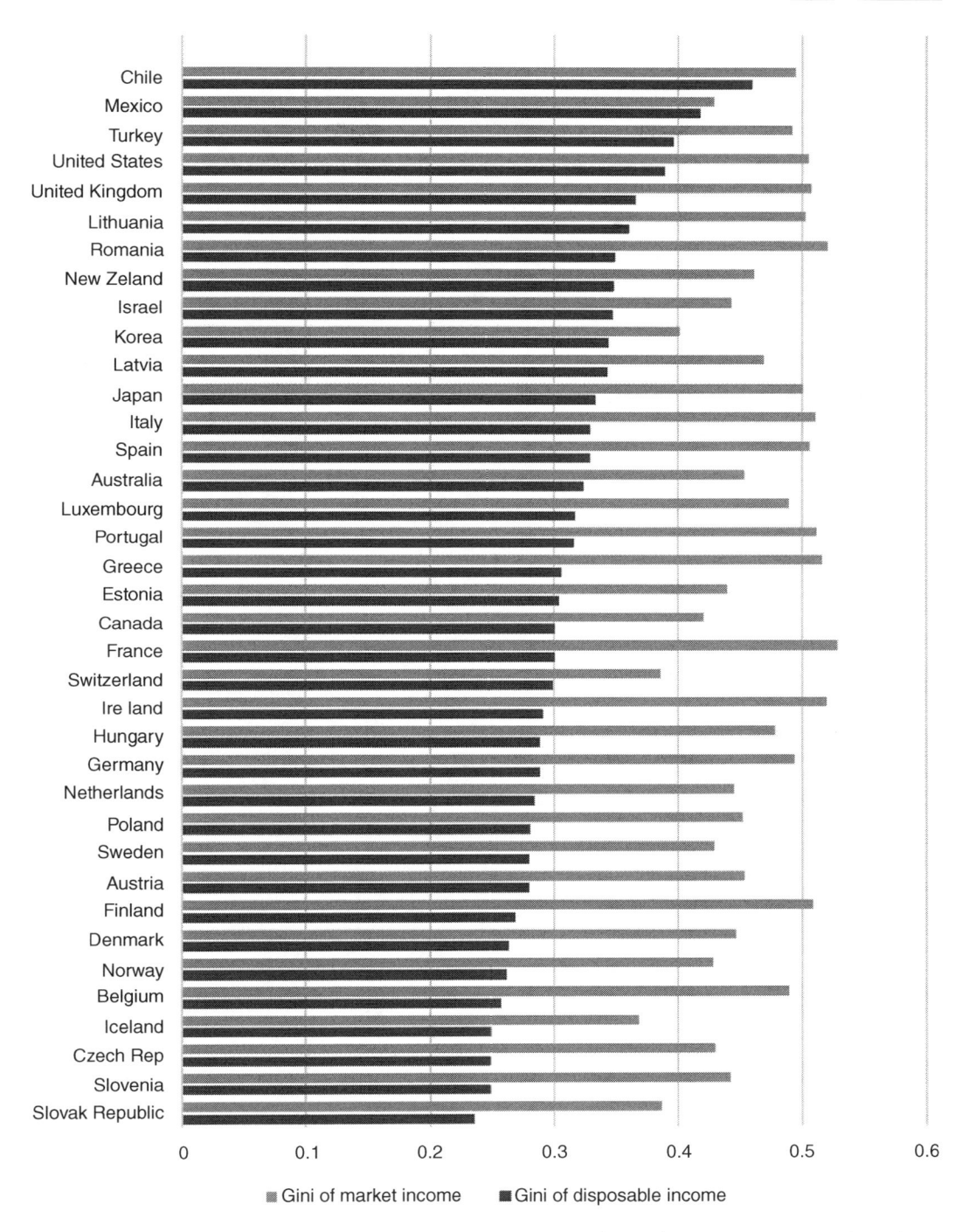

Figure 4.1 Effect of taxes and transfers on Gini coefficient of OECD countries, 2018 or latest data
Source: OECD, StatLink, Income Distribution Database, https://stats.oecd.org/Index.aspx?DataSetCode=IDD.

The Gini coefficient of disposable income does not tell us which taxes and welfare payments produce the equalising result. There is significant variation between the tax structures of different countries. For example, France has high taxes on consumption and high social security taxes, but relatively low reliance on the income tax. Highly egalitarian countries like Sweden and Finland have relatively low taxes on capital and heavy taxes on wages and consumption. Australia and New Zealand do not levy social security taxes and tax capital relatively lightly; these countries largely deliver tax equity through targeted transfer payments and progressive income tax rates on labour income.

The Gini coefficient that measures progressivity of the tax-transfer system ignores the effects of other government expenditures on social goods like housing, health or education, which may have a significant equalising effect. Other kinds of policy may increase equality in society through so-called pre-distributional rather than re-distributional effects.[31] Predistributional policies alter the distribution of market incomes through changing the framework regulation or settings in the market. Examples include land reform that distributes land ownership; or regulation of the labour market, for example by legislating a minimum wage.

Substantive Equity, Rights and Discrimination in Tax Law

Discussions of equity in tax law rarely refer to issues of human rights, or to gender, racial or other discriminatory issues that have long been analysed in other areas of law. It is generally accepted that formal discrimination has no place in tax law and so 'explicitly racial, religious, or sexual ground for differential treatment would not be allowable'.[32] Apart from outlawing formal discrimination, most 'rights-based' analyses of equity in taxation tend to be limited to the narrow (but still important) issue of due process for taxpayers. We return to this issue in Chapter 9.

Given broad patterns of economic disadvantage and subordination in society, and the breadth of the impact of taxation, it should not be surprising that tax law, like other law, 'sustains and deepens patterns of social inequality'.[33] The focus on formal neutrality led scholars to ignore the substantive discriminatory effects of tax systems and the systemic discursive, ideological or normative effects of taxation that may reinforce, or undermine, social and

---

[31] Martin O'Neill, 'Power, Predistribution, and Social Justice' (2020) 95 *Philosophy* 63–91; Jacob S Hacker, 'The Institutional Foundations of Middle-Class Democracy' in *Priorities for a New Political Economy: Memos to the Left* (London: Policy Network, 2011), 33–8.
[32] Murphy and Nagel, *The Myth of Ownership* (see n 25), 166.
[33] Lisa Philipps, 'Discursive Deficits: A Feminist Perspective on the Power of Technical Knowledge in Fiscal Law and Policy' (1996) 11(1) *Canadian Journal of Law and Society* 141–76, 145.

ideological norms of the family, race or class. There has been increasing attention paid to some of these dimensions of tax equity through a growing body of 'critical' tax scholarship.[34]

Critical tax scholars draw on approaches to law and sociological inquiry to address intersecting strands of race, gender or sexuality in tax law and to analyse how tax law (like all law) contributes to constructing the very fabric of society.[35] This scholarship also demonstrates the substantive, and structural, disadvantages produced by formally neutral tax law as it applies in different social, legal and economic contexts

Feminist tax scholars have long emphasised the need for public provision to improve economic outcomes for women while pointing to the 'gendered dynamics of tax policy' that undermine gender equality.[36] Take the example of the appropriate tax rate for wages versus capital gains. Claire Young pioneered a gendered tax expenditure analysis which showed that in Canada, lighter taxation of capital gains than wages disproportionately benefits men over women, exacerbating the gender inequality in distribution of income – based on the reality that women own fewer investment assets and derive fewer and smaller capital gains than men.[37] The intersecting discriminatory effects of tax-transfer systems on women's labour income, which are a significant disincentive to women's market work, is explained in Chapter 5.

Critical race scholarship provides insights into the racially discriminatory effects of tax laws. In the United States, significant academic research has led to policy recommendations aimed at alleviating racially discriminatory effects of the US tax system at all levels, from local property taxes, to the federal income tax.[38] The Tax Policy Center, a US think tank, has begun to collect and analyse tax return data on the intersection of race with marital status, age and

---

[34] Antony Infanti and Bridget Crawford (eds.), *Critical Tax Theory: An Introduction* (Cambridge, UK: Cambridge University Press, 2010); Karen B Brown and Mary Louise Fellows, *Taxing America* (New York: New York University Press, 1996).

[35] Antony Infanti, *Our Selfish Tax Laws* (Cambridge, MA: MIT Press: 2018); Tsilly Dagan, 'The Currency of Taxation' (2016) 84 *Fordham Law Review* 2537–64.

[36] See Kim Brooks, Asa Gunnarson, Lisa Philipps and Marie Wersig (eds.), *Challenging Gender Inequality in Tax Policy Making: Comparative Perspectives* (London: Hart Publishing, 2011); Lisa Philipps, 'Tax Law and Social Reproduction: The Gender of Fiscal Policy in an Age of Privatization' in Brenda Cossman and Judy Fudge (eds.), *Privatization, Law and the Challenge to Feminism* (Toronto: University of Toronto Press, 2002), 41; Miranda Stewart (ed.), *Tax, Social Policy and Gender: Rethinking Equality and Efficiency* (Canberra: ANU Press, 2017).

[37] Claire Young, 'Taxing Times for Women: Feminism Confronts Tax Policy' in Richard Krever (ed.), *Tax Conversations* (Amsterdam: Kluwer Law International, 1997), 261–92.

[38] Beverly Moran and William Whitford, 'A Black Critique of the Internal Revenue Code' (1996) *Wisconsin Law Review* 751–820; Dorothy A Brown, *The Whiteness of Wealth: How the Tax System Impoverishes Black Americans – And How We Can Fix it* (New York: Crown, 2021); Chye-Ching Huang and Roderick Taylor, *How the Federal Tax Code Can Better Advance Racial Equity* (Washington, DC: Center on Budget and Policy Priorities, 2019), www.cbpp.org/sites/default/files/atoms/files/7-25-19tax.pdf.

other indicators.[39] This analysis may become possible in future, as President Biden, on taking office in January 2021, issued an Executive Order calling for all federal agencies, including the Internal Revenue Service, to collect data to support racial equity in policy making and outcomes.[40]

Life Course and Intergenerational Equity

One other perspective on tax equity is useful to introduce at this point. This is an approach that considers the effects of taxes and transfers over the life course and across generations. Most measures of inequality of income or wealth, and of distributional effects of taxes and transfers, such as the Gini coefficient, are **static**. These measures provide a snapshot of the distribution for individuals or households at a point in time.

Taxes paid to (and transfers received from) government change substantially over the life course of individuals. A **dynamic** approach to equity and efficiency would consider the life course distributional and behavioural effects of taxation. Most individuals are 'net beneficiaries' of private or public support at some points in their lifetime, and 'net taxpayers' or contributors of taxation at other points in their lifetime. This approach can be extended to analyse the effects of policy for intergenerational equity.

One approach to equity over the life course that takes account of the social and economic context of individuals draws on the concept of 'capabilities' developed by Amartya Sen.[41] The concept of capabilities is similar to 'human capital', a concept referenced from time to time in tax policy. However, capabilities is a much richer concept, connecting human attributes and skills to life course needs of individuals, and linking these to human rights and agency of individuals to 'do and be' during their lifetime. Sen argued that 'the true measure of human development is that a person has the 'capabilities' necessary to leading the kind of life they value and have reason to value' so that 'capabilities allow an individual to fully function in society'.[42]

The capabilities approach supports a focus on the individual as an 'end in themselves', so that any one person's 'capabilities' must be equally regarded with the capabilities of others. Berik et al express three components of capabilities:

---

[39] See Tax Policy Center, 'Racial Disparities and the Income Tax System' (30 January 2020), https://apps.urban.org/features/race-and-taxes/.

[40] President Biden (US), Executive Order on Advancing Racial Equity and Support for Underserved Communities Through the Federal Government (20 January 2021), www.whitehouse.gov/briefing-room/presidential-actions/2021/01/20/executive-order-advancing-racial-equity-and-support-for-underserved-communities-through-the-federal-government/.

[41] Amartya Sen, *Development as Freedom* (Oxford: Oxford University Press, 1999); Miranda Stewart, 'Gender Equity in Australia's Tax System: A Capabilities Approach' in Brooks et al, *Challenging Gender Inequality in Tax Policy Making* (see n 36), 53–74.

[42] Sen, *Development as Freedom* (see n 41), 17.

Human well-being requires at a minimum adequate provisioning (through inter-connected paid labor and unpaid care activities and entitlements from the state or community); capabilities (the ability to do or be, based on provisioning); and agency (the ability to participate in decision making so as to shape the world we live in).[43]

The capabilities approach was further developed by Martha Nussbaum in her theory of social justice for women.[44] Individual capabilities need to be fostered throughout one's life. To achieve this requires an equitable distribution of the burden and cost of care, so that care is provided to all and that all are responsible for it. Because humans are 'animal beings whose lives are characterized by profound neediness as well as by dignity',

> a good society must arrange to provide care for those in a condition of extreme dependency, without exploiting women as they have traditionally been exploited, and thus depriving them of other important capabilities.[45]

It is particularly important to emphasise women as individuals with capabilities in discussing taxes and transfers. This is because women are frequently invisible in tax policy discourse and data by being embedded within a 'joint' spousal or household unit. Through the collection of revenues for public provision and redistribution, tax law can support the equitable distribution of the cost of care. For example, a policy of public childcare provision, or paid parental leave, shares the cost of care of infants or young children, relieving the burden on women (and families in general).

A particular focus of life course analysis is the design of tax policy for retirement savings and the distribution of wealth, which are important issues in an era of longevity and population ageing. We return to some of these issues in Chapter 5 (on work and family) and Chapter 6 (on savings and investment).

Efficiency

Optimal Tax Theory and Incentives

The principle of efficiency requires that taxes should not distort the allocation of resources in a market economy. This assumes that the market economy will achieve the social welfare-maximising allocation of resources in a world without taxes. Individuals will choose to produce and consume, work, save and invest, based on the price generated in the market, to a level that maximises their subjective well-being or welfare. Individual responses to taxation are 'microeconomic' but in aggregate, at the 'macroeconomic' level,

---

[43] Günseli Berik, Yana van der Meulen Rodgers and Stephanie Seguino, 'Feminist Economics of Inequality, Development, and Growth' (2009) 15(3) *Feminist Economics* 1–33, 2.
[44] Martha Nussbaum, 'Capabilities and Social Justice' (2002) 4(2) *International Studies Review* 123–35.
[45] Ibid., 134.

they imply a misallocation of resources that generates deadweight loss. The aim is to design the tax system so that across all consumers and producers, the resulting market equilibrium maximises social welfare while distribution can be addressed through the use of transfers funded by taxation.

Optimal tax theory was developed in the 1970s, largely by James Mirrlees, building on earlier work of Frank Ramsey and others.[46] Optimal tax theory aims to raise a given level of government revenue while improving aggregate social welfare.[47] Welfare in this usage refers to the utilitarian concept in welfare economics, of the overall well-being of the population. As all taxes distort market behaviour and reduce the level of production and consumption below the optimum for social welfare, the goal of optimal tax theory is to 'optimise' the system to achieve efficiency and redistribution. The 'first-best' and least distorting theoretical solution would be to require everyone to pay a lump-sum tax and to use the revenue to finance public goods and redistribution. However, in the real world this is neither possible nor desirable. Optimal tax theory recognises that taxes cannot be perfectly efficient and that 'second best' (or 'third best') solutions are needed.

This 'economic approach to tax design' was explicitly adopted in the Mirrlees Review in 2010.[48] The review asserted that its main purpose was not to engage with questions of the overall level of public spending, redistribution or taxation, but rather to achieve the optimal tax design while minimising its welfare-reducing economic effects. Therefore, the review aimed 'for a given distributional outcome' to ensure that 'the negative effects of the tax system on welfare and economic efficiency' should be minimised.[49]

The incentive effects of taxation are illustrated in a basic model of a market transaction in Figure 4.2a (supply and demand equilibrium price with no tax) and after a tax is introduced, in Figure 4.2b (supply and demand equilibrium price with tax). When a tax is introduced, the revenue goes to the government, but the imposition of the tax causes changes in pricing and consumer behaviour. A proportion of the 'surplus' or consumer and producer benefit from the market transaction is lost at the new 'taxed' equilibrium. Figure 4.2b shows that the seller (producer) responds to the tax by increasing the price of the good (the supply curve/line moves upward on the chart). In response, the buyer (consumer) purchases less of the taxed good or service.

---

[46] Mirrlees, 'An Exploration in the Theory of Optimal Income Taxation' (see n 20).
[47] This discussion draws on Graeme Cooper, Michael Dirkis, Miranda Stewart and Richard J Vann, *Income Taxation: Commentary and Materials* (Sydney: Thomson Reuters, 2020), chapter 1, incorporating contributions from Professor Patricia Apps, University of Sydney.
[48] Mirrlees et al, *Tax by Design* (see n 1), 21. The Review does an excellent description of the general approach; see also Peter Abelson, *Public Economics* (Sydney: Applied Economics, 2018), https://appliedeconomics.com.au/wp-content/uploads/2021/10/public-economics-principles-and-practice-book-by-peter-abelson.pdf, chapters 27 and 28.
[49] Mirrlees et al, *Tax by Design* (see n 1), 22.

Efficiency

(a) Basic model: economics of a tax

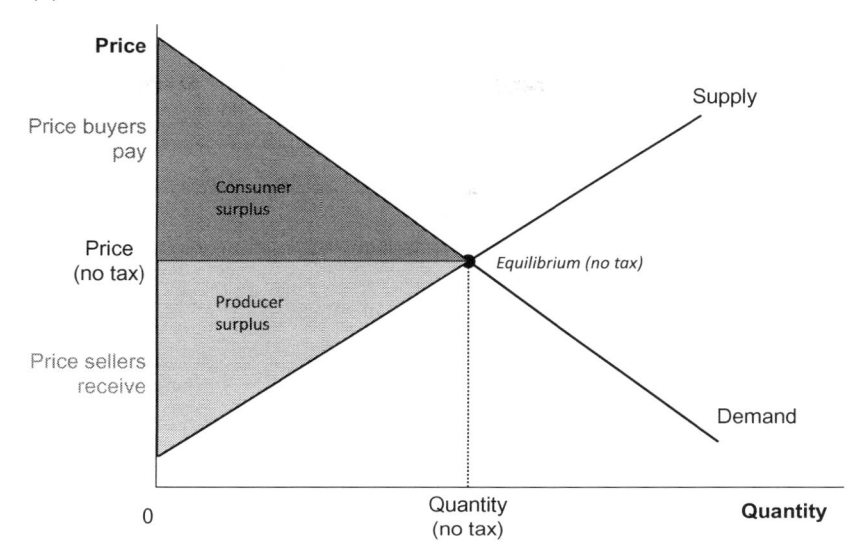

(b) Basic model: economics of a tax

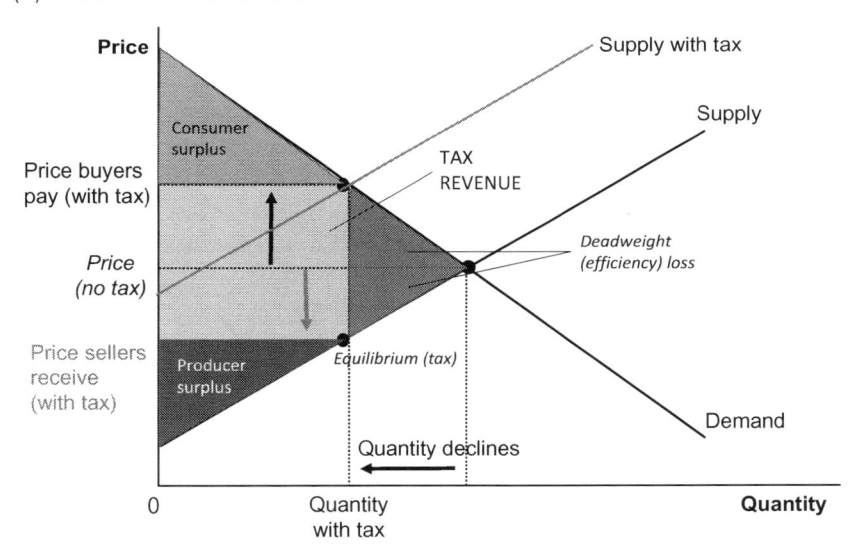

Figure 4.2 (a, b) Basic model – economics of a tax

The tax creates a **wedge** between the market price paid by the buyer (for a good, or an hour of work) and the market price received by the seller. A new equilibrium is produced that lowers the quantity of the good produced and consumed below the optimum for social welfare (which was achieved in a world with no taxes). Individual responses to taxation in aggregate reveal a misallocation of resources that generates a loss in welfare called the **deadweight loss** or **excess burden** of the tax.[50]

The size of the response of the seller in reducing supply and of the response of the consumer to the increased price depends on the **elasticity** of consumer demand for the good. This is an empirical question. If consumers continue to buy the good even at the higher price including the tax, then this indicates that consumer demand has low or zero elasticity. The consumer would bear the tax and the producer would continue to produce the same quantity of the good as before. There would be little or no deadweight loss and the equilibrium with a tax is equal or close to the equilibrium without a tax. This would be an efficient tax.

However, the consumer may decide not to purchase the good at the new price but instead may choose to **substitute** another good or prefer no consumption at all. This is called the **substitution effect** of the tax. If consumer demand is highly elastic, the producer would bear some of the burden of the tax because they cannot raise the price to the extent of the tax, so the quantity of the good is reduced producing a deadweight loss. This implies that the tax is inefficient. In the extreme case (none of the good purchased at all, at the higher price) there would be a large deadweight loss and there would also be no tax collected.

Optimal tax theory calls for us to determine the 'optimal' tax rate and base by considering the elasticity of response to taxation. The response of taxpayers that is emphasised in most applications of optimal tax theory is the substitution effect. A taxpayer may alter his or her economic behaviour in response to taxes by substituting another economic activity for the taxed activity. This is most obvious when considering the effects of a tax on demand and supply of a product, as illustrated in the model in Figure 4.2.

An example from history is the 'window tax' levied in England in various forms from the seventeenth to the nineteenth century.[51] The 'window tax' was thought to be an improvement over the pre-existing 'hearth tax', which required inspectors to enter the house and count the hearths. However, a widespread response to the tax was to brick up the windows or construct homes with fewer windows. This reduced amenity including light and air for those who lived in the houses, with serious health consequences especially in the slum housing in which poor tenants lived.[52] From an equity perspective,

---

[50] Abelson, *Public Economics* (see n 48), chapter 27; Mirrlees et al, *Tax by Design* (see n 1), 29.
[51] Smith, *Wealth of Nations* (see n 4), Book V, Chapter II, Part II, Article 1: 'The window-tax, as it stands at present January 1775), over and above the duty of three shillings upon every house in England, and of one shilling upon every house in Scotland, lays a duty upon every window, which, in England, augments gradually from twopence, the lowest rate, upon houses with not more than seven windows, to two shillings, the highest rate, upon houses with twenty-five windows and upwards'.
[52] Wallace Oates and Robert Schwab, 'The Window Tax: A Case Study in Excess Burden' (2015) 29(1) *Journal of Economic Perspectives* 163–80. The window tax may have originated in France,

the window tax was also problematic. While a window tax should fall heavier on the rich who have more windows in their houses, it was inequitable between house owners because it had no clear relation to the underlying value of the property. A low-valued house in the countryside might have more windows than a high-valued house in the city.

Optimal tax theory suggests that the tax rate should be high on goods or services with a low price elasticity (consumers will not reduce their consumption) and low on goods with a high price elasticity (consumers will respond by substituting other consumption or activity). If a consumer has a strong preference for good A, and it is not easily substituted with good B, they will continue to purchase good A, to the extent that they can afford it, even if the price increases. Consumer demand has low elasticity and this means that a higher tax can be levied without any negative efficiency effects. This has apparently perverse implications. As basic goods (food, housing, clothing) are usually considered to be necessities and are not able to be substituted, this implies as a matter of policy that a tax on necessities is preferable to a tax on luxuries, which are easily substitutable. A tax on luxuries may be difficult to enforce and may cause a change in consumption demand towards untaxed goods or services, whether that be a different product; a different jurisdiction; or obtaining the goods illegally, by smuggling or through avoidance or evasion of the tax.

The substitution effect is also commonly used in analysing the (dis)incentive effect of a tax on work (labour supply); and the (dis)incentive effects of a tax on saving or on the choice of investment by a taxpayer. For example, a taxpayer facing a tax rate on labour income may choose to substitute another, untaxed or lower taxed activity in place of the taxed work. A taxpayer seeking to invest capital may choose to invest in a lower taxed asset, such as a home that is exempt from taxation, rather than a higher taxed asset such as a bank account. In the context of open borders, a taxpayer may choose to work or invest in another lower taxed jurisdiction.

A countervailing effect, relevant especially when considering the incentive effects of taxes on work, is the **income effect**. If an individual seeks to maintain a level of after-tax income, they may work harder or seek a greater return from economic activity if a tax is imposed. Put bluntly, an individual who needs money will work, even if some of the income is taxed away; therefore, the income effect operates in the opposite direction to the substitution effect. The outcome of the income effect on the supply of labour, investment or saving by taxpayers depends, again, on elasticities of response. One topic on which significant empirical evidence has been collected is the labour

although it may be an apocryphal story that 'French doors', invented around the seventeenth century, were created to avoid the tax. Many other, fully substantiated examples of behaviour in response to taxes are given in Joel Slemrod and Michael Keen, *Rebellion, Rascals and Revenue: Tax Follies and Wisdom through the Ages* (Princeton, NJ: Princeton University Press, 2021).

supply elasticity of women and men; we return to this in our discussion of tax, work and family in Chapter 5.

The Principle of Neutrality

To address the deadweight loss generated by taxes, a 'rule of thumb' applied in many tax policy processes is that taxation should be **neutral** between choices.[53] In some tax reviews, **neutrality** is the central principle adopted for tax design. This is a useful principle where a taxpayer may have various alternative choices available; the most efficient tax system would ideally be neutral between these choices.

A comprehensive income tax that treats all forms of income or gain equally will be neutral with respect to the type or source of income derived. In this regard, the goal of 'neutrality' may lead to different recommendations to optimal tax theory, which recommends differential tax rates depending on the elasticity of taxpayer response. In any real tax system, there are numerous examples of differential tax treatment: these may include exemptions from the tax base, the progressive rate structure, timing differences for different asset investments, the realisation requirement that permits deferral of recognition of gain, and different tax treatment of different legal entities or persons, which are non-neutralities in the tax system. In Chapter 6, we discuss the diversity of nominal or effective tax rates for different forms of saving in many tax systems.

An important feature of tax reform processes is the battle between those who seek to introduce targeted tax provisions to encourage specific activities (or, perhaps, benefit vested interests), or to achieve fairness goals; and those who seek to **broaden the tax base** by eliminating or reducing differences in tax treatment, reducing distortions in market allocation of work or saving and potentially enabling taxes to raise the same revenue at a lower rate.

It seems likely that tax systems became more efficient when **broad-based** income or consumption taxes were successfully levied in the first half of the twentieth century. Broad-based taxes reduce the return to economic activity in a general way, rather than applying to specific goods or activities.[54] In contrast, earlier tax systems were composed of diverse taxes with different economic effects. Land taxes and taxes on inheritance, which were dominant forms of taxation in previous centuries, were relatively efficient as these tax bases were immobile and governments had access to information and were able to enforce these taxes. The array of specific taxes or excises on goods,

---

[53] Mirrlees et al, *Tax by Design* (see n 1), 22.
[54] Tony Atkinson and Joseph Stiglitz formalised the proof that a broad-based consumption or income tax is more efficient than differential commodity tax rates: 'The Design of Tax Structure: Direct versus Indirect Taxation' (1976) 6 *Journal of Public Economics* 55–75.

sumptuary taxes and early forms of tax on specific kinds of income or endowment were not so efficient, and also led to an array of taxpayer approaches to avoid these taxes. One may speculate that the increase in administrative capability that enabled governments to levy more efficient broad-based taxes was necessary before they were able to raise more taxes from the population while still benefiting from economic growth.

The emphasis on elasticity of taxpayer response in optimal tax theory challenges the 'neutrality' concept and runs counter to the comprehensive income tax benchmark that aims to tax all sources of income equally. We consider these issues further in Chapter 5 (taxes on work), Chapter 6 (taxes on saving and investment) and Chapter 7 (corporate and business taxation).

Finally, we need to consider potential **trade-offs between efficiency and equity**, which are frequently referred to in tax policy debates. Higher tax rates that aim to increase progressivity and redistribution may deter productive economic behaviour, such as work, saving or investing, creating deadweight loss that reduces the 'size of the pie'. However, lower tax rates may be less equitable. In the example of a tax on goods, the recommendation of optimal tax theory to tax necessities higher, or at least equal to, luxuries is regressive. This is one reason why economists argue that a flat tax rate applicable to all goods and services is a good compromise. In most countries, compromises are made in tax design, including exempting basic food or health care from a consumption tax base. As rich people also buy necessities, the exemption undermines the effectiveness of the tax and may not be as redistributive as is often assumed. The main approach of optimal tax theory to this issue is that the tax should be designed optimally and distributional issues should be dealt with through government transfers. However, dealing with all distributional issues through the welfare (or transfer) system brings its own challenges and faces many political and institutional constraints.

Taxes, Externalities and Market Failure

Differences in tax treatment that encourage taxpayers to change their economic behaviour might be the result of deliberate policy, for example, incentives for saving for retirement or for particular types of business investment. From a budgetary perspective, a specifically designed tax incentive should be treated as a 'tax expenditure' (as explained in Chapter 3). Whether it has the intended behavioural effect will depend on the response of taxpayers. Differences in tax treatment may also (even frequently) be unintended, and these can generate tax planning opportunities that undermine the tax base. One example is the different tax treatment of different legal entities, or different financial investments such as debt and equity that we observe in most tax systems. We discuss the issue of tax arbitrage and tax planning in Chapter 9.

Externalities are costs or benefits not accounted for in the market, so that the cost or benefit does not accrue to the firm or person carrying on the activity. So-called negative externalities or spillovers imply that costs will be higher than the market determines, while positive externalities or spillovers imply greater economy or social benefit than the market return to an activity.

Negative externalities or 'market failure' may be caused by incomplete information; truncated property rights; or imperfect competition, for example, produced through monopoly power in the market.[55] In response, it may be appropriate for taxes to be designed with the intention of altering economic incentives for behaviour and 'correcting' the market. Market failure is the main justification for lower taxes or subsidies to support innovation or research and development by businesses (see Chapter 7) or for higher taxes on some commodities. Other approaches to address negative externalities are subsidies, government regulation or direct governmental provision.

Taxes have been designed in many countries to address the negative externalities of pollution or health costs that are not fully priced in the market. Specific taxes intended to drive behavioural change to achieve better social or environmental impacts are called **Pigouvian taxes**.[56] These taxes can be levied to raise prices on goods and services that have negative externalities, including taxes on fuel, tobacco and alcohol, or on pollution. The most important such environmental tax would be a carbon tax, or carbon pricing scheme, which increases the price of pollution by carbon so as to reduce or prevent climate change. The empirical evidence is clear that a carbon tax or emissions price is the best economic incentive to change behaviour in this way.[57] More recently, taxes on sugar or meat have been proposed to achieve animal rights, health or environmental goals.[58] The increased prices are intended to change behaviour of consumers, who it is hoped will substitute other options that produce lower carbon emissions

Challenges and Limits of Efficiency Analysis

Economic modeling and efficiency analysis provides a useful way of understanding how tax systems affect behaviour, which can guide tax policy.

---

[55] See, e.g. Abelson, *Public Economics* (see n 48), 58.
[56] Janet Milne, 'Environmental Taxes and Fees: Wrestling with Theory' in Larry Kreiser, Soocheol Lee, Kazuhiro Ueta, Janet E Milne and Hope Ashiabor (eds.), *Environmental Taxation and Green Fiscal Reform* (Northampton, MA: Edward Elgar, 2014), 5–24.
[57] Rohan Best, Paul Burke and Frank Jotzo, *Carbon Pricing Efficacy: Cross-country Evidence*, CCEP Working Paper 2004 (Canberra: Australian National University, 2020), https://ccep.crawford.anu.edu.au/sites/default/files/publication/ccep_crawford_anu_edu_au/2020-06/wp_2004.pdf.
[58] E.g. Senarath Dharmasena and Oral Capps Jr, 'Intended and Unintended Consequences of a Proposed National Tax on Sugar-Sweetened Beverages to Combat the US Obesity Problem' (2012) 21(6) *Health Economics* 669–94.

However, caution is required for various reasons. First, and fundamentally, the comparison of the 'taxed' world with a hypothetical 'no-tax' world in the basic economic model ignores both the benefit of government and the imperfections of the market. In all circumstances that matter in the real world, the market would not exist without government, while the preferences of individuals, and the choices available to them in markets, are deeply structured by regulation. Few markets are perfectly efficient, externalities are pervasive, and there is widespread evidence of economic rents and mis-pricing of risk.[59]

Second, tax policy debates tend to overstate the importance of substitution effects of taxation and understate the importance of income effects. It is difficult to measure behavioural responses empirically. Measuring elasticity of response requires quasi-experimental approaches or large data sources on consumers and prices. However, studies of the elasticity of taxable income using administrative tax data have shown that the elasticity of response to taxes by individuals is often lower than expected, and that taxpayers who substitute other activities in response to tax rates may do so through tax planning rather than changing the underlying economic activity.[60]

Third, optimal tax theory makes the simplifying assumptions that all individuals have the same utility function and that all individuals behave rationally and in their own 'self-interest', pursuing their own 'preferences' in the market. However, individuals may act altruistically or may not act in their own economic self-interest, narrowly defined. The feminist critique of economics and law highlights the limited and gendered nature of 'rational economic man'.[61] Advances in behavioural economics demonstrate that individuals often do not respond 'rationally' to economic incentives, and this is relevant in important ways to tax policy.[62] One example is that individual rationality may be limited by cognitive biases such as short-term thinking, which are relevant in considering how to design tax policy for retirement saving.

Fourth, while tax policy acknowledges the imperfections of markets in the use of Pigouvian taxes, it otherwise tends to ignore them. Macroeconomic models of tax systems or tax reforms often make broad assumptions about elasticities and markets. Macroeconomic models usually apply a single labour supply elasticity to a household, but individuals inside a household may have very different elasticities.[63] The failure to differentiate individuals inside the

---

[59] Abelson, *Public Economics* (see n 48), part 2.
[60] Emmanuel Saez, Joel Slemrod and Seth H Giertz, 'The Elasticity of Taxable Income with Respect to Marginal Tax Rates: A Critical Review' (2012) 50(1) *Journal of Economic Literature* 3–50.
[61] See, e.g. Martha Fineman and Terence Dougherty, *Feminism Confronts Homo Economicus: Gender, Law and Society* (Ithaca, NY: Cornell University Press, 2005).
[62] See, e.g. B Douglas Bernheim, Stefano Dellavigna and David Laibson (eds.), *Handbook of Behavioral Economics: Foundations and Applications* (Amsterdam: North-Holland, 2018).
[63] This weakness was identified early on by Patricia Apps, *A Theory of Inequality and Taxation* (Cambridge, UK: Cambridge University Press, 1981); Patricia Apps and Ray Rees, 'Taxation and the Household' (1988) 35(3) *Journal of Public Economics* 355–69.

household means that optimal tax analyses may incorrectly estimate work responses to taxes with unfortunate efficiency and equity effects.

Finally, optimal tax theory, like all other tax theoretical approaches, frequently runs into political obstacles when applied to tax reform. While it aims to take account of both efficiency and equity, there is a tendency to assume that all distributional issues can be solved through transfers or other public expenditure. This ignores political and institutional structures that constrain government action in these fields, and leave the delivery of equity through the tax law as the 'least bad' or only politically available option. Recommendations from optimal tax theory may be too uncertain to provide governments with a stable foundation for tax reform. If the economy, or taxpayer preferences, change then ideally tax rates also change, but constantly 'optimising' or recalibrating tax policy in a way similar to the constant marginal resetting of interest rates by central banks is not viable. Tax reforms are difficult to achieve and frequent change may itself produce unintended negative political or economic consequences. The adage 'an old tax is a good tax' reflects that stability in a tax system is valuable and hard won by governments.

Opening the Borders of the Tax State

Tax Policy in a Global Economy

We discuss the tax state in international context in Part III. Here, we highlight some effects of opening the borders of the state and its economy for tax policy. Opening the borders permits mobility of trade, labour and capital and this upends many and requires us to change how we think about the fiscal bargain between taxpayers and the state.

The concept of comprehensive income assumes a single government levying taxation, capable of defining and taxing net economic gain of individuals in a way that is just, efficient and equitable. Classic optimal tax theory also assumes a single government facing a single budget constraint and seeks to design efficient taxation to raise a given level of revenue for that government.[64] However, as Michael Keen and David Wildasin observe:

> There is a fundamental difference between tax design in a many-country world and in a single country. In the latter case, there is naturally only a single government budget constraint to consider. In many-country settings, in contrast, each government will have its own distinct revenue constraint: that, indeed, is close to being a definition of an independent sovereign state. The countries of the world do not pool their tax revenues.[65]

---

[64] Michael Keen and David Wildasin, 'Pareto-Efficient International Taxation' (2004) 94 *The American Economic Review* 259–75, 259.
[65] Ibid., 260.

Optimising tax systems to maximise economic growth in a global economy will depend on how states and taxpayers interact, strategically or otherwise, across borders. There is a debate among tax economists about whether governments should seek to optimise global welfare, or to focus on national welfare, and in either case, how such a goal can be achieved.

Opening the borders also fundamentally changes the bargain between taxpayers and the state. In the closed tax state, 'the polity and the economy are perfect mappings of each other with respect to geography, membership, and the extent of trade and resource allocation'.[66] The fiscal constitution proposed by Geoffrey Brennan and James Buchanan sought to constrain a Leviathan 'revenue-maximising' government under the assumption of closed borders. Taxes fall on the locals who also receive the benefit of public goods and redistribution. Opening the borders introduces the option of exit. Taxpayers may 'vote with their feet', departing to another jurisdiction with taxes or public goods that suit them better. This changes the internal dynamics of the political bargain and establishes the conditions for tax competition between states.

Opening the borders may also cause us to reassess our principles of tax justice.[67] Absent a global sovereign, or a global pool of revenues to be distributed through a decision-making process among nations, there is no ability to do 'lump-sum transfers' to achieve fairness. This removes one of the basic assumptions of optimal tax theory in the international context. The principles of horizontal and vertical equity depend on the existence of a government responsible for redistribution among its taxpayer-citizens. Opening the borders challenges a government's ability to deliver distributive justice, as a result of tax competition or difficulties in enforcement of tax on mobile factors. It also requires us to re-examine who is included in the redistributive bargain of the state, and to ask whether individuals in one state have an obligation of redistribution to individuals in another state – and if so, how such a redistribution can be achieved, absent a world government. These tax justice questions are a subset of questions about how to achieve global justice, including between governments or between people globally, considered in the philosophical literature.[68]

---

[66] Geoffrey Brennan and James M Buchanan, *The Power to Tax: Analytical Foundations of a Fiscal Constitution* (Cambridge, UK: Cambridge University Press, 1980), 168.

[67] Tsilly Dagan, *International Tax Policy: Between Competition and Cooperation* (Cambridge, UK: Cambridge University Press, 2018).

[68] For contrasting views see Gillian Brock, *Global Justice: A Cosmopolitan Account* (Oxford: Oxford University Press, 2009); Thomas Nagel, 'The Problem of Global Justice' (2005) 33(2) *Philosophy and Public Affairs* 113–47. An attempt to discuss the tax aspects of global redistribution is in Miranda Stewart, 'Redistribution between Rich and Poor Countries' (2018) 72(4–5) *Bulletin of International Taxation* 297–309.

Supply-side Tax Policy

As discussed in Chapter 2, the 1980s came to be seen as the 'decade of tax reform'. Tax systems today are still recognisably the result of widespread tax changes during this period. The general approach drew on optimal tax theory concerning the disincentive effect of taxes, combined with the general principle of neutrality against a comprehensive income benchmark. This generated an overall approach to reform that became known as **supply-side tax policy**. The approach, crudely expressed, aimed to lower tax rates on labour and capital, and shift the tax base towards consumption. This was justified by arguments that tax policy needed to address mobility in an increasingly global economy, and that tax cuts would increase the supply of capital and business investment and skilled labour and thereby generate economic growth which would enable any loss in tax revenue from lower tax rates to be recovered.

The tax reforms of the 1980s responded to a perceived economic crisis for many governments, as explained in Chapter 2. The narrative is expressed in a report of the 35th conference of the International Institute for Public Finance, held in Italy in 1979, which announced that 'the fiscal state is at a critical point'. It identified the pressing problems for tax systems across economic, distributive and administrative fields:[69]

> [I]n countries where the tax burden has reached extremely high levels, people realize that it cannot be further raised, escaping economic drawbacks such as the strangling of incentives to produce and invest, the reduction of saving propensity and the reappearance of a barter economy. . . .
>
> [T]he progressivity of the fiscal system is jeopardized by two factors:
>
> (i) the fiscal apparatus must resort, by now, to raising indirect taxes, for the levels of the income taxes are already at the feasible maximum;
> (ii) international havens and various devices, considerable parts of the profits of the big companies and of high personal incomes as well as inheritances avoid taxation, which hits then, with its severe official progressivity, high-earned incomes, like salaries of top managers.
>
> Furthermore, taxpayer revolts are gaining momentum in many countries; anti-tax parties are blossoming, pleas for tax-cuts – justified not by short-run stabilisation reasons, but by the very principle of refusing high tax rates – have electoral appeal.

---

[69] Francesco Forte and Emilio Giardina, 'The Crisis of the Fiscal State' in Karl W Roskamp and Francesco Forte (eds.), *Reforms of Tax Systems* (Detroit: Wayne State University Press, 1981), 1–9.

A Tax Mix Switch from Income to Consumption?

Income taxes in many countries in the 1970s omitted much of the comprehensive income tax base, which had nonetheless been widely perceived as an ideal benchmark for the tax system. Many income taxes applied a lower tax rate, or no tax at all, to capital gains and did not tax foreign source income, increasing the attractiveness of hiding income in tax havens offshore. Governments enacted tax incentives to encourage business investment in plant and equipment as a part of industrial policy, which permitted fast write-offs of capital assets, and provided other concessions. These far from perfect income taxes were in reality an 'uneasy compromise'[70] or 'unwieldy hybrid'[71] of income and consumption taxes.

The 1980s saw the end of consensus about the comprehensive income tax as the benchmark for tax systems.[72] US scholars, policymakers and politicians, who had for so long favoured a progressive income tax, entered into a debate that continues today, about the merits of shifting to a consumption tax base.[73] This approach resonated with the supply-side recommendation for lower tax on capital to encourage investment and saving.

Tax reformers proposed that governments should increase consumption taxes, while reducing income taxes, leading to a tax mix switch. Some advocated a full conversion of the income tax to a consumption tax base. In 1977, the US Treasury published *Blueprints for Basic Tax Reform*, the result of a year-long study led by David Bradbury.[74] This report canvassed the possibility of a shift from an income tax to a consumption tax, which Bradbury later argued in a foundational book, *Untangling the Income Tax* (1981). In the United Kingdom, the *Meade Report* published in 1978 proposed a shift from the personal income tax to a personal expenditure tax with a cash flow business tax, all with lower tax rates than the system at the time.[75]

The new emphasis on consumption tax was spurred by the success of the indirect broad-based consumption tax in the form of a value added tax (VAT) in European countries. The VAT had been established as a requirement for membership in the European Economic Community (EEC) in the early 1960s. The United Kingdom replaced its pre-existing sales taxes with the VAT in

---

[70] Henry J Aaron, Harvey Galper, and Joseph A Pechman (eds.), *Uneasy Compromise: Problems of a Hybrid Income-Consumption Tax* (Washington, DC: Brookings Institution, 1988).

[71] John Kay and Mervyn King, *The British Tax System*, 5th ed (Oxford: Oxford University Press, 1990), https://ifs.org.uk/docs/kay_king.pdf, 225.

[72] Walter Hettich and Stanley Winer, 'The Shifting Foundations of Tax Reform' (1985) 38(4) *National Tax Journal* 423–45.

[73] See, e.g. Joseph Pechman (ed.), *What Should Be Taxed: Income or Expenditure?* (Washington, DC: Brookings Institution, 1980); Joseph Bankman and David Weisbach, 'Reply: Consumption Taxation Is Still Superior to Income Taxation' (2007) 60 *Stanford Law Review* 789–802.

[74] US Treasury, *Blueprints for Tax Reform* (see n 1).

[75] Institute of Fiscal Studies, *The Structure and Reform of Direct Taxation* (London: IFS, 1978). Subsequently, John Kay and Mervyn King published *The British Tax System* in 1978, now in its fifth edition, 1990, which was influential in spreading this message (see n 71).

1973 when it joined the EEC and the VAT has spread around the world since then. Today, the United States is the only wealthy country without a VAT. Reasons include political opposition by state governments that traditionally levied sales taxes and a conflict between Republicans who opposed the VAT as potentially leading to bigger government and Democrats who opposed the VAT on the grounds that it was regressive.[76]

The tax ideas of the 1980s were consolidated in governmental and independent tax reviews and spread around the globe through a process of cross-fertilisation of ideas between experts and the growing influence of the Organisation for Economic Co-operation and Development (OECD) and the International Monetary Fund, as well as through direct policy transfer between governments. There appeared to be a consensus of the experts and it was suggested that 'the tax systems of the major developed countries, if not all countries, will increasingly tend to resemble each other'.[77]

Ultimately, expert recommendations for a consumption or cash flow tax base were rejected and the income tax prevailed, albeit with some important changed parameters and with lower tax rates. Tax reforms tended to broaden the base of the income tax, eliminating some tax expenditures, accelerated depreciation and special rules. This was partly because the political goal of lowering rates for individuals and corporations required revenue to be raised in other ways, which necessitated a broader tax base. This 'broad base low rate' approach to tax reform became identified with the following main elements (with many differences in detail as enacted in different countries):

- Emphasis on efficiency and economic growth over equity, 'growing the pie';
- Lower personal tax rates to encourage labour supply and saving;
- Lower corporate tax rates and corporate-shareholder integration to encourage business investment;
- Lower flat rates on some capital income and gains, exemption of home ownership from taxation and concessions for retirement saving, which together incorporated some consumption tax elements in the base;
- Removing some tax expenditures, or addressing gaps, loopholes and special provisions in the tax base to raise revenue while imposing lower rates; and
- Some countries increased broad-based consumption taxes such as the VAT.

Tax economists were disappointed in the reform outcomes of the 1980s. John Kay and Mervyn King observed the 'apparent paradox' that while economists had increasingly favoured the merits of a consumption tax, policy nonetheless seemed to favour the income tax. Kay and King

---

[76] Daniel Shaviro, 'Simplifying Assumptions: How Might the Politics of Consumption Tax Reform Affect (Impair) the End Product?' in John W Diamond and George R Zodrow (eds.), *Fundamental Tax Reform: Issues, Choices, and Implications* (Cambridge, MA: MIT Press, 2008), 75–124; Kathryn A James, *The Rise of the Value-Added Tax* (New York: Oxford University Press, 2015).

[77] Cedric Sandford, *Successful Tax Reform: Lessons from an Analysis of Tax Reform in Six Countries* (Bath: Fiscal Publications, 1993), 222.

suggested that academic expertise played an important role in persuading policymakers to move towards 'fiscal neutrality', but 'the fact that the present system is called an income tax led policy-makers to think that the measures required to move to a comprehensive income tax involved less upheaval than those necessary for the transition to an expenditure tax'.[78] This remark may underestimate the wisdom of political choices about taxation. Successful tax states of the twentieth century had relied significantly on progressive income taxation, to the extent that this system has become quasi-constitutional in nature. A reform leading to the upheaval of the income tax would potentially undermine this stable political bargain; it could indeed be revolutionary.

Two decades into the twenty-first century, the hybrid nature of the income tax system in most successful tax states remains. Tax rates and other details have been frequently reformed, and each country has a different definition of the tax base, but the income tax has demonstrated considerable resilience to tax reform efforts and political and economic challenges. Nonetheless, many governments, with the exception of the United States, have enacted, expanded or increased the tax rate for the VAT. Overall, tax revenues remained stable, or even increased up to the Global Financial Crisis of 2008.

However, the reforms of the 1980s and 1990s, especially lower tax rates combined with economic globalisation, did lead to increasing income and wealth inequality, which became a matter of growing political and public concern (we discuss this in Chapter 6). In the international arena, governments increasingly engaged in tax competition to attract foreign investment, while tax avoidance or planning opportunities in personal and corporate income taxation in the global, digital economy were becoming apparent. This time, governments had less room to move in reducing rates and broadening bases to counter tax avoidance and rebuild a fiscal consensus.

Governments in the twenty-first century seem more cautious about doing major tax reform, at least in a domestic context. A wave of tax reviews, including the Mirrlees Review in the United Kingdom (published 2010, initiated in 2006), the Review of Australia's Future Tax System (published 2009, initiated in 2008) and the New Zealand Tax Working Group Review (2010, established in 2009), did not lead to fundamental change.[79] Attempts to 'operationalise' such reviews since then have generally been aborted.

In general, the supply-side approach to efficiency remains in these reviews but it is clear that the effects for of tax reform for equity and economic growth were more contested. Some queried the supply-side premise that zero, or low, tax rates on capital would always be more efficient and presented evidence that progressivity and/or higher marginal tax rates could be both efficient and

---

[78] Kay and King, *The British Tax System* (see n 71), 224.
[79] See n1. These reviews were compared by Chris Evans, 'Reflections on the Mirrlees Review: An Australasian Perspective' (2011) 32(3) *Fiscal Studies* 375–93.

equitable. The much wider use of empirical evidence and data about tax and transfer systems has supported scepticism about incentives and been kinder to the role of government and public provision than we saw in the 1980s.

Today, governments are grappling with the economic and fiscal crisis generated by the COVID-19 pandemic. While crisis may be a good time to initiate reform, there is little sign of major tax reform in response, so far. The exception may be the achievement of some reforms in the international arena, regarding the taxation of multinational enterprises. We discuss these developments in a globalised and digitalised economy in Part III.

Resilience of the Tax State

This final part of Chapter 4 introduces the concept of **resilience** of the tax state. Resilience evokes an ability to withstand, or respond coherently to external and internal shocks to the system. This enables the system as a whole to have capacity to return to a stable equilibrium, or alternatively to adapt to changing economic, social and legal circumstances in a way that maintains coherence and stability of the tax state. The concept of resilience was first developed by those studying ecological and social systems.[80] It is of increasing relevance in a world facing the drastic global effects of climate change, demographic changes such as declining fertility and population ageing, and slow economic growth.[81]

Systems theory suggests that a resilient system has the capacity to adapt to change and restore its equilibrium; or it may help us to identify when a system is reaching a tipping point that will move it into a new equilibrium. In the ecological context resilience is used to talk about ecosystems that are pushed over a threshold. In the financial context, resilience was widely referenced after the Global Financial Crisis, responding to widespread concern about the banking system, which had been essentially globalised during the 1990s. Without adequate controls on bank capital, or limits on consumer debt and currency flows at national or global levels, the crisis spread rapidly across the globe.

Systems theorists use the metaphor of a ball in the bowl illustrated in Figure 4.3. In this metaphor, changes impact upon the system, it faces shocks and disturbances, but if the ball does not reach the threshold, it will roll back and stabilise in the existing equilibrium. If a shock causes the ball to reach the threshold, this is a tipping point; the previous system equilibrium is no longer stable and a new equilibrium may be established.

---

[80] Brian Walker and David Salt, *Resilience Practice: Building Capacity to Absorb Disturbance and Maintain Function* (Washington, DC: Island Press, 2012).

[81] Richard Reid and Linda Botterill, 'The Multiple Meanings of "Resilience": An Overview of the Literature' (2013) 72(1) *Australian Journal of Public Administration* 31–40.

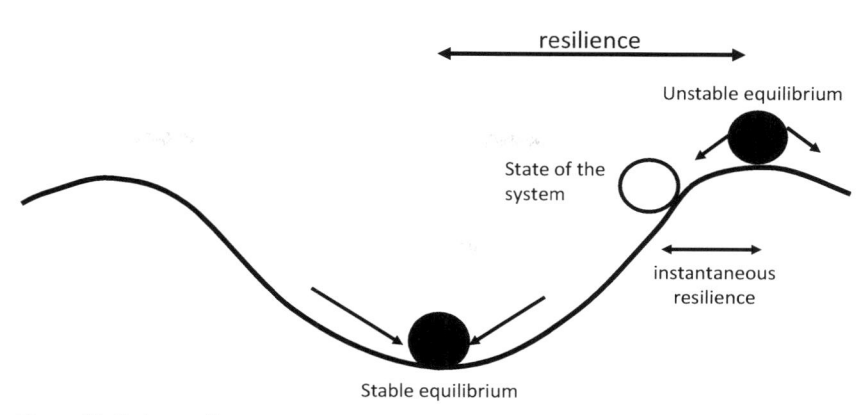

Figure 4.3 System resilience
Source: Brian Walker, 'Transforming Australia to Remain Resilient', Municipal Association of Australian Cities (December 2015), www.mav.asn.au/events/event-presentations/resilient-communities.

We can think about the 'tax state' and its system of taxation as a legal-economic-political-administrative set of relations and resources, a self-organising system that connects public and private resources across the economy and polity. There is a wide variety in tax systems, but they all have the common purpose of raising revenues to finance government. Recalling the goal expressed in Chapter 1 of taxation for a good democracy, a resilient tax system should support stable democratic government, as well as achieving policy goals of adequacy and sustainability of revenues to both 'grow the pie' and to redistribute it, through governmental action in public goods and redistribution.

A complex system incorporates continual variation and novelty, as system components change or new elements come into the system. Resilience is the capacity of a system to accommodate and absorb new elements or shocks and still retain its fundamental identity or character. A complex system also has interacting and interdependent components that operate and react with influences inside and outside the system. For example, the tax system interacts in a myriad of ways with the local and international economy, and with the population of individuals, families, employees and small and large businesses. Some threats to tax system resilience are illustrated in Box 4.1.

Applying a systems resilience perspective, it is not surprising that successful tax states have several major taxes that operate simultaneously across different aspects of the economy: income tax, consumption or sales taxes and social security taxes, as well as numerous specific taxes including customs and excise, real estate transaction taxes, and inheritance, wealth and land taxes. The concurrent operation of several taxes appears to be more resilient, even if some taxes do not themselves raise much revenue, and even if some taxes, or aspects of the tax system, are inefficient or inequitable. From an administrative

Box 4.1 Threats to tax system resilience

In tax systems today, threats to resilience arise from both internal and external changes and trends. These potential threats to the resilience of tax systems are all discussed in more detail elsewhere in the book:

- Some kinds of work are increasingly being done by independent contractors – the 'uberisation' of work in the 'gig' economy. Systems of tax collection such as pay-as-you-go withholding on wages are more difficult to apply to independent contractors or sole traders. Governments need to learn how to extend withholding and reporting systems to intermediary digital platforms to capture a fair share of income and consumption tax from these workers.
- Individuals are increasingly purchasing goods and digital services online from global intermediary platforms, instead of in shops. Governments need to extend their consumption tax laws, and develop new modes of collection and enforcement, to capture consumption tax from these sales that take place in the cloud and offshore.
- Tax states depend mainly on income and consumption taxes that fall on individuals who work. Ageing populations have fewer working age people relative to dependent older people. Lower fertility reduces the number of taxpaying workers, but also opens up opportunities to expand the labour tax base by bringing more women into the taxed market economy. As the dependency ratio changes, tax bases may need to shift away from wages and consumption, towards wealth, or assets, in order to fund growing needs of the ageing population.
- In a global digital economy, income from intangible assets such as intellectual property, brands and innovation, is increasingly mobile and can escape the corporate tax base. Governments need to learn to cooperate across borders to tax mobile capital income effectively; this may even lead to development of some kinds of global taxation.

and legal perspective, multiple taxes may also facilitate enforcement processes such as data triangulation and withholding from intermediaries, thereby operating to reinforce the system as a whole.

A resilient tax system should have the ability to adapt to economic, technological and social changes such as globalisation, digitalisation and population ageing; the shift of value from physical to intangible assets, and from goods to services; and changes to the legal and physical processes of work and investment. It should be able to recover and reorient in response to changes in taxpayer behaviour, tax planning and avoidance, ensuring continued generation of revenues while not impeding economic activities or preventing political legitimacy. This may be done through technological, legal, bureaucratic or policy-oriented changes in the system.

Finally, we can contrast 'resilience' to 'optimisation' of the tax system. A key observation of resilience thinking is that fully optimising a system may make it less resilient. To achieve resilience, a system requires some redundancy, and this implies some multiplicity, inefficiency or overlap of methods or components. We should expect that we cannot fully optimise the tax system, in part because we cannot predict which elements may collapse or fail. Tax system maintenance is a dynamic and continual social and economic process – the maintenance of the tax state itself.

Part II
Tax Law in Context

5

Tax, Work and Family

> The effects of the income tax on work effort are by no means obvious.
> Richard A Musgrave and Peggy Musgrave, *Public Finance in Theory and Practice*

The Income Tax on Wages

The Importance of Taxing Labour

The tax state of the twentieth century succeeded because it harnessed tax revenues from workers. The application of income taxes on wages, social security taxes levied on workers and employers, and broad-based consumption taxes was impossible before the existence of a mass labour market delivering wages higher than subsistence level. When waged work became widespread in the industrialising economies of the twentieth century, governments gradually overcame barriers to successful taxation of labour income.

Fundamentally, governments had to obtain a political mandate to establish taxation that was widely perceived as fair and legitimate to finance the public goods and social transfers that workers sought from government. Equally important was the development of administrative systems that could identify taxpayers and collect the wage tax. This required the establishment of a fiscal bargain with employers that would support pay-as-you-go withholding and contributory systems of social security that could deliver payments especially cash transfers. As explained in Chapter 4, both taxes and transfers are relevant for analysing the tax burden on labour income and the redistributive effect of taxation.

Taxes on workers remain crucial to financing tax states today. A study of the European Union-28 countries (including the United Kingdom) finds that half of all taxation is collected from labour income, ranging from a low of 35 per cent in Cyprus to a high of 58 per cent in Sweden.[1] Only one third of this arises from direct income taxes, with two thirds of labour taxes in Europe

---

[1] European Commission Directorate-General for Taxation and Customs Union, *Taxation Trends in the European Union* (2019 edition) (Luxembourg: Publications Office of the European Union, 2019), 25.

being collected in social security contributions and payroll taxes. Workers also bear the lion's share of consumption taxes such as the value added tax (VAT) or goods and services tax (GST), which provide close to one third of government revenues (as shown in Chapter 2).

An important reason for growth of revenues from taxing wages during the twentieth century was that the return to labour – the share of the economy benefiting workers – increased. The combination of universal voting in democracies, the increase of labour power through organisation, high marginal income tax rates, and expansive public expenditures increased the return to labour in most developed countries relative to capital.[2] The social insurance approach to financing welfare, pensions and unemployment payments for workers bolstered the tax state.

The early twenty-first century has seen a reversal of some of these economic effects and policies that started more than a century ago. These include a reduction in labour power relative to employers, the shift of workers into gig and casualised working contracts, stagnating wages and fiscal constraints on public expenditure and cash transfers that benefit workers. When these trends are combined with an ageing population and lower fertility and a trend to reduce tax rates on capital and on high-income workers, we can identify increasing risks to the resilience of the labour tax base itself.

From the Poll Tax to the Progressive Income Tax

A much older form of taxation of work was achieved through 'poll', 'head' or 'hearth' taxes. Poll taxes were usually a flat sum per person (almost always, adult males) or per 'household head' (adult males with spouse, children and others in the household), counted in a census or population register. In small communities, a poll tax was simply an equal contribution to government by all male able-bodied members of the community and was usually combined with a tax on property There are mentions of a poll tax in both old and new testaments in the bible.[3]

While formally equal, poll taxes are regressive, falling heaviest on those with the lowest income. Not surprisingly, although widespread, they are also unpopular. Bonney observes, 'it was the celebrated third English poll tax of 1380–1 which precipitated the Peasants' Revolt of 1381: this was a tax of

---

[2] Erik Bengtsson, Enrico Rubolino and Daniel Waldenstrom, *What Determines the Capital Share over the Long Run of History?*, IZA Discussion Paper No 13199 (Bonn: Institute of Labor Economics, 2020).

[3] Exodus 30:12; Matthew 17:24–27 refer to taxes levied under Moses and by the Romans; Robert Couzin, 'A Modern Look at the Roman Imperial "Jewish Tax"' (2017) 65(2) *Canadian Tax Journal* 333–52. Direct taxes such as poll taxes were considered equivalent to slavery in the classical Greek world: David F Burg, *A World History of Tax Rebellions: An Encyclopedia of Tax Rebels, Revolts, and Riots from Antiquity to the Present* (New York: Routledge, 2004), xv.

a shilling per head on all adults over fifteen years, except for genuine beggars'.[4] The lesson of unpopularity of poll taxation had to be relearned in 1990, after the Poll Tax Riots against the per-head local tax introduced by Prime Minister Margaret Thatcher in the United Kingdom. The riots led to the withdrawal and modification of the tax to improve fairness but the episode is said to have contributed to Prime Minister Thatcher's political demise.[5]

The English Parliament, once it gained control of taxation, limited the application of poll taxes. The poll tax of 1667 applied only to the wages of public officers and servants (a 5 per cent tax) and receipts of legal and medical practitioners (a 10 per cent tax, subject to a standard deduction of one third of receipts for expenses).[6] However, revenue needs led to continued imposition of poll taxes by governments. The *ancien regime* in France introduced a *capitation tax* on heads of households in 1695 as well as the *dixieme*, a 10 per cent income tax.[7] Adam Smith observed that a poll tax on 'bondmen employed in cultivation' had been historically common all over Europe.[8] Smith criticised the *capitation* and the poll tax as being inequitable, arbitrary and uncertain.

In contrast, early income taxes had exemptions that excluded basic wage earners. Prime Minister Pitt's 1799 income tax covered income from 'trades, professions, pensions, stipends, employments and vocations'[9] at a rate of 10 per cent, with a basic exemption and various other deductions.[10] Most wage earners had incomes well below the exemption. O'Brien concludes 'A workman could, in fact, legally enjoy an annual income from his labour and property of up to £80 before being assessed to tax'.[11]

During the nineteenth century, the taxation of labour income gradually shifted towards proportional tax rates. The Russian poll tax was replaced with a modern system of income and excise taxes.[12] In Prussia and other German

---

[4] Richard Bonney (ed.), *Economic Systems and State Finance* (Oxford: Clarendon Press, 1995), 474.
[5] B Guy Peters, *The Politics of Taxation: A Comparative Perspective* (Cambridge, MA: Blackwell, 1991).
[6] Ibid., 139.
[7] Bonney, *Economic Systems and State Finance* (see n 4), 474.
[8] Adam Smith, *An Inquiry into the Nature and Causes of Wealth of Nations* (London: Methuan, first published 1776, compilation by Edward Cannan, 1904, of 5th ed, 1789), www.econlib.org/library/Smith/smWN.html, Book V, Part II, Article II, 'Taxes on Profit, or Upon the Revenue Arising from Stock', Article IV, 'Capitation Taxes'.
[9] Bonney, *Economic Systems and State Finance* (see n 4), 487.
[10] The Triple Assessment levied tax on 'Annual Income' at a 10 per cent rate on incomes over £200 reducing to an exemption for incomes of less than £60. To use the exemption, taxpayers were required to provide a declaration as to their income: 39 Geo. II c. 13 s64 (1799) (UK): Peter Harris, *Income Tax in Common Law Jurisdictions: From the Origins to 1820* (Cambridge, UK: Cambridge University Press, 2006), 384, 406.
[11] PK O'Brien, 'British Incomes and Property in the Early Nineteenth Century' (1959) 12(2) *Economic History Review* Second Series 255–67, 260.
[12] Yanni Kitsonis, *States of Obligation: Taxes and Citizenship in the Russian Empire and Early Soviet Republic* (Toronto: University of Toronto Press, 2014).

states, a 'graduated capitation tax' which was 'halfway between a poll tax and a primitive income tax' was introduced, a step on the road towards the income tax adopted in 1891.[13]

Poll taxes remained as an instrument of social control, especially in the colonies and on slave owners. During European colonial expansion, poll taxes were used coercively to enforce labour for plantations and mines. The French colonist of Madagascar, Joseph Gallieni, intended a poll tax as an 'educational' tax – the 'impot moralisateur' – designed to 'teach the natives the value of work'.[14] The commodification of labour through the poll tax contributed to create a market economy in which natives would spend surplus on consumer goods while contributing a portion of their labour income to the government. In the early twentieth century, as the property voting franchise was ended in many countries, poll taxes were sometimes used to control access to the democratic process. The relationship between taxes, voting and citizenship was most explicitly demonstrated in the United States where a 'poll tax' was literally required to be paid to vote, a mechanism used to exclude poor and black people from voting.[15]

By the end of the nineteenth century, the theory and practice of progressivity in taxation was widely debated and countries were experimenting with variations of progressive rates.[16] Arguments for progressive taxation led to a rereading of Smith's Maxim of tax equality (extracted in Chapter 4) to support taxation based on ability to pay:

> It was relatively easy to justify graduation [in tax rates] by the huge intellectual authority of Smith, through a shift in the reading of his maxim to suggest that ability increased with the size of income, and that enjoyment was determined by the marginal value of each additional pound of income. This new reading of Smith was in accord with the writing of leading economists such as Marshall, Edgeworth and Pigou.[17]

An early innovator of a progressive labour income tax was New Zealand, which in 1891 enacted a law to tax income derived from 'the exercise of any profession, employment, or vocation of any kind, or from any salary, wages,

---

[13] Edwin RA Seligman, 'Progressive Taxation in Theory and Practice' (1908) 9(4) *American Economic Association Quarterly*, 3rd Series 1–334, 131–2.

[14] David Graeber, *Debt: The First 5,000 Years* (Brooklyn, NY: Melville House Printing, 2011), 50–1.

[15] Christopher J Bryant, Without Representation, No Taxation: Free Blacks, Taxes, and Tax Exemptions between the Revolutionary and Civil Wars' (2015) 21 *Michigan Journal of Race and Law* 91–123, discusses the complex interaction of taxation, freedom and voting, explaining how slave states imposed a tax on free blacks, while non-slave states sometimes provided an exemption from tax for free blacks, because they did not have the right to vote.

[16] Seligman, 'Progressive Taxation in Theory and Practice' (see n 13), 3.

[17] Martin Daunton, *Trusting Leviathan: The Politics of Taxation in Britain, 1799–1914* (New York: Cambridge University Press, 2001), 338–9.

allowances, pension, stipend, or charge or annuity....'.[18] A high threshold applied, and low progressive tax rates of 2.5 and 5 per cent.

When workers were included in the income tax, it became necessary to consider deductions for expenses incurred in generating income from work. The concept of comprehensive income proposed by Henry Simons with its focus on 'net gain' requires that work-related expenses are deductible, but personal consumption expenses are not. The boundary between personal and business expenses is often problematic and different countries draw the line around work-related expenses differently.

A classic example of an expense that has a clear nexus to work, but is also inherently personal, is the cost of commuting to work. In most countries, the cost of commuting is not deductible, although some countries including Germany, France and the Netherlands have legislated to provide a deduction or credit for this cost.[19] Similarly, the cost of childcare is usually treated as a non-deductible personal cost. A deduction for these types of expense would undermine the tax base and deliver an upside-down subsidy benefiting those with higher incomes more; cash transfers or public provision may be more effective. The larger contemporary issue may be that of deducting costs associated with the home, as during the COVID-19 pandemic, and in future, people work increasingly from home using digital technologies.

The Genius of Pay-as-you-go Withholding

The income tax did not become an effective 'mass tax' on the population until wage withholding was implemented, around the time of World War II, mostly as a response to increased revenue needs. Wage withholding systems dramatically expanded the technical and information capability of governments to collect labour taxes, leveraged through the delegation of the calculation and collection of tax to private intermediaries: employers.

In Canada, wage withholding was introduced in a 1942 'national defence tax' which increased the number of tax returns filed from 31,130 to 2.25 million and income tax revenues by 1,700 per cent by 1945.[20] In the United States, the Current Tax Payment Act of 1943 embedded wage withholding in the 'Victory Tax', and ultimately in the entire income tax.[21] This occurred

---

[18] Land and Income Assessment Act 1891 (New Zealand).
[19] See the discussion in Hugh J Ault, Brian J Arnold and Graeme Cooper, *Comparative Income Taxation*, 4th ed (Alphen aan den Rijn, Netherlands: Wolters Kluwer, 2020), Kindle Book, Loc 10180.
[20] Colin Campbell, 'JL Ilsley and the Transformation of the Canadian Tax System: 1939–1943' (2013) 61(3) *Canadian Tax Journal* 633–70; Jinyan Li, Arjin Choi and Cameron Smith, 'Automation and Workers: Re-Imagining the Income Tax for the Digital Age' (2020) 61(1) *Canadian Tax Journal* 99–124.
[21] Anuj Desai, 'What a History of Tax Withholding Tells Us about the Relationship between Statutes and Constitutional Law' (2014) 108(3) *Northwestern University Law Review* 859–904, 887.

after the enactment of the New Deal social security taxes in 1935, which had already 'forced employers to create managerial processes to deal with this new tax'.[22]

An earlier US attempt to introduce withholding in its 1916 income tax met with opposition from employers and banks and was replaced by a system of 'information at source', in which information about employees or income recipients would be provided to the revenue authority by the intermediary. Withholding transformed the relationship between American workers, their employers and the tax system, supporting the massive increase in income taxpayers from 7 million to 42 million between 1940 and 1945.[23] So fundamental is it to the financing of the US government that the withholding tax statute has been argued to be quasi-constitutional in nature.[24]

The UK Pay As You Earn system was introduced in 1944 to counter widespread evasion which had been a response to dramatically higher standard wartime tax rates. The British system was a 'final' withholding system. It 'changed income tax from a lump sum, payment-in-arrear system to a cumulative withholding tax, by requiring employers to calculate the tax due for each employee, deduct it from wages and pay it over to government each month'.[25] This approach means that even today, most British taxpayers do not need to file a tax return. In other pay-as-you-go systems, such as that adopted in Australia, the personal income tax return with expected refund from reconciling the tax withheld with income after deductions, has become a ritual, despite the significantly greater complexity of this system for most taxpayers.

Tax Rates and Work Incentives

In Chapter 4, we discussed the economic efficiency effects of the income tax on the supply of labour, arising from the **substitution** and **income effects** on incentives for individuals to do market work subject to taxation. A progressive marginal tax rate structure applied to individuals, which increases tax rates on labour as income rises, may generate changes in economic behaviour such as the substitution of a non-taxed activity instead of taxed work. Tax rates may create an incentive to work fewer hours or a disincentive to work more hours. On the other hand, if an individual needs a certain level of income in order to maintain their living standard (or pay the rent), they may work harder, for more hours, to achieve the required level of income after tax. This income effect works in the opposite direction to the substitution effect.

---

[22] Ibid., 895.
[23] Carolyn Jones, 'Class Tax to Mass Tax: The Role of Propaganda in the Expansion of the Income Tax During World War II' (1988–89) 37 *Buffalo Law Review* 685–737.
[24] Desai, 'What a History of Tax Withholding Tells Us about the Relationship between Statutes and Constitutional Law' (see n 21).
[25] Christopher Hood, 'British Tax Structure Development as Administrative Adaptation' (1985) 18(1) *Policy Sciences* 3–19, 14.

The decision margin for individuals facing a tax on labour supply comprises a choice to work earning market wages, subject to a tax, or to use their time (and skill) in some other way. Traditionally, economists called this the 'work-leisure' choice. However, in most situations individuals do not choose between 'work' and 'leisure' in the ordinary meaning of that word, but rather between (taxed) market work, and (untaxed) household work or home production such as childcare; between (taxed) work and (untaxed) education; or between work in the (taxed) formal economy or in the (untaxed) informal or cash economy. In all these situations, the wage tax reduces the after-tax income that individuals receive for hours or days of work, and so presents a disincentive to work, or an incentive to substitute other activities.

The classic 'marginal' analysis applied to workers facing a labour supply decision is to consider the marginal tax rate on the next dollar of income, or next hour worked; this is called the **intensive margin**.[26] For example, how likely is it that a worker will choose to do one hour of overtime work (based on after-tax return from the wage they will earn), or instead go to the beach? This decision is affected by the **marginal effective tax rate** (METR) faced by the worker on that hour of work.

In many situations, individuals do not face a marginal choice to work just one more hour, but instead have little or no flexibility in their work choices. An individual may face a stark choice about whether to work at all – to take a job – or to do unpaid care work in the home (if someone else can support that person), or to rely on unemployment benefit, if available. This 'bigger' choice is called the **extensive margin**. The relevant tax rate for a labour supply decision at the extensive margin is the **average tax rate**, or total tax paid as a share of total taxable income. This is sometimes called the **participation tax rate**, as it reflects the entire tax paid on labour income and the after-tax disposable income derived from work. Examples of the labour supply choice at the extensive margin are a choice to work in another jurisdiction, with lower tax than the home jurisdiction, or a choice to work in the illegal or informal economy.

It is increasingly common for individuals to face a choice whether to work part time or full time, or to take extra shifts in a week. In this more flexible work environment, the **effective average tax rate** on the next day of work, or **daily METR**, may be relevant to the decision. Workers are unlikely to do such complex calculations about after-tax return in real life. But it is plausible to assume that workers know what money they will have left over after working (their disposable income) and this informs their decision to work.

It is often suggested in tax policy debates that a higher tax rate on high-income earners will discourage work and this is inefficient; not surprisingly,

---

[26] Richard Blundell, Antoine Bozio and Guy Laroque, 'Extensive and Intensive Margins of Labour Supply: Work and Working Hours in the US, the UK and France' (2013) 34(1) *Fiscal Studies* 1–29.

such an argument is used to justify lowering marginal tax rates. At the extreme, this seems likely to be true: If you were taxed at a 90 per cent tax rate on your labour income, you might be very likely to change your economic behaviour to some untaxed activity – or rebel against the tax. However, there is little empirical evidence that the top tax rates applicable to labour income in most successful tax states stop people working. These tax rates are usually between 40 and 50 per cent; rather, the evidence suggests a relatively low elasticity of labour supply for workers facing those tax rates. This makes sense once it is understood that top tax rates usually apply to people who are *already* working full time at a high-wage job. The labour supply decision most top-earning individuals face is not, 'Should I work for another hour (tax at the top rate)?' but rather, 'Should I stay in or leave my job, thereby drastically reducing my income?' Some workers are highly mobile and may choose to work in another jurisdiction; we return to this issue in Chapter 10. However, what we are more likely to see in behavioural responses to taxes at higher wages is attempts to negotiate remuneration with lower taxed stock, options, or other fringe benefits; or tax planning, such as attempts to shift income into lower taxed entities such as corporations or to lower taxed family members.

The Design of Progressive Tax Rates

There are many ways in which progressive tax rates may be implemented in practice. Modern progressive tax rates usually apply in stepped increments at thresholds, from a zero rate up to a maximum. Some rate structures commence from the first dollar, with no tax-free threshold, but provide personal or family benefits or exemptions to deliver a basic minimum living standard for individuals. As income tax is levied on nominal income, inflation may have a significant effect. This is illustrated in Box 5.1.

An example of the progressive rate structures for a single individual in the income taxes of Germany and Australia is shown in Figure 5.1. The rate structures in these two countries are remarkably similar, but Germany has a linear increasing rate across the middle range of the rate structure. The top marginal income tax rate in each country is almost the same (the figure applies to individuals and excludes surcharges, such as the Medicare levy in Australia and provincial and local additions in Germany), although the top Australian tax rate applies at a lower threshold than in Germany. Average wages in each country are also similar,[27] and average workers face a marginal income tax rate of about 32 per cent in each country.

---

[27] OECD, 'Average Wages', https://data.oecd.org/earnwage/average-wages.htm, accessed 7 March 2022.

Box 5.1 Progressive tax rates, inflation and bracket creep

One policy concern about progressive tax rates is the effect of inflation. Income taxes are usually levied on a nominal basis. When prices increase because of a decline in value of the currency, the imposition of tax on nominal wages that are declining in purchasing power becomes an important issue. Inflation leads to higher tax collections based on a nominal tax base, while raising the effective tax rate on real income. In a progressive tax rate structure, inflation can cause 'bracket creep'.

Assume a weekly salary of $100 and an annual inflation rate of 5 per cent. The salary will purchase $100 worth of goods and services at the beginning of the year, but only $95 worth at the end of the year because inflation erodes the purchasing power of the salary. An income tax of 40 per cent applied to the wage of $100 per week raises $40 in tax, which generates a higher effective tax rate of 42 per cent on the 'real' purchasing power of $95 at the end of the year.

If a nominal wage is increased to keep up with inflation, this may push a taxpayer into a higher marginal tax bracket, while merely maintaining their purchasing power. Assume an income tax with a marginal rate of 25 per cent up to a threshold of $50,000 and a marginal rate of 40 per cent for income from $50,001. A taxpayer with an annual salary of $48,000 receives a wage increase of $2,400 to keep up with annual inflation of 5 per cent, so has a salary of $50,400 the following year. This pushes the taxpayer into the higher tax bracket and they would face a rate of 50 per cent on $400 of this increase. If the tax bracket were adjusted for the annual inflation of 5 per cent, it would have been raised to $55,000 in the ensuing year and the taxpayer would continue to face the lower tax rate of 25 per cent even after the nominal wage increase.

Some governments have indexed tax brackets to inflation, especially in response to very high inflation during the 1970s. In the United States, the federal income tax brackets were indexed to inflation in the Economic Recovery Tax Act of 1981. The United Kingdom, Canada (since 2000), France (in part) and Sweden also index tax brackets to inflation.[28] Other countries periodically adjust their tax brackets or reduce tax rates to respond to inflation, in a more political exercise. In an era when tax rates have flattened, wages stagnated and inflation is low, the pressure of bracket creep has lessened; still, this remains an important issue in ensuring political acceptability of progressive income taxes on workers.[29]

The Tax Burden on Labour Income

Today, significant policy attention is focused on the effective average tax rate, sometimes called the tax 'wedge' or 'burden' on labour income. One policy issue is the potential disincentive effect on employment, or on businesses

---

[28] Ault et al, *Comparative Income Taxation* (see n 19).
[29] Other elements of the nominal income tax may also need to be adjusted in times of high inflation, but this is not a straightforward task. It was a particular focus of tax policy during the 1970s when inflation was high in many OECD countries. See Victor Thuronyi, 'Adjusting Taxes for Inflation' in Victor Thuronyi (ed.), *Tax Law Design and Drafting: Vol 1* (Washington, DC: International Monetary Fund, 1996, revised 2012), chapter 13, www.imf.org/external/pubs/nft/1998/tlaw/eng/ch13.pdf.

Personal income tax rates for single taxpayers
Germany 2020 & Australia 2020–1

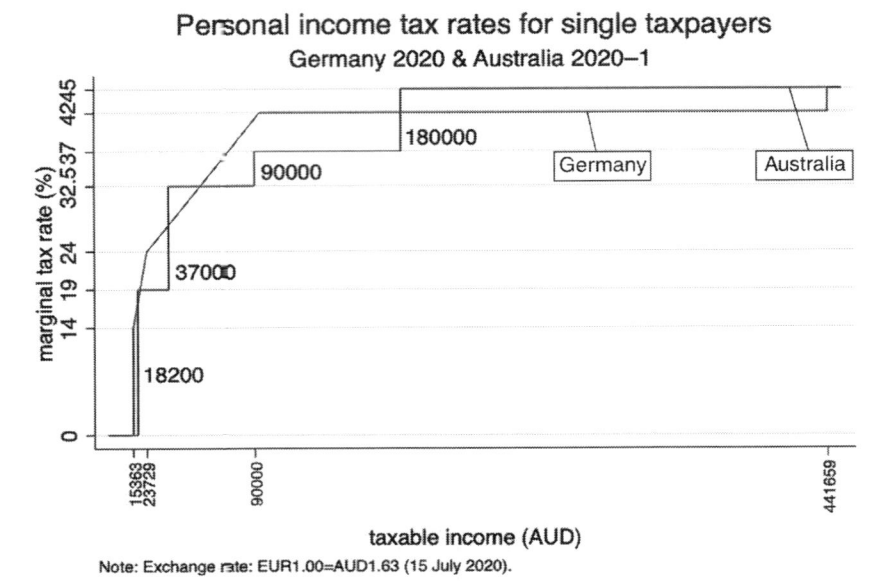

[Figure: chart showing marginal tax rate (%) on y-axis with values 0, 14, 19, 24, 32.537, 4245 and taxable income (AUD) on x-axis with thresholds 18200, 37000, 90000, 180000; separate lines for Germany and Australia; x-axis labels 15363/23729, 90000, 441659]

Note: Exchange rate: EUR1.00=AUD1.63 (15 July 2020).

Figure 5.1 Personal income tax rates for single taxpayers in Germany and Australia
Source: Mathias Sinning, Tax Rates of Income Tax Law in Germany (2020) and Australian (2020–21), Expressed in Australian Dollars.

employing workers.[30] The effective average tax rate on labour income is the total tax paid as a share of the employee wage, including income tax and social security contributions paid by both employers and employees.

The annual publication of the Organisation for Economic Cooperation and Development (OECD), *Taxing Wages*, presents information about the tax burden on average wages in each jurisdiction.[31] It reveals a wide range across countries, from below 10 per cent to above 50 per cent. This is shown, broken down into income tax and employee and employer social security contributions, in Figure 5.2 for selected countries.

Figure 5.2 shows that the average tax burden as a share of wage cost in the OECD is just over 35 per cent, of which income tax comprises about one third, and social security contributions from employees and employers comprise two thirds. However, in Denmark, the entire wage tax burden, while close to the OECD average, is payable in income tax. New Zealand has a much lower tax burden on average wages of 18 per cent, collected through the income tax, which is the only tax on labour income. The tax burden on labour income in Germany is almost 50 per cent, which is one of the highest in the OECD, in contrast to Australia, which has a wage tax burden of 28 per cent. This different average tax burden arises although, as indicated in Figure 5.1, marginal income tax rates in Australia and Germany are very similar. The

---

[30] OECD, *Revenue Statistics 2019* (Paris: OECD, 2019), chapter 1, figure 1.5, www.oecd.org/economy/revenue-statistics-2522770x.htm.
[31] OECD, *Taxing Wages* (Paris: OECD Publishing, 2020), https://doi.org/10.1787/20725124

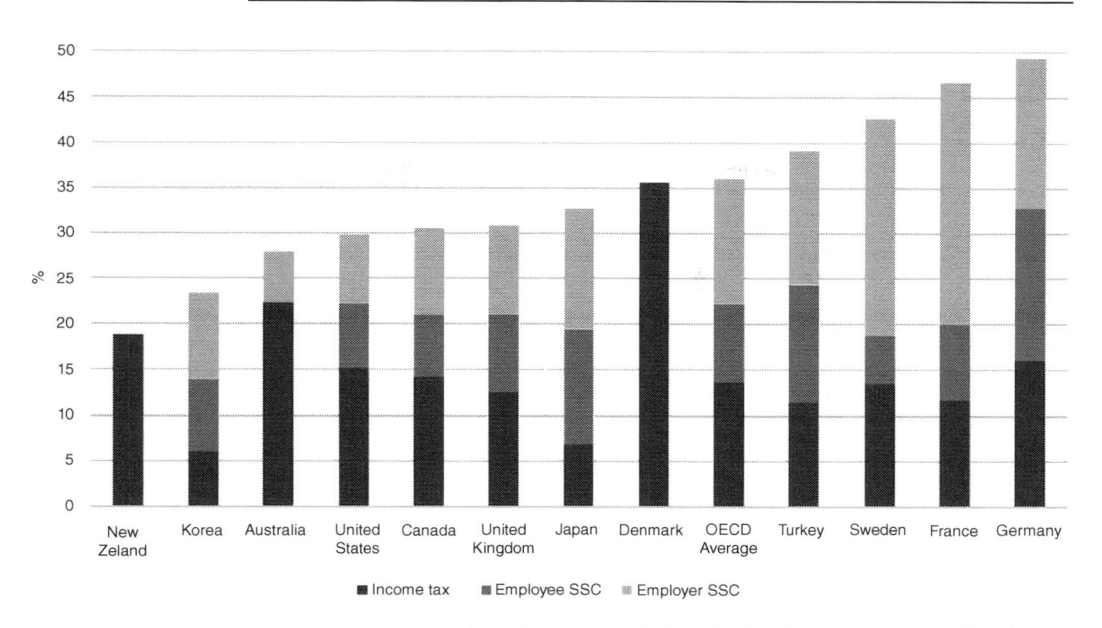

Figure 5.2 Income tax and social security contributions (SSC) as share of wage cost, selected OECD countries, 2019
Source: Selected Data from OECD, Taxing Wages 2020, Figure 5.2, www.oecd-ilibrary.org/taxation/taxing-wages/volume-/issue-_047072cd-en.

explanation is that Germany has much higher social security taxes, while Australia's mandatory retirement savings contributions by employers and employees are contributed into private superannuation funds, and are therefore not revealed in the tax statistics. If taken into account, they would push up the tax burden on the average wage by about two percentage points. The tax treatment of saving for retirement and the financing and means testing design of the age pension is an important element of the system of labour taxation over the life course; we return to discuss this in Chapter 6.

The Tax Unit

History of the Tax Unit and Women's Economic Independence

So far, the discussion of income tax on labour income has assumed that the taxpayer is an individual worker subject to tax. However, workers who pay taxes do not live in splendid isolation. As explained in Chapter 4, over the life course of a paradigmatic 'worker-taxpayer', taxes and transfers ebb and flow as workers are raised as dependent children, study, work and themselves have spouses and families, care for elders and become dependent again themselves in old age. Consequently, the way in which the tax system recognises spouses and dependants is an important element in its legal design, and its legal, distributional and economic effects.

In some countries, the income tax unit is a joint unit for spouses or a family, instead of an individual unit. One tax return is filed for the joint income of the couple, usually by combining and then splitting the income between them, while sometimes applying a different rate scale to combined income. The seemingly innocuous question of the tax unit has been a controversial issue in tax policy debates over the last century.[32] This is because it raises fundamental social issues about the family and women's economic independence. Before the twentieth century, women in many countries were denied the right to vote and to own property. In Britain, on marriage the property of a woman was passed to her husband. Building on pre-existing property and marriage laws, many income taxes historically applied a joint unit, or a single tax return for the 'head of household', assumed to be the adult male breadwinner. In the British income tax, the income of a married woman was deemed to be her husband's, so she was under the head of household in a legal and tax 'couverture'.[33]

During the twentieth century, reform of property and marriage laws gradually recognised married women as individuals able to hold property and earn their own income, but income tax laws were slow to follow. In 1920, Lillian Knowles, a member of the British Royal Commission into Income Tax, argued for individual taxation of husband and wife, while Sydney Webb advocated an alternative 'family quotient' approach.[34] The individual tax unit was finally adopted in the United Kingdom in 1990, but it still applies some joint or 'married' allowances. Civil law systems of property and marriage in Europe also underpinned the family or joint tax unit, based on laws that permitted splitting of income and assets between spouses during marriage and on divorce. France applies the income tax to the *foyer fiscal*, including the income of household members beyond spouses. Towards the end of the twentieth century, the trend in OECD tax systems was 'an almost one-way move from joint to individual taxation.'[35] Still, in 2019 a joint unit (sometimes optional) applied in Belgium, France (which aggregates family income including that of children or other relatives), Germany, Greece, Ireland, Luxembourg, Poland, Portugal, Spain, Switzerland and the United States. Some countries tax labour income to individuals but apply a joint unit to couples with 'interdependent' business income (Israel), or capital income and assets (Iceland, Finland and the Netherlands).[36]

---

[32] See, e.g. John G Head and Richard Krever (eds.), *Tax Units and the Tax Rate Scale* (Melbourne: Australian Tax Research Foundation, 1996); Maria Teresa Soler Roch (ed.), *Family Taxation in Europe* (Boston: Kluwer Law International, 1999).

[33] Kathleen Lahey, 'The "Capture" of Women in Law and Fiscal Policy: The Tax/Benefit Unit, Gender Equality, and Feminist Ontologies' in Kim Brooks, Åsa Gunnarson, Lisa Philipps and Maria Wersig (eds.), *Challenging Gender Inequality in Tax Policy Making* (London: Hart Publishing, 2011) 11–36, 18–19.

[34] Martin Daunton, *Just Taxes: The Politics of Taxation in Britain, 1914–1979* (New York: Cambridge University Press, 2002), 112ff.

[35] Ken Messere, 'Taxation in Ten Industrialized Countries over the Last Decade: An Overview' (1995) 10 *Tax Notes International* 512–35, 518.

[36] OECD, *Taxing Wages* (see n 29), Part II, Country Details (2019).

In Germany, there has always been a family tax unit; however, its form changed as a result of a famous decision of the Constitutional Court in 1958.[37] The earlier German income tax law aggregated the income of spouses, and taxed the aggregated income at the same progressive rate as applied to an individual with the same income. The court ruled that this approach violated the right to equality and the protection of marriage and the family in the Constitution.[38] Instead, the court recommended splitting the income of the couple between the two individuals (husband and wife) in the marriage, an approach upheld in a subsequent decision and still adopted today.[39]

The US income tax law, when first enacted, applied an individual tax unit. It was amended to permit a joint tax return in 1948, after a Supreme Court case permitting income splitting between members of a couple in states that applied civil community-property laws to marriage and divorce.[40] Today, a complicated rate structure in the United States establishes different rates for married and single taxpayers depending on their circumstances.

Australia, New Zealand and Canada applied the income tax to individuals from the early twentieth century. In 1975, a major review of the tax system by the Asprey Committee affirmed Australia's individual tax unit, stating that 'the right to be taxed as an individual has always been accorded in Australia'.[41] In contrast, Canada's Carter Tax Commission of 1966 recommended a family tax unit be introduced on the basis that equity should be considered by comparing families, but this recommendation was not adopted.[42]

Where a joint or couple unit is applied, a further issue arises: who should be recognised as a couple or family? The struggle during the late twentieth century by lesbian and gay couples for legal recognition, including the right to marry, also had implications for the tax unit. Today, many countries have amended their tax laws to extend recognition to same-sex couples, where a joint unit is applicable.[43]

---

[37] Joachim Lang, 'Germany' in Soler Roch (ed.), *Family Taxation in Europe* (see n 32), 55–70; Maria Wersig, 'Overcoming the Gender Inequalities of Joint Taxation and Income Splitting: The Case of Germany' in Brooks et al, *Challenging Gender Inequality in Tax Policy Making* (see n 33), 213–32, 216.

[38] BVerfG of 17 January 1957, BVerfGE 6, 55 (Germany).

[39] BVerfG of 3 November 1982, BVerfGE 61, 319, 347 (Germany).

[40] Laura Ann Davis, 'A Feminist Justification for the Adoption of an Individual Filing System' (1988) 62 *Southern California Law Review* 197–252; Edward J McCaffery, 'Taxation and the Family: A Fresh Look at Behavioral Gender Biases in the Code' (1993) 40 *UCLA Law Review* 983–1060.

[41] Commonwealth of Australia Taxation Review Committee, *Full Report January 31 1975* (1975) 134 [10–16], https://adc.library.usyd.edu.au/data-2/p00087.pdf.

[42] Canada Privy Council Office, *Report of the Royal Commission on Taxation. Vol 3: Taxation of Income: Part A, Taxation of Individuals and Families/Kenneth LeM Carter, Chairman* (Ottawa: Privy Council Office, 1966).

[43] Marie Digoix, *Same-Sex Families and Legal Recognition in Europe. European Studies of Population: Vol 24* (Cham: Springer International Publishing, 2020). Equal marriage rights – and the tax consequences that follow – also apply in Europe, Australia, New Zealand, Canada, many states in the United States and other countries.

The Tax Unit, Equity and Efficiency

Feminist tax theorists pioneered a tax discrimination analysis that argued for an individual unit on efficiency and equity grounds.[44] A key reason for this trend was changing demographic patterns, especially the increased participation of women in the workforce.

The rules about the tax unit, combined with personal and family exemptions, allowances and transfers, mark a gendered boundary between the 'taxed' market and 'untaxed' private or domestic family life. Home production is not subject to the income tax, although in a comprehensive income tax applied to individuals, it would be taxable.[45]

A system of joint taxation and progressive rates will effectively overtax the income of the secondary earner in a couple (usually the wife/mother, with a lower wage, less secure work and the social option of choosing to look after children at home). This is because the secondary earner's income is effectively 'on top' of the primary earner's income in the joint unit.[46] This is both inequitable, taxing the secondary earner at a higher rate than a comparable individual, and inefficient, as it creates a disincentive for the secondary earner to earn market income. This consequence applies whether the joint unit is legally enacted in the tax system, or is the unit for delivery of family benefits in the transfer system (as discussed later).

In comparing families with equivalent household income, applying a joint unit privileges a breadwinner-homemaker family structure when compared with a dual-income family. In the breadwinner-homemaker family, the spouse specialising in home production and childcare is untaxed; she is supported by the husband's taxed market income. This contrasts with a family in which both spouses work in the market, both are taxed on earned income and the family must pay for childcare costs.

An implicit assumption of the joint tax unit is that it reflects the equal sharing of income or consumption in the household. However, a wide variety of financial arrangements exist within couples.[47] The distribution of income, consumption and the tax burden will depend on intra-household bargaining and on the contribution to home production and market income of each

---

[44] See, e.g. Patricia Apps, Elizabeth Svage and Glen Jones, 'Tax Discrimination by Dependent Spouse Rebates or Joint Taxation' (1981) 53 *The Australian Quarterly* 262–79; Alicia H Munnell, 'The Couple versus the Individual under the Federal Personal Income Tax' in Henry J Aaron and Michael J Boskin (eds.), *The Economics of Taxation* (Washington, DC: Brookings Institution, 1980), 247–78.

[45] Nancy Staudt, 'Taxing Housework' (1995) 84 *Georgetown Law Journal* 1571–647.

[46] Alexander Bick and Nicola Fuchs-Schundeln, 'Quantifying the Disincentive Effects of Joint Taxation on Married Women's Labor Supply' (2017) 107(5) *American Economic Review* 100–4.

[47] Edith Gray and Ann Evans, 'Do Couples Share Income? Variation in the Organisation of Income in Dual-earner Households' (2008) 43(3) *Australian Journal of Social Issues* 441–57; Supriya Singh and Jo Lindsay, 'Money in Heterosexual Relationships' (1996) 32(3) *Journal of Sociology* 57–69; Marjorie E Kornhauser, 'Love, Money, and the IRS: Family, Income-sharing, and the Joint Income Tax Return' (1993) 45(1) *Hastings Law Journal* 63–111.

member in the couple.[48] Empirical studies have established that once women have their first child, their labour supply is far more **elastic** than male labour supply in response to tax rates.[49] There is little difference in labour supply elasticity for young men and women leaving school or education for work, although women face a gender wage gap from their first employment. However, once women bear children they are far more likely to leave the labour force, or work part time, 'specialising' in home production in response to the higher effective tax rate that they face on paid work. In sum, the efficiency aspect of the argument for a lower tax rate on women's work is simply this:

> According to optimal taxation theory, a benevolent government should tax individuals who have a more elastic labor supply less. The labor supply of women is more elastic than the labor supply of men. Therefore, tax rates on labor income should be lower for women than for men.[50]

It is estimated that in Germany and Belgium, moving from a joint tax unit to an individual tax unit would increase women's work hours by 25 to 35 per cent.[51] In response to these findings, the European Parliament has called for the elimination of joint or family-based provisions in the tax laws of all EU member states and their replacement with individual based rules.[52]

The Tax-transfer Unit and Childcare Costs

Governments use income tax laws and transfer laws to deliver allowances and exemptions for workers and their dependants, payments for the cost of children or for childcare, or tax credits aimed at 'making work pay'. Tax deductibility mainly benefits higher income families. Transfer payments for children or childcare are often means tested based on a joint unit to identify the threshold of income for eligibility or to target benefits to low income families. This limits, government expenditure on benefits. Where countries apply an individual unit in the income tax but a joint unit for income testing of benefits in the transfer system, this produces a 'quasi-joint' unit for couples, especially with children.

---

[48] Yuriy Andrienko, Patricia Apps and Ray Rees, 'Gender Bias in Tax Systems Based on Household Income' (2015) 117–18 *Annals of Economics and Statistics* 141–55.

[49] See, e.g. Bick and Fuchs-Schundeln, 'Quantifying the Disincentive Effects of Joint Taxation' (see n 46); Alberto Alesina, Andrea Ichino and Loukas Karabarbounis, 'Gender-based Taxation and the Division of Family Chores' (2011) 3 *American Economic Journal* 1–40.

[50] Alesina et al, 'Gender-based Taxation' (see n 49), 1.

[51] Bick and Fuchs-Schundeln, 'Quantifying the Disincentive Effects of Joint Taxation' (see n 46), 102.

[52] European Parliament, *Resolution on Gender Equality and Taxation Policies in the EU*, 2018/20195 (INI), No. 5, 6, 10; Åsa Gunnarson, *Gender Equality and Taxation – International Perspectives*, Copenhagen Business School Law Research Paper Series No 20-29 (Frederiksberg, Denmark: Copenhagen Business School, 2020).

The combination of progressive income tax rates and income-testing of benefits in a joint unit may generate high **marginal effective tax rates** on secondary earners that reduce their net gain from working. If the cost of caring for children is not socially provided, it is mothers (not fathers) who generally leave the labour force or reduce their working hours, and care for children at home. Therefore, net childcare costs add to the effective tax on women's work.[53] Box 5.2 and Figure 5.3 present an example from Australia, illustrating the combined effects of the unit of assessment in the income tax and transfer system; income thresholds; tax rates; and means testing for family payments and the childcare subsidy.[54]

Across the OECD, women's careers are one third shorter, on average, than men's and are much more likely to involve part time work.[55] The life course effect is a loss to the individual woman and to society as a whole in economic growth and taxes.

As well as adopting an individual tax unit, policy responses include means testing of transfers on individual income of the second earner; delivery of universal free (or almost free) childcare; paid parental leave; and regulation addressing the gender wage gap and workplace discrimination against fathers who take on caring responsibilities. In Germany, attempts to move away from joint taxation because of the discriminatory effect on women's work have faced difficulties because of the Constitutional framework. As the main issue is the tax bias against women's work in families with children, Germany has instead commenced providing heavily subsidised or free childcare.[56] A recent analysis finds that this boosts both fertility and women's workforce participation.[57]

---

[53] Olivier Thevenon, *Drivers of Female Labour Force Participation in the OECD*, OECD Social, Employment and Migration Working Papers No 145 (Paris: OECD, 2013), 34; Marian Fink, Jitka Janová, Danuše Nerudova, Jan Pavel, Margit Schratzenstaller, Friedrich Sinderman-Sienkiewicz and Martin Speilauer, '(Gender-differentiated) Effects of Changes in Personal Income Taxation' (2019) 54(3) *Intereconomics: Review of European Economic Policy* 146–54 www.intereconomics.eu/contents/year/2019/number/3/article/gender-differentiated-effects-of-changes-in-personal-income-taxation.html.

[54] See further Miranda Stewart, 'Gender Inequality in Australia's Tax-transfer System' in Miranda Stewart (ed.), *Tax, Social Policy and Gender: Rethinking Equality and Efficiency* (Canberra: ANU Press, 2017), 1–32.

[55] OECD, *The Pursuit of Gender Equality: An Uphill Battle* (Paris: OECD Publishing, 2017), 168, http://dx.doi.org/10.1787/9789264281318-en.

[56] European Commission, 'Germany – Early Childhood and School Education Funding' (2021), https://eacea.ec.europa.eu/national-policies/eurydice/content/early-childhood-and-school-education-funding-31_en, accessed 14 March 2022.

[57] Hanna Wang, 'Fertility and Family Leave Policies in Germany: Optimal Policy Design in a Dynamic Framework' (2019), https://sistemas.colmex.mx/Reportes/LACEALAMES/LACEA-LAMES2019_paper_320.pdf.

Box 5.2 Example of high effective tax rates on women's work

The Australian income tax is levied on an individual unit but Australian welfare benefits (cash transfers) for families with children are means tested on joint income. The childcare subsidy, a payment that is the main public financial support for childcare, is also means tested on joint income.

Assume Jess is a mother of two young children, aged two and three, who wishes to re-enter the labour market. Jess has taken time out to have children, perhaps utilising parental leave and being supported by her breadwinner partner who continues to work full time. If Jess worked full time, she will earn median female full-time weekly earnings and her partner earns median male full-time weekly earnings.

As a result of Jess returning to work, once she earns over the tax-free threshold of $18,200, she will begin to pay income tax on individual income at progressive marginal tax rates of 19 per cent rate and 32.5 per cent plus the Medicare levy of 2 per cent. Her partner already pays income tax on his wage. As a result of her earnings, the family will lose some family benefits, which are phased out based on joint income at a rate of 20 to 30 cents for each dollar over certain thresholds. The family must also pay for childcare. The childcare subsidy covers 85 per cent of the hourly childcare fee subject to a cap. It is phased out tested on joint income above a threshold.

Figure 5.3 presents the net gain from working for Jess, for each cumulative day on which she chooses to go back to work. The net gain for each day of work is represented by the dotted line, which is produced by the combination of income tax and loss of benefits on Jess's incremental salary if she returns to work, ranging from one day a week (part time) to five days a week (full time). The bars for each day represent the combination of earnings, family and childcare payments that increase Jess's income (above the x axis), and the tax paid, childcare cost and loss of family and childcare subsidies (below the x axis); these provide the daily net gain from work for Jess. It can be seen that on Day 1, Jess takes home $94 out of daily earnings of $190; however, on each of Days 2 to 5 of work, Jess takes home less than $35 out of her earnings: this is an effective tax rate in excess of 80 per cent on Jess's work.

It is hardly surprising that the extremely high effective tax rate illustrated in Figure 5.3 has a disincentive effect on labour supply. It is rational, at least in the short term, for Jess to choose to stay home or work only part time, and 'specialise' in care while the children are young. For families with children aged under five in Australia, it is overwhelmingly mothers who are not in the workforce (37.6 per cent of mothers compared to 6 per cent of fathers), or who work part time (62 per cent of mothers in the workforce compared to 8 per cent of fathers).[58]

---

[58] Australian Bureau of Statistics '4125.0 – Gender Indicators, Australia, Sep 2018' (25 September 2018), www.abs.gov.au/AUSSTATS/abs@.nsf/Lookup/4125.0Main+Features1Sep%202018?.

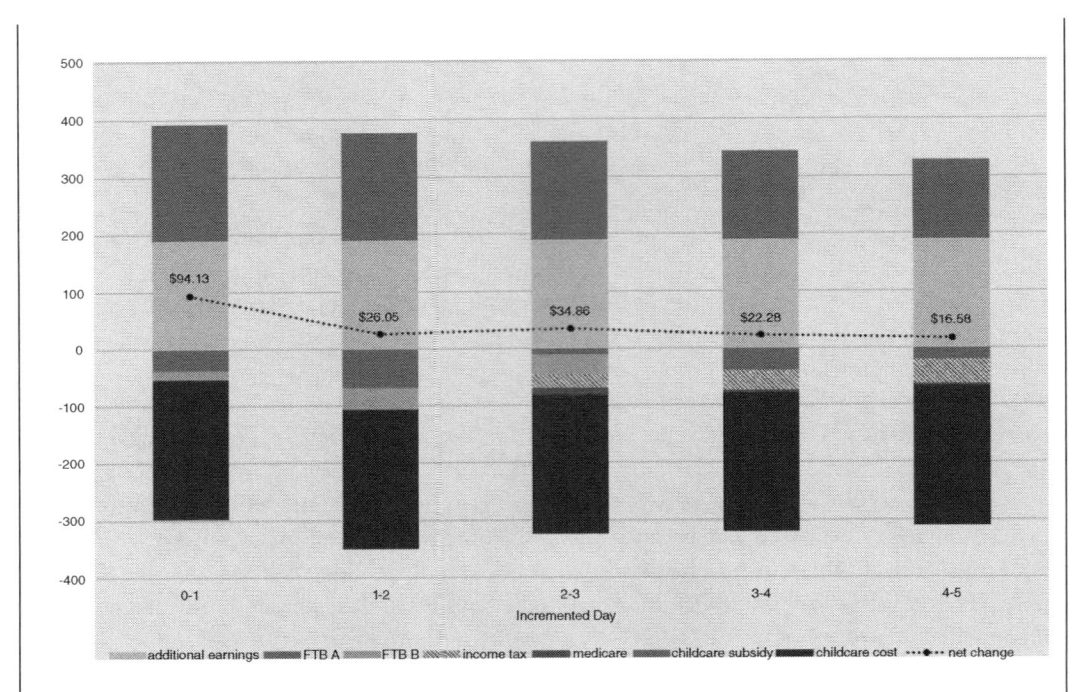

Figure 5.3 Marginal effective tax rate on second earner, cameo example, Australia, 2018
Note: FTB A is Family Tax Benefit A. FTB B is Family Tax Benefit B. These are payments delivered as cash transfers to families that satisfy income and eligibility tests.
Source: David Plunkett and Peter Martin, Data from David Plunkett Model of METRs in the Australian Income Tax and Transfer System (2018), https://ravebydave.blogspot.com/.

Taxing the Top 1 Per Cent

Tax rates became more progressive, and higher, in many countries between the 1930s and the 1960s. This was driven partly by fairness concerns and partly by the need for war finance. During World War II, top rates reached 90 per cent in the United Kingdom, Australia and the United States, as a result of surtaxes (the government also controlled much of the economy in many countries during this time).

This period also saw a significant drop in inequality of income and wealth, from high levels at the end of the nineteenth century. In some countries, tax rates had been escalated in response to activism about inequality, at the high point of consensus support for progressivity. In Sweden, tax rates were raised and progression increased as a product of the 'hot, leftish equality debate in the late 1960s', which had the main goal of redistribution of

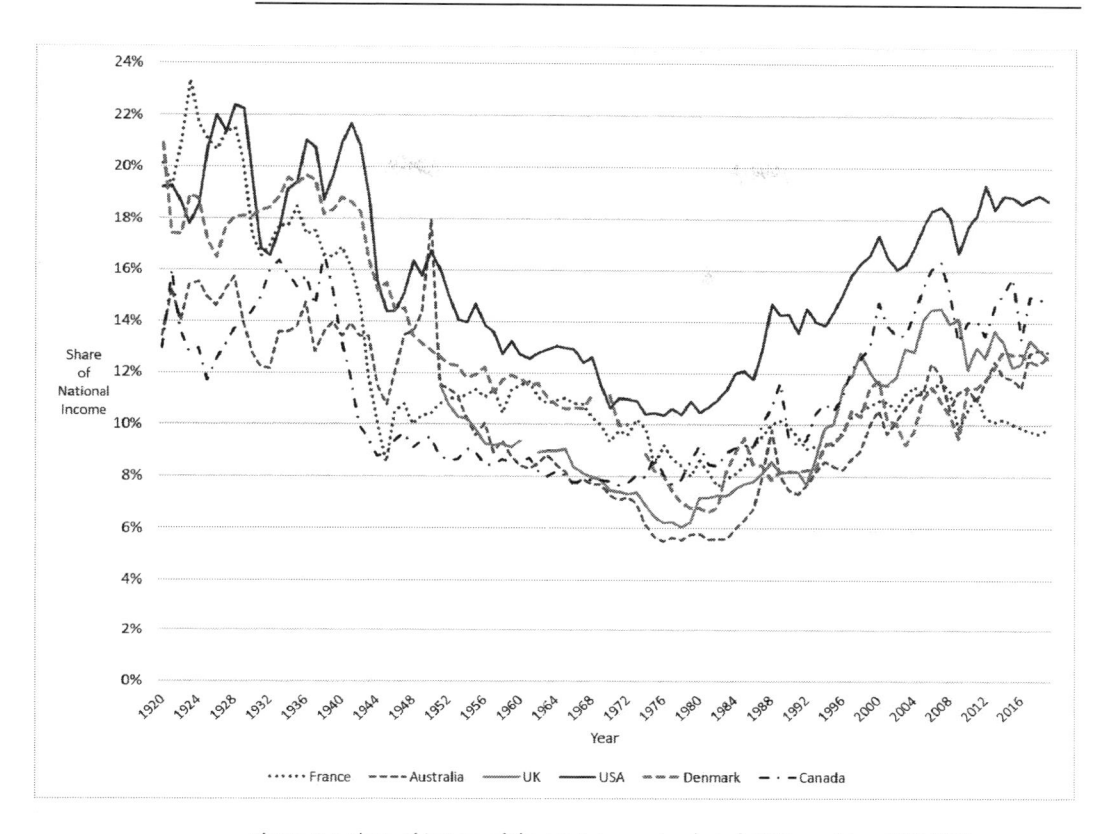

Figure 5.4 Share of income of the top 1 per cent, selected OECD countries, 1920–2019
Source: World Inequality Database, https://wid.world/.

earnings.[59] This progressive agenda was derailed in part by the high inflation of the 1970s, which pushed ordinary wages up the progressive tax rate structure in rapid 'bracket creep' that significantly increased the tax burden. Higher marginal tax rates also made tax avoidance much more attractive, and generated a significant tax planning response.

In recent years, there has been renewed attention to increasing inequality of income and wealth and to the role of tax rates in addressing inequality, drawing on empirical research that traced the long-run changes in income inequality.[60] Figure 5.4 shows the change in the share of income of the top 1 per cent across

---

[59] Dorothea Stromberg, 'Successes and Failures in Recent Swedish Tax Policy' in Karl W Roskamp and Francesco Forte (eds.), *Reforms of Tax Systems* (Detroit, MI: Wayne State University Press, 1981), 121–34, 122.

[60] Antony Atkinson and Thomas Piketty (eds.), *Top Incomes over the Twentieth Century: A Contrast between Continental European and English Speaking Countries* (Oxford: Oxford University Press, 2010); Thomas Piketty, *Capital in the Twenty-First Century*, trans. Arthur Goldhammer (Cambridge, MA: Harvard University Press, 2014); Thomas Piketty and Emmanuel Saez, 'Income Inequality in the United States, 1913–1998' (2003) 118 *Quarterly*

five countries, over the twentieth century. The top 1 per cent in the United States, United Kingdom and Canada owned as much as 20 per cent of the income in the 1920s, declining to below 10 per cent in the 1960s, then increasing again in the 1980s. The share of the top 1 per cent in total income grew significantly between 1981 and 2012, more than doubling in the United States (from 8 per cent in 1981 to 20 per cent in 2012), and nearly doubling in several other OECD member states.[61] Today, the top 10 per cent of the income distribution in most OECD countries owns between 20 to 35 per cent of income.[62]

An important cause of the growing share of income of the top 1 per cent was the 1980s supply-side tax reforms, which were summarised in Chapters 2 and 4. Governments reduced top income tax rates from above 60 per cent in many countries to below 50 per cent, flattened the overall tax rate structure and lowered tax rates on capital income and gains. Antony Atkinson and Andrew Leigh suggest that reductions in tax rates contributed one third to one half of the increase in top incomes since the 1980s.[63]

A large share of income in the top 1 per cent comprises labour income, reflecting high wages of skilled professionals, executives, sports stars and other highly paid individuals. However, estimates of income inequality based on income tax data understate the income of the top 1 per cent, and top 0.1 or 0.01 per cent, because these cohorts derive most of their income from capital. Capital gains are excluded from most income inequality statistics, which also exclude income owned and controlled in separate corporate entities. The shifting of income between the individual and corporate tax bases is discussed further in Chapter 7. One Canadian study indicates that including income of corporations that are closely controlled by top income earners would increase incomes significantly at the top of the distribution, indicating a more unequal distribution of income.[64]

For some countries that apply an individual tax unit and collect tax data disaggregated by gender, we can identify the share of women and men in the top 1 per cent. Women comprised between 13 per cent and 25 per cent of the top 1 per cent in Spain, Denmark, Canada, Norway, Italy, Australia, the United Kingdom and New Zealand.[65] The small share of women in top

---

Journal of Economics 1–39; Antony Atkinson and Andrew Leigh, 'The Distribution of Top Incomes in Five Anglo-Saxon Countries over the Long Run' (2013) 89 *Economic Record* 31–47.

[61] OECD, *Focus on Top Incomes and Taxation in OECD Countries: Was the Crisis a Game Changer?* (Paris: OECD, 2014), www.oecd.org/social/OECD2014-FocusOnTopIncomes.pdf.

[62] Carlotta Balestra and Richard Tonkin, *Inequalities in Household Wealth across OECD Countries: Evidence from the OECD Wealth Distribution Database*, OECD Statistics Working Papers 2018/1 (Paris: OECD, 2018), https://dx.doi.org/10.1787/7e1bf673-en , figure 2.9.

[63] Atkinson and Leigh, 'The Distribution of Top Incomes' (see n 60), 15.

[64] Michael Wolfson, Mike Veall, Neil Brooks and Brian Murphy, 'Piercing the Veil: Private Corporations and the Income of the Affluent' (2016) 64(1) *Canadian Tax Journal* 1–30.

[65] Miranda Stewart, Sarah Voitchovsky and Roger Wilkins, 'Women and Top Incomes in Australia' in Miranda Stewart (ed.), *Tax, Social Policy and Gender* (Canberra: ANU Press, 2017), 257–91, 266.

income cohorts reflects the gender pay gap, and women working part time, as well as deriving less capital income and owning fewer assets.

Thomas Piketty has suggested that the high marginal tax rates in place before the 1980s performed a regulatory function, keeping top salaries down.[66] High marginal tax rates may have effectively controlled senior executive remuneration in corporations; when tax rates were lowered, this 'regulatory' effect was removed. High tax rates may have prompted the development of employee stock options and other forms of non-salary remuneration with tax-preferred treatment.

The use of taxes to achieve regulation of executive salaries was attempted in a referendum in San Francisco (Proposition L) that passed the 'Overpaid Executive Tax'. Rather than increasing the individual tax rate, this proposal adds a 0.1 per cent surcharge to company business taxes if top executives earn 100 times more than their 'typical local worker'.[67]

Challenges for the Progressive Tax on Labour Income

Income Splitting

The income tax on labour income, and social security taxes that apply to wages, face a range of challenges in the twenty-first century. Some of these challenges have a long history. The treatment of deductions in the income tax and the potential for income splitting are problems inherent in the structure of a progressive income tax law.

Other challenges are new, or have grown significantly as technological and demographic changes have taken hold, with potential to undermine resilience of the tax-transfer system. Demographic trends will lead to fewer people of working age which may have a significant effect on the labour tax base in future. This is one reason why enabling the female labour supply in the workforce is critical to future stability of the system, as well as supporting gender equality. The stagnation of wages relative to the return to capital means that tax systems that rely on wage taxation will become less effective over time. The automation and digitisation of work accelerates this trend, undermining both revenues and equity in labour taxation.

As already explained, the individual tax unit and progressive tax rates are equitable and efficient, especially when we take into account different labour supply elasticities of men and women. However, this tax structure inevitably creates an incentive for individuals with lower taxed family members to split their income, gaining a tax advantage. Income splitting essentially involves the transfer of income from a taxpayer with a high marginal tax rate to another

---

[66] Piketty, *Capital in the Twenty-First Century* (see n 60), 423.
[67] Cyrus Farivar, 'San Francisco Voters Pass "Overpaid Executive Tax"', NBCNews, 6 November 2020, www.nbcnews.com/business/business-news/san-francisco-voters-pass-overpaid-executive-tax-n1246644.

person with a nil or low marginal rate. Overall, the income is subject to lower tax and this benefit can be shared between the high- and low-rate taxpayers. Income splitting introduces a 'joint' or family unit into the tax law, even if the formal unit is the individual.

Replacing the progressive rate structure with a flat tax rate with no tax-free threshold, applicable to all individuals, would remove the incentive to split income. This is an argument in favour of flattening the income tax rate on labour income, but it would undermine equity and would likely be perceived as overtaxing middle-income earners and undertaxing high-income earners. The compromise is to design and effectively administer rules to protect the integrity of the individual tax unit and progressive rate structure.

The inequity produced by income splitting was explained by Justice Lionel Murphy of the High Court of Australia in a case about splitting of the income of a solicitor (who was a partner in a partnership) with his spouse:

> The Act is based on graduation of tax for individual taxpayers and the evident legislative policy is to require those who are more financially able (as measured by their income) to pay at a higher rate than those less able ... it should not be construed to impute an intention to Parliament to have its main purpose defeated by an income splitting device which tends to defeat its policy of graduated tax rates, is available only to the professional and commercial classes, and allows the burden of taxation to be shifted increasingly from those taxpayers most able to afford it to those less able.[68]

Justice Murphy was in dissent, and income splitting of professional income was upheld by the High Court of Australia, and remains a common tax planning strategy today. Income splitting may also be achieved through the disposition of income-producing property to a family member or to a trust for their benefit, or through the sharing of business, professional or services income between family members. To be successful as a tax strategy, income splitting requires that the spouse and other family members are economically dependent on the taxpayer. As Judith Grbich observed, the notion of 'ordinary family dealings' constitutes the taxpayer and 'his' spouse in a traditional hierarchical and gendered fashion.[69]

The characterisation of income splitting arrangements as 'ordinary family dealings' historically saved them from classification as tax avoidance in various countries.[70] Today, most income tax laws adopt some anti-avoidance rules to limit income splitting of labour income, especially between parents and minor children. Such rules are effective if well administered, but they add complexity

---

[68] *Federal Commissioner of Taxation* v *Everett* (1980) 143 CLR 440 (Australia).
[69] Judith Grbich, 'The Tax Unit Debate Revisited: Notes on the Critical Resources of a Feminist Revenue Law Scholarship' (1991) 4 *Canadian Journal of Women and the Law* 512-38, 516.
[70] *Federal Commissioner of Taxation* v *Newton* [1958] AC 450; (1958) 32 ALJR 187 (Privy Council) (Australia).

to the tax law. Canada provides an example of a country with an individual income tax unit and rules to counter income splitting, either by applying a high tax rate, or by attributing the income back to the earner or asset owner. In 2018, the Canadian rules were extended to apply to what the Canada Revenue Agency calls 'income sprinkling' with adult children, a recognition of the longer dependence of young people on their families even in adulthood, for example while studying at university.[71]

Capitalisation of Labour Income

A progressive tax rate on labour income, in a system that applies a lower tax rate to capital income or gain, or to corporations, generates a further incentive to convert labour income into capital income, or to earn it in an entity rather than directly. This occurs in a variety of ways. Tax laws frequently permit the remuneration of inventors or executives with stock options eligible for capital gain, deferred or concessional tax treatment. Managers of venture capital and hedge funds in the United States and some other countries may be permitted to apply 'capital gain' treatment to their managerial income, or 'carried interest' in the fund (see further Chapter 7). Individuals who provide services as independent contractors rather than employees may have the option to incorporate their activities, accessing the lower tax rate applied to corporations.

The capitalisation of labour income undermines the progressive tax rate structure and creates horizontal inequity between workers facing the regular marginal tax rate schedule and those who get a tax break. It also generates a tax planning opportunity that may cost significant tax revenue. The significant effect on the tax system of 'shifting' of income out of the personal income tax into a lower taxed corporate income tax is explained in Chapter 7.

Taxing the Gig Economy

The formal structure of employment which is the basis for wage withholding and the progressive income tax is also undermined by the 'gig' economy. All tax laws that apply to income from work must wrestle with the distinction between employees and independent contractors. Income tax law intersects with labour and contract law, sometimes relying on existing legal categories, at other times overriding these with specific statutory rules.

This issue has become increasingly important as the institutionalised labour relations of the twentieth century have been unwound in the twenty-first century, as more individuals move into self-employment and engage in individual contracting, variable hours contracts and informal work activities. The

---

[71] Canada Revenue Agency, 'Income Sprinkling' (10 July 2019), www.canada.ca/en/revenue-agency/programs/about-canada-revenue-agency-cra/federal-government-budgets/income-sprinkling.html.

reliance of tax law on categories generated in other laws may create significant problems.[72] A recent comparative text observed:

> The tax treatment of employees and independent workers differs significantly for all the countries studied here. For most countries, expenses deductible by employees are restricted compared to expenses deductible by independent workers. Also, salaries and wages paid to employees are subject to withholding at source by employers, whereas most payments to independent workers are not. For countries with schedular systems, employment income is included in a different schedule than business income derived by independent workers. Thus, all the countries require rules to distinguish between employees and independent workers ... In some countries, the distinction is based on the distinction in the country's labor law (either statutory or case law); in others, there is a special distinction for purposes of tax law. In some countries, the distinction is dependent on the facts and circumstances of each case, while in others it is based on a limited number of factors, such as the amount of control exercised by the payer on a worker.[73]

Employers and employees arbitrage the tax benefits achieved by shifting their bargain outside withholding and social security systems (see a discussion of tax arbitrage in Chapter 9). The flexibility of contracting may suit some workers, who utilise these arrangements to reduce their taxes. However, contractor relationships may also be exploitative rather than a choice by workers. Employers can avoid labour law obligations as well as tax, workers' compensation, sick leave and social security payments, if they shift employees outside these formal systems.

The digital economy accelerates and disperses these effects through the use of multisided platforms that facilitate one-time contracting for unique or single services between individuals. Is an individual who is driving a car service such as Uber an employee, or in a sole proprietor business? A recent case in the United Kingdom and legislation in California have established Uber and Lyft drivers as 'employees' of the platform companies.[74] Another consequence of this changing work environment is a loss of benefits, for example, the large number of 'non-standard' or 'self-employed' workers who do not have paid sick leave, which has been a challenge for public health in response to the COVID-19 pandemic.[75]

---

[72] Judith Freedman, 'Employment Status, Tax and the Gig Economy – Improving the Fit or Making the Break?' (2020) 31(2) *King's Law Journal* 194–214.
[73] Ault et al, *Comparative Income Taxation* (see n 19), Kindle Book, Loc 7922.
[74] *Uber BV, Uber London LTD, Uber, Britannia Britannia LTD v Aslam, Farrar, Dawson and Others* (2017) Appeal No UKEAT/0056/17/DA, Employment Appeal Tribunal (UK); California Assembly Act 5 (2019) (US: California), codifying *Dynamex Operations W v Superior Court - 4 Cal. 5th 903, 232 Cal Rptr 3d 1, 416 P.3d 1* (2018) (US); now reversed by Proposition 22, which exempts app-based drivers from the law. Proposition 22 included various protections for drivers, but they will still be required to pay their own income taxes.
[75] OECD, *Paid Sick Leave to Protect Income, Health and Jobs through the COVID-19 Crisis*, OECD Policy Brief (Paris: OECD, 2 July 2020).

The COVID-19 pandemic may have accelerated these changes. The pandemic revealed that independent contractors and personal service companies who may have avoided social insurance contributions and employment taxes needed government support, while widespread working from home also poses challenges to basic concepts of income and expenses in the tax law.

It is difficult to define and tax the income of individuals in the sharing economy, such as those who do home maintenance jobs via a digital services platform, or rent a room in their house through Airbnb. Are these microbusinesses, or disguised employee–employer relationships? Is consumption tax, such as VAT, applicable to the supply? The answer to these questions in different countries may depend on the scale of the activity and design of thresholds in income and consumption taxes.

Digitalisation has enlarged the scale of barter, gift or 'sharing' transactions. The swopping of home-grown vegetables, car pooling, or payment and bartering for babysitting or small-scale sales of second-hand goods have long been untaxed, usually because these are perceived as *de minimis*, or because it is not possible to enforce the income tax on such dealings without unacceptable interventions into private or home life. The scale of such activities has been expanded by 'peer-to-peer sharing' facilitated by digital platform companies. These 'bring producers, providers, and consumers of goods and services together, in exchange for a fee ... informal pooling, renting, and borrowing arrangements are not new, access to the Internet and mobile technology means that the scale, scope, frequency, and transformative potential of such sharing transactions have reached an unprecedented degree'.[76]

Microbusinesses today access a range of customers beyond local or family-based relations. This blurs the boundary between business and hobby, private and market, employee and contractor and provides fertile ground for 'tax opportunism' by both individuals and the digital platforms, with potential to disrupt the tax base. Opportunities for tax minimisation arise from different administrative requirements, falling below thresholds for reporting systems or taxation, and rapid change and mobility in and out of platforms or systems that makes workers harder to track.[77] The issues overlap with taxing not-for-profits or social enterprises, discussed in Chapter 8.

A goal of tax policy is to produce horizontal equity between those who are earning income in similar ways, not to distort decision-making and to encourage compliance.[78] The gig economy undermines the fairness goal of taxing individuals with the same income equally (horizontal equity) while privatising the costs and risks of work, rather than ensuring such risks are publicly shared through the tax and transfer system. The solution is to extend tax obligations to the digital

---

[76] Shu-Yi Oei and Diane Ring, 'Can Sharing Be Taxed?' (2016) 93 *Washington University Law Review* 989–1069, 997–8; Li, Choi and Smith, 'Automation and Workers' (see n 20).
[77] Oei and Ring, 'Can Sharing Be Taxed?' (see n 76).
[78] Freedman, 'Employment Status, Tax and the Gig Economy' (see n 72), 212–13.

platform that facilitates such tailored commercial dealings. This could include the extension of withholding obligations for tax or social contributions by deduction at source, and imposing information obligations on platforms. Currently, there is a 'transparency gap' in information about workers operating on a digital platform, which will require law reform to overcome.[79]

The technological leap represented by intermediary platforms has generated some of the same issues as arose for the introduction of withholding on employers close to a century ago. Governments are highly motivated to protect the labour tax base and it is to be expected that tax authorities will increasingly harness the data capabilities of digital intermediaries in a new fiscal bargain with business or employers. This will require investment in expanded data systems by governments. Some success has been achieved for consumption taxation, as explained in Chapter 10. The taxation of the global multinational enterprises which operate the digital platforms such as Uber, Facebook or Airbnb, raises the separate challenge of levying corporate tax (see Chapter 11).

Automation and Taxing Robots

Robots or artificial intelligence may augment or replace jobs, but they essentially represent the capitalisation of labour. In an income tax, the cost of labour is a deductible expense for the business. Social security or payroll taxes, or contributory payments for workers' compensation or health insurance, are a fixed cost, whereas the personal income tax applies to labour income in the hands of the worker. If the number of workers can be reduced or workers can be removed from the 'books' of the company, business costs go down.

Treating robots as if they were human – levying a tax on 'their' labour – might superficially appear to level the playing field between robots and people. But robots are not people, they are capital investments. Capital costs of machinery or intellectual property are usually depreciable over time in an income tax, although in many tax systems immediate expensing is available for some capital costs. One idea is to tax the 'intensity' of automation, measured by jobs lost or disrupted, by the capital–labour ratio of the firm, or by the input cost of automation components.[80] Some have argued that a robot tax can be optimal because of structural transitions for skills of workers.[81] However, it is not clear that this is either desirable or feasible. A robot tax would move business tax policy in the opposite direction to current trends to permit 'expensing' or accelerated deductions for business

---

[79] Celeste Black, 'The Future of Work: The Gig Economy and Pressures on the Tax System' (2020) 68(1) *Canadian Tax Journal* 69–97, 86.

[80] See, e.g. Vincent Doi and Glendon Goh, *Taxation of Automation and Artificial Intelligence as a Tool of Labour Policy*, SMU Centre for AI & Data Governance Research Paper No. 2019/01 (1 November 2018), https://ssrn.com/abstract=3322306.

[81] Joao Guerreiro, Sergio Rebelo and Pedro Teles, *Should Robots Be Taxed?*, NBER Working Paper 23806 (Cambridge, MA: National Bureau of Economic Research, 2020).

capital investment to support innovation including new technologies. The structural shift of economic return from labour to capital, which has contributed to growing income inequality, cannot all be blamed on robots, but is a trend over several decades. A robot tax levied on corporations may slow the adoption of new technologies, but its incidence will fall indirectly on others in the economy. This issue is discussed in Chapter 7.

Ultimately, it seems undesirable to focus our efforts on taxing capital more highly where that capital is invested in new technology (which may have a chance, at least, of improving welfare), rather than taxing capital more effectively across the economy as a whole. A better, though politically difficult, approach is to increase taxation on capital derived by individuals and to redistribute revenues more fairly to workers, including those affected by automation, through the provision of transfers and public goods such as education.

Basic Income

Concept and Justification of a Basic Income

In the last part of this chapter on taxation of work, we address the issue of a universal basic income (UBI) and how to finance it with taxation. As explained in Chapter 2, the delivery of social support is a core function of successful tax states, which provide cash transfers to support individuals who are unemployed or receive low wages. There is significant diversity in the design of payments for the unemployed or low-income workers, but most payment systems are means tested to target them to the lowest income individuals. Tax credits, cash transfers and the minimum wage are all used by governments in respect of work and income support. Some countries have established 'work credits', for example the Earned Income Tax Credit in the United States, which is one of the largest US welfare programs in its federal system and is delivered through the tax code.[82] The UK Government has in the last few years carried out an extensive reorganisation of welfare payments, aiming to replace working credit and other benefits with a Universal Credit.[83] The new rules aim to integrate tax and welfare benefits and are intended to help 'make work pay' and to relieve poverty.

The withdrawal rates and conditions of all types of targeted income support payment may generate high marginal effective tax rates on labour income, creating 'poverty traps' in the system for low-income workers. This may not be an issue for workers who are choosing to take a full-time job. However, it is

---

[82] Tax Policy Center, 'What Is the Earned Income Tax Credit?' in *Key Elements of the U.S. Tax System, Briefing Book* (Washington, DC: Tax Policy Center, 2021), www.taxpolicycenter.org/briefing-book/what-earned-income-tax-credit.

[83] Centre for Social Justice, *Universal Credit* (London: Centre for Social Justice, October 2017), www.centreforsocialjustice.org.uk/core/wp-content/uploads/2017/10/Universal_Credit_Report.pdf.

increasingly an issue for workers who engage in insecure, seasonal, part-time or casual work.[84]

A different approach may be to provide a UBI, with or without a job guarantee as proposed by some, to help ensure the economic security of workers. There is growing interest in a UBI as a response to concerns about labour market disruptions, a lack of economic security of workers and inequality of income. The fiscal response of many governments to the COVID-19 pandemic brought the idea of universal income support for individuals to the forefront, as economic shutdowns prevented people from working and many more people have relied on government payments of unprecedented universality and size.

A simple definition of a UBI is 'an income unconditionally paid to all on an individual basis, without means test or work requirement'.[85] Most UBI proposals seek to provide an adequate income set at a high enough level to protect against poverty, although the unit of payment, level and need for conditions or eligibility requirements are all debated in the literature.

A UBI may also be described as a 'negative income tax' or a 'demogrant'. Viewing the tax-transfer system as a whole, an individual with income below a certain level should receive a payment (the UBI or 'negative' tax), but as their earned or private income increases, they should smoothly transition to paying income tax. To achieve this ideally requires a flat rate to apply to both withdrawal of the UBI and taxation of earned income generating quite a different system from most income taxes with progressive tax rates.

The concept of a UBI has antecedents dating back centuries, but it was substantially developed in the early twentieth century.[86] The concept has appealed to left and right on the political spectrum. A UBI was suggested by Bertrand Russell and won some public support in both the United Kingdom and Canada, and by the Henry George League in the 1920s. In the United Kingdom, Lady Juliet Rhys-Williams, a Conservative, made a case for a UBI in an influential *Pamphlet* released in 1942. Her proposal aimed to provide income security for workers in the market and in the home – especially, women who were raising children:[87]

---

[84] Jane Millar and Peter Whiteford, 'Timing It Right or Timing It Wrong: How Should Income-Tested Benefits Deal with Changes in Circumstances?' (2020) 28(1) *Journal of Poverty and Social Justice* 3–20, comparing systems in Australia and the United Kingdom.

[85] Luke Martinelli, *The Fiscal and Distributional Implication of Alternative Universal BI Schemes in the UK*, IPR Working Paper (Bath: Institute for Policy Research, 2017), 4; Antony Painter and Chris Thoung, *Creative Citizen, Creative State: The Principled and Pragmatic Case for a Universal Basic Income* (London: Royal Society for the Encouragement of Arts, Manufactures and Commerce, 2015), 4, www.thersa.org/discover/publications-and-articles/reports/basic-income; Amitai Etzioni and Alex Platt, *Basic Income: The Social Contract Revisited* (Oxford: The Foundation for Law, Justice and Society, 2008), 2.

[86] Guy Standing, *Basic Income: And How We Can Make It Happen* (UK: Pelican, 2017).

[87] Juliet Rhys-Williams, *Something to Look Forward to* (1942) extracted and expanded in *Taxation and Incentive* (London: William Hodge and Co, 1953); see Peter Sloman, 'Beveridge's

The prevention of want must be regarded as being the duty of the State to all of its citizens, and not merely to a favoured few. In short, we must abolish the Means Test, and provide benefits equal to those now paid out of unemployment assistance to every individual man, woman and child in the whole country. ... Family Allowances are not a species of charity, but rather a form of wages paid by the State to the parents of the next generation, in return for services rendered to future citizens. They form, in short, a social contract, not a dole.

In the United States, Milton Friedman proposed a negative income tax to replace other welfare programs.[88] A libertarian case may be made for a UBI that suggests that it will support deregulation and increase individual freedom.[89] Variants were proposed in official inquiries in the 1970s in Australia and the United Kingdom. There were experiments with negative income taxes in Canada and the United States in the 1970s and at one stage, it appeared such a scheme would be enacted by the US federal government.[90] More recent experiments with UBI have been financed by Silicon Valley entrepreneurs.[91] A two-year trial in Finland was terminated early, but studies indicate that there were positive effects on economic security and well-being, and no negative employment effects.[92]

Designing a Basic Income[93]

There is not scope to address all the issues about basic income here. This part discusses three main issues. First is the imperative of financing a UBI with taxation. Most UBI proposals have a fiscal cost that is much higher than the cost of current transfer (income support) systems. A UBI would require higher levels of taxation on some or all tax bases of income, consumption and wealth. The higher taxation required for a basic income will itself have efficiency and equity effects that must be considered in any UBI design.

Rival: Juliet Rhys-Williams and the Campaign for BI, 1942–55' (2015), www.repository.cam.ac.uk/bitstream/handle/1810/251445/Sloman%202015%20Contemporary%20British%20History.pdf.

[88] Milton Friedman, *Capitalism and Freedom* (Chicago: University of Chicago Press, 1962).

[89] Daniel Hemel and Miranda Fleischer, 'Atlas Nods: The Libertarian Case for a Basic Income' (2017) *Wisconsin Law Review* 1189–271.

[90] David H Freedman, 'Basic Income: A Sellout of the American Dream' *MIT Technology Review*, 13 June 2016, www.technologyreview.com/2016/06/13/159449/basic-income-a-sellout-of-the-american-dream/, 5.

[91] Ibid., 7.

[92] Joseph Zeballos-Roig, 'Finland's Basic-Income Trial Found People Were Happier, But Weren't More Likely to Get Jobs', World Economic Forum (8 May 2020), www.weforum.org/agenda/2020/05/finlands-basic-income-trial-found-people-were-happier-but-werent-more-likely-to-get-jobs/.

[93] David Ingles, Ben Philips and Miranda Stewart, 'From Guaranteed Minimum Income to Basic Income: What Might It Look Like?' in Peter Saunders (ed.), *Revisiting Henderson: Poverty, Social Security and Basic Income* (Melbourne: Melbourne University Press, 2019), 377–400.

Table 5.1. Basic income with 50 per cent flat tax

Citizen		Annual income	Private income per week	UBI per week	Tax paid per week	Disposable income per week	Average tax rate (%)
A	Destitute	0	0	$500	0	$500	0
B	Minimum wage	$34,000	$650	$500	650*0.5 = $325	500 + 325 = $825	28
C	Top 10 per cent	$90,000	$1,700	$500	1,700*0.5 = $850	500+ 850 = $1,350	38.6
D	Top 1 per cent	$240,000	$4,600	$500	4,600*0.5 = $2,300	500 + 2,300 = $2,800	45

Source: Author (annual and weekly incomes are illustrative only, derived from Australian wage data). UBI is assumed to be $500/week or $26,000 per year (two thirds of the Australian minimum wage). The UBI is not taxable. The average tax rate is calculated as a share of total income including the UBI.

Second, the concern is frequently raised about the 'welfare for all' provided by a UBI. However, it is easily demonstrated that a UBI financed with an income tax on earnings would be progressive. Table 5.1 presents an example of a UBI funded by a proportionate tax rate of 50 per cent on earned income (the UBI is not taxed) It shows that the rich are large net contributors and the poor are large net beneficiaries of a UBI designed in this way.

A UBI financed by a proportionate tax as illustrated in Table 5.1 will 'smooth' effective marginal tax rates at lower incomes, which may be high because of the means testing of welfare benefits. However, it will impose a higher marginal and average tax rate on the wages of many middle-income workers than current systems in most countries. An alternative approach may be to finance a UBI in part with higher taxes on wealth, which would be progressive and enable lower tax rates on labour income.

The third issue is the effect of a UBI, and associated taxes to finance it, on efficiency, specifically work incentives. This is a complex question because of the interaction of income and substitution effects for the whole population of working age taxpayers. Will the receipt of a UBI discourage people from paid work, as they have enough income to live on (the **income effect**)? Or will higher tax rates on labour income required to finance the UBI discourage people from work (the **substitution effect**)?

Modelling during the 1970s by Mirrlees showed that a negative income tax can be optimal depending on the responsiveness of individual labour supply and the degree of progressivity desired in the system.[94] UBI

---

[94] James A Mirrlees. 'An Exploration in the Theory of Optimum Income Taxation' (1971) 38 (2) *The Review of Economic Studies* 175–208. But see Jon Gruber and Emmanuel Saez, *The Elasticity of Taxable Income: Evidence and Implications*, NBER Working Paper No 7515 (Cambridge, MA National Bureau for Economic Research, 2000).

experiments provided mixed evidence about the impact on work incentives, but in general they demonstrate that disincentives are minor and identified increased well-being among the populations benefiting from the UBI.[95] Experiments in the United States in the 1960s showed that primary earners did not reduce hours of work very much, whereas hours worked by secondary earners (usually, mothers) fell by 10–15 per cent, as women used some of the money to increase time caring for children.[96]

---

[95] Robert A Moffitt, 'The Negative Income Tax and the Evolution of US Welfare Policy' (2003) 17 (3) *Journal of Economic Perspectives* 119–40, 129; Rosanna Scutella, *Moves to a BI-Flat Tax System in Australia: Implications for the Distribution of Income and Supply of Labour*, University of Melbourne Working Paper No 5/04 (Melbourne: Melbourne Institute of Applied Economic and Social Research, 2004); Ugo Colombino, 'Is Unconditional BI a Viable Alternative to Other Social Welfare Measures?' (2019) 128 *IZA World of Labor* 7 https://doi.org/10.15185/izawol.128.v2, 8.

[96] Colombino, 'Is Unconditional BI a Viable Alternative' (see n 95). Negative implications originally drawn from the data in these experiments may have been based on improper interpretation or poor experimental design.

6

Taxation of Saving and Wealth

> The luxuries and vanities of life occasion the principal expense of the rich, and a magnificent house embellishes and sets off to the best advantage all the other luxuries and vanities which they possess. A tax upon house-rents, therefore, would in general fall heaviest upon the rich; and in this sort of inequality there would not, perhaps, be anything very unreasonable.
>
> Adam Smith, *Wealth of Nations*

Taxing Capital

The Complex Role of Capital

The question of how to tax capital – including personal saving or wealth – has long been debated in academic, policy and political spheres. This is largely because of the complex role of capital itself in the economy. Spencer Bastani and Daniel Waldenstrom recently observed:

> There is substantial academic and political dispute regarding the appropriate role of taxes on capital in the tax system. Perhaps this is not that surprising given the complex nature of capital. Capital is needed to fund investments in the economy, it serves as a vehicle for individuals to transfer resources across time, and it can provide consumption benefits, as in the case of housing wealth. Furthermore, capital can be transmitted across generations and it can be moved across jurisdictions.[1]

The taxation of capital is, in most people's minds, fundamentally connected to inequality in the distribution of capital income and wealth. When asked the question, who owns capital, most people assume it is owned by 'the rich'. In the time of Adam Smith and even towards the end of the nineteenth century, only a small proportion of the population owned wealth. Early in the twentieth century, income taxes in countries including the United Kingdom, Australia and New Zealand applied higher tax rates to 'unearned income' from property

---

[1] Spencer Bastani and Daniel Waldenstrom, 'How Should Capital Be Taxed? Theory and Evidence from Sweden' (2020) 34(4) *Journal of Economic Surveys* 812–46, 812; see Jane Gravelle, *The Economic Effects of Taxing Capital Income* (Cambridge, MA: MIT Press, 1994).

or capital than to labour income. It was strongly felt as a matter of policy and politics that the higher tax rate on 'unearned' income was 'desirable and just'.[2]

Today, the opposite applies in most successful tax states. Progressive tax rates apply to labour income but capital income and gains are often taxed at lower rates, while a variety of exemptions, concessions and reduced tax rates apply to saving. The lower tax on capital income and gains is combined with a corporate tax rate that is almost always lower than the top marginal income tax rate (see further Chapter 7). Wealth and inheritance taxes have been repealed or significantly reduced in many countries since the 1980s.

The twentieth century saw the democratisation of wealth. While the situation differs widely across countries, a majority of the population in many successful tax states will own a home at some point during their lifetime (albeit purchased with mortgage debt) and have private savings in a retirement fund or other financial and property investments. This adds complexity to the question of how to tax capital, in the context of a broader suite of policy measures concerning public and private provision for individuals over the life course.

Governments seek to encourage saving to provide for economic security in retirement and for home ownership, often with generous tax concessions. Older people own more wealth than younger people, as they have accumulated it over a life course of working. Older generations have also benefited from decades of economic growth, rises in asset prices and substantial tax concessions for saving in many countries. Increased asset prices, especially of the home, means that some older people are asset-rich but income-poor. For young people, access to wealth is increasingly defined as a policy challenge, with calls to provide relief to younger people of working age who struggle to gain access to housing and other saving, and to tax the accumulated wealth of older generations.

Saving and investment may also be influenced by other tax rules, especially the ability to obtain income tax deductions for the interest on debt to finance income-producing investments. The middle class relies on debt to build wealth; this makes them vulnerable to falls in asset values so that the middle class increasingly relies on governments to maintain asset values that are at risk in financial crises.[3] Similar political constraints may apply to tax policy, making it difficult to limit or remove tax concessions for saving where these benefit the middle class in general.

---

[2] Martin Daunton, *Just Taxes: The Politics of Taxation in Britain, 1914–1979* (New York: Cambridge University Press, 2002), 116.

[3] Jeffrey Chwieroth and Andrew Walter, *The Wealth Effect: How the Great Expectations of the Middle Class Have Changed the Politics of Banking Crises* (Cambridge, UK: Cambridge University Press, 2019).

Inequality of Income and Wealth

Despite the dramatic expansion of the middle class in developed countries, capital income and wealth remain unequally distributed both within countries and across the globe. There are some very rich people, and they are very much richer than the rest of the population; there is also a share of the population that does not have any assets. Figure 6.1 shows the share of income, and share of wealth, owned by the top 10 per cent of households in member states of the Organisation for Economic Cooperation and Development (OECD). It shows that the top 10 per cent of the income distribution own between 20 to 35 per cent of income. As explained in Chapter 5, income inequality statistics based on tax data include income from work and services but do not usually take account of capital gains or of income and assets held in controlled corporations or other entities, thereby also understating inequality.

Wealth is much more concentrated than income. The measurement of wealth inequality is difficult because many governments do not collect wealth taxes or annual wealth statistics. Most wealth statistics are collected through surveys on a household (not individual) basis, and rely on accurate declarations of wealth in the survey. There is evidence that high-wealth households under-declare income and wealth, concealing it from tax authorities and in surveys.[4] Therefore, reported statistics on wealth are likely to understate inequality.

The top 10 per cent of the wealth distribution own between 35 and 80 per cent of wealth in member states (Figure 6.1). The United States has the most unequal wealth distribution but other countries including Germany, Denmark and the Netherlands also have highly unequal wealth distributions. On average, the top 20 per cent of the population in OECD countries own 80 per cent of financial wealth, 60 per cent of real estate wealth and about 40 per cent of other non-financial wealth. This means that the top 20 per cent also derives the majority of capital income and gains arising from these assets.[5]

Theory of Taxing Saving

It will be recalled that the comprehensive income tax applies to consumption plus the accretion to net wealth in a fiscal period such as a year (see Chapter 1). This means that in a comprehensive income tax, the return to saving is taxable at standard tax rates on an accrual basis, whether or not it is realised.

For example, if you own shares that were valued at $100 at the beginning of the year, and $120 at the end of the year, your taxable income would include

---

[4] Annette Alstadsaeter, Niels Johannesen and Gabriel Zucman, 'Tax Evasion and Inequality' (2019) 109(6) *American Economic Review* 2073–103; OECD, *Taxation of Household Savings* (Paris: OECD, 2018), www.oecd.org/ctp/taxation-of-household-savings-9789264289536-en.htm, 125.

[5] OECD, Income and Wealth Distribution Databases, www.oecd.org/social/income-distribution-database.htm, accessed 16 March 2022. The same result is obtained using the European Central Bank Household Finance and Consumption Survey (2016).

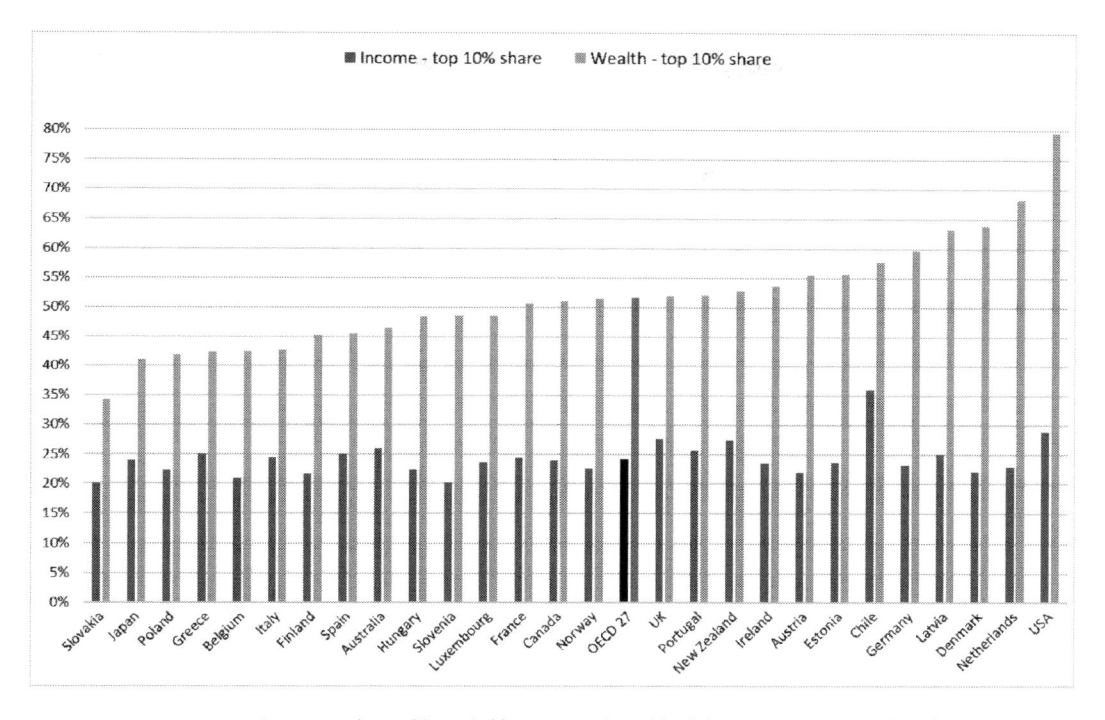

Figure 6.1 Share of household income and wealth of the top 10 per cent, selected OECD countries, 2015

Source: OECD, Income Distribution Database and Wealth Distribution Database, see www.oecd.org/social/income-distribution-database.htm.

the accretion to value of $20 (or would be reduced by a loss in value), even though you have not sold the shares. A comprehensive income tax would also apply to 'imputed' income, being the market value of services or property received in kind. The most important example for the purpose of taxing saving is 'imputed rent' that reflects the benefit that you derive from living in your own home (we return to this later).

Saving is usually analysed by economists as consumption that is deferred from one fiscal period to another. If you earn a dollar today, and save it instead of spending it, you can spend (consume) your saved dollar plus any earnings on it tomorrow. Economic modelling can extend the analysis of saving from just two periods of time across several years, or over a life cycle or multiple generations. The dynamic character of saving and its equivalence to consumption over time explains why 'capital income taxation stands right at the centre of a key tax policy issue: should the personal tax base be income or consumption?'[6]

---

[6] David White, 'The Impact of Economic Theory on Capital Gains Tax Reform Proposals' in Michael Littlewood and Craig Elliffe (eds.), *Capital Gains Taxation: A Comparative Analysis of Key Issues* (New York: Elgar Publishing, 2017), 30–80, 41.

As explained in Chapter 4, during the 1980s 'decade of tax reform', many experts advocated a switch from an income tax to a consumption tax base. The dominant expert view was that a consumption tax is the most efficient tax base because it does not tax the return to saving. This makes it 'neutral' between saving and spending, so that it does not distort the choice whether to save or spend.[7] In contrast, the income tax is said to 'double tax' the return to saving by taxing the return to saving across two periods, thereby creating a disincentive to save. The approach of exempting the return to saving conflicted with the comprehensive income approach of Henry Simons but found support in the optimal tax theory of the 1970s. It resonated with supply-side tax policy that argued in a more simplistic fashion for a reduction of taxes on capital to boost investment.[8]

An equity argument may also be made in favour of removing the 'double tax' on saving, which relies on assessing distributive justice over the life course, rather than at a single point in time. The theory of saving over the life course developed by Franco Modigliani suggests that savings accumulated during the life course, mostly through earning income from work, are consumed (or 'dissaved') in retirement.[9] This justifies a consumption tax approach, which redistributes income earned in one period of life for individuals to another period, enabling smoothing of life course consumption. This theory also finds justification in an older moral tradition praising the virtue of prudence over prodigality. Modigliani claimed that 'it is because of this relation between saving and productive capital that thrift has traditionally been regarded as a virtuous, socially beneficial act'.[10]

A century earlier, John Stuart Mill had said that savings should not be 'double taxed' while money 'spent in unproductive consumption pays only once' and 'a just and wise legislation would abstain from holding out motives for dissipating rather than saving the earnings of honest exertion'.[11] Mill was particularly concerned about the person 'who has no means of providing for old age ... except by saving from income' and argued that they 'should have the tax remitted on all that part of his income which is really and bona fide

---

[7] Nicholas Kaldor, *An Expenditure Tax* (London: Allen & Unwin, 1955); David Bradford, 'The Case for a Personal Consumption Tax' in Joseph Pechman (ed.), *What Should Be Taxed: Income or Expenditure?* (Washington, DC: Brookings Institution, 1979), 75–113.

[8] These various economic theories are discussed by Bastani and Waldenstrom, 'How Should Capital Be Taxed?' (see n 1).

[9] Franco Modigliani, 'Life-Cycle, Individual Thrift, and the Wealth of Nations' (1976) 76(3) *American Economic Review* 297–313; Franco Modigliani, 'The Role of Intergenerational Transfers and Life-Cycle Saving in the Accumulation of Wealth' (1998) 2(2) *Journal of Economic Perspectives* 15–20.

[10] Modigliani, 'Life-Cycle, Individual Thrift, and the Wealth of Nations' (see n 9), 313.

[11] John Stuart Mill, *Principles of Political Economy* (London: Longmans, 1848), www.econlib.org/library/Mill/mlP.html?chapter_num=1#book-reader, chapter 2, paragraph 2. See also Thomas Hobbes, *Leviathan* (London: Pelican Classics, [1651], 1968), Project Gutenberg eBook, www.gutenberg.org/files/3207/3207-h/3207-h.htm.

applied to that purpose'.[12] In the nineteenth century, Mill's approach to excluding the return to saving from tax likely was progressive. In his time, the rich had an annual income from their wealth on which to live throughout their lifetime. In contrast, those who had to 'save' income for the future were less wealthy.

More generally, how a government taxes its citizens and delivers expenditures is intimately linked to the life course. In a stylised way, we can present the life cycle effects for individuals of government taxes and transfers as follows. Children and young people are net recipients of benefits in care and time from individuals in private families and from public provision. When children become adults, they work and derive market income during the middle years of life, when individuals contribute taxes to finance government and redistribution. During this time, individuals enjoy growing private income for consumption and saving, and purchase assets. As individuals age and retire from the workforce, they earn less income and therefore pay less tax, while drawing down on private savings. In old age, individuals are net recipients of transfers from the state in old age.

One approach to presenting this 'life story' of taxes and transfers is through 'national transfer accounts', which bring together data on public taxes and transfers across the population. This approach can be combined with data on private contributions to dependants. Public taxes include income and social security taxes, while public transfers include welfare or cash payments to households. Private transfers include financial transfers and expenses, which may be identified through surveys, and transfers of time to care for dependants (most of which is provided by women), which may be quantified through time use survey data. A recent study of social policy in several European countries presented the distribution of public and private resource transfers between generations over the life course.[13] Figure 6.2 shows that infants and children receive the largest net transfers when both household and public transfers are taken into account. These transfers comprise mostly net private money and time transfers and some public subsidies. Working-age people are net contributors of public taxes and private transfers; and the elderly receive large net public transfers and little net private transfers. When net private transfers of time are taken into account, the elderly overall receive fewer transfers than the very young. The black line indicates the 'total life cycle deficit', or net balance of all resources received at any life stage.

Empirical evidence confirms that saving and wealth have strong life cycle characteristics. Figure 6.3 shows the distribution of wealth with respect to age,

---

[12] Ibid.
[13] Róbert Iván Gál, Pieter Vanhyusse and Lili Vargha, 'Pro-Elderly Welfare States within Child-Oriented Societies' (2018) 25(6) *Journal of European Public Policy* 944–58. See also United Nations, National Transfer Accounts manual, https://www.un.org/en/development/desa/population/publications/development/NTA_Manual.asp.

150   Taxation of Saving and Wealth

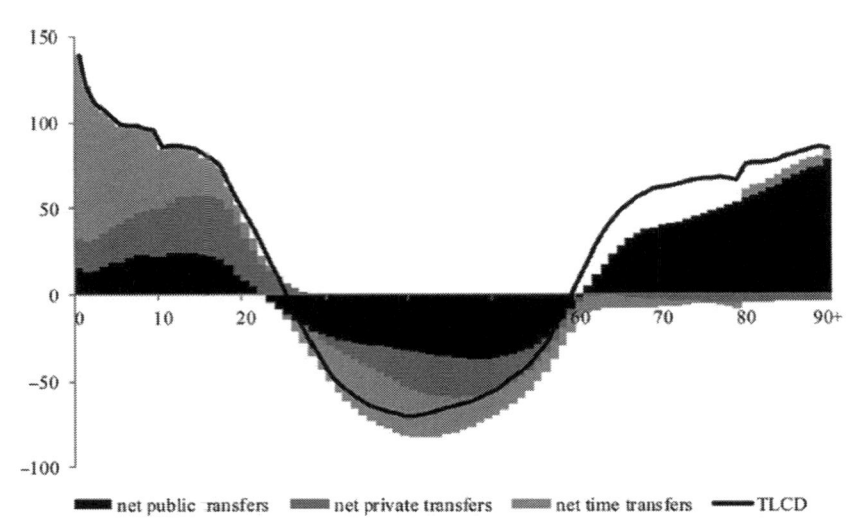

Figure 6.2 Per capita public, private and net time transfers by age, selected European countries, 2016
Note: TLCD is transfer life course deficit. It represents the net deficit in public and private transfers of money and time at different ages through the life course.
Source: Róbert Iván Gál, Pieter Vanhyusse and Lili Vargha, 'Pro-Elderly Welfare States within Child-Oriented Societies' (2018) 25(6) *Journal of European Public Policy* 944–58, Figure 2

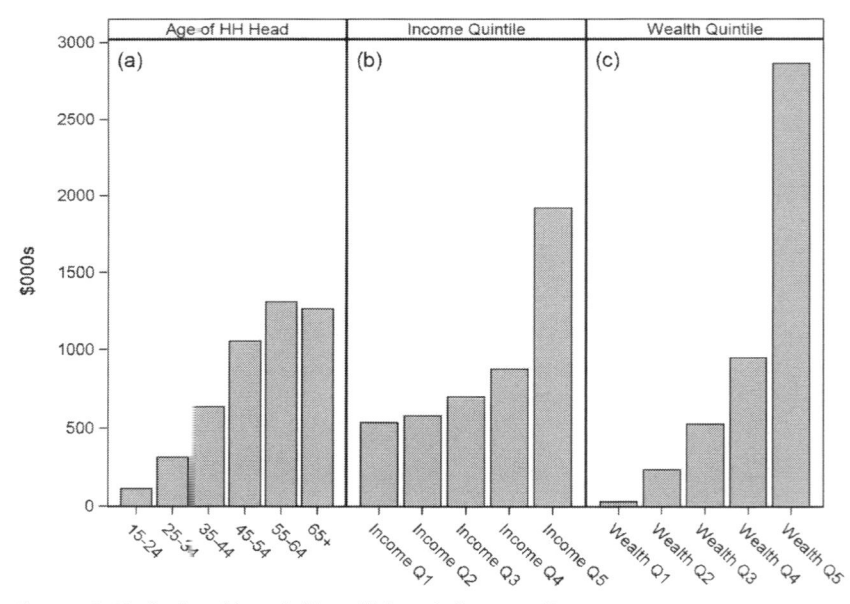

Figure 6.3 Distribution of household wealth by quintiles, Australia, 2017
Source: Ben Phillips, ABS Survey of Income and Wealth (2017).

income and wealth, in Australia. Figure 6.3(a) shows the life cycle distribution of wealth: people accumulate wealth as they age. Figure 6.3(b) shows that wealth is distributed unequally with respect to income quintiles but also indicates that some low-income households have significant wealth (largely

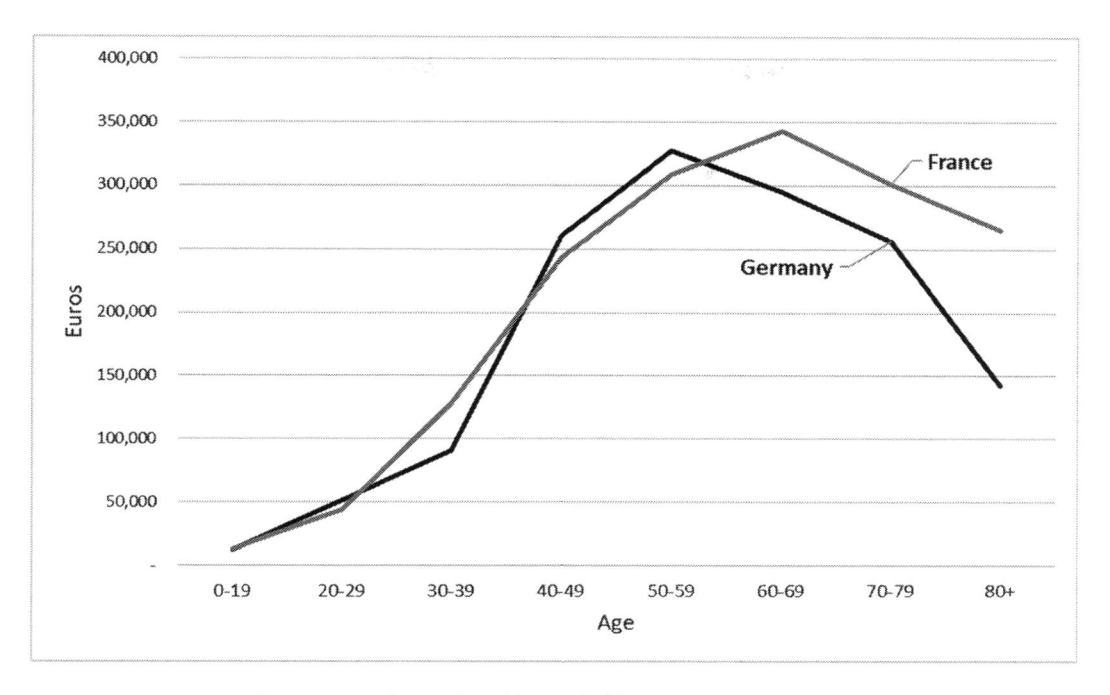

Figure 6.4 Distribution of wealth over the life course, Germany, France, 2015
Source: Carlotta Balestra and Richard Tonkin, *Inequalities in Household Wealth across OECD Countries: Evidence from the OECD Wealth Distribution Database*, OECD Statistics Working Papers 2018/1 (Paris: OECD, 2018), https://dx.doi.org/10.1787/7e1bf673-en, Data from Figure 6.4.

representing asset-rich but income-poor older people). Figure 6.3(c) shows the uneven distribution of wealth across households by wealth quintile.

The distribution of wealth over the life course in Germany and France is shown in Figure 6.4. It shows the distribution of the amount of average wealth by age. If the Modigliani model of saving and consumption perfectly reflected life course saving, there would not be any savings left to pass to heirs (unless the ability to leave bequests is deliberately designed into the system). Figure 6.4 show that at older ages, many households still own a substantial amount of wealth; older generations own more wealth in France than in Germany, but in each country, a significant minority of individuals do not consume all of their wealth by the end of life. Bearing in mind the unequal distribution of wealth, most end-of-life wealth is owned by people at the top of the wealth distribution.

To counter this intergenerational inequality arising from the mismatch of saving and consumption over the life course, an inheritance tax could be applied to capture the excess benefit received by high-income households. Alternatively, it would be more equitable to tax capital income and wealth to a greater extent during the life course to prevent increasingly unequal outcomes through the accumulation of wealth and bequests across generations.

The Hybrid Income-Consumption Tax

Early iterations of optimal tax theory on saving were based on a simple and uniform assumption that all inequality in capital income arose from inequality in earning ability of individuals.[14] There would be no need to tax capital income, if non-linear income tax on ability could be levied by governments. Following these theoretical developments, and the innovation of Nicholas Kaldor on the expenditure tax, the UK Meade report in 1978 advocated a personal expenditure tax.[15]

The 1980s 'supply-side' tax reforms retained the income tax, but in general with lower tax rates on capital. Some countries adopted a schedular or 'dual' income tax approach, which taxed capital at lower rates than labour, but in a more coherent way than in the past. These developments marked a move away from the comprehensive income benchmark. The income tax in most countries today is a 'hybrid' income-consumption tax.

In the 1990s, Jane Gravelle observed that the economic case for removing tax on capital altogether held true only on the basis of narrow parameters, producing at best ambiguous results.[16] The reasons for this include heterogeneity in capital returns, so that different kinds of investment produce different returns, which is now accepted in the literature; uncertainty about future earnings; and the importance of economic rents.

More recently, there has been a partial circling back towards support for taxing capital income taxation on efficiency and equity grounds. The Australian Henry Tax Review of 2009 stated that 'comprehensive income taxation, under which all savings income is taxed the same as labour income, is not an appropriate policy goal or benchmark'.[17] The Review did not propose to eliminate taxation of capital income but to tax it 'at a lower rate than labour income' in accordance with the principle that imposing tax on capital income 'creates a bias against savings, particularly long-term savings'.[18] In the United Kingdom, the Mirrlees Review of 2008 accepted that it would be efficient and equitable to impose some level of tax on capital income.[19] The underlying research by James Banks and Peter Diamond has been widely influential.[20]

---

[14] James A Mirrlees, 'An Exploration in the Theory of Optimum Income Taxation' (1971) 38(2) *The Review of Economic Studies* 175–208; Antony Atkinson and Joseph E Stiglitz, 'The Design of Tax Structure: Direct versus Indirect Taxation' (1976) 6(1-2) *Journal of Public Economics* 55-75.

[15] Institute of Fiscal Studies, *The Structure and Reform of Direct Taxation* (London: IFS, 1978).

[16] Gravelle, *Taxing Capital Income* (see n 1), 32.

[17] Australian Treasury, *Australia's Future Tax System: Final Report* (Canberra: Commonwealth of Australia, 2010), Part 1, 32.

[18] Ibid., 32.

[19] Mirrlees Review, *Reforming the Tax System for the 21st Century*, 2 vols (Oxford: Oxford University Press, 2010), www.ifs.org.uk/publications/mirrleesreview.

[20] James Banks and Peter Diamond, 'The Base for Direct Taxation' in Stuart Adam, Tim Besley, Richard Blundell, Stephen Bond, Robert Chote, Malcolm Gammie, Paul Johnson, Gareth Myles

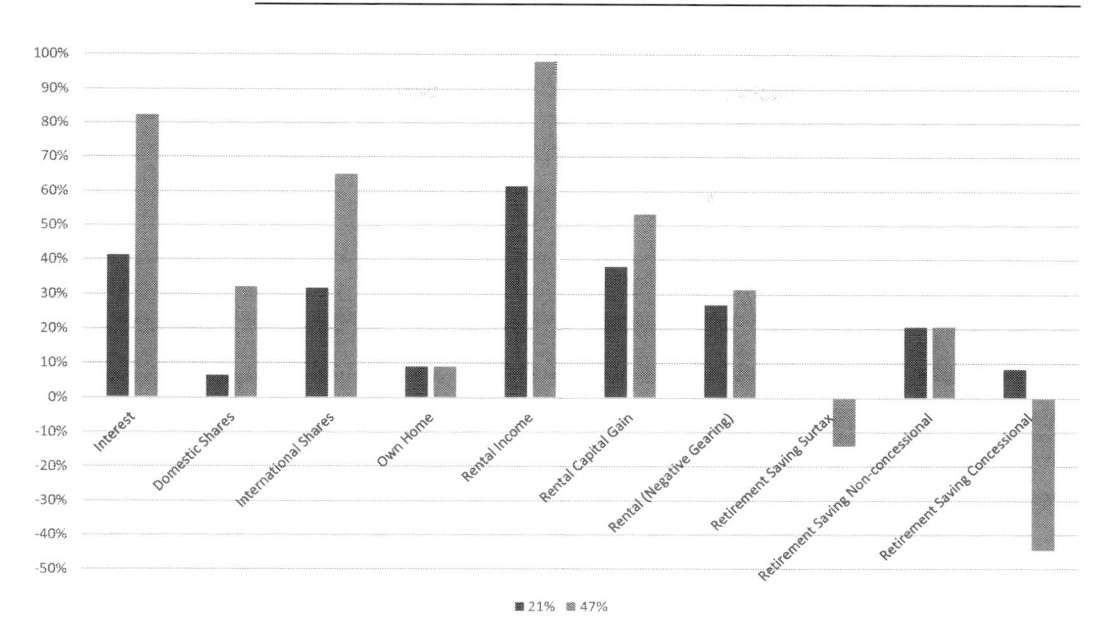

Figure 6.5 Marginal effective tax rates on different asset classes, Australia, 2020
Note: Assumptions include a constant real pre-tax rate of return of 3 per cent; annual inflation of 2 per cent; an investment period of 20 years; stamp duty of 4 per cent on property transactions; land tax of 0.4 per cent on investment property; and earnings in superannuation taxed at 10 per cent.
Source: Peter Varela, Robert Breunig and Kristen Sobeck, The Taxation of Savings in Australia: Theory, Current Practice and Future Policy Directions, Tax and Transfer Policy Institute (TTPI) Policy Report No. 01-2020 (Canberra: TTPI, Australian National University, 2020), Adapted from Figure 3.2.

A better policy goal may be neutrality across different forms of saving, as a potential improvement over existing systems that evince widely divergent tax rules for different asset classes, which may distort saving and investment choices. The diversity in tax rates on different forms of saving under the Australian income tax is illustrated in Figure 6.5.

Figure 6.5 shows the **marginal effective tax rate** (METR) of investing in different assets, over a 20 year period with real return of 3 per cent and inflation of 2 percent. The chart shows a '47%' taxpayer on the top marginal rate, and a '21%' moderate taxpayer. The METR takes account of taxes at central and subnational levels of government. For example, both high- and moderate-income individuals face an METR of only 9 per cent on owning their own home for 20 years (this reflects stamp duty on the home). However, high-income taxpayers who invest in concessionally taxed superannuation benefit from a *negative* 45 per cent tax rate, equivalent to a subsidy, while

and James M Poterba (eds.), *Dimensions of Tax Design. Mirrlees Review: Vol 1* (Oxford: Oxford University Press, 2010), 548–674, https://ifs.org.uk/publications/5223.

moderate-income taxpayers actually pay tax of about 8 per cent on concessional superannuation. This is because of the very high value of deductions for contributions to superannuation for high-income earners.

Economic Rent

An important reason to tax capital income and gains is that some part of the return to capital comprises 'economic rent'. The concept of 'rents' from land was well known from feudal times; as sovereigns began to extend the tax base, land-rents were an obvious place to start. Adam Smith advocated the taxation of 'ground-rents' on land, and 'house-rents' on the benefit of living in your own home. John Stuart Mill also advocated taxation of economic rent:[21]

> Suppose that there is a kind of income which constantly tends to increase, without any exertion or sacrifice on the part of the owners: those owners constituting a class in the community, whom the natural course of things progressively enriches, consistently with complete passiveness on their own part. In such a case it would be no violation of the principles on which private property is grounded, if the state should appropriate this increase of wealth, or part of it, as it arises. This would not properly be taking anything from anybody; it would merely be applying an accession of wealth, created by circumstances, to the benefit of society, instead of allowing it to become an unearned appendage to the riches of a particular class.

> Now this is actually the case with rent. The ordinary progress of a society which increases in wealth, is at all times tending to augment the incomes of landlords; to give them both a greater amount and a greater proportion of the wealth of the community, independently of any trouble or outlay incurred by themselves. They grow richer, as it were in their sleep, without working, risking, or economizing. What claim have they, on the general principle of social justice, to this accession of riches? In what would they have been wronged if society had, from the beginning, reserved the right of taxing the spontaneous increase of rent, to the highest amount required by financial exigencies?

To achieve this, Mill argued that there needed to be a benchmark valuation of land and then, after a period of economic and population growth, the accretion to value – the 'rent' – could be fully appropriated, or at least heavily taxed using a land tax

The concept of economic rent, or an unearned 'accession of wealth' remains the theoretical basis for land value taxation. Theorists have sought to distinguish 'economic rent' from other elements of the return to capital; essentially, rent is conceived as the return to endowments, monopolies or unique technological and market advantages generating an economic return above the 'normal return'. Economic rent has returned to the centre of debates about

---

[21] Mill, *Principles of Political Economy* (see n 11), chapter 2, paragraph 5.

taxing capital to individuals and corporations, reflecting the growth in returns to assets and monopolies in the twenty-first century. David White notes that 'modern normative theory ... commonly distinguish[es] between two, three or four constituent parts of capital income':

- the 'normal return', which compensates investors for deferring their consumption, sometimes also known as the 'risk-free return', the 'return to waiting' or the 'safe rate of interest';
- the 'return to risk taking', which compensates investors for bearing *ex ante* risk when their return on a project is uncertain, sometimes referred to as the expected 'risk premium';
- the 'supernormal return', which compensates investors for their unique skills or ideas, and is sometimes known as 'economic profit' or 'inframarginal returns'; and
- the *ex post* 'unexpected return' from (good or bad) luck, which is the difference between the actual and the expected return'.[22]

The Mirrlees Review proposed to tax above-normal capital income and gains of individuals at a relatively high rate, but provide a rate of return allowance, that would remove the 'normal return' to saving from tax.[23] While many have supported the concept, it has not been implemented. For corporations, the taxation of economic rent, 'supernormal' and 'unexpected return' are explored further in Chapters 7 and 11.

Capital Gains Tax

Taxation of Capital Gains Compared to Income

The income tax is levied on 'capital income', which includes the 'flow' of income from investments such as rent, royalties, interest or dividends. Historically determined legal concepts of income and capital underpin mature income tax systems.[24] A 'source' or 'flow' concept of income grew up in the civil law jurisdictions including Germany and France (and was adopted in Canada); a 'trust' concept of income developed in the Anglosphere or

---

[22] White, 'The Impact of Economic Theory on Capital Gains Tax Reform Proposals' (see n 6), 39; Henry J Aaron, Leonard E Burman and C Eugene Steuerle (eds.), *Taxing Capital Income* (Washington, DC: Urban Institute Press, 2007); Alan J Auerbach, 'The Future of Capital Income Taxation' (2006) 27 *Fiscal Studies* 399–420.

[23] Mirrlees Review, *Reforming the Tax System for the 21st Century* (see n 19).

[24] Hugh J Ault, Brian J Arnold and Graeme Cooper, *Comparative Income Taxation*, 4th ed (Alphen aan den Rijn, Netherlands: Wolters Kluwer, 2020); Viktor Thuronyi, Kim Brooks and Borbála Kolozs, *Comparative Tax Law*, 2nd ed (Alphen aan den Rijn, Netherlands: Wolters Kluwer, 2016).

Commonwealth countries including the United Kingdom, New Zealand and Australia.[25]

A key difference between 'source' and 'trust' concepts relates to the treatment of income and gains from a business. In civil law countries, for example Germany and Japan, gains sourced from a business are subject to tax, but personal or investment gains may not be taxable. In Anglo countries including the United Kingdom, Australia, New Zealand, South Africa and Canada, even business gains could be treated as 'capital' not 'income', and may not be subject to tax. The United States is unusual as its income tax has always been interpreted to encompass a broad concept of income that included 'any realised accession to wealth' including capital gains.[26]

Legislative reform was often needed to bring personal capital gains into the tax base; this was done in many countries as part of late twentieth century base-broadening tax reforms.[27] Despite this general trend, there is significant variation between the capital gains tax rules of different countries which adopt diverse solutions to challenges in defining the base and rate.[28] The taxation of capital gains complicates income tax legislation, dramatically expanding the length of tax statutes.

The realisation basis applied in most capital gains taxes provides a clear point in time when the gain can be identified and measured and cash is available for the taxpayer to pay the tax. However, the realisation approach means that timing of taxation of capital gain becomes to a greater or lesser extent a choice of the taxpayer. This creates an opportunity for tax planning, including offsetting of losses and gains. Tax laws usually quarantine capital losses to capital gains, to limit the opportunities to reduce income tax with losses. Wealthy taxpayers can defer the realisation of capital gain to the future, when the owner may face a lower tax rate, for example in retirement, or when passing assets to heirs on death. Taxpayers may also face a sudden increase in tax rate and quantum from realising a large 'one-off' capital gain in a single year; some tax laws 'average' the tax payable to ameliorate this problem.

The direct yield of revenue from capital gains taxes is relatively low in most countries, in the order of less than 1 per cent of gross domestic product (about 3 to 4 per cent of total tax revenues).[29] Why, then, levy a capital gains tax? The main reason is equity; high-income earners derive a substantial proportion of their income from capital, which would otherwise escape taxation. The second reason is to protect the labour and capital income tax base, by preventing the conversion of those kinds of income into untaxed capital gain.

---

[25] Thuronyi et al, *Comparative Tax Law* (see n 24).
[26] Ibid.
[27] For example, the United Kingdom in 1965, Canada in 1972 and Australia in 1985: Michael Littlewood, 'Capital Gains Taxes – A Comparative Survey' in Littlewood and Elliffe, *Capital Gains Taxation* (see n 6), 1–29, 2.
[28] Chris Evans and Cedric Sandford, 'Capital Gains Tax – The Unprincipled Tax' (1999) 5 *British Tax Review* 387–405.
[29] Littlewood and Elliffe, *Capital Gains Taxation* (see n 6), 6.

Most countries apply a lower tax rates to capital gains than to earned income, or in some cases to other forms of capital income. Many countries also apply extensive exemptions for capital gains on the home, small businesses and various other categories. In the United States, successive legislatures enacted rules to lower the tax rate applicable to so-called long-term capital gains. A few countries do not tax personal capital gains at all; a recent attempt to enact a capital gains tax in New Zealand failed, despite support from a Review committee and many tax experts.[30]

One argument in favour of a lower tax rate on capital gain is to compensate the taxpayer for the 'inflationary' element of the gain, as tax is levied on a nominal basis. Inflation can make a significant difference. However, this overtaxation is offset by the value of deferral arising because capital gains taxes apply only when gains are realised, which has the effect of undertaxation. Another argument in favour of lowering tax on capital gains is that the tax deters investors from realising or selling their assets, creating a 'lock-in' effect.

These questions have long been debated. Henry Simons observed in 1938 that gains and losses from investment assets 'present one of the most prominent and most controversial issues of income taxation'; even at that time, the issue was dealt with in a variety of ways in different jurisdictions, but tax experts had little inclination 'to approve or defend the existing arrangements' in any country.[31] The same applies today; few experts wholeheartedly approve of the current law and policy applicable to capital gains in their jurisdiction.

President Biden's 2022 US budget proposed to tax capital gains like ordinary income, at standard progressive marginal tax rates.[32] Experts likely would approve the higher rate, but not all would approve of taxation of capital gains like other types of income, for the reasons outlined previously: 'lock-in', inflation effects and volatility in tax rates. Another approach to mitigate such effects is to provide an annual, or lifetime, exemption for each individual's capital gains.[33] This solution would require keeping track of capital gains tax data over time, in a taxpayer's administrative or personal records, but as tax data systems improve, this may be less of a concern.

Accrual Taxation of Capital Gains

A comprehensive income tax approach would seek to shift the realisation based capital gains tax to taxing accrued value in each year the asset is owned.

---

[30] Ibid.
[31] Henry C Simons, *Personal Income Taxation: the Definition of Income as a Problem of Fiscal Policy* (Chicago: University of Chicago Press, 1938), 148.
[32] President Biden (US), Office of Management and Budget, *Budget of the US Government* (Washington, DC: Office of Management and Budget, 2022), www.whitehouse.gov/omb/budget/.
[33] Evans and Sandford, 'Capital Gains Tax' (see n 28).

The challenges of 'accrual' taxation include valuation and cash flow, and this is why it is not done as a general rule in most income taxes.[34] Valuation of an asset should be easy for listed shares but is much harder for privately owned businesses, intangible assets and assets located offshore. Cash is needed to pay the tax, unless the taxpayer has another source of income, can borrow to pay the tax or can defer payment, perhaps subject to an interest charge.

Some countries apply an accrual approach to the asset portfolios of banks and financial institutions, which already account on an accrual basis. However, it is more difficult to apply to other forms of assets. Property taxes (discussed later) apply on measured value at a point in time, not on realisation of the asset, so the approach is not infeasible.

A 'mark to market' approach identifies and values the asset with reference to specific market indicators at a point in time each year. This could easily work for shares or securities listed on a stock exchange, as the data about share price are freely available on a daily basis. The need to borrow or find funds to pay the tax remains. There may also be incentive effects on taxpayer investment portfolio choice, if listed shares were taxed in this way but other assets are not.

An alternative accrual approach deems a rate of return to an asset portfolio, based on a measure of real market return, and includes the deemed return in assessable income in each year. A deemed return approach to taxing capital income is adopted in the Netherlands applying its 'Three Box' approach (Box 6.1). This requires some formulas, but it may be no more complex than the many special rules that apply in other countries for taxing capital income and gains.

A deemed rate of return is one way to tax wealth, and reveals the relationship between an income tax and a wealth tax. For example, assume an asset that cost $100 has a real rate of return (disregarding inflation) of 5 per cent, or $5 per year. An income tax of 30 per cent on the 5 per cent return to the investment (tax of $1.50) is equivalent to a 1.5 per cent wealth tax on the value of the asset.

Dual Income Tax

Another schedular approach to taxing capital income is the so-called dual income tax adopted in the early 1990s in the Nordic countries of Sweden, Norway and Finland, and to a lesser extent Denmark.[35] The dual income tax

---

[34] Deborah J Schenk, 'An Efficiency Approach to Reforming a Realisation-based Tax' (2004) 57 *Tax Law Review* 503–48 concluded that reform of taxation of capital gains in the United States is not worthwhile because tax planning or substituted investments would likely remain, so reforms would increase complexity without increasing revenue.

[35] Peter Birch Sorenson, 'From the Global Income Tax to the Dual Income Tax: Recent Tax Reforms in the Nordic Countries' (1994) 1 *International Tax and Public Finance* 57–79, 57; Leif Mutén, 'Dual Income Tax: The Scandinavian Experience' in John Head and Richard Krever (eds.), *Company Tax Systems* (Melbourne: Australian Tax Research Foundation, 1997), 271–84.

Box 6.1 The Netherlands 'box' system – back to the future

The Netherlands taxes some capital income and gains applying a deemed rate of return in its 'Box' system introduced in 2001, in which income of investors is grouped into three 'Boxes'. The deemed rate of return approach was a 'return to the 1892 roots of the Netherlands income tax system' – which taxed a deemed yield to assets, instead of relying on realisation of income.[36]

Box 1 includes income from employment, active business, some pensions, and owner-occupied housing. Relevant expenses and allowances are deducted, and progressive income tax rates are applied. For home ownership, a deemed imputed income is included, calculated at up to 0.6 per cent annually of the valuation of the home up to about €1 million; for homes with a value that exceeds that amount, €6540 plus 2.35 per cent of market value above the threshold is included.

Box 2 includes dividends and capital gains from 'substantial' shareholdings (ownership of more than 5 per cent of a class of shares), taxed at a flat rate of 26.25 per cent. Deductions and losses from such shareholdings are restricted to be offset in Box 2.

Box 3 includes all other investment income, including capital gains and dividends on small (portfolio) shareholdings. A weighted notional yield is calculated based on a fictional 'savings' and 'investment' portion of the assets and is taxed at a flat rate of 30 per cent. For 2020, the weighted notional savings yield is 0.06 per cent (reflecting very low government bond rates), and the weighted notional investment yield is 5.33 per cent. Taxpayers are also given a deemed 'weighting' of the 'savings' and 'investment' components of the portfolio, based on a threshold value of investment assets in the year. A 15 per cent tax applies to companies paying dividends, and a credit for this tax can be offset against the Box 3 tax owed. The deemed approach means that actual income, gains, deductions and losses from Box 3 investments are ignored for tax purposes.

The 'Box' system has been subject to various modifications since it was established. The deemed return approach tends to overtax those who hold low yielding cash investments and to undertax those who hold equity or other investments. The Netherlands Government proposed in the 2020 budget to remove the deemed 'weighting' of saving and investment portions and to apply the Box 3 approach to actual asset holdings. This would have reduced tax for those who hold substantial savings; however, the proposal did not proceed because it would leave those with relatively low savings worse off.

applies progressive tax rates to labour income and active business income (such as sole proprietors) and a proportionate rate, lower than the top marginal progressive rate, to capital income and gains. There is no tax-free threshold for taxing capital income and gains.

[36] Kees van Raad and Frank Pötgens, 'The Netherlands' in Ault et al, *Comparative Income Taxation* (see n 24), Kindle Book, Loc 5553; *Source*: Marnix Schellekens, *Netherlands – Individual Taxation – Country Tax Guides* (Amsterdam: IBFD Tax Research Platform), https://research.ibfd.org, accessed 4 October 2020, Section 1.5; Marnix Schellekens, 'Government Changes Course on Box 3 Reform', https://research.ibfd.org, accessed 4 October 2020.

The move to adopt the dual income tax and abandon the 'old ideal of a global income tax' was a surprising departure from previous tax policy in the Nordic states, which had relied on a broad income tax base with steep progressive rates.[37] The key reasons were pressure for exemptions and a recognition of the excessive role that deductions, especially for interest on debt, played in respect to income from capital, as it was used in 'tax arbitrage' by high-rate taxpayers. Economic globalisation and pressure to lower tax rates on capital also played a part.

Bastani and Waldenstrom, drawing on the Swedish experience, argue that despite complexities, the Nordic dual income tax system which taxes labor income progressively and capital income at a proportional rate represents a reasonable trade-off between optimal tax principles and administrative feasibility. It recognises that the labor and capital income tax bases respond differently to taxation, and have different distributional implications. The proportionality of the capital income tax avoids issues connected with tax planning and tax arbitrage.[38] A recent Australian report argues in favour of introducing a 'modular' approach in place of the purportedly comprehensive, but in practice highly disparate and regressive approach to taxing savings in the current income tax law (as shown in Figure 6.5).[39]

The benefit theory of taxation provides a further justification for the dual income tax. In an era where those who derive capital income and gains can be said to have benefited most from economic globalisation and state regulation to support capital, and while wages in the middle stagnate, the dual income tax together with the corporate tax may succeed in ensuring a basic contribution to government by the owners of capital. While there are concerns about its lower, flat rate relative to the progressive rate on labour income, the broad base and lack of a tax-free threshold for capital income may make the dual income tax more effective at taxing capital income and gains than other systems. Frans Vanistendael suggests that in a context of irreversible economic globalisation and technological change, the dual income tax could even save democracies and prevent revolutions, because 'it guarantees taxation of capital income at a level that is comparable to that of the tax burden on labour and professional income, taking away the perception that rich capitalists will escape taxation'.[40]

---

[37] Mutén, 'Dual Income Tax' (see n 35).
[38] Bastani and Waldenstrom, 'How Should Capital Be Taxed?' (see n 1), 66.
[39] Peter Varela, Robert Breunig and Kristen Sobeck, *The Taxation of Savings in Australia: Theory, Current Practice and Future Policy Directions*, TTPI Policy Report No. 01-2020 (Canberra: Tax and Transfer Policy Institute, Australian National University, 2020), https://taxpolicy.crawford .anu.edu.au/sites/default/files/uploads/taxstudies_crawford_anu_edu_au/2020-07/20271_ anu_-_ttpi_policy_report-ff2.pdf.
[40] Frans Vanistendael, 'Democracy, Revolution and Taxation' (2017) 71(8) *Bulletin for International Taxation*.

Taxing Retirement Saving[41]

Retirement Incomes Policy

In most countries, income for retirement is provided by a combination of public and private provision. Support in old age is a public policy issue of major and growing importance in the context of an ageing population in most developed countries. It is therefore important that the public and private retirement savings and payment systems be designed coherently to achieve a fair and efficient outcome over the life course of individuals.

Private retirement saving may be done through regulated retirement savings funds or accounts, which are often subject to concessional tax treatment, or through personal investments in the home, shares and other investment assets. Public need-based pensions and contributory social security systems may be funded from consolidated revenue and general taxation, or by social security taxes that are contributed to a separate government fund. Age pensions and the cost of aged care are the largest social welfare expenditures of government, while tax concessions for retirement saving have a large fiscal cost relative to the normal income tax benchmark.

Subsidies delivered through the tax system for private retirement saving may be estimated as 'tax expenditures' (as explained in Chapter 3). Retirement savings tax concessions are large and regressive, delivering most benefit to middle- and higher income taxpayers, who are more able to save. On the other hand, public support for retirement through an age pension or social security system is generally neutral or redistributive in nature, benefiting low-income people especially when funded through a progressive income tax.

Income or Consumption Approach

A comprehensive income tax benchmark for retirement saving requires that contributions to saving are taxed at the individual tax rate; earnings or the return on retirement saving are also taxed at that rate; and payouts to the individual on retirement are exempt. This is sometimes called a tax-tax-exempt (TTE) system. At the other end of the spectrum, a consumption tax benchmark is achieved by exempting contributions to a retirement fund and earnings in the fund, and taxing at the time when savings are paid out to the retired individual. This is called an exempt-exempt-tax (EET) system. The EET system is sometimes called a 'postpaid' consumption tax approach. An alternative model would tax contributions and exempt earnings and payouts from a retirement fund in a tax-exempt-exempt (TEE) system, sometimes called a 'prepaid' consumption tax approach.

---

[41] This section draws in part on David Ingles and Miranda Stewart, 'Reforming Australia's Superannuation Tax System and the Age Pension to Improve Work and Savings Incentives' (2017) *Asia & the Pacific Policy Studies* https://doi.org/10.1002/app5.184.

Table 6.1. Benchmarks for taxation of retirement saving

	Contributions to fund	Earnings in fund	Payouts from fund	
Comprehensive income tax	Tax	Tax	Exempt	TTE
Postpaid consumption tax	Exempt	Exempt	Tax	EET
Prepaid consumption tax	Tax	Exempt	Exempt	TEE
Rate of return allowance	Tax	Low tax	Exempt	TtE

These different approaches are illustrated in Table 6.1, which also indicates the effect of the 'rate of return' approach to saving proposed by the Mirrlees review. If a flat, or proportionate, tax rate is applied, the EET and TEE approaches are equivalent over an individual's life course. This is because the present value of tax on payouts is the same as the tax that would otherwise be paid on earnings. However, if tax rates are progressive, the effect may be different, depending on the tax rate applied to an individual when they contribute to a retirement fund (which could be a high rate, for example applied to a high wage earner), and the tax rate when they receive a retirement payout (which could be a much lower rate).

Concessional taxation of retirement savings aims to encourage private saving for retirement. For tax incentives to result in increased net savings, they must generate a rise in voluntary private savings that is greater than the cost to the public inherent in the tax breaks. There is, however, little evidence that tax concessions for retirement saving produce increased overall net saving. Lisa Marriott summarised the literature:

> [M]ost studies conclude that tax incentives affect the allocation of household portfolios, but the effect on the amount saved is less clear ... Typically research finds that only a small amount of retirement savings are 'new' savings and the policies are an expensive form of encouraging saving ... tax incentives are successful in increasing levels of savings through the tax-preferred vehicle, but this does not necessarily result in increased levels in overall savings.[42]

Hybrid Tax Systems for Retirement

In reality, all countries have hybrid, and often complex, systems for taxing retirement saving. Many countries apply a deduction for contributions, or a lower rate on earnings, for retirement savings that are preserved until a person's retirement.

For example, the United States has a complicated array of savings options for individuals. These include private retirement savings accounts such as Roth IRAs (Individual Retirement Accounts), which are taxed on a TEE basis,

---

[42] Lisa Marriott, *The Politics of Retirement Savings Taxation: A Trans-Tasman Comparison* (Sydney, NSW: CCH Australia, 2010), 203.

and other retirement fund options, such as 401k plans, which are taxed on an EET basis.[43] Savers are advised to maximise their 401k plan before shifting to the Roth IRA, reflecting the assumption that the EET approach is more concessional, as the tax rate the individual will face on retirement is likely to be lower than the tax rate they face during their working life.

In Australia's private compulsory superannuation savings system, contributions by the employer, employee or self-employed are deductible up to a threshold, and contributions and earnings are taxed at 15 per cent in the fund. Pension or lump-sum benefits at retirement age are exempt from tax. This system may be even more generous than a consumption tax benchmark, which would fully exempt contributions and earnings but would tax payouts at individual marginal rates. The diverse concessional tax treatment of different elements of the Australian superannuation tax regime is shown in Figure 6.5.

Both public and private retirement savings or social security systems that rely on work-based contributions produce unequal outcomes based on gender.[44] Systems that provide tax deductibility for contributions or earnings deliver an 'upside-down' subsidy that provides most benefit to high-income earners who work full time through their working lives. Systems that depend on contributions from paid work inevitably discriminate against individuals, mostly women, who have interrupted working lives because they spend time out of the workforce to care for dependants, or work only part time, as well as facing a gender pay gap. Taking account of the different position of women in the social and economic context, the best policy to ensure women's economic security over their life course and in old age would be to reduce tax subsidies for private retirement saving significantly and use the tax funds to support the public age pension.

Taxing the Home

The Role of Home Ownership

Home ownership is a key element of household saving in many developed countries. Housing is both an investment and consumption good, accessed by individuals in differing capacities: as home owners, landlords and tenants. Housing is included in the tax bases of a number of different taxes that include income tax, consumption taxes such as a value added tax, land tax, wealth and inheritance taxes, property tax, conveyance duties and betterment taxes.[45]

---

[43] Benjamin Silver and Michael Slomovics, 'Retiring the 401(k): A New Framework for Retirement Savings' (2021) 39 *Yale Law and Policy Review Inter Alia* 1–26.
[44] Therese Jefferson, 'Women and Retirement Pensions: A Research Review' (2009) 15(4) *Feminist Economics* 115–45, https://doi.org/10.1080/13545700903153963.
[45] Miranda Stewart, 'Taxation Policy and Housing' in Susan J Smith et al (eds.), *International Encyclopedia of Housing and Home* (Amsterdam: Elsevier, 2012), 152–66; Miranda Stewart (ed.), *Housing and Tax Policy* (Sydney: Australian Tax Research Foundation, 2010).

These taxes are levied at various levels of local, provincial or central government. Many countries also provide exemptions or concessions for owner-occupied housing. Tax rules for housing may have complex interactions with pension systems, public housing and housing subsidy programs.

Early taxes on homes in Europe included a 'hearth tax' and a 'window tax'.[46] The window tax was intended to be progressive as the rate increased with the number of glass windows and hence, more or less, with the wealth of the home owner. However, Adam Smith argued in 1776 that window taxes were arbitrary, inefficient and inequitable in practice.[47] Instead, he proposed a tax on 'house-rents', meaning the 'rental' value of a home as being both efficient and equitable; this would be combined with a tax on land, or 'ground-rents', reflecting the value of the land itself. This would evolve into the income tax on imputed rent in many countries.

Today, in many developed countries, a high proportion of individuals live in their own home (ranging from approximately 40 per cent to more than 70 per cent).[48] As house prices have risen over decades of economic growth, especially in large cities, home ownership has contributed to increasing household wealth, and to increasing wealth inequality. Historically, home ownership has been more important in the 'New World' countries such as Canada, Australia and the United States and relatively less important in the United Kingdom and continental Europe, where long-term rentals, tenant protection and social or public housing were much more widespread.

Optimal tax theory suggests that an efficient tax would be high on goods that have a low price elasticity, but low on goods with a high price elasticity (see Chapter 4). It is generally considered that housing has a low price elasticity of demand because it is a necessity; this suggests that it should be relatively heavily taxed. However, housing tenure – rental versus ownership – may be quite elastic in response to taxation. Taxation may therefore distort the demand for and supply of different types of housing. Subsidies or tax concessions for home ownership may be justified on the grounds of positive externalities, for example, if this promotes stronger communities and a built environment that is better maintained. However, subsidies to home ownership may increase the possibility of bubbles or busts in the housing market. These subsidies also have an upside-down effect, producing inequity between those

---

[46] Lydia M Marshall, 'The Levying of the Hearth Tax, 1662–1688' (1936) 51(204) *The English Historical Review* 628–46; Andrew E Glantz, 'A Tax on Light and Air: Impact of the Window Duty on Tax Administration and Architecture, 1696–1851' (2008) 15(2) *Penn History Review* 1–23. See the discussion of (in)efficiency of the window tax in Chapter 4.

[47] Adam Smith, *An Inquiry into the Nature and Causes of the Wealth of Nations* (London: Methuan, 1776), www.econlib.org/library/Smith/smWN.html, Book V, Part II, Article 1, 'Taxes Upon the Rent of Houses'.

[48] John Doling, 'Housing Tenures Trends' in Susan J Smith et al (eds.), *International Encyclopedia of Housing and Home* (Amsterdam: Elsevier, 2012).

who can afford to own their own home or purchase housing as an investment, and those who pay rent.

Imputed Rent and Capital Gains on the Home

In many countries, capital gains on sale of the home are not taxed, or benefit from high thresholds and lower rates than other gains. More fundamentally – but less visibly – the imputed rent from home ownership is not usually taxed and expenses and losses on the home will not be deductible (although an exception may apply for home mortgage interest). In contrast, landlords can usually deduct costs associated with the purchase and ownership of investments in housing to derive rental income, including maintenance, leasing costs and interest on debt.

To treat the different housing tenures of home owners and tenants equally, we should tax home owners on the 'imputed rent', which is the benefit of living in your home. Consider a tenant who pays rent to a landlord. The rent is a consumption item and is not tax deductible, so it is paid out of after-tax income: it is subject to tax. Alternatively, imagine that you are the landlord who rents out a home, deriving rental income that would be subject to income taxation. Living in your own home, you are, effectively, 'renting' to yourself; but this rent is not subject to tax as it is not realised.

Historically, many countries taxed the imputed rent from living in your own home. This likely reflected the reality that home ownership was historically achieved only by those with significant wealth or income. Most governments abolished the taxation of imputed rent during the last century (for example, Australia abolished it in 1922, the United Kingdom in 1963, France in 1966, Germany in 1987 and Sweden in 1991).[49] In some countries, a property tax has replaced income tax as the main way to tax the benefit from owner-occupied housing. The Netherlands and Switzerland are among the only countries that still tax imputed rent, although some countries including France and Spain, tax the imputed rent from a second residence.

The revenue, efficiency and distributional outcomes of taxing imputed rent will depend on other aspects of a country's tax system. In general, the exemption from tax for imputed rent will be the largest 'tax expenditure' or subsidy for home ownership, compared to the comprehensive income tax benchmark.

Home ownership has also generally been exempt from capital gains taxation, even after the income tax base was expanded to include capital gains in many countries. The United States was a significant exception, levying income tax on the gain from sale of the home above a high value threshold.

---

[49] Stewart, 'Taxation Policy and Housing' (see n 45).

The exemption of capital gains and imputed rent shifts the tax treatment of home ownership towards a 'prepaid' consumption tax (TEE), explained in Table 6.1. The overall effect is that the two largest investments of the middle class – home ownership and retirement savings accounts – tend to be taxed with a consumption tax approach, rather than an income tax approach. This subsidises these forms of investment relative to other forms of investment and also favours those with higher incomes.

While the homes of those at the top of the income distribution are more valuable and may enjoy more capital appreciation than lower value homes, the exemption from tax for home ownership benefits a broad range of people who buy houses when they are relatively young with the assistance of mortgage debt, and pay down the debt over the life cycle, so home equity is increased as people age.[50] The deduction for mortgage interest further extends the subsidy for home ownership and creates an incentive to borrow to purchase a more expensive home. The United States and the Netherlands are examples of countries that permit deductibility of home mortgage interest (most countries do not). The US home mortgage interest deduction has been estimated to be among the most expensive of US tax expenditures.[51] Distributionally, it benefits middle-income earners the most, as high-income earners can often purchase the home outright, while low-income earners can take on less debt and also face lower tax rates.[52]

Taxation of Wealth

Wealth Inequality

Wealth is extremely unevenly distributed within countries, as shown in Figures 6.1 and 5.3. There is increasing interest in taxation of wealth in the twenty-first century, as growing inequality in wealth has become an important political issue. The top 1 per cent own about 45 per cent of global wealth, while the top 10 per cent own more than 80 per cent; in contrast, the bottom 50 per cent of the world's population collectively owns less than 1 per cent of global wealth.[53]

Globally, a very high share of wealth is concentrated in the United States. There are an estimated 46 million USD millionaires worldwide, of which the

---

[50] James Poterba and Todd Sinai, 'Tax Expenditures for Owner-Occupied Housing: Deductions for Property Taxes and Mortgage Interest and the Exclusion of Imputed Rental Income' (2008) 98(2) *American Economic Review* 84–9.

[51] Leonard E Burman, Christopher Geissler and Eric J Toder, ' How Big Are Total Individual Income Tax Expenditures, and Who Benefits from Them?' (2008) 98(2) *American Economic Review* 79–83.

[52] Austin J Drukker, Ted Gayer and Harvey S Rosen, *The Mortgage Interest Deduction: Revenue and Distributional Effects* (Washington, DC: Tax Policy Center, 2018), 17.

[53] Credit Suisse, *Global Wealth Report 2019* (Credit Suisse Research Institute, 2019), 14.

Taxation of Wealth

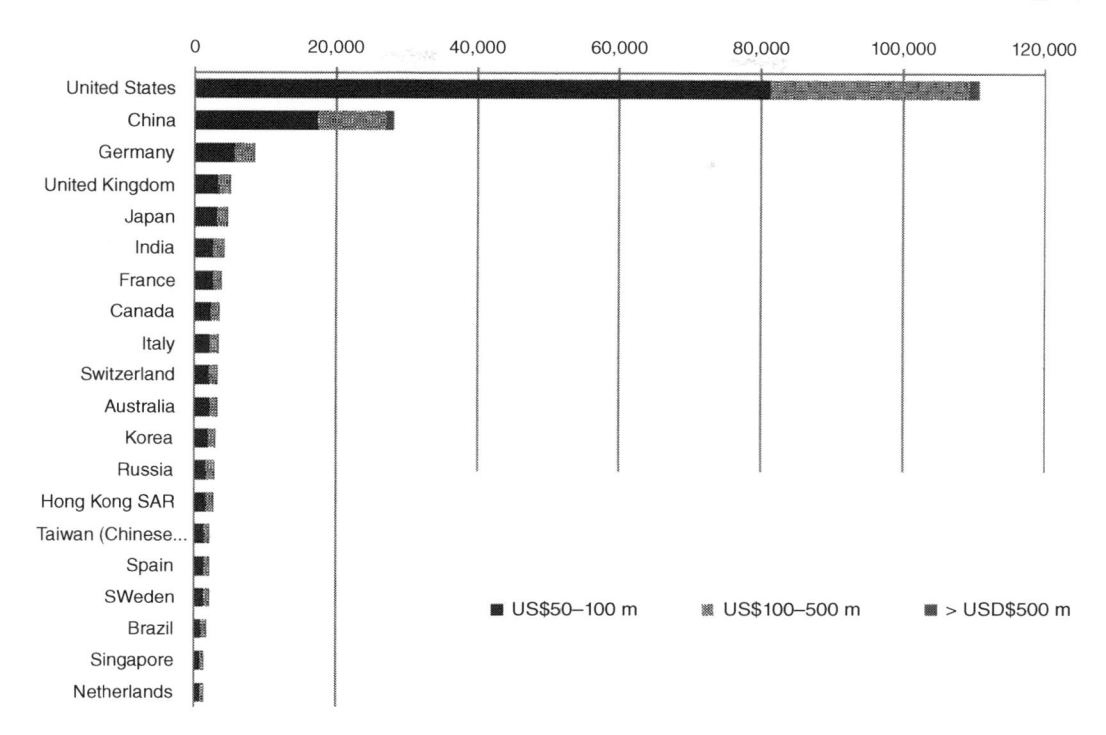

Figure 6.6 Ultra-high-net worth individuals, 2020
Source: Credit Suisse, Global Wealth Report 2019 (Credit Suisse Research Institute, 2019), Figure 6.6.

United States has 40 per cent, compared to 10 per cent in China PRC, 6 per cent in Japan, 5 per cent in each of Germany and the United Kingdom and 3 per cent in Canada.[54] Figure 6.6 shows that the rarefied air at the very top of the wealth distribution is breathed by fewer than 200,000 people, or 0.00001 per cent of the global population. There are an estimated 55,920 'ultra-high-net-worth' individuals with assets of at least US$100 million, the vast majority in the United States, with China a distant second. At the very top of the distribution are the billionaires, of whom there are only a few hundred.

Most of the wealth of the richest people in the world is held in shares of active corporate businesses. At the top, Jeff Bezos (Amazon) had wealth of US$131 billion in 2019, Bill Gates US$96.5 billion and Warren Buffet, US$82.5 billion.[55] These numbers, and those revealed in Figure 6.5, are, of course, extraordinary. However, it is important to get a realistic sense of scale of the assets controlled by the wealthiest individuals and the revenues that may be

---

[54] Ibid., 11.
[55] Newsweek, 'The Richest People on Earth', 13 January 2020, citing Statista: Forbes: The World's Billionaires 2019, www.newsweek.com/bill-gates-net-worth-wealth-since-microsoft-cascade-investment-bill-melinda-gates-foundation-1481482#slideshow/1559557.

raised from wealth taxation. Even confiscatory taxes on the world's richest people would finance only a fraction of government expenditure around the world for a small period of time.

For example, consider New Zealand, a country with 4 million people. In 2018-19 the annual budget of new Zealand was US$78 billion (NZ$119 billion). A complete confiscation of the wealth of Jeff Bezos would finance the government of New Zealand for less than two years (any realistic wealth tax would apply at a much lower rate, and raise a very much smaller amount of revenue). To provide another comparison, the largest private foundation in the world, the Bill and Melinda Gates Foundation, has about US$50 billion under management (see further Chapter 8). The Gates Foundation distributes about US$5 billion a year, or 6 per cent of the New Zealand government's annual budget.

Justification for Taxation of Wealth

Recalling that comprehensive income is equivalent to consumption plus the accrual of wealth in a period of time (see Chapter 1), the taxation of wealth provides another base enabling governments to harness a proportion of private net gain for public good. However, as illustrated, the case for wealth taxation does not rest on its ability to fund tax states at the scale to which we have become accustomed. Tax states have been able to harness large revenues in an efficient and fair way by taxing flows of income and consumption out of labour earnings and capital investment on an annual basis. Wealth taxation applies to stocks not flows and it will always contribute a small proportion of revenues relative to these broad-based taxes.

In the ageing populations of most OECD member states, wealth is increasingly concentrated among older generations (see Figure 6.4). This is a consequence of the accumulation of savings over the life course. This trend has become more pronounced in the recent decades because of increasing asset and consumer prices, combined with stagnating wages and slow economic growth. Intragenerational wealth inequality is also increasing. Older people without wealth (and especially who do not own their own home) face the risk of falling into poverty or homelessness, while an increasing share of younger generations may never be able to afford home ownership.

A recent study of wealth taxation in the United Kingdom summarised evidence that 'the young today have less wealth (in real terms) than older generations had at the same age'.[56] In 2015 in the United Kingdom, those aged 65 or older held 55 per cent of wealth, up from 32 per cent in 2000, while those aged 18 to 44 held 15 per cent of wealth, down from 25 per cent in 2000.[57]

---

[56] Arun Advani, Emma Chamberlain and Andy Summers, *Is It Time for a UK Wealth Tax? Initial Report* (London: UK Wealth Tax Commission, 2020), 9.

[57] Ibid.

A US study observed that 'baby boomers and the generation that preceded them currently own $84 trillion, or 81 per cent of all US household wealth – wealth that will before long be inherited by their children and other beneficiaries'.[58] In Australia, in 2016 those aged 65 or older owned nearly four times as much wealth as those aged 25 to 34, compared to about two and a half times as much in 1994.[59] Tax policy settings contribute to this increasingly skewed distribution of wealth and the growing social divide associated with it in the changed conditions of this century. The taxation of wealth is therefore an important tool to address inequality and to limit or reverse increasing concentrations of wealth.

A broad-based consumption tax can help to tax accumulated wealth. When a person is 'dissaving', by spending down their life course saving in retirement, a consumption tax would capture revenues on the accumulated wealth. David Bradford observed that 'amounts withdrawn from past accumulation are subject to tax' under a consumption tax.[60] Therefore, 'a tax based on consumption is in an important sense a tax on wealth ... [t]his fact makes a consumption approach an attractive one from the point of view of taxing according to ability to pay'. A shift from an income tax to a personal consumption or expenditure tax would have the effect of a one-off tax on accumulated wealth before the tax mix change; this would be both efficient and equitable.[61] However, it must be remembered that the equivalence between a wealth tax and a consumption tax assumes that wealth will be consumed during a person's life. Contrary to this assumption, savings are increasingly being passed to the next generation in bequests because they are not fully consumed during the life course.

A wealth tax does not capture economic rents, or the excess return to wealth. Based on the theory that it is efficient to tax economic rent or the above-normal rate of return, an income tax on capital income will be more efficient and raise more revenue than a wealth tax (Box 6.2).

Wealth taxation performs a regulatory function in addition to raising some revenue on a broader tax base. A wealth tax may help to control excesses of wealth holdings that generate inequality, and it may perform an important administrative function of providing information to governments about the

---

[58] Lily Batchelder, 'Tax the Rich and Their Heirs: How to Tax Inheritances More Fairly' *New York Times*, 24 June 2020; Lily Batchelder and David Kamin, *Taxing the Rich: Issues and Options*, SSRN Working Paper (2019), https://ssrn.com/abstract=3452274.

[59] Grattan Institute, *Generation Gap: Ensuring a Fair Go for Younger Australians* (Carlton, Victoria: Grattan Institute, 2019), 6 (figure 1.1).

[60] David Bradford, *Untangling the Income Tax* (Cambridge, MA: Harvard University Press, 1986), 18.

[61] Stuart Adam and Helen Miller, *The Economics of a Wealth Tax* (London: Wealth Tax Commission, 2020), 5.

> **Box 6.2 Taxing the return to wealth**
>
> Assume an investment of $100 with a 5 per cent real rate of return, $5 each year. A wealth tax of 1.5 per cent on this investment would raise $1.50 in tax. This is equivalent to an income tax of 30 per cent on the return of $5 from the investment.
>
> If the person with the $100 investment consumed all of the $5 return in goods and services in the year derived, then a consumption tax of 30 per cent would be equivalent to the income tax levied in that year.
>
> A lower wealth tax of 1 per cent of $100 ($1) would be equivalent to an income tax of 20 per cent on the $5 return ($1).
>
> Now assume the $100 investment delivered a normal rate of return of 5 per cent, and an above-normal rate of return (economic rent) of 20 per cent ($20). In this scenario, a wealth tax of 1 per cent (on $100) would still only capture $1 on taxation. However, an income tax of 20 per cent applied to both the normal and the above-normal return would capture $5 in tax.
>
> A rate of return allowance could be provided to exempt the normal rate of return of $5, and tax only the $20 in excess return generating $4 in tax. This would still raise more revenue than the wealth tax. The example suggests that a capital income tax would be more effective, and efficient, than a wealth tax in these circumstances.[62]

wealth holdings of its taxpayers. Piketty suggests that information might even be the primary function of a global wealth tax. Statistics about wealth, produced for tax returns may be important to 'promote democratic and financial transparency: there should be clarity about who owns what assets around the world'. In this regard, a wealth tax 'would be more in the nature of a compulsory reporting law than a true tax'.[63]

Emmanuel Saez and Gabriel Zucman have proposed a progressive wealth tax in the United States. They argue that addressing excessive wealth concentration is necessary to prevent the corrosive effect of wealth inequality on democratic institutions and policymaking – the social contract – in America.[64] The arguments of Saez and Zucman, and others, are similar to arguments made 150 years ago for a graduated property tax (encompassing both real and personal property) as a 'curb to predatory wealth'.[65] Ultimately, the most persuasive justification for a wealth tax is to support a democratic society and ensure a fair distribution of power, as well as assets, in that society.

---

[62] Ibid., 5.
[63] Thomas Piketty, *Capital in the Twenty-First Century*, trans. Arthur Goldhammer (Cambridge, MA: Harvard University Press, 2014), 518–19.
[64] Emmanuel Saez and Gabriel Zucman, *Progressive Wealth Taxation*, Brookings Papers on Economic Activity (Washington, DC: Brookings Institution, Fall 2019), 437–533, 438.
[65] WV Marshall, *A Curb to Predatory Wealth*, 2nd ed (1847; New York: RF Fenno, 1912), http://hdl.handle.net/2027/uc2.ark:/13960/t1sf2q66q.

Net Wealth Tax

A wealth tax may be levied on a person's net wealth on a regular or occasional basis during their lifetime, or on a transfer of wealth by gift or inheritance at death.[66] Net wealth is the value of assets at a point in time, less any liabilities. A wealth tax could be an annual impost on the value of net assets, or could be designed as a one-off levy intended to capture a significant return from existing wealth holdings. For example, the government of Argentina proposed a one-off wealth taxation to deal with the fiscal crisis produced by the COVID-19 pandemic. A one-off levy could be efficient especially if unannounced, as it could capture previously accumulated excess returns, without changing investment behaviour of taxpayers.[67]

Governments in the OECD historically levied net wealth taxes, and some continue to do so, although in most OECD member states, net wealth taxes have been repealed.[68] In France *l'impot sur les grandes fortunes* was introduced in 1945 and became the 'solidarity tax' in 1989; it was limited solely to real estate in 2017.[69] Norway has levied an annual wealth tax since 1892, with a rate of 0.85 per cent (0.15 per cent to the central government and 0.7 per cent to local government), applicable over a threshold of €150,000 per year per individual, on a household tax base. The base includes wealth in trusts, shares and houses, with various discounts or concessional valuation rules. In 2020, the Norwegian wealth tax raised EUR 1.6 billion, or 1.1 per cent of total revenue.[70]

The progressive wealth tax proposed by Saez and Zucman for the United States would have a relatively high rate of 6 per cent for billionaires, which they estimate would apply to the top 0.1 per cent of the population. They argue that this wealth tax would raise revenues of up to US$120 billion 'with perfect enforcement', and would restore progressivity at the top of the US income and wealth distribution.[71]

Challenges in designing a net wealth tax include valuation of assets; liquidity (the cash flow constraint for payment of the tax); how to capture wealth held by family members such as children and wealth held in trusts or corporations; and obtaining information to enable enforcement and counter avoidance and evasion. It is likely that an annual wealth tax may need to be

---

[66] Rebecca S Rudnick and Richard K Gordon, 'Taxation of Wealth' in Viktor Thuronyi (ed.), *Tax Law Design and Drafting: Vol 1* (Washington, DC: International Monetary Fund, 1996, revised 2012), www.imf.org/external/pubs/nft/1998/tlaw/eng/ch10.pdf.

[67] Ibid.

[68] OECD, *The Role and Design of Net Wealth Taxes in the OECD*, OECD Tax Policy Studies No 26 (Paris: OECD Publishing, 2018), https://doi.org/10.1787/19900538.

[69] Marine Dupas, *Wealth Tax: France*, Wealth Tax Commission Background Paper 134 (London: Wealth Tax Commission, 2020).

[70] Bettina Banoun, *Wealth Tax: Norway*, Wealth Tax Commission Background Paper 138 (London: Wealth Tax Commission, 2020).

[71] Saez and Zucman, *Progressive Wealth Taxation* (see n 64).

combined with a gift or inheritance tax and the wealth of family members especially minor children must be included in the base. As a wealth tax would likely generate significant responses by taxpayers to avoid the tax, enforcement would require significant transnational cooperation between governments.

Inheritance Tax

In the United States, United Kingdom, Japan and many European countries, inheritance tax continues to play a role in the tax system, although it only raises a relatively small proportion of overall revenues. Estate or inheritance taxes are generally supported by tax economists. The Meade Committee in the United Kingdom stated that inherited wealth is 'a proper subject for heavier taxation on grounds both of fairness and of economic incentives'.[72] From an equity perspective, inheritance of wealth undermines equality of opportunity, so an inheritance tax is considered to equalise advantages between those who inherit wealth and those who do not. An inheritance tax may lead to more consumption and less saving during the life course and may generate more charitable donations, if these are deductible against the wealth transfer tax. These behavioural responses may not be problematic, and both would contribute to reducing wealth concentration.

The liberal economists of the nineteenth century supported an inheritance tax. Mill argued that a progressive inheritance tax is an acceptable tax on capital:

> It is not the fortunes which are earned, but those which are unearned, that it is for the public good to place under limitation ... I conceive that inheritances and legacies, exceeding a certain amount, are highly proper subjects for taxation; and that the revenue from them should be as great as it can be made without giving rise to evasions, by donation *inter vivos* or concealment of property, such as it would be impossible adequately to check. The principle of graduation ... that is, of levying a larger percentage on a larger sub, though its application to general taxation would be in my opinion objectionable, seems to me both just and expedient as applied to legacy and inheritance duties.[73]

The inheritance of wealth is a legal event that provided a useful 'tax handle' for governments, enabling identification and valuation of assets and a point in time for taxation on the transfer of title to heirs. Today, this means that inheritance taxes often only apply to estates that require registration or 'probate' in common law jurisdictions, which may be only a fraction of all

---

[72] Institute of Fiscal Studies, *The Structure and Reform of Direct Taxation* (London: IFS, 1978), 318, cited in James A Mirrlees, Stuart Adam, Tim Besley, Richard Blundell, Stephen Bond, Robert Chote, Malcolm Gammie, Paul Johnson, Gareth Myles and James M Poterba, *Tax by Design* (Oxford: Oxford University Press, 2011), https://ifs.org.uk/publications/5353, 356.

[73] Mill, *Principle of Political Economy* (see n 11), Book II, chapter 1 section 6, [542].

assets that pass on death; this may pose difficulties in enforcement of inheritance taxes.

There are various different designs of inheritance taxation. An estate or bequest tax is applied to the deceased who passes the assets to heirs; alternatively, the tax could apply to the individual who inherits the asset. The Mirrlees Review advocated effective taxation of gifts or inheritances of wealth as 'an important complement to an appropriate tax treatment of lifetime savings'.[74] An inheritance tax usually includes housing and other assets as part of the tax base, although concessions may apply for the home inherited, or lived in, by a surviving spouse or dependent family member.

The UK inheritance tax applies to the deceased estate at a rate of 40 per cent of assets above a tax-free allowance of £325,000, a threshold that has not changed for more than a decade. In contrast, the US estate and gift tax has a high threshold of US$11.58 million (gross assets and combined taxable gifts), excluding property passed to a surviving spouse. In the UK inheritance tax, there are exemptions for farming property (leading to increasing numbers of wealthy families owning farms), and for passing the home and some assets to a surviving spouse. The high rate and relatively low threshold makes the inheritance tax unpopular. A major loophole in the UK inheritance tax is the failure to tax lifetime (*inter vivos*) gifts that are made at least seven years before the date of death. The Mirrlees Review advocated an inheritance tax that would apply instead to the recipient of bequests or gifts, based on their total receipts over the life course (by *inter vivos* gift or at death). Despite their theoretical advantages, inheritance taxes in practice are often criticised because they have too many exclusions, are complex or easily avoided, or have thresholds that are too low – affecting the middle of the distribution– or too high, failing to capture adequate return from the wealthy.

The 1980s saw a significant reduction in rates or even repeal of inheritance taxes in many countries. Australia's estate and gift duties were repealed in 1981. New Zealand does not levy an inheritance tax. In the United States and United Kingdom, a 'step up' in basis to market value on death in the income tax significantly rewards holding capital assets until they can be passed on to heirs. Even in countries that levy inheritance tax, the assumption that the estate tax captures gain on death is less true than in previous times.[75] In Canada, the passing of assets on death is a deemed disposal that attracts tax based on market value. This suggests a possible alternative reform, being to extend the capital gains tax to apply to gains on death.

---

[74] Mirrlees et al, *Tax by Design* (see n 72).
[75] Tax Policy Center, 'What Is the Difference between Carryover Basis and Step Up Basis?' in *Key Elements of the U.S. Tax System, Briefing Book* (Washington, DC: Tax Policy Center, 2020), www.taxpolicycenter.org/briefing-book/what-difference-between-carryover-basis-and-step-basis.

The process of reduction of inheritance or wealth taxes during the late twentieth century may be the strongest evidence that the era of supply-side reforms that commenced in the 1980s successfully reduced taxes on capital for the benefit of the wealthy. This has likely contributed to increased wealth inequality and these changes are politically difficult to reverse or modify. Tax systems have shifted to a new equilibrium that is less efficient, fair and resilient, so that today governments find themselves in the position of undertaxing wealth and assets, despite concern about inequality and government debt. It is not surprising that there is increasing attention being paid to wealth taxes by scholars and some politicians, but moving to a system that taxes wealth more highly remains challenging politically.

Land and Property Taxation

We turn finally to a brief discussion of the taxation of land, one of the most important assets available to governments as a tax base. Land taxes are levied on a measure of the value of land or property, periodically or at a point in time, such as at the time of transfer of the land. Usually, land and property taxes apply to the gross value of land and do not take account of liabilities. Valuation methods vary widely, and land taxes may apply to unimproved, improved or market value depending on the jurisdiction. An annual land tax is a specific form of annual wealth tax.

Historically, land and property taxation was of great importance. Land is immovable, so provides a revenue base that cannot be shifted out of the jurisdiction. At a time when there were few other good 'tax handles', property taxes imposed on assessed land or building value generated a significant proportion of government revenues. To establish a successful land tax, methods of identification, registration and valuation of land are required. The technology of geometric land surveys and cadastres was developed in the eighteenth century in the Italian domain.[76] It spread across Europe and enabled establishment of a viable land tax in France, Austria and large parts of the German confederation. Tax administrators applied and refined the Italian model, communicating across borders through personal contacts and informal networks, developing a 'governmental science' of land taxation.[77]

The US economist and political scientist Henry George was famous for his advocacy for the 'single tax' base of land. The 'Single Taxers' became an important social and political movement in the late nineteenth century.[78] George argued that the 'economic rent' arising from land could be confiscated

---

[76] Christine Lebeau, 'Regional Exchanges and Patterns of Taxation in 18th Century Europe: The Case of the Italian Cadastres' in Holger Nehring and Florian Schui (eds.), *Global Debates about Taxation* (London: Palgrave Macmillan, 2007), 21–35.

[77] Ibid., 29.

[78] Henry George, *Progress and Poverty* (New York: Appleton, 1879).

(or taxed very highly) by the state. However, in practice land and property taxation never rose to the level he recommended. Land tax was not sufficient to fund the size of government that was reached in successful tax states during the twentieth century, which relied on broad-based taxation of income and consumption. Today, land taxation remains an important element of the tax system, but economic rents or super-profits are less tied to land, and are becoming increasingly mobile and intangible in the global digital economy. Policy attention has turned to harnessing the economic rents of multinational enterprises through the corporate tax.

Property and land taxation today is usually levied at the local government level, where it operates substantially as a user-charge or benefit tax for local services. In many countries, local property taxes are the main tax levied on home ownership. Property tax is typically an annual levy on a periodically updated assessed site value. Some countries also impose a general land tax, or taxes such as stamp duties on real property transactions. These transaction taxes are calculated as a percentage of price or market value of the house when sold, which is a convenient time to collect the tax.

The politics and administration of property taxation can be fraught with difficulty. The most significant challenge is maintaining the currency of land valuation against the powerful interests of existing land-holders. In California, the story of Proposition 13, the popular ballot initiative that slashed property taxes by keeping the valuation of property at low market values, is a salutary lesson in the unpopularity of property tax.[79] O'Sullivan et al suggest:

> the property tax has always been among the least popular of taxes. There are three essential reasons for this persistent unpopularity. First, it is a highly visible tax that a property owner often has to pay directly – it is not hidden in the manner of a sales tax or value-added tax. Second, it is a tax on wealth, not income. Not all taxpayers with highly valued property also have high incomes. This naturally leads to resentment and social tension. Finally, the property tax is typically based on estimated market value and not on a particular transaction. This leads to disputes between taxpayers and assessors over the true value of the property. Moreover, in most jurisdictions, assessments are conducted on regular cycles which allows for additional inequities to creep in during an often lengthy assessment cycle.[80]

Many of these problems with property tax existed in Germany, where property taxes are levied at the provincial level. The Federal Constitutional Court found that the valuation rules for property taxes, which relied on decades old assessed values that differed across different states, led to unjustifiable inequality of treatment. Some assessed values of property had not been updated since

---

[79] Proposition 13 was passed in 1978. See Arthur O'Sullivan, Terri A Sexton and Steven M Sheffrin, *Property Taxes & Tax Revolts: The Legacy of Proposition 13* (Cambridge, UK: Cambridge University Press, 1995).
[80] Ibid., 11.

the 1960s in western Germany, and since the 1930s in eastern Germany. The government proposed a reform that aims to apply a new national valuation measure to property.[81] The valuation approach for residential properties will be based on the deemed future income for the property, discounted by an interest rate. This approach indirectly captures some tax on imputed income from the home, which otherwise goes untaxed in the income tax. The property tax will subject the land valued in this way to tax at a basic federal rate with a local multiplier, and will provide revenues to local governments in Germany.

---

[81] 'Current Status of Implementation of the German Property Tax Reform', *German Tax Monthly* (Frankfurt: KPMG, October 2021), 3–4, https://assets.kpmg/content/dam/kpmg/de/pdf/Themen/2021/09/german-tax-monthly-october-2021-kpmg.pdf.

7

Corporate and Business Taxation

The corporation income tax is one of the most fascinating species produced by the process of economic legislation around the world.

Arthur C Harberger, quoted by David Bradford, *Untangling the Income Tax*

Why Tax Corporations?

Corporations Are Important

Policy discussions about the corporate tax often begin with the fundamental question: Why tax corporations?[1] Reuven Avi-Yonah observed that corporations are 'everywhere' and 'nowhere' in economic and social life.[2] The corporation is treated as a separate taxpayer in most income tax laws. Yet, like other intermediary business and investment vehicles, it is a legal fiction or construct. A corporation cannot bear the economic burden of a tax: a theory of ability to pay cannot be directly applied to a corporation.[3]

Before considering the economic and legal design of the corporate tax, it is worth identifying some political and historical reasons why governments tax corporations. Essentially, governments tax corporations because corporations are important. Sijbren Cnossen put it this way:

---

[1] James A Mirrlees, Stuart Adam, Tim Besley, Richard Blundell, Stephen Bond, Robert Chote, Malcolm Gammie, Paul Johnson, Gareth Myles and James M Poterba, *Tax by Design. Mirrlees Review: Vol 2* (Oxford: Oxford University Press, 2011), https://ifs.org.uk/publications/5353, 408.

[2] Reuven S Avi-Yonah, 'Corporations, Society, and the State: A Defense of the Corporate Tax' (2004) 90(5) *Virginia Law Review* 1193–255, 1194–5. The agency theory of the corporation has today given way to more sophisticated institutional approaches such as stakeholder or community theories: see Oliver E Williamson and Sidney G Winter (eds.), *The Nature of the Firm: Origins, Evolution, and Development* (New York: Oxford University Press, 1993); Lynn Stout, 'The Economic Nature of the Corporation' in Francesco Parisi (ed.), *Oxford Handbook of Law and Economics. Vol 2: Private and Commercial Law* (Oxford: Oxford University Press, 2017), 343–8; Thomas Donaldson and Lee Preston, 'The Stakeholder Theory of the Corporation: Concepts, Evidence and Implications' (1995) 20(1) *Academy of Management Review* 65–91; David Ciepley, 'Beyond Public and Private: Towards a Political Theory of the Corporation' (2013) 107(1) *American Political Science Review* 139–58.

[3] Kim Brooks, 'Learning to Live with an Imperfect Tax: A Defence of the Corporate Tax' (2003) 36 *University of British Columbia Law Review* 621.

Corporation taxes are important because corporations are social and economic institutions of great impact. As separate legal entities, corporations have the power to contract, the right to hold and convey title to property, the capacity to sue and to be sued, and the authority to make rules and bylaws. Corporations have a life independent of the lives of their shareholders, they beget offspring, called subsidiaries, and, in principle, corporations are legally immortal. ...

The social and economic importance of the 'invention' of the corporate form of business organisation has rightly been compared to the discovery of steam and electricity. Corporations have reshaped the world in which we live. In most countries, a large part of the national produce is generated in the corporate sector and its activities exercise a profound influence on the remainder of the economy. Modern industrial development is absolutely unthinkable without the corporate business form in which capital and labour are combined for mutually beneficial productive purposes. Without exaggeration, the corporation may be characterised as the 'central economic institution of modern society'.[4]

History also matters. Governments tax corporations because they have done so for a long time. Peter Harris traced the history of the corporate tax in Great Britain to 1450, when a tax was applied to 'manors, lands, tenements, rents, services, offices, fees, annuities, profits, and commodities temporal' in the hands of 'persons corporate'.[5] Subsequent taxes applied to guilds, collectives and the 'mysteries' of trades whether 'corporate or incorporate'.[6] The poll tax of 1667 to fund the English War with France and the Netherlands applied to corporations, while the first British income tax of 1799 taxed both corporations and shareholders.[7]

In Sweden, taxes on corporations date from the nineteenth century and were significantly increased through the first half of the twentieth century.[8] The US 'corporate excise tax' was introduced in 1909 and there were earlier taxes on 'corporate' organisations.[9] Japan levied income tax on 'corporate income' from 1899, and the first German Corporate Income Tax Act was

---

[4] Sijbren Cnossen, 'The Role of the Corporation Tax in OECD Member Countries' in John G Head and Richard Krever (eds.), *Company Tax Systems*, Conference Series No 18 (Melbourne: Australian Tax Research Foundation, 1997), 49–84, 49, citing Richard Goode, *The Corporation Income Tax* (New York: John Wiley, 1951) and Edward Mason, 'Corporation' in David L Sills (ed.), *International Encyclopedia of the Social Sciences: Vol 3* (New York: Macmillan and Free Press, 1968), 396.

[5] Peter Harris, *Income Tax in Common Law Jurisdictions: From the Origins to 1820* (Cambridge, UK: Cambridge University Press, 2006), 49.

[6] Ibid., 67–8.

[7] Ibid., 139; 413.

[8] Dan Johansson, Mikael Stenkula and Gunnar Du Rietz, 'Capital Income Taxation of Swedish Households, 1862–2010' (2015) 63(2) *Scandinavian Economic History Review* 154–77 https://doi.org/10.1080/03585522.2014.980314; Leif Mutén, 'The Development of Capital Income Taxation in Sweden 1928–2002' (2003) 44 *Scandinavian Studies in Law* 259–75.

[9] Steven A Bank, 'Entity Theory as Myth in the Origins of the Corporate Income Tax' (2001) 43 *William and Mary Law Review* 447, 497–8.

enacted in 1920.[10] A similar history is apparent in Canada[11] and New Zealand.[12]

A third reason why governments tax corporations is because it is clear in many cases that corporations are owned and managed by the wealthy and therefore the corporate tax is progressive. This is also a reason why the corporate tax is politically popular.

A fourth, more prosaic but still important reason is that the corporate tax is necessary to prevent the avoidance of personal income tax by shifting income into corporations.

Finally, the corporate tax is one way in which governments seek to regulate capitalism. The 1909 US corporate tax aimed to regulate corporate entities with the goal of protecting investors, at a time before federal securities and investment disclosure regulation was established.[13] A regulatory approach justified the corporate tax as the price to be paid for the privilege of conducting business in a legal form that provided limited liability and other advantages to investors.[14] The administration of the tax would provide information that governments initially intended to make publicly available to investors, although this 'publicity' aspect was soon shut down as a result of corporate lobbying. Today, we see the reappearance of this function of the corporate tax; while corporate tax rates continue to trend downward, corporate tax reporting obligations, information exchange and regulation escalate in a global context.

While governments have always taxed corporations, tax experts, whether they are lawyers, economists or accountants, have often criticised the corporate tax. Kim Brooks observes that 'attacks on the corporate tax are not new ... such attacks have recurred at fairly regular intervals over the history of the corporate tax. The objections that businesspeople might have to the tax are obvious, but economists, who agree on little else, also have been almost unanimous in opposing the tax'. Brooks observes that Henry Simons, the founder of the 'comprehensive income tax', abhorred separate corporate taxes, while 'tax law scholars have also generally opposed the separate corporate tax

---

[10] Hugh J Ault, Brian J Arnold and Graeme Cooper, *Comparative Income Taxation*, 4th ed (Alphen aan den Rijn, Netherlands: Wolters Kluwer, 2020).

[11] J Harvey Perry, *Taxes, Tariffs and Subsidies. A History of Canadian Fiscal Development: Vol 1* (Toronto: University of Toronto Press, 1955); Richard Bird, *The Corporate Income Tax in Canada: Does its Past Foretell Its Future?* SPP Research Papers 9(38) (Calgary: University of Calgary, 2016).

[12] Annie Cho, 'The Five Phases of Company Taxation in New Zealand: 1840–2008' (2008) 14 *Auckland University Law Review* 150–75.

[13] Marjorie E Kornhauser, 'Corporate Regulation and the Origins of the Corporate Income Tax' (1990) 66(1) *Indiana Law Journal* 53–136.

[14] Jane Gravelle, 'The Corporate Income Tax – A Persistent Policy Challenge' (2011) 11 *Florida Tax Review* 73–96.

and have suggested that it should be replaced with a form of tax that integrates the corporate and shareholder level taxes'.[15]

Politicians and policymakers are conscious of the importance of corporations in business enterprise and economic growth and have long been concerned that the corporate tax should not stifle innovation, appetite for risk and business investment. The speech of the Australian Prime Minister on introducing the first federal corporate income tax of 1915 illustrates this concern and could easily be made today:

> At this juncture it is of the utmost importance that we shall do nothing to discourage enterprise; on the contrary, we must do all that we can to encourage it. ... Modern production is conducted largely, if not mainly, through the agency of companies ... It is thus obvious that a tax which pressed heavily on companies would tend to retard production.[16]

Complexity of the Corporate Tax

Corporations pose major challenges for tax policy, law and administration and the corporate tax is usually the most complex tax in the armoury of governments. A key reason is the diversity of corporations and their activities. Corporations range from small and closely held proprietary companies that deliver personal services, or trade on a small scale, to large multinational corporate groups operating in countries around the world. Corporations may operate new businesses or be mature public listed firms; they may be venture capital-funded start-ups or the 'unicorns', the massive privately owned businesses of the tech world, or may be owned in whole or part by governments. The corporate tax law must apply to all these different kinds of corporation; alternatively, special and targeted rules must be developed to deal with their different characteristics. Either approach generates complexity for at least some corporations and their owners, and for the tax administration and profession.

The corporate tax requires rules to deal with the diverse modes of finance and investment in the corporate form. This includes shareholders investing equity, and creditors investing debt. The investors in corporations are themselves extremely diverse, ranging from individuals to other businesses, widely held pension funds and banks, residents and non-residents, all of which have different tax profiles. Corporations may be a vehicle for investment owned by a single individual or family; for a joint venture involving unrelated parties; in combination with other legal entity forms such as trusts and partnerships; or in corporate groups of hundreds of wholly owned subsidiaries.

---

[15] Brooks, 'Learning to Live with an Imperfect Tax' (see n 3), 625–6.
[16] Prime Minister Hughes (Cth), Second Reading Speech, Income Tax Assessment Bill 1915, House of Representatives, Australian Parliament (18 August 1915), Hansard, 5843.

The corporate tax must also provide rules for the vicissitudes of corporate operation: the tax treatment of profits and losses; investment in different forms of assets, trading stock and employees and transactions with shareholders including dividends, returns of capital, stock options and share buybacks. Corporations grow or shrink in scale of operations, turnover and profit; distribute profits or reinvest earnings; generate losses; go into liquidation; and engage in endless processes of merger and acquisition, divestment and spin-off with other corporations and their investors.

Finally, the design of the corporate tax is inextricably connected with the design of rules for international taxation because the corporation is the main vehicle for international direct investment. International tax rules are directed to establishing the nexus of corporations and their profits to different countries, in order to establish tax jurisdiction. This might be where the corporation is legally established or where its owners, managers, employees, plant, assets, finances or consumers are located (we return to this issue in Chapter 11). The domestic tax rules for income and expenses of corporations may have different effects across borders, generating double taxation or opportunities for non-taxation.

Despite these complexities, a corporation is a good 'tax handle'.[17] The separate legal entity status of the corporation facilitates tax administration. A corporation presents an opportunity for a government to identify, locate and tax profit because it is registered, has an address, owns assets, rents or owns premises, buys and sells goods and services, has a bank account and pays employees. There are far fewer corporations than individuals in most country tax systems and they are often easier to identify and pursue through investigation and audit processes. Under accounting and legal principles, corporations must annually report net profit or loss and corporations that are listed or over a certain size must often report at least some financial, profit and tax information to shareholders and the public. Corporations are subject to many regulatory regimes that can generate data that are useful to triangulate tax enforcement. Because of these features, corporations have themselves become the vehicle for enforcement of many other taxes, especially withholding taxes on employees, and consumption taxes such as the value added tax (VAT).

At the same time, the separate entity status of the corporation presents a wide range of opportunities for tax planning and avoidance. These include the use of small-scale owner-operated corporations as a vehicle to avoid the personal income tax on consultancy or services income; the abuse of bankruptcy processes to avoid paying tax debts; 'letter box' corporations in tax havens; and the proliferation of subsidiary corporations located in low tax

---

[17] Christopher Hood, 'British Tax Structure Development as Administrative Adaptation' (1985) 18(1) *Policy Sciences* 3–31.

jurisdictions around the world, which are an essential element in multinational enterprise tax planning.

Corporate Tax Revenues and Rates

Figure 7.1 shows corporate tax revenue as a percentage of total taxation, and as a percentage of gross domestic product (GDP) for selected Organisation for Economic Co-operation and Development (OECD) member states. It shows that there is wide variation in the share of corporate tax in total taxation across countries, although there is less variation in corporate tax as the share of GDP; most countries are fairly close to the OECD average of about 3 per cent.

As shown in Figure 7.1, France, Sweden, Germany and Denmark have among the highest tax levels in the OECD but the corporate tax in these countries raises below 7 per cent of tax revenues. The United States also raises a relatively small share of revenue from the corporate tax. In contrast, Australia raises 13.5 per cent and Mexico raises 21.8 per cent of total taxation from the corporate tax. Some small countries, especially Luxembourg, also

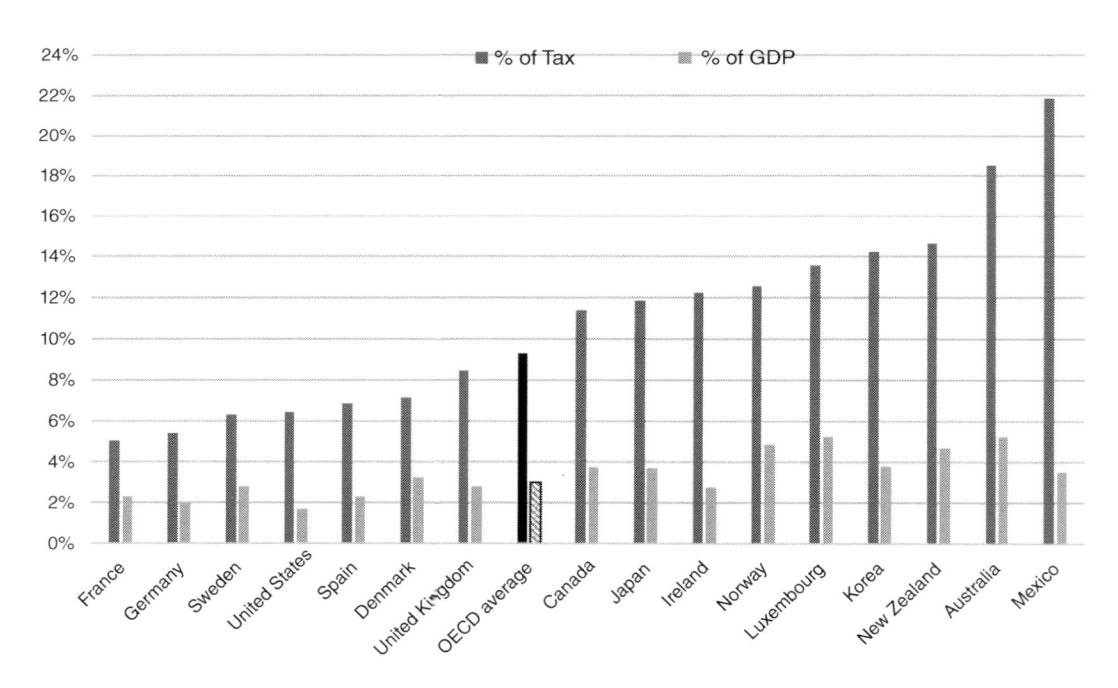

Figure 7.1 Corporate income tax, share of total taxation and of GDP, selected OECD countries, 2017
Source: OECD, Corporate Tax Revenues, www.oecd-ilibrary.org/taxation/data/revenue-statistics/comparative-tables_data-00262-en.

have a large corporate tax share. This is because Luxembourg is an international hub for corporate capital.

Until the 1980s, corporate tax rates averaged 50 per cent or higher in OECD member states. Today's global average is closer to 25 per cent and trending downwards. For example, Denmark, Sweden and Finland have relatively low corporate tax consistent with the Nordic dual income tax model for taxing personal savings and investment, discussed in Chapter 6.

Corporate tax rate trends for 2000 to 2021 are shown in Figure 7.2. The average corporate tax rate in the OECD has come down from 45 per cent in 1980 to 23 per cent in 2021. The United States cut its federal corporate tax rate from 35 per cent to 21 per cent in the Tax Cuts and Jobs Act of 2017. Other countries to reduce corporate tax rates in recent years include the United Kingdom (19 per cent); China (25 per cent); Canada (26.5 per cent); and Australia, on small and medium business corporations (25 per cent, while retaining a 30 per cent rate on large corporations). Ireland has long had a low rate of 12.5 per cent. Australia, Japan and Germany now sit at the top of the range for large corporations. As discussed further in Chapter 11, governments are cooperating to establish an effective minimum tax of 15 per cent on profits of large multinational enterprises.

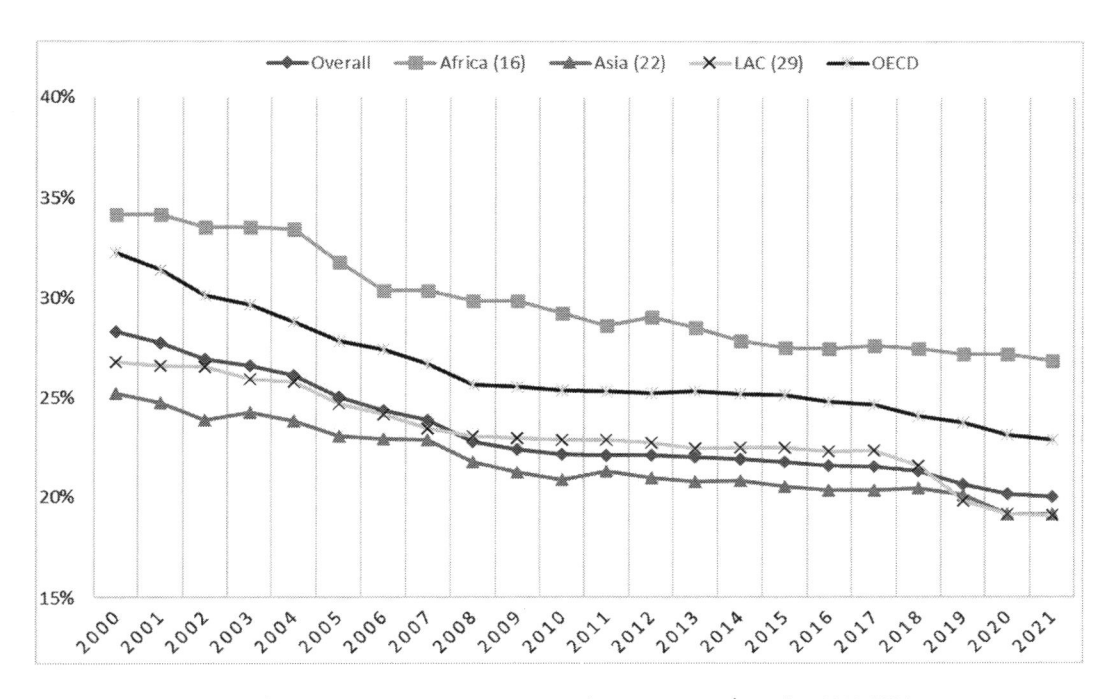

Figure 7.2 Average statutory corporate income tax rates by region, 2000–2021
Note: LAC indicates Latin American and Caribbean jurisdictions. Chart ignores zero-rate jurisdictions
Source: OECD, Corporate Tax Statistics 2021, Figure 6.

Although corporate tax rates have come down, the level of corporate revenues across the OECD has remained relatively stable. There are several reasons for this. First, corporate tax revenue depends on both the rate and the base – the definition of corporate profit subject to tax. If the definition of corporate taxable profit is broad, then more tax will be collected even at a lower tax rate.

Second, corporate tax revenue is partly a function of a country's corporate-shareholder tax system. For example, in Australia and New Zealand, shareholders receive a tax credit against their personal income tax on dividends where corporate tax was previously paid. In these systems, higher corporate tax is collected but a significant proportion is refunded to shareholders in the personal income tax system.

Third, corporate tax revenues depend on the level of profit or return to capital generated in the corporate sector, compared to the return generated in other business entity forms or in the hands of individuals. The return to the corporate sector has increased over time in many countries. This is partly in response to the decline in corporate tax rates relative to personal income tax rates, which creates an incentive to derive profits in the corporate form.

Incidence of the Corporate Tax

The economic incidence of the corporate tax is one of the thorniest issues in public finance.[18] As explained in Chapter 1, the burden of corporate tax must fall on real people and cannot be borne by the legal fiction of the corporate entity. The incidence of the corporate tax may fall on shareholders (or owners of capital generally), workers (or labour generally, through lower wages), managers (through lower wages) or consumers (through higher prices).

One view of corporate tax incidence, which has dominated through much of the history of the corporate tax, is that the burden falls on the shareholders who own the corporation. This characterises the corporate tax as a withholding tax on the shareholder and it underpins the design of tax rules for corporate distributions in many countries. For example, corporate tax rules may permit a deduction for dividends, or apply the tax only to income at the corporate or shareholder level.[19] For small, closely held or family-owned corporations, this approach seems plausible; there is a clear nexus between ownership and control by the shareholders and the corporate entity's underlying profits.

---

[18] There is a wide literature. See e.g. Head and Krever, *Company Tax Systems* (see n 4); David Bradford, *Untangling the Income Tax* (Cambridge, MA: Harvard University Press, 1986); George Zodrow, International Taxation and Company Tax Policy in Small Open Economies' in Iris Claus, Norman Gemmell, Michelle Harding and David White (eds.), *Tax Reform in Open Economies: International and Country Perspectives* (Cheltenham: Edward Elgar, 2010).

[19] Harris, *Income Tax in Common Law Jurisdictions* (see n 5), 413.

This view was generalised to show that the corporate tax falls on capital in general in a famous analysis by Arnold Harberger in 1962.[20] Harberger showed (under various strong assumptions) that the corporate tax in the long run falls on capital, through changes to capital asset values and to the return to capital in the economy. Essentially, if the return to corporate activity is reduced by a tax relative to other forms of capital, investment will shift out of the corporate sector into other sectors; over time this will tend to equalise the after-tax return to capital across the economy.

An alternative theory that grew up in the twentieth century, and paradoxically became known as the 'classical' theory, sought to treat the corporation not as an aggregate of other interests but as a separate person. The corporate tax applied to profits of the legal entity, and any distribution by way of dividends would be separately taxed in the hands of shareholders under the personal income tax. Where profits were entirely retained and reinvested in the corporation, this ensured a single level of tax on that profit. However, where profits were distributed, the classical system 'double taxed' those profits.

Some argued in support of 'classical' or 'double' taxation of corporate profits because of the powerful role of the corporations in the economy.[21] In many countries the classical corporate tax system had a more pragmatic rationale, as a response to greater revenue needs of government during and after World War II. There were also reasons of international tax allocation that made the 'classical' system attractive, as the country where the corporation did business could tax the profit and dividends were taxed when distributed to shareholders, in their country of residence.

By the 1980s, there were growing concerns that the tax on corporations, and capital in general, was too high and was an obstacle to business investment. There were also concerns about fairness. The classical system generated a tax bias towards debt to finance investment because interest on debt was deductible but dividends were taxed at an effective rate exceeding the marginal tax rate of the shareholder, violating principles of horizontal and vertical equity. This created an incentive for corporations to retain profits instead of distributing them, or to find creative ways to distribute value out of the corporation in forms other than a dividend. Corporations did significant tax planning to avoid the corporate tax at domestic and international levels.

Box 7.1 presents examples of shifting income between the corporate and personal income tax systems, in response to tax rates. These examples demonstrate that the owners and controllers of closely held corporations may, indeed, bear the corporate tax – or perceive that they do – and respond to it

---

[20] Arnold C Harberger, 'The Incidence of the Corporation Income Tax' (1962) 70(3) *Journal of Political Economy* 215–40.
[21] Gerhard Colm, 'The Corporation and the Corporate Income Tax in the American Economy' (1954) 45 *American Economic Review* 486–503.

Box 7.1 Income shifting between the corporate and personal income tax systems

The US corporate tax provides an illustration of the shifting of privately owned business activity, or business income, out of corporations into lower taxed entities. From the 1980s until 2017, the United States had a corporate tax rate of 35 per cent, significantly higher than the tax rate on the income and capital gains of many investors. The corporate tax applied to 'C-corporations', which are traditional corporations, but not to pass-through entities, including partnerships, 'S-corporations' and limited liability corporations (LLCs).

Despite its relatively high corporate tax rate, the United States has raised relatively low revenue from the corporate tax, and those revenues declined over several decades: 'the most striking feature of the corporate tax is its diminished importance'.[22] An explanation is that business income was being earned *outside* the corporate sector. The US Treasury estimates that by 2011, 54 per cent of US business income was earned in pass-through entities compared to 21 per cent in 1980.[23] Taxpayers had shifted business activity and income out of the corporate form into pass-through entities enabling taxation at the individual level.

Taxpayers may shift income or activity the other way, out of the personal income tax base into the corporate tax. In the United Kingdom in 2002, the starting tax rate for small corporations was lowered to zero. The number of incorporations per week increased by more than half. The zero rate was eliminated in 2006 and the rate of increase dropped off. The UK corporate tax rate is today significantly lower than top marginal tax rates on labour income; overall, the use of corporations has trended up, relative to other business forms.[24] The lesson is that a zero rate on corporate profit is an undesirable policy that will lead to significant tax base shifting to avoid the personal income tax.

Another illustration is provided from Finland, which in response to European tax law developments in 2005 introduced a 'classical' tax system in place of the shareholder 'imputation credit' that had previously applied. This increased the tax rate on dividends. There was a strong response by the owners of private firms, who moved to paying themselves wages, which would be deductible for the company and taxable to the recipient, instead of paying dividends, which were more highly taxed.[25]

---

[22] Jane Gravelle, 'Corporate Income Tax: Incidence, Economic Effects and Structural Issues' in John G Head and Richard Krever (eds.), *Tax Reform in the 21st Century* (Alphen aan den Rijn, Netherlands: Wolters Kluwer, 2009), 355–84, 357.

[23] Michael Cooper, John McClelland, James Pearce, Richard Prisinzano, Joseph Sullivan, Danny Yagan, Owen Zidar and Eric Zwick, *Business in the United States: Who Owns It and How Much Tax Do They Pay?*, Working Paper 104/2015 (Washington, DC: Department of the Treasury, Office of Tax Analysis, 2011), www.treasury.gov/resource-center/tax-policy/tax-analysis/Documents/WP-104.pdf.

[24] Claire Crawford and Judith Freedman, 'Small Business Taxation' in Stuart Adam, Tim Besley, Richard Blundell, Stephen Bond, Robert Chote, Malcolm Gammie, Paul Johnson, Gareth Myles and James M Poterba, *Dimensions of Tax Design. Mirrlees Review: Vol 1* (Oxford: Oxford University Press, 2010), 1028–99, https://ifs.org.uk/publications/5228.

[25] Jarko Harju and Tuomas Matikka, *Business Owners and Income-Shifting Between Tax Bases: Empirical Evidence from a Finnish Tax Reform*, CESifo Working Paper No 5090 (2014), https://ssrn.com/abstract=2536285.

accordingly. However, for widely held corporations with significant and diverse economic activity, the question is more difficult. Who benefits from a lower corporate tax rate, or suffers from a higher one? In large firms where management is separated from shareholders, do managers obtain the benefit of a lower corporate tax rate, or tax planning to reduce the rate, instead of shareholders – perhaps in higher executive compensation?

The analysis of corporate tax incidence may change if we assume mobility of capital across borders. In Chapter 4, we introduced the impact of opening the borders, or economic globalisation, on tax policy. This is particularly important when thinking about the corporate tax. Numerous studies carried out since the 1980s suggest that in a 'small open economy', the burden of the corporate tax falls partly on labour, and not only on capital. An implication of this analysis is that a higher corporate tax may drive down wages, or cause unemployment in a country; or, conversely, a lower corporate tax may increase jobs or wages.[26] The analysis of countries as 'small open economies' assumes that the country cannot influence the global return to capital (most countries cannot), and that the marginal investor seeks the best global after-tax return. Where a country levies a corporate tax, this marginal investor requires a higher rate of return to compensate for the tax. In a global market, capital can flow to a lower taxed jurisdiction that offers a higher after-tax return. As there are fewer investments that meet the required higher rate of return in the higher taxing jurisdiction, this leads to a drop in inbound investment, which implies lower economic growth, fewer jobs or lower wages.

Integrating Corporate and Shareholder Tax

In response to the theory that the corporate tax is borne by shareholders, governments developed corporate-shareholder tax systems with the aim of alleviating the 'double taxation' on corporate profits. Some of these recalled the 'dividend-deduction' system that operated in early income taxes. Others applied a new approach, of a tax credit for shareholders that 'imputed' corporate tax to them, and then offset the corporate tax against their individual tax on the dividend. During the 1990s, 24 out of 28 OECD member states had enacted some form of dividend relief, including a full or partial 'imputation' credit system or a lower rate on dividend income.[27] In the ensuing

---

[26] See, e.g. Alan J Auerbach, *Who Bears the Corporate Tax? A Review of What We Know*, NBER Working Papers Series No 11686 (Cambridge, MA: National Bureau of Economic Research, 2006); a recent study using German data is Nadja Dwenger, Pia Rattenhuber and Viktor Steiner, 'Sharing the Burden? Empirical Evidence on Corporate Tax Incidence' (2019) 20(4) *German Economic Review* e107–e140, https://doi.org/10.1111/geer.12157.

[27] Cnossen, 'The Role of the Corporation Tax in OECD Member Countries' (see n 4).

Table 7.1. Corporate-shareholder tax systems

	Classical system	Imputation tax credit	Dividend exemption	Half inclusion	Low flat rate	Dual income tax
Company						
Taxable income	100	100	100	100	100	100
Company tax	30	30	30	30	30	30
After-tax company income	70	70	70	70	70	70
Shareholder						
Dividend	70	70	70	70	70	70
Imputation gross up	Na	30	Na	Na	Na	Na
Income	70	100	0	35	70	70
Income tax	35	50	0	17.5	17.5 (a)	21 (b)
Imputation credit	Na	30	Na	Na	Na	Na
Net shareholder tax	35	20	0	17.5	17.5	21
Shareholder income after tax	35	50	70	52.5	52.5	49
Total tax	65	50	30	47.5	47.5	51
Effective tax rate	65 per cent	50 per cent	30 per cent	47.5 per cent	47.5 per cent	51 per cent

Note: Assumed company tax rate is 30 per cent and shareholder tax rate is 50 per cent. (a) low flat rate, assumed shareholder tax rate is 25 per cent. (b) dual income tax, assumed shareholder tax on capital income is 30 per cent. The dual income tax system that operates in the Nordic states is explained in Chapter 6.
Source: Adapted from Table 3, Richard J Vann, 'General Report' in *Trends in Company/Shareholder Taxation: Single or Double Taxation? Cahiers de Droit Fiscal International: Vol 88a* (Rotterdam: International Fiscal Association, 2003), 21–70, 29.

decade, continual flux occurred in the design of corporate-shareholder tax systems but most governments did not return to the classical system.[28]

Today, countries adopt a wide variety of corporate-shareholder tax systems, all of which aim, to some degree, to alleviate the double tax on corporate profit. Table 7.1 presents an example to illustrate the effect for profits taxable

---

[28] Richard J Vann, 'General Report' in *Trends in Company/Shareholder Taxation: Single or Double Taxation? Cahiers de Droit Fiscal International: Vol 88a* (Rotterdam: International Fiscal Association, 2003), 21–70, 23.

at an assumed company tax rate of 30 per cent and dividends paid to a shareholder with an assumed personal tax rate of 50 per cent. Each of the 'integration' methods of dividend imputation, half inclusion, dual income and flat rate systems ensure that taxation under the corporate-shareholder system approximates the shareholder tax rate of 50 per cent. However, the classical system 'overtaxes' and the dividend exemption 'undertaxes' the shareholder. Table 7.1 does not address the extraction of value from the corporation by a share sale that will usually generate a capital gain. As explained in Chapter 6, in most countries this is taxed at a lower rate. The reduced tax rate on capital gain mitigate the 'double tax' effect produced from taxing gain on the sale of shares.

A corporate-shareholder dividend imputation system has numerous advantages.[29] Taxation on profits is collected from the corporation, but the personal tax rate applies for domestic individual investors on distributed dividends. The imputation system reduces the bias towards companies retaining their profits, rather than distributing them as dividends, and eliminates the bias towards debt and against equity.

The major challenge to corporate-shareholder integration, especially imputation systems, arises from the globalisation of the economy, and the opening of national borders to capital flows.[30] Governments are not prepared to give a tax credit to foreign shareholders for domestic tax, or give a credit for foreign corporate tax that would be, in effect, a transfer to the treasury of the foreign jurisdiction. The Court of Justice of the European Union (EU) found in a series of cases that the denial of an imputation credit for foreign corporate tax discriminates against cross-border capital investment, breaching the free movement of capital.[31] This spelled the end of imputation systems in Europe. Faced with potentially large revenue losses, by the early 2000s, most EU member states had abolished or limited their imputation credit systems for both domestic and foreign shareholders.

Some countries outside the EU have retained an imputation credit system including Australia and New Zealand. This is one reason why Australia collects a much higher proportion of corporate tax than most other developed countries. However, a consequence of the 'small open economy' theory of corporate tax incidence explained previously is that tax relief for dividends of

---

[29] Michael J Graetz and Alvin C Warren, 'Integration of Corporate and Shareholder Taxes' (2016) 69(3) *National Tax Journal* 677–700, https://dx.doi.org/10.17310/ntj.2016.3.07, viewed imputation systems favourably especially in the context of the former US corporate tax rate of 35 per cent; this may have become moot since the US corporate tax rate was lowered to 21 per cent.
[30] Vann, 'General Report' (see n 28).
[31] Ibid.

domestic shareholders provides a subsidy for domestic investors. Clemens Fuest and Bernd Huber explain this logic:

> in a small open economy ... The marginal shareholder in domestic firms is a foreign shareholder. This implies that the level of real investment is not affected by the taxation of domestic dividend income at the household level. A reduction in the tax burden on dividends is therefore merely an undesirable subsidy on domestic asset holdings... which is inefficient for the economy as a whole.[32]

On the other hand, the dividend imputation system in Australia has the advantage that it encourages Australian companies with domestic shareholders to pay Australian corporate tax.[33] This is because Australian investors, including the very large pension investment funds, benefit from imputation credits and favour investments in large Australian corporations that pay Australian tax.

The Corporate Tax on Economic Rents

Chapter 6 introduced the concept of 'economic rent' as a component of the return to capital representing the 'above normal' return. Most economists agree that the return to extraction of non-renewable resources, such as oil and gas or minerals, is an 'economic rent' that should be taxed, for example by a royalty that operates as a price for access to the resource. One suitable role for the corporate tax is to tax economic rents, or above-normal returns, derived from market power, such as the ability to extract a higher price from a monopoly. A tax on economic rents is generally considered to fall on the owner of rents, or the monopolist, in the case of the corporate tax.

Revisiting the debate about corporate tax incidence nearly 50 years after his 1962 article, Harberger observed that we can think of the return to the monopolist as itself like a 'privately imposed, privately collected excise tax on the monopolized product or products'.[34] The extraction of value by the monopolist wrongly co-opts the economic return that should go to consumers in the market, or to governments as sovereign actors. Apart from resources extraction – where a royalty can do quite well – Harberger concluded that there is no easy way to tax monopoly profits, except by a corporate income tax.

---

[32] Clemens Fuest and Bernd Huber, *The Optimal Taxation of Dividends in A Small Open Economy*, CESifo Working Paper Series No 348 (2000), 2.

[33] Catherine Ikin and Alfred Tran, 'Corporate Tax Strategy in the Australian Dividend Imputation System' (2013) 28(3) *Australian Tax Forum* 523-53; Rodney Brown, Yongdoek Lim and Chris Evans, 'The Impact of Full Franking Credit Refundability on Corporate Tax Avoidance' (2020) 17(2) *eJournal of Tax Research* 134-67.

[34] Arnold C Harberger, 'The Incidence of the Corporation Income Tax Revisited' (2008) 61(2) *National Tax Journal* 303-12.

However, the corporate income tax applies to the 'normal return' to investment as well as to economic rents. This has led to policy proposals that would relieve the corporate tax on the 'normal return', while retaining or even increasing it on economic rents. We discuss these proposals later. First, it is useful to explore the definition of the tax base for business investment, to which we turn next.

Taxation of Business Investment

Tangible and Intangible Business Assets

The tax treatment of investment in plant, equipment, buildings, intellectual property and other business assets is a significant issue in any income tax law. The income tax rules for business assets usually apply to businesses in all forms, not only corporations.

Under a comprehensive income tax, a business expense that acquires a short-term benefit or asset is immediately deductible, while an expense to acquire a benefit or asset lasting for a period longer than one fiscal year is deductible over the life of the benefit obtained. This permits a deduction for the decline in value of long-lived assets such as machinery, equipment or buildings over their effective lives, which may range from only a couple of years for a computer or phone that quickly becomes obsolete to several decades for heavy machinery, aircraft and buildings. Most income tax laws also permit a write-off over time for the cost of intellectual property including copyright (for example, applying to books, artistic works or computer software code), patents, trademarks, business names and registered designs. No depreciation should be permitted for an asset that does not depreciate, such as land.

A government that wishes to stimulate investment in new equipment, or promote the development of patents, might provide a write-off for these costs that is faster than their effective life. For example, a government might legislate for immediate deductibility or 'expensing' of the cost of a particular kind of business asset, or even deliver a subsidy by providing an investment allowance or credit of more than 100 per cent. The higher the corporate tax rate, the more such a deduction is worth to the taxpayer. The main benefit for the taxpayer of business expensing or 'accelerated' depreciation is timing, enabling earlier deduction of costs than would otherwise be permitted. This moves the corporate income tax along a spectrum towards a 'consumption' or 'expenditure' benchmark.

On the other hand, a government might seek to broaden the corporate tax base by reining in deductions for depreciating assets. A study of the corporate tax reforms of the 1980s and 1990s in 16 countries including members of the EU and the G7 concluded that 'the most common reform to corporate income taxes in these countries has been to lower tax rates and to broaden tax bases'.[35] This was measured through an analysis of the **marginal effective tax rate** (METR), which calculates the after-tax cost of capital for corporate investment in different sectors, taking account of the rate and the definition of the base, including deductions for investment in assets, and the tax treatment of the cost of financing business investment.[36] The study demonstrated the wide diversity of after-tax cost of investment across countries. The removal of some of these special rules and incentives was one way in which governments succeeded in maintaining revenue from the corporate tax as rates declined.

Tax Policy for Innovation and Entrepreneurship

Debates about innovation, entrepreneurship and economic growth date to the beginnings of capitalism. In 1803, French economist Jean-Baptiste Say described entrepreneurs as those who shift 'economic resources out of an area of lower and into an area of higher productivity and greater yield'.[37] Say recognised that the production of new goods and services involves risk and the entrepreneur takes upon themselves 'the immediate responsibility, risk, and conduct of a concern of industry, whether upon his own or a borrowed capital'.[38] A century later, Joseph Schumpeter identified the broader economic implications of entrepreneurship, which he described as an innovative activity that leads to the creation of new products, services or industries. This, in turn, cause the demise of older, established ones in a 'process of industrial mutation' reflected in his famous phrase 'creative destruction'.[39]

The argument to subsidise innovation, including through the tax system, assumes that economic growth is in part a product of technological progress in new or more advanced physical or intangible investments, or through research and development (R&D) by firms. Where innovation is harnessed by businesses to contribute to the more efficient use of labour and capital, this increases productivity. Innovation-led growth is thought to be aided by entrepreneurial (and risky) investments that may generate higher returns, and may require venture capital.[40] Policymakers should support innovative

---

[35] Michael P Devereux, Rachel Griffith and Alexander Klemm, *Corporate Income Tax Reforms and International Tax Competition* (Warwick: Centre for Economic Policy Research, University of Warwick, 2002).
[36] Mervyn A King and Don Fullerton (eds.), *The Taxation of Income from Capital* (Chicago: University of Chicago Press, 1984).
[37] Quoted in Peter F Drucker, *Innovation and Entrepreneurship* (New York: Harper Business, 1985), 21.
[38] Jean Baptiste Say, *A Treatise on Political Economy; or the Production, Distribution, and Consumption of Wealth*, 4th ed (Kitchener, Ontario: Batoche Books, 2010), 128.
[39] Joseph A Schumpeter, *Capitalism, Socialism and Democracy* (London: Routledge, 1994), 83.
[40] Duanjie Chen, Franck Lee and Jack M Mintz, *Taxation, SMEs and Entrepreneurship*, OECD Science, Technology and Industry Working Papers No. 2002/09 (Paris: OECD Publishing, 2002), https://doi.org/10.1787/013245868670.

activities that lead to economic development that can produce social surplus, and where 'market failure' arises because the private returns to innovation cannot be harnessed or the risk is too high. On this theory, innovation or new knowledge has some of the features of a public good.

Taxation reduces the return to the risk-taking entrepreneur, so it is not surprising that taxes are perceived to be a disincentive to entrepreneurship or to investing in R&D or new technologies. The challenge for policymakers is how to identify, and reward, taxpayers who are doing things that governments want to support, while not reducing taxes for activities that do not deliver the hoped-for social surplus from innovation.

Tax incentives for innovation are directed to one of the following goals:[41]

1. Reduce the cost of capital investment in tangible assets of a specified or general kind, for example, through investment allowances, accelerated depreciation or immediate expensing of costs;
2. Provide tax concessions for specific investments in research or technical innovation, even if this will not immediately generate income;
3. Reduce the cost of equity finance, by allowing a credit or deduction for equity investment or capital contributions;
4. Share the risk of loss from investments, for example, by permitting upfront use of tax losses against other income, providing credits or refunds for losses or permitting trading of losses to taxable parties;
5. Reduce tax on economic gain derived from a successful investment, for example, by a lower tax rate or exemption for the gain on sale or public offering of a venture capital business, or by reducing the tax rate on profit generated by defined businesses.

Tax law relies on proxies to identify entrepreneurs or activities that should be eligible for these types of concessions; but proxies are difficult to define because it is difficult to define entrepreneurship.[42] Proxies for innovation or entrepreneurship that are adopted in tax laws include (1) small business; (2) new business; (3) technological or science-driven business operations defined by sector or activity; (4) the ownership or investment in intellectual property, as a measure of innovation; (5) the level of risk (higher risk may be indicated, for example, by the extent of business losses); and (6) growing business (for example, measured by growth in size, turnover or market over time). All of these proxies are prone to inaccuracy. There is, therefore, a significant risk that tax policy to support entrepreneurship and innovation will be overinclusive,

---

[41] Miranda Stewart, 'Venture Capital Taxation in Australia and New Zealand' (2005) 11 *New Zealand Journal of Taxation Law and Policy* 216–49; Cameron Rider, Lillian Hong, Ann O'Connell, Miranda Stewart and Michelle Herring, *Taxation Problems in the Commercialisation of Intellectual Property*, IPRIA Report 2006/01 (Parkville: Intellectual Property Research Institute of Australia, 2006).

[42] Wolfgang Hölzl, 'The Economics of Entrepreneurship Policy: Introduction to the Special Issue' (2010) 10 *Journal of Industry, Competition and Trade* 187–97.

subsidising businesses that do not merit the subsidy, or underinclusive, failing to support worthy and innovative businesses.

Small Business

Small and medium-sized enterprises (SMEs) represent the majority of firms in most countries. SMEs employ the majority of workers and contribute valuable social capital, which is not usually recognised in the metric of economic growth or taxable corporate profits. They are diverse in respect to industries and in terms of their profitability and potential for growth.[43]

Many countries offer tax concessions to SMEs. Some are aimed at reducing tax compliance and regulatory costs, while others are subsidies, such as a lower corporate tax rate; the ability to tax deduct business investment 'up front' on an expense or cash flow basis; or tax credits for micro-businesses. Rationales include that these tax concessions support employment or that small businesses are innovative and entrepreneurial.

Claire Crawford and Judith Freedman identify the heterogeneity of the small business sector across entity form, industry, activity, ownership, financing and risk, as a major challenge for tax law design.[44] They advocate a more neutral treatment of different forms of business activities, by size and by legal form, in place of the proliferation of special tax rules for small business that are seen in the United Kingdom and many other jurisdictions. Concessional taxation of small business generates planning margins that promote tax avoidance and increase complexity. If concessions are to be applied, Crawford and Freedman suggest that deductions for the cost of business assets, or provision of an allowance for corporate equity would produce fewer distortions or incentives to convert labour income into capital income in small firms.

Empirical evidence discredits the proxy of 'small business' as a useful indicator of a 'true' entrepreneur. Most small businesses stay small – they do not grow as they mature, so they do not add jobs through this process.[45] New, rather than small, businesses create new jobs – 'it is not "small-ness" that is driving net job creation, it is relative "new-ness"'.[46] New or young firms that do not survive are also responsible for lots of job destruction; but if they survive, they tend to grow faster than other small businesses. A constant flow

---

[43] OECD, *Strengthening SMEs and Entrepreneurship for Productivity and Inclusive Growth* (Paris: OECD, 2019), https://doi.org/10.1787/c19b6f97-en.
[44] Crawford and Freedman, 'Small Business Taxation' (see n 24).
[45] William Gale and Samuel Brown, 'Small Business, Innovation, and Tax Policy: A Review' (2013) 66(4) *National Tax Journal* 871–92, 877.
[46] Ibid.; see, e.g. Luke Hendrickson, Stan Bucifal, Antonio Balaguer and David Hansell, *The Employment Dynamics of Australian Entrepreneurship*, Research Paper 4/2015 (Office of the Chief Economist, Australian Government Department of Industry and Science, 2015), 7.

of new entrepreneurial ventures is therefore assumed to be good for the economy. In sum, tax policy focused on encouraging entrepreneurship may not be the same as tax policy to support small firms.

Start-ups and Venture Capital

Start-up enterprises may have difficulty communicating their (current and future) value to potential investors. The riskiness of these enterprises is illustrated by their high failure rate but the rewards from the small percentage of successes may be much higher than the normal market return.[47] The OECD gives three reasons why 'market failure' may result for financing of start-up enterprises and so a subsidy may be necessary:[48]

1. They rely heavily on created intangible assets, confidential information and trade secrets, which may be difficult to value;
2. They have 'negative cash flows', and there may not be the prospect of positive cash flow for some years;
3. They are small, depend on the skills and expertise of particular talented individuals and have uncertain operating environments.

The income tax law operates to make the government a 'partner' in all businesses, by enabling deductibility of business losses against other income. Usually, losses can be carried forward to be offset against profits of the business in a future year. However, if a business fails it may not be possible to claim the loss deduction. In response to these concerns, measures in support of venture capital have been applied in different countries.[49] Tax concessions may take the form of 'front-end incentives', such as a tax deduction or credit for the cost of investment whether or not it is successful; or 'back-end incentives', which reward a successful investment with a lower tax rate. For example, an 'angel investor' tax credit is a 'front-end' incentive for the investor who makes capital available, or lowers the cost of capital, for the entrepreneur. Employee remuneration of the inventor or key personnel in start-ups may be subsidised by providing tax concessions for remuneration in employee stock options.[50] This kind of tax subsidy reduces the cost of labour to the business.

---

[47] Ronald J Gilson, 'Engineering a Venture Capital Market: Lessons from the American Experience' (2003) 55 *Stanford Law Review* 1067–103, 1076, refers to a high variance of returns on venture capital-backed companies, with half the total return provided by only 6.8 per cent of the investments and over a third resulting in loss. Another common rule of thumb is the 'one in 10' rule, whereby one investee company out of 10 produces a significant return, while the others produce losses or only break even.

[48] Chen et al, *Taxation, SMEs and Entrepreneurship* (see n 40).

[49] Stephen Barkoczy and Daniel Sandler, *Government Venture Capital Incentives: A Multi-jurisdiction Comparative Analysis* (Sydney: Australian Tax Research Foundation, 2007).

[50] Ronald J Gilson and David M Schizer, 'Understanding Venture Capital Structure: A Tax Explanation for Convertible Preferred Stock' (2003) 116 *Harvard Law Review* 874–916.

Front-end tax incentives also front-load the cost to the government, when the chances of a successful investment may be small. They may increase the number of venture capital investments but these may not be of high quality. They also generate opportunities for tax planning. An upfront tax deduction can be marketed to high-income taxpayers such as lawyers and doctors, like other mass marketed tax schemes aimed at generating deductions, without necessarily generating productive investment. This presents significant risks for policymakers and tax administrators.

A 'back-end incentive' rewards 'winners' who derive actual gains from risky investments.[51] It is less costly to government but it may motivate fewer investments overall. The risk for government is that lower tax rates can be harnessed for less productive investment. This is the main problem with the generalized back-end incentive enacted in most countries, which is simply a reduction in the capital gains tax rate, as explained in Chapter 6. A lower capital gains tax rate also provides an incentive to convert other business or labour income into capital gain, ultimately lowering the tax on the return to *labour*. The problem is illustrated by the controversy about US tax treatment of 'carried interest' on private equity funds, discussed in Box 7.2.

Research and Development

The case for R&D tax concessions rests on the goal of innovation-led economic growth and on the assumption of market failure, that is, firms do less R&D than is socially optimal. Governments fund innovation by spending money directly on scientific research in universities, the military, or governmental institutions. Governments also provide direct grants to businesses to carry out R&D. More than half of governmental support for R&D in many countries is provided through the tax system (examples are provided in Table 7.2).[52] However, some governments do not apply R&D tax incentives, instead delivering support through grants and public investment – Germany and New Zealand are examples of this approach.

An argument made in support of tax incentives for R&D is that they leave to the market, or private enterprise, the choice about what kind of research to do rather than the government 'picking winners' by funding particular kinds of research. Whether this makes any appreciable difference to outcomes,

---

[51] Harvey S Rosen, 'Entrepreneurship and Taxation: Empirical Evidence' in Vesa Kanniainen and Christian Keuschnigg (eds.), *Venture Capital, Entrepreneurship and Public Policy*, CESifo Seminar Series (Cambridge, MA: MIT Press, 2005).
[52] Silvia Appelt, Matej Bajgar, Chiara Criscuolo and Fernando Galindo-Rueda, *The Effects of R&D Tax Incentives and Their Role in the Innovation Policy Mix*, OECD Science, Technology and Industry Policy Papers No. 92 (Paris: OECD, 2020), https://read.oecd.org/10.1787/65234003-en?format=pdf, 1.

> **Box 7.2 Hedge funds and the carried interest controversy**
>
> One controversial tax concession in the United States is the capital gains treatment for so-called 'carried interest' of venture capital and private equity fund managers.[53] Fund managers may be remunerated with a carried interest in the profit of the fund, for example, 20 per cent of the profit. This is their main financial reward above a 2 per cent of assets management fee.
>
> There is no special tax concession for carried interest in US tax law. However, US income tax rules for venture capital entities have the result that the 20 per cent carried interest is treated as 'long-term capital gain' taxed at half the ordinary income tax rate. If this profit share were treated as remuneration for management services, it would be taxed at progressive rates, likely at the top US marginal income tax rate of 39.6 per cent.
>
> In 2008, Victor Fleischer published an influential law review article suggesting that the taxation of carried interest is a tax loophole that disguises labour income as capital gain, benefiting fund managers who are in the top 0.1 per cent of individual taxpayers, and costing billions in tax revenue.[54] More than a decade later, numerous legislative bills have been introduced into the US Congress aiming to remove the carried interest concession. President Obama and subsequently President Biden have supported its removal.[55] So far, the loophole remains.
>
> The 'carried interest' controversy illustrates the difficulty in characterisation of private equity compensation as a payment for services, or a reward for risk. It also demonstrates how a tax loophole can be generated through the interaction of ordinary tax law provisions – and how difficult it can be to eliminate from the tax code.

empirical studies into the effectiveness of R&D tax incentives suggest that there is a marginal benefit from the incentives – that is, the incentives create 'additionality', or extra R&D above what would have been done without the subsidy.[56]

Like all tax incentives, R&D incentives generate significant tax planning risks, for example, encouraging businesses to 'relabel' non-R&D business activity to attract the concession. Another possibility is that R&D incentives become yet another an element in multinational tax planning. Instead of carrying out new R&D, businesses may simply 'relocate' R&D activities into jurisdictions that offer more generous concessions. A related phenomenon is the adoption of lower tax rates on intellectual property in so-called patent boxes. We discuss these issues in Chapter 11.

---

[53] Donald Marples, *Taxation of Carried Interest* (Washington, DC: Congressional Research Service, 9 July 2020), https://crsreports.congress.gov/product/pdf/R/R46447.

[54] Victor Fleischer, 'Two and Twenty: Taxing Partnership Profits in Private Equity Firms' (2008) 83(1) *New York University Law Review* 1–59.

[55] Andrew R Sorkin, Jason Karaian, Sarah Kessler, Michael J de la Merced, Lauren Hirsch and Ephrat Livni, 'Private Equity's Favorite Tax Break May Be in Danger' *New York Times*, 12 June 2021, www.nytimes.com/2021/04/23/business/dealbook/carried-interest-biden.html.

[56] Appelt, Bajgar, Criscuolo and Galindo-Rueda, *The Effects of R&D Tax Incentives* (see n 52).

Table 7.2. Tax concessions for research and development

Country	Concession	Qualifying R&D	Rates	Limitation of benefits	Preferences for SMEs or new firms	Treatment of excess credits or deductions
Australia	R&D tax credit	Current R&D, depreciation of equipment	40 per cent (above corporate tax rate of 30 per cent)	Threshold and ceiling for R&D expenditure	45 per cent credit rate and refund for SMEs with turnover less than $20m	Carry-forward; refund for SMEs
France	R&D tax credit	Current R&D, depreciation of equipment	30 per cent (below €100m), 5 per cent above	Threshold for R&D expenditure	SME immediate refund	Carry-forward; refund after three years for large firms
Israel	Accelerated depreciation	Machinery and equipment, buildings	Two or four time standard rates	Deduction for subcontracted R&D	Na	Indefinite carry-forward
Japan	R&D tax credit	Current R&D, depreciation of equipment, buildings	10 per cent	Ceiling for R&D expenditure	Na	Na
Norway	R&D tax credit	Current R&D, machinery and equipment	18 per cent	Ceiling for R&D expenditure	20 per cent rate for SMEs	Refundable in following year
Spain	R&D and Innovation tax credit	Current R&D, machinery and equipment, intangibles	25 per cent; various other rates	Ceiling on R&D benefits and refund	Na	Refund, unlimited carry-forward
United Kingdom	R&D tax allowance or credit	Current R&D	130 per cent (SMEs), 11 per cent (large firms)	Ceiling on tax relief	130 per cent for SMEs	Refund, unlimited carry-forward

Source: Table B.1, Silvia Appelt, Matej Bajgar, Chiara Criscuolo and Fernando Galindo-Rueda, *The Effects of R&D Tax Incentives and Their Role in the Innovation Policy Mix*, OECD Science, Technology and Industry Policy Papers No 92 (Paris: OECD, 2020), https://read.oecd.org/10.1787/65234003-en?format=pdf

Directions for Corporate Tax Reform

The Business Cash Flow Tax

The revolution in optimal tax theory from the 1970s onwards generated a range of proposals for corporate tax reform in the academic and policy literature. The literature is vast and complex, and will not be fully explored, but some corporate tax reform proposals are outlined here. The 'idealised' versions of these proposals have not generally been enacted by governments, although some governments have enacted reforms inspired by these proposals.

Most corporate tax reform proposals aim to reform the tax base, not simply lower tax rates. They usually aim to retain, or even increase, tax on economic rents earned in corporations, while removing tax from the 'normal return' to capital or reducing the tax on investment. Another goal is to equalise the tax treatment of debt and equity, removing a significant bias that arises because interest on debt is deductible, but dividends are not.

The business cash flow tax permits full expensing and loss offset for the cost of capital or business investment. This shifts the base towards a consumption tax.[57] This recalls the debates about how to tax personal savings discussed in Chapter 6 and requires us to consider the underlying benchmark for the corporate tax: should it be the comprehensive income tax, or a consumption tax? In the international context, these proposals have been developed into a destination cash flow corporate tax (see Chapter 11).

In a VAT, wages are taxable and not eligible for input credits (unlike other business inputs). The business cash flow tax, in which all business investment is 'expensed', permits the deduction of wages from the base.

A cash flow tax is, in theory, simpler than an income tax because all base calculations are on a 'cash in, cash out' basis: the difference between payments and receipts is the tax base. This avoids the issue of how to treat capital expenditure and capital gains of businesses, which generates significant complexity and uncertainty for both taxpayers and the revenue.

The business cash flow tax base can be designated as business sales minus purchases of real assets and services, ignoring financial assets and services. This is sometimes called the 'real' or R-base cash flow tax.[58] Interest expense would not be deductible and asset depreciation would be replaced with a deduction for investment expenditure when incurred. An alternative cash flow tax base is called an RF cash flow tax. This aims to incorporate financial transactions – borrowing and lending – into the tax base, providing a deduction for costs of financing and including returns in income. Both the R and R+F cash flow taxes narrow the tax base by providing a deduction for the present value of investment costs. In theory, the cash flow tax applies to economic rents but exclude the

---

[57] Peter Wilson, *An Analysis of a Cash Flow Tax for Small Business*, New Zealand Treasury Working Paper 02/27 (Wellington: New Zealand Treasury, 2002), 3.
[58] Institute of Fiscal Studies, *The Structure and Reform of Direct Taxation* (London: IFS, 1978).

normal return and for this reason, for a given tax rate, it is considered to be more efficient than the corporate income tax. However, the narrower base of a cash flow tax would cause a revenue loss, so a higher tax rate is required to achieve a given revenue.

The United States has a history of proposals for enacting a business cash flow or consumption-based tax to replace the corporate income tax.[59] The Bush Tax Reform Advisory Panel of 2005 proposed the Growth and Investment Tax, a business-level cash flow tax under which capital expenditure and wages would be deductible, but not dividends and interest.[60] The main reason for the attractiveness of these proposals to US tax experts and policymakers is the lack of a federal broad-based consumption tax, like a VAT or GST, in contrast to most other successful tax states.

Allowance for Corporate Equity

The corporate income tax can be modified to tax economic rents through providing an allowance for corporate equity (ACE). This would address the distortion in the corporate income tax between debt and equity. An ACE system has been recommended for Canada,[61] by the Mirrlees Review in the United Kingdom,[62] and by the Tax and Transfer Policy Institute in Australia.[63]

The ACE is no longer in the theoretical realm. Belgium has adopted an ACE and several other countries have variants, while Austria is considering implementing an ACE.[64] It is not clear if these policy experiments will be stable; one reason is that for a given revenue yield, the ACE requires a higher tax rate because normal returns are exempted. However, the global trend for corporate tax rates is downward, so raising the corporate tax rate is difficult to achieve.

---

[59] Robert Hall and Alvin Rabushka *The Flat Tax* (Stanford, CA: Hoover Institution Press, 2007); see also the Bradford X-Tax: Bradford, *Untangling the Income Tax* (see n 18); David Bradford, 'Blueprint for International Tax Reform' (2001) 46 *Brooklyn Journal of International Law* 1449–63; John Due, 'Should the Corporation Income Tax Be Replaced by the Value Added Tax?' (1964) 57 *Proceedings of the Annual Conference on Taxation under the Auspices of the National Tax Association* 431–40.

[60] US President's Advisory Panel on Federal Tax Reform, *Simple, Fair and Pro-growth: Proposals to Fix America's Tax System* (2005), https://home.treasury.gov/system/files/131/Report-Fix-Tax-System-2005.pdf.

[61] Robin Boadway and Neil Bruce, 'A General Proposition on the Design of a Neutral Business Tax' (1984) 24 *Journal of Public Economics* 231–9.

[62] Mirrlees et al, *Tax by Design* (see n 1).

[63] Kristen Sobeck, Robert Breunig and Alex Evans, *Corporate Income Taxation in Australia: Theory, Current Practice and Future Policy Directions*, Tax and Transfer Policy Institute (TTPI) Policy Report No. 01-2022 (Canberra: TTPI, Australian National University, 2022), https://taxpolicy.crawford.anu.edu.au/sites/default/files/uploads/taxstudies_crawford_anu_edu_au/2022-03/ttpi_corporate_income_tax_report.pdf.

[64] Elke Asen, 'Austria Is Mulling an Allowance for Corporate Equity' *Tax Foundation* (23 July 2020), https://taxfoundation.org/austria-corporate-equity-tax-allowance/.

The ACE starts with the normal definition of corporate income and subtracts an allowance – a percentage of book equity – which is designed to reflect either the risk-free or the 'normal' rate of return. An alternative is to permit corporations to deduct an imputed rate of return (a notional risk-free return on capital) on their entire book asset base (debt plus equity). Actual interest is not deductible. This design of an ACE is, in theory, economically equivalent to an R-base cash flow tax. It also shares the drawbacks of that system, as it hurts heavily indebted firms and largely exempts the financial sector. The financial sector would need to be taxed separately. As a matter of transition, the ACE could be applied only to 'new' investment, to prevent a windfall benefit for 'old' investment.

To be fully neutral, the ACE system 'requires the transformation of the personal income tax into a personal consumption tax, which comprehensively exempts the normal return to capital'.[65] The Mirrlees Review recommended that the ACE at the corporate level be accompanied by a rate of return allowance that exempts the normal return in the personal income tax. One study found that an ACE would be welfare-improving if the reduction in corporate tax receipts was made up by increased consumption taxation; if, however, the corporate tax rate was increased to cover the cost, welfare was reduced.[66]

One challenge for designing an ACE is to identify the rate of return that determines the amount of the allowance. The risk-free or 'normal' return is generally proxied by a government bond rate, but corporations are very diverse and this is unlikely to be suitable for all businesses. An ACE may not fully equalise the tax treatment of debt and equity, but only mitigate the debt bias.[67] Because it essentially provides a new deduction in the corporate income tax system, the ACE is vulnerable to tax planning, and this seems to have been experienced in some countries, including Italy.[68] Concerns about the ACE benefiting multinational enterprises have resulted in a 'plethora of legislative amendments' to limit the risk.[69]

Comprehensive Business Income Tax

An alternative approach is the comprehensive business income tax (CBIT), which includes all income and permits deductions for expenses and

---

[65] Sijbren Cnossen, *Tackling Spillovers by Taxing Corporate Income in the European Union at Source*, CESifo Working Paper No 5790 (Munich: CESifo Group, 2015), 11.

[66] Ruud de Mooij and Michael P Devereux, 'Alternative Systems of Business Tax in Europe: An Applied Analysis of ACE and CBIT Reforms' (2011) 18 *International Tax and Public Finance* 93–120, https://link.springer.com/article/10.1007/s10797-010-9138-8.

[67] Ann Kayis-Kumar, 'Thin Capitalisation Rules: A Second-Best Solution to the Cross-Border Debt Bias?' (2015) 30(2) *Australian Tax Forum* 299–355.

[68] Massimo Bordignon, Silvia Giannini and Paolo Panteghini, *Reforming Business Taxation: Lessons from Italy*, SIEP Working Paper (Pavia: Società Italiana di Economia Pubblica, 2000), 13.

[69] Kayis-Kumar, 'Thin Capitalisation Rules' (see n 67).

depreciation of capital investment, except interest expense (the cost of financing). The CBIT broadens the corporate tax base and removes the debt-equity bias by eliminating interest deductibility. The corporate tax rate could be lowered as a CBIT can raise more revenue at a lower tax rate. However, the CBIT taxes the normal return and is therefore considered to be less efficient than approaches that seek to tax only the economic rent.

The CBIT was proposed by the US Treasury in the early 1990s.[70] It would be combined with full integration between the corporate and personal income tax by disallowing the deduction for interest costs and exempting dividend and interest income and capital gains at the personal level. It has the advantage of uniformity and sufficient revenue at a standard rate applying to all business entities, whether or not incorporated, and it can be combined with the dual income tax on personal savings and investment, discussed in Chapter 6.

However, the CBIT raises a number of complexities including the treatment of financial institutions and noncorporate firms. Economic depreciation for capital assets remains; this is a source of complexity but, on the other hand, also an additional policy lever. Some studies suggest that the best results may be gained by combining the CBIT with immediate expensing of business capital investment.[71] It may also be possible to combine an ACE and the CBIT to achieve financing neutrality (and lower corporate tax rates).[72] One proposal has supported a CBIT in the EU context to standardise the effective tax rate on various forms of capital income; this would create a flat tax rate on interest and dividend income, which is a form of dual income tax.[73] Withholding taxes on interest and dividends would be gradually raised to the dual income tax rate.

A Hybrid, Messy but Essential Tax

From its origins, debates about the corporate tax have concerned two main issues: first, who and what corporations represent; and second, 'whether the modern corporation was the central engine of productivity, which tax policy should reinforce, or whether it was an economic predator, which tax policy could and should tame'.[74]

In place of further tax rate cuts to stimulate competitiveness, governments today seem inclined to enact targeted incentives for the cost of business

---

[70] US Treasury, *Integration of the Individual and Corporate Tax Systems: Taxing Business Income Once* (Washington, DC: US Government Printing Office, 1992), 40.
[71] Doina Radulescu and Michael Stimmelmayr, *ACE vs CBIT: Which Is Better for Investment and Welfare?*, CESifo Working Paper No 1850 (Munich: CESifo, 2006), 3.
[72] de Mooij and Devereux, 'Alternative Systems of Business Tax in Europe' (see n 66).
[73] Cnossen, 'Tackling Spillovers by Taxing Corporate Income in the European Union at Source' (see n 65).
[74] W Elliot Brownlee *Federal Taxation in America* (Cambridge, UK: Cambridge University Press, 2004), 49–53, cited by Gravelle, 'The Corporate Income Tax' (see n 14), 79.

investment, especially on intangibles and R&D. These policies are especially attractive as governments seek to increase business investment in the COVID-19 pandemic. They shift corporate taxes along the spectrum from an income towards a consumption tax base, but it seems less likely that governments will proceed further to reform corporate tax systems by introducing an ACE or cash flow tax. As Edward Kleinbard observed, 'basically, theory is all very nice, but it turns out to be impossible in practice to distinguish among risk-adjusted normal returns, ex-post returns to risk, and true economic rents'.[75]

Ultimately, the corporate tax is a compromise of many policy goals. Despite this, it is an important element of the tax system for most successful tax states. The corporate tax raises some revenue and counters excessive market power and return in the corporate sector. It provides an essential bulwark to the personal income tax system and ensures some taxation of capital. It also gives tax administrators a useful handle for administration of the tax system. A risk of abandoning the corporate income tax is that economic rents of all sorts will be undertaxed. This matters for resource-producing countries, but also for all countries around the world where business generates super-profits from increasingly globalised and digitalised markets. We return to discuss the corporate tax in a globalised digitalised economy in Chapter 11.

---

[75] Edward Kleinbard, 'Capital Taxation in an Age of Inequality' (2017) 90 *Southern California Law Review* 590–682, 593.

8

Tax, Charity and Philanthropy

Whereas lands, tenements, rents, annuities, profits, hereditaments, goods, chattels, money and stocks of money have been heretofore given ... some for relief of aged, impotent and poor people, some for maintenance of sick and maimed soldiers and mariners, schools of learning, free schools and scholars in universities, some for repair of bridges, ports, havens, causeways, churches, seabanks, and highways, some for education and preferment of orphans, some for or towards relief, stock or maintenance for houses of correction, some for marriages of poor maids, some for supportation, aid and help of young tradesmen, handicraftsmen and persons decayed; and others for relief or redemption of prisoners or captives ...

Preamble to the *Statute of Charitable Uses* (Statute of Elizabeth), 1601

Charity and Government

The Boundaries of Tax and Charity

Tax law constitutes the boundaries of charities, the market and the state which operate in a 'jumbled mixed economy'.[1] Charities are a subset of the not-for-profit sector, sometimes called the 'third sector' to distinguish it from the market and the state. The charitable tax exemption sets the border of the tax state with the charitable sector. Its political, or ethical, justification recognises, as Evelyn Brody suggests, that charities are in a sense 'co-sovereign' with the state.[2]

The tax law also delineates the other important boundary around the charitable sector between public benefit and private gain. A not-for-profit organisation must not be carried on for private gain of its owners or members. To be eligible for the tax exemption, a charity or not-for-profit must carry out purposes that are of public benefit for the population or a class of it, as defined by law. Any surplus or 'profit' derived from activities or investments of a not-for-profit organisation must ultimately be applied to its defined purpose.

---

[1] Kathleen D McCarthy, 'Blurring the Boundaries. A Review Essay' (2010) 52 *Comparative Studies in Society and History* 939–46, 939.
[2] Evelyn Brody, 'Of Sovereignty and Subsidy: Conceptualizing the Charity Tax Exemption' (1997) 23 *Journal of Corporation Law* 585–630.

Most commonly, an exemption is provided from income and corporate taxation, while other concessions may apply, for example in consumption taxes such as the value added tax or in property tax. Taxation and regulatory regimes also establish prudential, activity and reporting restrictions for not-for-profits. Many governments also provide a concession for donations to charity, such as a tax deduction or credit. In so doing, the tax law reduces the cost to the individual and delivers a subsidy to the charitable purpose selected by the donor.

Governments and charities are similar, in that both deliver goods and services for public benefit. This includes many social goods such as education, health and social welfare (as discussed in Chapter 2). Charities also play an important role in civic, social, business and political life. The distinction between public and private goods in a charity law context was expressed by Matthew Harding as follows:[3]

> The idea behind this distinction is that private goods – education and health care are classic examples – have a character such that it is not possible for everyone to enjoy them at the same time, whereas public goods – clean air or a free society, for instance – have a character such that everyone may access and enjoy them simultaneously. A purpose might benefit the public according to the public benefit test of charity law either because it entails the provision of an excludable private good to a class of persons that is in some relevant sense a public class, or because it stands to realise a non-excludable public good.

The Size of the Not-for-profit Sector

The not-for-profit sector is large and diverse in most developed countries. The sector operates across a wide range of areas including education, social services, health care, housing and community development, culture and recreation, labour, business, the environment, religious congregations and international aid and development.[4] As well as charities, not-for-profits include community and sporting associations; clubs and societies in which members combine resources for their mutual benefit; political parties; unions and business organisations; local councils and quasi-governmental actors; and trading cooperatives and collectives.[5]

---

[3] Matthew Harding, *Charity Law and the Liberal State* (Cambridge, UK: Cambridge University Press, 2014), 14.
[4] Bernard Enjolras, Lester M Salamon, Karl Henrik Sivesind and Annette Zimmer, *The Third Sector as a Renewable Resource for Europe: Concepts, Impacts, Challenges and Opportunities* (London: Palgrave Macmillan, 2018), 57. See also the Johns Hopkins Comparative Nonprofit Sector Project (1991–2017), http://ccss.jhu.edu/research-projects/comparative-nonprofit-sector-project/, accessed 16 March 2022.
[5] David Moore, Katerina Hadzi-Miceva and Nilda Bullain, 'A Comparative Overview of Public Benefit Status in Europe' (2008) 11(1) *International Journal of Not-for-Profit Law* 5–35, 5; Anne-Marie Piper (ed.), *Charity Law: Jurisdictional Comparisons* (London: Thomson Reuters, 2012).

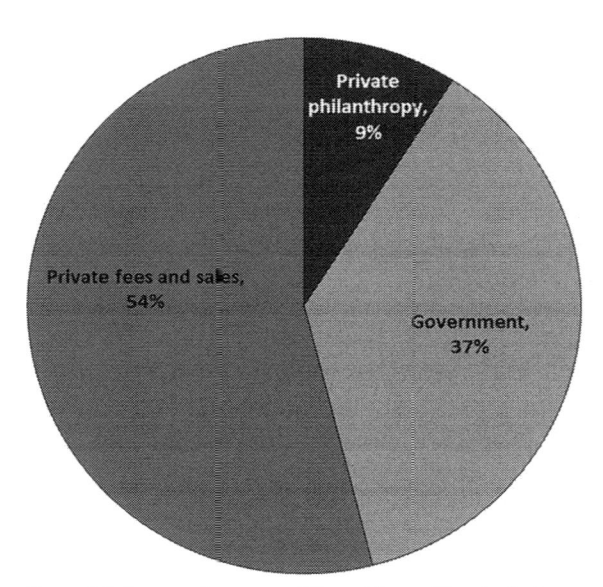

Figure 8.1 Sources of revenue of the not-for-profit sector in Europe, 2014
Source: Bernard Enjolras, Lester M Salamon, Karl Henrik Sivesind and Annette Zimmer, *The Third Sector as a Renewable Resource for Europe: Concepts, Impacts, Challenges and Opportunities* (London: Palgrave Macmillan, 2018), Figure 3.4.

It is estimated that the United States has 1.5 million charities contributing an estimated $1 trillion to the economy, about 5 per cent of gross domestic product.[6] Charities reported $1.4 billion in revenue and nearly $2.6 billion in assets in 2009.[7] Charities in Europe employ more than 7 per cent of the workforce, nearly half as many employees as the government, while the entire not-for-profit sector employ 10 per cent of the workforce. There were 29 million full-time equivalent workers in the sector, of which 45 per cent were paid and 55 per cent were volunteers. This was the same size as the workforce in each of the trade and manufacturing sectors – so the not-for-profit sector has been described as an 'enormous economic engine'.[8]

The not-for-profit sector derives revenues from a variety of sources. While private philanthropy attracts most attention, it accounts for a relatively small share of revenues for the sector. Figure 8.1 shows the main sources of revenue of the not-for-profit sector in Europe. Philanthropy comprises 9 per cent of sector revenue in Europe, fees and sales of goods and services, membership dues and investment income account for 54 per cent, and government grants,

---

[6] National Center for Charitable Statistics (US), 'The Nonprofit Sector Brief 2019' (18 June 2020), https://nccs.urban.org/project/nonprofit-sector-brief.
[7] Molly F Sherlock and Jane G Gravelle, *An Overview of the Nonprofit and Charitable Sector* (Washington, DC: Congressional Research Service, 2009), http://digitalcommons.ilr.cornell.edu/key_workplace/685.
[8] Enjolras et al, *The Third Sector as a Renewable Resource for Europe* (see n 4).

contracts and reimbursements for services make up the balance.[9] In the United States, revenue from fees and services made up about half of total revenue of not-for-profits; government grants provided about 30 per cent of revenue and about 20 per cent came from donations and investment income.[10]

Organisations in the not-for-profit sector operate in an array of legal entity forms, including unincorporated associations, corporations of various forms, cooperatives, mutual associations, trusts and funds. The diversity of the sector's operations, legal form, services and revenues poses a challenge for not-for-profit taxation and regulation.

The Tax Privilege of Charity

Origins and Justification of the Charitable Exemption

The law and regulation of charity in the United Kingdom and other common law countries predates the income tax law. The definition of 'charity' originates in the Preamble to the English *Statute of Charitable Uses of 1601* (the Statute of Elizabeth) refined by subsequent case law. The main purposes are relief of poverty, religion, education and other purposes 'of public benefit'.

The establishment of a formal charity law by Queen Elizabeth I was an act of governmental control, seeking to encourage such private activity for public benefit while establishing the rules under which it should be conducted. The Statute of Elizabeth was intended to regulate charitable trusts and organisations against 'a background of fraud and neglect by charitable trustees'.[11] The Statute of Elizabeth was also an element of the Poor Law that was intended to regulate poverty relief, which had been previously managed by local governments.[12] It has been suggested that the government hoped that private giving would finance poverty relief.[13]

Two centuries later, when the income tax law was introduced, it established the boundaries of charitable activity through the grant of the 'privilege' of exemption.[14] In the United States, Canada, Australia and New Zealand, a tax exemption for charities was included from the earliest income tax law at the

---

[9] Ibid., 58.
[10] Sherlock and Gravelle, *An Overview of the Nonprofit and Charitable Sector* (see n 7).
[11] Harding, *Charity Law* (see n 3), 9; Gareth Jones, *History of the Law of Charity 1532–1827* (Cambridge, UK: Cambridge University Press, 1969), chapter 3; James J Fishman, 'Encouraging Charity in a Time of Crisis: The Poor Laws and the Statute of Charitable Uses of 1601' (2005), http://dx.doi.org/10.2139/ssrn.868394.
[12] Rhodri Davies, *Public Good by Private Means: How Philanthropy Shapes Britain* (London: Charitable Aid Foundation Alliance Publishing Trust, 2015).
[13] Paul Slack, *The English Poor Law 1531–1782* (Cambridge, UK: Cambridge University Press, 1995).
[14] Harding, *Charity Law* (see n 3), 9.

turn of the twentieth century. As the century progressed, the delivery of social welfare was largely taken over by governments. Charities continued to operate many activities, including schools and private hospitals, but these were eclipsed by the extent of state provision. This was most obviously the case regarding income support for poverty relief. However, by the end of the century, charities and other not-for-profits had again expanded their activities, as they took on service provision of many social welfare functions. The ancient role of charities in 'relieving the burdens of government' became more important,[15] as governments sought to limit the growth of the tax state (see Chapter 3). The big difference from earlier times was that charities were primarily funded by government for the outsourced delivery of health, education and homelessness services.

The growth of funding directed to not-for-profits through government procurement processes raises important questions about the accountability and control of public expenditure, as is the case for all outsourced service delivery. In providing these services, not-for-profits operate to alleviate poverty but they have little scope to do broader public policy work to address poverty or other social needs in a systematic way.[16] They may also be constrained from engaging in public or political debate about social welfare.

The public welfare role of charities is one important justification for the charitable tax exemption. Another justification is a political concept of public benefit, to support pluralism in a liberal democratic society.[17] Pluralism may refer to the decentralisation of decision-making power to citizens, the recognition of minority preferences or a more diverse economic and social life that is encouraged by the tax exemption.[18] Other social values arguably promoted by the exemption include individual freedom, initiative and responsibility through reinforcing socially desirable conduct, enshrining the independence of the charitable sector,[19] and promoting altruism.[20]

One approach to estimating the fiscal cost of the charitable exemption is to treat it as a government subsidy to support charity in delivering public

---

[15] John D Colombo and Mark A Hall, *The Charitable Tax Exemption* (Boulder, CO: Westview Press, 1995), 5.

[16] Michael Chesterman, 'Foundations of Charity Law in the New Welfare State' (1999) 62(3) *Modern Law Review* 333–49; Holger Schoneville, 'Poverty and the Transformation of the Welfare (State) Arrangement: Food Banks and the Charity Economy in Germany' (2018) 16(2) *Social Work and Society* https://ejournals.bib.uni-wuppertal.de/index.php/sws/article/view/570.

[17] Harding, *Charity Law* (see n 3); Lawrence M Stone, 'Federal Tax Support of Charities and Other Exempt Organizations: The Need for a National Policy' (1968) 20 *University of Southern California School of Law Tax Institute* 27, 45.

[18] David A Brennen, 'A Diversity Theory of Charitable Tax Exemption: Beyond Efficiency, through Critical Race Theory, toward Diversity' (2006) 4(1) *Pittsburgh Tax Review* 1–54.

[19] David G Duff, 'Tax Treatment of Charitable Contributions in Canada: Theory, Practice, and Reform' (2004) 42(1) *Osgoode Hall Law Journal* 47, 50–70, 63.

[20] Rob Atkinson, 'Altruism in Nonprofit Organizations' (1990) 31 *Boston College Law Review* 501–639.

goods.[21] The concept of a 'tax expenditure', introduced in Chapter 3, could be applied to estimate the revenue forgone from the exemption. The revenue forgone will depend on how tightly the definition of charity is drawn and whether any limits are set on its application to various revenue sources.

However, the benchmark for estimating a tax expenditure in the income tax is taxable *private* income. It is not straightforward to apply this benchmark to charities that have a purpose of *public* benefit, with a non-distribution rule. The difficulty of applying the benchmark and estimating the revenue foregone under the tax exemption means that the charitable exemption is not treated as a tax expenditure in the United States or in Australia.

Since the 1990s, governments have paid renewed attention to the regulation of charities and the not-for-profit sector. This led to significant reforms in some countries including legislating a definition of charity for the first time in Australia and the United Kingdom. Independent regulators have been established in the United Kingdom, New Zealand and Australia.[22] Despite all this policy attention, the exemption from tax for charities and not-for-profits has remained largely intact.

Commercial Activities of Not-for-profits

The expansion of not-for-profits into activities that generate fees for goods and services has blurred the boundary between charitable activities, which are exempt, and commercial and for-profit activities, which are normally taxable.[23] Weisbrod observed that a commercial charity 'sounds like a paradox'.[24] The literature suggests several possible concerns about charities engaging in commerce, including risks to reputation, 'mission drift', financial or capital risks and operational challenges.[25]

---

[21] Miranda Perry Fleischer, 'Subsidizing Charity Liberally' in Matthew Harding (ed.), *Research Handbook on Not-for-Profit Law* (New York: Edward Elgar, 2018), 418–43; Rob Atkinson, 'Theories of the Federal Income Tax Exemption for Charities: Thesis, Antithesis and Synthesis' in Paul Bater, Frits W Hondius and Penina Kessler Lieber (eds.), *The Tax Treatment of NGOs: Legal, Fiscal, and Ethical Standards for Promoting NGOs and Their Activities* (The Hague: Kluwer Law International, 2004), 253–84; Kerrie Sadiq and Catherine Richardson, 'Tax Concessions for Charities: Competitive Neutrality, the Tax Base and "Public Goods" Choice' (2010) 25(4) *Australian Tax Forum* 401–16.

[22] Matthew Harding, Ann O'Connell and Miranda Stewart (eds.), *Not-for-Profit Law: Theoretical and Comparative Perspectives* (Cambridge, UK: Cambridge University Press, 2014); Harding, *Research Handbook on Not-for-Profit Law* (see n 21).

[23] Joyce Chia and Miranda Stewart, 'Doing Business to Do Good: Should We Tax the Business Profits of Not for Profits?' (2012) 33 *Adelaide Law Review* 335–70.

[24] Burton A Weisbrod, 'The Nonprofit Mission and Its Financing: Growing Links between Nonprofits and the Rest of the Economy' in Burton A Weisbrod (ed.), *To Profit or Not to Profit: The Commercial Transformation of the Nonprofit Sector* (Cambridge, UK: Cambridge University Press, 2000), 1–22, 11–12.

[25] See, e.g. Brenda Zimmerman and Raymond Dart, *Charities Doing Commercial Ventures: Societal and Organizational Implications* (Toronto: Trillium Foundation, 1998), chapter 3, http://epe.lac-bac.gc.ca/100/200/300/cprn/english/cdc_e.pdf.

Allowing not-for-profits to generate untaxed business profits raises concerns about eroding the tax base.[26] Another concern is to prevent tax avoidance by commercial entities or individuals shifting otherwise taxable activity into an untaxed form. Governments may also wish to ensure horizontal equity or competitive neutrality in a 'level playing field' between tax-exempt charitable businesses and taxable commercial businesses.

One policy response is to levy income tax on revenue from commercial activities of charities. Cases that raised the issue in Australia and the United States, and the US policy response, are discussed in Box 8.1. The rationale may be to prevent a charity being diverted from its altruistic goals so that decisions begin to be made on a commercial rather than a charitable basis.[27] However, defining commercial activities of a charity that should be so taxed is not straightforward. For example, many fees for goods and services delivered by charities are 'mission-linked', that is, connected to the service or activity that is at the core of the organisation's purpose of public benefit. Charitable hospitals, housing organisations or schools may charge fees or co-payments for educational, health and housing services that are provided by them. Some commercial activities are *de minimis* or marginal activities, for example, the sale of postcards in a cathedral.[28]

The most controversial question is whether the exemption causes an uneven playing field with taxable businesses. Many US scholars argue that the charitable tax exemption should not affect the behaviour of an organisation when deciding how to set its prices and minimise its costs; it is in the interests of charities to charge the full market price, so as to generate more revenue to fund charitable activities. Imposing a tax on 'unrelated' business activities may encourage charities to confine their commercial activities to 'related' areas, causing disproportionate harm to competitors in those areas, rather than carrying on other businesses.[29] In Australia, three policy reviews since the 1990s have concluded that the tax exemption for trading income of not-for-profits does not violate competitive neutrality sufficiently to warrant such a policy response, and an attempt to introduce such a tax failed.[30]

It has been observed that, 'with the decline of the welfare state, charitable organisations are expected to do more with the same resources. Reliance on

---

[26] Sadiq and Richardson, 'Tax Concessions for Charities' (see n 21).
[27] Zimmerman and Dart, *Charities Doing Commercial Ventures* (see n 25).
[28] Raymond Dart, 'Charities in Business, Business in Charities, Charities and Business – Mapping and Understanding the Complex Non-profit/Business Interface' (2004) 18 *Philanthropist* 181–98, 182–3; Chitvan Trivedi, 'A Social Entrepreneurship Bibliography' (2010) 19 *Journal of Entrepreneurship* 81–5.
[29] Rose-Ackermann, 'Unfair Competition' (see n 32).
[30] Chia and Stewart, 'Doing Business to Do Good' (see n 23).

Box 8.1 Taxing the business income of charities

A corporation that carried out only business activities but was successful in obtaining a charitable tax exemption was the subject of an Australian case, *Federal Commissioner of Taxation* v *Word Investments Ltd* (2008) 236 CLR 204 (High Court of Australia). The corporation operated a funeral business for profit and did not itself carry on any charitable activities. However, under the terms of its constitution, it was required to, and did, distribute all profits to an affiliated missionary organisation which was a tax-exempt religious charity. Religious charities are not eligible to receive deductible gifts in Australia (in contrast to many other countries). Therefore, the company sought an exemption on the basis that it was, itself, a charity.

The High Court upheld the applicant's eligibility for the charitable exemption because the objects listed in its constitution were directed towards a sole purpose of 'advancing religion in a charitable sense'. The court held that 'Word endeavoured to make a profit, but only in aid of its charitable purposes. To point to the goal of profit and isolate it as the relevant purpose is to create a false dichotomy between characterisation of an institution as commercial and characterisation of it as charitable'.[31] The case comes close to an acceptance that passing income to another eligible charity is sufficient for eligibility.

A similar 'destination of income' approach was taken by the US courts in *CF Mueller Co. v Commissioner*, 190 F.2d 120 (3rd Cir. 1951). The tax-exempt New York University owned a macaroni factory that passed all of its profits to the university and contributed to funding the NYU Law School among other things.[32] This case led to the introduction of the US 'unrelated business income tax' or UBIT in the 1950s.

The UBIT applies to tax business income of a charity that is unrelated to its charitable mission, less attributable deductions.[33] The merits of the UBIT have been widely debated.[34] The US experience suggests that introducing a UBIT does a relatively poor job of protecting the tax base. The rule requires line drawing between passive investment and business activity and generates tax planning margins, including the strategic allocation of business expenses to 'unrelated' profits to reduce the tax liability. Despite the long history of UBIT in the United States, other governments, including Australia, have not enacted a similar rule, although some deny charitable status for not-for-profits that do commercial activity.

---

[31] *Federal Commissioner of Taxation* v *Word Investments* (2008) 236 CLR 204, 219 (High Court of Australia).

[32] *CF Mueller Co.* v *Commissioner*, 190 F.2d 120 (3rd Cir. 1951) (US); Weisbrod, 'The Nonprofit Mission and Its Financing' (see n 24), 11–12; and see Ian Murray, 'Charitable Fundraising through Commercial Activities: The Final Word or a Pyrrhic Victory?' (2008) 11(2) *Journal of Australian Taxation*, 138–207, 193–5.

[33] Internal Revenue Code (US) § 511; Ethan Stone, 'Adhering to the Old Line: Uncovering the History and Political Function of the Unrelated Business Income Tax' (2005) 54 *Emory Law Journal* 1475–556.

[34] John D Colombo, 'Commercial Activity and Charitable Tax Exemption' (2002) 44 *William and Mary Law Review* 487–567; Boris I Bittker and George K Rahdert, 'The Exemption of Nonprofit Organizations from Federal Income Taxation' (1976) 85 *Yale Law Journal* 299–358; Henry B Hansmann, 'Unfair Competition and the Unrelated Business Income Tax' (1989) 75 *Virginia*

donations alone will, in many cases, be insufficient'.[35] The best approach to minimising the commercialisation of charity is enforcing the delivery of genuine public benefit rather than limiting the approach to raising funds.

Social Enterprise

A social enterprise may be loosely described as a commercial organisation that aims to generate a profit alongside, or by carrying out, a 'social' or public benefit purpose.[36] The growth of digital platforms for crowd funding has made non-traditional market or social enterprises easier to establish, and the challenge of identifying the taxability (or potential tax deductibility) of contributions more difficult. The concept of 'social enterprise' became popular in the early 2000s and has been described as a 'site of contestation' about 'relationships between 'the social' and 'the economic'.[37] Social enterprises are 'hybrids', combining 'diverse elements, such as goals of profit and of social value creation, elements which were traditionally housed in separate, and separately taxed, entities, or to blur the lines among public sector, private for-profit and charitable sectors'.[38] Some types of social enterprise aim to generate lower profits than a normal business while achieving other goals, such as environmentally sustainable activities or organic and fair trade farming.

The United States has seen the most innovative use of business entities to achieve social purposes.[39] New hybrid entities, such as L3C 'low-profit' companies and 'B' (benefit) corporations, are intended to be more flexible than charitable entities in permitting commercial purposes and activity, while also seeking to embed social, environmental and other public good purposes in the business. To date, as Mayer and Ganahl explain, 'none of these hybrid entities, whether the L3C, the benefit corporation, the flexible purpose corporation, or the other forms in the United States and in Europe, enjoy the tax

---

Law Review 605–35; Susan Rose-Ackermann, 'Unfair Competition and Corporate Income Taxation' (1982) 34 *Stanford Law Review* 1017–39; Richard Steinberg, '"Unfair" Competition by Nonprofits and Tax Policy' (1991) 44 *National Tax Journal* 351–64; James R Hines Jr, 'Nonprofit Business Activity and the Unrelated Business Income Tax' in James M Poterba (ed.), *Tax Policy and the Economy: Vol 13* (Cambridge, MA: MIT Press, 1999), 57–84.

[35] *Federal Commissioner of Taxation v Word Investments Ltd* (2006) 64 ATR 482 (Federal Court of Australia), 497.

[36] Janelle A Kerlin, 'A Comparative Analysis of the Global Emergence of Social Enterprise' (2010) 21 *Voluntas* 162–79.

[37] Jo Barraket and Nicholas Collyer, 'Mapping Social Enterprise in Australia: Conceptual Debates and Their Operational Implications' (2010) 16(2) *Third Sector Review* 11–28, 25; see Trivedi, 'A Social Entrepreneurship Bibliography' (see n 28).

[38] Sheila Killian and Philip O'Regan, 'Taxation and Social Enterprise: Constraint or Incentive for the Common Good' (2018) 10(1) *Journal of Social Entrepreneurship* 1–18, https://doi.org/10.1080/19420676.2018.1517103.

[39] Lloyd Hitosi Mayer and Joseph R Ganahl, 'Taxing Social Enterprise' (2014) 66(2) *Stanford Law Review* 387–442.

preferences that governments commonly extend to charitable nonprofits'.[40] They conclude that it would be a mistake to extend tax exemptions to social enterprises because balancing public benefit and flexibility would be too difficult:

> either the federal government would not be able to ensure that the recipient hybrids would in fact provide the public benefits that justify providing these kinds of tax benefits in the first place, or the restrictions the federal governments or state governments would have to impose to ensure such public benefits would undermine the very flexibility that is the main attraction of these hybrid forms.[41]

Tax planning can achieve a significantly reduced tax burden, for example, through the combination of taxable and tax-exempt entities. One possible approach is to permit joint ventures between charitable tax-exempt organisations and business enterprises.

Tax and Philanthropy

The Deduction for Charitable Giving

The income tax deduction for philanthropic giving reduces the tax payable by individuals and corporations that donate to eligible charities. In a system with progressive income tax rates, a deduction provides a larger tax concession to high-income earners than to low-income earners. Some country tax laws also provide an exclusion from capital gains tax for donations of property and deductions or exemptions from wealth or inheritance taxes for charitable donations.

A charitable gift is required by law to be a genuine gift and not be made by the taxpayer in the expectation of benefit or to earn income. However, the voluntary and discretionary character of a charitable donation suggests it is a form of personal consumption that would not be deductible in the comprehensive income tax.[42] The philanthropic tax deduction may be analysed as a subsidy provided by the government to encourage charitable giving and therefore, indirectly, to support the charitable sector. The state effectively contributes a portion of the donation equal to the tax rate.

In contrast to the charitable exemption, the revenue forgone from the philanthropic deduction can be relatively easily estimated as a tax expenditure. The US Treasury estimated the revenue forgone from deductibility of charitable gifts by individuals and corporations to non-profit educational institutions, hospitals and other purposes to exceed $45 billion in 2019.[43] This

---

[40] Ibid., 403.
[41] Ibid., 422.
[42] David G Duff, 'Tax Treatment of Charitable Contributions in a Personal Income Tax: Lessons from Theory and Canadian Experience' in Harding et al, *Not for-Profit Law* (see n 22), 204.
[43] US Treasury, *Analytical Perspectives on the Budget* (2020), chapter 16, table 16-3, 195.

ranked in the top 10 largest tax expenditures in the United States. Estimates of what economists call the 'price-elasticity of giving' vary widely but indicate that the deduction does encourage philanthropy.[44]

An important justification for the tax deduction, as for the charitable exemption, is to support a wide set of social and civil society choices by individuals. However, governments have expressed concern from time to time about the removal of the expenditure from government supervision and control. In the nineteenth century, William Gladstone, Chancellor of the Exchequer of Britain, argued that the deduction was undemocratic, opaque and inadequately regulated, stating: 'If we have the right to give public money, we have no right to give it in the dark. We are bound to give it with discrimination; bound to give it with supervision; bound as a constitutional Parliament, if the Hospitals are to receive a grant, to bring them within some degree of control'.[45] Gladstone failed in his attempt to limit the charitable tax deduction.

The deduction gives high-income donors a higher benefit and thereby privileges their choices about the organisations or purposes that should receive more funds. The pluralist justification for the deduction may be undermined by the 'upside down' nature of the subsidy. Canada has replaced the deduction with a tax credit for donations to eligible charities, producing a more equal result.[46] The credit could be designed to be 'refundable' so that if it exceeds the tax owed, the individual receives a grant. Another approach would be for the government to directly provide a matching grant of all or some of the donation.

As a matter of principle, if we accept that the 'taxpayer-voter' participates in deciding what government should spend taxes on, as discussed in Chapter 2, the philanthropic deduction accords the votes of high-income donors more weight than the votes of low-income donors and completely 'disenfranchises' the lowest income donors who pay no tax.[47]

Private Foundations and 'Big Philanthropy'

It has long been possible for charitable trusts with specific purposes to be established in common law jurisdictions. Tax-exempt trusts or foundations have become an increasingly important means by which wealthy people manage their donations to charitable purposes. Donor-controlled funds are

---

[44] Duff, 'Tax Treatment of Charitable Contributions in a Personal Income Tax' (see n 42), citing John Peloza and Piers Steel, 'The Price Elasticities of Charitable Contributions: A Meta-Analysis' (2005) 24 Journal of Public Policy and Marketing 260–72.

[45] David Owen, English Philanthropy 1660–1960 (Cambridge, MA: Harvard University Press, 1964).

[46] David G Duff, 'Charitable Contributions and the Personal Income Tax: Evaluating the Canadian Credit' in Jim Phillips, Bruce Chapman and David Stevens (eds.), Between State and Market: Essays on Charities Law and Policy in Canada (Montreal: McGill-Queen's University Press, 2001), 407–56.

[47] Duff, 'Tax Treatment of Charitable Contributions in a Personal Income Tax' (see n 42), 217.

widespread in the United States, where they have been described as a 'unique American answer to the problem of excess wealth in a society with limited income redistribution'.[48] In 2010, US foundations were estimated to control more than $600 billion in assets.[49]

Many famous private foundations were established a century ago, including the Carnegie Foundation in 1911, the Rockefeller Foundation in 1913 and the Ford Foundation in 1936. These foundations provide significant public benefit; nonetheless, they remain under private direction to a very large degree. As directors of the foundation, family members may have a greater voice in determining the public good than ordinary people who do not have such resources. The highly visible role of 'billionaire philanthropists' is epitomised by the Bill and Melinda Gates Foundation, established in 2000. The Gates Foundation comprises two charitable trusts now with US$50 billion in endowment, with Bill and Melinda Gates and Warren Buffett as trustees.[50] The foundation reports grants in excess of $54 billion since its inception, about $5 billion each year.

One writer describes the largest US foundations as 'immense tax-exempt private corporations dealing in good works' where the decision about 'good' is made by the controllers of the foundation.[51] This could be perceived as a challenge to democratic governance. Alternatively, it may protect the use of funds for public benefit from corrupt or incompetent governments or enable provision of international public goods such as the elimination of disease which nation states have failed to achieve. Emmanuel Saez and Gabriel Zucman take the former view and propose that donor-controlled funds such as the Bill and Melinda Gates Foundation should be subject to a progressive annual wealth tax 'until the time that such funds have been spent or moved fully out of the control of the donor'.[52]

Private foundations in the United States are subject to regulatory requirements including a 5 per cent distribution requirement and a 2 per cent 'excise' tax each year.[53] The minimum distribution requirement was introduced in

---

[48] Helmut K Anheier and Stefan Toepler, 'Philanthropic Foundations. An International Perspective' in Helmut K Anheier and Stefan Toepler (eds.), *Private Funds, Public Purpose. Philanthropic Foundations in International Perspective* (New York: Kluwer, 1999), 3–23.

[49] Paolo Barbetta, Luca Colombo and Gilberto Turati, 'Regulating European Grant-Making Foundations. Lessons from the USA Experience?' (2015) 37(5) *Journal of Policy Modeling* 763–81.

[50] Bill and Melinda Gates Foundation, 'Foundation Fact Sheet', www.gatesfoundation.org/about/foundation-fact-sheet, accessed 16 March 2022.

[51] Joanne Barkan, 'Big Philanthropy vs Democracy' (2013) 60(4) *Dissent* 47–54. See further Robert Reich, Chiara Cordelli and Lucy Bernholz (eds.), *Philanthropy in Democratic Societies: History, Institutions, Values* (Chicago: University of Chicago Press, 2016).

[52] Emmanuel Saez and Gabriel Zucman, *Progressive Wealth Taxation*, Brookings Papers on Economic Activity (Washington, DC: Brookings Institution, Fall 2019), 437–533.

[53] Carolyn Levine and Richard Sansing, 'The Private Foundation Minimum Distribution Requirement and Public Policy' (2014) 36(1) *Journal of the American Taxation Association* 165–80.

1969 in response to evidence that foundations tended to accumulate assets without distributing sufficient funds.[54] Internal governance and donation decisions should be transparent, consistent with the expectations for transparency of charitable activities and of government budgeting, for public benefit.

In the last two decades, the US model of private foundations has spread to other countries, as governments seek to encourage the wealthy to increase philanthropy, with the carrot of retaining family control over donor decisions. In Australia, legislation for private ancillary funds was introduced in 2001 and the number and size of funds has been steadily growing; today, annual donations are about AU$2.5 billion and funds have an average size of $3 million. These funds operate by distributing grants to other charitable organisations, usually with a minimum distribution requirement, such as 5 per cent of asset value. The initial contribution of assets into the foundation is tax-deductible, delivering a substantial upfront benefit to high-income or wealthy individuals.

Charities, Tax Avoidance and Evasion

One reason that Prime Minister Gladstone sought to end the tax exemption for charities was the ability it offered taxpayers of the Victorian era to avoid taxation by 'covenanting' a bequest at a future time to a named charity.[55] There is an inevitable risk of tax avoidance where concessional tax treatment is made available to taxpayers. As the not-for-profit sector has grown, and wealth inequality has increased (see Chapter 6), the opportunity and temptation for tax avoidance provided by charitable exemptions and deductions have also increased. Donors may extract private benefit in fees or property or fail to distribute for charitable purposes. There are examples of charities agreeing to participate in tax shelters established by private individuals for their own benefit. For example, a charity might be a tax-exempt counterparty to a transaction, 'monetising' a portion of their tax exemption in exchange for enabling a deduction for the taxpayer.[56]

In 2009, the Organisation for Economic Co-operation and Development (OECD) prepared a report on tax evasion and fraud through charities, which it stated was a serious and increasing risk in many countries.[57] The report

---

[54] Barbetta et al, 'Regulating European Grant-Making Foundations' (see n 49), 779, describe prudential requirements in Italy and Germany that do not always have clear requirements for distributions.

[55] Davies, *Public Good by Private Means* (see n 12), Kindle Book, Loc 2425-6; Owen, *English Philanthropy 1660–1960* (see n 45).

[56] See, e.g. Daryll K Jones, 'When Charity Aids Tax Shelters' (2001) 12(4) *Florida Tax Review* 770–830.

[57] OECD, *Report on Abuse of Charities for Money-Laundering and Tax Evasion*. Tax Crimes and Money Laundering Sub-Group of Working Party No. 8 (Paris: OECD, 2009), www.oecd.org/tax/exchange-of-tax-information/42232037.pdf, based on information provided by governments of 19 countries.

presents many examples of the use of a charity for evasion or fraud, including participation in a scheme for the personal benefit of organisers or directors; concealing salaried employees as volunteers; issuing receipts for payments that are not true donations; and manipulating the value of donated assets. The art market is notorious for the last, as wealthy taxpayers seek to donate artworks or other valuable property to public galleries, universities or other tax-exempt or governmental institutions.

In a Canadian case concerning abuse of tax credits for an art donation program, the court found in favour of the Minister of National Revenue.[58] In this case, Mr Roher had participated, with others, in an art donation program in which he paid CAN$383,937 into the program and claimed $2.3 million in donation tax credits over the period 1998 to 2004. The donee institutions were complicit in providing a donation receipt for more than twice the monetary contribution. The Federal Court of Appeal affirmed that the market value of donated art was the monetary contribution, not the stated value of each item of art, thereby limiting the tax credit to the money actually donated.

The Globalisation of Charity

Tax and Charity across National Borders

Charities and philanthropy now reach across national borders in a global 'third sector' that compares in size to some states. The commercialisation and globalisation of charity are interconnected, as illustrated by the title of the bestseller, *Philanthrocapitalism: How Giving Can Save the World*.[59] The not-for-profit sector operates across borders in two main ways: organisations may do activities across borders and charitable gifts may be donated across borders.[60]

There is a lack of good data about the level of global philanthropic financial flows.[61] However, more than 100 philanthropic foundations from around the world, of which the Gates Foundation is the largest, delivered a total of US$24 billion to support the United Nations Sustainable Development Goals in the period 2013–15.[62] The growth of global charitable and philanthropic entities

---

[58] *Roher v Canada* (2019) 2019 FCA 313; affirming 2019 TCC 17 (Tax Court of Canada).
[59] Matthew Bishop and Michael Green, *Philanthrocapitalism: How Giving Can Save the World* (New York: Bloomsbury Press, 2009).
[60] Ineke A Koele, *International Taxation of Philanthropy: Removing Tax Obstacles for International Charities* (Amsterdam: IBFD Publications, 2007), 1–2.
[61] See, e.g. the Special Issue on Global Philanthropy (2011) 13(1–2) *The International Journal of Not-for-Profit Law*.
[62] OECD, *Private Philanthropy for Development* (Paris: OECD Publishing, 2018), https://doi.org/10.1787/9789264085190-en. Larger estimates by other organisations aggregate cross-country flows and include remittances, e.g. the estimate of US$64 billion from the Hudson Institute Center for Global Prosperity, *The Index of Global Philanthropy and Remittances 2016* (Washington, DC: Hudson Institute, 2017).

has been called a 'global associational revolution'.[63] This may have been prompted by an apparent crisis of nation states who seem unable 'to cope on [their] own with the social welfare, developmental, and environmental problems that face nations today'.[64] It has also been stimulated by enhanced communications and an expansion in the middle class in developed countries.

Historically, English charity law did not confine 'benefit to the public' territorially. The foundational British case, *Commissioners for Special Purposes of the Income Tax* v *Pemsel* [1891] AC 531 (House of Lords) upheld a charitable trust for 'maintaining, supporting, and advancing the missionary establishments among heathen nations of the Protestant Episcopal Church'. Another interesting example is an Australian case that upheld a trust to fund a prize for a musical competition between composers from Austria (in Europe); the court held that music was of 'universal interest' so that its advancement abroad had 'a sufficient nexus with the benefit of a substantial section of our public'.[65]

Many governments have legislated to limit the exemption and philanthropic deduction to charities within national borders, with the common exception of to international organisations that provide benefits such as disaster or poverty relief, international aid or defence. In contrast, the United States allows a deduction for donations by individuals to charitable foundations that donate overseas on certain conditions of domestic control.[66]

Dissolving the Borders of Charity in the European Union

We can gain an insight into the consequences for the tax state of transnational charity by considering a series of cases about charities crossing borders in the European Union. These cases applied the freedoms of the Treaty on the

---

[63] Lester M Salamon, Helmut K Anheier, Regina List, Stefan Toepler, S. Wojciech Sokolowski et al (eds.), *Global Civil Society: Dimensions of the Nonprofit Sector* (Baltimore, MD: Johns Hopkins Center for Civil Society Studies, 1999), 3, 4; and see Koele, *International Taxation of Philanthropy* (see n 60), 4.

[64] Lester M Salamon, Helmut K Anheier et al, 'Civil Society in Comparative Perspective' in Salamon et al (eds.), *Global Civil Society* (see n 63), 3–39, 4.

[65] *Re Lowin; Perpetual Trustee Co Ltd* v *Robins* [1967] 2 NSWR 140 (Supreme Court of New South Wales, Australia), 1456. See Gino E Dal Pont and Stefan Petrow, *Law of Charity* (LexisNexis Butterworths, 2010), 75–6 [3.53].

[66] Koele, *International Taxation of Philanthropy* (see n 60), 13; Paul Bater, 'Introduction: International Tax Issues Relating to Non-Profit Organisations and Their Supporters' in Paul Bater, Frits Hondius and Penina Kessler Lieber (eds.), *The Tax Treatment of NGOs: Legal, Fiscal, and Ethical Standards for Promoting NGOs and Their Activities* (The Hague: Kluwer Law International, 2004), 1–29; David Moore and Douglas Rutzen, 'Legal Framework for Global Philanthropy: Barriers and Opportunities' (2011) 13(1–2) *The International Journal of Not-for-Profit Law* www.icnl.org/resources/research/ijnl/legal-framework-for-global-philanthropy-barriers-and-opportunities; Sabine Heidenbauer, Sigrid Hemels, Brigitte Muehlmann, Miranda Stewart, Otmar Thoemmes and Tina Tukic, 'Cross-Border Charitable Giving and Its Tax Limitations' (2013) 67 *Bulletin for International Taxation* 611–25.

Functioning of the European Union ('EU Treaty'), especially the free movement of capital under Article 63 of the EU Treaty. The first case, *Centro di Musicologia Walter Stauffer* (C-386/04) [2006] ECR I-8203 ECLI:EU:C:2006:568 (CJEU) ('*Stauffer*'), concerned an Italian charity that derived rental income from properties it owned in Germany. The Court of Justice of the European Union (CJEU) decided that Germany was obliged to recognise the tax-exempt status of the Italian charity, as it was comparable with German charitable organisations and should not be discriminated against based on the free movement of capital.

The approach in *Stauffer* was affirmed in *Missionswerk Werner Heukelbach eV v Belgium* (C-25/10) ECR [2011] ECR I-00497, ECLI:EU:C:2011:65, in relation to estate duty. A Belgian woman made a bequest to a religious organisation in Germany. Belgian estate duty applied at rates up to 80 per cent, but a lower rate of 7 per cent would apply to a donation to a not-for-profit organisation resident in Belgium. The Belgian authorities levied duty at the top rate. The CJEU held that this breached the free movement of capital and the lower rate should be applied.

The CJEU has also required governments to recognise tax deductibility of donations across borders. In *Persche v Finanzamt Lüdenscheid* (C-318/07) [2009] ECR 2009 I-00359, ECLI:EU:C:2009:33, a German taxpayer donated a gift to a charitable institution resident in Portugal and claimed a deduction against his German income tax. The German tax authority disallowed the deduction in accordance with German tax law because the institution was not a German charitable organisation. The CJEU ruled that charitable donations, including in-kind gifts, are subject to the treaty rule establishing free movement of capital, so Germany was prohibited from denying the deduction for donations to a charity in another EU member state if the deduction would have qualified had it been a domestic charity.

It is notable that the CJEU in these decisions treats philanthropic activities in the same way as market activities, as a flow of 'capital' within the single market. However, the charitable sector is normatively distinct from the market economy, and so this analogy does not logically follow, or at least, may be worthy of analysis. The CJEU does not recognise the fiscal cost to the government of the tax concession or assess the benefit of charities for the government providing the concession. While the CJEU acknowledges that allowing a tax deduction or exemption may encourage charities to take on the burden of governmental responsibilities, the loss of tax revenues resulting from extending the concession abroad was not a justification for breaching the freedoms in the EU Treaty.[67] Finally, the CJEU rejects the argument that a

---

[67] Case C-318/07, *Persche v Finanzamt Lüdenscheid* (C-318/07) [2009] ECR 2009 I-00359, ECLI: EU:C:2009:33, [45]–[46]. See also Case C-10/10, *European Commission v Austria* [2011] ECR I-5389.

state could not exercise 'effective fiscal supervision' across the border.[68] Today, this seems less of a concern, as there are several ways in which oversight could be achieved, by requiring reporting, registration with the domestic authority or imposing obligations of proof on the donor or the charity.[69]

These decisions of the CJEU essentially dissolved the national boundaries of charity by applying the logic of the single market. Governments were permitted to define what organisations would qualify for tax exempt status, or benefit from deductible gifts, but must extend the tax advantage to all similar institutions in the European Union and European Free Trade Association region. Lilian Faulhaber highlights the stark choice available for the treasury departments of EU member states following these cases: 'either eliminate subsidies to their domestic institutions or residents, or subsidise the institutions and residents of other member states on equal terms'.[70]

It is a testament to the importance of charities and other not-for-profits that the reaction of most EU member states has been to expand tax concessions rather than eliminate them. Some countries have extended a deduction for donations to eligible organisations worldwide, not just within the EU. However, other countries, including France and Germany, have retained limitations about benefit for their own residents, or country reputation, that may even breach the *Persche* decision.[71] The governments of EU member states may also seek to support their domestic not-for-profits by direct spending or grants, rather than by tax deductions, to avoid the effect of these decisions.

Tax, Charity and Global Public Benefit

The charitable exemption and deduction for philanthropy are intended to deliver public benefit to residents of the tax state, while sharing the cost across the taxpaying population. The reach of charitable and philanthropic activity across borders challenges our definition of who benefits and who should pay, and increases the difficulty of ensuring accountability and enforcement for charity that takes place outside the jurisdiction.

There are good arguments for extending charitable tax concessions across borders including positive spill-overs for people and governments – the cooperative funding from governmental and philanthropic sources to support research into a vaccine is an illustration of this. If the rationale for tax concessions is liberal pluralism, then we should respect and support the

---

[68] Case C-386/04, *Centro di Musicologia Walter Stauffer* (C-386/04) [2006] ECR I-8203 ECLI:EU:C:2006:568 (CJEU), [49].
[69] Ineke A Koele, 'Tax Privileges of NGOs and Their Benefactors: A Landlocked Privilege?' in Bater et al, *The Tax Treatment of NGOs* (see n 66), 326.
[70] Lilian V Faulhaber, 'Charitable Giving, Tax Expenditures, and Direct Spending in the United States and the European Union' (2014) 39 *Yale Journal of International Law* 87–129, 103.
[71] Ibid., 105.

decisions of donors and charities to determine where and how to fund public good for the benefit of regional or global communities of the 'public'. This is widely recognised in the extension of donor and charity exemptions for international development, disaster relief and environmental organisations.

Yet we also need to acknowledge the borders of the tax state. Most governments see their first responsibility to be provision of public goods to their own population within their own territory and face increasing fiscal constraints in providing these public goods. The EU has not succeeded to date in its attempts to harmonise taxation or to raise significant taxes for the EU as a whole. Nor has it succeeded in creating a standardised European charitable foundation that would have tax-exempt status.[72] Difficulties were faced in all areas including defining suitable public purposes and appropriate regulation, while the proposal for EU tax-exempt status was so controversial that it was dropped entirely. If we remove the territorial borders of charity before establishing a firm framework for transnational co-operation in taxation, we may undermine the pursuit of public benefit by governments and charities in a global context.

---

[72] Oonagh B Breen, 'European Non-profit Oversight: The Case for Regulating from the Outside in' (2016) 91 *Chicago-Kent Law Review* 991–1020.

9

Administration, Compliance and Avoidance

> So much ingenuity has been used in inventing methods whereby less taxes would be paid that we have been obliged from time to time to change our revenue laws to meet these evasions, and at the present time it is evident that further modifications should be made. There is, therefore, an ever-recurring succession of problems of taxation in both small and great matters, which have inevitably become complex and intricate.
>
> US Congressman William Green, quoted by Graeme Cooper, 'The Taming of the Shrewd: Identifying and Controlling Income Tax Avoidance'

Tax Administration

Certainty and Convenience in Taxation

In the Maxims of Adam Smith, extracted in Chapter 4, the requirement of *certainty* (Maxim II) was considered by Smith to be the most important. In eighteenth-century Britain, Smith was concerned about preventing arbitrariness and limiting the coercive power of the sovereign. Smith was also concerned about the *convenience* of taxation. He strongly criticised the taxes of his time for exposing taxpayers to 'much unnecessary trouble, vexation and oppression' and being 'so much more burdensome to the people than they are beneficial to the sovereign'. He said some taxes were payable at an 'inconvenient' time, while applauding other taxes levied when the taxpayer would have the funds to pay.[1] Finally, Smith expressed concern about abuse of power by tax inspectors, bemoaning the 'frequent visits and the odious examination of the tax-gatherers', with their expensive 'perquisites' and the temptation through their office to 'insolence' and corruption.

Today, protection against arbitrariness in taxation in most democratic states is ensured by the constitutional requirement that taxation must be imposed by the legislature (not by executive fiat) and administered through

---

[1] Adam Smith, *An Inquiry into the Nature and Causes of Wealth of Nations* (London: Methuan, first published 1775, compilation by Edward Cannan, 1904, of 5th ed, 1789), www.econlib.org/library/Smith/smWN.html, Book V, Part II, 'Of Taxes'.

the due process of law. The definition of a 'tax' establishes the scope of legitimate taxing power, for example, by distinguishing taxation from fines, penalties or the taking of property that requires compensation. The principles of certainty and convenience require the protection of taxpayer rights and procedural fairness in collection, investigation, review and appeal. Certainty also remains a goal of tax law drafting, although this often seems difficult to achieve. The lack of legal certainty is most noted, and controversial, in the context of debates about tax avoidance and anti-avoidance rules. We explore some of these issues in this chapter as well as discussing approaches to tax administration, compliance and avoidance.

Administrative Elements for Effective Taxation

Tax administration is constrained by what is feasible. Taxes are most effective when applied to good 'tax handles' that can be counted and collected by the state, given its capability.[2] The levying of customs tariffs on trade was feasible when ships arrived in a limited number of controlled ports, once governments could secure the ports and administer the counting and taking of a share of trade, or money in its place. The identification, valuation and taxation of land became possible on invention of the cadastre and establishment of reliable registers of land sales.[3]

Successful tax states have been able to adapt to changing social and economic structures by occupying new tax 'niches' for 'convenient fiscal exploitation'; this helps to explain the growth of some kinds of taxation and not others, even where the taxes adopted do not meet an economic or distributional ideal.[4] As market economies became more complex and differentiated, governments learned how to implement more sophisticated taxes on new forms of financial dealings and gains. Principles of accounting evolved and governments learned how to levy taxation on the abstract concepts of flows of income, net profit, or value added. The massive increase in broad-based income tax and consumption tax during the twentieth century was built through successful adoption of these elements of tax administration. Therefore, 'tax policy is really tax-systems policy':

> A tax system is a set of rules, regulations, and procedures that (1) defines what events or states of the world trigger tax liability (tax bases and rates), (2) specifies who or what entity must remit that tax and when (remittance rules), and (3) details procedures for ensuring compliance, including

---

[2] Christopher Hood, 'British Tax Structure Development as Administrative Adaptation' (1985) 18 (1) *Policy Sciences* 3–31, 28–9.
[3] Christine Lebeau, 'Regional Exchanges and Patterns of Taxation in 18th Century Europe: The Case of the Italian Cadastres' in Holger Nehring and Florian Schui (eds.), *Global Debates about Taxation* (London: Palgrave Macmillan, 2007), 21–35.
[4] Hood, 'British Tax Structure' (see n 2), 28–9.

information-reporting requirements and the consequences (including penalties) of not remitting the legal liability in a timely fashion (enforcement rules).[5]

It will be recalled from Chapter 1 that Paul McDaniel identified six elements necessary for an effective tax law: the tax unit; definition of the tax base; timing of taxation; valuation of the tax base; the tax treatment of firms; and boundaries of jurisdiction to tax. The administrative elements of a successful tax system were identified by Christopher Hood in his study of the British tax system, and the relationship with the necessary legal elements is striking:[6]

1. *Tax units:* An easily identifiable and stable population of taxpayers, or taxable objects, for example, a 'reliable ready-made' register of taxpayers or a cadastre of units of land.
2. *Tax channels:* The ability to assess and collect tax 'through a relatively small number of channels or bottlenecks at which administrative oversight can economically be applied', for example, at the time when a sale transaction must be registered.
3. *Tax base valuation:* A tax base defined by objective and easily ascertained values, for example, prices or wages that are published or recorded systematically.
4. *Tax data:* The ability to cross-check or triangulate data, for example, utilising data that are established for different administrative purposes, such as a land register, a register of deaths and inheritance, or wages where both employees and employers identify and record the payment.
5. *Tax enforcement:* The ability to carry out direct investigation and collection of tax, with suitable administrative, debt collection and asset seizure powers.
6. *Tax reinforcement:* The ability to 'reinforce' tax collection, for example through 'cross-sanctions' in different regulatory regimes, collection from third parties, or harnessing administrative capacity in different levels of government, or across jurisdictions.

A critical element that has extended governmental tax capacity is the ability to co-opt the resources of external actors to assist with tax collection. This has been achieved through systems of regulation of business and financial intermediaries and professional advisors, which are embedded in processes of data sharing and tax remittance. Tax administration conducted in this way is a successful implementation of 'regulatory capitalism', in which new regulatory techniques and interdependences 'increased delegation to business and professional self-regulation and to civil society, to intra- and international networks of regulatory experts, and increased regulation of the state by the state'.[7]

---

[5] Joel Slemrod and Christian Gillitzer, *Tax Systems* (Cambridge, MA: MIT Press, 2013), 10.
[6] Hood, 'British Tax Structure' (see n 2), 24.
[7] John Braithwaite, *Regulatory Capitalism: How It Works, Ideas for Making It Work Better* (Cheltenham: Edward Elgar, 2008), 11.

Governments rely on employers, corporations, financial institutions, tax professionals and, increasingly, digital platforms (such as Amazon or Google) to participate in various ways in tax system administration. The use of intermediary entities for withholding and remittance of taxes is usually backed by severe penalties for businesses that fail to comply. In this way, the state's capacity to govern 'is actually extended by the ability to enlist through negotiation the governance capabilities of other actors'.[8]

Examples of governments successfully harnessing intermediaries, technological and legal developments to support taxation include:

- The expansion of mass wage taxation using pay-as-you-go (PAYG) withholding from employers (discussed in Chapter 5). Governments collect on average 70 per cent of personal income tax by withholding at source;[9]
- Collection of account information from banks, or withholding of tax if the information is not provided;
- Withholding of taxes from the payers of dividends, interest, rents and royalties, especially when paid offshore; and from purchasers of shares and real estate;
- The application of a value added tax (VAT) on the intermediary businesses in the supply chain bringing them into the tax remittance system;
- The adoption of excise taxes at high rates on highly regulated goods, such as tobacco, alcohol and fuel, which can be collected at specific points of importation, production and sale; and
- The trend to levy digital services taxes or extend corporation tax or VAT through collections from large multinational enterprises that supply digital services in a jurisdiction (we return to these developments in Part III).

The administrative element is *necessary* but not *sufficient* to ensure successful taxation. A tax that could be easily administered may be rejected by the populace – perhaps for that very reason. On the other hand, all countries appear to have some taxes that collect little revenue, are inefficient, or are rather poorly administered but that have an established base and clientele – an economic niche – and so continue to exist. Examples include specific agricultural levies or financial transaction taxes.

The Rise of the Tax Authority

Successful tax administration requires a well-ordered, trained and remunerated bureaucracy. At the time of Adam Smith, the growth of 'state bureaucracy

---

[8] Ibid., 34.
[9] OECD, *Tax Administration 2019: Comparative Information on OECD and Other Advanced and Emerging Economies* (Paris: OECD Publishing, 2019), https://doi.org/10.1787/74d162b6-en, 71.

for extracting revenue, particularly the capacity to implement increasingly standardized taxation ... helped make the state the most significant economic actor at the time and the key organizer of world-scale economic operations'.[10] The success of the modern tax state owes much to the development of a bureaucracy that was not dependent on ad hoc rewards, such as commissions or tax farming for its income, and that had suitable technological, legal and financial skills. Today, the tax authority is one of the largest and most efficient agencies in government. In 2019, the Australian Taxation Office (ATO) had over 21,000 employees for a total population of 25 million (14 million individual taxpayers) and total tax revenue of AU$404.6 billion.[11] Her Majesty's Revenue and Customs (HMRC) in the United Kingdom had over 61,000 employees in 2019, for a total population of 65 million (31.6 million individual taxpayers) and total tax revenue of £636.7 billion.[12]

Tax authorities have been so successful that they are frequently utilised to carry out non-tax functions for governments.[13] These include the administration of student loans, research and development incentives, family benefits or child support, and collection and payment of compulsory social security or retirement contributions. The fiscal response to the COVID-19 pandemic in countries around the world has been largely delivered by tax authorities. The tax system presents many opportunities to speed up payments out of government – such as VAT refunds or cash payments and to slow down payments into government – such as income tax instalments.

The main steps in a tax administration process are illustrated in Figure 9.1. The 'assessment' and 'processing payments' stage includes collection of revenues through withholding and remittance, or instalment payment systems. Risk-based audit systems have ensured collection of significant tax revenues from businesses and individuals. Tax enforcement now involves the extensive use of data analytics and risk analysis, examining patterns of taxpayer behaviour over time and across sectors in the economy. Tax dispute management includes both formal and informal or alternative dispute resolution methods, such as mediation, informal review, negotiated settlements and even

---

[10] Saskia Sassen, *Territory, Authority, Rights: From Medieval to Global Assemblages* (Princeton, NJ: Princeton University Press, 2006), 19.
[11] Australian Taxation Office, *Annual Report 2019–20* (Canberra: ATO, 2020), www.ato.gov.au/uploadedFiles/Content/CR/Downloads/Annual_Report_2019-20/annual_report_2019-20.pdf.
[12] Her Majesty's Revenue and Customs, *Annual Report 2019 to 2020* (London: HMRC, 2020), https://assets.publishing.service.gov.uk/government/uploads/system/uploads/attachment_data/file/932874/HMRC_Annual_Report_and_Accounts_2019_to_2020__Print_.pdf.
[13] OECD Forum on Tax Administration, *Tax Administration in OECD and Selected Non-OECD Countries,* Comparative Information Series (2010) (Paris: OECD, 2011), www.oecd.org/tax/forum-on-tax-administration/publications-and-products/comparative/CIS-2010.pdf, 15, indicating that two thirds of tax authorities had been given non-tax functions.

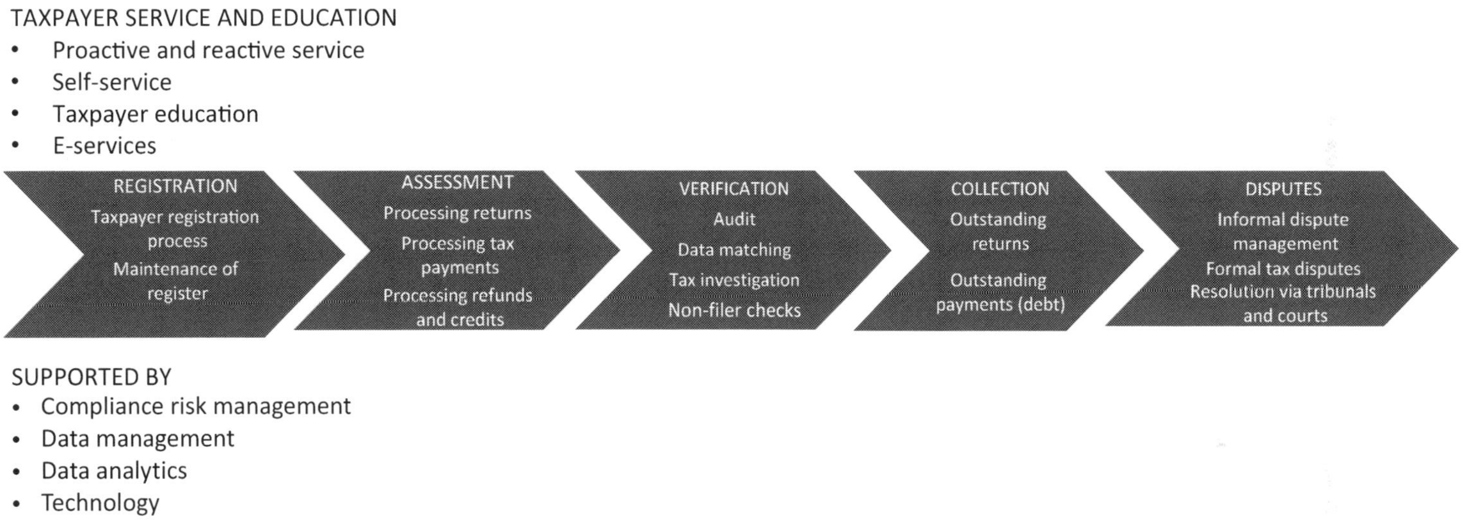

TAXPAYER SERVICE AND EDUCATION
- Proactive and reactive service
- Self-service
- Taxpayer education
- E-services

REGISTRATION
Taxpayer registration process
Maintenance of register

ASSESSMENT
Processing returns
Processing tax payments
Processing refunds and credits

VERIFICATION
Audit
Data matching
Tax investigation
Non-filer checks

COLLECTION
Outstanding returns
Outstanding payments (debt)

DISPUTES
Informal dispute management
Formal tax disputes
Resolution via tribunals and courts

SUPPORTED BY
- Compliance risk management
- Data management
- Data analytics
- Technology

Figure 9.1 Tax administrative functions
Source: Adapted from OECD, *Tax Administration 2017* (OECD: Paris, 2017), Figure 6.1.

arbitration are becoming more widespread, especially for international taxation of large corporate taxpayers.[14]

Investment in tax administration is money well spent for governments. A study of 58 countries including Organisation for Economic Co-operation and Development (OECD) member states observed that the tax administrations of these states:

> are large and complex organisations employing [in total] around 1.6 million staff. They deal with the tax affairs of around 810 million personal income tax and corporate taxpayers who contact tax administration in excess of 500 million times via telephone, in-person, e-mail or paper and generate more than 1.6 billion online contacts. And the tax administrations do this on a combined operating budget amounting to around EUR 71 billion, equivalent to less than 1% of total revenues collected.[15]

The extensive powers of tax authorities have not gone unnoticed by taxpayers or politicians There has been a proliferation of bodies that carry out political and administrative oversight of tax authorities, in a kind of 'meta-regulation' of the state by the state. These bodies are frequently established in response to demands by taxpayers and may include representatives of business or professional advisors. For example, the HMRC Board includes non-executive members currently or formerly of large companies such as Rolls Royce, Anglo-American and eBay. Business participants bring significant expertise but there is a risk of negative public perception if there is significant business engagement. Many governments have established bureaucratic complaints systems, such as ombudsmen, while tax authorities report regularly to the parliament and the public. The Australian Inspector-General of Taxation has the role of investigating and reporting on the administration of tax laws, including systems dealing or communicating with the public generally, or with particular people and organisations.[16]

A summary of the institutions that oversee the tax authorities in Australia, the United Kingdom, Canada and New Zealand is in Table 9.1. Recent inquiries by these institutions investigated diverse matters including the regulation of tax practitioners, administration of capital gains tax, compliance arrangements with large corporations, response to tax evasion and criminal attacks, the effective management of tax reliefs, data systems, tobacco smuggling, and a range of internal business transformation, public management and human resources issues.

---

[14] See, e.g. G Tony Pagone, *Tax Disputes* (Annandale, NSW: Federation Press, 2018); Pasquale Pistone and Jan JP de Goede (eds.), *Flexible Multi-tier Dispute Resolution in International Tax Disputes* (Amsterdam: IBFD, 2020).
[15] OECD, *Tax Administration 2019* (see n 9), 21.
[16] Inspector-General of Taxation Act 2003 (Cth) (Austl).

Table 9.1. Oversight of tax authorities

	Australian Tax Office	United Kingdom HM Revenue and Customs	Canada Revenue Agency	New Zealand Inland Revenue Department
Performance audits and reviews by an independent external agency	Australian National Audit Office Inspector-General of Taxation	National Audit Office	Office of the Auditor General of Canada	Controller and Auditor-General
Service complaints from taxpayers	Inspector-General of Taxation	The Adjudicator's Office Parliamentary & Health Service Ombudsman	Office of the Taxpayer's Ombudsman Office of the Privacy Commissioner of Canada	Office of the Ombudsman
Parliamentary inquiries on Annual Reports of the tax authority	House Standing Committee on Tax and Revenue Senate Estimates Committee	House of Commons, Public Accounts Committee Treasury Select Committee	None	Finance and Expenditure Committee
Parliamentary inquiries on specific issues of administration	House Standing Committee on Tax and Revenue Senate Standing Committee on Economics	House of Lords, Select Committee on Economic Affairs House of Commons, Treasury Select Committee	House of Commons, Standing Committee on Finance	Finance and Expenditure Committee
Tax law simplification	None	Office for Tax Simplification	None	Taxpayers Simplification Panel
Board responsible for oversight of tax authority	None	HMRC Board	Board of Management	None (Board structure is internal)

Source: Author compilation from various sources.

Tax Compliance and Evasion

Quasi-voluntary Compliance

Tax administration relies heavily on voluntary compliance.[17] This is better understood as 'quasi-voluntary compliance', a term invented by Margaret Levi in her groundbreaking study, *Of Rule and Revenue*.[18] Successful tax states, almost by definition, have achieved quasi-voluntary compliance in taxation.

Obtaining a true indication of the level of compliance – or evasion – is impossible but tax authorities seek to measure levels of compliance in various ways. These include analysis of the tax gap (discussed later), taxpayer opinion surveys, and analysis of administrative data on filing, income reporting and payment. The OECD reports on-time tax payments for selected jurisdictions for personal income tax exceeding 87 per cent, employer PAYG withholding exceeding 95 per cent, corporate income tax exceeding 91 per cent and VAT exceeding 92 per cent.[19] Only a small fraction of individual or corporate tax returns are audited (as low as 1 to 3 per cent in many cases), or are subject to disputes and collection challenges; yet it appears that most tax is collected, most of the time.

Tax evasion is usually defined as the fraudulent misstatement of taxable income, expenses, credits or other tax matters to evade the payment of tax. It encompasses failure to file a tax return or declare income, overstatement or falsification of deductible expenses, false claims for tax credits, or the use of fake transactions and sham entities. Tax evasion is subject to civil and criminal penalties. Tax authorities may investigate, amend or issue default assessments, seize or freeze assets, levy penalties and interest and seek prosecution for fraud leading to criminal convictions, fines and imprisonment.

While tax evasion is as old as taxes, systematic research into tax compliance and evasion as a social and governance process began in the 1970s. There is a wide literature on tax compliance, evasion and regulatory approaches, in legal, economic, behavioural, sociological, ethical and political disciplines. Academic research centres funded by tax authorities and other research sources have led some of this work, including the Australian Centre for Tax System Integrity established by Professor Valerie Braithwaite at the Australian National University from 1999 to 2006,[20] and the Tax Administration Research Centre established in 2013 at the University of Exeter in the United Kingdom.[21]

---

[17] OECD, *Tax Administration 2019* (see n 9), 34.
[18] Margaret Levi, *Of Rule and Revenue* (Berkeley, CA: University of California Press, 1988).
[19] OECD, *Tax Administration 2019* (see n 9), table D.18.
[20] See legacy website: http://ctsi.org.au/, accessed 16 March 2022.
[21] Tax Administration Research Centre, University of Exeter, 'About TARC', https://tarc.exeter.ac.uk/thecentre/abouttarc/, accessed 1 April 2022.

One question of interest to tax authorities and policymakers is *why* people comply with or evade taxation. The answer to this question could help in improving revenue collection or identifying the effectiveness of different enforcement approaches. Tax authorities are intensely engaged in the design of administrative and regulatory approaches that best achieve revenue targets. Administration of the tax law should also support an efficient, fair and sustainable tax system. Fundamentally, the question is political – why do people engage in the necessary cooperative social activity that sustains successful tax states? Where people do *not* comply, the consequent 'evasion' of a tax may amount to a tax revolt. Taxation has often appeared to be the 'last straw' that triggers political rebellions from the French Revolution, to the War of American Independence, to the London riots against the poll tax of Margaret Thatcher in 1990.[22] Despite the last example, tax revolts rarely happen in successful tax states, although tax evasion and avoidance remain constant challenges.

The classic economic model of tax evasion explored the effect of deterrence combining the likelihood of detection and the severity of punishment if the evader was caught.[23] This model assumed taxpayers rationally weigh these elements in deciding whether to evade a tax. Another possibility is that ideology, morality or beliefs are important determinants of taxpayer behaviour. Contesting both of these explanations, Levi argued that governments seek quasi-voluntary compliance by negotiating a fiscal bargain with taxpayers because it is ultimately too costly to collect taxes solely by coercion.[24] Rulers (governments) must adopt strategies of cooperation that go further than coercion, deterrence or ideological norms, as explained in the following extract.[25]

> One way that rulers can reduce the costs of enforcement is to create or encourage situations where taxpayers engage in quasi-voluntary compliance. It is *voluntary* because taxpayers choose to pay. It is *quasi*-voluntary because the noncompliant are subject to coercion – if they are caught. The fact that compliance is not only a matter of principle distinguishes quasi-voluntary compliance from ideological compliance. Taxpayers make a calculated decision based on the behavior of others. Nor is quasi-voluntary compliance purely self-interested behavior. It cannot be accounted for solely by coercion and only rarely by positive selective incentives.
>
> Quasi-voluntary compliance will occur only when taxpayers have confidence that (1) rulers will keep their bargains and (2) the other constituents will keep

---

[22] See Joel Slemrod and Michael Keen, *Rebellion, Rascals and Revenue: Tax Follies and Wisdom through the Ages* (Princeton, NJ: Princeton University Press, 2021); David F Burg, *A World History of Tax Rebellions: An Encyclopedia of Tax Rebels, Revolts, and Riots from Antiquity to the Present* (New York: Routledge, 2004).
[23] Michael G Allingham and Agnar Sandmo, 'Income Tax Evasion: A Theoretical Analysis' (1972) 1 *Journal of Public Economics* 323–38.
[24] Levi, *Of Rule and Revenue* (see n 18), 51.
[25] Ibid., 52–4 (extracts).

theirs. Taxpayers are strategic actors who will cooperate only when they can expect others to cooperate as well. ... To create and maintain quasi-voluntary compliance, rulers search for noncoercive strategies that produce a high level of constituent cooperation. They must create confidence in their credibility and their capacity to deliver promised returns for taxes. They must convince taxpayers that taxpayer contributions make a difference in producing desired goods. They must coordinate the actions of taxpayers so that each perceives others doing their share, too.

I argue that rulers can increase compliance by demonstrating that the tax system is fair. A perception of exploitation – that is, an unfair contract – promotes noncompliance. ... Quasi-voluntary compliance rests on the effectiveness of sanctions when enough constituents are already cooperating. Rulers can then focus scarce resources on those constituents most likely to be noncompliant. Most rulers calculate that the marginal cost of universal enforcement is too high. Most are willing to tolerate imperfect enforcement as long as they can ensure that there is relatively general compliance ...

Tax payment may not always appear 'voluntary' to the individual taxpayer. In a PAYG system, the employee has little choice in the matter; nor does the customer in a value-added business supply chain for levying of VAT. However, some level of political consent of the employee or customer is broadly assumed. Specifically, a cooperative approach backed by coercion must be implemented by negotiation with the intermediary firms who will do the withholding and remitting of tax. Most firms decide that it is in their interest to maintain good relations with tax authorities in respect of the tax to be remitted for employees and on customer sales. They may take a different approach to their own business tax compliance.

During the 1970s, social scientists grew interested in the apparently growing 'behavioural problem' of tax evasion in many countries in the context of high tax rates, avoidance scandals and large fiscal deficits in many countries.[26] Researchers investigated the personal characteristics of tax evaders, in their social context and financial situation. They also analysed taxpayer culture and 'morale' including trust in government in general, in the tax authority, or in other taxpayers, and attitudes or beliefs about the fairness of the tax system.[27] Empirical methods include surveys of taxpayers, which aimed to identify the extent of tax evasion and attitudes to it, and social science experiments in the 'lab', often using students as subjects, as was the case for much other research into deterrence and compliance for other kinds of law.[28]

---

[26] Russell H Weigel, Dick J Hessing and Henk Elffers, 'Tax Evasion Research: A Critical Appraisal and Theoretical Model' (1987) 8 *Journal of Economic Psychology* 215–35.
[27] See, e.g. Benno Torgler, *Tax Morale and Compliance: Review of Evidence and Case Studies for Europe*, World Bank Policy Research Working Paper 5922 (Washington, DC: World Bank, 2010).
[28] Benno Torgler, 'Speaking to Theorists and Searching for Facts: Tax Morale and Tax Compliance in Experiments' (2002) 16(5) *Journal of Economic Surveys* 657–83.

Studies of attitudes to tax evasion tend to produce the result that the majority of people state that tax evasion, like corruption, is not justifiable. Women are more likely than men to state that tax evasion is never justifiable and the evidence suggests that women are more likely to be tax compliant.[29] Trust in government is an important indicator of compliance. Many people consider that tax evasion is justifiable if tax rates are too high; the tax system is unfair; a large portion of the money collected is wasted; or the government discriminates because of religion, race or ethnic background.

While taxpayer attitudes matter, one of the most important indicators of likelihood to evade (or avoid) taxes is taxpayer *opportunity*. A self-employed business owner has significantly more opportunity to evade taxation than a wage earner. Individuals with capital income are more able to evade taxation, for example by hiding the income in offshore bank accounts. It is sometimes assumed that high-income taxpayers are more likely to do 'avoidance' or 'planning' than evasion, while low-income taxpayers may operate 'off the books' in cash or fail to file returns. However, recent evidence suggests that where the opportunity exists, wealthy individuals do significant evasion. Using massive leaks from offshore financial institutions including the HSBC Switzerland 'Swiss Leaks' and the 'Panama Papers' of Mossack Fonseca, as well as tax amnesty data from the Swedish tax authority, high levels of tax evasion were estimated for the top 0.01 per cent of the income distribution who hold a lot of income and assets offshore.[30]

Self-assessment and Responsive Tax Regulation

Towards the end of the twentieth century, many tax authorities shifted towards a 'self-assessment' system and away from a traditional bureaucratic system of receipt, checking and handling of paper tax returns. There was a recognition that the bureaucratic process was unable to respond to the much larger number of taxpayers filing returns and the increasing complexity of the tax law, while absorbing resources that would be better targeted towards providing help to taxpayers who sought to comply, and taking enforcement action against non-compliant taxpayers.[31]

In the context of self-assessment, tax authorities have sought to learn from the compliance and evasion literature to structure their enforcement approaches so as to maximise quasi-voluntary compliance for taxpayers with different

---

[29] Benno Torgler and Neven Valev, 'Gender and Public Attitudes towards Corruption and Tax Evasion' (2010) 28(4) *Contemporary Economic Policy* 554–68.

[30] Annette Alstadsaeter, Niels Johannesen and Gabriel Zucman, 'Tax Evasion and Inequality' (2019) 109(6) *American Economic Review* 2073–103.

[31] See, e.g., Paul J Keating, *A Full Self Assessment System of Taxation: A Consultative Document* (Canberra: Australian Taxation Office, 1990). In the United Kingdom, self-assessment was introduced in 1996 for self-employed and business taxpayers, as most wage earners do not file returns: Simon James, 'Self-assessment and the UK Tax System' (1997) 13 *Australian Tax Forum* 205–26.

A New Approach to Tax Compliance

Figure 9.2 Example of regulatory practice with ATO compliance model
Source: Valerie A Braithwaite, 'A New Approach to Tax Compliance' in Valerie A Braithwaite (ed.), *Taxing Democracy* (Aldershot: Ashgate, 2003), 1–11, Figure 1.1.

propensities to comply or evade. This has led to application of 'responsive' regulation that adjusts the approach to the posture, psychology or situation of the taxpayer.[32] An example is the ATO Compliance Model of the early 2000s, built on research by the Australian Centre for Tax System Integrity. An illustration of the model 'pyramid' of tax compliance is in Figure 9.2, which aligns regulatory strategies with the motivational postures of taxpayers.[33] The self-assessment system is intended to free resources for educating and supporting the mass of compliant taxpayers at the bottom of the pyramid and responding to the minority of non-compliant or hostile taxpayers at the top of the pyramid.

Tax practitioners have a significant role to play in advising taxpayers and steering them towards more or less compliant tax strategies. Taxpayers operate with tax practitioners in social and administrative networks that lead to compliance, or non-compliance, based on a combination of opportunity, peer and

---

[32] John Braithwaite, 'The Essence of Responsive Regulation' (2011) 44 *UBC Law Review* 475–520; Robert Baldwin and Julia Black, 'Really Responsive Regulation' (2008) 71(1) *Modern Law Review* 59–94.

[33] Valerie A Braithwaite, 'A New Approach to Tax Compliance' in Valerie A Braithwaite (ed.), *Taxing Democracy* (Aldershot: Ashgate, 2003), 1–11.

social effects.[34] Tax practitioners are adaptive or 'contingent' and may change tax compliance behaviour depending on context. There has been a growing focus by tax authorities on regulation of such 'tax intermediaries', including legal and accounting tax professionals, investment banks and financial advisors.[35]

There has been a growing influence of 'nudge' and behavioural economics approaches in tax administration.[36] Taxpayers or tax practitioners who are 'contingent' in their behaviour may be open to nudges and can be a key target group for the application of behavioural approaches to regulation. These approaches have been tested in the administrative 'real world', applying randomised controlled trials.[37] Applying choice architecture in the area of tax compliance is premised on the basis that taxation is a legal obligation. Therefore, the focus is not whether the state should influence individual decision-making about whether or not to pay tax, but how best to encourage individuals to do so.[38] Most behavioural research has focused on individual taxpayers. The provision of information, default withholding or payment systems ('opt-out' rather than 'opt-in') and making it easy to pay taxes are all important to improving tax compliance.

Good design interventions for tax payment should enhance the legitimacy of the overall tax system and respect taxpayer rights, as well as satisfying payment and collection goals. This is because underpinning a behavioural and 'make it easy' approach to tax compliance are laws that structure the rights and duties of the revenue authority and the taxpayer.[39] Tax law in substance and procedure is usually (and usually should be) formal and uniform, with clearly defined categories, powers, accountability and review mechanisms. The stability, predictability and respect for rights of law is a strength but it may limit adaptation to behaviourally driven, flexible and personalised payment systems.

Box 9.1 describes approaches to taxpayer rights taken by the United Kingdom, the United States, and the European Commission.

[34] Elea Wurth and Valerie Braithwaite, 'Tax Practitioners and Tax Avoidance: Gaming through Authorities, Cultures and Markets' in Nigar Hashimzade and Yuliya Epifantseva (eds.), *Routledge Companion on Tax Avoidance Research* (Abingdon: Routledge, 2017), 320–39.

[35] OECD Forum on Tax Administration, *Study into the Role of Tax Intermediaries* (Paris: OECD, 2008), www.oecd.org/tax/administration/39882938.pdf

[36] Richard Thaler and Cass Sunstein, *Nudge* (New Haven, CT: Yale University Press, 2008). See discussion in Emily Millane and Miranda Stewart, 'Behavioural Insights in Tax Collection: Getting the Legal Settings Right' (2019) 16(3) *eJournal of Tax Research* 500–35.

[37] The United Kingdom was a leader in establishing a 'Behavioural Insights' or 'Nudge' unit in government, which did significant work on taxes and charges. Other research has been done by scholars with the Australian Taxation Office, see, e.g. Christian Gillitzer and Mathias Sinning, 'Nudging Businesses to Pay Their Taxes: Does Timing Matter?' (2020) 169 *Journal of Economic Behavior and Organization* 284–300; and see Giulia Mascagni, 'From the Lab to the Field: A Review of Tax Experiments' (2018) 32(2) *Journal of Economic Surveys* 273–301.

[38] Simon James, 'Taxation and Nudging' in Morris Altman (ed.), *Handbook of Behavioural Economics and Smart Decision-making: Rational Decision-making within the Bounds of Reason* (Cheltenham: Edward Elgar, 2017), 317–30, 324.

[39] Millane and Stewart, 'Behavioural Insights in Tax Collection' (see n 36).

Box 9.1 Taxpayer rights

To demonstrate their commitment to cooperative compliance and due process, some tax authorities, or legislatures, have established 'charters' of taxpayer rights. In the United Kingdom, the first Charter of taxpayer rights was established in the 1980s, and later put on a legislative footing. In Australia, the Taxpayers' Charter was instituted as an administrative document in 1996.[40] In 2015, the OECD found that taxpayer rights were formally defined in 45 out of 55 tax administrations surveyed, of which about three quarters were based in legislation and the remainder were administrative documents.[41]

In the United States, the National Taxpayer Advocate, an independent office within the Internal Revenue Service (IRS), has been a high-profile advocate of taxpayer rights and responder to taxpayer complaints. Following a proposal from former Advocate Nina Olsen, the IRS adopted a Taxpayer Bill of Rights in 2014.[42] The Advocate reports to the US Congress each year on 'at least ten of the most serious problems encountered by taxpayers, legislative and administrative recommendations for solving those problems, and a discussion of the year's ten most frequently litigated tax issues'.[43] In a recent report, the Advocate stated bluntly that 'the IRS does not have sufficient resources to provide quality service. Due to antiquated technology, a smaller workforce, and an increased workload, the IRS cannot provide quality service without additional funding'.[44]

The European Commission published Guidelines for a Model European Taxpayers' Code in 2016.[45] It sets out principles about the rights and responsibilities of both taxpayers and tax administrations, in respect of the following:

- Lawfulness and legal certainty
- Non-discrimination and equality of taxpayers
- Presumption of honesty
- Courtesy and consideration
- Respect of law
- Impartiality and independence
- Fiscal secrecy and data protection
- Privacy
- Representation.

The Code also includes guidelines that address information, guidance and services to taxpayers, and set expectations of conduct in assessment, audit and dispute processes.

---

[41] OECD, *Tax Administration 2017: Comparative Information on OECD and Other Advanced and Emerging Economies* (Paris: OECD, 2017), https://doi.org/10.1787/tax_admin-2017-en, figure 3.4.
[42] Internal Revenue Service (US), Taxpayer Bill of Rights (24 February 2022), www.irs.gov/taxpayer-bill-of-rights.
[43] Taxpayer Advocate Service (US), Reports to Congress, https://taxpayeradvocate.irs.gov/reports.
[44] National Taxpayer Advocate (US), *Annual Report to Congress* (Washington, DC: Taxpayer Advocate Service, 2019), https://taxpayeradvocate.irs.gov/reports/2019-annual-report-to-congress.
[45] European Commission Directorate-General for Taxation and Customs Union, *Guidelines for a Model for a European Taxpayers' Code* (Brussels: European Commission, 2016), https://ec

Tax Data and Automation

Information 'is at the heart of modern tax systems'.[46] The insatiable thirst for information of tax authorities has increased commensurately with the number of taxpayers, types of tax and level of taxation. As indicated in Figure 9.1, it is a basic principle of administrative design that taxpayers have individual tax file registration numbers. The OECD observes that 'the active management of "tax registers" remains a priority area for tax administrations'.[47] Successful tax authorities put significant effort into the authentication and protection of taxpayer identities, and they may also be subject to privacy and data protection laws in their jurisdiction. The European Union is undoubtedly the leader in privacy protection and the *General Data Protection Regulation* (EU, 2016/679) that came into force in 2018 applies to all tax authorities in the European Union.

Tax authority powers gradually expanded during the twentieth century, empowering them to demand information from taxpayers, or from third parties (such as banks, employers or contractors), about their own or others' income, assets and financial transactions. Tax authorities have wide powers to request books and records and to access premises of taxpayers. However, these powers are subject to legal limits in many countries.[48] More than half of the 58 administrations surveyed in 2019 by the OECD had the ability to enter business premises, but only nine were authorised to enter the home of a taxpayer without consent or a judicial warrant. Even where such powers are available, it is important to use them sparingly, to protect trust in the authorities. Tax authorities can usually demand information about taxpayers from other government agencies or from third parties.[49] The most common source for verification of taxpayer data today is computerized data-matching that utilises information accessed from third parties including corporations, employers and financial institutions and cross-checks this against data supplied by the taxpayer.[50]

The externalisation of many functions to private actors has generated highly efficient tax administration, but it has increased compliance costs in money and time for many individuals and businesses. Empirical research since the 1990s demonstrates high average costs of compliance. In 2004 Joel Slemrod

---

.europa.eu/taxation_customs/system/files/2016-11/guidelines_for_a_model_for_a_european_taxpayers_code_en.pdf.

[46] Slemrod and Gillitzer, *Tax Systems* (see n 5), 11; Christopher Hood, 'The "Tax State" in the Information Age' in TV Paul, G John Ikenberry and John Hall (eds.) *The Nation-State in Question* (Princeton, NJ: Princeton University Press, 2003), 213–33.

[47] OECD, Tax Administration 2019 (see n 9), 74.

[48] See, e.g. Pasquale Pistone (ed.), *Tax Procedures* (Amsterdam: IBFD, 2020); Tonny Schenk-Geers, *International Exchange of Information and the Protection of Taxpayers* (Alphen aan den Rijn, Netherlands: Kluwer Law International, 2009); Roman Seer and Isabel Gabert (eds.), *Mutual Assistance and Information Exchange* (Amsterdam: IBFD, 2010).

[49] OECD, Tax Administration 2019 (see n 9), 87.

[50] Ibid.

and Jon Bakija estimated the total annual cost of enforcing and complying with the US corporate and personal income tax to be US$135 billion, or as much as 10 per cent of income tax revenues collected that year.[51]

Some taxpayers – such as individual wage earners – have little compliance cost, especially where they do not need to file returns, as in Japan, the United Kingdom and New Zealand. However, compliance costs are quite large for many firms and studies indicate they are regressive, falling heaviest on small business.[52] Reasons for high compliance costs include a 'messy' tax base and heavy and frequent information, withholding and reporting obligations. Political pressures tend to drive tax systems towards complexity, for example, to enact targeted rules for particular industries, or complex integrity rules. Taxpayers also expend time and resources minimising taxes through tax planning (discussed later).

Adam Smith's Maxim of 'convenience' may have a renaissance in the digital era, although this may come at a cost of increased surveillance and threats to privacy. Governments are rapidly adopting 'e-filing' and 'e-payment' systems; those that have initiated these systems report e-filing in excess of 70 per cent for individuals and 80 per cent for businesses, while e-payment systems applicable in many countries at similar levels.[53]

These digital developments may change the terms of the cooperative compliance bargain between the tax authority and business intermediaries. Digitalisation and cloud computing are removing the need for data to be compiled by the intermediary and reported in special processes. Instead, the tax authority may have full and instant access to wage and tax reporting. An example is 'single touch payroll' instituted by the ATO in 2018, which provides automated real time access to wage and retirement contributions data. The information can be cross-checked with bank records for employees and the employer.[54]

The effective operation of automated or algorithmic systems of administration may generate a higher risk of administrative error, with sometimes devastating effects on individuals and businesses. To date, problems affecting large numbers of people have been more visible in the context of welfare payments than in the tax system. A salutary lesson for tax authorities was produced by the Australian debacle of aggressive privatised pursuit of erroneous 'robo-debts', involving the issue of automated debt notices to thousands of

---

[51] Joel Slemrod and Jon Bakija, *Taxing Ourselves: A Citizens' Guide to the Debate over Taxes*, 5th ed (Cambridge, MA: MIT Press, 2017), 164.

[52] Philip Lignier and Chris Evans, 'The Rise and Rise of Tax Compliance Costs for the Small Business Sector in Australia' (2012) 27(3) *Australian Tax Forum* 615–72.

[53] OECD, *Tax Administration 2019* (see n 9), 80.

[54] Single Touch Payroll requires businesses to report wages, PAYG withholding and superannuation to the ATO each time the business pays its employees, on or before the day on which the payment is made: ATO, 'Single Touch Payroll' (4 November 2021), www.ato.gov.au/General/Other-languages/In-detail/Information-in-other-languages/Single-Touch-Payroll/.

individuals, for allegedly overpaid social security payments. After failing to heed earlier legal advice, the government lost in court cases which confirmed that the automated system generated outcomes that were not in accordance with law, leading to mass settlement of claims and a Senate inquiry.[55] Significant challenges have also been encountered in the United Kingdom's attempt to implement a Universal Credit for low-income workers and the unemployed. These examples raise broader challenges of timing, payment and errors in administration of tax-transfer systems using automation.[56]

A perennial issue for tax authorities, practitioners and taxpayers has been the increasing complexity and size of the tax law itself. There is a large literature on tax law drafting and interpretation, and there have been various attempts by governments to simplify tax legislation.[57] However, it is difficult to get agreement even on what 'simplicity' means for tax law. This has led to new agencies for 'reducing red tape' and 'law simplification' that aim to tame this aspect of tax complexity, as illustrated in Table 9.1.

Tax Planning and Avoidance

The Ubiquity of Tax Planning

Taxation is an element of all economic transactions: 'the taxing authority is an uninvited party to all contracts. The taxing authority brings to each of its 'forced' ventures with taxpayers a set of contractual terms (tax rules)'.[58] If a deal is profitable, the tax authority 'shares' in the profit by the amount of tax due; if a deal is unprofitable and a loss is made, the tax authority 'shares' in the loss. One response to a tax is to change economic behaviour: for example, to work less, or to invest in a more tax-favoured vehicle, as discussed in previous chapters. Another response is to do tax planning to minimise the tax paid.

Tax planning aims to legally maximise the after-tax return to the taxpayer, while tax avoidance and tax evasion minimise tax in ways that the law proscribes. Individuals and businesses carry out tax planning as an integrated element of business strategy and profit maximisation. This is acknowledged by

---

[55] Parliament of the Commonwealth of Australia, Senate Inquiry, 'Centrelink's Compliance Program', www.aph.gov.au/Parliamentary_Business/Committees/Senate/Community_Affairs/Centrelinkcompliance, accessed 24 March 2022.

[56] Jane Millar and Peter Whiteford, 'Timing It Right or Timing It Wrong: How Should Income-Tested Benefits Deal with Changes in Circumstances?' (2020) 28(1) *Journal of Poverty and Social Justice* 3–20.

[57] A survey is in Margaret McKerchar, Kristen Meyer and Stewart Karlinsky, 'Making Progress in Tax Simplification: A Comparison of the United States, Australia, New Zealand and the United Kingdom' in Margaret McKerchar and Michael Walpole (eds.), *Further Global Challenges in Tax Administration* (Bath, Fiscal Publications, 2006), 359–75.

[58] Myron L Scholes, Mark A Wolfson, Merle M Erickson, Michelle L Hanlon and Edward L Maydew, *Taxes & Business Strategy, Global Edition*, 5th ed (Harlow: Pearson Education, 2015), 22.

courts of various jurisdictions. During the 1960s, Justice Harlan of the United States Supreme Court stated:

> [T]he tax laws exist as an economic reality in the businessman's world, much like the existence of a competitor. Businessmen plan their affairs around both, and a tax dollar is just as real as one derived from any other source.[59]

Tax laws produce many opportunities or margins for tax planning because they treat different business or investment activities, legal entities, types of income or gain, types of expense or loss, types of asset and types of contracting differently. Such opportunities may be the result of complicated or special rules, or they may arise from structural features of the tax law. Taxpayers may do tax planning that uses some of these features while achieving their main economic goal but with a lower tax burden. For example, a taxpayer in a progressive tax system may be able to earn the income him or herself, and then arrange for their dependent family member receive some of it, and be taxed at a lower rate than the taxpayer. This income splitting if legally achieved would generate an overall lower taxed outcome for the taxpayer and their family, as explained in Chapter 5. Alternatively, taxpayers may seek out tax-favoured treatment of a course of action, or type of income or entity.

The ubiquity of opportunities for tax planning might suggest that tax planning is very widespread, while the availability of professional advice to assist in tax planning suggests the value of planning opportunities. However, tax minimisation is not free; it also has costs and risks. Some costs of tax planning are obvious: the cost of tax advice and time; the risk that an anti-avoidance rule will apply; costs of countering enforcement, litigation, and ultimately penalties and interest if the taxpayer ends up in a dispute with the revenue authority; and social and reputational costs. Other costs are less obvious, arising from the economic and price effects of tax planning.

Tax planning may become a widespread or *mass* activity of individual taxpayers, for example, through leveraging investments with tax-deductible interest (illustrated in Box 9.2 about passive loss tax shelters). Individual and corporate tax planning became increasingly 'mass marketed', financialised and widespread during the 1990s, leading to a strong although often delayed response by tax authorities.[60] In this situation, to protect the tax base, tax authorities and legislatures seek to shut down the tax planning through changes to the tax law and strict enforcement.

---

[59] *CIR v Brown* (1965) 380 US 563 (US). This was subsequently quoted by the Australian High Court in *Federal Commissioner of Taxation v Spotless Services Ltd* (1996) 186 CLR 404 (High Court of Australia); the existence of the commercial or business purpose did not prevent application of the GAAR in that case.

[60] US Treasury, *The Problem of Corporate Tax Shelters – Discussion, Analysis and Legislative Proposals* (Washington DC: Department of the Treasury, 1999); Joseph Bankman, 'An Academic's View of the Tax Shelter Battle' in Henry J Aaron and Joel Slemrod (eds.), *Crisis in Tax Administration* (Washington, DC: Brookings Institution Press, 2004), 9–37.

Box 9.2 Passive investment losses as a tax shelter

An example of a general rule that may generate a tax shelter is the rule for deductibility of interest expense, which is a normal element of most income tax laws. Combined with other features of the tax law, such as high marginal tax rates on income and lower, deferred capital gains tax rates on the sale of assets, and where financing is widely available, this may generate planning that has a high revenue cost.

Interest deductions on borrowings to invest in real estate or other investments may be large, while the level of debt is largely within the control of the taxpayer. The interest, with other expenses, may exceed the income generated by the asset. The 'passive loss' generated by a debt-financed investment may shelter other income such as salary from high tax rates. The tax on any gain on disposal of the investment is deferred into the future, when the asset is finally sold. Deferral of tax on the gain reduces the net present value of the tax due, while a capital gain is usually taxed at a lower rate than ordinary income.

These features existed in the US income tax law in the 1970s. In the 1986 base-broadening tax reform, the United States introduced 'passive activity loss rules' to halt the widespread use of such losses. The high marginal rates that applied at the time provided an incentive for tax planning because a loss deduction was worth the marginal tax rate (at a tax rate of 60 per cent a loss of $100 is worth $60 in tax). The 'passive activity loss rules' quarantine the deduction to passive income, shutting down this tax shelter.[61]

The US 'passive activity loss rules' are specific integrity rules that shut down tax minimisation behaviour but at the same time introduce a new tax planning margin into the law. The passive loss rules add complexity and a certain amount of arbitrariness to the law, but they serve the purpose of protecting the intent and coherence of the tax system.

Other countries also have rules to address the tax shelter of passive losses. The dual income tax levied in Nordic states, discussed in Chapter 6, generally limits investment losses to be offset only against investment gains. This schedular approach prevents using investment losses to shelter active business or work income from tax.

In contrast, Australian tax law has no passive loss limitation rule. A widespread tax planning strategy by individual investors is to 'negatively gear' rental property investments producing a loss that shelters other income from tax. The net rental loss is a result of deductions for interest, depreciation and other holding costs that exceed rent from the property. More than 2 million Australians (out of a tax filing population of 14 million) invest in at least one rental property and more than half of these investments generate a rental loss. The overall fiscal result is estimated to be *negative*, amounting to a $3 billion revenue loss in the 2016–17 tax year.[62]

---

[61] Internal Revenue Code (US) s 469; Hugh J Ault, Brian J Arnold and Graeme Cooper, *Comparative Income Taxation*, 4th ed (Alphen aan den Rijn, Netherlands: Wolters Kluwer, 2020), Part 6.3.

[62] Australian Taxation Office, 'Taxation Statistics 2016–17', table 8 and chart 10 (24 September 2020), www.ato.gov.au/About-ATO/Research-and-statistics/In-detail/Taxation-statistics/Taxation-statistics—previous-editions/Taxation-statistics-2016-17/?anchor=Individuals#Chart10.

An important element of tax planning is the ability for taxpayers to contract with each other to their mutual advantage, at the expense of the revenue. This is called 'tax arbitrage'. This may be done between 'related' parties, such as two companies in the same corporate group. The separate legal entity status of the corporation facilitates such tax planning, whether at a small or global scale. For example, a self-employed individual may establish a consultancy business in a corporation subject to a lower tax rate than the personal tax rate. The individual has established two taxable persons (themselves and the corporation) that face different tax rates but controls both entities and can plan the derivation of income and payments from the corporation to themselves to minimise taxation (see Chapter 5). A multinational enterprise conducted in a corporate group with subsidiaries in high and low tax jurisdictions around the world is a tax planning behemoth, able to control transactions, trade, assets and value across all of these legal entities and jurisdictions.

Dealing in tax advantages may also take place between unrelated parties. An employee negotiating a salary package with an employer may seek to receive a portion of the remuneration as a tax-favoured benefit instead of salary, for example, a car that receives a concessional valuation, or stock options that permit deferral of tax. The employer may be indifferent (the remuneration is deductible either way); or may favour the deal as it reduces employer costs. Alternatively, the employer may face more cost and administration as a result of the deal, so that the employer will agree to remuneration delivered in the way preferred by the employee only if the cost is lowered.

The ideal tax arbitrage is for a low tax rate or exempt taxpayer to trade with a high tax rate taxpayer. Assume taxpayer A, facing a zero tax bracket, is eligible for a tax deduction of $100, but this deduction has no immediate value to A, who will not pay tax in any event. If A can trade their $100 deduction to taxpayer B in the 40 per cent tax bracket for an upfront price of, say, $35, then both A and B will be better off, but less tax will be paid. Such a trade could be done by leasing a depreciating asset eligible for the deduction to the other person, in exchange for an upfront lease payment.

Innovations in econometric methods and access by researchers to large scale anonymised taxpayer data have led to new findings about tax planning, or the 'elasticity of taxable income' of taxpayers.[63] This seeks to measure how 'elastic' taxpayers are in changing their behaviour in response to tax rates or special provisions such as tax exemptions in the tax system. Taking advantage of discontinuities or 'notches' in the tax system, such as the threshold for tax rate bands in the progressive rate structure, or changes in tax rates over time,

---

[63] Slemrod and Gillitzer, *Tax Systems* (see n 5), 79; Emmanuel Saez, Joel Slemrod and Seth H Giertz, 'The Elasticity of Taxable Income with Respect to Marginal Tax Rates: A Critical Review' (2012) 50(1) *Journal of Economic Literature* 3–50.

researchers can identify how taxpayers who have similar characteristics change their behaviour when faced with a change in a tax rate.[64]

Tax elasticity research confirms that individual wage earners subject to PAYG withholding have a taxable income elasticity of close to zero. In contrast, self-employed business owners and investors have a much greater elasticity of taxable income, confirming their greater propensity and opportunity to do tax planning. The existence of related parties also facilitates tax planning. For example, one study found that self-employed taxpayers who are members of a couple are much more responsive to tax rates, with a taxable income elasticity of close to one.[65]

Tax Shelters

Governments often use tax incentives to encourage particular activities or investments. In Chapter 7, tax incentives to support innovation, research and development and entrepreneurship were discussed. These incentives are *intended* to change taxpayer behaviour to achieve their policy goal of more innovative research by businesses. This poses the risk that the tax incentive will overreach and will be more wasteful than productive. The policy decision is a balancing act:

> Success is achieved when the tax rules subsidize activities that benefit society as a whole more than they benefit the individuals engaging directly in the activities. ... Although the deadweight costs associated with time spent in tax planning may seem socially wasteful, the relevant question is how much waste would exist using alternative means to achieve the same social goals.[66]

Distinguishing a 'productive' innovation or social policy response from a tax planning response is difficult. The tax law can appear conflicted between promoting economic or social policy goals through tax concessions on the one hand, and trying to prevent tax avoidance utilising opportunities for tax minimisation with a range of general and ad hoc rules.

Tax-favoured treatment may also be unintended, sometimes described as a 'loophole' that facilitates tax planning and operates as a 'tax shelter', as illustrated in Box 9.2. Taxpayers adapt their behaviour to the opportunities available to them, and magnify the results by borrowing and diversification of investments.

Whatever the reason for differential tax treatment, every boundary or category in the tax law produces a margin that may facilitate tax planning. This should, at the least, lead to caution in policymakers as to whether tax

---

[64] Saez et al, 'The Elasticity of Taxable Income' (see n 63).
[65] Nazila Alinaghi, John Creedy and Norman Gemmell, *Do Couples Bunch More? Evidence from Partnered and Single Taxpayers in New Zealand*, Working Papers in Public Finance, No 02/2020 (Wellington: Victoria School of Business and Government, Victoria University of Wellington, New Zealand, 2020).
[66] Scholes et al, *Taxes & Business Strategy* (see n 58).

incentives can succeed in achieving goals. Tax reform proposals aimed at 'broadening the base' and 'neutrality' to eliminate special treatment have the merit that they may reduce the available margins for tax planning.[67] A similar argument can be made for reducing and flattening tax rates, as higher and graduated tax rates make tax planning more attractive.

Anti-avoidance Approaches

Legal Definitions of Tax Avoidance

Tax avoidance is difficult to define. It is an arrangement or transaction that satisfies the technical requirements of the tax statute, but reduces tax in a way that is against the spirit or policy of the law.[68] The puzzle of a transaction in accordance with law that must be prohibited because it reduces tax is the crux of the problem of defining tax avoidance. One approach emphasises the 'contrived' or 'artificial' aspects of avoidance transactions.[69] An economic definition of tax avoidance is: 'taxpayer efforts to reduce their tax liability that do not alter their consumption basket other than due to income effects'.[70] This implies intentional efforts by taxpayers to minimise tax liabilities while maintaining the economic substance of their activities. This definition is similar to legal definitions that seek to emphasise the 'substance' instead of legal form of the transaction.

One recently developed concept is 'aggressive tax planning'.[71] The OECD Forum on Tax Administration has defined aggressive tax planning by multinational enterprises as having the following elements:

> Planning involving a tax position that is tenable but has unintended and unexpected tax revenue consequences. Revenue bodies' concerns relate to the risk that tax legislation can be misused to achieve results which were not

---

[67] See, e.g. Natasha Sarin, Lawrence Summers and Joe Kupferberg, *Tax Reform for Progressivity: A Pragmatic Approach*, Hamilton Project/Brookings Institution Working Paper 2020/1 (Washington, DC: Brookings Institution, 2020); Tristram Sainsbury and Robert Breunig, *The Australian Tax Planning Playbook: Vol 1*, TTPI Working Paper 1/2020 (Canberra: Tax and Transfer Policy Institute, Australian National University, 2020), https://taxpolicy.crawford.anu.edu.au/publication/ttpi-working-papers/16280/australian-tax-planning-playbook-volume-1.

[68] Chris Evans, 'Containing Tax Avoidance: Anti-avoidance Strategies' in John G Head and Richard Krever (eds.), *Tax Reform in the 21st Century*: (Alphen aan den Rijn, Netherlands: Kluwer Law International, 2009), 529–60.

[69] Rebecca Prebble and John Prebble, 'Does the Use of General Anti-avoidance Rules to Combat Tax Avoidance Breach Principles of the Rule of Law? A Comparative Study' (2010) 55 *Saint Louis University Law Journal* 21–45; Graeme Cooper (ed.), *Tax Avoidance and the Rule of Law* (Amsterdam: IBFD Publications, 1997).

[70] Slemrod and Gillitzer, *Tax Systems* (see n 5), 53.

[71] OECD, *Seoul Declaration: Third Meeting of the OECD Forum on Tax Administration (14–15 September 2006)* (Paris: OECD, 2006), www.oecd.org/tax/administration/37415572.pdf; Annet Wnyana Oguttu and Ann Kayis-Kumar, 'Curtailing Aggressive Tax Planning: The Case for Introducing Mandatory Disclosure Rules in Australia' (2019) 17(1) *eJournal of Tax Research* 83–104 (part 1); and (2020) 17(2) 233–57 (part 2).

foreseen by the legislators. This is exacerbated by the often lengthy period between the time schemes are created and sold and the time revenue bodies discover them and remedial legislation is enacted.

Taking a tax position that is favourable to the taxpayer without openly disclosing that there is uncertainty whether significant matters in the tax return accord with the law. Revenue bodies' concerns relate to the risk that taxpayers will not disclose their view on the uncertainty or risk taken in relation to grey areas of law (sometimes, revenue bodies would not even agree that the law is in doubt).[72]

Concerns about aggressive tax planning, and the role of tax practitioners and investment banks in this process were among the drivers of the G20-OECD Base Erosion and Profit Shifting (BEPS) project that we discuss in Chapter 11.

The features or strategies that appear time and again in income tax avoidance schemes (and are important in tax planning generally) include:

- income splitting between high tax rate and low tax rate entities through bargaining or where jointly controlled;
- transfer pricing (shifting profits or losses between associated entities);
- inflating values of assets such as trading stock or depreciating assets, so as to achieve a step-up in cost for a tax deduction;
- timing alteration, for example, bringing forward the recognition of expenses or deferring the recognition of income;
- conversion of a receipt from one form of income to another form of (lower taxed) income, for example, ordinary income to capital gains;
- conversion of an expense from non-deductible to deductible, for example, private to business or capital to revenue in nature;
- obtaining a tax benefit at no or little economic cost or commercial risk, for example, using non-recourse debt in a 'round robin' or circular transaction to generate a tax deduction, or claiming a tax loss that was not 'suffered' economically by the taxpayer; and
- shifting location, for example, establishing the source of income or residence for tax purposes in a low-tax jurisdiction instead of a high-tax jurisdiction.

Tax laws deal with tax avoidance in three main ways: through specific or targeted anti-avoidance rules enacted in the tax statute (sometimes called 'SAARs' or 'TAARs'); through judicial doctrines or approaches to interpretation; and through statutory general anti-avoidance rules (GAARs). The gradual accretion of SAARs and TAARs in the tax statute adds significantly to its complexity in many countries; the US passive activity loss rules discussed in Box 9.2 are an example. These integrity rules are necessary to ensure

---

[72] OECD, *Study into the Role of Tax Intermediaries* (see n 35), Glossary.

resilience of the system but they increase complexity and administrative and compliance costs.

Judicial Anti-avoidance Doctrines

The judiciary play an important role in the application of the tax rules, including specific and general anti-avoidance rules. Tax rules are statutory law that must be applied and interpreted in a 'positivist' sense, without recourse to external morality or other justification.[73] Judges and lawyers rely, explicitly or implicitly, on theories of textual analysis and statutory interpretation applicable in their jurisdiction. Legal values of consistency, coherence and certainty are important in interpreting the tax law, managing disputes and litigating tax cases.

One important issue is whether judicial emphasis is placed on a 'literal' interpretation of statutory words, or on the meaning of those words interpreted with reference to Parliamentary intent, evidenced in the 'spirit' or 'policy' of the provision. The judiciary must also establish the facts and ascertain the effect of the legal arrangements of the taxpayer. Here, a court's approach to the 'substance' or form of the legal transaction is important. The adoption of a 'purposive' interpretive approach to the statute, or applying an 'economic substance' approach to a transaction, can go a long way to addressing tax avoidance. Last, but not least, the judiciary play a role that might be thought of as cultural or normative despite the strictures of legal positivist interpretation: that is, the judiciary has a role in establishing societal and taxpayer attitudes with respect to payment of tax under the law.

In the United States, 'courts have traditionally sought to determine the legislative purpose for a specific statute in order to determine whether the statute's plain meaning is unreasonable'[74] – implying a 'substantive' or purposive approach. In other jurisdictions, there may be uncertainty about how the judiciary will approach the textual analysis of tax law. Brian Arnold has suggested that 'there is considerable confusion in Canada concerning the doctrine of substance over form', with courts in some cases emphasising 'commercial and economic realities', and in other cases respecting the taxpayer's 'legal' relationships.[75]

Courts have developed specific judicial doctrines that may strike down tax avoidance schemes. These include civil law doctrines of *fraude á la loi*, *fraus*

---

[73] See, e.g. Leslie Green, 'Legal Positivism' in Edward N Zalta (ed.), *The Stanford Encyclopedia of Philosophy* (Stanford, CA: Stanford University Press, 2003).
[74] Hugh J Ault, 'United States' in Ault et al, *Comparative Income Taxation* (see n 65), Kindle Book, Loc 7462.
[75] Brian J Arnold, 'Canada' in Ault et al, *Comparative Income Taxation* (see n 65), Kindle Book, Loc 2309.

legis, *abus de droit*, *simulation* and the common law doctrine of sham transactions.[76] A concept of abuse of law has been applied by the Court of Justice of the European Union.[77]

The word 'sham' is used in a popular way to refer to fake or disguised transactions, similar to a deliberate fraud.[78] A doctrine of sham transactions is applied by courts across the common law world, including the United Kingdom, Australia, Canada, New Zealand, India, South Africa and the United States. Judges use phrases such as 'trompe l'oeil';[79] suggesting a legal form established in written documentation and other evidence as a cloak to hide the real transaction and its tax consequences. For example, an arrangement may purport to be a business partnership at law, but it is in reality an employee–employer relationship.[80] A letter-box company in a tax haven may be the alter ego of another person.[81]

US courts established early in the twentieth century a 'sham transaction' doctrine aimed at overriding the form of transactions and reflecting their economic substance for tax purposes. More generally, 'US courts use a variety of judicially-created doctrines, such as the sham doctrine, the step transaction doctrine, the economic substance doctrine' to address tax avoidance transactions.[82] In 2010, the US government codified its economic substance doctrine and imposed strict legislative penalties for violation.[83] In general, it appears that judicial doctrines applied case by case are too narrow and cumbersome to address tax avoidance schemes.

Statutory General Anti-avoidance Rules

It is increasingly common for governments to legislate a statutory GAAR that gives the tax authority power to override the effect of other provisions of the tax

---

[76] Miranda Stewart, 'Sham Transactions and Tax Avoidance' in Nigar Hashimzade and Yuliya Epifantseva (eds.), *The Routledge Companion to Tax Avoidance Research* (London: Routledge, 2017), 48–57; Edwin Simpson and Miranda Stewart (eds.), *Sham Transactions* (Oxford: Oxford University Press, 2013).

[77] Rita de la Feria and Stefan Vogenauer (eds.), *Prohibition of Abuse of Law: A New General Principle of EU Law* (Oxford: Hart Publishing, 2011).

[78] See, e.g., CBC, 'Isle of Sham: Tales from a Canadian Tax Haven', www.taxfairness.ca/en/news/isle-shamtales-canadian-tax-haven, accessed 16 March 2022.

[79] *Antle* v *R* (2010) 2010 DTC 7304 (Canada; French report).

[80] In Australia: *Cam & Sons Pty Ltd* v *Sargent* (1940) 14 ALJ 162 (High Court of Australia); in the United States, e.g. *ASA Investerings Partnership* v *Commissioner* 201 F.3d 505 (DC Cir. 2000) (US).

[81] See, e.g. James Kessler, 'What Is (and What Is Not) a Sham' (2020) 9.2.2 *Offshore & International Tax Review*, www.khpplc.co.uk/client-area/review/907/OITR-Vol922-What-is-and-what-is-not-A-Sham-James-Kessler-QC.

[82] Joshua Blank and Nancy Staudt, 'Sham Transactions in the United States' in Simpson and Stewart, *Sham Transactions* (see n 76), 68–85, 69.

[83] Internal Revenue Code (US), Section 7701(o).

law.[84] New Zealand has had a statutory GAAR in its income tax law since 1891, and Australia since 1915. In other countries, a GAAR is relatively recent. In the United Kingdom, after a long period of development of judicial doctrines and considerable uncertainty about their effect, the GAAR was introduced in 2013 following the Aaronson Report.[85]

Modern statutory GAARs emphasise the objective facts and taxpayer purpose, and focus on the economic or commercial substance of a transaction as opposed to its legal form. Many GAARs require a hypothesis of an alternative transaction that would result in higher tax, which is evidence of a purpose to achieve the lower tax outcome. If conditions are met, a GAAR usually authorizes the tax authority to void or deny a transaction and in some cases to reconstruct a new transaction that is subject to more tax in the jurisdiction. The extent of tax authority power under a GAAR varies significantly between countries. It may be argued that, where a GAAR is applied, this is an indication of a flaw in the existing core structure that should be remedied with more general reform.[86]

The GAAR operates to set the boundaries of acceptable behaviour under the core rules of the tax law. This function is illustrated by the 'double reasonableness' test in the UK GAAR. The rule applies if a 'tax arrangement' is found to be 'abusive'. A tax arrangement will be 'abusive' if it is an arrangement 'the entering into or carrying out of which cannot reasonably be regarded as a reasonable course of action in relation to the relevant tax provisions, having regard to all the circumstances'. Judith Freedman explains:

> This is the central 'double reasonableness' test. It is seeking to provide a norm of 'acceptability'. It is not for the judge (or the GAAR panel) to decide what they think would have been reasonable, rather they are to decide what could have been 'reasonably regarded as reasonable'.[87]

When applied, a statutory GAAR subjects a taxpayer to more tax than would otherwise apply under the law in respect of the relevant structure or transaction. Does this mean the statutory GAAR breaches the rule of law? The question has been explored by various commentators.[88] The better view is

---

[84] Michael Lang, Jeffrey Owens, Pasquale Pistone, Alexander Rust, Josef Schuch and Claus Staringer (eds.), *GAARs – A Key Element of Tax Systems in the Post-BEPS World* (Amsterdam: IBFD, 2016).

[85] Finance Act 2013 (UK) Part 5; see Judith Freedman, 'United Kingdom' in Lang et al, *GAARs – A Key Element of Tax Systems* (see n 84), 741–64; Graham Aaronson, *GAAR Study: A Study to Consider Whether a General Anti-avoidance Rule Should Be Introduced into the UK Tax System* (London: Her Majesty's Treasury, 2011).

[86] Richard Krever, 'General Report: GAARs' in Lang et al, *GAARs – A Key Element of Tax Systems* (see n 84), 1–20 [1.10].

[87] Freedman, 'United Kingdom' (see n 85), [37.2.1].

[88] See, e.g. Cooper, *Tax Avoidance and the Rule of Law* and Prebble and Prebble, 'Does the Use of General Anti-Avoidance Rules to Combat Tax Avoidance Breach Principles of the Rule of Law?' (see n 69).

that the GAAR does not breach the rule of law, but is rather a 'meta-rule', sometimes called an organic or constitutional rule. The GAAR saves the tax law from excessive formality, bringing it into closer alignment with economic facts of taxpayers and their dealings. Thus, it operates 'as a kind of gateway that makes tax law (which is otherwise autonomous) vulnerable to the influence of other systems, in particular the economic system'.[89] This is necessary to protect the coherence of the tax law.

The Tax Gap

Governments seek to quantify tax evasion, including the informal or cash economy, through the identification and measurement of the 'tax gap'.[90] Some tax authorities publish a tax gap analysis, including Australia, the United Kingdom, Canada, Denmark, Finland, Sweden and the United States; others do internal analysis to support administrative functions.[91] The tax gap may be approached from a top-down 'macro' perspective, or from an empirical, bottom-up perspective. No data approach is fully comprehensive. For example, random audits will capture a lot of information about the taxpayer population but cannot provide information about those who are not in the system at all.

A tax gap can be defined as the difference between the total theoretical liability of a tax and the actual tax revenue collected in a period. The total theoretical liability is an estimate of the expected tax on the assumption that all liable taxpayers fully complied with all of their obligations. The tax gap may be generated through an 'administration and compliance' gap or a 'law and policy' gap. The policy gap may also be analysed as 'tax expenditures' or departures from a benchmark tax system, as defined in Chapter 3. This is illustrated in Figure 9.3. The 'compliance gap' is more commonly called the 'tax gap'; however, in many developed countries, the 'policy gap' may be more important in revenue forgone.

The UK HMRC annual tax gap report has the purpose of providing a foundation for understanding and responding to non-compliance, and to provide information to the public about compliance in the tax system.[92] The report estimates the UK tax gap to be 4.7 per cent, or £31 billion in 2018–19. This is lower than in previous reports dating back to 2006, with HMRC

---

[89] Geraldine Hikaka and John Prebble, 'Autopoiesis and General Anti-avoidance Rules' (2010) 21 *Critical Perspectives on Accounting* 549–59, 551.

[90] Neil Warren and Richard Highfield, *Mind the (Tax) Gap! It Is Bigger and More Complex than You Think*, UNSW Business School Research Paper (Sydney: University of New South Wales, 2020); and see International Monetary Fund, *Current Challenges in Revenue Mobilization: Improving Tax Compliance* (Washington, DC: IMF, April 2015), www.imf.org/external/np/pp/eng/2015/020215a.pdf.

[91] The OECD reports that 31 of 58 surveyed jurisdictions do some tax gap analysis, and 18 publish some of the results: OECD, *Tax Administration 2019* (see n 9), 35.

[92] Her Majesty's Revenue and Customs, *Measuring Tax Gaps 2020 edition* (London: HMRC, 9 July 2020).

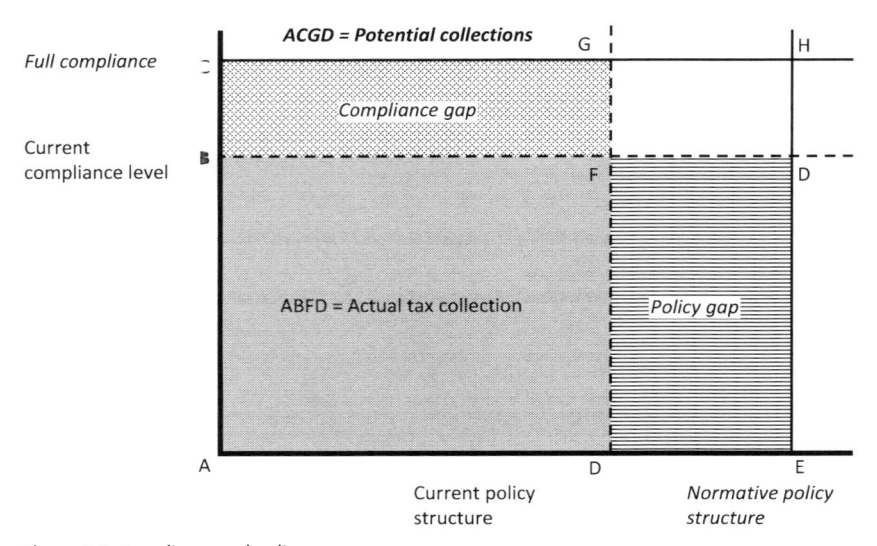

Figure 9.3 Compliance and policy gaps
Source: International Monetary Fund, *Current Challenges in Revenue Mobilization: Improving Tax Compliance* (Washington, DC: IMF, April 2015), www.imf.org/external/np/pp/eng/2015/020215a.pdf.

reporting a downward trend from 7.5 per cent in 2005–06, the first year in which it reported.

The HMRC tax gap report summarises the types of taxpayer, types of tax and types of behaviour generating the tax gap. The largest tax gap is estimated to be by small businesses. This is the sector with the most individual choice that is least embedded in a network of withholding and data cross-checking – in contrast to individual wage earners and large businesses.

Part III
The Tax State in the Global Digital Era

10

Tax Jurisdiction

The Individual and the State

> The proprietor of land is necessarily a citizen of the particular country in which his estate lies. The proprietor of stock is properly a citizen of the world, and is not necessarily attached to any particular country.
>
> Adam Smith, *Wealth of Nations*

Tax Jurisdiction

The Borders of the Tax State

The Treaty of Westphalia of 1648 divided up the territory of Europe in 'a political imaginary that mapped the world as a system of mutually recognizing, sovereign territorial states'.[1] The successful assertion of tax jurisdiction was a critical element of the 'organizing logics' of the sovereign state.[2] In the eighteenth century, Adam Smith considered taxation to be essential to make Britain a 'great nation' in an international order of other nations. In the second half of the twentieth century, the nation state operated in what Nancy Fraser termed the 'Keynesian-Westphalian' frame,[3] built on a market economy. This 'tax and welfare state' was actively interventionist in the economy and had a core role of redistribution. Taxation was territorially and economically bounded, and claims for distribution were mostly internal, or domestic, claims on the state. International law recognised the right of other tax states to exist applying their own sovereign representative and distributional frame. However, the national border causes difficulties for the relationship between tax law and economic reality. Economic globalization since the 1980s has created new challenges for tax policy, as explained in

---

[1] Richard Falk, 'Revisiting Westphalia, Discovering Post-Westphalia' (2002) 6(4) *Journal of Ethics* 311–52.
[2] Saskia Sassen, *Territory, Authority, Rights: From Medieval to Global Assemblages* (Princeton, NJ: Princeton University Press, 2006), 10.
[3] Nancy Fraser, 'Reframing Justice in a Globalizing World' in David Held and Ayse Kaya (eds.), *Global Inequality: Patterns and Explanations* (Cambridge, UK: Polity Press, 2007), 252–68, 252

Chapter 4. As John Prebble observed, 'A gain does not recognise national borders. Borders are created by humans'.[4]

The allocation of tax jurisdiction between countries through a combination of unilateral tax laws, bilateral treaties and multilateral treaty models was argued by Avi-Yonah to amount to an 'international tax system' or customary law of international tax.[5] This international tax system included a principle of avoiding double taxation, and a principle that income should be taxed once (somewhere). The former principle is widely adopted but the latter has been highly contested. However, Sunita Jogarajan dates to the League of Nations an international tax principle of 'tax once, and only once'.[6]

This chapter focuses on the jurisdiction to tax individuals on the basis of 'residence' and 'source', reflecting their physical presence or the connection to the state of labour or capital income or assets that they control. Chapter 11 turns to consider tax jurisdiction over corporations and the challenge for states of taxing multinational enterprises in a global digital economy.

Tax jurisdiction is constrained by the administrative or practical limits of state capability to enforce taxation. It has never been the case that sovereigns could successfully tax all their 'subjects' as legally defined. Ideally, we would align the legal jurisdiction to tax reasonably closely to the boundaries of 'enforcement jurisdiction'.[7] To achieve this, simplicity and 'rough justice' approaches are usually to be favoured.[8] Governmental ability to enforce taxes is dynamic, with the potential to change through political, technological and economic developments. Governments have the potential to enhance their administrative capability in the international sphere by cooperating with each other. The engagement of states in international tax regulation is an expression of national sovereignty; cooperation between governments in taxation may enhance sovereignty through enhancing the taxing capacity of the state.

Residence and Source

The tax concepts of residence and source have legal roots in the international law concepts of jurisdiction *in personam* of a sovereign over individuals, and jurisdiction *in rem*, over economic activity, real property or other assets within

---

[4] John Prebble, 'Why Is Tax Law Incomprehensible?' (1994) 4 *British Tax Review* 380–93, 384. Of course, gains, too, are created by humans.
[5] Reuven S Avi-Yonah, *International Tax as International Law* (Cambridge, UK: Cambridge University Press, 2009).
[6] Sunita Jogarajan, *Double Taxation and the League of Nations*, Cambridge Tax Law Series (Cambridge, UK: Cambridge University Press, 2018).
[7] Walter Hellerstein, 'Jurisdiction to Tax in the Digital Economy: Permanent and Other Establishments' (2014) 68(6–7) *Bulletin for International Taxation* 346–51.
[8] H David Rosenbloom, 'Where's the Pony? Reflections on the Making of International Tax Policy' (2009) 57(3) *Canadian Tax Journal* 489–503, 496–7.

the territory.[9] Tax residence is a two-way bargain. The state comprises its territory and its population, who are essential to its continuing existence. The definition of 'residence' aims to retain taxpayers and their economic production, consumption and wealth within its borders. The residence jurisdiction matches our expectation that 'what makes a given collection of individuals into fellow subjects of justice is their shared residence on the territory of a modern state and/or their membership in the political community that corresponds to such a state'.[10]

States assert 'source' jurisdiction to tax the economic return to individuals from work, business or investment in their territory or by identifying some relationship between the income generated and the state. One early approach, which still has resonance today, is Edwin Seligman's concept of 'economic allegiance' to the tax state, which requires us to consider 'where is wealth acquired, where does it exist, where do the property rights become enforceable, and where is the wealth disposed of'.[11] The first three elements of this concept refer to income, gains or assets, while the last implies that consumption or expenditure in the jurisdiction may support source taxation.

Consistently with international law, states have 'the right to exercise jurisdiction and the duty to recognise the same right of other States'.[12] This interstate bargain is usually implemented by allocating to the residence state the primary right to tax worldwide income *and* the primary responsibility to recognise the right of other states to tax income from economic activities with a sufficient nexus to their own jurisdiction. The residence state has the responsibility to eliminate 'double tax', or relieve tax on income where it is taxed by the other jurisdiction (for example, by an exemption or credit). This is because the residence state 'stands in a position to see the entirety of the taxpayer's income and therefore is best situated to avoid international double taxation'.[13]

A state may assert tax jurisdiction based on the political nexus of citizenship (no successful tax state relies *only* on citizenship as the basis of tax jurisdiction). This derives from a theory of personal allegiance to the sovereign which predates the nation state. International lawyer Philip Jessup observed that sovereignty based on citizenship is 'both older and newer than the territorial

---

[9] Yoram Margalioth, 'Taxation, International' in *Max Planck Encyclopedias of International Law* (Oxford: Oxford University Press, 2011).

[10] Fraser, 'Reframing Justice in a Globalizing World' (see n 3), 255.

[11] Edwin RA Seligman, *Double Taxation and International Fiscal Cooperation* (New York: Macmillan, 1928), 112–13.

[12] Frederick A Mann, 'The Doctrine of International Jurisdiction Revisited after 20 Years' in *Collected Courses of the Hague Academy of International Law: Vol 186* (The Hague: Hague Academy of International Law, 1984), http://dx.doi.org/10.1163/1875-8096_pplrdc_A9789024731770_01, 20.

[13] H David Rosenbloom, 'What's Trade Got to Do with It' (1994) 49 *Tax Law Review* 593–8, 596.

theory', suggesting that 'the history of all laws opens with an entirely personal conception of law: every man possessed only the rights and duties with which the laws of his own tribe, city, or class invested him, and could not be judged by any other'.[14] Jessup concluded that 'territoriality of jurisdiction' is a rule of convenience 'not a requirement of justice or even a necessary postulate of the sovereignty of the State'.[15]

Wei Cui asked whether 'residence' and 'source' might be considered as 'empty' rules, operationalised by states to assert and define their taxing jurisdiction in relation to each other.[16] That is, a government may define a taxpayer over which the government asserts 'worldwide' tax jurisdiction as a 'resident', and may define the income that it chooses to tax (regardless of whether the person deriving it is 'resident') as having a 'source' in its jurisdiction.[17] However, the content of these terms is not only established by the government's *assertion* of jurisdiction, as an exercise of economic and state power in relation to its own people and to other states. A better approach, while acknowledging the difficulties, is to follow Jessup in an analysis of the concepts of 'residence' and 'source' as *rules of convenience* in establishing tax jurisdiction.[18]

We can combine Jessup's concept of jurisdictional *convenience* with Seligman's concept of *economic allegiance* to identify the following principles of tax jurisdiction:

- The duty or obligation of the taxpayer to the state, largely derived from the benefit obtained from the state by the taxpayer;
- the taxpayer's right to just taxation, based on ability to pay, and the obligation and ability of the state to deliver just taxation to the taxpayer;
- the ability of the state to administer and of the taxpayer to comply with the tax; and
- the duty of states to each other in permitting the legitimate exercise of tax jurisdiction involving the preceding elements.

It is important to emphasise that these principles relate to *people* and their relationship with the tax state. Entities such as corporations are legal fictions that may be proxies for both economic activity and taxing authority. We therefore will need to consider tax jurisdiction in different ways for individuals and corporate entities. We may also need to consider jurisdiction differently for different types of economic return, such as active income (business profits and labour income), passive income (capital, or investment income and gains),

---

[14] Philip Jessup, *Transnational Law* (Cambridge, MA: Harvard University Press, 1956), Part II, 41.
[15] Ibid., 44.
[16] Wei Cui, 'Minimalism about Residence and Source' (2017) 38 *Michigan Journal of International Law* 245–69.
[17] Ibid., 254.
[18] Jessup, *Transnational Law* (see n 14), 41.

consumption, or stocks and transfers of wealth, based on the market activity and the constraints on state action in each case.

Tax Treaties

International tax rules are established by many states in their domestic tax law – that is, tax jurisdiction is primarily established unilaterally. However, tax treaties also play an important role in managing the tax relations between states. Bilateral tax treaties have been the dominant mode of international tax cooperation between states since the nineteenth century, negotiated on the principle of reciprocity between two sovereign nations.[19]

The diversity of national tax systems and state economic circumstances have been considered as the reason, and justification, for bilateralism in tax treaties.[20] The twentieth century saw a significant increase in income taxes in many countries. This led the League of Nations to commission a series of reports on double taxation in the 1920s and to the first model treaties that formed the basis of a small network of bilateral tax treaties, mostly in Europe.[21] The Four Economists, who produced their report in 1923, considered whether a multilateral convention could be produced.[22] Seligman saw multilateralism as a way for countries with similarities in their tax systems to cooperate.[23] However, treaty negotiation was ultimately established in the pathways of bilateralism.[24]

The first Organisation for Economic Co-operation and Development (OECD) Model Convention was published in 1963. The Committee on Fiscal Affairs was established in 1971 and it produced the first Model Convention with Commentary in 1977.[25] The Model Convention was most recently updated in 2017.[26] In 1991, the approach to updating the Model and

---

[19] Sunita Jogarajan, 'Prelude to the International Tax Treaty Network: 1815–1914 Early Tax Treaties and the Conditions for Action' (2011) 31(4) *Oxford Journal of Legal Studies* 679–707.

[20] H David Rosenbloom and Stanley Langbein, 'United States Tax Treaty Policy: An Overview' (1981) 19 *Columbia Journal of Transnational Law* 359–406, 366.

[21] Jogarajan, *Double Taxation and the League of Nations* (see n 6), 3.

[22] GWJ Bruins, L Einaudi, ERA Seligman and J Stamp, *Report on Double Taxation: Submitted to the Financial Committee* (1923) extracted in Jogarajan (see n 6), 19.

[23] Seligman, *Double Taxation and International Fiscal Cooperation* (see n 11), 170.

[24] Thomas Rixen and Ingo Rohlfing, 'The Institutional Choice of Bilateralism and Multilateralism in International Trade and Taxation' (2007) 12 *International Negotiation* 389–414; Ekkehart Reimer and Alexander Rust (eds.), *Klaus Vogel on Double Taxation Conventions*, 4th rev ed (Alphen aan den Rijn, The Netherlands: Kluwer Law International, 2015), 1.

[25] OECD, 'Draft Double Taxation Convention on Income and on Capital' (1963), www.oecd-ilibrary.org/taxation/draft-double-taxation-convention-on-income-and-capital_9789264073241-en; OECD, 'Model Double Taxation Convention on Income and Capital' (1977), www.oecd-ilibrary.org/taxation/model-double-taxation-convention-on-income-and-capital_9789264055919-en.

[26] OECD, 'Model Convention with Respect to Taxes on Income and on Capital' (latest edition 2017), with Commentary, www.oecd.org/tax/model-tax-convention-on-income-and-on-capital-full-version-9a5b369e-en.htm.

Commentary was made 'ambulatory'. Recently, the views of non-OECD member states on the OECD Model and its revision have been encouraged. The purpose of the Model Convention and Commentary is 'to clarify, standardise, and confirm the fiscal situation of taxpayers who are engaged in commercial, industrial, financial, or any other activities in other countries through the application by all countries of common solutions to identical cases of double taxation'.[27] The OECD, with a relatively small number of 38 member states, has the capacity to make rules binding on its members but does not usually do so, preferring a consensus-based approach.[28]

The United Nations Model Convention is also influential, especially for treaty negotiation between developing and developed countries.[29] The UN, with 193 member states, may claim a mandate for the widest representation in terms of multilateral taxation. Since 1980, the UN Committee of Experts on International Cooperation in Tax Matters for the Economic and Social Council (ECOSOC) has produced the UN Model Convention.[30] The Committee was established in 2004 and meets twice a year.[31] The Committee has 25 members including experts in tax policy and administration appointed by governments with four-year terms. It provides non-binding recommendations updates the UN Model, and has prepared a toolkit and manual on tax treaty negotiation between developing and developed nations. However, the Committee has insufficient resources to act as a global multilateral tax institution despite suggestions that the UN should have this role.[32] As a result of both of these model conventions, 'the treaty based international tax regime already has multilateral features laced into its fundamental network-like structure'.[33]

The bilateral approach was successful in supplementing national tax laws to establish a stable framework for international taxation to relieve double taxation, remove barriers to investment and achieve fairness for individual and

---

[27] Reimer and Rust, *Klaus Vogel on Double Taxation Conventions* (see n 24), 1.
[28] Jonathan Schwarz, *Schwarz on Tax Treaties* (Alphen aan den Rijn, Netherlands: Kluwer Law International, 2018), 2.
[29] United Nations Economic and Social Council, 'Model Double Taxation Convention between Developed and Developing Countries' (2017), with Commentary, www.un.org/esa/ffd/wp-content/uploads/2018/05/MDT_2017.pdf.
[30] Ibid. See UN, 'Charter of the United Nations' 1 UNTS XVI (26 June 1945), art 681, www.un.org/en/about-us/un-charter; UN ECOSOC, 'UN Tax Committee', www.un.org/development/desa/financing/what-we-do/ECOSOC/tax-committee/tax-committee-home, accessed 29 March 2021.
[31] UN ECOSOC, 'ECOSOC Resolution 2004/69 on "Committee of Experts on International Cooperation in Tax Matters" (E/2004/INF/2/Add.3, page 14)' (11 November 2004), www.un.org/development/desa/financing/document/ecosoc-resolution-200469-committee-experts-international-cooperation-tax-matters.
[32] See, e.g. Sudharshan Kasturirangan, 'The United Nations Tax Committee as a Player in the International Tax Policy Discussion' in Anna Binder and Viktoria Wöhrer (eds.), *Special Features of the UN Model Convention* (Vienna: Linde Verlag, 2019), 3–24.
[33] Yariv Brauner, 'McBEPS: The MLI – The First Multilateral Tax Treaty That Has Never Been' (2018) 46 *Intertax* 6–17, 7.

corporate taxpayers. However, bilateral treaty negotiation is slow and secretive and it has always been partial. Over time, the bilateral tax treaty network generated fragmentation, gaps and special rules. These created an international tax environment ripe for treaty shopping and international tax arbitrage. In 2001, Victor Thuronyi proposed a multilateral tax treaty to replace the bilateral network, which he described as 'ossified' and 'weak' in the face of tax planning by multinational enterprises and wealthy individuals.[34]

In respect of transnational tax administration, bilateral treaties have largely been overtaken by multilateral agreements. Recent developments in the G20-OECD Base Erosion and Profit Shifting (BEPS) project suggest a renewed approach of multilateralism to achieve some international tax goals; we discuss this in Chapter 11.

Residence of Individuals

Defining Tax Residence

The concept of tax residence grew out of the older international law concept of domicile.[35] In 1927 the Four Experts advising the League of Nations observed that 'the tendency of modern fiscal law is to consider that all persons domiciled in a State should be liable to the same taxation therein whatever their nationality may be'.[36] Poll taxes, the forerunner to income taxes on labour as explained in Chapter 5, were residence-based taxes on local inhabitants.[37] For example, in the Colony of Connecticut, 'the duty of every inhabitant to contribute towards the support of the colony was based upon the theory of benefit received by reason of the existence of the government'.[38]

Criteria to determine residence include physical presence, place of birth, family, social and economic connections, intention and legal connection to the state. Tax residence is reassessed every year to establish the worldwide income base subject to tax but these factors taken together evoke a concept of belonging and build a life cycle element into the annual snapshot of tax status.

An individual may have more than one 'residence' based on these factors. Bilateral tax treaties establish criteria to resolve conflicts, based on the OECD Model Tax Convention Article 4. The Article 4 tiebreaker sets out

---

[34] Victor Thuronyi, 'International Tax Cooperation and a Multilateral Tax Treaty' (2001) 26(4) *Brooklyn Journal of International Law* 1641–81.
[35] Bernard H Oxman, 'Jurisdiction of States' in *Max Planck Encyclopedias of International Law* (Oxford: Oxford University Press, 2007), [10].
[36] Jogarajan, *Double Taxation and the League of Nations* (see n 6), 287.
[37] Peter Harris, *Income Tax in Common Law Jurisdictions* (Cambridge, UK: Cambridge University Press, 2006), 171.
[38] Frederick R Jones, *History of Taxation in Connecticut: 1636–1776*. Johns Hopkins University Studies in Historical and Political Science 14th Series No 8 (Baltimore, MD: Johns Hopkins Press, 1896), 15; in Harris, *Income Tax in Common Law Jurisdictions* (see n 37).

a hierarchical list of criteria including possessing a 'home' that is permanently available to the individual; having closer 'personal and economic relations'; 'centre of economic interests' or 'centre of vital interests'; or the place of 'habitual abode', or habitual stay ('*séjourne de façon habituelle*').[39] These criteria are intended to be 'of such a nature that there can be no question but that the person concerned will satisfy it in one State only, and at the same time it must reflect such an attachment that it is felt to be natural that the right to tax devolves upon that particular State'.[40] Despite this, the issue may be difficult to resolve and tax authorities or courts may fall back on economic connections, similar to a 'source' concept. Nationality may be a last resort means of deciding jurisdiction.

Justification for Residence Taxation

The justification for residence taxation relies on both the ability to pay principle and the benefit theory of taxation. This is explained by Brian Arnold as follows:[41]

> If two residents have equal amounts of income, they should be subject to the same tax burden, even if one resident's income is derived totally from domestic sources while the other's income is derived exclusively from outside the country. This equity justification is based on the assumption that all residents of a country derive significant personal benefits from the country, in the form of public goods and services, that justify taxing them irrespective of the source of their income. Thus, an individual who lives in a country may derive benefits from its infrastructure (roads and public safety), legal system, social welfare system, and education system even where all the individual's income is earned outside that country. The neutrality justification is that a country should not create a tax incentive for its residents to work or invest outside the country. If the foreign source income of residents is not subject to residence country tax, residents have an incentive to earn low-taxed foreign source income in preference to domestic source income, and this incentive is detrimental to the domestic economy.

The critical element of 'benefit', in Peggy Musgrave's words, is that nation states are '*serving populations* with common purposes and interests'. It is this *service* of the state to its people that entitles it to 'a degree of tax sovereignty over the tax treatment of the income-earning activities abroad of their residents'.[42] The service of the state to its people can be linked to the 'life cycle' character of the definition of 'residence' as it encompasses expenditures on

---

[39] OECD, 'Model Tax Convention on Income and on Capital 2017, Commentary on Article 4' https://doi.org/10.1787/mtc_cond-2017-en
[40] Ibid.
[41] Brian J Arnold, *International Tax Primer*, 4th ed (Alphen aan den Rijn, Netherlands: Kluwer Law, 2019), 39–40.
[42] Peggy Musgrave, 'Sovereignty, Entitlement, and Cooperation in International Taxation' (2001) 26 *Brooklyn Journal of International Law* 1335–56, 1336 (emphasis added).

health, housing, education, welfare, the legal system and physical infrastructure to the resident over their life course.

The ability to pay principle as set out by Arnold requires consideration of the income tax base. If we apply the benchmark of comprehensive income, all income of the taxpayer should be aggregated, no matter where it is derived, so it can be taxed at progressive rates. Many countries explicitly recognise ability to pay in rules that provide residents with a tax-free threshold, basic exemption or personal and family allowances. Non-residents who are taxable on income sourced in the jurisdiction are often not accorded such benefits, as they should be accorded ability to pay by their own 'residence' state, which should also protect them from double taxation on foreign source income.

New Residents, Departing Residents

Rules about tax residence must address the mobility of individuals between states. States evince a tendency to *extend* the definition of residence – and hence their tax jurisdiction. Many states assert jurisdiction on the basis of physical presence in the jurisdiction for a minimum period of time. Often, a minimum of half a year (183 days) is the requirement but there are many variations.

For example, the United States applies a complex 'substantial presence test' requiring a minimum of 31 days during the current year, and 183 days during the three-year period that includes the current year and the two years immediately prior, counting all the days present in the current year; one out of three of the days present in the first year before the current year, and one out of six of the days present in the second year before the current year.[43] The United States also asserts a 'residence' jurisdiction over 'green card holders' who have the right to live and work in the country.

Applying such tests, new arrivals, or those in the jurisdiction for a relatively short time, for example on working visas, may easily become tax residents. These individuals benefit from the infrastructure, economy and laws of the state while they are there, but they lack the 'life cycle' connection that justifies benefit jurisdiction over residents. The promise to new migrants, which comes with tax obligations, is often purely economic: access to jobs or other opportunities to earn income. Newly arrived tax residents may not be eligible for the full protection of the welfare state or such benefits as free health, childcare or education for many years after their arrival. Indeed, the social state is often more tightly bounded than the tax state. Governments frequently add residence time periods, visa requirements and contributory obligations to ration the provision of social services to new arrivals, while their tax systems remained tied to residence determined annually. This has been a particular

---

[43] Internal Revenue Service (US), *Substantial Presence Test*, updated 27 October 2021, www.irs.gov/individuals/international-taxpayers/substantial-presence-test.

issue in the European Union (EU), because of the free movement of persons. Since the 1990s, some EU states tightened access to social services, while others expanded access to all who could demonstrate residence, thereby continuing to align the benefits of government with tax obligations.[44]

A recent trend is for governments to make it more difficult for departing individuals to shed their residence status. The United Kingdom has made individual tax residence more 'adhesive' than in the past.[45] Other countries also have 'clinging' residence rules, which seek to tax an individual for a period of years after they depart the jurisdiction, especially when a resident departs for a zero or low tax jurisdiction.[46]

Some states have broadened tax residence while narrowing the tax obligations that go with it, with the goal of attracting high-income or wealthy individuals to become residents in a deal sweetened with lower taxes. These states 'buy in' such individuals and apply specific investment or business requirements; it is presumed that the new residents, while paying lower income taxes, will contribute to the domestic economy or through other taxes such as consumption tax or property tax.[47] The number of jurisdictions enacting tax incentives to attract individuals to become residents seems to be increasing. Governments implementing these programs abrogate the worldwide jurisdiction of the residence state, while permitting individuals to claim residence that would enable them to avoid the worldwide taxing jurisdiction of other states. This could be considered to run counter to the duty of states not to interfere with the ability of other states to assert taxing jurisdiction.

The Citizen-Taxpayer

Citizenship as a basis for tax jurisdiction has the value that it makes explicit the link between tax and democracy. Citizenship will often be a good proxy for identifying the benefit of government that has accrued to the individual, including those who grew up in a jurisdiction even if they depart as adults to live elsewhere. Despite these advantages, the United States is an outlier in

---

[44] There is a wide literature; see, e.g. Maurizio Ferrera, *The Boundaries of Welfare: European Integration and the New Spatial Politics of Social Protection* (Oxford: Oxford University Press, Oxford Scholarship Online, 2005), https://oxford.universitypressscholarship.com/view/10.1093/0199284660.001.0001/acprof-9780199284665.

[45] Her Majesty's Revenue and Customs, *Guidance Note RDR3: Statutory Residence Test* (2014), www.gov.uk/government/publications/rdr3-statutory-residence-test-srt. The 'adhesive' approach has been recommended for Australia by the Board of Taxation, *Reforming Individual Tax Residency Rules – A Model for Modernisation* (March 2019), https://taxboard.gov.au/consultation/reforming-individual-tax-residency-rules-a-model-for-modernisation.

[46] Allison Christians, 'Buying In: Residence and Citizenship by Investment' (2017) 62 *Saint Louis University Law Journal* 51–71; for example, France (in tax treaty with Monaco); Spain (in relation to tax havens); and Finland, 64.

[47] Ibid.

asserting jurisdiction to tax its citizens on their worldwide income. The US citizenship jurisdiction dates to the origins of the US income tax in 1913.[48] The benefit theory was the main justification adopted by the US Supreme Court in *Cook v Tait* 265 US 47 (1924), where the taxpayer was a US individual who moved to Mexico. The court upheld the taxation of worldwide income of citizens as constitutional based on the relationship of citizen and state: 'the government, by its very nature, benefits the citizen and his property wherever found and, therefore, has the power to make the benefit complete'.[49]

Some international lawyers queried whether personal allegiance justifies the 'economic allegiance upon which the principle of taxation is founded'.[50] In practice, other governments are not much troubled by the rule; they will assert jurisdiction to tax the US citizen resident in their own jurisdiction, leaving the United States to manage its political and tax relationship with its own 'extraterritorial' citizens.

There has been criticism of the citizenship tax on the basis that in today's era of global mobility of individuals, it is anachronistic and unjust.[51] The rule is mostly strongly criticised today by expatriate US citizens, especially those who have lived their whole lives elsewhere but are citizens of the United States by birth. The jurisdictional reach of US citizenship taxation was a relatively minor irritant, unenforced and unenforceable, during much of the twentieth century. This changed when the United States extended its power to tax offshore financial income through the Foreign Account Tax Compliance Act 2010 (FATCA), which has broad application. The choice to renounce citizenship is open to US citizens but conditions are strict especially for individuals with assets. (See discussion in Boxes 10.5 and 10.6).[52]

Jurisdiction over Labour Income

Source of Labour Income

Income from work is taxable by the 'source' jurisdiction defined to be the place where the work is performed. The nexus is determined by physical presence in

---

[48] With earlier antecedents: Michael S Kirsch, 'Taxing Citizens in a Global Economy' 82 (2007) *New York University Law Review* 443–530.
[49] *Cook v Tait* 265 US 47 (1924), 56 (Supreme Court) (US).
[50] Mann, *The Doctrine of International Jurisdiction Revisited after 20 Years* (see n 12), 24; although later concluding that citizenship-based taxation is acceptable: Frederick A Mann, *Further Studies in International Law* (Oxford: Clarendon Press, 1990), 14, in Kirsch, 'Taxing Citizens in a Global Economy' (see n 48), fn 114.
[51] Allison Christians, 'A Global Perspective on US Citizenship Taxation' (2017) 38(2) *Michigan Journal of International Law* 193–243, 202; Ruth Mason, 'Citizenship Taxation' (2016) 89 *Southern California Law Review* 169–240; Reuven S Avi-Yonah, 'The Case Against Taxing Citizens' (2010) 58 *Tax Notes International* 389–94, 389; contra Kirsch, 'Taxing Citizens in a Global Economy' (see n 48).
[52] Internal Revenue Service (US), *Expatriation Tax*, updated 22 July 2021, www.irs.gov/individuals/international-taxpayers/expatriation-tax.

the jurisdiction and by the legal contract for performance of services. The location of the contract is amenable to tax planning, but in today's era of increasing remote or digital work, the reliance on a physical presence arguably presents more of a challenge to the tax jurisdiction.

The key administrative constraint for taxation of labour income is whether the tax may be collected through withholding from the employer or recipient of services, or whether the taxpayer has personal responsibility to file a return and pay tax as an independent contractor. The challenge of distinguishing employees and independent contractors, discussed in Chapter 5, resurfaces at the international level. States take different approaches to the legal (or tax) definitions of employee and contractor. Many other issues arise, including time limits and thresholds for taxation; levying of tax rates on net or gross basis (treatment of expenses); identifying the entity or individual who is responsible for tax payment; and applying the tax treaty rules. The treaty models establish a variety of approaches, described succinctly by Brian Arnold as a 'mess'.[53] The interaction of some of these rules is illustrated in Box 10.1, presenting the example of a mobile professor.

An extreme example of a mobile worker is presented by sports people or entertainers who earn income around the world. Tax treaties usually set a rule that they are taxable by withholding at a flat rate on a gross basis if they earn any amount from activities in a country. This supports source taxation, but it creates a risk for the taxpayer of excessive taxation, as they face significant expenses and may face different rates and rules about expenses, or gross withholding across countries.[54] It may require multiple tax filings for tax compliance around the world. A common response of internationally active sports people and entertainers is to have their tax residence in a tax haven. Essentially, they are not taxable anywhere on a residence basis, but only on a 'source' basis on income earned around the world.

Transnational Workers

A different problem arises for transnational workers who have a tax residence different from the place where they work. This may cause a mismatch between the tax rates on labour income in the source country, and the worker's entitlement to a tax-free threshold or family allowance in the residence country. Conflicts of tax residence and source for transnational workers have generated numerous cases in the Court of Justice of the European Union (CJEU).

---

[53] Brian J Arnold, 'The Taxation of Income from Services under Tax Treaties: Cleaning Up the Mess' (2010) 65(2) *Bulletin for International Taxation*.
[54] Ibid., [2.3.6], [2.3.9].

> **Box 10.1 The mobile professor**
>
> A professor travels to teach a course for two weeks in a state different from their place of residence. The professor may be taxable on a source basis on the fee earned in the state in which they teach the course (the 'source' state). If the professor is employed by a university in that state, the university may be responsible for withholding and remitting the tax to the government. The jurisdiction to tax the professor on the teaching fee is able to be enforced, even though they are present for only two weeks, because of the local university that is required to withhold the tax.
>
> The professor remains a resident in their home state, taxable on a worldwide basis including the teaching fee. The 'residence' state relies on the professor to provide the necessary information to relieve double tax. If tax was withheld in the source state, the professor has an incentive to declare their income to the residence state, so that they can claim a tax credit or exemption because of the foreign tax.
>
> If the professor contracted to teach as an independent contractor rather than as an employee, the remuneration is likely to fall outside the withholding rules of the 'source' state, without special provision. Jurisdiction to tax is also limited by model tax treaty rules, which state that an independent contractor would be taxable on professional services performed in a state only if they are present there for a substantial period (e.g. 183 days), or have a fixed base in that state. This would not be satisfied by the professor, so the state in which they teach the course may not have jurisdiction to tax the fee. The professor should declare the fee in their tax return for their state of residence.
>
> The treaty rules for taxing independent professional services tend to favour the residence state, which retains worldwide jurisdiction to tax. However, the tax authority of the residence state relies on the professor to inform it about the fee derived from the foreign university. Without voluntary compliance by the professor, or cooperation with the source state, it may be difficult for the residence state to find out about the fee and to enforce its taxing rights.

Case C-279/93, *Schumacker* ECLI:EU:C:1995:31 (CJEU) upset the standard approach to tax jurisdiction, despite direct taxes on workers being within the exclusive authority of member states.[55] Mr Schumacker was a tax resident of Belgium who derived most of his income from work in Germany; in Belgium, he derived insufficient income earned to take the family circumstances into account. German income tax was withheld at source by the German employer, but Mr Schumacker was considered by the German tax authority to

---

[55] See e.g. Peter J Wattel, 'Progressive Taxation of Non-Residents and Intra-EC Allocation of Personal Tax Allowances: Why Schumacker, Gilly and Gschwind Do Not Suffice' (2000) 40(6) *European Taxation* 210–23, 214–15; Giorgio Beretta, 'Cross-border Mobility of Individuals and the Lack of Fiscal Policy Coordination among Jurisdictions (Even) after the BEPS Project' (2019) 47(1) *Intertax* 91–112.

be ineligible for the German married tax unit because he was not resident in Germany. Consequently, the income tax owed by him was higher than that owed a taxpayer with a similar family situation who was resident in Germany. The CJEU found this to be a breach of equal treatment required to establish the free movement of people in the EU. To add to the complexity, Mr Schumacker's spouse received unemployment benefits from their home state of Belgium. Full spousal 'splitting' under the German rules would require this Belgian income of the spouse to be taken into account. It was accepted that Germany could take into account the unemployment income of the spouse in calculating the base for joint taxation in Germany.

Schumacker effectively transferred the obligation to recognise ability to pay of the residence state (Belgium) to the source state (Germany). The CJEU recognised a kind of 'virtual residence', where an individual who works in one member state but resides in a second member state earns income 'entirely or almost exclusively from the work performed in the first state and does not receive in the second state sufficient income to be subject to taxation there in a manner enabling his personal and family circumstances into account'.[56] The argument of the German tax authority that this would undermine the 'cohesion' of residence taxation was rejected. Complexity of tax administration was not considered a barrier in an era of mutual cooperation and exchange of tax information in the EU.

The CJEU took the analysis further in *X* v *Staatssecretaris van Financiën* ECLI:EU:C:2017:102 where the taxpayer resident in Spain earned 60 per cent of his income in the Netherlands and 40 per cent in Switzerland. The CJEU upheld the taxpayer's claim to deduct the loss on his residence in Spain against his Dutch income, while still being treated as a 'non-resident' of the Netherlands. In these circumstances, it would be more appropriate to spread the obligation to recognise personal or family circumstances across all three states – but this implies harmonisation of such rules.[57] Where family circumstances are addressed in social welfare rather than tax law, the issue might be resolved differently. These tax issues have not been uniformly resolved in the EU despite some decades of court decisions and national responses.[58]

One solution is to apply a hybrid approach to the taxation of transnational workers. The US citizenship rule is alleviated for individuals who work in a foreign jurisdiction by an exemption for wage income of non-resident citizens up to a threshold of $107,600 in 2020, plus an allowance

---

[56] Case C-279/93, *Schumacker* ECLI:EU:C:1995:31 (CJEU), Ruling para [2].
[57] Wattel, 'Progressive Taxation of Non-Residents' (see n 55), 214–15.
[58] Federica Pitrone, 'Tax Residence of Individuals within the European Union: Finding New Solutions to Old Problems' (2016) 8(3) *World Tax Journal* 357–77.

for some costs of paying for a home in another country.[59] In Canada, a non-resident worker who derives 90 per cent or more of their income from Canadian employment is eligible for personal exemptions or tax credits, including for their spouse and dependants. In Australia, a flat rate of 15 per cent applies for earnings of temporary workers on 'working holiday' or 'seasonal worker' visas, even if they would satisfy the ordinary definition of 'resident'. The 15 per cent rate is a compromise between resident status (tax-free threshold and progressive rates) and non-resident tax status (normally taxed at 32.5 per cent from the first dollar).[60]

Taxing the 'Brain Drain'

A well-known issue in development policy concerns the 'brain drain' from the large-scale migration of skilled workers, often from developing to developed countries. The opening of borders to migration during the 1960s and 1970s, and the dramatic reduction in cost of travel and communications, increased the 'brain drain' significantly.[61]

A worker who migrates permanently from one country to another will pay taxes in the host country as a resident on worldwide income and not in their country of origin unless they have assets there. The host country benefits from the human capital and work of the migrant, as well as their taxes. The origin country loses the human capital and tax revenue, but it contributed at least some of the cost of early education, health and other benefits for the migrant when growing up. Family members in the origin country may benefit from remittances, which we consider later; these improve family well-being and relieve the origin country of some fiscal obligations to its own residents. The transnational migration therefore creates a complex redistribution of economic and fiscal benefit between countries.

One response is a 'brain drain tax'.[62] Jagdish Bhagwati and William Dellalfar proposed a 10 per cent tax on the incomes of professional immigrants, for a period of 10 years after immigration to the United States. The

---

[59] Internal Revenue Service (US), *Foreign Earned Income Exclusion*, updated 8 December 2021, www.irs.gov/individuals/international-taxpayers/foreign-earned-income-exclusion.
[60] See Canada Revenue Agency, *Seasonal Agricultural Workers Program* RC4004(E) Rev. 20, modified 23 December 2021, www.canada.ca/en/revenue-agency/services/forms-publications/publications/rc4004/seasonal-agricultural-workers-program.html#P73_2779; Australian Taxation Office, https://www.ato.gov.au/Individuals/coming-to-australia-or-going-overseas/coming-to-australia/working-holiday-makers/. If the worker is a 'resident' and from a treaty country this may breach the non-discrimination clause: *Addy v Commissioner of Taxation* [2021] HCA 34.
[61] Yariv Brauner, 'Brain Drain Taxation as Development Policy' (2010) 55 *Saint Louis University Law Journal* 221, http://scholarship.law.ufl.edu/facultypub/169.
[62] Jagdish N Bhagwati and William Dellalfar, 'The Brain Drain and Income Taxation' (1973) 1 *World Development* 94–100.

United States would collect the tax and remit it to the country of origin. A more recent proposal is for the country of origin to levy the tax, to be collected by the host country and remitted to the country of origin. The host country would provide the immigrant with a credit for that tax against its own income tax (as for work done in a 'source' country).[63] To date, no brain drain tax has been implemented anywhere in the world.

The brain drain tax challenges the justice of the 'residence' tax rule for workers who migrate from poor to rich countries. However, there is dispute about its design, purpose and economic effects. A brain drain tax would require high levels of transnational cooperation between the host and origin states. It is intended to deliver equity across borders, but it might undermine both horizontal and vertical equity in the host country if it produced a higher effective tax rate on new immigrants than on other workers earning the same wage, unless it was fully offset in the host country's own tax system. Advocates of the brain drain tax have responded to the critique of inequity by arguing that the tax would be small relative to the much higher lifetime wages earned by the migrant in the host country. However, such a tax would likely be unpopular with migrants themselves.

It might be argued that the origin country government does not deserve the tax because it did not provide sufficient benefits for the individual who chose to depart the jurisdiction. This may be because the origin country did not have the resources to provide such benefits. A more general argument that supports a brain drain tax is sovereignty represented by the citizenship of the migrant in the origin state.

If the 'brain drain' tax is intended to compensate the origin country for the loss of human capital and to support its economic development, it is justifiable only if the revenues are applied to support those goals.[64] This proposal recalls budgeting for earmarked funds, discussed in Chapter 2. The transfer of revenues from host country to origin country is similar to a transfer of aid, detached from the social and political process of tax payment from individuals to government. See Box 10.2 for an illustration of earmarking a brain drain tax to higher education.

On the other hand, the country of origin might seek to enact preferential taxation or a tax incentive to encourage a reversal of the brain drain, as has been done in Israel.[65] One might query, why only returning migrants? Why not seek to attract all kinds of skilled workers into the jurisdiction with lower taxes? This tax policy suggests that 'nation building' or cultural and social goals of the government dominate the economic or fiscal aspects of seeking skilled professionals to return 'home'.

---

[63] Matthew J Lister, 'A Tax-credit Approach to Addressing Brain Drain' (2017) 62 *Saint Louis University Law Journal* 73–84.
[64] Brauner, 'Brain Drain Taxation' (see n 61), 257.
[65] Ibid., 266.

Box 10.2 A brain drain tax for higher education

A 'brain drain' tax could be 'earmarked' to investment in education in a region or globally. A levy could be collected from a skilled migrant worker in the host jurisdiction and paid to the origin country to repay the investment, especially in tertiary education that prepares skilled migrants for working in the global economy.[66]

A possible model is a tax that is contingent on income earned by the educated worker. The approach of income-contingent government loans for higher education is adopted in various countries. In Australia and New Zealand, university fees are funded with government loans and repayment is deferred until graduates start to earn income. The repayments are collected through the pay-as-you-go withholding system for wage taxation. In Australia, if the graduate never earns more than a threshold wage, the loan is never due and collectable. The loan does not carry interest but is indexed to inflation.

When higher education loans were introduced in Australia in the 1980s, there was no obligation for graduates to repay the debt if they resided overseas, even if they earned high wages in a foreign country. In New Zealand, income-contingent student loans are interest-free but if a student leaves the country, loans start to carry interest and minimum repayments are required. Not surprisingly, enforcement was a major challenge. For some graduates living and working overseas, the accruing education debt they owed in New Zealand was a disincentive to return home.

Since 2016 Australia has amended its laws to enforce collection of higher education debt from graduates who earn income and reside in another country. The New Zealand and Australian tax authorities signed an agreement to share information on graduates who owe student loans and live in the other country. New Zealand statistics indicate that about 15 per cent of those who owe student loans live outside the country, of whom about 70 per cent are in Australia. In the ensuing year, the tax authorities identified matching records for about 85,000 individuals.[67]

The next step in cooperation would be for the Australian tax authority to collect NZ education debts and remit them to the NZ government and vice versa. However, as most Australian graduates travel elsewhere in the world (rather than New Zealand), Australia needs to seek cooperation from tax authorities in the United States, United Kingdom and other attractive jurisdictions to enforce its higher education loans on graduates living elsewhere.

This model of cross-border collection of government loans could be developed into a broader scheme. Governments could commit to collecting education-related debts for other countries. A further extension of the concept could be to use the higher education levy to provide an educational fund for the region, or to invest in higher education institutions to benefit the region as a whole. This takes a 'slice' of the benefit of government – higher education – and seeks to finance it by taxing higher income mobile workers who have benefited from that education. The system would operate as a partial 'brain drain' tax.

---

[66] This concept is explored in Bruce Chapman, Philip Clarke, Timothy Higgins and Miranda Stewart, 'Income Contingent Collection of a "Brain Drain Tax": Theory, Policy and Empirical Potential' (2015) 54(2) *Population Review* 13–27. Financing higher education in an era of global mobility is discussed in Thomas Lange, 'Public Funding of Higher Education When Students and Skilled Workers Are Mobile' (2009) 65(2) *FinanzArchiv* 178–99.

[67] OECD, *Tax Administration 2019: Comparative Information on OECD and Other Advanced and Emerging Economies* (Paris: OECD Publishing, 2019), https://doi.org/10.1787/74d162b6-en, 99.

Tax Jurisdiction in a Global Remittance Economy

Many transnational workers work in another country on a long-term basis. Over many years, they remit a large share of their labour income earned in the host jurisdiction to family in the home jurisdiction.[68] Remittance workers may be in a very different position from 'brain drain' migrants. Many are on visas with limited or no rights to permanent residence and no right to bring their family to the host country. Despite these circumscribed rights, remittance workers are liable to income tax on their earnings in the host country. Even illegal migrant workers often pay significant income tax in the country where they work and reside.[69]

Usually, remittances will be treated as intra-family gifts that are not taxable in the home jurisdiction and are not eligible for a deduction in the host jurisdiction. The host jurisdiction benefits from the labour that it needs for its economy and from the income tax of migrant workers. The family back home benefits from the remittance, and it is generally considered that the remittance supports investment and consumption in the economy of the origin country. Policymakers tend to argue against the home jurisdiction taxing remittances.[70] However, a case can be made for modification of the tax rules in this global economy of work and family, to enable the home government to receive some tax on the labour income of remittance workers.[71]

One approach would permit the worker to deduct the remittance from income for host country tax purposes and the origin country to include it in the income of recipient family member(s). This would permit 'income splitting' of the migrant worker's labour income between family members in a transnational context. As explained previously, the family unit was recognised 'across borders' in the *Schumacker* case in the EU. Chapter 5 presented an argument that income splitting in the family unit undermines the progressive individual income tax, undertaxing home production and creating a disincentive for women to work in the market economy. However, in the international context, it may be fair and efficient to permit income splitting. We could recognise the remittance as a 'partnership' distribution to the spouse, who is

---

[68] The size of remittance flows is difficult to estimate because of unofficial channels, but in 2017 they were estimated at about $596 billion, of which $450 billion flowed to developing economies: Dilip Ratha, 'What Are Remittances?' *Finance & Development*, www.imf.org/external/Pubs/FT/fandd/basics/pdf/ratha-remittances.pdf, accessed 24 March 2022.

[69] Congressional Budget Office (US), *The Impact of Unauthorized Immigrants on the Budgets of State and Local Governments* (Washington, DC: CBO, 2007) estimates that about 50 to 75 per cent of illegal migrants pay income taxes and other taxes in the United States.

[70] See, e.g. Dilip Ratha, Supriyo De and Kirsten Schuettler, 'Why Taxing Remittances Is a Bad Idea', World Bank Blogs, 24 March 2017, https://blogs.worldbank.org/peoplemove/why-taxing-remittances-bad-idea.

[71] Ariel Stevenson, 'Recovering Lost Revenue through Taxation of Transnational Households' (2016) 34(1) *Berkeley Journal of International Law* 100–56.

an active partner in the transnational exchange of labour. The remittance would be non-taxable (or deductible) to the worker in the host country. To prevent avoidance, this could be combined with a 'subject to tax' rule in the host country. Alternatively, the host country could provide a credit to the remittance worker for the tax paid by the worker's family in the home country. All of these approaches require strong regulation of remittances and close coordination between the tax authorities of each country.

Finally, we can observe that a portion of the labour income tax base of developed countries is 'mobile' in the opposite direction through 'outsourcing' and 'offshoring' of service, back office and information technology work to countries with lower wages but increasingly educated populations, such as India, the Philippines and Indonesia.[72] Rather than being framed as an issue of labour taxation, this is usually framed as an issue of mobility of corporate capital, which we discuss in Chapter 11.

Mobility of the Working Elite

The high-income working elite comprising skilled professionals, technicians, inventors, financiers, performers and sports people are likely to be attractive workers in any jurisdiction; earning high wages, they are exposed to relatively high marginal tax rates. This leads to the argument that governments should reduce tax rates or flatten the progressivity of the rate structure to attract, or retain, elite workers. Rather than a 'brain drain', this may be better analysed as a global 'brain circulation': for example, Jinyan Li observes that Canada is concerned about a 'brain drain' to the United States but has a 'brain gain' from the rest of the world.[73]

Economic theory suggests that skilled workers will respond to high taxes on their labour income using their 'exit' option. The empirical evidence is mixed. Studies suggest that the after-tax income differential between the country of origin and the host country affects skilled worker migration.[74] There is a high elasticity of response for some kinds of workers, such as sports people, with differences depending on whether people are entering or exiting a jurisdiction.[75] 'Superstar' inventors are responsive to taxes, but local

---

[72] See, e.g. Leslie P Willcocks, Mary C Lacity and Chris Sauer (eds.), *Outsourcing and Offshoring Business Services* (Cham: Springer, 2017).

[73] Jinyan Li, *International Mobility of Highly Skilled Workers in the Canadian Context: Tax Barriers and Reform Options*, Commissioned Reports, Studies and Public Policy Documents Paper 55 (2009), http://digitalcommons.osgoode.yorku.ca/reports/55

[74] Peter Egger and Doina M Radulescu, 'The Influence of Labour Taxes on the Migration of Skilled Workers' (2009) 32(9) *The World Economy* 1365–79, https://doi.org/10.1111/j.1467-9701.2009.01213.x.

[75] Henrik Kleven, Camille Landais, Mathilde Munoz and Stefanie Stantcheva, 'Taxation and Migration: Evidence and Policy Implications' (2020) 34(2) *Journal of Economic Perspectives* 119–42.

'superstars' are relatively inelastic: there may be an increase of 1 per cent in domestic 'superstar' inventors for a 10 per cent reduction in the top tax rate.[76] However, a top tax rate reduction was found to increase migration into a country of foreign 'superstars' by as much as 26 per cent.

Various countries have enacted tax discounts for skilled immigrants, including Belgium, Denmark, Finland, Italy, the Netherlands and Sweden.[77] However, policymakers face a challenge in balancing the contribution of inventors or other skilled migrants to economic growth, relative to the overall loss in tax revenue, horizontal and vertical equity. Generalised top rate cuts will undermine progressivity and revenue and may have only a small effect on the margin, while delivering lower taxes to 'inframarginal' skilled workers who are already in the jurisdiction.

The mobility of skilled labour in response to taxes is further complicated by digitalisation and the rise in remote working by 'digital nomads' who live in one jurisdiction but work remotely for employers or clients in other jurisdictions.[78] As global travel has been drastically curtailed and 'work from home' has become a necessity during the COVID-19 global pandemic this trend has increased. Box 10.3 looks at the example of the 'digitalised' professor.

Some skilled workers, and some remittance workers, access zero or low tax jurisdictions (for example, oil and gas engineers who work in the Middle East), or seek to take advantage of the various 'residence attraction' schemes to locate their residence in a lower taxed location. Yet despite evidence of mobility at the margin, it seems that the majority of skilled workers prefer to stay in their countries of origin. The home bias of most workers is exacerbated by COVID-19; the desire of skilled expatriates to return 'home' has become stark in the pandemic.[79] Those who migrate and have choices available to them will choose their destination on the basis of many factors, of which lifestyle, safety, family and opportunities for their children likely dominate tax.

---

[76] Ufuk Akcigit, Salomé Baslandze and Stefanie Stantcheva, 'Taxation and the International Mobility of Inventors' (2016) 106(1) *American Economic Review* 2930–81.

[77] Alejandro Esteller-Moré, Amedeo Piolatto and Matthew D Rablen, 'Taxing High-Income Earners: Tax Avoidance and Mobility' in Nigar Hashimzade and Yuliya Epifantseva (eds.), *The Routledge Companion to Tax Avoidance Research* (London: Routledge, 2018), 304–19.

[78] Svetislav Kostić, 'In Search of the Digital Nomad – Rethinking the Taxation of Employment Income under Tax Treaties' (2019) 11(2) *World Tax Journal* 189–225. Kostić's main example concerns an individual who travels the world and works where they please, while retaining tax residence in one country. After (and even before) COVID-19, one wonders how many such individuals exist; the more likely example is the individual who lives permanently in one state but works for an employer or clients in another state.

[79] The queue of thousands of expatriates seeking to return to Australia and New Zealand is illustrative: see, e.g. Zach Hope, 'Brain Gain: Half of Australian Expats Are Back Home, and They've Brought Their Talents with Them', *The Age*, 27 March 2021, www.theage.com.au/national/victoria/brain-gain-half-of-australian-expats-are-back-home-and-they-ve-brought-their-talents-with-them-20210327-p57ek5.html.

Box 10.3 The digitalised professor

Varying the example in Box 10.1 of the professor teaching abroad, assume the professor stays home in their country of residence and teaches the course online or remotely to students at a university in another country paid by a foreign university. Does the foreign state still have the primary right to tax the income?

This will depend on an analysis of where the teaching is 'performed'. Is this where the teacher is located (the residence state), or where the students are located, or both, or neither? If the place of performance cannot be identified, the source of income may be identified by the location of the contract and payment, which may be able to be altered at the choice of the professor or the university.

Just as important is the question of which state has capability to enforce taxation. As before, if this is an employment relationship and there is a withholding obligation, the foreign tax authority could enforce source taxation by withholding from the university employer in that state. However, if this is an independent contractor relationship, the foreign state may not have legal jurisdiction to tax.

The residence state of the professor may not be able to enforce taxation, even if it has jurisdiction; it is dependent on a voluntary declaration of the foreign income, or evidence in the professor's bank account of the receipt of funds. If the foreign state taxes the income at a non-trivial rate, the professor has an incentive to declare the income to the residence tax authority, so as to claim an exemption or credit.

Cross-border Retirement Saving

Tax systems may be an impediment to mobility but the issue may not be primarily, or exclusively, about high tax rates. The tax problems faced by skilled workers include the double taxation of non-cash remuneration, savings and pensions.[80] The complexity that results from navigating multiple tax systems is another important factor. The taxation of cross-border retirement saving may be particularly difficult to resolve, either generating double taxation or non-taxation. Box 10.4 presents an example.

A country seeking to encourage skilled workers, inventors or executives to locate or work in its jurisdiction could permit them to receive some of their labour income in the form of a capital return. In the international context, capital income is usually taxed on a 'residence' rather than a 'source' basis and often attracts lower tax rates. Another approach is to accord such workers an exemption or lower tax rate on foreign savings or assets, exempting them from the worldwide taxing basis usually appliable for residents.

An example is a special tax rule for 'temporary' residents working in Australia, who are eligible for the tax-free threshold and are taxed on their worldwide labour income, but only on their Australian source, not foreign, capital income. The rule provides a concession for foreign expatriates who

---

[80] Li, *International Mobility of Highly Skilled Workers in the Canadian Context* (see n 73).

Box 10.4 Retiring from cold countries to warm countries

An increasingly important tax issue for mobile workers is tax treatment of retirement savings.[81] This raises jurisdictional questions that sometimes conflict with tax policy for retirement discussed in Chapter 6. Which country bears the fiscal cost of the subsidy for retirement saving during a person's working life, and then has the right to tax payouts on retirement, if the worker has migrated in the meantime? Which country has the obligation to pay a pension from a social security fund or general revenues, if the worker did not contribute to the tax system of that country during their working life?

The growing importance of this issue is illustrated by the termination of bilateral tax treaties of Sweden with each of Greece and Portugal in 2021. The main issue was the treaty allocation of taxing rights on pensions received by retired people exclusively to the residence country.[82] Retirees from Sweden would become tax residents of Greece or Portugal, and would no longer pay any tax on their pension income in Sweden. The country of retirement might even go further and offer lower tax rates or special concessions to attract retirees.

The countries have announced that the treaties will be renegotiated but it is not easy to identify a better jurisdictional rule. The residence basis for taxing the age pension may be difficult to remove without challenging the fundamental norm of tax residence.

One approach is to use citizenship as an identifier of jurisdiction in relation to retirees, or exiting residents (this is already done for some capital income, as discussed later in this chapter). Sweden could assert citizenship jurisdiction over the pensions of its exiting pensioners. However, this may cause those exiting to abandon Swedish citizenship and it provides an incentive for the receiving countries to offer citizenship to them. An alternative might be to negotiate a right to tax pension income that would remain with Sweden for a period of years after departure from the jurisdiction.

have offshore assets, protecting foreign savings from tax. The worldwide basis was thought to discourage multinational enterprises from bringing in skilled personnel and locating in Australia.[83] The personal tax concession was aligned with government policy to attract corporate investment into the country.

Jurisdiction over Capital Income

Mobility of Capital

The primary right to tax capital income of individuals is allocated to the 'residence' country which asserts jurisdiction on a worldwide basis. The

---

[81] Some of these issues are explored in Beretta, 'Cross-border Mobility of Individuals' (see n 55).
[82] IBFD News, 'Sweden Proposes Terminating Tax Treaty with Greece, Sweden Proposes Terminating Tax Treaty with Portugal' (23 March 2021).
[83] Parliament of the Commonwealth of Australia, Senate, 'Revised Explanatory Memorandum, Taxation Laws Amendment Bill (No. 2) 2003 (Cth)', 2003, http://www5.austlii.edu.au/au/legis/cth/bill_em/tlab2200320s5/memo1.html.

'source' country retains limited rights to tax capital income, such as dividends, interest and royalties, usually by applying a withholding tax on the gross payment. The rate of withholding taxes is often reduced by bilateral tax treaties based on the OECD or UN model. The residence country has the duty to alleviate double taxation by granting a credit or exemption in respect of source taxation of capital income.

The mobility of capital has long posed a challenge to the administrative capability of residence states to enforce taxation. Adam Smith was aware of the fiscal implications of capital mobility of 'stock' compared to land. He observed that:[84]

> land is a subject which cannot be removed; whereas stock easily may. The proprietor of land is necessarily a citizen of the particular country in which his estate lies. The proprietor of stock is properly a citizen of the world, and is not necessarily attached to any particular country. He would be apt to abandon the country in which he was exposed to a vexatious inquisition, in order to be assessed to a burdensome tax, and would remove his stock to some other country where he could either carry on his business, or enjoy his fortune more at his ease. By removing his stock he would put an end to all the industry which it had maintained in the country which he left. Stock cultivates land; stock employs labour. A tax which tended to drive away stock from any particular country would so far tend to dry up every source of revenue both to the sovereign and to the society. Not only the profits of stock, but the rent of land and the wages of labour would necessarily be more or less diminished by its removal.

Governments could obtain little information about the value or location of revenue arising from mobile 'stock' without a 'severe inquisition'. In this circumstance it was inevitable, in Smith's view, that taxes on 'stock' would be arbitrary and levied at relatively low rates:

> The nations, accordingly, who have attempted to tax the revenue arising from stock, instead of any severe inquisition of this kind, have been obliged to content themselves with some very loose, and, therefore, more or less arbitrary, estimation. The extreme inequality and uncertainty of a tax assessed in this manner can be compensated only by its extreme moderation, in consequence of which every man finds himself rated so very much below his real revenue that he gives himself little disturbance though his neighbour should be rated somewhat lower.[85]

Today, we can identify two main aspects of capital mobility across borders: (1) the exit from a jurisdiction of a resident who owns capital (whether in or out of the jurisdiction); and (2) the exit or accumulation of capital outside the

---

[84] Adam Smith, *An Inquiry into the Nature and Causes of Wealth of Nations* (London: Methuan, first published 1776, compilation by Edward Cannan, 1904, of 5th ed, 1789), www.econlib.org/library/Smith/smWN.html, Book V, Chapter II, Part 1, Article II, 'Tax on Profit, or Upon the Revenue Arising from Stock'.

[85] Ibid.

> **Box 10.5 Exit taxes**
>
> The departure of residents who own capital from a jurisdiction may be partly addressed by 'exit taxes' levied at the border. An 'exit tax' may be levied when individuals become non-residents, on the gain in capital assets that accrued during their time as a resident.[86] Another approach is for the origin state to assert taxing jurisdiction over income for a period of time after departure, an approach by which 'residence' countries extend their tax jurisdiction towards a 'citizenship' threshold.
>
> The US government applies an exit tax on wealthy US individuals who move abroad and renounce their citizenship, above a threshold with the potential for deferral of the tax until sale in some circumstances.[87] Australia treats exit by the individual as a capital gains 'realisation' event, levying capital gains tax on accrued gain in assets on exit, with the exclusion of land located in Australia.
>
> Treating exit from the tax jurisdiction as a realisation aims to achieve fairness primarily on the basis of the benefit theory, as it applies in respect of gain accrued during the time that the individual was resident. It likely also supports taxation on the basis of ability to pay, on the basis that higher income taxpayers are more likely to own assets and are more likely to be mobile. However, exit taxes also impose a barrier, or friction, that may have disincentive effects for labour mobility, thereby undermining the efficiency case for migration in general.
>
> Some countries apply a citizenship rule to extend tax jurisdiction in certain circumstances, although they would normally apply a residence basis for jurisdiction. For example, the Netherlands extends its inheritance tax to citizens for 10 years after they terminate residence, an approach that has been held not to contravene the free movement of capital in the EU.[88]

jurisdiction that is owned or controlled by residents in the jurisdiction. In Adam Smith's time, the individual 'stock' owner, a 'citizen of the world', would likely exit the jurisdiction, taking their capital with them. Today, this may be partly addressed by 'exit' taxes (see Box 10.5).

The second form of capital mobility is more important. As Reuven Avi-Yonah has argued in the US context, the relevant question 'is whether individual US residents and citizens can escape the income tax on dividends, interest and capital gains by moving their capital overseas without moving themselves'.[89]

The difficulty in taxing mobile capital is so great that many early income taxes pragmatically adopted an exclusive source, or 'territorial', base for the income

---

[86] Beretta, 'Cross-border Mobility of Individuals' (see n 55), 99.
[87] Internal Revenue Code (US) section 877A, introduced in 2008 to replace a 10-year 'trailing tax' on renouncing citizenship.
[88] Case C-513/03, *Heirs of MEA van Hilten*, 45–52 (2006), ECR 2006 I-01957, ECLI:EU: C:2006:131 (CJEU).
[89] Reuven S Avi-Yonah, *And Yet It Moves: A Tax Paradigm for the 21st Century*, Law and Economics Research Paper Series, Paper 12-008 (Ann Arbor, MI: Michigan Law School, University of Michigan, 2012).

tax. Most tax states broadened the income tax base to cover worldwide income during the middle of the twentieth century, but a territorial base continued to apply in Israel until relatively recently, and it still applies in Singapore, Hong Kong, Malaysia and some other countries. Where legal jurisdiction to tax worldwide income is established, the administrative constraint remained a serious impediment. Even if the individual remains in the 'residence' state, finding out about income and assets located elsewhere was extremely difficult, and collecting tax on that income or assets held offshore even more so.

The Terrain of 'Offshore'

The mobility of capital would not be an issue, at least from an international tax system perspective, if capital held 'offshore' was taxed in another jurisdiction, consistently with the 'single tax' principle proposed by Avi-Yonah and others. The fundamental problem is that 'offshore' refers to the holding of income or assets in low or nil tax jurisdictions, or 'tax havens' so that it escapes taxation in any country.

Tax havens are both a fiscal and a geopolitical phenomenon. The terrain of 'offshore' is a product of global capitalism and state regulation, combined with the unwinding of empires from an earlier era and the building of new states after World War II.[90] Governments of successful tax states were instrumental in creating tax havens out of a mix of former colonies, nation states, territories and dependencies during the middle and late twentieth century. This produced 'an archipelago-like landscape of distinct legal spaces – sometimes carved out within a national territory, sometimes located in smaller territorial units on the margins of more sizable states, sometimes hosted in city-states'.[91]

Why did the successful 'tax states' of the twentieth century establish an international tax system that made it difficult to enforce the residence tax base. Why did they legislate for bank secrecy that hid information from tax authorities and refuse to cooperate in cross-border tax enforcement, hampering their own ability to collect income tax on offshore assets? In this opaque environment, the reality was that governments could not collect taxes on offshore capital income unless taxpayers voluntarily complied. As the income tax base was broadened and tax rates increased during the twentieth century, it became increasingly attractive to earn and accumulate capital income offshore. More and more people – not just the very rich – accessed these opportunities. Residents of tax states found a myriad of creative ways to hold funds offshore, including through anonymised savings vehicles such as numbered bank accounts, in separate corporations or trusts, or utilising bearer shares and

---

[90] Vanessa Ogle, 'Archipelago Capitalism' (2017) 122(5) *American Historical Review* 1431–58, and see references in fn23, 1437.

[91] Ibid., 1432. See also Jason C Sharman, *Havens in a Storm: The Struggle for Global Tax Regulation* (Ithaca, NY: Cornell University Press, 2006).

nominee shareholders, as well as layers of companies to obscure ownership, supported by a new 'offshore finance' industry and professional advisors.

Some tax havens were a dependency of a larger neighbour: the Isle of Man, Gibraltar and the Channel Islands with the United Kingdom; Monaco with France; Andorra with France and Spain; San Marino with Italy; and Liechtenstein with Switzerland. These jurisdictions retained older state and financial structures (and did not enact income taxes), while around them the European states developed substantial tax systems:

> The distinguishing feature of European tax havens ... is that they tend to be small anachronistic formations. Originally, these jurisdictions did not set themselves purposefully to establish laws that would attract tax evaders; rather, it was the other way around: the world around them launched on a course that has led to an unprecedented rise in taxation and regulation. These small and conservative states refused to follow suit.[92]

Tax havens combine a legally recognised geographic territory with legal entity forms and relationships, some old, repurposed and adapted and some new, designed for holding anonymous and secure wealth in those jurisdictions. Usually, legal entities are established through incorporation or settlement in that jurisdiction. Suitable entities include the trust with its ancient history in common law jurisdictions, separating legal control from beneficial ownership of assets and income;[93] holding vehicles like nominee corporations; and investment forms such as anonymous bank accounts, bearer shares and bonds.

Tax havens also exist within states that are otherwise high taxing jurisdictions. Switzerland developed substantial taxes on its domestic population, in line with other European tax states. At the same time, Switzerland built an 'offshore' financial economy through its centuries-old and highly regarded banking system, for which it legislated strict bank secrecy in 1934 (the breach of which was a criminal offence). Between the 1950s and 1980s, a second wave of legal and territorial reconfiguration produced a new set of tax havens. The city states of Singapore and Hong Kong established themselves as low tax locations for foreign direct investment and free trade, with cheap wages for manufacturing and strong rule of law. The Grand Duchy of Luxembourg reinvented itself as a banking and financial centre after the decline of its steel industry in the 1970s.

---

[92] Ronen Palan, 'Trying to Have Your Cake and Eating It: How and Why the State System Has Created Offshore' (1998) 42 *International Studies Quarterly* 635–44, 638; Sharman, *Havens in a Storm* (see n 91), 22.

[93] Katy Barnett, 'Offshore Trusts in the South Pacific: How Far Can the Concept of the Trust Be Stretched before It Breaks?' in Ying Khai Liew and Matthew Harding (eds.), *Asia-Pacific Trusts Law: Vol 1: Theory and Practice in Context* (Oxford: Hart Publishing, 2021), 353–80, *Bloomsbury Collections*, http://dx.doi.org/10.5040/9781509934829.ch-019.

Other small states, especially the 'islands in the sun', sought to become offshore financial centres as a pathway towards economic independence. This was promoted as a pathway to economic development by former colonial masters, and by the International Monetary Fund and World Bank, in places as diverse as the Bahamas, the Cayman Islands, the Netherlands Antilles and the British Virgin Islands, and in the Pacific, the Cook Islands and Vanuatu:

> The offshore world emerged on a more significant scale precisely at the moment when these state-based projects began to assume their greatest importance. It consisted of multiple elements and enclaves: tax havens, with their relaxed regulations and minimal taxes; flags of convenience registries, which allowed a ship whose owner lived in one country to be registered under and subject to the laws of another country; offshore financial markets and banking institutions, which offered investors advantages absent in national financial markets; and foreign trade or special economic zones, which provided incentives designed to attract foreign investment. This archipelago-like landscape allowed free-market capitalism to flourish on the sidelines of a world increasingly dominated by larger and more interventionist nation-states.[94]

Developed country governments tolerated, and even promoted, havens despite their known use for tax avoidance by their own residents or those of other countries. The geopolitics may be illustrated by the example of Vanuatu, formerly the New Hebrides jointly administered by Britain and France. Decolonisation was on the agenda during the 1970s, and was ultimately achieved in 1980, supported by the British but with French opposition. Vanuatu had no income tax and became a popular tax haven for Australians who sought to avoid income and estate taxes. In 1974, Australian Prime Minister Gough Whitlam urged British Prime Minister Harold Wilson to take steps to shut down the tax haven status of Vanuatu. Wilson refused, on the basis that Britain had to prioritise the territory's economic development and independence over other consequences.[95]

From Eurobonds to Offshore Bank Accounts

One reason why tax havens were actively constructed and fostered by tax states was because, in a world of capital controls, governments and multinational enterprises increasingly relied on them as global hubs for capital raising. The most well-known example is the Eurobond market, which started in the Netherlands in the 1960s, and was granted a stamp duty concession by the UK government to encourage this global financial business to relocate to the City of London.

---

[94] Ogle, 'Archipelago Capitalism' (see n 90), 1433.
[95] The National Archives, Prime Minister's Office, PREM16/18, letter, Harold Wilson to Gough Whitlam, 30 August 1974, discussed by Ogle, 'Archipelago Capitalism' (see n 90), 1444.

Eurobonds were anonymous 'bearer bonds' that provided a way for borrowers to raise US dollar denominated debt on global financial markets, outside US currency controls. The 'principal concerns of the Eurobond investor [were] for the freedom from withholding tax in the source country, and for the maintenance of anonymity, so that tax may be avoided in his own country'.[96] US corporate borrowers were keen to access foreign capital but the United States imposed a 30 per cent withholding tax on interest paid offshore to non-resident investors (reduced under some tax treaties). US corporations accessed the offshore Eurobond market by issuing bearer bonds through finance subsidiaries located in the Netherlands Antilles, a tax haven that was included in the US-Netherlands bilateral tax treaty with a zero withholding tax rate. Governments, including state and local governments in the United States, were also major borrowers on the Eurobond market.

In the early 1980s, the United States took action to address Eurobonds but it quickly abandoned attempts at regulation. Instead, the US legislated to establish *itself* as a tax haven for debt capital. It did this by enacting an exemption for outbound 'portfolio interest' paid by US borrowers to non-resident lenders. This reduced the cost of capital for US borrowers, sidestepping the Eurobond market and encouraging large capital flows into the United States.

Tax havens were attractive for a growing number of middle and high-income taxpayers in high taxing states who used bank accounts to evade tax in the residence country. The use of secret offshore bank accounts has a long history. It has been estimated that between World War I and World War II, Switzerland received between 5 and 10 per cent of French GDP in financial capital, largely from French citizens whose wealth transfer to Switzerland was facilitated by French banks.[97] When most governments abandoned capital controls in the 1980s, giving a new push to economic globalisation, the terrain of 'offshore' was well established and ready to take advantage of dramatically increased flows of cross-border saving by individuals. This was made even easier when banking markets globalised in the 1990s.

Bringing 'Offshore' into the Tax Jurisdiction

Extending Legal Jurisdiction to Offshore Holdings

The terrain of 'offshore' is constructed by both territorial and legal entity boundaries. The residence state must legislate to cross these boundaries, if it is to succeed in asserting jurisdiction to tax offshore income.

---

[96] Andrew W Shoyer, 'Tax Treatment of Interest Paid to Foreign Investors – Policy and Practice Concerns' (1985) 11 *International Tax Journal* 283, 294.
[97] Ogle, 'Archipelago Capitalism' (see n 90), 1436, fn 17.

The basic rule of residence jurisdiction requires worldwide income earned directly by a resident individual, such as interest on an offshore bank account, to be assessed to tax. Ultimately, it was the access to 'offshore' tax evasion by the middle class, revealed in scandals including the 'Panama Papers' and UBS and HSBC 'Swiss Leaks', combined with the Global Financial Crisis, that finally led governments to cooperate with each other in tax administration. However, it is relatively easy for taxpayers to avoid this basic rule by holding income and assets *indirectly*, through an offshore company or trust. The separate legal entity is a different taxpayer who is resident in a different jurisdiction.

Governments must extend the worldwide residence tax base to include income derived through controlled offshore entities. This may be done through anti-avoidance rules, such as those discussed in Chapter 9. It may also be achieved through rules that attribute income in foreign controlled entities to resident individuals. We focus on the examples of the United States, and the United Kingdom, both countries whose governments progressively enacted tax rules through the twentieth century to keep up with individual tax planning using entities in tax havens.

The US worldwide income tax, with a credit for foreign tax, was enacted early in the twentieth century. In 1934, the US Congress enacted domestic personal holding company rules aimed at what the Congress said was 'the most prevalent form of tax avoidance practiced by individuals with large incomes' – 'incorporated pocketbooks'.[98] At the time, the corporate tax rate was 13.5 per cent and the top personal income tax rate was 63 per cent, creating a strong incentive for wealthy individuals to hold investments in controlled corporations. In 1937, the US Congress extended these rules to capital income in foreign personal holding companies of US taxpayers.[99]

A foreign personal holding company had a foreign residence (it was usually incorporated in a foreign jurisdiction), was more than 50 per cent owned or controlled by a group of five or fewer US individuals and derived capital income including interest, dividends, royalties and gains that were subject to little or no tax in the foreign jurisdiction. The rule required US shareholders to include in their US tax return on an accrual basis their pro rata share of the income in the foreign company, although the income was not distributed to them as a dividend.

After World War II, the US Congress turned its attention to the use of offshore trusts, enacting in 1954 the 'grantor trust' rules that remain in the Internal Revenue Code today.[100] These rules seek to tax the US grantor (or

---

[98] Monica Gianni, 'PFICs Gone Wild!' (2014) 29 *Akron Tax Journal* 29–64, 43.
[99] Ibid., 45.
[100] H Brian Holland, Lloyd W Kennedy, Stanley S Surrey and William C Warren, 'Proposed Revision of the Federal Income Tax Treatment of Trusts and Estates – American Law Institute Draft' (1953) 53 *Columbia Law Review* 316–73.

settlor) who controls the trust. The next development occurred in the 1960s, as part of a major overhaul of the US tax code. In 1962, the US Congress enacted foreign investment company rules that aimed to address foreign corporations being used to avoid US taxation, which the Congress identified as an increasingly serious problem.[101] The foreign investment company rules applied accrual taxation of US shareholders on their foreign investment company income, unless the corporation elected to distribute at least 90 per cent of its taxable income each year to its US shareholders. Capital gains on sales of foreign investment company shares were treated as taxable income subject to ordinary tax rates.

The 1962 reform brought controlled foreign corporations (CFCs) into the US tax jurisdiction so as to ensure that offshore income would be taxed on an 'accrual' basis where it was not distributed into the United States by a dividend. The CFC rules enacted in 'Subpart F' of the Internal Revenue Code (where they remain today) were the first such rules in the world and a model for CFC rules enacted elsewhere.

A CFC is a foreign corporation of which more than 50 per cent by vote or value is owned by US shareholders, each owning at least 10 per cent of the foreign corporation. A US shareholder of a CFC is taxed on an accrual basis on their pro rata share of CFC income. The CFC rules targeted capital, or passive, income including foreign personal holding company income, foreign base sales and services income. Tax on active business income, and some forms of foreign sales income could be deferred (we return to this in Chapter 11).

In 1986, a new set of personal foreign investment company (PFIC) rules were enacted. This remains a central regime addressing offshore tax avoidance or evasion by US individuals. The PFIC rules aim to eliminate the benefit of tax deferral by holding income in a foreign corporation that has majority passive income and to eliminate the tax advantage of holding income in a foreign fund compared to a domestic fund. The rules are extremely broad and levy a higher tax on foreign investments than on US investments in various situations. A US shareholder may elect for mark to market taxation of its foreign investments or may elect to have PFIC income distributed.

This cursory summary of a complex and layered set of US tax rules reveals the steps that must be taken in order to bring the terrain of 'offshore' into the worldwide residence jurisdiction. First, the legislature must enact rules to override the separate legal personality of the corporation or trustee. Second, these rules must authorise tracing to identify the ultimate beneficial owners and controllers through a chain of entities. Third, the legislature must extend the concept of the taxable person and taxable income to include income accrued in the offshore controlled entity, overriding the 'realisation' principle

---

[101] HR Rep No. 87-1447, at 72 (1962).

of the income tax and the border of the foreign jurisdiction, where the income legally remains in the hands of the entity.

Somewhat similar changes were made through the last century in the United Kingdom, with a focus on trusts rather than companies. The UK Parliament began to legislate to tax income in offshore trusts in the 1920s, through a series of rules with similar aims to the US grantor trust rules. The legislative changes were a reaction to court decisions that permitted strategies to shift income into separate offshore entities. This was only moderately successful, as Mark Brabazon explains:

> Parliament responded by enacting anti-avoidance rules, the broad strategy of which was to attribute shifted income back to the grantor. A cat-and-mouse game ensued as wealthy taxpayers, their lawyers and accountants thought up new forms of lawful tax avoidance (as it was characterized), to which the Revenue responded by urging Parliament to stem the leakage of tax by plugging each new scheme and eventually its foreseeable variants. The rules were laid down in stages, the most important of which date from 1922, 1936, 1938 and 1946. This settlements legislation, as it was known, was substantially revised in 1995 and rewritten a decade later as part of the tax law rewrite project. It is still extraordinarily complex.[102]

Without rules that perform the function of the US foreign accrual legislation or UK settlements rules, a residence jurisdiction with an open economy essentially permits well-advised individuals to remove capital from the tax jurisdiction, and gives up the terrain of 'offshore' for private benefit. However, foreign income accrual rules are notoriously complex to administer and comply with, and it was not until late in the twentieth century that they were more widely adopted across countries.

In the 1980s, such rules to counter tax haven activity of individuals and corporations were a subject of proceedings of the International Fiscal Association[103] and the OECD began to pay attention to the issue.[104] Governments began to legislate various types of targeted or general rules to address offshore structures where these came to the attention of the revenue authority. In the 1990s, CFC and foreign investment trust rules began to be more widely adopted. These rules established *legal* jurisdiction to tax but they only solve the first step of the challenge of taxing offshore. They require *enforcement*, to which we turn next.

---

[102] Mark Brabazon, *International Taxation of Trust Income* (Cambridge, UK: Cambridge University Press, 2019), [2.2.3].

[103] Brian J Arnold (ed.), *Taxation of Domestic Shareholders on Undistributed Income of Foreign Corporate Affiliates: Objectives, Techniques, and Consequences* (Deventer: Kluwer Law and Taxation Publishers, 1987).

[104] OECD, *International Tax Avoidance and Evasion: Four Related Studies* (Paris: OECD, 1987).

A History of Non-cooperative Sovereigns

Historically, cooperation between states on tax administration was minimal.[105] Concerns about growing international tax evasion informed attempts at a Model tax convention after World War I, but ultimately the League of Nations focused on relieving double taxation and not on cooperation to stamp out tax evasion.[106]

Although worldwide residence income taxation became firmly established in the twentieth century, administrative cooperation between tax states lagged. Tax authorities could not identify offshore holdings without the ability to obtain and verify information from other governments, or from banks or businesses subject to foreign laws. There was little political will to overcome these limitations. In the 1980s, despite governments building the legal infrastructure for taxation of individuals on offshore income, international administrative cooperation remained in the narrow pathways laid down by bilateral negotiation.[107] Where information was accessible, cross-border enforcement was hampered by the sheer burden of storing and sharing paper tax records and slow communications. Sol Picciotto concluded that only an 'embryonic world tax administration' had been developed because tax administrators were too 'heterogenous, informal and over-secretive' for cooperation to succeed.[108]

In 1988, the OECD and the Council of Europe sought to address this through a new multilateral Convention on Mutual Administrative Assistance in Tax Matters (the 'Administrative Convention'), for signature of member states. The Administrative Convention entered into force on 1 April 1995 but the effort fizzled as many states failed to sign or ratify the treaty (the United Kingdom did not sign until 2007). In the 1990s, the OECD, at the behest of the G7, again attempted to tackle the use of tax havens.[109] We return to discuss tax competition in Chapter 11; suffice to say here that this project also failed to achieve its ambitious goals. Instead, the United States urged the G7 and OECD to 'refocus' its attention on the exchange of information so as to counter tax evasion.[110]

The OECD built a campaign for the amendment of bilateral tax treaties to support administrative exchange, and for negotiation of Tax Information

---

[105] The history of exchange of tax information across borders has been examined in depth by others. See, e.g. Roman Seer and Isabel Gabert (eds.), *Mutual Assistance and Information Exchange* (Amsterdam: IBFD, 2010); Steven A Dean, 'The Incomplete Global Market for Tax Information' (2008) 49(3) *Boston College Law Review* 605–72. The first recorded bilateral tax treaty in 1843 did aim to support tax administrative cooperation between France and Belgium: Jogarajan, 'Prelude to the International Tax Treaty Network' (see n 19), 679.

[106] Jogarajan, *Double Taxation and the League of Nations* (see n 6).

[107] Sol Picciotto, *International Business Taxation: A Study in the Internationalization of Business Regulation* (London: Weidenfeld & Nicolson, 1992).

[108] Ibid.

[109] OECD, *Harmful Tax Competition* (Paris: OECD, 1998).

[110] US Treasury, 'Treasury Secretary Paul H O'Neill, Statement at the Pre-G-7 Press Conference' (Press Release PO-464, 5 July 2001).

Exchange Agreements (TIEAs) with tax havens to enable access to information about residents' offshore income. In 2003, the OECD established a new Global Forum on Transparency and Exchange of Information for Tax Purposes that included member states, tax havens and other states that wished to join. This effort built on the incremental success of the first EU Savings Directive in 2003 in response to the use of offshore bank accounts by residents of EU member states.[111] The EU Savings Directive 2003/43/EC established information exchange, with the alternative of withholding of taxes (for example between Germany and Switzerland). Incremental progress was made in bilateral cooperation, but by 2008 there were still only 44 TIEAs signed globally.

The Era of Bank Secrecy Is Over

The Global Financial Crisis of 2008, which occurred around the same time as various tax avoidance scandals were being reported, changed the dynamic permanently.[112] The crisis led to fiscal challenges for governments (although relatively minor compared to the global fiscal impact of the COVID-19 pandemic). This focused policy attention on the failure of banks in the global economy. In 2009 the G20 London Summit proclaimed that 'the era of bank secrecy is over'.[113]

The first, inspired step by the G20-OECD was to open the Administrative Convention to signature by all countries. By the end of 2021, 144 jurisdictions had signed the Administrative Convention and it had entered into force in more than 130 countries, including 17 jurisdictions covered by territorial extension.[114] (See Box 10.6 for a discussion of the different path taken by the United States.) Today, the Administrative Convention is the main international legal framework for transnational tax cooperation, providing a legal basis for all kinds of tax information exchange (by request, spontaneous and automatic), and a range of other forms of administrative cooperation and tax collection across borders. This process also demonstrated that multilateralism may be possible. The Administrative Convention filled many gaps in the legal framework for international tax administration, and updated pre-existing or incomplete bilateral regimes. Implementation by states in practice requires a bilateral

---

[111] European Commission, Directive 2003/48/EC of 3 June 2003 on taxation of savings income in the form of interest payments.
[112] Miranda Stewart, 'Transnational Tax Information Exchange Networks: Steps Towards a Globalized, Legitimate Tax Administration' (2012) 4(2) *World Tax Journal* 152–79.
[113] G20, *Global Plan for Recovery and Reform: The Communiqué from the London Summit* (2 April 2009), www.g20.utoronto.ca/2009/2009communique0402.html.
[114] OECD and Council of Europe, The Multilateral Convention on Mutual Administrative in Tax Matters Amended by the 2010 Protocol (2011). See www.oecd.org/ctp/exchange-of-tax-information/convention-on-mutual-administrative-assistance-in-tax-matters.htm.

> **Box 10.6 The United States goes it alone: FATCA**
>
> The Administrative Convention was signed but not ratified by the United States. Instead, the United States has taken a unilateral path that achieves some of the same goals and has sometimes led, or prompted, global cooperative developments. An example is the Financial Account Tax Compliance Act 2010 (FATCA) rules that prompted establishment of the CRS for sharing data on bank accounts of individuals around the world, endorsed in 2013.
>
> FATCA requires banks and financial institutions in foreign jurisdictions to provide information about US account holders to the Internal Revenue Service (IRS), or withhold and remit a 30 per cent withholding tax on income derived by those account holders.
>
> The imposition of legal obligations to disclose account holder information on banks and financial institutions that are outside US tax jurisdiction has led to the description of FATCA as extraterritorial. Banks and financial institutions are bound by account holder confidentiality rules that would not apply to disclosures to the tax authority of another country unless specifically permitted by law or treaty.[115]
>
> To achieve the implementation of FATCA, the United States has engaged directly in bilateral treaty negotiation with countries where banks are located.[116] To date, the United States has entered into 113 bilateral FATCA agreements, with more than 100 in force by June 2021.[117] The approach adopted is an administrative agreement, not a binding international treaty, that commits the foreign government to collect information on the financial accounts of US citizens from its domestic financial institutions and banks, and then to remit this information automatically to the IRS. In some agreements, the United States commits to provide automatic exchange of information to the other country about the accounts of their residents in US banks. Through this process, the IRS has enlarged its capability to identify, quantify and collect taxes on the investment income of its domestic residents and citizens and its approximately seven million offshore citizens.

memorandum of understanding, or agreement between the tax authorities of different countries. For example, based on Article 6 of the Administrative Convention, there are over 4,500 bilateral exchange relationships activated with respect to more than 110 jurisdictions committed to automatic information exchange, under the Common Reporting Standard (CRS) established by the OECD.[118]

The EU updated its earlier efforts in tax administrative cooperation in Council Directive 2010/24/EU of 16 March 2010 concerning mutual assistance for the recovery of tax claims, and Council Directive 2011/16/EU on tax

---

[115] Steven A Dean and Rebecca M Kysar, 'Introduction: Reconsidering the Tax Treaty' (2016) 41 *Brooklyn Journal of International Law* 967–72.
[116] US Treasury, 'Foreign Account Tax Compliance Act', https://home.treasury.gov/policy-issues/tax-policy/foreign-account-tax-compliance-act, accessed 23 March 2022.
[117] Ibid.
[118] OECD, 'International Framework for the CRS', www.oecd.org/tax/automatic-exchange/international-framework-for-the-crs/, accessed 23 March 2022.

administrative cooperation. Directive 2014/107/EU mandated automatic exchange, consistently with the CRS. These have been further updated by Council Directive 2021/514 (DAC7), which encompasses tax cooperation and automated information reporting.

The exchange of information rules are monitored by the Global Forum, which today has 162 members, making it the largest tax forum in the world (outside the United Nations itself).[119] The Global Forum's unglamorous, but seemingly relentless, peer review of country laws concerning exchange of information, bank secrecy and automated data sharing continues a decade after it was established and seems to have brought the majority of governments up to a reasonable base standard.[120]

Collecting Tax across Borders

Tax authorities must go further in cooperation if they aim to collect tax across borders. The traditional 'revenue rule' of international law mandates that sovereigns will not enforce taxes of other sovereigns. The revenue rule has a long history in common law and civil law countries.[121]

The rule is abolished by provisions in the Administrative Convention. The OECD has included Article 27 in its Model Convention supporting bilateral agreement for mutual assistance in collection of taxes.[122] In the EU, fomer Directive 2010/24/EU and DAC7 override the revenue rule.[123] However, there is a long way to go before the revenue rule is abolished completely. About half of the signatories to the Administrative Convention have entered a reservation on assistance in tax debt recovery.[124] A significant minority of signatories also

---

[119] OECD, 'Global Forum on Transparency and Exchange of Information for Tax Purposes', www.oecd.org/tax/transparency/, accessed 28 March 2022.

[120] OECD, *Transparency and Exchange of Information for Tax Purposes: Multilateral Co-operation Changing the World: 10th Anniversary Report* (Paris: OECD, 2019), www.oecd.org/tax/transparency/global-forum-10-years-report.pdf

[121] Philip Baker, Ernst Czakert, Arie van Eijsden, Maria AG Ruiz and Liselott Kana, 'International Assistance in the Collection of Taxes' (2011) 65 *Bulletin for International Taxation* 281–7.

[122] Jennifer Roeleveld, 'Article 27: Assistance in the Collection of Taxes' in Pasquale Pistone (ed.), *Global Tax Treaty Commentaries* (Amsterdam: IBFD Tax Research Platform, 2019), [1.1.1].

[123] Louise Parker, 'Mutual Assistance in the Collection of Taxes' (2017) 71(9) *Bulletin for International Taxation* 1.

[124] Council of Europe, 'Reservations and Declarations for Treaty No 127 – Convention on Mutual Administrative Assistance in Tax Matters'. The US 'will not provide assistance in the recovery of any tax claim ... pursuant to Article 11 ... of the Convention'; see www.coe.int/en/web/conventions/full-list?module=declarations-by-treaty&numSte=127&codeNature=0, accessed 27 March 2022. This causes problems for enforcement of some US taxes; see Walter Hellerstein, 'The Rapidly Evolving Universe of US State Taxation of Cross-Border Online Sales after *South Dakota v Wayfar, Inc.*, and Its Implications for Australian Businesses' (2020) 18 *eJournal of Tax Research* 320–49, 345.

Box 10.7 Collecting tax across borders

How and when does cross-border tax debt collection happen, and how much is collected? Most countries do not publish adequate data. One situation in which tax debts may be collected from offshore is where residents have migrated but still owe tax to their previous residence state.

Denmark estimates that in 2016 there were 75,490 individuals resident abroad who had tax debts owing to the Danish government. The government collected DKK 66.6 million from 4,936 persons in 2013, DKK 244.5 million from 18,678 persons in 2014, DKK 164.6 million from 16,010 persons in 2015 and DKK 147.5 million from 8,071 persons in 2016.[125] The data do not show the countries, treaties or process of collection, and suggest that mutual assistance techniques are not yet being widely used.

In another example, the tax authority of the Netherlands was able to do direct enforcement to enforce taxes owed by a large number of farmers who had emigrated from the Netherlands while still owing a tax debt. Through close liaison between the two tax authorities, the Netherlands authority directly approached the emigrant taxpayers supported by the local tax authority. Ultimately, about 90 per cent of the tax owed was paid.[126]

---

maintain a reservation on the service of documents in their jurisdiction. Even the stance of the OECD is still rather negative: the Model Commentary to Article 27 contains numerous reasons why countries should *not* include the Article in a bilateral treaty, including whether it will provide balanced and reciprocal benefits to both states; whether there is sufficient trade and investment between the states to justify such assistance, whether revenue agencies will be able to effectively provide the assistance and whether taxpayer rights will be sufficiently protected.

The Japanese tax authority has identified that 86 per cent of financial account balances reported to it under the CRS were from jurisdictions that had not yet agreed to do mutual assistance in tax collection.[127] Japan has, consequently, advocated for a global standard for tax recovery assistance. Even where the legal framework to support cross-border tax debt collection exists, there remain challenges for effective collection. A government that is requested to provide assistance in collection may choose not to prioritise the tax, and collection may be lengthy and difficult, even between neighbouring states or within Europe. Box 10.7 discusses some examples.

---

[125] Parker, *Mutual Assistance* (see n 123), 7.
[126] Baker et al, *International Assistance in the Collection of Taxes* (see n 121), 286.
[127] OECD Forum on Tax Administration, *OECD FTA Tax Debt Management Network Workshop, Report of the Presentations, 4–5 March 2020* (Paris: OECD, 2020), www.oecd.org/tax/forum-on-tax-administration/events/report-fta-workshop-tax-debt-management-network.pdf.

Taxpayer Rights in a Global Context

In the new world of transnational tax administration, the risks for taxpayer rights and privacy increase. An important reason for slow progress in sharing tax information a century ago, expressed by the League of Nations, was a fear that countries were establishing 'an extension beyond national frontiers of an organized system of fiscal inquisition'.[128] Many have expressed concerns about how to protect taxpayer rights and privacy where information is provided to other countries.[129] Multilateral and bilateral tax administrative treaties and EC Directives contain provisions for due process and the confidentiality of taxpayer information. However, once information is exchanged the treaties rely on national tax laws to protect taxpayers. There is a complex web of jurisdictions and different laws, and treaty provisions on information exchange are worded in a variety of ways. Without a world tax administration or global privacy agency, there is no overarching enforcement of privacy in transnational information exchange.

Another issue relates to the forum for appeal if a taxpayer is concerned that either due process in transnational income gathering has not been carried out or that privacy is breached. The EC regime sets out rules for appeal in respect of cross-border enforcement of tax debts, dividing jurisdiction between the requesting state (for substantive tax law appeals) and the requested state (in relation to the enforcement itself); even so, one can envisage significant complexity and difficulties for taxpayers in seeking to carry out appeals in different forums.

Taxpayer rights have become a focus of comparative research including by the IBFD Observatory on the Protection of Taxpayers' Rights, which produces a yearbook explaining and comparing issues in taxpayer rights across more than 40 jurisdictions around the world.[130] The annual report expresses a concern that transnational administration has led to a deterioration in procedural fairness for taxpayers, even as governments have increasingly acknowledged taxpayer rights in domestic tax systems (as discussed in Chapter 9). Arthur Cockfield suggested a 'global taxpayer bill of rights' as a means of increasing trust and confidence in increasingly globalised and digitalised tax administration.[131]

---

[128] League of Nations, 'Double Taxation and Tax Evasion: Report – Document C.216.M.85 (London, April 12th, 1927)' in *Legislative History of United States Tax Conventions: Vol 4 Sec 1: League of Nations* (Washington, DC: US Government Printing Office, 1962), 25.

[129] IBFD, *IBFD Yearbook on Taxpayers' Rights 2019* (Amsterdam: Observatory on the Protection of Taxpayers' Rights, 2020), www.ibfd.org/sites/default/files/2021-06/2019%20IBFD%20Yearbook%20on%20Taxpayers%27%20Rights%20%28final%29_0.pdf.

[130] IBFD, *IBFD Yearbook on Taxpayers' Rights 2020* (Amsterdam: Observatory on the Protection of Taxpayers' Rights, 2021), www.ibfd.org/sites/default/files/2021-09/2020%20IBFD%20Yearbook%20on%20Taxpayers'%20Rights%20(1).pdf.

[131] Arthur Cockfield, 'Sharing Tax Information in the 21st Century: Big Data Flows and Taxpayers as Data Subjects' (2019) 67(4) *Canadian Tax Journal* 1179–99.

VAT on E-commerce and the One-stop Shop

The focus in this chapter has been on the income tax. However, the most innovative developments in transnational tax administration have occurred in the sphere of consumption tax, specifically, the value-added tax (VAT) or goods and services tax (GST) enacted in about 170 countries around the world. The spread of the VAT was in part driven by the World Trade Organization principles for free trade.[132] The removal of export taxes was achieved by the *destination principle* that allocates tax jurisdiction for the VAT to the place of residence of the consumer. The destination principle was adopted uniformly in the European Union, and generally around the world.[133]

In the 1980s, cross-border shopping was limited to mail-order businesses and locations where shoppers could physically cross the border, such as tourist shopping in border towns in parts of Europe and between Canada and the United States. Most imported goods were supplied to domestic businesses that sold them to resident consumers. Many VAT laws sought to tax the importation by applying a 'reverse charge' mechanism that puts the obligation to remit the tax on the importing business in the jurisdiction, instead of the offshore supplier. For outbound sales, a refund of input tax credits was delivered to the exporter. Direct cross-border purchases by consumers were usually ignored, although tax credits were sometimes provided for tourists who took purchases home with them.

After the first internet-based shopping systems were established in the 1990s, the OECD responded to this new phenomenon with the 1998 Ottawa Taxation Framework for global e-commerce.[134] The Ottawa Framework enshrined the destination principle and established the goal of neutrality between domestic and foreign supplies. The OECD also established Working Party No. 9 on Consumption Taxes, which engaged with countries outside the OECD and with non-governmental organisations and businesses.[135] The Ottawa Framework

---

[132] Miranda Stewart, 'Global Trajectories of Tax Reform: The Discourse of Tax Reform in Developing and Transition Countries' (2003) 44(1) *Harvard International Law Journal* 139–90.

[133] There is significant diversity among 'real' VATs around the world, which differ from the benchmark 'ideal' VAT, including in implementation of the destination principle: see Kathryn James, *The Rise of the Value-Added Tax* (New York: Oxford University Press, 2015); Kathryn James and Thomas Ecker, 'Relevance of the OECD International VAT/GST Guidelines for Non-OECD Countries' (2017) 32 *Australian Tax Forum* 317–76, 335.

[134] OECD, *Electronic Commerce: Taxation Framework Conditions*. A Report by the Committee on Fiscal Affairs, Ottawa (8 November 1998) (Paris, OECD, 1998), www.oecd.org/ctp/consumption/1923256.pdf.

[135] Arthur Cockfield, 'The Rise of the OECD as an Informal "World Tax Organization" through National Responses to E-Commerce Tax Challenges' (2005–6) 6 *Yale Journal of Law & Technology* 136–87, 160–1; OECD, *Implementation of the Ottawa Taxation Framework Conditions* (Paris: OECD, 2003), www.oecd.org/tax/administration/20499630.pdf; OECD, *Electronic Commerce: Taxation Framework Conditions* (see n 134); OECD, *Electronic*

required Business-to-Consumer (B2C) supplies to be taxed in the place of consumption and Business-to-Business (B2B) supplies to be taxed in the place of the recipient business. Practical difficulties of valuation and administration still prevented governments from levying tax on inbound sales of goods to onshore consumers below a value threshold. Most VAT laws did not apply to tax inbound digital services provided directly to consumers.

The mass expansion of digital commerce forced governments to extend the VAT jurisdiction to digital supplies from offshore. The rise of the global sales platforms such as eBay, Amazon or Alibaba; global digital content delivery in music, film, books and news by Netflix, Disney and Apple; and the invention of entirely new forms of digital services such as Facebook and Twitter, led to increased governmental concern about a loss of VAT revenue and an unfair playing field for domestic businesses. While there is variation among VATs in EU member states, EC Directive 2006/112/EC established fundamental parameters for the VAT base and rate in each country.[136] The multilateral basis for the VAT enabled the EU to respond quickly to tax issues arising from cross-border digital commerce. The EU Directive on e-commerce was issued in 2002.[137] This led to early commitments to comply by digital firms such as Amazon and AOL/TimeWarner.[138]

In 2015, the Global Forum on VAT brought together more than 100 countries to confirm that residence of the consumer is the trigger for taxation of offshore supplies and to propose that tax be withheld and remitted by the offshore platform or seller.[139] The residence of the consumer either for delivery, or payment (e.g. a credit card) would provide the administrative and legal proxy to identify which jurisdiction had the right to collect tax on the sale.[140]

This has been implemented in the EU and various other countries, despite initial resistance from the digital companies. The most interesting new development is the EU 'One-Stop Shop' for VAT which launched on 1 July 2021 after a postponement for six months because of the COVID-19 pandemic.[141] The new regime follows a pilot 'Mini-One Stop Shop' from 2015,

---

Commerce: The Challenges to Tax Authorities and Taxpayers (Paris: OECD, 1997), www.oecd.org/tax/treaties/1923232.pdf.

[136] EU Council Directive 2006/112/EC (28 November 2006).

[137] EU, 'Council Directive 2002/38/EC Amending Directive 77/338/EEC as regards the Value Added Tax Arrangements Applicable to Radio and Television Broadcasting Services and Electronically Supplied Services' (2002) 128 *Official Journal of European Communities* 40.

[138] Cockfield, 'The Rise of the OECD as an Informal "World Tax Organization"' (see n 139), 160–1.

[139] OECD, 'Recommendation of the Council on the Application of Value Added Tax/Goods and Services Tax to the International Trade in Services and Intangibles' OECD/LEGAL/0430 (27 September 2016), https://legalinstruments.oecd.org/en/instruments/OECD-LEGAL-0430.

[140] OECD, *International VAT/GST Guidelines* (Paris: OECD Publishing, 2017), https://read.oecd.org/10.1787/9789264271401-en?format=pdf, p. 66, Guidelines 3.5 and 3.6.

[141] European Commission Directorate-General for Taxation and Customs Union, *Explanatory Notes on VAT E-commerce Rules*, Council Directive (EU) 2017/2455, 2019/1995, Council Implementing Regulation (EU) 2019/2026 (Brussels: European Commission, September

which the EU claims as a success.[142] Essentially, businesses declare and pay VAT in one jurisdiction, and the revenue is remitted by that tax authority to other jurisdictions in the EU.

Towards Transnational Tax Administration

A sign of institutionalisation of transnational tax administrative networks is the increased engagement of businesses, such as banks doing financial information reporting to governments. The example of FATCA, and the broader obligation for banks to provide data on taxpayer accounts to revenue authorities, illustrates this phenomenon. From the perspective of government, this enables outsourcing of costs of administration to intermediaries. FATCA requires foreign banks to internalize the costs of administration of tax information exchange about their customers. In the VAT context, the challenge of collection remains for offshore digital supplies and sales. The EU One-Stop-Shop embeds governments and businesses in an EU-wide system of VAT returns and collection. The OECD aims to establish collection rules for digital platforms for the collection of VAT for multiple tax jurisdictions.

Tax authorities are connected through automated and digitised networks of databases and communications that could not have been predicted two decades ago. The events of 2009 turned out to be a tipping point into a new equilibrium enabling systematic transnational tax administration. The developments of the last decade have changed the rules of the game for taxation of capital income of individuals across borders, shrinking previously strong institutions such as bank secrecy in favour of revenue authorities.[143] As well as the financial crisis and political scandals of tax evasion, at least two other factors enabled this transition. First, the explosion of digital technologies of the previous decade made it feasible to achieve mass, secure sharing of data between governments. Second, the OECD, with the G20, opened its legal and administrative systems to non-member states in the Global Forum and Administrative Convention. One reason for the success of the Convention is that it provides a framework under which governments may enter into bilateral arrangements to implement specific elements, without implementing other elements, yet still participating in multilateral processes for tax cooperation.

2020), https://vat-one-stop-shop.ec.europa.eu/document/download/3372e2f2-d5ec-46ea-a2ac-97bc4f5ec634_en and other resources at https://ec.europa.eu/taxation_customs/business/vat/vat-e-commerce/resources_en.

[142] EC, 'Modernising VAT for Cross-border E-commerce', https://ec.europa.eu/taxation_customs/business/vat/vat-e-commerce/modernising-vat-cross-border-e-commerce_en, accessed 14 March 2022.

[143] Simon Steinlin and Christine Trampusch, 'Institutional Shrinkage: The Deviant Case of Swiss Banking Secrecy' (2012) 6 *Regulation & Governance* 242–59, https://doi.org/10.1111/j.1748-5991.2012.01128.x.

The administrative, technological, and political coverage of transnational tax administration is neither globally inclusive nor completely effective. Developing countries have benefited very little from the administrative progress of the last decade. However, transnational tax cooperation comprises a growing 'pattern of regular and purposive relations among like government units working across the border', in 'a dense web of relations that constitutes a new transgovernmental order'.[144] Cross-border tax avoidance and evasion continue, while new forms of 'offshore' may be created. One concern is the use of cryptocurrencies, to enable tax evasion and money laundering.[145] Another concern is the failure of most governments to enact effective reporting regimes to identify beneficial ownership of offshore trusts, nominee companies and opaque funds in tax havens. The US Congress may have provided leadership on some aspects of this important issue with its Corporate Transparency Act, effective from January 2021, which requires reporting by US corporations about who owns or controls them to the Financial Crimes Enforcement Network of the US Treasury.[146]

There are risks even in the context of the new automated information sharing regimes. A recent study suggests that governments which provide 'citizenship-for-sale' are facilitating evasion of information obligations.[147] The researchers find evidence that when opening a bank account in the country in which an individual has acquired a new citizenship by investment (such as Dominica or Cyprus), the individual may use the citizenship documents to imply residence in that country, rather than in their actual country of residence. The automated information platforms will collect bank account information and (wrongly) send it to the place where citizenship was purchased. Governments may be able to address this by putting pressure on the 'citizenship-for-sale' countries to release the information, or by requiring banks to ask more questions about residence.

Transnational tax administrative networks evince a kind of 'regulation up' from national to the global, as governments legalise and institutionalize bureaucratic and data processes across borders.[148] Two decades ago, Henk Vording and Koon Caminada observed that 'meaningful international tax cooperation may well require that in the near future, a substantial part of

---

[144] Anne-Marie Slaughter, *A New World Order* (Princeton, NJ: Princeton University Press, 2004), 14.

[145] Omri Marian, 'Are Cryptocurrencies Super Tax Havens?' (2013) 112 *Michigan Law Review First Impressions* 38–48.

[146] See, e.g. Transparency International US Office, https://us.transparency.org/news/beneficial-ownership-registry-considerations/, accessed 1 April 2022.

[147] Dominika Langenmayr and Lennard Zyska, *Escaping the Exchange of Information: Tax Evasion via Citizenship-by-Investment*, CESifo Working Paper 8956 (Munich: CESifo Group, March 2021).

[148] Samuel Barrows, 'Racing to the Top ... at Last: The Regulation of Safety in Shipping' in Walter Mattli and Ngaire Woods (eds.), *The Politics of Global Regulation* (Princeton, NJ: Princeton University Press, 2009), 189–210.

national tax administrations' efforts is to provide services to other national tax administrations'.[149] Cooperation between tax states requires resources, but it also extends the tax state's capacity to govern (while undermining some elements of capacity of tax havens).[150] In the next chapter, we discuss the taxation of capital held in corporations and the dynamic negotiation of territory and power between multinational enterprises and tax states.

---

[149] Henk Vording and Koon Caminada, 'Tax Co-ordination: Crossing the Rubicon?' in Dirk A Albregtse, Arij L Bovenberg and LGM Stevens (eds.), *Er zal geheven worden!, Opstellen aangeboden aan Prof. Dr S. Cnossen* (Deventer: Kluwer, 2001), 335–45.

[150] Linda Weiss, 'The State-augmenting Effects of Globalization' (2005) 10(3) *New Political Economy* 345–53.

11

States and Corporations in the Global Digital Economy

The power of a large transnational corporation approximates that of the government of a medium-sized country.

Sijbren Cnossen, 'The Role of the Corporation Tax in OECD Member Countries'

Competition and Cooperation of Tax States

Tax Sovereignty

Taxation is a sovereign function of the state, 'constrained to a limited extent' under various international and supranational rules, including European Union (EU) law, World Trade Organization (WTO) law, bilateral tax treaties and (possibly) customary international law.[1] However, sovereignty on its own cannot explain much about how states behave in the international tax context. Tax competition is usually presented as an exercise of sovereignty by tax states. Yet cooperation in an international order of states is also an exercise of sovereignty. The more fundamental question concerns in what circumstances tax competition, or tax cooperation, would be beneficial or detrimental for tax states or for global welfare.

The influential Tiebout hypothesis suggests that decentralised taxation and spending on public goods combined with full mobility of taxpayers would maximise economic welfare for all.[2] If we assume that taxation and public goods are confined by state borders and cross-border mobility of trade, investment and migration is perfect, we can model the 'idealised Tiebout world of competing governments, each of which supplies some public goods to its

---

[1] Wolfgang Schön, 'National Sovereignty and Taxation' in Thomas Cottier and Krista N Schefer (eds.), *Elgar Encyclopedia of International Economic Law* (Cheltenham: Edward Elgar, 2017), III.70.

[2] Charles M Tiebout, 'A Pure Theory of Local Expenditures' (1956) 64 *Journal of Political Economy* 416–24. The hypothesis has been much debated but it remains influential; see, e.g. Robin Boadway and Jean-Francois Tremblay, 'Reassessment of the Tiebout Model' (2012) 96 (11–12) *Journal of Public Economics* 1063–78; Edward J Huck, 'Tiebout or Samuelson: The 21st Century Deserves More' (2004) 88 *Marquette Law Review* 185–93.

citizens, public goods whose benefits do not spill over beyond the boundaries of the individual polity'.[3] In this model, tax competition between governments enhances welfare because mobile citizens can choose the government that delivers the public goods they desire. Governments must deliver the public goods desired by citizens more efficiently, limiting a tendency to maximise revenue.[4]

The impact on tax policy of opening the borders of the tax state to a global economy was discussed in Chapters 2 and 4. In respect of trade and investment, there has been more than one wave of economic globalisation, which has been a feature of capitalist expansion since the nineteenth century.[5] For our purposes in analysing the impact on taxation, we can consider two stages of globalisation in the twentieth century. The first stage involved the expansion of global trade in goods by removing barriers and lowering tariffs after World War II. The fiscal consequences of this process were relatively easy to manage for many tax states. By the 1960s, as shown in statistics presented in Chapters 1 and 2, tax states had succeeded in harnessing revenues from taxes on domestic income and consumption, while the share of revenue raised from customs and excise had long ago declined. By the time the WTO was established in 1995, trade taxes were a small fraction of revenues of these countries.[6]

A greater challenge to tax states arose from the wave of economic globalisation in investment and financial flows in the late twentieth century. Tax states faced widespread fiscal, economic and currency crises in the 1970s, as discussed in Chapter 2. During the 1980s, many governments removed capital controls and floated their currencies. Foreign direct investment dramatically expanded. Outbound investment into developing countries (including China), with low wages and other costs, was attractive for large corporations especially from the United States, Europe and Japan. Large-scale foreign direct investment led to the development of global value chains around the world and the agglomeration of value in multinational enterprises (MNEs) operating in multiple jurisdictions.

This wave of economic globalisation generated economic growth which produced buoyant tax revenues for many governments, even as they reduced tax rates. It also led to the 'decade of tax reform' explained in Chapter 4. By the 1990s, globalisation shifted towards financial capital and global trade in services, intellectual property and other intangible assets. The internet arrived

---

[3] Geoffrey Brennan and James M Buchanan, *The Power to Tax: Analytical Foundations of a Fiscal Constitution* (Cambridge, UK: Cambridge University Press, 1980), 172.
[4] Ibid., 171.
[5] Giovanni Arrighi, *The Long Twentieth Century* (London: Verso, 1994); Jean-Bernard Auby, *Globalisation, Law and the State* (Oxford: Hart Publishing, 2017).
[6] Julia Cagé and Lucie Gadenne, 'Tax Revenues and the Fiscal Cost of Trade Liberalization, 1792–2006' (2018) 70 *Explorations in Economic History* 1–24. In contrast, many developing and newly independent states were unable to raise sufficient revenues from domestic consumption and income taxes to replace the revenue lost from tariff reductions during the 1980s and 1990s.

and digitalisation of the economy rapidly increased, providing new paths for global trade and investment Globalisation and digitalisation produced much greater mobility of goods, investment and information.

Many of the assumptions about mobility that underpin Tiebout's theory do not hold perfectly in the real world. People are much less mobile than capital, and the extent of capital mobility is highly variable. Investors have a 'home' bias, while market information is asymmetric and often inadequate. Foreign direct investment depends on many country-specific factors, including resources, rule of law, education of the workforce, transport, the location of consumers and geopolitical security. However, some assumptions of Tiebout's model do hold in the global context. Mobility *has* increased, but the governmental functions of taxation and expenditure to fund public goods and redistribution remain 'deeply decentralized', although nation states are 'interdependent'.[7]

In this context, tax competition by states has become increasingly apparent. Governments lower taxes with the goal of attracting, or retaining, desirable people, capital or economic activities in a jurisdiction. These international effects are in stark contrast to the traditional model of the tax state in isolation:

> The implicit traditional conception of states sees them as powerful sovereigns that operate in a closed economy with the capacity to make and enforce mandatory rules, impose taxes, and set redistribution. However, in many ways, states have come to resemble actors in a competitive global market, where their ability to govern is increasingly shaped by the international supply and demand of resources and the elasticity of taxpayers' choices.[8]

Tax competition puts downward pressure on taxes on mobile capital, or skilled or high-income individuals, while governments that need revenue retain or even increase taxes on immobile factors, such as ordinary consumers. The downward trend of corporate tax rates is illustrated in Figure 7.2 in Chapter 7.

Sven Steinmo in his landmark study of the US, Swedish and UK tax systems at the start of the 1990s, suggested that 'the excesses and abuses of tax policy, on the one hand, and the growing internationalization of the world economy, on the other, imposes a new set of constraints on tax policy makers'.[9] The threat of exit increases the power of 'marginal' taxpayers who are more mobile. This drives taxes down on these taxpayers who would shift their capital investment, residence or labour offshore. The lower taxes also benefit 'inframarginal' taxpayers, who would not leave, at greater cost to revenue without enhanced efficiency. The downward pressure on revenue may make it more

---

[7] Tsilly Dagan, *International Tax Policy: Between Competition and Cooperation* (Cambridge, UK: Cambridge University Press, 2018), 44.
[8] Ibid., 13.
[9] Sven Steinmo, *Taxation and Democracy: Swedish, British and American Approaches to Financing the Modern State* (New Haven, CT: Yale University Press, 1993), 21.

difficult for governments to deliver public goods or redistribution, undermining equity and reducing trust or community values. Tsilly Dagan calls this the 'tragic choice' of the tax state as it weighs the dilemmas of exit and voice, efficiency and redistribution.[10]

The challenge in resolving these issues may have arisen, as Philip Genschel and Thomas Rixen suggest, from the 'normative settlement' of the transnational tax order early in the twentieth century, which 'simultaneously created a demand' for a transnational legal solution for tax competition 'and hindered the supply of such a solution'.[11] The focus on double tax relief produced an apparently stable order of tax jurisdiction based on residence and source. The success of this transnational legal order to relieve double taxation 'inadvertently invigorated tax competition. It opened new options for taxpayers to reduce their tax bills through cross-border tax arbitrage and left national governments free to vie for inbound tax arbitrage flows by aggressive low-tax strategies'.[12] At the same time, it constrained the legal and political space for curbing tax competition in which there were strong vested interests (among states and capital).

Cooperation between states to regulate tax competition may be both feasible and beneficial. Tsilly Dagan argues against the cartelisation of international tax by a group of rich countries, as likely being unjust to low-income countries and detrimental for overall global welfare.[13] However, the question is not so much whether there should be *any* regulation, as the extent and type of regulation. It seems likely that cooperative multilateral regulation of the international tax framework would make us better off.[14]

Harmful Tax Competition

In 1996, the G7 called upon the Organisation for Economic Co-operation and Development (OECD) to pursue multilateral measures to counter the distorting effects of tax competition on investment and financing decisions and the consequences for national tax bases. This led to the 1998 report, *Harmful Tax Competition – An Emerging Global Issue* prepared by its Committee on Fiscal Affairs.[15] In 2000, the sequel report, *Towards Global Tax Cooperation*, identified potentially harmful tax practices or 'preferential regimes' of OECD member states and published an official 'blacklist' of 35 'uncooperative tax

---

[10] Dagan, *International Tax Policy* (see n 7).
[11] Philipp Genschel and Thomas Rixen, 'Settling and Unsettling the Transnational Legal Order of International Taxation' in Terence C Halliday and Geoffrey Shaffer (eds.), *Transnational Legal Orders* (Cambridge, UK: Cambridge University Press, 2015), 154–84.
[12] Ibid., 155.
[13] Dagan, *International Tax Policy* (see n 7).
[14] Ibid.
[15] OECD, *Harmful Tax Competition* (Paris: OECD, 1998).

havens' (see Chapter 10). The report proposed that OECD member states would take 'coordinated' and 'defensive' measures 'swiftly and effectively against jurisdictions that persist in their harmful tax practices'.[16]

The OECD campaign to regulate tax competition did not achieve these goals, largely because of dissension within its own ranks.[17] Luxembourg and Switzerland, whose banking and financial centre regimes were directly affected, dissented from the report, breaking with the usual consensus approach in the OECD. There was also criticism of the OECD campaign from the ranks of 'offshore' financial centres that found allies among international organisations including the Commonwealth secretariat and the International Monetary Fund (IMF). The reaction indicated how many small and newly independent states had adopted the low tax financial centre pathway to economic development, and how much they would be affected by a change in approach of rich countries. Ultimately, the United States, which had supported the project under President Clinton, withdrew its support under newly elected President Bush. US Treasury Secretary Paul O'Neill said:[18]

> I share many of the serious concerns that have been expressed recently about the direction of the OECD initiative. I am troubled by the underlying premise that low tax rates are somehow suspect and by the notion that any country, or group of countries, should interfere in any other country's decision about how to structure its own tax system. I also am concerned about the potentially unfair treatment of some non-OECD countries. The United States does not support efforts to dictate to any country what its own tax rates or tax system should be, and will not participate in any initiative to harmonize world tax systems.

The Harmful Tax Competition project revealed a lack of consensus about whether tax competition was really 'harmful'; the suggestion sat uneasily with the dominant paradigm in favour of competition and the liberalisation of global flows of capital and trade. However, many argued that tax competition was generating a race to the bottom that would leave all governments, and their citizens, worse off and may even contribute to the fiscal crisis of the welfare state.[19]

At the end of the twentieth century, regulatory scholars John Braithwaite and Peter Drahos contrasted the failure of international tax cooperation with the apparent success of cooperation between states on other aspects of international business regulation. Braithwaite and Drahos concluded that the dominant mode of reciprocal bilateralism between states had generated an

---

[16] OECD, *Towards Global Tax Cooperation* (Paris: OECD, 2001), 24, https://doi.org/10.1787/9789264184541-en.

[17] Jason C Sharman, *Havens in a Storm: The Struggle for Global Tax Regulation* (Ithaca, NY: Cornell University Press, 2006), 1.

[18] US Treasury, 'Treasury Secretary O'Neill Statement on OECD Tax Havens' (Press Release PO-366, 10 May 2001).

[19] Reuven S Avi-Yonah, 'Globalization, Tax Competition and the Fiscal Crisis of the Welfare State' (2000) 113(7) *Harvard Law Review* 1573–676.

international tax structure of 'polycentric, regulatory diversity' between 'rogue fiscal sovereigns'.[20] The ad hoc approach of states to cooperation on taxation was no match for the 'monocentric complexity' of MNEs that have the ability to plan tax outcomes across hundreds of subsidiaries and different jurisdictions, leading to a genuine erosion of state sovereignty'.[21]

Yet while tax rates came down, contrary to forecasts of a 'race to the bottom', there seemed instead to be a 'race to the middle' in tax revenues.[22] Governments succeeded in maintaining, or even increasing, tax revenues but the structure of tax systems shifted in response to globalisation. Taxes on less mobile consumption and labour increased in some countries. Lower tax rates on corporations likely contributed to increased investment using corporations, and greater returns to capital, sustaining tax revenues.

While the regulation of tax competition, through cooperation between states, seems likely to improve global welfare, we should also be aware that tax competition is only one aspect of 'systems competition' between states for resources, skilled labour or capital.[23] If tax competition is curtailed through cooperation between states, then competition in other forms of fiscal, labour or economic policy may become more pronounced.

Corporate Tax Policy in a Global Economy

Corporate Tax Jurisdiction

In the international context, the corporate tax has multiple functions, just as it does in the domestic context. Importantly, as emphasised in Chapter 7, a corporation is not a real person and it cannot bear the burden of corporate tax, which must be shifted to investors, consumers or workers. The corporate tax operates as a proxy for taxing the foreign owners of corporations on profits from their inbound investments in a country. This can be understood as a return to the source or production country for the benefit of access to

---

[20] John Braithwaite and Peter Drahos, *Global Business Regulation* (Cambridge, UK: Cambridge University Press, 2000), 107.
[21] Ibid., 108–9.
[22] John Hobson, 'Disappearing Taxes or "Race to the Middle"?' in Linda Weiss (ed.), *States in the Global Economy: Bringing Domestic Institutions Back In* (Cambridge, UK: Cambridge University Press, 2003), 37–57; Rachel Griffith, James Hines and Peter B Sorenson, 'International Capital Taxation' in Stuart Adam, Tim Besley, Richard Blundell, Stephen Bond, Robert Chote, Malcolm Gammie, Paul Johnson, Gareth Myles and James M Poterba (eds.), *Dimensions of Tax Design. Mirrlees Review: Vol 1* (Oxford: Oxford University Press, 2010), 914–1027, https://ifs.org.uk/publications/5227. See also Duane Swank and Sven Steinmo, 'The New Political Economy of Taxation in Advanced Capitalist Economies' (2002) 46 *American Journal of Political Science* 642–55; Michael P Devereux, Rachel Griffith and Alexander Klemm, *Corporate Income Tax Reforms and International Tax Competition*, Warwick: Centre for Economic Policy Research University of Warwick, 2002).
[23] Hans-Werner Sinn, *The New Systems Competition* (Malden, MA: Blackwell Publishing, 2003).

economic advantages and legal protections in that country. The corporate tax also collects a return for governments on location-specific economic rents, such as the return to resource extraction. The corporate tax might indirectly enable collection of tax on consumers in a market jurisdiction, or might be an indirect (and perhaps unintended) tax on labour in the home jurisdiction. The corporate tax is a vehicle for delivering subsidies or incentives for investment in the international as in the domestic context.

Debates about capital mobility largely, though not exclusively, refer to *corporate mobility*. Governments 'compete for the activities of mobile multinational firms, which have access to valuable proprietary assets, rather than simply for mobile capital. ... such firms make discrete investment choices: for example, whether to export to a new market or to produce locally, or where within a new location to site a new production facility'.[24]

The model of states as small open economies in a global context (explained in Chapter 4) implies that corporate taxes should trend to zero. This assumes that corporate investment is perfectly mobile, which is unlikely to be true.[25] We also need to consider the worldwide corporate tax environment. If the corporate tax rate in different countries is similar, then tax becomes less relevant for the marginal foreign investor; the 'closed economy' model might quite reasonably apply in this case.

The concepts of 'residence' and 'source' are generally applied to establish the nexus of corporate taxpayers to the state, as they are for individual taxpayers. These concepts roughly match the traditional distinction in corporate tax policy between *capital-exporting* (residence) countries, oriented towards outbound capital investment; and *capital-importing* (source) countries, which seek to encourage inbound capital investment. Public finance scholars have attempted to devise principles of capital export or capital import 'neutrality' that would enable identification of the ideal international tax system, as explained in Box 11.1.

Today, it is recognised that governments apply a hybrid policy approach, seeking to design corporate tax policy that will support both inbound and outbound investment, in a global context in which other governments are seeking to do the same. This is illustrated in the following statement from a 2004 Australian policy review:

> As Australia has integrated into the global marketplace, investment by Australian firms in other countries has increased sharply. This is part of a worldwide trend. ... It is becoming increasingly important that the Australian

---

[24] Devereux et al, *Corporate Income Tax Firms and International Tax Competition* (see n 22), 452–53.
[25] Kimberly A Clausing, 'In Search of Corporate Tax Incidence' (2012) 65(3) *Tax Law Review* 433–72 surveys various studies and conducts her own empirical analysis.

Box 11.1 Corporate tax neutrality

In the 1960s, drawing on economic theories of foreign direct investment, Peggy Richman (Musgrave) developed the concepts of 'capital export neutrality' (CEN) and 'capital import neutrality' (CIN) with the aim of providing a rational economic basis for allocating jurisdiction for corporate tax.[26]

CEN aims to *maximise the pre-tax return* to an investment no matter where it takes place (the global return to investment). A tax system will satisfy CEN if an investor faces the same effective tax rate no matter where they invest globally. CEN is achieved by residence taxation of the investor's worldwide income, if foreign tax rates that are credited by the residence country are equal to or lower than domestic tax rates. If the foreign tax rate is higher than the domestic tax rate, CEN would require refundability of foreign tax credits to taxpayers, something that no government is willing to do as it essentially transfers funds from one treasury to another.

CIN aims to equalise the *after-tax return* to investment around the world (the global return to saving). CIN holds if all investments into one jurisdiction face the same effective tax rate, no matter where the investor is located. This is achieved by source taxation of all investments at the same rate, with full relief provided by the residence country.

Both CEN and CIN would be satisfied if there was a single global tax system, or a fully harmonised global system so that the same tax rate and tax base applied in every country in the world. That is, global welfare could be maximised if we had a world government and taxing authority. However, in a world where different countries each levy their own corporate tax, it is impossible to achieve both CEN and CIN.

Scholars since Musgrave have argued for various other 'neutralities' such as 'national neutrality' or 'capital ownership neutrality' that seek to reflect the behaviour of governments in setting tax policy unilaterally. However, 'none of the standards proposed fits all cases and tax policy cannot feasibly be calibrated to have different rules for different cases'.[27]

The most important critique of the classic models of corporate tax neutrality is that they ignore a crucial third type of tax territory – the 'offshore' tax haven, which we introduced in Chapter 10. In a world with tax havens, it is impossible to optimise global welfare, absent a global minimum tax.[28]

---

[26] Peggy Richman, *Taxation of Foreign Income: An Economic Analysis* (Baltimore, MD: Johns Hopkins Press, 1963); Peggy Musgrave, *United States Taxation of Foreign Investment: Issues and Arguments* (Cambridge, MA: International Tax Program, Harvard Law School, 1969); Michael P Devereux, 'Taxation of Outbound Direct Investment: Economic Principles and Tax Policy Considerations' in John G Head and Richard Krever (eds.), *Tax Reform in the 21st Century* (Alphen aan den Rijn, Netherlands: Wolters Kluwer, 2009), 499–523, 502–3. On the challenge of neutralities, see Daniel Shaviro, 'Why Worldwide Welfare as a Normative Standard in US Tax Policy?' (2006–7) 60 *Tax Law Review* 155–78.

[27] Rosanne Altshuler, 'Lessons from the Study of Taxes and the Behavior of US Multinational Corporations' in Iris Claus, Norman Gemmell, Michelle Harding and David White (eds.), *Tax Reform in Open Economies* (London: Edward Elgar, 2010), 61–77; Shaviro, 'Why Worldwide Welfare as a Normative Standard in US Tax Policy?' (see n 27).

[28] Altshuler, 'Lessons from the Study of Taxes and the Behavior of US Multinational Corporations' (see n 28).

domestic economy offer an attractive investment location for foreign companies. It is also becoming increasingly important that Australian companies are able to invest competitively in international markets. The taxation system should not impede either of these objectives.[29]

The residence of a corporation establishes jurisdiction to tax worldwide income and, as for individuals, the residence country is responsible for providing an exemption or credit for foreign tax in respect of business income that is taxed elsewhere. Residence is also a condition of access to benefits under a bilateral tax treaty of the residence country.

Despite the assertion of jurisdiction over worldwide income, most governments tax only the profits of business activities conducted within their territory. This is achieved by providing an exemption for foreign business income or for dividends from foreign subsidiaries that carry on active businesses. Consequently, the corporate income tax on business investment is effectively levied on a territorial, not worldwide, basis.

The territorial system (taxing at the location of the business) was applied early in the twentieth century in many countries, in line with a realist approach to enforcement of tax jurisdiction. During the mid-twentieth century, in part because governments sought increased revenue, many corporate tax systems shifted to a 'classical' mode in which both the company and shareholders were taxed (as discussed in Chapter 7). At the same time, the base was expanded, in some countries at least, to worldwide income with a credit for foreign taxes. The territorial (exemption) approach reappeared during the 1980s, as governments sought to encourage increased inbound and outbound investment.

Taken to its full extent, the worldwide income approach requires the application of corporate tax to income accrued in controlled foreign corporations (CFCs) offshore. The United States pioneered CFC rules in 1962 (as discussed in Chapter 10). However, the rules were never fully comprehensive, being enacted with an exemption for active foreign business income derived in foreign corporations. This supported outbound investment by US corporations, facilitating the development of US-based MNEs. Over time, further types of foreign business and sales income were carved out from the application of the US CFC rules, permitting deferral of taxation on global income of US MNEs that was not repatriated to US shareholders. The territorial approach to corporate tax was confirmed in the Tax Cuts and Jobs Act 2017, which also removed the deferral concession for offshore global income of US MNEs (the regime may be subject to further reforms under President Biden).

---

[29] Australian Treasury Board of Taxation, *Review of International Tax Arrangements: Vol 1* (Parkes, ACT: Australian Treasury Board of Taxation, 2004), 29. See Miranda Stewart, 'Australia's Hybrid International Tax System: A Limited Focus on Tax and Development' in Karen B Brown (ed.), *Taxation and Development – A Comparative Study* (New York: Springer, 2017), 17–42.

The Legal Fiction of Corporate Residence

Governments have effectively harmonised the form of the corporation so that it is today universally recognised by states, a move that has been crucial for global capitalism.[30] A standardised concept of corporate 'residence' has also become 'one of the cornerstones of corporate income taxation, both in domestic and international law'.[31]

The definition of corporate 'residence' for tax purposes is usually based on the legal place of incorporation or the place of management or control of the corporation. It does not take much scrutiny to work out that corporate residence bears little relationship to the ordinary meaning of 'residence' of an individual. As explained by Lord Loreburn in *De Beers Consolidated Mines Ltd v Howe (Surveyor of Taxes)* [1906] A.C. 455 HL, 458, because a corporation 'in a natural sense does not reside anywhere, some artificial test must be applied'.[32] John Prebble observed:[33]

> If, despite logic, it is possible for companies in law to have a substantive connection with a geographical locality, that connection can only be in terms of residence of shareholders, directors, or employees, or in terms of the place or places where directors or employees carry out their work for the company.
>
> Humans must have spent at least *some* time in the jurisdictions where they were born, but (to the extent that companies are capable of having a substantive connection with any geographical place) companies may have no substantive connection at all with the place of their incorporation. The result is that the place-of-incorporation test of corporate residence for some companies reaches a result that is purely formal and devoid of any substance.
>
> The solution is only a little happier when courts or legislatures try to compose substantive corporate residence rules. They employ expressions like, 'where the company's real business is carried on', and 'where what we should call the head office in popular language is, and where the business of the company is really directed', and 'centre of management'. These expressions relate to the actions of people or, in the case of 'head office', to the bricks and mortar that surround some of the people in question. At least the expressions relate current facts (of

---

[30] Katharina Pistor, *The Code of Capital: How the Law Creates Wealth and Inequality* (Princeton, NJ: Princeton University Press, 2019) explores the broader effects of global standardisation of the legal form of the corporation and of financial transactions such as debt and equity investment.

[31] Edoardo Traversa (ed.), *Corporate Residence and Mobility*, EATLP International Tax Series No 16 (Amsterdam: IBFD, 2017), 1.

[32] This case is the origin of the 'central management and control' test in common law jurisdictions; see John F. Jones and Johann Hattingh, 'De Beers Consolidated Mines Ltd v Howe (1906): Corporate Residence: An Early Attempt at European Harmonisation' in Dominic de Cogan and John Snape (eds.), *Landmark Cases in Revenue Law* (Oxford: Hart Publishing, 2019), 67–90, Bloomsbury Collections, http://dx.doi.org/10.5040/9781509912285.ch-003.

[33] John Prebble, 'Ectopia, Tax Law and International Taxation' (1997) 5 *British Tax Review* 383–403, 389–90.

human action and place) to another fact (geographical jurisdiction). In this respect, the expressions are part of a law that more closely reflects reality than a law that turns on the location of a formal act of incorporation that may have occurred many years ago. But, nevertheless, the relationship of fact to fact is via an intermediate step that comprises a fiction: the corporation itself.

The challenge of locating corporate residence has increased in an era of digital corporate management, which has only been exacerbated by the COVID-19 pandemic. It is difficult to envisage directors flying to corporate board meetings located in specific jurisdictions around the world in future, so even the practical test of central or effective management and control may become increasingly difficult to locate. As explained in Box 11.2, MNEs may become untethered from their country of establishment.

Corporate residence is paradoxically 'both reinforced and eroded by the evolution of the global economy, in particular the development of multinational firms and the digitalisation of the management and operating activities of companies'.[34] The corporate form that always comes with a tax 'residence' is ideally suited for the distribution of the ownership of assets and the construction of transactions within a MNE, through controlled subsidiaries with specialised activities and relationships, located in high tax and low tax territories around the world. The importance of separate entity status of the corporation for international tax planning by US-headquartered MNEs is reinforced by the US 'check-the-box' tax regulations, introduced in 1997.[35] The 'check-the-box' regulations enable US parent companies to override, or 'look through', subsidiaries when this was suitable for tax planning purposes, while in other circumstances continuing to recognise their separate legal status.

For a closely controlled (private, or family owned) corporation, looking through the separate entity enables the allocation of tax jurisdiction based on the residence of the shareholders who control it. The taxation of income accrued in closely controlled foreign entities, discussed in Chapter 10, is an important element of tax law to counter international tax planning by resident individuals.

In contrast, most large MNEs are widely held by thousands of individuals and corporations around the world, directly or through investment and pension funds, banks, insurance companies, private trusts, or even sovereign wealth funds acting on behalf of whole countries. A recent study exhaustively examined a range of data in an attempt to identify who owns Apple Inc and other US-

---

[34] Traversa, *Corporate Residence and Mobility* (see n 31), chapter 1 near fn 59. See also Wolfgang Schön, 'International Tax Coordination for a Second Best World (Part I)' (2009) 1 *World Tax Journal* 67–70.

[35] Internal Revenue Code (US) Treas. Reg. § 301.7701-3 ('Classification of certain business entities') under which a US corporation can elect, by checking a box on the return, to have a foreign wholly owned subsidiary treated as if it does not exist for purposes of US corporate income tax liability.

Box 11.2 Untethering the MNE from the nation state

For most of the twentieth century, the investments of a nationally headquartered corporation beyond the boundaries of its 'home' or residence state were perceived as an extension of state power that would benefit or enhance economic interests of the 'home' state. A large business conducted through a corporate group, headquartered in one country and with substantial investments in subsidiary corporations in other jurisdictions, was perceived as 'nationally' representative.[36] For example, Caterpillar was perceived as a US company, or Toyota as a Japanese company.

Today, the corporation operating internationally has developed into the flexible, mobile, and globally proliferating form of the MNE. Mihir Desai suggests that in these conditions, 'the center cannot hold. The archetypal multinational firm with a particular national identity and a corporate headquarters fixed in one country is becoming obsolete as firms continue to maximise the opportunities created by global markets. National identities can mutate with remarkable ease and firms are unbundling critical headquarters functions and reallocating them worldwide'.[37]

An MNE may detach itself from the 'home' jurisdiction in numerous ways, such as shifting its legal entity to a new tax residence, or transferring intellectual property or other valuable assets offshore. An MNE may be 'dual-listed' across stock exchanges in different jurisdictions, for example, the mining group BHP-Billiton, which became listed in both the United Kingdom and Australia (it has recently begun a process to unwind the 'dual' structure).[38]

The tax residence of the head corporation of an MNE may be changed to a different jurisdiction by a reverse takeover or 'corporate inversion'. From the 1980s until the US enacted anti-inversion rules and subsequently the US corporate tax rate was lowered from 35 per cent to 21 per cent, there were numerous 'inversions' of US corporations to locate headquarters in low-taxed jurisdictions.

In 2015, the pharmaceutical group Pfizer entered into a US$160 billion inversion agreement with Ireland-based pharmaceutical corporation Allergan. The headquarters of the merged group would be in Ireland facing a favourable 12.5 per cent tax rate. The deal was terminated following introduction of anti-inversion rules in the US tax code, so Pfizer remains headquartered in the United States.[39]

based MNEs.[40] It failed to identify what proportion of these MNEs was owned in the United States and what proportion was owned internationally; the corporations themselves could not identify or locate all of their shareholders.

There are well-known instances of significant private control by individuals of global MNEs. For example, in early 2022, Elon Musk owned about 17 per

---

[36] Mihir A Desai, 'The Decentering of the Global Firm' (2009) 32 *The World Economy* 1271–90, https://doi.org/10.1111/j.1467-9701.2009.01212.x.
[37] Ibid.
[38] See BHP, 'Unified Corporate Structure', www.bhp.com/about/our-businesses/unified-corporate-structure, accessed 24 March 2022.
[39] Michelle C Neely and Larry D Sherrer, 'A Look at Corporate Inversions, Inside and Out' (2017) *The Regional Economist* 1–3, www.stlouisfed.org/~/media/publications/regional-economist/2017/first_quarter_2017/corporate_inversions.pdf.
[40] Chris Sanchirico, 'As American as Apple Inc: International Tax and Ownership Nationality' (2015) 68 *Tax Law Review* 207–74.

cent of Tesla, and Jeff Bezos owned about 10 per cent of Amazon.[41] These multibillionaires could be taxed directly on the value of their shares, if governments wished to do so. However, the residence of these individuals in the United States is a poor indicator of whether the United States should have jurisdiction to tax the profits of Tesla or Amazon, which operate and derive revenues in countries around the world.

In sum, the residence of a corporation is becoming 'less and less credible as a proxy to the place of income-generating economic activity and will remain largely uncoordinated at the international level'.[42] We should, therefore, seek to reduce its importance in the international allocation of jurisdiction to tax profits. National policymakers can only address this by establishing coherent rules that draw aside the 'corporate veil' and address the location of assets and of international income.[43]

Source and Permanent Establishment

The 'source' jurisdiction for corporate tax aims to allocate taxing rights to net gain generated from business activity in a jurisdiction that reaches the threshold of a permanent establishment (PE). The PE is the main way in which the international tax regime pierces the corporate veil and establishes a taxable nexus for business income.

Effective taxation requires the further step of calculating the profit to be attributed and taxed to the PE. The rules for allocating corporate profits to a PE or subsidiary doing business in a country rely on the 'arm's length' principle. This is intended to bring the tax allocation of profits in line with the commercial profits that would be expected to be recognised in an commercial transaction (OECD Model Convention Articles 7 and 9). The arm's length principle was developed as a convenient way to ensure that 'transfer prices' on intra-group contracts would reflect commercial reality.

The source jurisdiction also has primacy in levying a withholding tax on gross outbound payments of certain kinds of 'passive' return to investment such as interest, rents, dividends or royalties. The rate of withholding tax is usually limited by bilateral tax treaties in accordance with the OECD or United Nations (UN) model conventions. Governments have generally taken steps to ensure that rents and gains from land in their jurisdiction, including

---

[41] See Robert Frank, 'Elon Musk Unloaded $22 Billion of Tesla Stock – and Still Owns More Now than a Year Ago', CNBC, 15 February 2022, www.cnbc.com/2022/02/15/elon-musk-unloaded-billions-of-tesla-stockand-still-owns-more-than-last-year.html; Kerry Dolan, 'Jeff Bezos Just Sold 2 Billion Worth of Amazon Stock', Forbes, 4 November 2021, www.forbes.com/sites/kerryadolan/2021/11/04/jeff-bezos-just-sold-2-billion-worth-of-amazon-stock/.
[42] Traversa, *Corporate Residence and Mobility* (see n 31), chapter 1 near fn 83.
[43] Scott Wilkie, 'New Rules of Engagement? Corporate Personality and the Allocation of "International Income" and Taxing Rights' in Brian J Arnold (ed.), *Tax Treaties after the BEPS Project: A Tribute to Jacques Sasseville* (Toronto: Canadian Tax Foundation, 2017), 349–72.

mining rights, are taxable there, although for many countries the interposition of a corporate legal entity (or two) located offshore may successfully break the nexus even for gains on land.

The traditional definition of PE in OECD model convention Article 5 requires a 'fixed place' through which the business of the enterprise is carried on, or the existence of a 'dependent' agent in the jurisdiction habitually exercising authority on behalf of the enterprise. The assumption is that a threshold of business activity 'determines the circumstances in which the foreign enterprise can be considered sufficiently integrated into the economy of the state to justify taxation in that state'.[44] Examples include a mine site, factory, or an office where services are provided. The UN model convention developed to support capital-importing developing countries applies a lower threshold, including, for example, the use of substantial equipment in the jurisdiction.

The PE concept and arm's length principle establish a taxing nexus that should, based on the principles of tax jurisdiction proposed in Chapter 10, enable *convenient* taxation that is reasonably certain and that is capable of being enforced by the jurisdiction where the business or assets are located. This has become more difficult as value is increasingly found in intangible assets such as intellectual property, securities, trademarks or brands. The legal source of income from intangibles may be based on various factors such as the location of the payer; the place of the contract, funds payment or other legal transactions; or some indirect identification of the underlying economic activity that produced the income.[45] All of these elements may be uncertain, arbitrary or easily manipulated.

The mere selling of goods or services into a jurisdiction from an offshore location, including ancillary activities such as warehousing of goods onshore before delivery, was excluded from the traditional definition of PE. This was amended as part of the OECD Base Erosion and Project Shifting (BEPS), discussed later. The traditional definition of PE did not permit taxing jurisdiction merely because a country was on the 'market' for consumer goods or services from foreign sellers. This is one way in which the proxies for determining PE and its taxable profits in current international tax rules are no longer accepted as a good reflection of economic substance, or a suitable basis for allocating tax jurisdiction (we return to this later).

Stateless Income

Tax havens are widely used to lower the global taxes of MNEs, as long as this is not too costly for them (through anti-avoidance rules, enforcement activity,

---

[44] OECD, *Addressing the Tax Challenges of the Digital Economy: Action 1 Final Report* (Paris: OECD, 2014), 39, www.oecd-ilibrary.org/taxation/addressing-the-tax-challenges-of-the-digital-economy_9789264218739-en.

[45] John Prebble, 'Why Is Tax Law Incomprehensible?' (1994) 4 *British Tax Review* 380–93, 384.

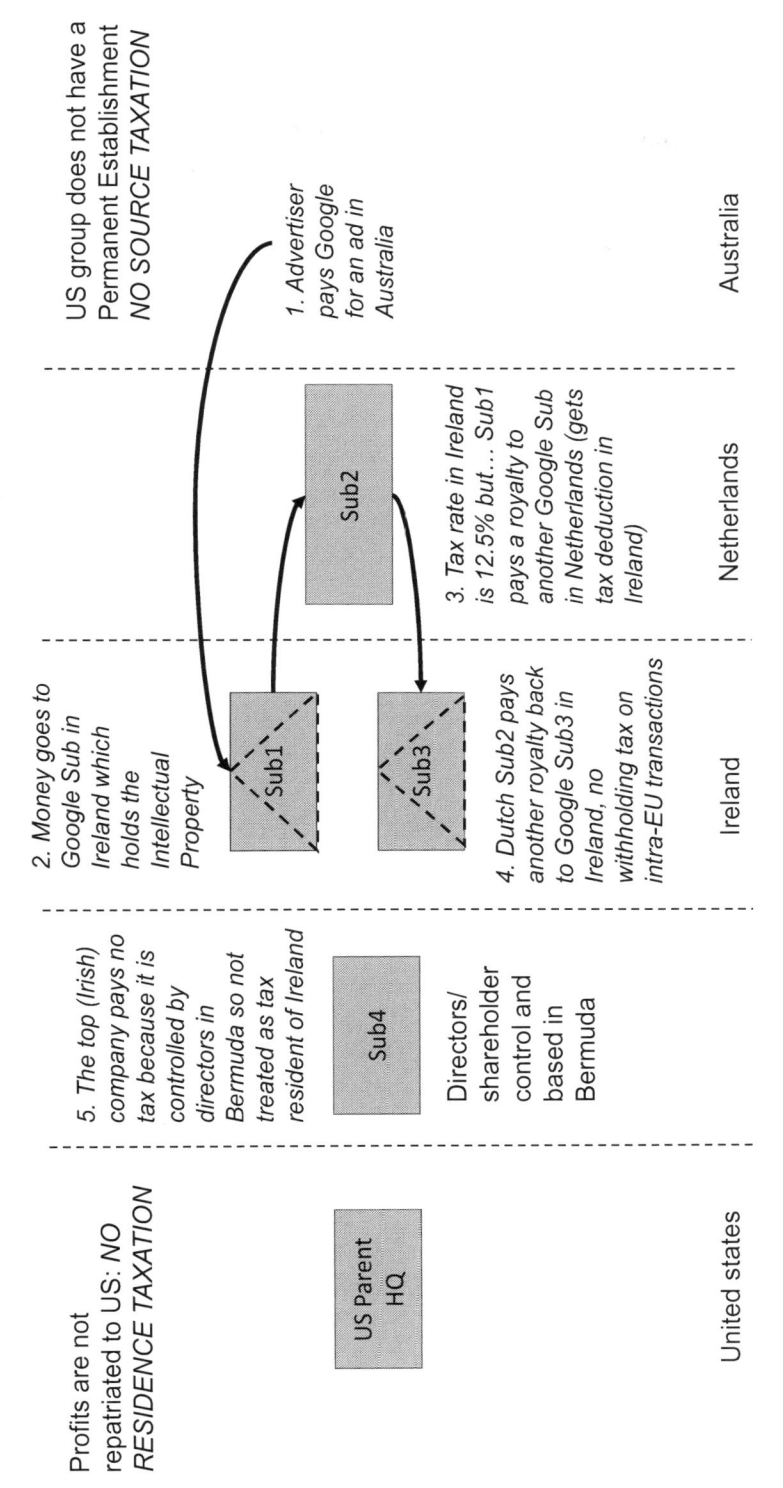

US group does not have a Permanent Establishment
NO SOURCE TAXATION

1. Advertiser pays Google for an ad in Australia

3. Tax rate in Ireland is 12.5% but... Sub1 pays a royalty to another Google Sub in Netherlands (gets tax deduction in Ireland)

2. Money goes to Google Sub in Ireland which holds the Intellectual Property

4. Dutch Sub2 pays another royalty back to Google Sub3 in Ireland, no withholding tax on intra-EU transactions

5. The top (Irish) company pays no tax because it is controlled by directors in Bermuda so not treated as tax resident of Ireland

Directors/shareholder control and based in Bermuda

Profits are not repatriated to US: *NO RESIDENCE TAXATION*

| United states | Ireland | Netherlands | Australia |

US Parent HQ — Sub4 — Sub1 — Sub3 — Sub2

Figure 11.1 Double Irish-Dutch Sandwich tax planning structure

transaction costs or reputational damage, for example). In Edward Kleinbard's influential article titled 'Stateless Income',[46] he analysed the ability of MNEs to locate income or profit in tax havens that are neither the residence jurisdiction of the parent company or the source jurisdiction where economic activity is located, thereby reducing their taxes and generating 'tax rents'.[47] This undermines both residence and source taxation and 'changes everything':

> Stateless income tax planning enables savvy multinational firms to capture tax rents, by deflecting high-tax source country pretax returns to very low-tax jurisdictions. Stateless income planning also enables firms effectively to do the same with residence pretax returns through arbitrage, by locating a disproportionate amount of debt in the residence country.[48]

One example of a tax structure that generates 'stateless income' is the so-called Double Irish-Dutch Sandwich adopted by various US MNEs, including Google, in the first decade of the twenty-first century. This is illustrated in Figure 11.1. While now past its use-by date for various reasons, including tax reform in Ireland and the United States, it provides a useful illustration of some key elements of international tax planning. These include the combined effects of separate corporate entity status, or 'checking the box' to ignore that status; high and low tax jurisdictions; payments for valuable intangible property; transfer pricing; and the role of tax havens.

The Double Irish-Dutch Sandwich involved subsidiary companies located in Ireland, which had a low company tax rate of 12.5 per cent; the Netherlands, which operated as a conduit jurisdiction because of generous headquarters rules and low withholding tax in the US-Netherlands tax treaty; and Bermuda, a long-standing tax haven. The country where the advertising revenue is earned (where the consumer 'clicks' on Google) does not have jurisdiction to tax, because the activities do not rise to the level of a PE (there is no physical presence). The jurisdictions in which the fee or royalty passes through Sub1 and Sub2 may take a small tax payment, but the payments are deductible when they leave the jurisdiction. Although incorporated in Ireland, Sub3 is not a tax resident of Ireland, or of any other jurisdiction, because of the 'residence' rules of Ireland and, Bermuda and the United States. The United States, where the parent entity is located, did not (at the time) have jurisdiction to tax because profits were not repatriated. The 'check-the-box' rules meant that the United States ignored Sub1 and Sub3 and perceived the royalty payments as received by Sub2, which meant that the US CFC rules did not apply.

An MNE may respond to taxes by doing tax planning, as illustrated in Figure 11.1, or by moving economic investment to a different country. The

---

[46] Edward Kleinbard, 'Stateless Income' (2011) 11(9) *Florida Tax Review* 700–66.
[47] Ibid., 704.
[48] Edward Kleinbard, 'The Lessons of Stateless Income' (2011) 65(1) *Tax Law Review* 99–172, 135.

difficulty that economists have in finding an empirical relationship between corporate tax competition, wages and jobs may be partly explained by the effectiveness of international tax planning by MNEs.[49] The ability of MNEs to separate their taxable income, and corporate tax payable, from their real investments might actually be protecting jobs and wages in higher tax jurisdictions. This implies that the global marginal investor really matters: in a race to the bottom in corporate tax rates, 'real' investment might actually flee to a lower taxed jurisdiction.

The availability of tax havens and the opportunity to do international tax arbitrage between different approaches to corporate residence, PE and profit allocation rules, advantages enterprises that can operate or restructure globally compared to those that cannot. This may have contributed to the agglomeration of capital investment in MNEs and the distribution of assets and value-chains around the world. It suggests that the success of MNEs is not only a function of corporate synergies or global efficiency of production, but is also a product of their success in tailoring tax systems, adapting concepts of residence, source and taxable value to achieve lower global taxation. We turn now to recent attempts to reform international taxation of MNEs in the global digital economy.

Base Erosion and Profit Shifting

The BEPS Project

After the Global Financial Crisis of 2008, having achieved some success in its efforts to build tax administrative cooperation, the G20 with the OECD turned its attention to the role of tax havens in corporate international tax planning and avoidance. The focus on MNEs may have taken some pressure off governments facing budget deficits and enacting fiscal austerity measures at home. Attention shifted from individual tax evasion to the evidence from 'Panama Papers' and other leaks that corporations also took advantage of tax havens. Widespread public concern about corporate tax avoidance was fuelled by reports from non-government organisations[50] and Parliamentary and congressional public inquiries.[51] Governments began to pay increased attention to

---

[49] Clausing, 'In Search of Corporate Tax Incidence' (see n 25).
[50] ActionAid UK, *Addicted to Tax Havens* (Chard: ActionAid UK, 2012), www.actionaid.org.uk/sites/default/files/doc_lib/addicted_to_tax_havens.pdf.
[51] See, e.g., Parliament of the United Kingdom Public Accounts Committee, 'Tax Avoidance: The Role of Large Accountancy Firms: Follow-up' (6 February 2015), https://publications.parliament.uk/pa/cm201415/cmselect/cmpubacc/1057/105706.htm; Parliament of the Commonwealth of Australia, Senate Economic References Committee, 'An Inquiry into Tax Avoidance and Aggressive Minimization by Corporations Registered in Australia and Multinational Corporations Operating in Australia', www.aph.gov.au/Parliamentary_Business/Committees/Senate/Economics/Corporatetax45th, accessed 24 March 2022.

'stateless income', 'double non-taxation' and tax arbitrage facilitated by the tax treaties and laws of different jurisdictions.[52]

Some of the most prominent MNEs were in the public eye. In October 2010, a Bloomberg headline blared: 'Google 2.4 Per Cent Rate Shows How $60 Billion Is Lost to Tax Loopholes'.[53] Google's strategy relied on the 'Double-Irish Dutch Sandwich', illustrated in Figure 11.1. In 2012, Starbucks responded to public criticism and protests at its stores by announcing that it would pay £20 million in 'voluntary' tax, amid revelations that it had successfully avoided paying tax in the United Kingdom over the prior three years.[54] In 2013, the G20 leaders declared (in language reminiscent of the 1990s) that 'tax avoidance, harmful practices and aggressive tax planning have to be tackled'.[55]

The IMF also began to study the effects of international corporate tax planning, producing an influential report in 2014 which concluded that there was significant evidence of tax-motivated avoidance transactions by MNEs.[56] A literature review of empirical studies finds ample evidence for tax-motivated structures including transfer pricing; location of valuable intellectual property in low tax jurisdictions; tax treaty shopping; deferral; corporate inversions and location of headquarters companies; and thin capitalisation, shifting deductible interest payments to high tax jurisdictions while not affecting the overall debt exposure of the group.[57] Box 11.3 outlines these strategies that generate 'base erosion and profit shifting' (BEPS).

The OECD Action Plan on BEPS is summarised in Box 11.4. The Action Plan aimed to 'prevent governments losing corporate tax revenue, the emergence of competing sets of international standards, and the replacement of the current consensus-based framework by unilateral measures, which could lead to global tax chaos'.[58] After consulting on draft reports issued in 2014, the OECD presented final reports to the G20 finance ministers in October 2015.

---

[52] H David Rosenbloom 'International Tax Arbitrage and the International Tax System' (1998) 53 *Tax Law Review* 137–66; Kleinbard, 'Stateless Income' (see n 46).

[53] Jesse Drucker, 'Google 2.4% Rate Shows How $60 Billion Is Lost to Tax Loopholes' *Bloomberg Business Week*, 20 October 2010, www.bloomberg.com/news/articles/2010-10-21/google-2-4-rate-shows-how-60-billion-u-s-revenue-lost-to-tax-loopholes.

[54] Eric Pfanner, 'Starbucks Offers to Pay More British Tax Than Required' *New York Times*, 6 December 2012, www.nytimes.com/2012/12/07/business/global/07iht-uktax07.html?_r=0.

[55] G20, 'Saint Petersburg Declaration' (6 September 2013), www.g20.utoronto.ca/2013/2013-0906-declaration.html, para. 50.

[56] International Monetary Fund, *Spillovers in International Corporate Taxation*, IMF Policy Paper (Washington, DC: IMF, 2014).

[57] Sebastian Beer, Ruud de Mooij and Li Liu, *International Corporate Tax Avoidance: A Review of the Channels, Magnitudes, and Blind Spots*, International Monetary Fund Working Paper WP/18/168 (Washington, DC: IMF, 2018).

[58] OECD, *Action Plan on Base Erosion and Profit Shifting* (Paris: OECD Publishing, 2013), https://doi.org/10.1787/9789264202719-en.

> **Box 11.3 Base erosion and profit shifting by MNEs**
>
> International tax planning is facilitated not merely by the existence of zero rates, but through leveraging the *difference* between zero or low tax rates in some jurisdictions, and higher tax rates in other jurisdictions. This is achieved by locating subsidiaries in low tax jurisdictions, and establishing contracts that set prices for sales, services, licences or financial transactions between those subsidiaries and subsidiaries in high tax countries. In this way, profit shifting may occur through 'transfer pricing', which alters the price of internal corporate transactions, including sales of goods and services, licensing of intellectual property and financial transactions such as lending and insurance between subsidiary members of the group located in different jurisdictions.
>
> For example, a subsidiary in a higher taxing jurisdiction may pay large royalties for patents or trademarks, or a high fee for insurance or marketing, to another subsidiary located in a tax haven. The payments are deductible in the jurisdiction where business activity is taking place.
>
> Base erosion may occur through claiming large losses or deductions in higher tax jurisdictions, reducing the tax liability in that jurisdiction, and overall, for the corporate group. An example is thin capitalisation or debt shifting. This occurs when investment in a higher taxing jurisdiction is overleveraged, or charged at an excessive interest rate, generating interest payments that are tax deductible in that country and are paid to another group entity facing a lower tax rate. Overall, the group manages its debt globally and maintains a stable exposure to debt risk.
>
> International tax arbitrage or 'double non-taxation' may occur when transactions are characterised differently under the tax laws of two different jurisdictions. For example, interest on debt may be tax-deductible in the high-taxing country and the same transaction may be characterised as a tax-exempt dividend on equity in the recipient country. This could lead to an outcome in which no tax is payable in any jurisdiction.

Unlike the Harmful Tax Competition project of the 1990s, the G20-led BEPS project succeeded in achieving governmental action on many of its recommendations under these Actions. The G20 included the BRICS (Brazil, Russia, India, China and South Africa) who joined with other governments to promote the project. International business was engaged in close consultation. The BEPS recommendations were agreed through the usual OECD working process of consensus in working parties of OECD member states, expanded to include the BRICS and some other countries. The Actions required domestic tax reform in the states who agreed to the process, the ratification of a multilateral treaty to amend bilateral treaties and enhancement of multilateral systems of tax administrative cooperation. Countries participating in what is now called the Inclusive Framework on BEPS have committed to minimum standards and common approaches.

Despite many tax reforms arising from the BEPS project, it is difficult to assess how much the BEPS Actions have changed business as usual for taxpayers or governments, or whether they have led to increased tax payable by MNEs to

Box 11.4 The BEPS Action Plan

The BEPS Action Plan proposed 15 Actions for reform to achieve: (1) coherence; (2) substance; and (3) transparency in the international tax system.

Action 1 examined the core issue of the digital economy. The G20 and OECD were not able to reach a consensus on recommendations for the digital economy in 2015.

Coherence

These Actions aimed to prevent double non-taxation by addressing gaps or mismatches in the international tax system that might lead to no or low taxation.

Action 2 addressed hybrid mismatch transactions or entities that enabled different tax outcomes in two countries, generating double non-taxation.

Action 3 proposed strengthening CFC rules to capture foreign low-taxed income in controlled entities.

Action 4 sought to limit base erosion arising from thin capitalisation, or deductible interest deductions and other financial payments.

Action 5 aimed to counter harmful tax practices by requiring reform or removal in a peer reviewed process.

Substance

These Actions aimed to 'fix the flaws' in tax treaties that enabled international avoidance, by aligning taxing rights with economic substance.

Action 6 introduced a treaty anti-abuse rule.

Action 7 proposed rules to limit artificial avoidance of PE status.

Actions 8, 9 and 10 aimed to strengthen transfer pricing standards for intangible assets, and to modify the transfer pricing approach to risk and overcapitalisation of shell companies. However, the arm's length principle was reaffirmed.

Transparency and Enforcement

These Actions aimed to build the capacity of tax authorities to administer the international tax system in cooperation with each other.

Action 11 authorised the OECD to collect and evaluate data on BEPS.

Action 12 concerned disclosure of aggressive tax planning to tax authorities.

Action 13 increased requirements for transfer pricing documentation based on country-by-country (CbC) reporting.

Action 14 proposed strengthening mechanisms for dispute resolution between governments about double taxation, including the Mutual Authority Procedure (MAP) and mandatory binding arbitration.

Action 15 would enable the BEPS minimum standards (and other rules) through establishment of a Multilateral Instrument to amend bilateral tax treaties and implement the agreed reforms.

governments around the world.[59] This may be partly a function of timing; many BEPS measures commenced in 2017 or later, and there has been little time for empirical evaluation. Modelling the revenue impact of BEPS, and the potential effect of anti-BEPS measures, is difficult. However, one meta-analysis of various studies finds evidence of erosion of the US corporate tax base by about 17 per cent, while estimates in some other relatively high tax rate countries indicate fiscal impact of about 5 to 10 per cent of corporate tax revenues.[60]

Some aspects of the BEPS project suggest a shift in the principles underlying the international tax system and the increased interpenetration of domestic and international elements. The next part focuses on multilateralism in designing the new international corporate tax rules, the growth in transnational corporate tax administration, the rise in anti-avoidance rules in international tax, and the approach to so-called harmful tax practices and tax incentives.

Multilateralism in Corporate Tax

It has been observed that the BEPS project evinces a move towards multilateralism with the potential to transform international tax law.[61] One way it did this was the completely novel development of a multilateral treaty under Action 15, which would allow countries to swiftly amend bilateral tax treaties to implement the BEPS initiative.[62] The Multilateral Convention to Implement Tax Treaty Related Measures to Prevent Base Erosion and Profit Shifting, also known as the *Multilateral Instrument* (MLI), opened for signature in 2017 and entered into force on 27 June 2018. Important signatories outside the OECD include China, India, South Africa, Indonesia and Russia (but notably, not the United States). By 2021, the MLI had been signed by 95 jurisdictions (nearly 80 countries), with potential coverage of nearly 2000 bilateral tax treaties.

The MLI is bolted on top of the network of bilateral income tax treaties based on the OECD and UN Models. As a matter of international law, the MLI

---

[59] Catherine A Brown and Joseph Bogle, 'Treaty Shopping and the New Multilateral Tax Agreement – Is It Business as Usual in Canada?' (2020) 43(1) *Dalhousie Law Journal* 1–32. A series of policy briefs examining progress and governmental engagement on each of the 15 Actions is available at University of Melbourne, Melbourne School of Government, 'International Tax Design for the 21st Century', https://government.unimelb.edu.au/research/regulation-and-design/research-outputs/research-papers/international-tax-design-for-the-21st-century, accessed 24 March 2022.

[60] Beer et al, *International Corporate Tax Avoidance* (see n 57).

[61] Ruth Mason, 'The Transformation of International Tax' (2020) 114(3) *American Journal of International Law* 353–402; Pasquale Pistone, 'Coordinating the Action of Regional and Global Players during the Shift from Bilateralism to Multilateralism in International Tax Law' (2014) 6 *World Tax Journal* 1–9.

[62] OECD, *Action 15: A Mandate for the Development of a Multilateral Instrument on Tax Treaty Measures to Tackle BEPS* (Paris: OECD, 2015), www.oecd.org/ctp/beps-action-15-mandate-for-development-of-multilateral-instrument.pdf, para. 10.

is said to 'modify' covered tax agreements (Article 1).[63] The MLI is effective only in relation to notified tax treaties, provisions and rules to the depository hosted by the OECD. The implementation of the MLI is a Rubik's cube,[64] in which each country's choices interact with the choices of other countries. While it is intended that the MLI will apply to as many bilateral tax treaties as possible, there are numerous ways in which countries may limit or modify its application. This flexible approach has been suggested as a model for reform of the similarly large network of bilateral investment treaties around the world.[65]

Ruth Mason argues that the multilateralism (and substance) of BEPS 'reflected – and to a significant extent operationalised – major changes in the participants, agenda, institutions, norms, and legal instruments of international tax'.[66] These changes reveal, Mason suggests, growing agreement on an international norm of 'full taxation' of income (one may query if this is the same as the 'single tax' principle proposed by Avi-Yonah). It also indicates the establishment of minimum standards, for example in transfer pricing and anti-abuse. Others suggest that neither the BEPS project nor the MLI has changed the status quo:

> The core mission of the MLI is to support the current, bilateral treaties based international tax regime and to empower its hold on the tax world. This mission is consistent with BEPS that evolved into a political project primarily designed to preserve the institutional status of the OECD as the caretaker of the international tax regime.[67]

Multilateralism of the BEPS project has served to expand the role and influence of the OECD as an international institution. Developing countries, despite having an increasing voice in the Global Forum and Inclusive Framework on BEPS, have been unable to set the agenda or participate substantially in framing the rules.[68] Nonetheless, the increasing agitation by countries for full participation in forums negotiating multilateral rules, although scarcely achieved, legitimates multilateralism as a process for establishing international tax law.

---

[63] OECD Directorate for Legal Affairs, *Multilateral Convention to Implement Tax Treaty Related Measures to Prevent Base Erosion and Profit Shifting: Functioning under Public International Law* (Paris: OECD, 2015), paras 15–16; OECD, Explanatory Statement to The Multilateral Convention to Implement Tax Treaty Related Measures to Prevent Base Erosion and Profit Shifting (2016), www.oecd.org/tax/treaties/explanatory-statement-multilateral-convention-to-implement-tax-treaty-related-measures-to-prevent-BEPS.pdf, para 13.

[64] With credit to Professor Jan De Goede (IBFD), whose phrase this is.

[65] Wolfgang Alschner, 'The OECD Multilateral Tax Instrument: A Model for Reforming the International Investment Regime?' (2019) 45(1) *Brooklyn Law Journal* 1–73.

[66] Mason, 'The Transformation of International Tax' (see n 61), 354.

[67] Yariv Brauner, 'McBEPS: The MLI – The First Multilateral Tax Treaty that Has Never Been' (2018) 46(1) *Intertax* 6–17, 16.

[68] Irma Mosquera Valderrama, 'Legitimacy and the Making of International Tax Law: The Challenges of Multilateralism' (2015) 7 *World Tax Journal* 343–82.

Transnational Corporate Tax Administration

The expansion of transnational tax administration in the last decade was explained in Chapter 10. This has been extended to corporate tax through the BEPS project. The agreement for production and exchange of country-by-country (CbC) reporting of profits as a minimum standard (Action 13), the exchange of information on rulings that provide tax concessions, also a minimum standard (Action 5) and the optional agreement of a growing number of countries to binding dispute resolution processes at the international level (Action 14) are all important developments arising out of the BEPS Project.

The CbC report presents information about income, profits and tax paid by MNEs in every jurisdiction in which they operate, and enables this information to be shared between tax authorities. To achieve exchange of CbC reports, participating governments had to reform their domestic tax laws to require MNEs to submit the relevant information, and to agree the Common Reporting Standard (CRS) for automatic exchange of CbC reports.[69] The threshold for MNE obligations to provide CbC reports is global revenues in excess of €750 million. The rules apply only to large business, but nonetheless this threshold includes thousands of MNEs. The legislation to require profit reporting to support CbC reports has been adopted in more than 90 countries.[70] The OECD has issued guidance on the interpretation and implementation of CbC reporting, which aims to standardise reporting and ease administration and compliance. As a minimum standard, this Action is subject to peer review to ensure its prompt and accurate implementation.

The head entity of a corporate group must lodge the CbC report, Master file and Local file, with the head entity's tax authority. The Master file contains information about the MNE's business operations and international organisational structure, transfer pricing policies and how it allocates global income and economic activity within its group. The Local file contains in-depth information relating to specific transactions between the members of the MNE, allowing tax authorities to check these individual transactions within the context of the MNE's global operations. This includes information relating to the allocation of revenue, profit and taxes paid in individual jurisdictions in which the MNE operates. The CbC report also includes a list of entities within the MNE group

---

[69] See OECD, 'OECD Releases Peer Review Documents for Assessment of BEPS Minimum Standards (Actions 5 and 13)', 1 February 2017, www.oecd.org/tax/beps/oecd-releases-peer-review-documents-for-assessment-of-beps-minimum-standards-actions-5-and-13.htm and OECD, *Transfer Pricing Documentation and Country-by-Country Reporting: Action 13 – 2015 Final Report* (Paris: OECD, 2015), https://read.oecd.org/10.1787/9789264241480-en?format=pdf.

[70] OECD, 'OECD Releases Peer Review Documents' (see n 69); OECD, 'BEPS: Action 13 Country-by-Country Reporting', www.oecd.org/tax/beps/beps-actions/action13/, accessed 7 March 2022; OECD, *Transfer Pricing Documentation and Country-by-Country Reporting* (see n 69).

and their relevant tax jurisdictions, and the nature of the main business carried out by each entity.

The sharing of CbC reports is done under 'activated' bilateral exchange agreements. The first exchanges took place in June 2018. The OECD reported aggregated and anonymised data from CBC reports in July 2021, which provides information on the global activities of nearly 6000 MNE groups operating in more than 100 jurisdictions.

The US Internal Revenue Service has pioneered the publication of statistics based on CbC reports from US MNEs.[71] A recent study utilises CbC data to confirm significant misalignment of reported profit and tax paid by US-based MNEs.[72] The study finds that the CbC reports provide improved data on MNE activities, operations and profits around the globe, enabling better understanding of tax-motivated planning, and enforcement of tax laws. It also reports some interesting details, including the significance of the Cayman Islands in terms of profit allocation by US MNEs, and of Puerto Rico as a hub for the US pharmaceutical industry.

CbC reports are not available to the public. Non-government organisations, including the Tax Justice Network, have advocated for publication of CbC reports. Publication of profits in different jurisdictions is required for banks in the EU.[73] To date, studies provide mixed evidence of the impact of publicity on tax avoidance behaviour. One study finds that the number of subsidiaries of European banks in tax havens declined significantly and that reputational risk is a factor for some banks; however, the mandatory disclosure does not reduce tax haven presence across banks in general.[74] Other studies find little evidence of a decline in profit shifting or a reduction in tax avoidance since public CbC reporting began.[75]

A different institutional development is the growing acceptance of mandatory binding arbitration on international tax disputes by countries outside the EU (where it is already mandated). This has occurred through adoption of the arbitration clauses in the MLI and in bilateral tax treaties. Mandatory binding arbitration may apply where two governments cannot agree on tax allocation

---

[71] Internal Revenue Service (US), 'SOI Tax Stats – Country by Country Report', updated 12 January 2022, www.irs.gov/statistics/soi-tax-stats-country-by-country-report.

[72] Javier Garcia-Bernardo, Petr Jansky and Thomas Torslov, 'Multinational Corporations and Tax Havens: Evidence from Country-by-Country Reporting' (2021) 28 *International Tax and Public Finance* 1519–61, https://doi.org/10.1007/s10797-020-09639-w.

[73] European Commission Credit Requirement Directive IV of 2013 introduced following public advocacy; see, e.g. Jill Treanor, 'Avaaz Bank Tax Transparency Petition Attracts More than 200,000 Signatures', *The Guardian* online, 27 February 2013, www.theguardian.com/business/2013/feb/27/eu-tax-transparency-avaaz-petition.

[74] Eva Eberhartinger, Rafael Speitmann and Caren Sureth-Sloane, *Banks' Tax Disclosure, Financial Secrecy, and Tax Haven Heterogeneity*, WU International Tax Research Paper Series No 2020-01 (2021), https://ssrn.com/abstract=3523909.

[75] Preetika Joshi, Edmund Outslay, Anh Persson, Terry Shevlin and Arunh Venkat, 'Does Public Country-by-Country Reporting Deter Tax Avoidance and Income Shifting? Evidence from the European Banking Industry' (2020) 37 *Contemporary Accounting Research* 2357–97.

under a tax treaty, and effective 'double tax' has resulted for a taxpayer.[76] Most tax treaties contain a provision establishing the Mutual Agreement Procedure (MAP) in Article 25 of the OECD Model Convention. This enables the tax authorities of each jurisdiction to resolve treaty-related tax disputes. The OECD Model also contains Article 27 on arbitration, but historically many countries did not adopt this provision, as it is seen as a reduction of sovereignty.

During the BEPS project, taxpayers lobbied for arbitration to provide increased certainty and speed up MAP dispute resolution. While few, if any arbitrations actually take place, the mechanism operates as an incentive for tax authorities to settle disputes under MAP within required time limits, usually two years. The OECD has also stepped up its monitoring and reporting of the number of MAP disputes outstanding and settled on a regular basis. The Inclusive Framework Consensus on the digital economy calls for adoption of a binding dispute resolution process; this approach may be different from arbitration, but it is not yet clear what form it will take.

Tax authorities continue to strengthen cross-border engagement. One example is the Forum on Tax Administration, which includes representatives from 53 countries.[77] One Forum initiative, recently expanded in its membership, is the Joint International Task Force on Shared Intelligence and Collaboration, which now includes 42 tax authorities.[78] The Forum also established the International Compliance Assurance Program (ICAP) in December 2020.[79] ICAP aims to leverage CbC reporting, sharing data and managing multilateral risk assessment of MNEs 'to determine each group's specific international tax risks, including those related to transfer pricing and permanent establishment'.[80]

Anti-abuse Approaches[81]

The history and development of anti-abuse approaches in national tax laws, including statutory General Anti-Avoidance Rules (GAARs) was discussed in

---

[76] Michael Lang, Jeffrey Owens, Jasmin Kollmann and Laura Turcan (eds.), *International Arbitration in Tax Matters* (Amsterdam: IBFD, 2016).
[77] OECD Forum on Tax Administration, www.oecd.org/tax/forum-on-tax-administration/about/, accessed 28 March 2022.
[78] OECD Forum on Tax Administration, 'Joint International Taskforce on Shared Intelligence and Collaboration', http://www.oecd.org/tax/forum-on-tax-administration/about/jitsic/, accessed 28 March 2022.
[79] OECD Forum on Tax Administration, '2020 FTA "Amsterdam" Plenary Communique' (2020), www.oecd.org/tax/forum-on-tax-administration/events/2020/forum-on-tax-administration-communique-2020.pdf.
[80] Stephanie Soong Johnston, 'Multilateral Tax Risk Assessment Program to Exit Pilot Phase' (9 December 2020) *Tax Notes International*.
[81] This part draws on Sarah Blakelock and Miranda Stewart 'Australia's Evolving General Anti-avoidance Law' in Manuel Tron (ed.), *The Structure of Anti-avoidance Rules. Vol 100a: Cahiers*

Chapter 9. Historically, anti-abuse approaches have had much less prominence in the international context. When the BEPS project was initiated, there was ambiguity about whether it was acceptable for there to be 'double non-taxation' in the international sphere.[82] There was also uncertainty about whether tax minimisation achieved while strictly complying with tax laws and tax treaties, could be subject to national GAARs and other anti-abuse approaches.

The BEPS project has made clear, under Action 6 and the minimum standard included in the MLI, that tax treaties should aim prevent tax avoidance and evasion, as well as provide relief from double taxation. Action 6 mandated the inclusion of a treaty rule aimed at preventing abuse of tax treaties. The rule applies a principal purpose test (PPT), which would deny a treaty benefit 'if it is reasonable to conclude, having regard to all relevant facts and circumstances, that obtaining that benefit was one of the principal purposes of any arrangement or transaction that resulted directly or indirectly in that benefit', unless it is established that granting the benefit would be in accordance with the object and purpose of the Convention.

The PPT is intended to ensure that tax treaties provide benefits in respect of bona fide trade and investment, 'as opposed to arrangements whose principal objective is to secure a more favourable tax treatment'.[83] As discussed in Chapter 9, a judgment that a transaction is abusive requires a benchmark against which to determine the legitimacy of the relevant transaction. Unlike a domestic GAAR, the PPT cannot itself authorise a tax authority to levy more taxation but can only deny treaty benefits and thereby (indirectly) levy more tax on a cross-border transaction.

Some governments have taken steps to extend their domestic GAARs to international transactions, or to enact special anti-abuse taxes. The United Kingdom pre-empted the BEPS project and enacted its own 'diverted profits tax', nicknamed the 'Google tax', in 2015. Australia copied the approach, if not the detailed design, extending the Australian GAAR for large MNEs that enter into schemes to avoid tax by avoiding the attribution of business profits to a PE in Australia (the Multinational Anti-Avoidance Law) or diverting profits out of Australia (the Diverted Profits Tax).

Harmful Tax Practices

Finally, it is worth commenting on BEPS Action 5, which refreshed the OECD project on harmful tax competition of the 1990s. This is the most explicit

---

de droit fiscal international (70th International Fiscal Association Congress, Sdu Fiscale & Financiele Uitgevers) (Rotterdam: International Fiscal Association, 2018).

[82] Michael Lang, 'General Report' in *Double Non-taxation. Cahiers de droit international: Vol 89a* (Amsterdam: IBFD, 2004).

[83] OECD, *Preventing the Granting of Treaty Benefits in Inappropriate Circumstances: Action 6 Final Report* (Paris: OECD, 2015), https://doi.org/10.1787/9789264241695-en, supra n 16 at 68.

element in the BEPS project that addresses a potential 'race to the bottom' by tax regimes 'that unfairly erode the tax bases of other countries'. However, the Action 5 Report stated that this work 'is not intended to promote the harmonisation of income taxes or tax structures generally within or outside the OECD, nor is it about dictating to any country what should be the appropriate level of tax rates'.[84]

This apparent contradiction is addressed by the Action 5 report in two ways. The first is procedural. Action 5 established a process for identifying harmful tax regimes that should be closed down and requirements for disclosure, transparency and information exchange between countries, especially rulings that give tax concessions to taxpayers. The peer review of preferential regimes of OECD members and other countries in the BEPS project has led to the abolition of some regimes and provides a lever for negotiation to establish minimum standards for such regimes.

The second approach in the Action 5 report, as elsewhere in the BEPS project, is to turn to economic substance as a minimum requirement. The Action 5 report states:

> Action Item 5 specifically requires substantial activity for any preferential regime. . . . this requirement contributes to the second pillar of the BEPS project, which is to align taxation with substance by ensuring that taxable profits can no longer be artificially shifted away from the countries where value is created.[85]

This approach enables the broadening of the harmful tax practices work beyond just ring-fenced or discriminatory preferential regimes, which were the focus of the OECD Harmful Tax Competition Report in 1998.

A challenge for Action 5 was how to treat the expanding number of low-taxed 'patent boxes' around the world. In 1965, France established the first patent box, a rule that provided a preferential tax rate for income derived from patents or other intellectual property in the jurisdiction.[86] When Ireland joined the European Union in 1973, it introduced an exemption for the income from royalties on patents first registered in Ireland. These patent boxes aimed to encourage innovation and commercialisation of research and development, similarly to tax incentives for business discussed in Chapter 7. However, they quickly became a lightning rod for international tax planning,

---

[84] OECD, *Countering Harmful Tax Practices More Effectively, Taking into Account Transparency and Substance: Action 5: 2015 Final Report* (Paris: OECD, 2015), http://dx.doi.org/10.1787/9789264241190-en, 27. It has led to abolition of some 'harmful' regimes; see OECD, 'Progress towards a Fairer Global Tax System Continues as Additional Countries Bring Their Preferential Tax Regimes in Line with International Standards' (5 August 2021), www.oecd.org/tax/beps/progress-towards-a-fairer-global-tax-system-continues-as-additional-countries-bring-their-preferential-tax-regimes-in-line-with-international-standards.htm.

[85] OECD, *Countering Harmful Tax Practices More Effectively* (see n 84), 27.

[86] Edoardo Traversa and Alessandra Flamini, 'Chapter 6: Patent Boxes Before and After BEPS Action 5' in Pasquale Pistone and Dennis Weber (eds.), *The Implementation of Anti-BEPS Rules in the EU: A Comprehensive Study* (Amsterdam: IBFD, 2018).

as it was possible to locate patents of MNEs in these jurisdictions and so attract the low tax rate. Similar provisions were enacted in many other European countries, and 'became a tax competition tool'.[87]

In 2014, at the same time that it sought to counter corporate tax avoidance, the UK Government took a strongly competitive stance, reducing its company tax rate to 20 per cent and announcing a new patent box for intellectual property income. Concerns were raised by Germany and other countries regarding consistency with BEPS Action 5. Ultimately, agreement was reached on a substance test measured by expenditure on developing the intellectual property in the jurisdiction. If substance could not be established, patent boxes would have to be amended or abolished.

Meanwhile, the United States had extended tax to foreign low taxed income in the Tax Cuts and Jobs Act 2017 and established its own version of a patent box in its GILTI rule for Global Intangible Low Taxed Income, which set a minimum tax rate of just over 13 per cent on such income.[88] These events revealed the continuing downward trend in tax rates on valuable intangible assets. An anti-abuse approach was ultimately not enough to control the race to the bottom. This was one of the factors that led to the Inclusive Framework Consensus, which we discuss later.

This discussion of the BEPS project illustrates that governments simultaneously vacate the tax jurisdiction (create a patent box or enact a participation exemption) and assert and extend the tax jurisdiction (establish a digital services tax or expand the definition of permanent establishment).

The Global Digital Economy

The Tax Consequences of Digitalisation

From the advent of the internet in the mid-1990s, commercial activities began to be conducted as 'e-commerce', which included a 'wide array of commercial activities carried out through the use of computers, including online trading of goods and services, electronic funds transfers, online trading of financial instruments, and electronic data exchanges between companies and within a company'.[89] It became difficult to locate economic transactions geographically; the 'disjuncture between the geographical foundations of modern taxing

---

[87] Ibid.
[88] Jane Gravelle and Donald Marples, *Issues in International Corporate Taxation: The 2017 Revision* (Washington, DC: Congressional Research Service, updated 27 August 2021), 4.
[89] Richard L Doernberg, Luc Hinnekens, Walter Hellerstein and Jinyan Li, *Electronic Commerce and Multijurisdictional Taxation* (Alphen aan den Rijn, Netherlands: Kluwer Law International, 2001), 2. See also Arthur Cockfield, Walter Hellerstein, Rebecca Millar and Christophe Waerzeggers, *Taxing Global Digital Commerce* (Alphen aan den Rijn, Netherlands: Kluwer Law International, 2013).

systems, on the one hand, and the nonterritorial character of e-commerce on the other, is at the heart of the challenge that e-commerce poses to taxation'.[90]

In the twenty-first century, the scale and type of digitalised activities have dramatically increased. This combined with economic globalization to generate new forms of supercharged global mobility. These developments in turn led to the massive growth of digital companies, and suggestions of economic rents accruing to global digital commerce. Although the language of the 'digital' economy implies a comparison with a 'real' economy, the OECD observed that the digital economy is not at the margins of some real or physical economy, but, rather, that all of the economy is becoming digitized to some degree.

The BEPS Action 1 Report asserted that rules of nexus need to be revisited in this context but did not propose a solution.[91] Some of the issues had been identified in earlier work by the OECD and others on electronic commerce.[92] The OECD identified three phenomena facilitated by digitalisation that pose challenges to corporate tax:

– Scale without mass (the ability to have very large global consumer markets without a physical presence),
– Increased value and reliance on intangible assets (intellectual property), and
– The centrality of consumer data for large corporate revenues, profit and value.

The digital economy exacerbates pre-existing problems with transfer pricing and location of business activity, especially through the individualization of consumption and user experience. It moves away from mass industrial capitalism (dominant in the twentieth century) towards tailored services for which each consumer pays a unique price. This change is occurring at the same time that modular production, value chains and centralised IP make the production of such bespoke goods and services ever more efficient. Internally, each MNE also operates uniquely. Transfer pricing rules premised on comparable notions of identical products and market prices are less viable as all aspects of the tax analysis become 'case-by-case'. Transactions may be fully integrated within the MNE, or market prices for services and products are unique, so comparability loses its usefulness.

The most important development has been the rise of market jurisdictions. The jurisdictions where digital consumers are located are a site of massive revenue generation for large digital MNEs, but the government of the market

---

[90] Roland Paris, 'The Globalization of Taxation? Electronic Commerce and the Transformation of the State' (2003) 47(2) *International Studies Quarterly* 153–82, 162.
[91] OECD, *Addressing the Tax Challenges of the Digital Economy* (see n 44), 17.
[92] See, for example, OECD, *A Borderless World: Realising the Potential of Electronic Commerce* (Paris: OECD, 1998); Niv Tadmore, 'Source Taxation of Cross-border Intellectual Supplies – Concepts, History and Evolution into the Digital Age' (2007) 61(1) *Bulletin for International Taxation*.

jurisdiction may not have the ability to tax based on 'source' or nexus in the traditional sense of a PE. Governments became increasingly concerned about the lack of corporate tax being collected from sales within the jurisdiction. In Chapter 10, the developments in extending consumption tax to offshore digital platforms and service providers were noted. In contrast, the BEPS project had not delivered a solution for corporate taxation of profits arising from market jurisdictions. Moreover, the BEPS project focused on 'value creation' as a way to locate taxing nexus, which only loosely connected with the location of the ultimate consumer.[93]

Digital Services Taxes

Governments began to take unilateral action to levy tax on digital MNEs that accrued revenue from consumers or users in their jurisdiction. The new digital services taxes (DSTs) are a kind of excise on specific forms of revenue from advertising, or sales on digital platforms.[94] India was a first mover with its digital equalisation levy enacted in 2016. Soon after, France enacted a DST, followed by the United Kingdom and other European countries. In 2018, the European Commission proposed a common DST for Europe.[95] The US government grew concerned about the impact on US-based digital MNEs. Under President Trump, the US Trade Representative initiated a trade investigation into DSTs enacted by France, and later by Austria, India, Italy, Spain, Turkey and the United Kingdom, on the basis that these were discriminatory trade measures burdening US digital companies and are inconsistent with principles of international taxation.[96]

There is significant variation in the design of DSTs, but they tend to be levied at a low flat rate (e.g. 2 or 3 per cent) on gross revenues in connection with defined digital services for consumers or users in the jurisdiction. Usually, DSTs apply to large MNEs, for example, with revenues exceeding the €750 million threshold for CbC reporting. Covered digital services include online marketplaces enabling sales of goods and services, online advertising, social media digital interface services and search engines. The nexus is based on the presence of the user in the jurisdiction, usually by accessing an IP address used by the service recipient.

---

[93] See, e.g. Allison Christians, 'Taxing According to Value Creation' (2018) 90 *Tax Notes International* 1379–83.

[94] Chris Noonan and Victoria Plekhanova, 'Digital Services Tax: Lessons from the Section 301 Investigation' (2021) 2021(1) *British Tax Review* 83–115.

[95] European Commission 'Proposal for a Council Directive on the Common System of a Digital Services Tax on Revenues Resulting from the Provision of Certain Digital Services', COM (2018) 148 final, Brussels, 21.3.2018.

[96] Office of the US Trade Representative, 'USTR Announces, and Immediately Suspends, Tariffs in Section 301 Digital Services Taxes Investigations' (2 June 2021), https://ustr.gov/about-us/policy-offices/press-office/press-releases/2021/june/ustr-announces-and-immediately-suspends-tariffs-section 301-digital-services-taxes-investigations.

The DSTs are separate taxes to the corporate tax but have some interactions with it. For example, in France, the DST is deductible against the corporate tax. However, if the MNEs affected do not have a PE in France, they will not be liable to French corporate tax, so the deduction is useless for them, in contrast to French companies affected by the DST.

The enactment of DSTs has been criticised as likely to lead to chaotic and complex double taxation on gross revenues. DSTs have also been praised as a suitable levy to capture tax on the economic rents derived by large digital MNEs delivering to mass consumer markets.[97] DSTs have generated some tax revenue, but they also play a role in the geopolitical negotiations over reforming the corporate tax, most importantly between the United States and other countries.[98] As the process of negotiating a way to capture more tax revenue on the largest global corporations continues, it is clear that DSTs are not only unilateral tax policy, but are part of a complex bargaining process concerning global digital taxation, involving states, MNEs and multilateral forums such as the OECD and EU.

Destination-based Cash Flow Tax

As governments have sought to expand their tax jurisdiction based on the role of their populations as consumers of digitalised goods and services – the 'market' jurisdiction – tax theory has also moved towards the idea of consumption as the corporate tax base. The concept of a business cash flow tax was explained in Chapter 7. This concept, which is equivalent to a consumption tax with a deduction for wages, is extended to the international context by allocating tax jurisdiction to the 'destination' country where the ultimate consumer is located.

A destination-based cash flow tax (DBCFT) was put forward by some leading tax economists.[99] They argued that the DBCFT has several attractive properties. Because it taxes the consumer, who is assumed to be relatively immobile, it does not distort the scale and location of investment, ensures neutral treatment of debt and equity as sources of finance, is robust against avoidance through inter-company transactions, and would provide long term stability being resistant to tax competition amongst states. It would also achieve the taxation of economic rents in an open economy context.

---

[97] Wei Cui, 'The Digital Services Tax: A Conceptual Defense' (2019–20) 73 *Tax Law Review* 69–111; Daniel Shaviro, 'Mobile Intellectual Property and the Shift in International Tax Policy from Determining the Source of Income to Taxing Location-Specific Rents: Part One' (2020) *Singapore Journal of Legal Studies* 681–701.
[98] Office of the US Trade Representative, 'USTR Announces' (see n 95).
[99] Michael P Devereux, Alan J Auerbach, Michael Keen, Paul Oosterhuis, Wolfgang Schön and John Vella, *Taxing Profit in a Global Economy* (Oxford: Oxford University Press, Oxford Scholarship Online, 2021).

In 2016 a version of a DBCFT was put forward by some Republicans who sought to achieve US corporate tax reform.[100] The destination base would tax sales in the United States, but not overseas, in a similar manner to a destination-based VAT. Purchases or investment abroad would not be deductible. Hence, the corporate-level DBCFT would be levied on revenues, less expenditures, where a corporation's products are used rather than where the corporation is located or where the goods are produced, eliminating incentives to shift profits abroad. Ultimately, President Trump and Congressional Republicans rejected the DBCFT option and instead lowered the US corporate income tax rate to 21 per cent, while expanding deductions for business assets among many other changes in the Tax Cuts and Jobs Act of 2017.

While the DBCFT proposal continues to attract interest, no country has yet replaced a corporate income tax with a destination cash-flow tax. One reason why countries have not pursued this model is that it would significantly narrow the corporate tax base. Another reason is taxation of source-based economic rents. Resource-exporting countries such as Australia, Canada, Brazil or Indonesia are concerned to protect source taxation of profits on their resource sectors – as these reflect economic rents to a large degree and are part of the price for extraction of non-renewable resource. In addition to a corporate cash-flow tax, a separate resource tax would be needed to tax the mining sector[101]

The Inclusive Framework Consensus

The latest multilateral negotiations for corporate tax have been carried out in the G20-OECD Inclusive Framework, producing a Consensus on Pillar One and Pillar Two in October 2021.[102] The Inclusive Framework, comprising more than 140 jurisdictions, aims to establish an entirely new tax jurisdictional rule: a formula to allocate and tax some global profits of the largest MNEs in market countries (Pillar One). It also aims to ensure a minimum level of taxation where the diversity of tax rules applicable around the world results in non-taxation or very low taxation of corporate profits (Pillar Two).

The October 2021 consensus was achieved after President Biden, and Treasury Secretary Janet Yellen, expressed support of the United States for

---

[100] Scott Greenberg, 'Details of the House GOP Tax Plan', Tax Foundation (24 June 2016), https://taxfoundation.org/details-house-gop-tax-plan.

[101] An alternative is a resource rent tax to be applied to all companies: Robin Boadway and Jean-Francois Tremblay, *Corporate Tax Reform: Issues and Prospects for Canada*, Mowat Research #88 (Toronto: Mowat Centre, University of Toronto, 2014), 45–6.

[102] OECD/G20 Inclusive Framework on BEPS, *Statement on a Two-Pillar Solution to Address the Tax Challenges Arising from the Digitalisation of the Economy* (8 October 2021), www.oecd.org/tax/beps/statement-on-a-two-pillar-solution-to-address-the-tax-challenges-arising-from-the-digitalisation-of-the-economy-october-2021.htm.

the negotiations. A key to the international tax deal is the agreement by countries to drop unilateral measures such as DSTs.

Pillar One: Formulary Jurisdiction for Market Countries

Pillar One aims to ensure a fairer distribution of taxing rights to market countries for the largest MNEs, including digital companies, regardless of whether firms have a physical presence in the jurisdiction. The OECD estimates that taxing rights on more than US$100 billion profit will be reallocated to market countries each year. Pillar One will require a new multilateral tax treaty to establish the new taxing right and profit rules, and will 'turn off' existing provisions in domestic law and bilateral treaties that would prevent application of this taxing right. The introduction of formulary apportionment, even limited to residual digital profits of some MNEs, introduces an entirely novel approach to taxing corporate profits.

Pillar One applies to MNEs with global turnover exceeding €20 billion, reducing to €10 billion after 2030, and with profit above 10 per cent. It is estimated that this will cover only about the top 100 global MNEs. Apple, Microsoft, Amazon, Alphabet (Google) and Facebook are in the top 10 by market capitalisation. Other top 100 global companies are in traditional sectors including retail, cars, finance, pharmaceuticals and foods.[103] A portion of profit will be allocated to market jurisdictions where there is a minimum €1 million in revenue derived (for jurisdictions with small gross domestic product, this is lowered to €250,000). There is an exclusion for extractive industries and regulated financial services.

The amount to be taxable in the end-market jurisdiction is called 'Amount A', proposed to be 25 per cent of the residual profit of the MNE above the 10% routine profit. Negotiations also continue on 'Amount B' about profits of marketing and distribution hubs. Pillar One applies a global approach to determine the MNE's taxable profits, using consolidated group accounting profits. This global approach has the advantage of introducing a new 'tax handle' at the level of the MNE.

Pillar Two: Global anti-Base Erosion Rule

The Global anti-Base Erosion Rule (GloBE) is a set of interacting domestic tax rules to be enacted by participating countries, consistent with an international framework of model rules and guidance. These are the Income Inclusion Rule, Under Taxed Payment Rule and a treaty-based Subject to Tax Rule.

The GloBE applies to MNEs with revenues over a threshold of €750 million, including the resource and financial sectors. It will apply at a rate of 15 per cent determined on a 'country by country' basis. It requires the minimum effective rate of 15 per cent to apply in each jurisdiction. Enforcement of the GloBE will draw on data about MNE profits and entities in CbC reports,

---

[103] PWC, 'Global Top 100 Companies by Market Capitalisation' (March 2021), www.pwc.com/gx/en/services/audit-assurance/publications/global-top-100-companies.html.

explained previously. The GloBE may play an important role in constraining tax competition. However, it will exclude from tax an amount equal to at least 5 per cent of the value of tangible assets and payroll in a jurisdiction. This essentially permits tax competition where 'physical' assets and employees are located.

Implementation

Draft rules for Pillar One and Pillar Two have been released for consultation in 2022 but there are numerous issues to be resolved before either proposal can be implemented. For Pillar One, implementation will be through a multilateral treaty for signature at the earliest in 2023. For Pillar Two, participating jurisdictions will be required to carry out law reform to enact the rules, likely commencing in 2023, conforming with international model rules and standards. There may be development of mechanisms to coordinate over time. The process is intended to coordinate with removal of unilateral measures such as DSTs. A new dispute resolution system is intended to address potential disputes about Pillar One application.

The Inclusive Framework Two-Pillar solution, if it succeeds, will extend multilateral cooperation in international tax further than ever before. However, it is far from achieving a single, or harmonised, global corporate tax on MNEs. Even in the EU, which has established the most comprehensive regional tax cooperation, harmonisation of corporate tax rules has proved elusive. The project for a harmonised EU corporate tax has been on foot at least since the Ruding Report of 1992.[104] In 2001, the European Commission proposed a single consolidated corporate tax base.[105] It was proposed again in 2011, and the proposal was relaunched in 2016 as the Common Consolidated Corporate Tax Base (CCCTB). This was replaced in 2021 with the 'Business in Europe: Framework for Income Taxation' (BEFIT), which aims to implement the Two-Pillar consensus applying a formulary apportionment approach in the EU.[106] The United Kingdom was a strong opponent of the CCCTB and its departure from the EU may enable more agreement, although the parliaments

---

[104] European Commission, *Company Taxation in the Internal Market* {COM(01)582 final}, Commission Staff Working Paper (Brussels: EC, 23 October 2001), 8; Onno Ruding, *Report of the Committee of Independent Experts on Company Taxation* (Luxembourg: Office for Official Publications of the European Communities, 1992); Onno Ruding, 'Tax Harmonization in Europe: The Pros and Cons, The David R. Tillinghast Lecture' (2000) 54 *Tax Law Review* 101–10; Miranda Stewart, 'The David R Tillinghast Lecture: Commentary' (2000) 54 *Tax Law Review* 111–30; Hans-Werner Sinn, 'Tax Harmonization and Tax Competition in Europe' (1990) 34 *European Economic Review* 489–504.

[105] European Commission, 'Company Taxation: Commission Suggests Single Consolidated Tax Base' IP/01/1468 (23 October 2001), https://ec.europa.eu/commission/presscorner/detail/en/IP_01_1468.

[106] European Commission 'Proposal for a Council Directive on a Common Consolidated Corporate Tax Base' COM/2016/683 final (25 October 2016), https://eur-lex.europa.eu/legal-content/EN/TXT/HTML/?uri=CELEX:52016PC0683&from=en; European Commission, 'Communication on Business Taxation for the 21st Century' COM(2021)251final (18 May 2021).

of several other EU member states including Ireland, Sweden, Denmark, Malta, Luxembourg and the Netherlands also opposed the 2016 proposal. The vested interests of large corporate taxpayers may prevent cross-border harmonisation of the tax base, as this would reduce tax arbitrage opportunities, even though it may also reduce compliance costs.[107]

Tax competition about corporate tax between states in a global economy is fundamentally a competition between capital and labour: between achieving an adequate return to workers, whether that return is in wages, or in revenues that are redistributed, and the return to capital that is contained within the corporation and by high-income individuals. By enfolding 'offshore' tax havens inside the boundaries of the corporate group, MNEs combine juridical and territorial elements to extract value from labour and capital outside the jurisdictional boundaries of tax states. While states, acting competitively, take on some of the characteristics of corporations in the market, we could also say that MNEs take on some of the characteristics of states.

An effective response to tax competition that supports the welfare of citizens of tax states will require a renegotiation of the boundaries of the state and corporations. Reforms will need to deconstruct the border between 'offshore' havens and tax states, and 'pierce the veil' of the separate legal entity of the corporation, in its particularly malleable form of the MNE. Reforms may take the form of extending jurisdiction of either 'residence' or 'source' country into the terrain of 'offshore' or consolidating economic activity across the global MNE and allocating it based on nexus factors such as sales. Arnold Harberger argued that the economic rents of corporate giants operate like a tax on value that should go to consumers or to the public. Harberger identified the corporate tax as the best way to capture economic rents of MNEs.[108] We can see the beginning of some of these developments in the Two-Pillar Inclusive Framework consensus.

---

[107] Julie Roin, 'Taxation without Coordination' (2002) 31 *Journal of Legal Studies* 31 (2002) S61–S94.

[108] Arnold Harberger, 'The Incidence of the Corporation Income Tax Revisited' (2008) 61(2) *National Tax Journal* 303–12.

12

The Future Tax State

Though shaped by the tumultuous events of the decades, the essentials have remained intact: how to create a social environment which serves the dignity of the individual, not in splendid isolation but bound and enriched by membership in a community of shared rights and obligations.

Richard Musgrave, *Social Science, Ethics, and the Role of the Public Sector*

The Tax State's 'Good Twentieth Century'[1]

This book has explored the history and development of the tax state in achieving success in the twentieth century, through supporting and harnessing the returns to economic growth and delivering public goods and redistribution to its population.

In the successful tax state, taxation raises revenues to fund expenditures on public goods, redistribution and regulation. This helps to ensure that markets serve society and not the reverse. The historical survey in Chapter 2 shows that the governmental ability to raise taxation, to regulate market and social life and to spend those funds effectively evolved interdependently. Ideas developed as practice evolved. Theories of public goods arose when it became necessary to explain the scale of government and consider the failure of the market to deliver broad public benefit. Theories about the constraint of government arose when it became clear that public waste was widespread and government unable to maintain stability and coherence of the tax system.

Taxation is a social process that draws the boundaries of governmental, market and private spheres of life and that intimately affects individuals in their everyday lives. Chapter 3 placed taxation in the context of the political and social budgeting process of governments. Chapter 4 presented the evolution of tax principles of equity and efficiency, and emphasised 'resilience' of the tax state as a system of fiscal governance, in the face of many challenges over the last century. Part II of this book examined the role of taxation in

---

[1] Christopher Hood, 'The Tax State in the Information Age' in TV Paul, G John Ikenberry and John Hall (eds.), *The Nation-State in Question* (Princeton, NJ: Princeton University Press, 2003), 213–33, 215.

shaping our work and family lives, personal saving and investment, and how changes in all of these spheres, in the context of broader demographic trends, mean that taxation laws must also change if they are to remain effective and fair. It then examined taxation laws for many aspects of business and economic organisation, whether through for profit activities in corporations, business investment, innovation and entreprenurship, or not for profit activities in charities, and key challenges in tax administration, compliance and avoidance.

Christopher Hood asked, 'Is the twentieth-century advance of the tax state in the developed countries best seen as a historical aberration, from which we might expect a reversion to more historically normal levels? How should we interpret and explain the tax state's 'good twentieth century'?'[2] Hood posed this question in a collection that asked more generally about the fate of the nation state. It is a fundamental question for states that have come to be dependent on, and defined by, their ability to raise taxation.

For us, the question is, how well placed is the tax state for success in the twenty-first century? While we cannot predict the future based on the past, we can learn from the evolution of the tax state over the last century what has been called the 'energy' of history, its momentum, direction, power and interests that establish the future directions for tax.[3]

Hood suggested that three factors are necessary for continued success of the tax state. The first factor relates to the capacity of the tax state to produce a tax culture that sustains it. In a democracy, this is the ability to produce ruling electoral coalitions that achieve political consent to broad-based taxation to fund delivery of public goods and a fair distribution of economic returns. The second factor relates to quasi-voluntary compliance in the administrative tax state in a changing technological and economic context. Taxation laws support and limit the coercive power of governments. As they have developed through the twentieth century, governments succeeded in harnessing intermediaries in the market economy to do much of the work of tax collection for the dominant tax bases of income and consumption. Tax states rely on a stable fiscal bargain with intermediaries including employers, corporations, banks and the tax profession, as well as with the ultimate taxpayers.

The third factor identified by Hood is 'the existence of broader international conditions capable of sustaining or augmenting the tax state'.[4] This raises the global challenges discussed in Part III of the book, which explores how the increasing interdependence of governments in a globalised and digitalised economy challenges tax jurisdiction and its practical implementation.

---

[2] Ibid.
[3] Don Watson, *Recollections of a Bleeding Heart: A Portrait of Paul Keating* (Sydney: Random House, 2002), 75.
[4] Hood, 'The Tax State in the Information Age' (see n 1), 222.

Underpinning these factors for success of the tax state are changing social and economic conditions. Hood predicted, accurately, two decades ago that the intergenerational politics of the ageing population and low economic growth limit buoyancy in tax revenues and may 'prove more of a challenge for at least some states than was the industrial age'.[5]

Reassembling the Tax State for the Twenty-First Century

The Community of the Tax State

The tax state is assembled and its boundaries defined through the social process of taxation. Taxation laws define the base of income, consumption or wealth and in so doing draws lines between the private family and market labour; between taxes to fund government and charitable activities; between corporations and public investment; between the national and the global; and between taxpayers, and those who resist paying tax. The boundaries of the tax state have always been flexible and permeable, and may be adapted to a new equilibrium. The tax state is not fully coextensive with geographical territory, with the democratic state (citizenship) or with the welfare state. Governments are continually embroidering the boundaries of the tax state, in a changing pattern that brings in, or excludes, people, production and consumption over time.

There has never been full consent of the population in tax states; rather, they have succeeded even in the face of opposition, based on the ability to enact a political compromise and to operate with quasi-voluntary compliance from most of the people, most of the time. In the twenty-first century, some politicians, and even some governments, have expressed an ideological hostility to taxation as the basis for financing government. Sometimes this posture is more rhetorical than real, such as the advocacy in a previous UK election by Michael Gove to abolish the value added tax (VAT), a tax that finances one third of UK governmental functions.[6] Other politicians, such as President Trump in the United States, seemed intent on dismantling the tax system while turning to increasingly heavy reliance on debt to fund government expenditure. Over more than a decade, actions of the US Congress defunded the Internal Revenue Service, hollowing out its administrative capacity and causing the tax system to become less effective and more unfair.[7] President

---

[5] Ibid., 223–4.
[6] John Johnston, 'Michael Gove Pledges to Scrap VAT in Bid to Boost Post-Brexit Economy' (9 June 2019), www.politicshome.com/news/article/michael-gove-pledges-to-scrap-vat-in-bid-to-boost-postbrexit-economy.
[7] See, e.g. Paul Kiel and Jesse Elsinger, 'How the IRS Was Gutted', *ProPublica* and *The Atlantic*, 11 December 2018, www.propublica.org/article/how-the-irs-was-gutted. This trend has a longer history in the United States; e.g. Daniel A Smith, *Tax Crusaders and the Politics of Direct Democracy* (New York: Routledge, 1998), 21–3 on the problems caused by tax referenda that constrained the revenue capacity of US states.

Biden has to some extent reversed this trend. Whether he will succeed in financing expanded social and infrastructure expenditure with increased taxes remains to be seen, as he presides over a US Congress that continues its hostility towards taxation.

Tax changes since the 1980s in response to economic globalisation have contributed to the wholesale renovation of the state in accordance with a 'logic of discipline' that modified its structure and functions. These changes were 'not aimed simply at dismantling or shrinking the state but also at rebuilding government so that it would complement a liberalized and globalized economy'.[8] Such alterations of the role and activities of government likely generate innovation and increased economic activity (and hence growth) but may also undermine distributive justice in the shared community of the tax state. These changes also tend towards a shift of authority from government to the market that Sassen identifies as 'denationalisation'.[9] The tax state is changed through these processes, which operate increasingly in the service of capital, and less in the service of labour.

The 'logic' of fiscal discipline, discussed in Chapter 3 in the context of budgeting, continues to operate today, and will resurface after the COVID-19 pandemic. However, it seems increasingly necessary in the global digital era to rethink the fiscal compact between citizens and government. Tax states may have reached the limits of a strategy aimed at reducing taxes and constraining spending, especially through the privatisation of care and risk onto individuals.

As the twentieth century entered its last decade, Musgrave observed that 'changes in family structure will call for reconsideration of the taxable unit in the design of personal taxation. Ageing of the population and concern with medical care will increase the weight of social insurance and may widen the role of contributory taxes' and 'trends towards greater inequality in the pre-tax distribution of income may call for adjustments in tax structure, as may changing attitudes towards tax fairness'.[10] The need for more social protection and health care in an ageing population, and a response to increased inequality of income and wealth, are continuing challenges for the tax state. Tax states have the capability to reorient and renew social infrastructure for their changing populations, recognising the value contributed through care and household production as well as market production. Important levers to respond to these challenges discussed in this book include fair and efficient taxation of the work of individuals; sharing the cost of care, lightening the burden for women; and

---

[8] Alasdair Roberts, *The Logic of Discipline: Global Capitalism and the Architecture of Government* (Oxford: Oxford University Press, 2010), 4.
[9] Saskia Sassen, *Territory, Authority, Rights: From Medieval to Global Assemblages* (Princeton, NJ: Princeton University Press, 2006).
[10] Richard A Musgrave, 'Schumpeter's Crisis of the Tax State: An Essay in Fiscal Sociology' (1992) 2(2) *Journal of Evolutionary Economics* 89–113, 109.

taxing savings and investment more fairly over the life course, including by reorienting the tax system towards wealth and capital income.

The Interdependence of Tax Sovereignty

Globalisation and digitalisation are not limited to the economic sphere concerning mobility of goods, capital, labour or value between states or in the digital realm. They have led to increasing interconnectedness across all dimensions of human behaviour in global and digital space, in 'a process of increased density and frequency of international social interactions relative to local or national ones'.[11] This implies more interdependence between people and governments, not only more integrated markets. Inevitably, tax cooperation between governments will increase. Governments have begun, and will continue to adapt their tax systems to new transnational and global processes, building and strengthening multilateral institutions and harnessing the massive capabilities of intermediaries and technology in the global digital economy. Governments face the risk of declining tax capacity if they fail to cooperate or utilise digital resources.

The first two decades of the twenty-first century have demonstrated the tensions that exist in relations of tax states with each other, and with the untaxed terrain of 'offshore'. While it seems difficult for states to agree on new rules for international tax, states already cooperate in taxation in multiple ways. These include bilateral or multilateral treaties; the development of consensus-based international standards or peer-reviewed norms; policy transfer or copying of unilateral rules; judicial notice of foreign authorities and establishment of a body of international tax case law; and policy transfer through bureaucratic, academic and professional networks. International tax law has developed through these formal and informal channels, usually in an incremental way, but sometimes punctuated with new developments that may shifting international tax to a new equilibrium.

What is the effect on tax sovereignty? Genschel and Rixen divide tax sovereignty into three bases: legal sovereignty ('the exclusive right of national governments to make tax law'); administrative sovereignty ('the exclusive right to administer and enforce tax law') and revenue sovereignty ('the exclusive right to claim all tax revenue for the national budget').[12] They argue that all three bases of sovereignty cannot be simultaneously satisfied in the context of economic

---

[11] Sylvia Walby, *Globalization and Inequalities: Complexity and Contested Modernities* (London: Sage Publications, 2009), Kindle Book, Loc 847.
[12] Philipp Genschel and Thomas Rixen, 'Settling and Unsettling the Transnational Legal Order of International Taxation' in Terence C Halliday and Gregory Shaffer (eds.), *Transnational Legal Orders* (Cambridge, UK: Cambridge University Press, 2015), 154–84, 156.

globalisation. To address double tax and curb tax competition, government must 'pool tax sovereignty internationally', always 'sacrificing' either legal, administrative or revenue sovereignty to deal with the global challenge.

It is contestable whether cooperation across any of these dimensions reduces tax sovereignty. The concept of sovereignty at international law does not assume a state in isolation, but a state coexists with other states. Tax competition is not the only way for a state to express sovereignty. The engagement of states with each other in numerous and layered cooperative forums is also an expression of sovereignty of the state. What we see as the 'non-cooperation' in international tax during much of the twentieth century was the result of cooperation by governments to support the interests of capital, combined with significant practical limitations to their ability to collect taxation. In the twenty-first century, tax states can harness new and powerful modes of cooperation in tax law and administration. Chapter 10 explained how governments have taken steps towards increased cooperation in tax administration in the last decade, and Chapter 11 considered the latest developments of the Base Erosion and Profit Shifting (BEPS) project and the Inclusive Framework to tax multinational enterprises in the global digital economy. These developments are incomplete and imperfect, but they have potential to substantially alter the dynamics of international tax and the power of nation states with respect to global capital.

Tax competition and tax cooperation between states are often presented as mutually exclusive but these modes of state behaviour are not separable: they co-evolve or co-construct each other. Many tax states are simultaneously competing while also deeply integrating in administrative and even legal structures. While multilateral tax cooperation between states increases, we continue to see reductions in tax rates to attract innovation, investment and skilled labour. Rather than suggesting that states are 'losing' tax sovereignty by cooperating in a world where they have themselves created the conditions that drive down tax rates, it is more useful for us to understand how both tax competition and tax cooperation are produced through a dynamic process of unilateral, bilateral and multilateral actions of tax states.

Transnational Tax Law and Administration

Tax law and policy is a matter for nation states, but it is constantly influenced by cross-border tax policy learning and to an extent, the establishment of global tax norms that are widely applied in national tax law. One element is the constant flow of expert ideas and policies on taxation from one country to another. The extent to which tax laws change in response to policy transfer can be difficult to determine but there are significant cross-border influences and trends evident in policy, law (including the common law and statutory approaches) and tax administration. However, national tax systems will continue to differ in terms of the level and types of tax, and the details of rates and bases, not only in response to domestic politics but also because of pressure from multinational enterprises and high wealth investors, who benefit from continued diversity and complexity in national tax systems.

The achievement of transnational tax administration has required significant legal and institutional change in tax states. This will increase, as governments, just like businesses and individuals, take advantage of new technological opportunities. The prospect of transnational, or even global, tax administration raises questions about how to ensure effective governance, and accountability of tax authorities. As discussed in Chapter 9, the administrative constraint on taxation is fundamental and it has shaped the development of tax states seeking 'quasi-voluntary compliance' over time. The success of the tax state in the twentieth century is a consequence of governments harnessing modes of tax collection that are relatively convenient, relatively simple and less vexatious than alternative ways of raising revenue. It also relied on a bargain that provides the tax authority wide powers subject to significant oversight. Digitalised processes and expanding access to data in tax states offer significant benefits for easing compliance and administrative burdens but also lead to increased risks of error and concerns about privacy and taxpayer rights.

New international governmental and bureaucratic forums are being established to institutionalise transnational development of tax law and integration of tax administration; it will be challenging to ensure that these are sufficiently stable, respected and representative. Achieving fairness and legitimacy in multilateral tax rule-making requires attention to which countries set the agenda and make the decisions – and in whose interest the multilateral bargain operates.[13] Power may be located in developed countries, or blocs, such as the United States or the European Union, or may be in the international institutions themselves as they jockey for pre-eminence in multilateral tax law making processes.[14] A century ago, the League of Nations considered that 'tricky' issues in international tax were to be dealt with by a permanent international organisation.[15] There are various ways in which the Organisation for Economic Co-operation and Development (OECD), as collector of tax statistics, tax researcher and secretariat for the Global Forum and Inclusive Framework, has become a 'de facto' world tax organisation, or may be the best placed international organisation to do this role. However, to achieve this, the OECD will have to change in fundamental ways through expanded multilateralism.

---

[13] Allison Christians, 'BEPS and the New International Tax Order' (2016) 6 *Brigham Young University Law Review* 1603.
[14] Diane Ring, 'Who Is Making International Tax Policy? International Organizations as Power Players in a High Stakes World' (2009–10) 33 *Fordham International Law Journal* 649–722.
[15] Sunita Jogarajan, *Double Taxation and the League of Nations*, Cambridge Tax Law Series (Cambridge, UK: Cambridge University Press, 2018), 99.

Justice and Legitimacy of the Future Tax State

The theory of cosmopolitanism, or internationalism, provides a perspective on individuals as members of a global community.[16] It implies that our social and community obligations and the impact of taxes on individual well-being need to be considered across borders and not just within states. However, taxes as a political and legal matter are inextricably tied to states, as explored throughout this book. The justification of taxes on the theory of benefit derived under government and its legitimate authority to tax, as well as the achievement of tax justice based on ability to pay, depend on the taxpayer–state nexus.

Tsilly Dagan suggests that 'not only cosmopolitanism but also the statist theories of political justice mandate, that is they require, that for a multilateral regime established through cooperation to be justified it must improve or at least not worsen the welfare of the least well off citizens in all the cooperating states'.[17] Dagan is sceptical that this can be achieved and argues in favour of tax competition and continued decentralisation of tax systems. On the other hand, Ana Paula Dourado suggests that international tax justice requires multilateralism.[18] A justice approach could, in the suggestion of Dourado, involve 'a non-discrimination principle between mobile and immobile taxpayers and investment without forgetting that redistribution is one of the main states' budgetary functions, and in the current international tax system, redistribution is a function played by the state'.[19]

The benefit theory of taxation remains valuable in the current era as a foundational principle defining the obligation of all to contribute to government. This is because it requires us to address the political question of what the state, and hence taxes, are for and why we should pay them. In an era of globalisation, we need to rethink benefit of who, and by whom, through the tax state.

Justice in taxation is essential, but it is less clear that international tax policy should have as its main focus the delivery of tax justice. International tax policy probably cannot deliver on maximising the welfare of the worst off, in a Rawlsian framework, or a global welfare state. This is the remit of tax states, and is one of the reasons for their success. Nation states will continue to be best placed to achieve tax justice through provision of social welfare, public goods and market regulation, as well as progressive taxation. However, the twenty-first century is a global era. It will be necessary to find a way to redraw the boundaries of national tax systems support environmental sustainability

---

[16] Gillian Brock, *Global Justice: A Cosmopolitan Account* (Oxford: Oxford University Press, 2009).
[17] Tsilly Dagan, *International Tax Policy: Between Competition and Cooperation* (Cambridge, UK: Cambridge University Press, 2018).
[18] Ana Paula Dourado, 'Introduction: International Tax Multilateralism or Reinforced Unilateralism?' in Ana Paula Dourado (ed.), *International and EU Tax Multilateralism: Challenges Raised by the MLI* (Amsterdam: IBFD, 2020), 1–11, part 0.1.
[19] Ibid.

and a minimum level of social protection for all: that no one in the world will live in poverty.

For tax states, legitimacy is premised on the fiscal constitution, including the commitment of taxpayers to comply with justified taxation. The fiscal bargain is ensured by the rule of law, procedural fairness delivered to taxpayers, and accountability of the tax authority to the legislature.[20] In an international context, governments must ensure a legal basis for tax cooperation and the accountability of transnational tax administration to democratic institutions and the public more broadly. Achieving such legitimacy requires, at a minimum, transparency of governmental action. A new challenge for budgeting is how governments and citizens might design and participate in decision-making about taxing and spending beyond national borders. Budget processes that seek to connect revenues and the delivery of public goods and redistribution globally do not exist or are embryonic. These processes have the potential to reassemble the community of the tax state in a more stable, and just, system.

The success of the tax state in the twentieth century depended on its sovereign territorial and economic boundaries. The globalisation and digitalisation of the economy presents a fundamental challenge to the authority, structure and resilience of the tax state in the twenty-first century. Successful tax states rely mostly on the revenue from the personal income tax on wages, social security tax and consumption tax. These tax bases need strengthening and defending, while innovation in tax bases in both unilateral and multilateral approaches is possible.

The COVID-19 pandemic has revealed how interdependent the world has become. At the same time, we have seen a resurgence of nationalist fiscal policy by states. Governments through control of taxation, spending and the money supply actively engage in the economy to ensure the safety and welfare of their people – or fail to do so, privileging economic and global interests and excluding some classes of person from fiscal protection.

Some have called for a new fiscal compact to support expanded public investment, redistribution and a coordinated response to global taxes to address environmental crisis and poverty in future.[21] A transnational perspective on tax law requires us to 'deconstruct the various law-state associations'.[22] These constituent elements of the tax state – its territorial reach, population of taxpayers, legislative authority and domain of rights – are being reassembled

---

[20] Robert Baldwin, R *Rules and Government* (Oxford: Oxford University Press, 1995), 41ff; and see Bronwen Morgan and Karen Yeung, *An Introduction to Law and Regulation* (Cambridge, UK: Cambridge University Press, 2007), chapter 5.

[21] The Manifesto for the Democratization of Europe, led by Thomas Piketty and others, proposes a new tax and funding deal in the European Union: 'A Budget for Europe', http://tdem.eu/en/a-budget-for-europe/, accessed 26 March 2022.

[22] Peer Zumbansen, 'Defining the Space of Transnational Law: Legal Theory, Global Governance, and Legal Pluralism' (2012) 21 *Transnational Law & Contemporary Problems* 305–36, 311.

through numerous processes involving diverse actors in both domestic and international arenas. These processes sometimes strengthen and at other times weaken the tax state.

Tax law is constitutional in nature, supporting the fiscal bargain of tax states in their unique political and social conditions. This means it can be slow to change, even if some modifications or adaptations seem to be made quickly in response to national or global challenges. A century ago, Joseph Schumpeter argued that fiscal affairs are crucial 'at the turning points of epochs, when old forms die off and new structures emerge, times which always involve a crisis of the old fiscal methods'.[23] Tax states today may be at a tipping point to a new equilibrium that is less equal, and less congenial to democratic governance and effective delivery of public goods and redistribution. Governments as tax sovereigns must navigate two modes of interaction: the market mode of competition, and the regulatory mode of cooperation in relations with capital and labour and with other states in the global digital economy. Tax states must achieve a transformation of sovereignty understood to be the capability to tax, if they are to properly serve their people. This requires the reassembly of the constituent elements of the tax state to serve collective and individual ends in a global community of shared rights and obligations.

---

[23] Joseph A Schumpeter, 'The Crisis of the Tax State' [1918] (1954) 4 *International Economic Papers* 5–38, 3, trans. Wolfgang Stolper and Richard A Musgrave.

References

Aaron, Henry J, Leonard E Burman and C Eugene Steuerle (eds.), *Taxing Capital Income* (Washington, DC: Urban Institute Press, 2007)

Aaron, Henry J, Harvey Galper and Joseph A Pechman (eds.), *Uneasy Compromise: Problems of a Hybrid Income-Consumption Tax* (Washington, DC: Brookings Institution, 1988)

Aaronson, Graham, *GAAR Study: A Study to Consider Whether a General Anti-avoidance Rule Should Be Introduced into the UK Tax System* (London: Her Majesty's Treasury, 2011)

Abelson, Peter, *Public Economics* (Sydney: Applied Economics, 2018), https://appliedeconomics.com.au/wp-content/uploads/2021/10/public-economics-principles-and-practice-book-by-peter-abelson.pdf

ActionAid UK, *Addicted to Tax Havens* (Chard: ActionAid UK, 2012), www.actionaid.org.uk/sites/default/files/doc_lib/addicted_to_tax_havens.pdf

Adam, Stuart, Tim Besley, Richard Blundell, Stephen Bond, Robert Chote, Malcolm Gammie, Paul Johnson, Gareth Myles and James M Poterba (eds.), *Dimensions of Tax Design. Mirrlees Review: Vol 1* (Oxford: Oxford University Press, 2010), https://ifs.org.uk/publications/7184

Adam, Stuart and Helen Miller, *The Economics of a Wealth Tax* (London: Wealth Tax Commission, 2020)

Advani, Arun, Emma Chamberlain and Andy Summers, *Is It Time for a UK Wealth Tax? Initial Report* (London: Wealth Tax Commission, 2020)

Akcigit, Ufuk, Salomé Baslandze and Stefanie Stantcheva, 'Taxation and the International Mobility of Inventors' (2016) 106(1) *American Economic Review* 2930–81

Alesina, Alberto, Andrea Ichino and Loukas Karabarbounis, 'Gender-based Taxation and the Division of Family Chores' (2011) 3 *American Economic Journal: Economic Policy* 1–40

Alesina, Alberto, and Roberto Perotti, 'Fiscal Discipline and the Budget Process' (1996) 86 *American Economic Review* 401–7

Alinaghi, Nazila, John Creedy and Norman Gemmell, *Do Couples Bunch More? Evidence from Partnered and Single Taxpayers in New Zealand*, Working Papers in Public Finance, No 02/2020 (Wellington: Victoria School of Business and Government, Victoria University of Wellington, 2020)

Allingham, Michael G, and Agnar Sandmo, 'Income Tax Evasion: A Theoretical Analysis' (1972) 1 *Journal of Public Economics* 323–38

Alschner, Wolfgang, 'The OECD Multilateral Tax Instrument: A Model for Reforming the International Investment Regime?' (2019) 45(1) *Brooklyn Law Journal* 1–73

Alstadsaeter, Annette, Niels Johannesen and Gabriel Zucman, 'Tax Evasion and Inequality' (2019) 109(6) *American Economic Review* 2073–103

Altshuler, Rosanne, 'Lessons from the Study of Taxes and the Behavior of US Multinational Corporations' in Iris Claus, Norman Gemmell, Michelle Harding and David White (eds.), *Tax Reform in Open Economies* (London: Edward Elgar, 2010), 61–77

Anderson, Barry, 'The Changing Role of Parliament in the Budget Process' (2009) 9(1) *OECD Journal on Budgeting* 1–11

Andrienko, Yuriy, Patricia Apps and Ray Rees, 'Gender Bias in Tax Systems Based on Household Income' (2015) 117–18 *Annals of Economics and Statistics* 141–55

Angres, Leigh, and Jorge Salazar, *Discretionary Spending in 2018: An Infographic* (Washington, DC: Congressional Budget Office, 2019), www.cbo.gov/publication/55343

Mandatory Spending in 2018: An Infographic (Washington, DC: Congressional Budget Office, 2019), www.cbo.gov/publication/55344

Anheier, Helmut K, and Stefan Toepler, Philanthropic Foundations. An International Perspective in Helmut K Anheier and Stefan Toepler (eds.), *Private Funds, Public Purpose. Philanthropic Foundations in International Perspective* (New York: Kluwer, 1999), 3–23

Appelt, Silvia, Matej Bajgar, Chiara Criscuolo and Fernando Galindo-Rueda, *The Effects of R&D Tax Incentives and Their Role in the Innovation Policy Mix*, OECD Science, Technology and Industry Policy Papers No 92 (Paris: OECD, 2020), https://read.oecd.org/10.1787/65234003-en?format=pdf

Apps, Patricia, *A Theory of Inequality and Taxation* (Cambridge, UK: Cambridge University Press, 1981)

Apps, Patricia, and Ray Rees, 'Australian Family Tax Reform and the Targeting Fallacy' (2010) 43(2) *Australian Economic Review* 153–75

'Taxation and the Household' (1988) 35(3) *Journal of Public Economics* 355–69

Apps, Patricia, Elizabeth Savage and Glen Jones, 'Tax Discrimination by Dependent Spouse Rebates or Joint Taxation' (1981) 53 *The Australian Quarterly* 262–79

Arnold, Brian J, 'Canada' in Hugh J Ault, Brian J Arnold and Graeme Cooper, *Comparative Income Taxation*, 4th ed (Alphen aan den Rijn, Netherlands: Wolters Kluwer, 2020)

International Tax Primer, 4th ed (Alphen aan den Rijn, Netherlands: Kluwer Law, 2019)

'The Process of Tax Policy Formulation in Australia, Canada and New Zealand' (1990) 7 *Australian Tax Forum* 379–94

(ed.), *Taxation of Domestic Shareholders on Undistributed Income of Foreign Corporate Affiliates: Objectives, Techniques, and Consequences* (Deventer: Kluwer Law and Taxation Publishers, 1987)

'The Taxation of Income from Services under Tax Treaties: Cleaning Up the Mess' (2010) 65(2) *Bulletin for International Taxation*

Arrighi, Giovanni, *The Long Twentieth Century* (London: Verso, 1994)

Asen, Elke, 'Austria Is Mulling an Allowance for Corporate Equity', Tax Foundation (23 July 2020), https://taxfoundation.org/austria-corporate-equity-tax-allowance/

Ashiabor, Hope, Janet E Milne and Mikael Skou Andersen (eds.), *Environmental Taxation in the Pandemic Era. Vol 23: Critical Issues in Environmental Taxation Series* (Cheltenham: Edward Elgar, 2021)

Atkinson, Antony, and Andrew Leigh, 'The Distribution of Top Incomes in Five Anglo-Saxon Countries over the Long Run' (2013) 89 *Economic Record* 31–47

Atkinson, Antony and Thomas Piketty (eds.), *Top Incomes over the Twentieth Century: A Contrast between Continental European and English Speaking Countries* (Oxford: Oxford University Press, 2010)

Atkinson, Antony, and Joseph Stiglitz, 'The Design of Tax Structure: Direct versus Indirect Taxation' (1976) 6 *Journal of Public Economics* 55–75

Atkinson, Rob, 'Altruism in Nonprofit Organizations' (1990) 31 *Boston College Law Review* 501–639

'Theories of the Federal Income Tax Exemption for Charities: Thesis, Antithesis and Synthesis' in Paul Bater, Frits Willem Hondius and Penina Kessler Lieber (eds.), *The Tax Treatment of NGOs: Legal, Fiscal, and Ethical Standards for Promoting NGOs and Their Activities* (The Hague: Kluwer Law International, 2004), 253–84

Auby, Jean-Bernard, *Globalisation, Law and the State* (Oxford: Hart Publishing, 2017)

Auerbach, Alan J 'The Future of Capital Income Taxation' (2006) 27 *Fiscal Studies* 399–420

Who Bears the Corporate Tax? A Review of What We Know, NBER Working Papers Series No 11686 (Cambridge, MA: National Bureau of Economic Research, 2006)

Auerbach, Alan J, and Yuriy Gorodnichenko, *Fiscal Stimulus and Fiscal Sustainability*, NBER Working Paper 23789 (Cambridge, MA: National Bureau of Economic Research, 2017), www.nber.org/papers/w23789

Auerbach, Alan J, and Kent Smetters (eds.), *The Economics of Tax Policy* (New York: Oxford University Press, 2017)

Ault, Hugh J, 'United States' in Hugh J Ault, Brian J Arnold and Graeme Cooper, *Comparative Income Taxation*, 4th ed (Alphen aan den Rijn, Netherlands: Wolters Kluwer, 2020)

Ault, Hugh J, Brian J Arnold and Graeme Cooper, *Comparative Income Taxation*, 4th ed (Alphen aan den Rijn, Netherlands: Wolters Kluwer, 2020)

Australian Bureau of Statistics, '4125.0 – Gender Indicators, Australia, Sep 2018' (25 September 2018), www.abs.gov.au/AUSSTATS/abs@.nsf/Lookup/4125.0Main+Features1Sep%202018?

Australian Taxation Office, *Annual Report 2019–20* (Canberra: ATO, 2020), www.ato.gov.au/uploadedFiles/Content/CR/Downloads/Annual_Report_2019-20/annual_report_2019-20.pdf

'A-Life (ATO Longitudinal Information Files)' (2020), https://alife-research.app/info/overview, accessed 16 March 2022

'Single Touch Payroll' (4 November 2021), www.ato.gov.au/General/Other-languages/In-detail/Information-in-other-languages/Single-Touch-Payroll/

'Taxation Statistics 2016–17', table 8 and chart 10 (24 September 2020), www.ato.gov.au/About-ATO/Research-and-statistics/In-detail/Taxation-statistics/Taxation-statistics—previous-editions/Taxation-statistics-2016-17/?anchor=Individuals#Chart10

References

Australian Treasury, *2021 Intergenerational Report: Australia over the Next 40 Years* (Parkes, ACT: Commonwealth of Australia, June 2021), https://treasury.gov.au/sites/default/files/2021-06/p2021_182464.pdf

Australia's Future Tax System: Final Report (Canberra: Commonwealth of Australia, 2010)

Australian Treasury Board of Taxation, 'Reforming Individual Tax Residency Rules – A Model for Modernisation' (March 2019), https://taxboard.gov.au/consultation/reforming-individual-tax-residency-rules-a-model-for-modernisation

Review of International Tax Arrangements: Vol 1 (Parkes, ACT: Australian Treasury Board of Taxation, 2004)

Avi-Yonah, Reuven S, 'The Case Against Taxing Citizens' (2010) 58 *Tax Notes International* 389–94

'Corporations, Society, and the State: A Defense of the Corporate Tax' (2004) 90(5) *Virginia Law Review* 1193–255

'Globalization, Tax Competition and the Fiscal Crisis of the Welfare State' (2000) 113(7) *Harvard Law Review* 1573–676

International Tax as International Law (Cambridge, UK: Cambridge University Press, 2009)

And Yet It Moves: A Tax Paradigm for the 21st Century, Law and Economics Research Paper Series, Paper 12-008 (Ann Arbor, MI: Michigan Law School, University of Michigan, 2012)

Baker, Philip, Ernst Czakert, Arie van Eijsden, Maria AG Ruiz and Liselott Kana, 'International Assistance in the Collection of Taxes' (2011) 65 *Bulletin of International Taxation* 281–7

Balestra, Carlotta, and Richard Tonkin, *Inequalities in Household Wealth across OECD Countries: Evidence from the OECD Wealth Distribution Database*, OECD Statistics Working Papers 2018/1 (Paris: OECD, 2018), https://dx.doi.org/10.1787/7e1bf673-en

Baldwin, Robert, *Rules and Government* (Oxford: Oxford University Press, 1995)

Baldwin, Robert, and Julia Black, 'Really Responsive Regulation' (2008) 71(1) *Modern Law Review* 59–94

Ballarat Reform League, 'Taxation without Representation Is Tyranny', Eureka Stockade, Colony of Victoria, Australia, 11 November 1854

Bank, Steven A, 'Entity Theory as Myth in the Origins of the Corporate Income Tax' (2001) 43 *William and Mary Law Review* 447

Bank, Steven A, Kirk J Stark and Joseph J Thorndike, *War and Taxes* (Washington, DC: Urban Institute Press, 2008)

Bankman, Joseph, 'An Academic's View of the Tax Shelter Battle' in Henry J Aaron and Joel Slemrod (eds.), *Crisis in Tax Administration* (Washington, DC: Brookings Institution Press, 2004), 9–37

Bankman, Joseph, and David Weisbach, 'Reply: Consumption Taxation Is Still Superior to Income Taxation' (2007) 60 *Stanford Law Review* 789–802

Banks, James, and Peter Diamond, 'The Base for Direct Taxation' in Stuart Adam, Tim Besley, Richard Blundell, Stephen Bond, Robert Chote, Malcolm Gammie, Paul Johnson, Gareth Myles and James M Poterba (eds.), *Dimensions of Tax Design. Mirrlees Review: Vol 1* (Oxford: Oxford University Press, 2010), 548–674, https://ifs.org.uk/publications/5223

Banoun, Bettina, *Wealth Tax: Norway*, Wealth Tax Commission Background Paper 138 (London: Wealth Tax Commission, 2020)

Barbetta, Paolo, Luca Colombo and Gilberto Turati, 'Regulating European Grant-Making Foundations. Lessons from the USA Experience?' (2015) 37(5) *Journal of Policy Modeling* 763–81

Barkan, Joanne, 'Big Philanthropy vs Democracy' (2013) 60(4) *Dissent* 47–54

Barkoczy, Stephen, and Daniel Sandler, *Government Venture Capital Incentives: A Multi-jurisdiction Comparative Analysis* (Sydney: Australian Tax Research Foundation, 2007)

Barnett, Katy, 'Offshore Trusts in the South Pacific: How Far Can the Concept of the Trust Be Stretched before It Breaks?' in Ying Khai Liew and Matthew Harding (eds.), *Theory and Practice in Context. Asia-Pacific Trusts Law: Vol 1* (Oxford: Hart Publishing, 2021), 353–80, Bloomsbury Collections, http://dx.doi.org/10.5040/9781509934829.ch-019

Barraket, Jo, and Nicholas Collyer, 'Mapping Social Enterprise in Australia: Conceptual Debates and Their Operational Implications' (2010) 16(2) *Third Sector Review* 11–28

Barrows, Samuel, 'Racing to the Top ... at Last: The Regulation of Safety in Shipping' in Walter Mattli and Ngaire Woods (eds.), *The Politics of Global Regulation* (Princeton, NJ: Princeton University Press, 2009), 189–210

Bastable, Charles F, *Public Finance*, 3rd ed (London: Macmillan, 1903), www.econlib.org/library/Bastable/bastbPF.html

Bastani, Spencer, and Daniel Waldenstrom, 'How Should Capital Be Taxed? Theory and Evidence from Sweden' (2020) 34(4) *Journal of Economic Surveys* 812–46

Bastida, Francisco, and Bernardino Benito, 'Central Government Budget Practices and Transparency: An International Comparison' (2007) 85 *Public Administration* 667–716

Batchelder, Lily, 'Tax the Rich and Their Heirs: How to Tax Inheritances More Fairly', *New York Times*, 24 June 2020

Batchelder, Lily, and David Kamin, *Taxing the Rich: Issues and Options*, SSRN Working Paper (2019), https://ssrn.com/abstract=3452274

Bater, Paul, 'Introduction: International Tax Issues Relating to Non-Profit Organisations and Their Supporters' in Paul Bater, Frits W Hondius and Penina Kessler Lieber (eds.), *The Tax Treatment of NGOs: Legal, Fiscal, and Ethical Standards for Promoting NGOs and Their Activities* (The Hague: Kluwer Law International, 2004), 1–29

Batina, Raymond I, and Toshihiro Ihori, *Public Goods: Theory and Evidence* (New York: Springer, 2005)

Beer, Sebastian, Ruud de Mooij and Li Liu, *International Corporate Tax Avoidance: A Review of the Channels, Magnitudes, and Blind Spots*, IMF Working Paper WP/18/168 (Washington, DC: International Monetary Fund, 2018)

Belinga, Vincent, Dora Benedek, Ruud A de Mooij and John Norregaard, *Tax Buoyancy in OECD Countries*, IMF Working Paper No 14/110 (Washington, DC: International Monetary Fund, 2014)

Bengtsson, Erik, Enrico Rubolino and Daniel Waldenstrom, *What Determines the Capital Share over the Long Run of History?*, IZA Discussion Paper No 13199 (Bonn: Institute of Labor Economics, 2020)

Bentley, Duncan, 'Taxpayer Rights in Australia Twenty Years after the Introduction of the Taxpayers' Charter' (2016) 14(2) *eJournal of Tax Research* 291–318

Beretta, Giorgio, 'Cross-border Mobility of Individuals and the Lack of Fiscal Policy Coordination among Jurisdictions (Even) after the BEPS Project' (2019) 47(1) *Intertax* 91–112

Berik, Günseli, Yana van der Meulen Rodgers and Stephanie Seguino, 'Feminist Economics of Inequality, Development, and Growth' (2009) 15(3) *Feminist Economics* 1–33

Bernheim, B Douglas, Stefano Dellavigna and David Laibson (eds.), *Handbook of Behavioral Economics: Foundations and Applications* (Amsterdam: North-Holland, 2018)

Best, Rohan, Paul Burke and Frank Jotzo, *Carbon Pricing Efficacy: Cross-country Evidence*, CCEP Working Paper 2004 (Canberra: Australian National University, 2020), https://ccep.crawford.anu.edu.au/sites/default/files/publication/ccep_crawford_anu_edu_au/2020-06/wp_2004.pdf

Betts, Susan, Patrick De Mets, Rene Louis Ossa and Enrique Rojas, *Postcrisis Revenue Generation for Tax Administrations*, Special Series on COVID-19 (Washington, DC: International Monetary Fund, 28 July 2021), www.imf.org/-/media/Files/Publications/covid19-special-notes/en-special-series-on-covid-19-postcrisis-revenue-generation-for-tax-administrations.ashx

Bhagwati, Jagdish N, and William Dellalfar, 'The Brain Drain and Income Taxation' (1973) 1 *World Development* 94–100

BHP, 'Unified Corporate Structure', www.bhp.com/about/our-businesses/unified-corporate-structure, accessed 24 March 2022

Bick, Alexander, and Nicola Fuchs-Schundeln, 'Quantifying the Disincentive Effects of Joint Taxation on Married Women's Labor Supply' (2017) 107(5) *American Economic Review* 100–4

Bill and Melinda Gates Foundation, 'Foundation Fact Sheet', www.gatesfoundation.org/about/foundation-fact-sheet, accessed 16 March 2022

Bird, Richard, *The Corporate Income Tax in Canada: Does Its Past Foretell Its Future?*, SPP Research Papers 9(38) (Calgary: University of Calgary, 2016)

Bishop, Matthew, and Michael Green, *Philanthrocapitalism: How Giving Can Save the World* (New York: Bloomsbury Press, 2009)

Bittker, Boris I, and George K Rahdert, 'The Exemption of Nonprofit Organizations from Federal Income Taxation' (1976) 85 *Yale Law Journal* 299–358

Black, Celeste, 'The Future of Work: The Gig Economy and Pressures on the Tax System' (2020) 68(1) *Canadian Tax Journal* 69–97

Blakelock, Sarah, and Miranda Stewart, 'Australia's Evolving General Anti-avoidance Law' in Manuel Tron (ed.), *The Structure of Anti-avoidance Rules. Cahiers de droit fiscal international: Vol 103a* (70th International Fiscal Association Congress, Sdu Fiscale & Financiele Uitgevers) (Rotterdam: International Fiscal Association, 2018)

Blank, Joshua, and Nancy Staudt, 'Sham Transactions in the United States' in Edwin Simpson and Miranda Stewart (eds.), *Sham Transactions* (Oxford: Oxford University Press, 2013), 68–85

Blondal, Jon R, Dirk-Jan Kraan and Michael Ruffner, 'Budgeting in the United States' (2003) 3(2) *OECD Journal on Budgeting* 7–53

Blundell, Richard, Antoine Bozio and Guy Laroque, 'Extensive and Intensive Margins of Labour Supply: Work and Working Hours in the US, the UK and France' (2013) 34(1) *Fiscal Studies* 1–29

Boadway, Robin, and Neil Bruce, 'A General Proposition on the Design of a Neutral Business Tax' (1984) 24 *Journal of Public Economics* 231-9

Boadway, Robin, and Jean-Francois Tremblay, *Corporate Tax Reform: Issues and Prospects for Canada*, Mowat Research #88 (Toronto: Mowat Centre, University of Toronto, 2014)

'Reassessment of the Tiebout Model' (2012) 96(11-12) *Journal of Public Economics* 1063-78

Bonney, Robert (ed.), *Economic Systems and State Finance* (Oxford: Clarendon Press, 1995)

Bordignon, Massimo, Silvia Giannini and Paolo Panteghini, *Reforming Business Taxation: Lessons from Italy*, SIEP Working Paper (Pavia: Società Italiana di Economia Pubblica, 2000)

Bos, Frits, *The Dutch Fiscal Framework: History, Current Practice and the Role of the Central Planning Bureau* (The Hague: Central Planning Bureau, July 2007)

Boskin, Michael J. and Charles E McLure Jr (eds.), *World Tax Reform: Case Studies of Developed and Developing Countries* (San Francisco, CA: ICS Press, 1990)

Brabazon, Mark, *International Taxation of Trust Income* (Cambridge, UK: Cambridge University Press, 2019)

Bradford, David, 'Blueprint for International Tax Reform' (2001) 26 *Brooklyn Journal of International Law* 1449-63

'The Case for a Personal Consumption Tax' in Joseph Pechman (ed.), *What Should Be Taxed: Income or Expenditure?* (Washington, DC: Brookings Institution, 1979), 75-113

Untangling the Income Tax (Cambridge, MA: Harvard University Press, 1986)

Braithwaite, John, 'The Essence of Responsive Regulation' (2011) 44 *UBC Law Review* 475-520

Regulatory Capitalism: How It Works, Ideas for Making It Work Better (Cheltenham: Edward Elgar, 2008)

Braithwaite, John, and Peter Drahos, *Global Business Regulation* (Cambridge, UK: Cambridge University Press, 2000)

Braithwaite, Valerie A, 'A New Approach to Tax Compliance' in Valerie A Braithwaite (ed.), *Taxing Democracy* (Aldershot: Ashgate, 2003), 1-11

Brash, Donald T, 'New Zealand's Remarkable Reforms' (Speech, Annual Hayek Memorial Lecture, Institute of Economic Affairs, 4 June 1996)

Braun, Miguel, and Nicolás Gadano, 'What Are Fiscal Rules for? A Critical Analysis of the Argentine Experience' (2007) 91 *CEPAL Review* 53-66

Brauner, Yariv, 'Brain Drain Taxation as Development Policy' (2010) 55 *Saint Louis University Law Journal* 221 http://scholarship.law.ufl.edu/facultypub/169

'McBEPS: The MLI – The First Multilateral Tax Treaty that Has Never Been' (2018) 46 *Intertax* 6-17

Brauner, Yariv, and Michael McMahon (eds.), *The Proper Tax Base: Structural Fairness from an International and Comparative Perspective* (Alphen aan den Rijn, Netherlands: Wolters Kluwer, 2012)

Brauner, Yariv, and Miranda Stewart (eds.), *Tax, Law and Development* (Cheltenham: Edward Elgar, 2013)

van Brederode, Robert F, and Richard Krever (eds.), *Legal Interpretation of Tax Law*, 2nd ed (Alphen aan den Rijn, Netherlands: Wolters Kluwer, 2017)

Breen, Oonagh B, 'European Non-profit Oversight: The Case for Regulating from the Outside in' (2016) 91 *Chicago-Kent Law Review* 991–1020

Brennan, Geoffrey, and James M Buchanan, *The Power to Tax: Analytical Foundations of a Fiscal Constitution* (Cambridge, UK: Cambridge University Press, 1980)

Brennan, Geoffrey, and Loren Lomasky, 'Institutional Aspects of "Merit Goods" Analysis' (1983) 41(2) *FinanzArchiv/Public Finance Analysis* 183–206

Brennen, David A, 'A Diversity Theory of Charitable Tax Exemption: Beyond Efficiency, through Critical Race Theory, toward Diversity' (2006) 4 *Pittsburgh Tax Review* 1–54

Brewer, Mike, Emmanuel Saez and Andrew Shephard, 'Means Testing and Tax Rates on Earnings' in Stuart Adam, Tim Besley, Richard Blundell, Stephen Bond, Robert Chote, Malcolm Gammie, Paul Johnson, Gareth Myles and James M Poterba, *Dimensions of Tax Design. Mirrlees Review: Vol 1* (Oxford: Oxford University Press, 2010), 90–201, www.ifs.org.uk/publications/7184

British Museum, 'Support Notes for Tutors. ESOL Workshop: Origins of Writing', www.britishmuseum.org/sites/default/files/2019-11/Origins-of-writing-support-notes-for-teachers_final.pdf, accessed 18 March 2022

Brock, Gillian, 'Egalitarianism, Ideals, and Cosmopolitan Justice' (2005) 36 *Philosophical Forum* 1–30

Global Justice: A Cosmopolitan Account (Oxford: Oxford University Press, 2009)

Brody, Evelyn, 'Of Sovereignty and Subsidy: Conceptualizing the Charity Tax Exemption' (1997) 23 *Journal of Corporation Law* 585–630

Brooks, Kim, 'Learning to Live with an Imperfect Tax: A Defence of the Corporate Tax' (2003) 36 *University of British Columbia Law Review* 621

(ed.), *The Quest for Tax Reform Continues: The Royal Commission on Taxation Fifty Years Later* (Toronto: Thomson Carswell, 2013)

Brooks, Kim, Åsa Gunnarson, Lisa Philipps and Maria Wersig (eds.), *Challenging Gender Inequality in Tax Policy Making: Comparative Perspectives* (London: Hart Publishing, 2011)

Broome, Andre, 'Setting the Fiscal Policy Agenda: Economic News and Election Year Tax Debates in New Zealand' (2006) 24(2) *Law in Context* 60–77

Brown, Catherine A, and Joseph Bogle, 'Treaty Shopping and the New Multilateral Tax Agreement – Is It Business as Usual in Canada?' (2020) 43(1) *Dalhousie Law Journal* 1–32

Brown, Dorothy A, *The Whiteness of Wealth: How the Tax System Impoverishes Black Americans – And How We Can Fix It* (New York: Crown, 2021)

Brown, Karen B and Mary Louise Fellows, *Taxing America* (New York: New York University Press, 1996)

Brown, Rodney, Yongdeok Lim and Chris Evans, 'The Impact of Full Franking Credit Refundability on Corporate Tax Avoidance' (2020) 17(2) *eJournal of Tax Research* 134–67

Brownlee, W Elliot, *Federal Taxation in America* (Cambridge, UK: Cambridge University Press, 2004), 49–53

Bryant, Christopher J, 'Without Representation, No Taxation: Free Blacks, Taxes, and tax Exemptions between the Revolutionary and Civil Wars' (2015) 21 *Michigan Journal of Race and Law* 91–123

Burg, David F, *A World History of Tax Rebellions: An Encyclopedia of Tax Rebels, Revolts, and Riots from Antiquity to the Present* (New York: Routledge, 2004)

Burman, Leonard E, Christopher Geissler and Eric J Toder ' How Big Are Total Individual Income Tax Expenditures, and Who Benefits from Them?' (2008) 98 (2) *American Economic Review* 79–83

Burton, Mark, 'Citizens as Partners: Foundations for an Effective Tax System in the New Democratic Era' (2006) 24(2) *Law in Context* 169–93

Burton, Mark, and Kerrie Sadiq, *Tax Expenditure Management: A Critical Assessment* (Cambridge, UK: Cambridge University Press, 2013)

Cagé, Julia, and Lucie Gadenne, 'Tax Revenues and the Fiscal Cost of Trade Liberalization, 1792–2006' (2018) 70 *Explorations in Economic History* 1–24

Calmfors, Lars, *The Role of Independent Fiscal Policy Institutions*, CESifo Working Paper No 3367 (Munich: CESifo Group, February 2011)

Calmfors, Lars, and Simon Wren-Lewis, 'What Should Fiscal Councils Do?' (2011) 26 *Economic Policy* 649, 651–95

Campbell, Colin, 'JL Ilsley and the Transformation of the Canadian Tax System: 1939–1943' (2013) 61(3) *Canadian Tax Journal* 633–70

Campbell, John L, 'The State and Fiscal Sociology' (1993) 19 *Annual Review of Sociology* 163–85

Canada Privy Council Office, *Report of the Royal Commission on Taxation: Vol 3: Taxation of Income: Part A, Taxation of Individuals and Families/Kenneth LeM Carter, Chairman* (Ottawa: Privy Council Office, 1966)

Canada Revenue Agency, 'Income Sprinkling' (10 July 2019), www.canada.ca/en/revenue-agency/programs/about-canada-revenue-agency-cra/federal-government-budgets/income-sprinkling.html

'Seasonal Agricultural Workers Program RC4004(E) Rev. 22' (modified 23 December 2021), www.canada.ca/en/revenue-agency/services/forms-publications/publications/rc4004/seasonal-agricultural-workers-program.html#P73_2779

Cardoso, José Luis and Pedro Lains, 'Introduction' in *Paying for the Liberal State: The Rise of Public Finance in Nineteenth-Century Europe* (New York: Cambridge University Press, 2010), 1–26

(eds.), *Paying for the Liberal State: The Rise of Public Finance in Nineteenth-Century Europe* (New York: Cambridge University Press, 2010)

Carey, Peter, *The Tax Inspector* (New York: Vintage International, 1993)

Cashin, Cheryl, Susan Sparkes and Danielle Bloom, *Earmarking for Health: From Theory to Practice*, Health Financing Working Paper No 5 (Geneva: World Health Organisation, 2017)

CBC, 'Isle of Sham: Tales from a Canadian Tax Haven', www.taxfairness.ca/en/news/isle-shamtales-canadian-tax-haven, accessed 16 March 2022

Centre for Social Justice, *Universal Credit* (London: Centre for Social Justice, October 2017), www.centreforsocialjustice.org.uk/core/wp-content/uploads/2017/10/Universal_Credit_Report.pdf

Centre for Tax System Integrity, http://ctsi.org.au/, legacy website, accessed 16 March 2022

Chan, James L, 'Major Federal Budget Laws of the United States' in Siamack Shojai (ed.), *Budget Deficits and Debt: A Global Perspective* (Westport, CT: Praeger, 1999), 17–25

Chapman, Bruce, Philip Clarke, Timothy Higgins and Miranda Stewart, 'Income Contingent Collection of a "Brain Drain Tax": Theory, Policy and Empirical Potential' (2015) 54(2) *Population Review* 13–27

Charlesworth, Lone, *Welfare's Forgotten Past: A Socio-legal History of the Poor Law* (Abingdon: Routledge, 2010)

Chen, Duanjie, Franck Lee and Jack M Mintz, *Taxation, SMEs and Entrepreneurship*, OECD Science, Technology and Industry Working Papers No. 2002/09 (Paris: OECD Publishing, 2002), https://doi.org/10.1787/013245868670

Chesterman, Michael, 'Foundations of Charity Law in the New Welfare State' (1999) 62(3) *Modern Law Review* 333–49

Chia, Joyce, and Miranda Stewart, 'Doing Business to Do Good: Should We Tax the Business Profits of Not for Profits?' (2012) 33 *Adelaide Law Review* 335–70

Cho, Annie, 'The Five Phases of Company Taxation in New Zealand: 1840–2008' (2008) 14 *Auckland University Law Review* 150–75

Chohan, Usman, 'Independent Budget Offices and the Politics-Administration Dichotomy' (2018) 41(12) *International Journal of Public Administration* 1009–17

Christensen, Johan, 'Bringing the Bureaucrats Back in: Neo-liberal Tax Reform in New Zealand' (2012) 32(2) *Journal of Public Policy* 141–68

Christians, Allison, 'BEPS and the New International Tax Order' (2016) 6 *Brigham Young University Law Review* 1603

   'Buying In: Residence and Citizenship by Investment' (2017) 62 *Saint Louis University Law Journal* 51–71

   'A Global Perspective on US Citizenship Taxation' (2017) 38(2) *Michigan Journal of International Law* 193–243

   'Taxing According to Value Creation' (2018) 90 *Tax Notes International* 1379–83

Chwieroth, Jeffrey, and Andrew Walter, *The Wealth Effect: How the Great Expectations of the Middle Class Have Changed the Politics of Banking Crises* (Cambridge, UK: Cambridge University Press, 2019)

Ciepley, David, 'Beyond Public and Private: Towards a Political Theory of the Corporation' (2013) 107(1) *American Political Science Review* 139–58

Clausing, Kimberly A, 'In Search of Corporate Tax Incidence' (2012) 65(3) *Tax Law Review* 433–72

Cnossen, Sijbren, 'The Role of the Corporation Tax in OECD Member Countries: A Survey and Evaluation' in John G Head and Richard Krever (eds.), *Company Tax Systems*, Conference Series No 18 (Melbourne: Australian Tax Research Foundation, 1997), 49–84

   Tackling Spillovers by Taxing Corporate Income in the European Union at Source, CESifo Working Paper No 5790 (Munich: CESifo Group, 2015)

Cockfield, Arthur, 'The Rise of the OECD as an Informal 'World Tax Organization' through National Responses to E-Commerce Tax Challenges' (2005–6) 6 *Yale Journal of Law & Technology* 136–87

   'Sharing Tax Information in the 21st Century: Big Data Flows and Taxpayers as Data Subjects' (2019) 67(4) *Canadian Tax Journal* 1179–99

Cockfield, Arthur Walter Hellerstein, Rebecca Millar and Christophe Waerzeggers, *Taxing Global Digital Commerce* (Alphen aan den Rijn, Netherlands: Kluwer Law International, 2013)

Colm, Gerhard, 'The Corporation and the Corporate Income Tax in the American Economy' (1954) 45 *American Economic Review* 486–503

Essays in Public Finance and Fiscal Policy (New York: Oxford University Press, 1955)

'Theory of Public Expenditures' (1936) 183 *The Annals of the American Academy of Political and Social Science* 1–11

Colombino, Ugo, 'Is Unconditional Basic Income a Viable Alternative to Other Social Welfare Measures?' (2019) 128 *IZA World of Labor* https://doi.org/10.15185/izawol.128.v2

Colombo, John D, 'Commercial Activity and Charitable Tax Exemption' (2002) 44 *William and Mary Law Review* 487–567

Colombo, John D, and Mark A Hall, *The Charitable Tax Exemption* (Boulder, CO: Westview Press, 1995)

Commonwealth of Australia Taxation Review Committee, *Full Report January 31 1975* (1975), https://adc.library.usyd.edu.au/data-2/p00087.pdf

Congressional Budget Office (US), *The Impact of Unauthorized Immigrants on the Budgets of State and Local Governments* (Washington, DC: CBO, 2007)

Cooper, George, 'The Taming of the Shrewd: Identifying and Controlling Income Tax Avoidance' (1985) 85 *Columbia Law Review* 657–729

Cooper, Graeme, 'The Benefit Theory of Taxation' (1994) 11 *Australian Tax Forum* 397–509

Tax Avoidance and the Rule of Law (Amsterdam: IBFD Publications, 1997)

Cooper, Graeme, Michael Dirkis, Miranda Stewart and Richard J Vann, *Income Taxation: Commentary and Materials* (Sydney: Thomson Reuters, 2020)

Cooper, Michael, John McClelland, James Pearce, Richard Prisinzano, Joseph Sullivan, Danny Yagan, Owen Zidar and Eric Zwick, *Business in the United States: Who Owns It and How Much Tax Do They Pay?*, Working Paper 104/2015 (Washington, DC: Department of the Treasury, Office of Tax Analysis, 2011), www.treasury.gov/resource-center/tax-policy/tax-analysis/Documents/WP-104.pdf

Council of Europe, *Gender Budgeting: Practical Implementation. Handbook* (Strasbourg: Council of Europe, Directorate General of Human Rights and Legal Affairs, 2009)

'Reservations and Declarations for Treaty No 127 – Convention on Mutual Administrative Assistance in Tax Matters', www.coe.int/en/web/conventions/full-list?module=declarations-by-treaty&numSte=127&codeNature=0, accessed 27 March 2022

Couzin, Robert, 'A Modern Look at the Roman Imperial "Jewish Tax"' (2017) 65(2) *Canadian Tax Journal* 333–52

Crawford, Claire, and Judith Freedman, in Stuart Adam, Tim Besley, Richard Blundell, Stephen Bond, Robert Chote, Malcolm Gammie, Paul Johnson, Gareth Myles and James M Poterba, *Dimensions of Tax Design. Mirrlees Review: Vol 1* (Oxford: Oxford University Press, 2010), 1028–99, https://ifs.org.uk/publications/5228

Credit Suisse, *Global Wealth Report 2019* (Credit Suisse Research Institute, 2019)

Cui, Wei, *The Administrative Foundations of the Chinese Fiscal State* (Cambridge, UK: Cambridge University Press, 2022)
    'The Digital Services Tax: A Conceptual Defense' (2019–20) 73 *Tax Law Review* 69–111
    'Minimalism about Residence and Source' (2017) 38 *Michigan Journal of International Law* 245–69
'Current Status of Implementation of the German Property Tax Reform', *German Tax Monthly* (Frankfurt: KPMG, October 2021), 3–4, https://assets.kpmg/content/dam/kpmg/de/pdf/Themen/2021/09/german-tax-monthly-october-2021-kpmg.pdf
Dagan, Tsilly, 'The Currency of Taxation' (2016) 84 *Fordham Law Review* 2537–64
    International Tax Policy: Between Competition and Cooperation (Cambridge, UK: Cambridge University Press, 2018)
Dal Pont, Gino E, and Stefan Petrow, *Law of Charity* (New York: LexisNexis Butterworths, 2010)
Dart, Raymond, 'Charities in Business, Business in Charities, Charities and Business – Mapping and Understanding the Complex Non-profit/Business Interface' (2004) 18 *Philanthropist* 181–98
Daunton, Martin, 'Creating Legitimacy: Administering Taxation in Britain, 1815–1914' in José Luis Cardoso and Pedro Lains (eds.), *Paying for the Liberal State: the Rise of Public Finance in Nineteenth-Century Europe* (New York: Cambridge University Press, 2010), 27–56
    Just Taxes: The Politics of Taxation in Britain, 1914–1979 (New York: Cambridge University Press, 2002)
    Trusting Leviathan: The Politics of Taxation in Britain, 1799–1914 (New York: Cambridge University Press, 2001)
Davies, Rhodri, *Public Good by Private Means: How Philanthropy Shapes Britain* (London: Charitable Aid Foundation Alliance Publishing Trust, 2015)
Davis, Laura Ann, 'A Feminist Justification for the Adoption of an Individual Filing System' (1988) 62 *Southern California Law Review* 197–252
Davoodi, Hamid R, Paul Elger, Alexandra Fotiou, Daniel Garcia-Macia, Xuehui Han, Andresa Lagerborg, W Raphael Lam and Paulo Medas, *Fiscal Rules and Fiscal Councils: Recent Trends and Performance during the COVID-19 Pandemic*, IMF Working Paper WP/22/11 (Washington, DC: International Monetary Fund, 2022)
de la Feria, Rita (ed.), *VAT Exemptions: Consequences and Design Alternatives* (Alphen aan den Rijn, Netherlands: Wolters Kluwer, 2013)
de la Feria, Rita, and Stefan Vogenauer (eds.), *Prohibition of Abuse of Law: A New General Principle of EU Law* (Oxford: Hart Publishing, 2011)
de Mooij, Ruud, and Michael P Devereux, 'Alternative Systems of Business Tax in Europe: An Applied Analysis of ACE and CBIT Reforms' (2011) 18 *International Tax and Public Finance* 93–120, https://link.springer.com/article/10.1007/s10797-010-9138-8
Dean, Steven A, 'The Incomplete Global Market for Tax Information' (2008) 49(3) *Boston College Law Review* 605–72
Dean, Steven A, and Rebecca M Kysar, 'Introduction: Reconsidering the Tax Treaty' (2016) 41 *Brooklyn Journal of International Law* 967–72

Debrun, Xavier, and Keiko Takahashi, 'Independent Fiscal Councils on Continental Europe: Old Wine in New Bottles?' 9(3) *CESifo DICE Report* 44 (Munich: ifo Institut - Leibniz-Institut für Wirtschaftsforschung an der Universität München, 2011)

Desai, Anuj, 'What a History of Tax Withholding Tells Us about the Relationship between Statutes and Constitutional Law' (2014) 108(3) *Northwestern University Law Review* 859–904

Desai, Mihir A, 'The Decentering of the Global Firm' (2009) 32 *The World Economy* 1271–90 https://doi.org/10.1111/j.1467-9701.2009.01212.x

Devereux, Michael P, 'Taxation of Outbound Direct Investment: Economic Principles and Tax Policy Considerations' in John G Head and Richard Krever (eds.), *Tax Reform in the 21st Century* (Alphen aan den Rijn, Netherlands: Wolters Kluwer, 2009), 499–523

Devereux, Michael P, Alan J Auerbach, Michael Keen, Paul Oosterhuis, Wolfgang Schön and John Vella *Taxing Profit in a Global Economy* (Oxford: Oxford University Press, Oxford Scholarship Online, 2021), https://oxford.universitypressscholarship.com/view/10.1093/oso/9780198808060.001.0001/oso-9780198808060

Devereux, Michael P, Rachel Griffith and Alexander Klemm, *Corporate Income Tax Reforms and International Tax Competition* (Warwick: Centre for Economic Policy Research, University of Warwick, 2002)

Dharmasena, Senarath, and Oral Capps Jr, 'Intended and Unintended Consequences of a Proposed National Tax on Sugar-Sweetened Beverages to Combat the US Obesity Problem' (2012) 21(6) *Health Economics* 669–94

Digoix, Marie, *Same-Sex Families and Legal Recognition in Europe. European Studies of Population: Vol 24* (Cham: Springer, 2020)

Dincecco, Mark, 'Fiscal Centralization, Limited Government, and Public Revenues in Europe, 1650–1913' (2006) 69(1) *The Journal of Economic History* 48–103

Doernberg, Richard L, Luc Hinnekens, Walter Hellerstein and Jinyan Li, *Electronic Commerce and Multijurisdictional Taxation* (Alphen aan den Rijn, Netherlands: Kluwer Law International, 2001)

Dolan, Kerry, 'Jeff Bezos Just Sold 2 Billion Worth of Amazon Stock', Forbes, 4 November 2021, www.forbes.com/sites/kerryadolan/2021/11/04/jeff-bezos-just-sold-2-billion-worth-of-amazon-stock/

Doling, John, 'Housing Tenure Trends' in Susan J Smith et al (eds.), *International Encyclopedia of Housing and Home* (Amsterdam: Elsevier, 2012)

Donaldson, Thomas, and Lee Preston, 'The Stakeholder Theory of the Corporation: Concepts, Evidence and Implications' (1995) 20(1) *Academy of Management Review* 65–91

Dourado, Ana Paula, 'Introduction: International Tax Multilateralism or Reinforced Unilateralism?' in Ana Paula Dourado (ed.), *International and EU Tax Multilateralism: Challenges Raised by the MLI* (Amsterdam: IBFD, 2020), 1–11

Downes, Ronnie, and Sherie Nichol, *Designing and Implementing Gender Budgeting* (Paris: Public Governance Directorate, OECD, 2019), www.oecd.org/gov/budgeting/designing-and-implementing-gender-budgeting-a-path-to-action.pdf

Drucker, Jesse, 'Google 2.4% Rate Shows How $60 Billion Is Lost to Tax Loopholes', Bloomberg Business Week, 20 October 2010, www.bloomberg.com/news/articles/2010-10-21/google-2-4-rate-shows-how-60-billion-u-s-revenue-lost-to-tax-loopholes

Drucker, Peter F, *Innovation and Entrepreneurship* (New York: Harper Business, 1985)

Drukker, Austin J, Ted Gayer and Harvey S Rosen, *The Mortgage Interest Deduction: Revenue and Distributional Effects* (Washington, DC: Tax Policy Center, 2018)

Due, John, 'Should the Corporation Income Tax Be Replaced by the Value Added Tax?' (1964) 57 *Proceedings of the Annual Conference on Taxation under the Auspices of the National Tax Association* 431–40

Duff, David G, 'Benefit Taxes and User Fees in Theory and Practice' (2004) 54 *University of Toronto Law Journal* 391–447

'Charitable Contributions and the Personal Income Tax: Evaluating the Canadian Credit' in Jim Phillips, Bruce Chapman and David Stevens (eds.), *Between State and Market: Essays on Charities Law and Policy in Canada* (Montreal: McGill-Queen's University Press, 2001), 407–56

'Tax Policy and the Virtuous Sovereign: Dworkinian Equality and Redistributive Taxation' in Monica Bhandari (ed.), *Philosophical Foundations of Tax Law* (Oxford: Oxford University Press, 2017), 161–91, https://doi.org/10.1093/acprof:oso/9780198798439.003.0008

'Tax Treatment of Charitable Contributions in a Personal Income Tax: Lessons from Theory and Canadian Experience' in Matthew Harding, Ann O'Connell and Miranda Stewart (eds.), *Not for-Profit Law: Theoretical and Comparative Perspectives* (Cambridge, UK: Cambridge University Press, 2014), 199–231

'Tax Treatment of Charitable Contributions in Canada: Theory, Practice, and Reform' (2004) 42(1) *Osgoode Hall Law Journal* 47, 50–70

Dupas, Marine, *Wealth Tax: France*, Wealth Tax Commission Background Paper 134 (London: Wealth Tax Commission, 2020)

Dwenger, Nadja, Pia Rattenhuber and Viktor Steiner, 'Sharing the Burden? Empirical Evidence on Corporate Tax Incidence' (2019) 20(4)*German Economic Review* e107–e140, https://doi.org/10.1111/geer.12157

Eberhartinger, Eva, Raffael Speitmann and Caren Sureth-Sloane, *Banks' Tax Disclosure, Financial Secrecy, and Tax Haven Heterogeneity*, WU International Tax Research Paper Series No 2020-01 (2021), https://ssrn.com/abstract=3523909

Egger, Peter, and Doina M Radulescu, 'The Influence of Labour Taxes on the Migration of Skilled Workers' (2009) 32(9) *The World Economy* 1365–79 https://doi.org/10.1111/j.1467-9701.2009.01213.x 1365–79

Emerton, Patrick, and Kathryn James, 'The Justice of the Tax Base and the Case for Income Tax' in Monica Bhandari (ed.), *The Philosophical Foundations of Tax Law* (Oxford: Oxford University Press, 2017), 125–66, https://doi.org/10.1093/acprof:oso/9780198798439.003.0007

Emmerson, Carl, and Isabel Stockton, 'Rewriting the Fiscal Rules: IFS Green Budget' in Carl Emmerson, Paul Johnson and Ben Zaranko (eds.), *The IFS Green Budget* (London: Institute for Fiscal Studies, 2021), 147–82, https://ifs.org.uk/publications/15693

Enjolras, Bernard, Lester M Salamon, Karl Henrik Sivesind and Annette Zimmer, *The Third Sector as a Renewable Resource for Europe: Concepts, Impacts, Challenges and Opportunities* (London: Palgrave Macmillan, 2018)

Esteller-Moré, Alejandro, Amedeo Piolatto and Matthew D Rablen, 'Taxing High-Income Earners: Tax Avoidance and Mobility' in Nigar Hashimzade and Yuliya

Epifantseva (eds.), *The Routledge Companion to Tax Avoidance Research* (London: Routledge, 2018), 304–19

Etzioni, Amitai, and Alex Platt, *Basic Income: The Social Contract Revisited* (Oxford: The Foundation for Law, Justice and Society, 2008)

European Commission, 'Company Taxation: Commission Suggests Single Consolidated Tax Base' IP/01/1468 (23 October 2001), https://ec.europa.eu/commission/presscorner/detail/en/IP_01_1468

Company Taxation in the Internal Market {COM(01)582 final}, Commission Staff Working Paper (Brussels: EC, 23 October 2001)

'Germany – Early Childhood and School Education Funding' (2021), https://eacea.ec.europa.eu/national-policies/eurydice/content/early-childhood-and-school-education-funding-51_en, accessed 14 March 2022

'Modernising VAT for Cross-border E-commerce', https://ec.europa.eu/taxation_customs/business/vat/vat-e-commerce/modernising-vat-cross-border-e-commerce_en, accessed 14 March 2022

'Proposal for a Council Directive on a Common Consolidated Corporate Tax Base' COM/2016/683 final (25 October 2016), https://eur-lex.europa.eu/legal-content/EN/TXT/HTML/?uri=CELEX:52016PC0683&from=en

Public Finances in EMU-2010 (Brussels: Directorate-General for Economic and Financial Affairs, 2010)

Six-Pack? Two-Pack? Fiscal Compact? A Short Guide to the New EU Fiscal Governance (Brussels: Directorate-General for Economic and Financial Affairs, 14 March 2012), http://ec.europa.eu/economy_finance/articles/governance/2012-03-14_six_pack_en.htm

European Commission Directorate-General for Taxation and Customs Union, *Explanatory Notes on VAT E-commerce Rules*, Council Directive (EU) 2017/2455, 2019/1995, Council Implementing Regulation (EU) 2019/2026 (Brussels: European Commission, September 2020), https://vat-one-stop-shop.ec.europa.eu/document/download/3372e2f2-d5ec-46ea-a2ac-97bc4f5ec634_en

Guidelines for a Model for a European Taxpayers' Code (Brussels: European Commission, 2016), https://ec.europa.eu/taxation_customs/system/files/2016-11/guidelines_for_a_model_for_a_european_taxpayers_code_en.pdf

Taxation Trends in the European Union, (Luxembourg: Publications Office of the European Union, 2019)

European Union, 'Council Directive 2002/38/EC Amending Directive 77/338/EEC as regards the Value Added Tax Arrangements Applicable to Radio and Television Broadcasting Services and Electronically Supplied Services' (2002) 128 *Official Journal of European Communities* 40

Evans, Chris, 'Containing Tax Avoidance: Anti-avoidance Strategies' in John G Head and Richard Krever (eds.), *Tax Reform in the 21st Century* (Alphen aan den Rijn, Netherlands: Kluwer Law International, 2009), 529–60

'Reflections on the Mirrlees Review: An Australasian Perspective' (2011) 32(3) *Fiscal Studies* 375–93

Evans, Chris, John Hasseldine, Andrew Lymer, Robert Ricketts and Cedric Sandford, *Comparative Taxation: Why Tax Systems Differ* (Bath: Fiscal Publications, 2017)

Evans, Chris, and Cedric Sandford, 'Capital Gains Tax – The Unprincipled Tax' (1999) 5 *British Tax Review* 387–405

Fabian, Mark, and Robert Breunig (eds.), *Hybrid Public Policy Innovations: Contemporary Policy Beyond Ideology* (New York: Routledge, 2018)

Falk, Richard, 'Revisiting Westphalia, Discovering Post-Westphalia' (2002) 6(4), *Journal of Ethics* 311–52

Farivar, Cyrus, 'San Francisco Voters Pass "Overpaid Executive Tax"', NBCNews, 6 November 2020, www.nbcnews.com/business/business-news/san-francisco-voters-pass-overpaid-executive-tax-n1246644

Farrelly, Colin, 'Taxation and Distributive Justice' (2004) 2 *Political Studies Review* 185–97

Fasone, Cristina, and Elena Griglio, 'The Setting Up of the Fiscal Councils and the Perspectives for the National Parliaments: Comparing Belgium, Germany and the UK' in Bruno De Witte, Adrienne Heritier and Alexander H Trechsel (eds.), *The Euro Crisis and the State of European Democracy: Contributions from the 2012 EUDO Dissemination Conference* (Florence: European University Institute, 2013)

Faulhaber, Lilian V, 'Charitable Giving, Tax Expenditures, and Direct Spending in the United States and the European Union' (2014) 39 *Yale Journal of International Law* 87–129

Ferrera, Maurizio, *The Boundaries of Welfare: European Integration and the New Spatial Politics of Social Protection* (Oxford: Oxford University Press, Oxford Scholarship Online, 2005), https://oxford.universitypressscholarship.com/view/10.1093/0199284660.001.0001/acprof-9780199284665

Fineman, Martha, and Terence Dougherty, *Feminism Confronts Homo Economicus: Gender, Law and Society* (Ithaca, NY: Cornell University Press, 2005)

Fink, Marian, Jitka Janová, Danuše Nerudova, Jan Pavel, Margit Schratzenstaller, Friedrich Sinderman-Sienkiewicz and Martin Speilauer, '(Gender-differentiated) Effects of Changes in Personal Income Taxation' (2019) 54(3) *Intereconomics: Review of European Economic Policy* 146–54 www.intereconomics.eu/contents/year/2019/number/3/article/gender-differentiated-effects-of-changes-in-personal-income-taxation.html

Fishman, James J, 'Encouraging Charity in a Time of Crisis: The Poor Laws and the Statute of Charitable Uses of 1601' (2005), http://dx.doi.org/10.2139/ssrn.868394

Fleischer, Miranda Perry, 'Subsidizing Charity Liberally' in Matthew Harding (ed.), *Research Handbook on Not-for-Profit Law* (New York: Edward Elgar, 2018), 418–43

Fleischer, Victor, 'Two and Twenty: Taxing Partnership Profits in Private Equity Firms' (2008) 83(1) *New York University Law Review* 1–59

Forte, Francesco, and Emilio Giardina, 'The Crisis of the Fiscal State' in Karl W Roskamp and Francesco Forte(eds.), *Reforms of Tax Systems* (Detroit, MI: Wayne State University Press, 1981), 1–9

Frank, Robert, 'Elon Musk Unloaded $22 Billion of Tesla Stock – and Still Owns More Now than a Year Ago', CNBC, 15 February 2022, www.cnbc.com/2022/02/15/elon-musk-unloaded-billions-of-tesla-stockand-still-owns-more-than-last-year.html

Fraser, Nancy, 'Reframing Justice in a Globalizing World' in David Held and Ayse Kaya (eds.), *Global Inequality: Patterns and Explanations* (Cambridge, UK: Polity Press, 2007), 252–68

Freedman, David H, 'Basic Income: A Sellout of the American Dream' *MIT Technology Review*, 13 June 2016, www.technologyreview.com/2016/06/13/159449/basic-income-a-sellout-of-the-american-dream/

Freedman, Judith, 'Employment Status, Tax and the Gig Economy – Improving the Fit or Making the Break?' (2020) 31(2) *King's Law Journal* 194–214

'United Kingdom' in Michael Lang, Jeffrey Owens, Pasquale Pistone, Alexander Rust, Josef Schuch and Claus Staringer (eds.), *GAARs – A Key Element of Tax Systems in the Post-BEPS World* (Amsterdam: IBFD, 2016), 741–64

Friedman, Milton, *Capitalism and Freedom* (Chicago: University of Chicago Press, 1962)

Fuest, Clemens, and Bernd Huber, *The Optimal Taxation of Dividends in A Small Open Economy*, CESifo Working Paper Series No 348 (Munich: CESifo Group, 2000)

G20, 'Global Plan for Recovery and Reform: The Communiqué from the London Summit' (2 April 2009), www.g20.utoronto.ca/2009/2009communique0402.html

'Saint Petersburg Declaration' (6 September 2013), www.g20.utoronto.ca/2013/2013-0906-declaration.html

Gál, Róbert Iván, Pieter Vanhuysse and Lili Vargha, 'Pro-Elderly Welfare States within Child-Oriented Societies' (2018) 25(6) *Journal of European Public Policy* 944–58

Galbraith, John Kenneth, *A History of Economics: The Past as Present* (London: Penguin, 1987)

Gale, William, and Samuel Brown, 'Small Business, Innovation, and Tax Policy: A Review' (2013) 66(4) *National Tax Journal* 871–92

Garcia-Bernardo, Javier, Petr Jansky and Thomas Tørsløv, 'Multinational Corporations and Tax Havens: Evidence from Country-by-Country Reporting' (2021) 28 *International Tax and Public Finance* 1519–61 https://doi.org/10.1007/s10797-020-09639-w

Gaspar, Vitor, and Gita Gopinath, 'Fiscal Policies for a Transformed World', IMFblog, 10 July 2020, https://blogs.imf.org/2020/07/10/fiscal-policies-for-a-transformed-world/

Genschel, Philipp, and Thomas Rixen, 'Settling and Unsettling the Transnational Legal Order of International Taxation' in Terence C Halliday and Gregory Shaffer (eds.), *Transnational Legal Orders* (Cambridge, UK: Cambridge University Press, 2015), 154–84

George, Henry, *Progress and Poverty* (New York: Appleton, 1879)

Gianni, Monica, 'PFICs Gone Wild!'(2014) 29 *Akron Tax Journal* 29–64

Gillitzer, Christian, and Mathias Sinning, 'Nudging Businesses to Pay Their Taxes: Does Timing Matter?' (2020) 169 *Journal of Economic Behavior and Organization* 284–300

Gilson, Ronald J, 'Engineering a Venture Capital Market: Lessons from the American Experience' (2003) 55 *Stanford Law Review* 1067–103

Gilson, Ronald J, and David M Schizer, 'Understanding Venture Capital Structure: A Tax Explanation for Convertible Preferred Stock' (2003) 116 *Harvard Law Review* 874–916

Glantz, Andrew E, 'A Tax on Light and Air: Impact of the Window Duty on Tax Administration and Architecture, 1696–1851' (2008) 15(2) *Penn History Review* 1–23

Global Legal Monitor, 'China: Individual Income Tax Law Revised', Library of Congress (24 September 2018), www.loc.gov/law/foreign-news/article/china-individual-income-tax-law-revised-2/

Goldscheid, Rudolf, 'A Sociological Approach to Problems in Public Finance' in Richard A Musgrave and Alan T Peacock (eds.), *Classics in the Theory of Public Finance* (New York: Palgrave Macmillan, 1918, trans. Elizabeth Henderson; 1958), 202–13

State Socialism or State Capitalism (Vienna: Anzengruber Verlag, 1917)

Goode, Richard, *The Corporation Income Tax* (New York: John Wiley, 1951)

Gould, Andrew C, and Peter J Baker, 'Democracy and Taxation' (2002) 5 *Annual Review of Political Science* 87–110

Government of New Zealand Treasury Department, *The Wellbeing Budget 2019* (Wellington: Government of New Zealand, 30 May 2019), https://treasury.govt.nz/sites/default/files/2019-05/b19-wellbeing-budget.pdf

Graeber, David, *Debt: The First 5,000 Years* (Brooklyn, NY: Melville House Printing, 2011)

Graetz, Michael J, and Alvin C Warren, 'Integration of Corporate and Shareholder Taxes' (2016) 69(3) *National Tax Journal* 677–700 https://dx.doi.org/10.17310/ntj.2016.3.07

Grattan Institute, *Generation Gap: Ensuring a Fair Go for Younger Australians* (Carlton, Victoria: Grattan Institute, 2019)

Gravelle, Jane, 'Corporate Income Tax: Incidence, Economic Effects and Structural Issues' in John G Head and Richard Krever (eds.), *Tax Reform in the 21st Century* (Alphen aan den Rijn, Netherlands: Wolters Kluwer, 2009), 355–84

'The Corporate Income Tax – A Persistent Policy Challenge' (2011) 11 *Florida Tax Review* 73–96

The Economic Effects of Taxing Capital Income (Cambridge, MA: MIT Press, 1994)

Gravelle, Jane, and Donald Marples, *Issues in International Corporate Taxation: The 2017 Revision* (Washington, DC: Congressional Research Service, updated 27 August 2021)

Gray, Edith, and Ann Evans, 'Do Couples Share Income? Variation in the Organisation of Income in Dual-earner Households' (2008) 43(3) *Australian Journal of Social Issues* 441–57

Grbich, Judith, 'The Tax Unit Debate Revisited: Notes on the Critical Resources of a Feminist Revenue Law Scholarship' (1991) 4 *Canadian Journal of Women and the Law* 512–38

Green, Leslie, 'Legal Positivism' in Edward N Zalta (ed.), *The Stanford Encyclopedia of Philosophy* (Stanford, CA: Stanford University Press, 2003)

Greenberg, Scott, 'Details of the House GOP Tax Plan', Tax Foundation (24 June 2016), https://taxfoundation.org/details-house-gop-tax-plan

Gribnau, Hans, and Henk Vording, 'The Birth of Tax as a Legal Discipline' in Paul Harris and Dominic de Cogan, *Studies in the History of Tax Law: Vol 8* (London: Hart Publishing, 2017), 37–66

Griffith, Rachel, James Hines and Peter B Sorenson, 'International Capital Taxation' in Stuart Adam, Tim Besley, Richard Blundell, Stephen Bond, Robert Chote, Malcolm Gammie, Paul Johnson, Gareth Myles and James M Poterba, *Dimensions of Tax Design. Mirrlees Review: Vol 1* (Oxford: Oxford University Press, 2010), 914–1027, https://ifs.org.uk/publications/5227

Gruber, Jon, and Emmanuel Saez, *The Elasticity of Taxable Income: Evidence and Implications*, NBER Working Paper No 7515 (Cambridge, MA: National Bureau for Economic Research, 2000)

Gruen, Nicholas, 'Greater Independence for Fiscal Institutions' (2001) 1(1) *OECD Journal on Budgeting* 89–115

Guerreiro, Joao, Sergio Rebelo and Pedro Teles, *Should Robots Be Taxed?* NBER Working Paper No 23806 (Cambridge, MA: National Bureau for Economic Research, 2020)

Gunnarson, Åsa, *Gender Equality and Taxation – International Perspectives*, Copenhagen Business School Law Research Paper Series No 20-29 (Frederiksberg, Denmark: Copenhagen Business School, 2020)

Hacker, Jacob S, The Institutional Foundations of Middle-Class Democracy,' in *Priorities for a New Political Economy: Memos to the Left* (London: Policy Network, 2011), 33–8

Hall, Peter A, 'Policy Paradigms, Social Learning, and the State: The Case of Economic Policymaking in Britain' (1993) 25 *Comparative Politics* 275–96

Hall, Robert, and Alvin Rabushka, *The Flat Tax* (Stanford, CA: Hoover Institution Press, 2007)

Hansmann, Henry B, 'Unfair Competition and the Unrelated Business Income Tax' (1989) 75 *Virginia Law Review* 605–35

Harberger, Arnold C, 'The Incidence of the Corporation Income Tax' (June 1962) 70(3) *Journal of Political Economy* 215–40

'The Incidence of the Corporation Income Tax Revisited' (2008) (61)2 *National Tax Journal* 303–12

Harding, Matthew, *Charity Law and the Liberal State* (Cambridge, UK: Cambridge University Press, 2014)

(ed.), *Research Handbook on Not-for-Profit Law* (New York: Edward Elgar, 2018)

Harding, Matthew, Ann O'Connell and Miranda Stewart (eds.), *Not-for-Profit Law: Theoretical and Comparative Perspectives* (Cambridge, UK: Cambridge University Press, 2014)

Harju, Jarkko and Tuomas Matikka, *Business Owners and Income-Shifting Between Tax Bases: Empirical Evidence from a Finnish Tax Reform*, CESifo Working Paper No 5090 (Munich: CESifo Group, 2014), https://ssrn.com/abstract=2536285

Harris, Peter, *Income Tax in Common Law Jurisdictions: From the Origins to 1820* (Cambridge, UK Cambridge University Press, 2006)

Hayek, Friedrich, *The Road to Serfdom* (London: Routledge & Kegan Paul, 1944)

He, Wenkai, *Paths Toward the Modern Fiscal State* (Cambridge, MA: Harvard University Press, 2013)

Head, John G, 'On Merit Goods' (1966) 25(1) *FinanzArchiv* 1–29

Public Good and Public Welfare (Durham, NC: Duke University Press, 1969)

Head, John G and Richard Krever (eds.), *Company Tax Systems*, Conference Series No 18 (Melbourne: Australian Tax Research Foundation, 1997)

(eds.), *Tax Units and the Tax Rate Scale* (Melbourne: Australian Tax Research Foundation, 1996)

Heidenbauer, Sabine, Sigrid Hemels, Brigitte Muehlmann, Miranda Stewart, Otmar Thoemmes and Tina Tukic, 'Cross-Border Charitable Giving and Its Tax Limitations' (2013) 67 *Bulletin for International Taxation* 611–25

Hellerstein, Walter, 'Jurisdiction to Tax in the Digital Economy: Permanent and Other Establishments' (2014) 68(6-7) *Bulletin of International Taxation* 346-51

'The Rapidly Evolving Universe of US State Taxation of Cross-Border Online Sales after South Dakota v Wayfar, Inc., and Its Implications for Australian Businesses' (2020) 18 *eJournal of Tax Research* 320-49

Hemel, Daniel, and Miranda Fleischer, 'Atlas Nods: The Libertarian Case for a Basic Income' (2017) *Wisconsin Law Review* 1189-271

Hendrickson, Luke, Stan Bucifal, Antonio Balaguer and David Hansell, *The Employment Dynamics of Australian Entrepreneurship*, Research Paper 4/2015 (Canberra: Office of the Chief Economist, Australian Government Department of Industry and Science, 2015)

Her Majesty's Revenue and Customs, *Annual Report 2019 to 2020* (London: HMRC, 2020), https://assets.publishing.service.gov.uk/government/uploads/system/uploads/attachment_data/file/932874/HMRC_Annual_Report_and_Accounts_2019_to_2020__Print_.pdf

'Guidance Note RDR3: Statutory Residence Test' (2014), www.gov.uk/government/publications/rdr3-statutory-residence-test-srt

Measuring Tax Gaps 2020 edition (London: HMRC, 9 July 2020)

Hettich, Walter, and Stanley Winer, 'The Shifting Foundations of Tax Reform' (1985) 38(4) *National Tax Journal* 423-45

Hikaka, Geraldine, and John Prebble, 'Autopoiesis and General Anti-avoidance Rules' (2010) 21 *Critical Perspectives on Accounting* 549-59

Hines, James R, Jr, 'Non-profit Business Activity and the Unrelated Business Income Tax' in James M Poterba (ed.), *Tax Policy and the Economy: Vol 13* (Cambridge, MA: MIT Press, 1999), 57-84

Hobbes, Thomas, *Leviathan* (London: Pelican Classics, [1651], 1968), Project Gutenberg eBook, www.gutenberg.org/files/3207/3207-h/3207-h.htm

Hobson, John, 'Disappearing Taxes or "Race to the Middle"?' in Linda Weiss (ed.), *States in the Global Economy: Bringing Domestic Institutions Back in* (Cambridge, UK: Cambridge University Press, 2003), 37-57

Holland, H Brian, Lloyd W Kennedy, Stanley S Surrey and William C Warren, 'Proposed Revision of the Federal Income Tax Treatment of Trusts and Estates – American Law Institute Draft' (1953) 53 *Columbia Law Review* 316-73

Hölzl, Werner, 'The Economics of Entrepreneurship Policy: Introduction to the Special Issue' (2010) 10 *Journal of Industry, Competition and Trade* 187-97

Hood, Christopher, 'British Tax Structure Development as Administrative Adaptation' (1985) 18(1) *Policy Sciences* 3-31

'The "Tax State" in the Information Age' in TV Paul, G John Ikenberry and John Hall (eds.), *The Nation-State in Question* (Princeton, NJ: Princeton University Press, 2003), 213-33

Hope, Zach, 'Brain Gain: Half of Australian Expats Are Back Home, and They've Brought Their Talents with Them', *The Age*, 27 March 2021, www.theage.com.au/national/victoria/brain-gain-half-of-australian-expats-are-back-home-and-they-ve-brought-their-talents-with-them-20210327-p57ek5.html.

House of Lords (UK), Select Committee on Intergenerational Fairness and Provision, *Tackling Intergenerational Unfairness*, Report of Session 2017-19 (London:

Parliament of the United Kingdom, 2019), https://publications.parliament.uk/pa/ld201719/ldselect/ldintfair/329/329.pdf

Huang, Chye-Ching, and Roderick Taylor, *How the Federal Tax Code Can Better Advance Racial Equity* (Washington, DC: Center on Budget and Policy Priorities, 2019), www.cbpp.org/sites/default/files/atoms/files/7-25-19tax.pdf

Huck, Edward J, 'Tiebout or Samuelson: The 21st Century Deserves More' (2004) 88 *Marquette Law Review* 185–93

Hudson Institute Center for Global Prosperity, *The Index of Global Philanthropy and Remittances 2016* (Washington, DC: Hudson Institute, 2017)

IBFD, *IBFD Yearbook on Taxpayers' Rights 2019* (Amsterdam: Observatory on the Protection of Taxpayers' Rights, 2020), www.ibfd.org/sites/default/files/2021-06/2019%20IBFD%20Yearbook%20on%20Taxpayers%27%20Rights%20%28final%29_0.pdf

IBFD, *IBFD Yearbook on Taxpayers' Rights 2020* (Amsterdam: Observatory on the Protection of Taxpayers' Rights, 2021), www.ibfd.org/sites/default/files/2021-09/2020%20IBFD%20Yearbook%20on%20Taxpayers'%20Rights%20(1).pdf

IBFD News, 'Sweden Proposes Terminating Tax Treaty with Greece, Sweden Proposes Terminating Tax Treaty with Portugal' (23 March 2021)

Ikin, Catherine, and Alfred Tran, 'Corporate Tax Strategy in the Australian Dividend Imputation System' (2013) 28(3) *Australian Tax Forum* 523–53

Infanti, Antony, *Our Selfish Tax Laws* (Cambridge, MA: MIT Press: 2018)

Infanti, Antony, and Bridget Crawford (eds.), *Critical Tax Theory: An Introduction* (Cambridge, UK: Cambridge University Press, 2010)

Ingles, David, and Miranda Stewart, 'Australia's Company Tax: Options for Fiscally Sustainable Reform' (2018) 33(1) *Australian Tax Forum* 101–39

'Reforming Australia's Superannuation Tax System and the Age Pension to Improve Work and Savings Incentives' (2017) *Asia & the Pacific Policy Studies* https://doi.org/10.1002/app5.184

Ingles, David, Ben Philips and Miranda Stewart (2019) 'From Guaranteed Minimum Income to Basic Income: What Might It Look Like?' in Peter Saunders (ed.), *Revisiting Henderson: Poverty, Social Security and Basic Income* (Melbourne: Melbourne University Press) 377–400

Institute of Fiscal Studies, *The Structure and Reform of Direct Taxation* (London: IFS, 1978)

Internal Revenue Service (US), 'Expatriation Tax', updated 22 July 2021, www.irs.gov/individuals/international-taxpayers/expatriation-tax

'Foreign Earned Income Exclusion', updated 8 December 2021, www.irs.gov/individuals/international-taxpayers/foreign-earned-income-exclusion

'SOI Tax Stats – Country by Country Report', updated 12 January 2022, www.irs.gov/statistics/soi-tax-stats-country-by-country-report

'Substantial Presence Test', updated 27 October 2021, www.irs.gov/individuals/international-taxpayers/substantial-presence-test

'Taxpayer Bill of Rights' (24 February 2022), www.irs.gov/taxpayer-bill-of-rights

International Budget Partnership, *Open Budget Survey 2019*, 8th ed (Washington, DC: IBP, 2020), www.internationalbudget.org/wp-content/uploads/open-budget-survey-2017-report-english.pdf

International Monetary Fund, *Current Challenges in Revenue Mobilization: Improving Tax Compliance* (Washington, DC: IMF, April 2015), www.imf.org/external/np/pp/eng/2015/020215a.pdf

Spillovers in International Corporate Taxation, IMF Policy Paper (Washington, DC: IMF, 2014)

International Monetary Fund/OECD, *Tax Policy for Climate Change, IMF-OECD Report for the G20 Finance Ministers and Governors* (April 2021), www.oecd.org/tax/tax-policy/tax-policy-and-climate-change-imf-oecd-g20-report-april-2021.pdf

James, Kathryn, *The Rise of the Value-Added Tax* (New York: Oxford University Press, 2015)

James, Kathryn, and Thomas Ecker, 'Relevance of the OECD International VAT/GST Guidelines for Non-OECD Countries' (2017) 32 *Australian Tax Forum* 317–76

James, Simon, 'Self-assessment and the UK Tax System' (1997) 13 *Australian Tax Forum* 205–26

'Taxation and Nudging' in Morris Altman(ed.), *Handbook of Behavioural Economics and Smart Decision-making: Rational Decision-making within the Bounds of Reason* (Cheltenham: Edward Elgar, 2017), 317–30

Janssen, John, *New Zealand's Fiscal Policy Framework: Experience and Evolution*, Treasury Working Paper No 01/25 (Wellington: New Zealand Treasury Department, 2001)

Jefferson, Therese, 'Women and Retirement Pensions: A Research Review' (2009) 15(4) *Feminist Economics* 115–45 https://doi.org/10.1080/13545700903153963

Jessup, Philip, *Transnational Law* (Cambridge, MA: Harvard University Press, 1956)

Jogarajan, Sunita, *Double Taxation and the League of Nations*, Cambridge Tax Law Series (Cambridge, UK: Cambridge University Press, 2018)

'Prelude to the International Tax Treaty Network: 1815–1914 Early Tax Treaties and the Conditions for Action' (2011) 31(4) *Oxford Journal of Legal Studies* 679–707

Johansson, Dan, Mikael Stenkula and Gunnar Du Rietz, 'Capital Income Taxation of Swedish Households, 1862–2010' (2015) 63(2) *Scandinavian Economic History Review* 154–77 https://doi.org/10.1080/03585522.2014.980314

Johns Hopkins Comparative Nonprofit Sector Project (1991–2017), http://ccss.jhu.edu/research-projects/comparative-nonprofit-sector-project/, accessed 16 March 2022

Johnston, John, 'Michael Gove Pledges to Scrap VAT in Bid to Boost Post-Brexit Economy' (9 June 2019), www.politicshome.com/news/article/michael-gove-pledges-to-scrap-vat-in-bid-to-boost-postbrexit-economy

Johnston, Stephanie Soong, 'Multilateral Tax Risk Assessment Program to Exit Pilot Phase' (9 December 2020) *Tax Notes International*

Jones, Carolyn, 'Class Tax to Mass Tax: The Role of Propaganda in the Expansion of the Income Tax During World War II' (1988–89) 37 *Buffalo Law Review* 685–737

Jones, Daryll K, 'When Charity Aids Tax Shelters' (2001) 12(4) *Florida Tax Review* 770–830

Jones, Frederick R, *History of Taxation in Connecticut: 1636–1776*. Johns Hopkins University Studies in Historical and Political Science 14th Series No 8 (Baltimore, MD: Johns Hopkins Press, 1896)

Jones, Gareth, *History of the Law of Charity 1532–1827* (Cambridge, UK: Cambridge University Press, 1969)

Jones, John A, and Johann Hattingh, 'De Beers Consolidated Mines Ltd v Howe (1906): Corporate Residence: An Early Attempt at European Harmonisation' in Dominic de Cogan and John Snape (eds.), *Landmark Cases in Revenue Law* (Oxford: Hart Publishing, 2019), 67–90, Bloomsbury Collections, http://dx.doi.org/10.5040/9781509912285.ch-003

Joshi, Preetika, Edmund Outslay, Anh Persson, Terry Shevlin and Arunh Venkat. 'Does Public Country-by-Country Reporting Deter Tax Avoidance and Income Shifting? Evidence from the European Banking Industry' (2020) 37 *Contemporary Accounting Research* 2357–97

Joumard, Isabelle, Per Mathis Kongsrud, Young-Sook Nam and Robert Price, 'Enhancing the Cost Effectiveness of Public Spending: Experience in OECD Countries' (2004) (37) *OECD Economic Studies* 109–61

Kaldor, Nicholas, *An Expenditure Tax* (London: Allen & Unwin, 1955)

Kasturirangan, Sucarshan, 'The United Nations Tax Committee as a Player in the International Tax Policy Discussion' in Anna Binder and Viktoria Wöhrer (eds.), *Special Features of the UN Model Convention* (Vienna: Linde Verlag, 2019), 3–24

Kato, Junko, *Regressive Taxation and the Welfare State: Path Dependence and Policy Diffusion* (Cambridge, UK: Cambridge University Press: 2010)

Kay, John, and Mervyn King, *The British Tax System*, 5th ed (Oxford: Oxford University Press, 1990), https://ifs.org.uk/docs/kay_king.pdf

Kayis-Kumar, Ann, 'Thin Capitalisation Rules: A Second-Best Solution to the Cross-Border Debt Bias?' (2015) 30(2) *Australian Tax Forum* 299–355

Keating, Paul J, *A Full Self Assessment System of Taxation: A Consultative Document* (Canberra: Australian Taxation Office, 1990)

Keen, Michael, and David Wildasin, 'Pareto-Efficient International Taxation' (2004) 94 *The American Economic Review* 259–75

Kelton, Stephanie, *The Deficit Myth: Modern Monetary Theory and the Birth of the People's Economy* (New York: Public Affairs, 2020)

Kerlin, Janelle A, 'A Comparative Analysis of the Global Emergence of Social Enterprise' (2010) 21 *Voluntas* 162–79

Kessler, James, 'What Is (and What Is Not) a Sham' (2000) 9.2.2 *Offshore & International Tax Review*, www.khpplc.co.uk/client-area/review/907/OITR-Vol922-What-is-and-what-is-not-A-Sham-James-Kessler-QC

Keynes, John Maynard, *The General Theory of Employment, Interest and Money* (London: Macmillan, 1936)

Kiel, Paul, and Jesse Eisinger, 'How the IRS Was Gutted', *ProPublica* and *The Atlantic*, 11 December 2018, www.propublica.org/article/how-the-irs-was-gutted

Killian, Sheila, and Philip O'Regan, 'Taxation and Social Enterprise: Constraint or Incentive for the Common Good' (2018) 10(1) *Journal of Social Entrepreneurship* 1–18 https://doi.org/10.1080/19420676.2018.1517103.

King, Mervyn A, and Don Fullerton (eds.), *The Taxation of Income from Capital* (Chicago: University of Chicago Press, 1984)

Kirsch, Michael S, 'Taxing Citizens in a Global Economy' (2007) 82 *New York University Law Review* 443–530

Kitsonis, Yanni, *States of Obligation: Taxes and Citizenship in the Russian Empire and Early Soviet Republic* (Toronto: University of Toronto Press, 2014)

Klein, Martin, and Manfred JM Neumann, 'Seigniorage: What Is It and Who Gets It?' (1990) 126(2) *Weltwirtschaftliches Archiv* 205–21 https://doi.org/10.1007/BF02706356

Kleinbard, Edward, 'Capital Taxation in an Age of Inequality' (2017) 90 *Southern California Law Review* 590–682

'The Lessons of Stateless Income' (2011) 65(1) *Tax Law Review* 99–172

'Stateless Income' (2011) 11(9) *Florida Tax Review* 700–66

Kleven, Henrik, Camille Landais, Mathilde Munoz and Stefanie Stantcheva, 'Taxation and Migration: Evidence and Policy Implications' (2020) 34(2) *Journal of Economic Perspectives* 119–42

Koele, Ineke A, *International Taxation of Philanthropy: Removing Tax Obstacles for International Charities* (Amsterdam: IBFD Publications, 2007)

'Tax Privileges of NGOs and Their Benefactors: A Landlocked Privilege?' in Paul Bater, Frits Hondius and Penina Kessler Lieber (eds.), *The Tax Treatment of NGOs: Legal, Fiscal, and Ethical Standards for Promoting NGOs and Their Activities* (The Hague: Kluwer Law International, 2004), 323–38

Kornhauser, Marjorie E, 'Corporate Regulation and the Origins of the Corporate Income Tax' (1990) 66(1) *Indiana Law Journal* 53–136

'Love, Money, and the IRS: Family, Income-sharing, and the Joint Income Tax Return' (1993) 45(1) *Hastings Law Journal* 63–111

Kostić, Svetislav, 'In Search of the Digital Nomad – Rethinking the Taxation of Employment Income under Tax Treaties' (2019) 11(2) *World Tax Journal* 189–225

Krever, Richard, 'General Report: GAARs' in Michael Lang, Jeffrey Owens, Pasquale Pistone, Alexander Rust, Josef Schuch and Claus Staringer (eds.), *GAARs – A Key Element of Tax Systems in the Post-BEPS World* (Amsterdam: IBFD, 2016), 1–20

Kuhnle, Stein, and Anne Sander, 'The Emergence of the Western Welfare State' in Francis G Castles, Stephan Leibried, Jane Lewis, Herbert Obinger and Christopher Pierson (eds.), *The Oxford Handbook of the Welfare State* (Oxford: Oxford University Press, 2010), 73–92, https://doi.org10.1093/oxfordhb/9780199579396.003.0005

Lahey, Kathleen A, 'The "Capture" of Women in Law and Fiscal Policy: The Tax/Benefit Unit, Gender Equality, and Feminist Ontologies' in Kim Brooks, Åsa Gunnarson, Lisa Philipps and Maria Wersig (eds.), *Challenging Gender Inequality in Tax Policy Making* (London: Hart Publishing, 2011), 11–36

Lang, Joachim, 'Germany' in Maria Teresa Soler Roch (ed.), *Family Taxation in Europe* (Boston: Kluwer Law International, 1999), 55–70

Lang, Michael, 'General Report', in *Double Non-taxation. Cahiers de droit international: Vol 89a* (Rotterdam: International Fiscal Association, 2004)

Lang, Michael, Jeffrey Owens, Jasmin Kollmann and Laura Turcan (eds.), *International Arbitration in Tax Matters* (Amsterdam: IBFD, 2016)

Lang, Michael, Jeffrey Owens, Pasquale Pistone, Alexander Rust, Josef Schuch and Claus Staringer (eds.), *GAARs – A Key Element of Tax Systems in the Post-BEPS World* (Amsterdam: IBFD, 2016)

Lange, Thomas, 'Public Funding of Higher Education When Students and Skilled Workers Are Mobile' (2009) 65(2) *FinanzArchiv* 178-99

Langenmayr, Dominika, and Lennard Zyska, *Escaping the Exchange of Information: Tax Evasion via Citizenship-by-Investment*, CESifo Working Paper 8956 (Munich: CESifo Group, March 2021)

Lawsky, Sarah B, 'On the Edge: Declining Marginal Utility and Tax Policy' (2011) 95 *Minnesota Law Review* 904-52

League of Nations, 'Double Taxation and Tax Evasion: Report – Document C.216.M.85 (London, April 12th, 1927)' in *Legislative History of United States Tax Conventions: Vol 4 Sec 1: League of Nations* (Washington, DC: US Government Printing Office, 1962)

Lebeau, Christine, 'Regional Exchanges and Patterns of Taxation in 18th Century Europe: The Case of the Italian Cadastres' in Holger Nehring and Florian Schui (eds.), *Global Debates about Taxation* (London: Palgrave Macmillan, 2007), 21-35

Lee, Albert, and Martin Rabenort, 'The Changing Role of the Tax Professional' (2009) 20(8) *International Tax Review* 32-4

Leroy, Marc, *Taxation, the State and Society: The Fiscal Sociology of Interventionist Democracy. Public Action: Vol 7* (Brussels: PIE Peter Lang, 2011; trans. from the French edition, 2010)

Levi, Margaret, *Of Rule and Revenue* (Berkeley, CA: University of California Press, 1988)

Levine, Carolyn, and Richard Sansing, 'The Private Foundation Minimum Distribution Requirement and Public Policy' (2014) 36(1) *Journal of the American Tax Association* 165-80

Li, Jinyan, *International Mobility of Highly Skilled Workers in the Canadian Context: Tax Barriers and Reform Options*, Commissioned Reports, Studies and Public Policy Documents Paper 55 (2009), http://digitalcommons.osgoode.yorku.ca/reports/55

Li, Jinyan, Arjin Choi and Cameron Smith, 'Automation and Workers: Re-Imagining the Income Tax for the Digital Age' (2020) 61(1) *Canadian Tax Journal* 99-124

Lignier, Philip, and Chris Evans, 'The Rise and Rise of Tax Compliance Costs for the Small Business Sector in Australia' (2012) 27(3) *Australian Tax Forum* 615-72

Lister, Matthew J, 'A Tax-credit Approach to Addressing Brain Drain' (2017) 62 *Saint Louis University Law Journal* 73-84

Littlewood, Michael, 'Capital Gains Taxes — A Comparative Survey' in Michael Littlewood and Craig Elliffe (eds.), *Capital Gains Taxation: A Comparative Analysis of Key Issues* (Cheltenham: Elgar Publishing, 2017), 1-29

Lledó, Victor, Sungwook Yoon, Xiangying Fang, Samba Mbaye and Young Kim, *Fiscal Rules at a Glance: The IMF Fiscal Rules Dataset 1985-2015* (Washington, DC: International Monetary Fund, 2017)

Manifesto for the Democratization of Europe, 'A Budget for Europe', http://tdem.eu/en/a-budget-for-europe/, accessed 26 March 2022

Mann, Frederick A, 'The Doctrine of International Jurisdiction Revisited after 20 Years' in *Collected Courses of the Hague Academy of International Law: Vol 186* (The Hague: Hague Academy of International Law, 1984), http://dx.doi.org/10.1163/1875-8096_pplrdc_A9789024731770_01

Further Studies in International Law (Oxford: Clarendon Press, 1990)

Margalioth, Yoram, 'Taxation, International' in *Max Planck Encyclopedias of International Law* (Oxford: Oxford University Press, 2011)

Marian, Omri, 'Are Cryptocurrencies "Super" Tax Havens?' (2013) 112 *Michigan Law Review First Impressions* 38–48

Marples, Donald, *Taxation of Carried Interest* (Washington, DC: Congressional Research Service, 9 July 2020), https://crsreports.congress.gov/product/pdf/R/R46447

Marriott, Lisa, *The Politics of Retirement Savings Taxation: A Trans-Tasman Comparison* (Sydney, NSW: CCH Australia, 2010)

Marshall, Lydia M, 'The Levying of the Hearth Tax, 1662–1688' (1936) 51(204) *The English Historical Review* 628–46

Marshall, WV, *A Curb to Predatory Wealth* (1847; 2nd ed, New York: RF Fenno, 1912), http://hdl.handle.net/2027/uc2.ark:/13960/t1sf2q66q

Martin, Isaac William, Ajay Mehrotra and Monica Prasad, *The New Fiscal Sociology: Taxation in Comparative and Historical Perspective* (New York: Cambridge University Press, 2009)

Martinelli, Luke, *The Fiscal and Distributional Implication of Alternative Universal BI Schemes in the UK*, IPR Working Paper (Bath: Institute for Policy Research, 2017)

Mascagni, Giulia, 'From the Lab to the Field: A Review of Tax Experiments' (2018) 32(2) *Journal of Economic Surveys* 273–301

Mason, Edward, 'Corporation' in David L Sills (ed.), *International Encyclopedia of the Social Sciences: Vol 3* (New York: Macmillan and Free Press, 1968), 396

Mason, Ruth, 'Citizenship Taxation' (2016) 89 *Southern California Law Review* 169–240

'The Transformation of International Tax' (2020) 114(3) *American Journal of International Law* 353–402

Mayer, Lloyd Hitosi, and Joseph R Ganahl, 'Taxing Social Enterprise' (2014) 66(2) *Stanford Law Review* 387–442

McCaffery, Edward J, 'Taxation and the Family: A Fresh Look at Behavioral Gender Biases in the Code' (1993) 40 *UCLA Law Review* 983–1060

McCarthy, Kathleen D, 'Blurring the Boundaries. A Review Essay' (2010) 52 *Comparative Studies in Society and History* 939–46

McDaniel, Paul, 'Comments', in Joseph Pechman, *What Should Be Taxed: Income or Expenditure?* (Washington, DC: Brookings Institution, 1980), 282–3

McDaniel, Paul, and Stanley Surrey (eds.), *International Aspects of Tax Expenditures: A Comparative Study* (Cambridge, MA: Harvard University Press, 1985)

McKerchar, Margaret, Kristen Meyer and Stewart Karlinsky, 'Making Progress in Tax Simplification: A Comparison of the United States, Australia, New Zealand and the United Kingdom' in Margaret McKerchar and Michael Walpole (eds.), *Further Global Challenges in Tax Administration* (Bath: Fiscal Publications, 2006), 359–75.

McQuaig, Linda, *Behind Closed Doors: How the Rich Won Control of Canada's Tax System ... and Ended Up Richer* (Toronto: Viking, 1989)

Mehrotra, Ajay K, *Making the Modern American Fiscal State: Law, Politics, and the Rise of Progressive Taxation, 1877–1929* (New York: Cambridge University Press, 2013)

Messere, Ken, *Tax Policy in OECD Countries: Choices and Conflicts* (Amsterdam: IBFD Publishing, 1993)

'Taxation in Ten Industrialized Countries over the Last Decade: An Overview' (1995) 10 *Tax Notes International* 512–35

Mill, John Stuart, *Principles of Political Economy* (London: Longmans, 1848), www.econlib.org/library/Mill/mlP.html?chapter_num=1#book-reader

Millane, Emily, and Miranda Stewart, 'Behavioural Insights in Tax Collection: Getting the Legal Settings Right' (2019) 16(3) *eJournal of Tax Research* 500–35

Millar, Jane, and Peter Whiteford, 'Timing It Right or Timing It Wrong: How Should Income-Tested Benefits Deal with Changes in Circumstances?' (2020) 28(1) *Journal of Poverty and Social Justice* 3–20

Milne, Janet, 'Environmental Taxes and Fees: Wrestling with Theory' in Larry Kreiser, Soocheol Lee Kazuhiro Ueta, Janet E Milne and Hope Ashiabor (eds.), *Environmental Taxation and Green Fiscal Reform* (Cheltenham: Edward Elgar, 2014), 5–24

Mirrlees, James A, 'An Exploration in the Theory of Optimum Income Taxation' (1971) 38(2) *The Review of Economic Studies* 175–208

Mirrlees, James A, Stuart Adam, Tim Besley, Richard Blundell, Stephen Bond, Robert Chote, Malcolm Gammie, Paul Johnson, Gareth Myles and James M Poterba, *Tax by Design. Mirrlees Review: Vol 2* (Oxford: Oxford University Press, 2011), https://ifs.org.uk/publications/5353

Mirrlees Review, *Reforming the Tax System for the 21st Century*, 2 vols (London: Institute for Fiscal Studies, 2010), www.ifs.org.uk/publications/mirrleesreview

Mitchell, William, L Randall Wray and Martin Watts, *Macroeconomics* (London: Macmillan International, 2019)

Modigliani, Franco, 'Life-Cycle, Individual Thrift, and the Wealth of Nations' (1976) 76(3) *American Economic Review* 297–313

'The Role of Intergenerational Transfers and Life-Cycle Saving in the Accumulation of Wealth' (1998) 2(2) *Journal of Economic Perspectives* 15–20

Moffitt, Robert A, 'The Negative Income Tax and the Evolution of US Welfare Policy' (2003) 17(3) *Journal of Economic Perspectives* 119–40

Monson, Andrew, and Walter Scheidel (eds.), *Fiscal Regimes and the Political Economy of Premodern States* (New York: Cambridge University Press, 2015)

Moore, David, Katerina Hadzi-Miceva and Nilda Bullain, 'A Comparative Overview of Public Benefit Status in Europe' (2008) 11 *International Journal of Not-for-Profit Law* 5–35

Moore, David, and Douglas Rutzen, 'Legal Framework for Global Philanthropy: Barriers and Opportunities' (2011) 13(1–2) *The International Journal of Not-for-Profit Law* www.icnl.org/resources/research/ijnl/legal-framework-for-global-philanthropy-barriers-and-opportunities

Moran, Beverly, 'Adam Smith and the Search for an Ideal Tax System' in Isaac W Martin, Ajay Mehrotra and Monica Prasad (eds.), *The New Fiscal Sociology: Taxation in Comparative and Historical Perspective* (Cambridge, UK: Cambridge University Press, 2009), 201–15

Moran, Beverly I, and William Whitford, 'A Black Critique of the Internal Revenue Code' (1996) *Wisconsin Law Review* 751–820

Morel, Nathalie, Chloé Touzet and Michael Zemmour, 'Fiscal Welfare in Europe: Why Should We Care and What Do We Know So Far?' (2018) 28(5) *Journal of European Social Policy* 549–60

References

Morgan, Bronwen, and Karen Yeung, *An Introduction to Law and Regulation* (Cambridge, UK: Cambridge University Press, 2007)

Mosquera Valderrama, Irma, 'Legitimacy and the Making of International Tax Law: The Challenges of Multilateralism' (2015) 7 *World Tax Journal* 343–82

Mumford, Ann, *Fiscal Sociology at the Centenary: UK Perspectives on Budgeting, Taxation and Austerity* (London: Palgrave Macmillan UK, 2019)

Munnell, Alicia H, 'The Couple versus the Individual under the Federal Personal Income Tax' in Henry J Aaron and Michael J Boskin (eds.), *The Economics of Taxation* (Washington, DC: Brookings Institution, 1980), 247–80

Murphy, Liam, and Thomas Nagel, *The Myth of Ownership: Taxes and Justice* (Oxford: Oxford University Press, 2002)

Murray, Ian, 'Charitable Fundraising through Commercial Activities: The Final Word or a Pyrrhic Victory?' (2008) 11(2) *Journal of Australian Taxation* 138–207

Musgrave, Peggy, 'Comments on Two Musgravian Concepts' (2008) 32 *Journal of Economics and Finance* 340–7

'Sovereignty, Entitlement, and Cooperation in International Taxation' (2001) 26 *Brooklyn Journal of International Law* 1335–56

United States Taxation of Foreign Investment: Issues and Arguments (Cambridge, MA: International Tax Program, Harvard Law School, 1969)

Musgrave, Richard A, *The Future of Fiscal Policy: A Reassessment* (Leuven: Leuven University Press, 1978)

'The Nature of the Fiscal State: The Roots of My Thinking' in James M Buchanan and Richard A Musgrave, *Public Finance and Public Choice: Two Contrasting Visions of the State* (Cambridge, MA: MIT Press, 1999), 29–49

Public Finance in a Democratic Society. The Foundations of Taxation and Expenditure: Vol III (Northampton, MA: Edward Elgar, 2000)

'Schumpeter's Crisis of the Tax State: An Essay in Fiscal Sociology' (1992) 2(2) *Journal of Evolutionary Economics* 89–113

Social Science, Ethics, and the Role of the Public Sector (Cambridge, UK: Cambridge University Press, 1990)

The Theory of Public Finance: A Study in Public Economy (New York: McGraw-Hill, 1959)

Musgrave, Richard A, and Peggy Musgrave, *Public Finance in Theory and Practice*, 5th ed (New York: McGraw-Hill, 1989)

Musgrave, Richard A, and Alan T Peacock (eds.), *Classics in the Theory of Public Finance* (New York: Palgrave Macmillan, 1958)

Mutén, Leif, 'The Development of Capital Income Taxation in Sweden 1928–2002' (2003) 44 *Scandinavian Studies in Law* 259–75

'Dual Income Tax: The Scandinavian Experience' in John Head and Richard Krever (eds.), *Company Tax Systems* (Melbourne: Australian Tax Research Foundation, 1997), 271–84

Nagel, Thomas, 'The Problem of Global Justice' (2005) 33(2) *Philosophy and Public Affairs* 113–47

National Center for Charitable Statistics (US), 'The Nonprofit Sector Brief 2019' (18 June 2020), https://nccs.urban.org/project/nonprofit-sector-brief

National Taxpayer Advocate (US), *Annual Report to Congress* (Washington, DC: Taxpayer Advocate Service, 2019), https://taxpayeradvocate.irs.gov/reports/2019-annual-report-to-congress

Neal, Larry, 'Conclusion: The Monetary, Fiscal, and Political Architecture of Europe, 1815–1914' in José Luis Cardoso and Pedro Lains (eds.), *Paying for the Liberal State: The Rise of Public Finance in Nineteenth-Century Europe* (New York: Cambridge University Press, 2010), 279–302

Neely, Michelle C, and Larry D Sherrer, 'A Look at Corporate Inversions, Inside and Out' (2017) *The Regional Economist* 1–3, www.stlouisfed.org/~/media/publications/regional-economist/2017/first_quarter_2017/corporate_inversions.pdf

Nehring, Holger, and Florian Schui (eds.), *Global Debates about Taxation* (London: Palgrave Macmillan, 2007)

Newsweek, 'The Richest People on Earth', 13 January 2020, citing Statista: Forbes: The World's Billionaires 2019, www.newsweek.com/bill-gates-net-worth-wealth-since-microsoft-cascade-investment-bill-melinda-gates-foundation-1481482#slideshow/1559557

Nienaber, Michael, 'Germany Eyes Fiscal U-turn with New Debt to Finance Climate Plan', Reuters, 8 August 2019, www.reuters.com/article/us-germany-debt-exclusive/exclusive-germany-eyes-fiscal-u-turn-with-new-debt-to-finance-climate-plan-idUSKCN1UY1NS

Noonan, Chris, and Victoria Plekhanova, 'Digital Services Tax: Lessons from the Section 301 Investigation' (2021) 2021(1) *British Tax Review* 83–115

Norges Bank Investment Management, nbim.no/en/, accessed 16 March 2022

Nussbaum, Martha, 'Capabilities and Social Justice' (2002) 4(2) *International Studies Review* 123–35

O'Brien, Denis P (ed.), *The History of Taxation*, 8 vols (Brookfield, VT: Pickering & Chatto, 1999)

O'Brien, PK, 'British Incomes and Property in the Early Nineteenth Century' (1959) 12(2) *Economic History Review* Second Series 255–67

O'Connor, James, *The Fiscal Crisis of the State* (New York: St Martin's Press, 1973)

O'Neill, Martin, 'Power, Predistribution, and Social Justice' (2020) 95 *Philosophy* 63–91

O'Neill, Martin, and Shepley Orr (eds.), *Taxation: Philosophical Perspectives* (Oxford: Oxford University Press, 2018)

O'Sullivan, Arthur, Terri A Sexton and Steven M Sheffrin, *Property Taxes & Tax Revolts: The Legacy of Proposition 13* (Cambridge, UK: Cambridge University Press, 1995)

Oates, Wallace, and Robert Schwab, 'The Window Tax: A Case Study in Excess Burden' (2015) 29(1) *Journal of Economic Perspectives* 163–80

Obinger, Herbert, and Uwe Wagschal, 'Social Expenditure and Revenues' in Francis G Castles, Stephan Leibried, Jane Lewis, Herbert Obinger and Christopher Pierson (eds.), *The Oxford Handbook of the Welfare State* (Oxford: Oxford University Press, 2010), 333–52, https://doi.org10.1093/oxfordhb/9780199579396.003.0005

OECD, *Action 15: A Mandate for the Development of a Multilateral Instrument on Tax Treaty Measures to Tackle BEPS* (Paris: OECD, 2015), www.oecd.org/ctp/beps-action-15-mandate-for-development-of-multilateral-instrument.pdf

Action Plan on Base Erosion and Profit Shifting (Paris: OECD Publishing, 2013), https://doi.org/10.1787/9789264202719-en

Addressing the Tax Challenges of the Digital Economy: Action 1 Report (Paris: OECD, 2014), www.oecd-ilibrary.org/taxation/addressing-the-tax-challenges-of-the-digital-economy_9789264218789-en

'Average Wages', https://data.oecd.org/earnwage/average-wages.htm accessed 7 March 2022

'BEPS: Action 13 Country-by-Country Reporting', www.oecd.org/tax/beps/beps-actions/action13/, accessed 7 March 2022

A Borderless World: Realising the Potential of Electronic Commerce (Paris: OECD, 1998)

Budgeting and Public Expenditures in OECD Countries 2019 (Paris: OECD Publishing, 2019), https://doi.org/10.1787/9789264307957-en

Budgeting for the Future, Working Paper No 95 (Paris: OECD, 1997)

Consumption Tax Trends 2020 (Paris: OECD, 2020), www.oecd-ilibrary.org/taxation/consumption-tax-trends-2020_152def2d-en

Countering Harmful Tax Practices More Effectively, Taking into Account Transparency and Substance: Action 5: 2015 Final Report (Paris: OECD, 2015), http://dx.doi.org/10.1787/9789264241190-en

'Draft Double Taxation Convention on Income and on Capital' (1963), www.oecd-ilibrary.org/taxation/draft-double-taxation-convention-on-income-and-capital_9789264073241-en

Electronic Commerce: Taxation Framework Conditions. A Report by the Committee on Fiscal Affairs, Ottawa (8 November 1998),www.oecd.org/ctp/consumption/1923256.pdf

Electronic Commerce: The Challenges to Tax Authorities and Taxpayers (Paris: OECD, 1997), www.oecd.org/tax/treaties/1923232.pdf

'Fiscal Sustainability: The Contribution of Fiscal Rules' (2002) 72 *OECD Economic Outlook* 117–36

Focus on Top Incomes and Taxation in OECD Countries: Was the Crisis a Game Changer? (Paris: OECD, 2014), www.oecd.org/social/OECD2014-FocusOnTopIncomes.pdf

'Global Forum on Transparency and Exchange of Information for Tax Purposes', www.oecd.org/tax/transparency/, accessed 28 March 2022

Green Budgeting in OECD Countries (Paris: OECD Publishing, 2021), https://doi.org/10.1787/acf5d047-en

Harmful Tax Competition (Paris: OECD, 1998)

Implementation of the Ottawa Taxation Framework Conditions (Paris: OECD, 2003), www.oecd.org/tax/administration/20499630.pdf

'International Framework for the CRS',www.oecd.org/tax/automatic-exchange/international-framework-for-the-crs/, accessed 23 March 2022

International Tax Avoidance and Evasion: Four Related Studies (Paris: OECD, 1987)

International VAT/GST Guidelines (Paris: OECD Publishing, 2017)

Making Dispute Resolution Mechanisms More Effective: Action 14 Final Report (Paris: OECD, 2015), https://read.oecd.org/10.1787/9789264241633-en?format=pdf

'Model Convention with Respect to Taxes on Income and on Capital' (latest edition 2017), with Commentary,www.oecd.org/tax/model-tax-convention-on-income-and-on-capital-full-version-9a5b369e-en.htm

'Model Double Taxation Convention on Income and Capital' (1977), www.oecd-ilibrary.org/taxation/model-double-taxation-convention-on-income-and-capital_9789264055919-en

'Model Tax Convention on Income and on Capital 2017, Commentary on Article 4', https://doi.org/10.1787/mtc_cond-2017-en

'OECD Best Practices for Budget Transparency' (2002) 1(3) *OECD Journal on Budgeting* 7

'OECD Income and Wealth Distribution Databases', www.oecd.org/social/income-distribution-database.htm, accessed 16 March 2022

'OECD Releases Peer Review Documents for Assessment of BEPS Minimum Standards (Actions 5 and 13)', 1 February 2017, www.oecd.org/tax/beps/oecd-releases-peer-review-documents-for-assessment-of-beps-minimum-standards-actions-5-and-13.htm

'OECD.Stat', https://stats.oecd.org/, accessed 16 March 2022

'OECD Tax Statistics – Comparative Tables 1965–2018', https://doi.org/10.1787/data-00262-en

Paid Sick Leave to Protect Income, Health and Jobs through the COVID-19 Crisis, OECD Policy Brief (Paris: OECD, 2 July 2020)

Preventing the Granting of Treaty Benefits in Inappropriate Circumstances: Action 6 Final Report (Paris: OECD, 2015), https://doi.org/10.1787/9789264241695-en

Private Philanthropy for Development (Paris: OECD Publishing, 2018), https://doi.org/10.1787/9789264085190-en

'Progress towards a Fairer Global Tax System Continues as Additional Countries Bring Their Preferential Tax Regimes in Line with International Standards' (5 August 2021), www.oecd.org/tax/beps/progress-towards-a-fairer-global-tax-system-continues-as-additional-countries-bring-their-preferential-tax-regimes-in-line-with-international-standards.htm

The Pursuit of Gender Equality: An Uphill Battle (Paris: OECD, 2017), https://doi.org/10.1787/9789264281318-en

'Recommendation of the Council on the Application of Value Added Tax/Goods and Services Tax to the International Trade in Services and Intangibles' OECD/LEGAL/0430 (27 September 2016), https://legalinstruments.oecd.org/en/instruments/OECD-LEGAL-0430

Report on Abuse of Charities for Money-Laundering and Tax Evasion, Tax Crimes and Money Laundering Sub-Group of Working Party No 8 (Paris: OECD, 2009), www.oecd.org/tax/exchange-of-tax-information/42232037.pdf

Revenue Statistics 2019 (Paris: OECD, 2019), www.oecd.org/economy/revenue-statistics-2522770x.htm

'Revenue Statistics – Tax Structures', www.oecd.org/ctp/tax-policy/revenue-statistics-tax-structures.htm, accessed 16 March 2022

The Role and Design of Net Wealth Taxes in the OECD, OECD Tax Policy Studies No 26 (Paris: OECD Publishing, 2018), https://doi.org/10.1787/19900538

Seoul Declaration: Third Meeting of the OECD Forum on Tax Administration (14–15 September 2006) (Paris: OECD, 2006), www.oecd.org/tax/administration/37415572.pdf

Strengthening SMEs and Entrepreneurship for Productivity and Inclusive Growth (Paris: OECD, 2019), https://doi.org/10.1787/c19b6f97-en

Tax Administration 2017: Comparative Information on OECD and Other Advanced and Emerging Economies (Paris: OECD, 2017), https://doi.org/10.1787/tax_admin-2017-en

Tax Administration 2019: Comparative Information on OECD and Other Advanced and Emerging Economies(Paris: OECD Publishing, 2019), https://doi.org/10.1787/74d162b6-en

'Tax and Fiscal Policy in Response to the Coronavirus Crisis: Strengthening Confidence and Resilience' (updated 19 May 2020), www.oecd.org/coronavirus/policy-responses/tax-and-fiscal-policy-in-response-to-the-coronavirus-crisis-strengthening-confidence-and-resilience-60f640a8/

Tax Expenditures in OECD Countries (Paris: OECD, 2010), https://doi.org/10.1787/9789264076907-en

Taxation of Household Savings (Paris: OECD, 2018), www.oecd.org/ctp/taxation-of-household-savings-9789264289536-en.htm

Taxing Wages (Paris: OECD Publishing, 2020), https://doi.org/10.1787/20725124

Towards Global Tax Cooperation (Paris: OECD, 2001), https://doi.org/10.1787/9789264184541-en

Transfer Pricing Documentation and Country-by-Country Reporting: Action 13 – 2015 Final Report (Paris: OECD, 2015), https://read.oecd.org/10.1787/9789264241480-en?format=pdf

Transparency and Exchange of Information for Tax Purposes: Multilateral Co-operation Changing the World: 10th Anniversary Report (Paris: OECD, 2019), www.oecd.org/tax/transparency/global-forum-10-years-report.pdf

OECD Directorate for Legal Affairs, *Multilateral Convention to Implement Tax Treaty Related Measures to Prevent Base Erosion and Profit Shifting: Functioning under Public International Law* (Paris: OECD, 2015)

OECD Forum on Tax Administration, www.oecd.org/tax/forum-on-tax-administration/about/, accessed 28 March 2022

OECD Forum on Tax Administration, '2020 FTA "Amsterdam" Plenary Communique' (2020), www.oecd.org/tax/forum-on-tax-administration/events/2020/forum-on-tax-administration-communique-2020.pdf

'Joint International Taskforce on Shared Intelligence and Collaboration', www.oecd.org/tax/forum-on-tax-administration/about/jitsic/, accessed 28 March 2022

OECD FTA Tax Debt Management Network Workshop (March 2020), Report of the Presentations, 4–5 March 2020 (Paris: OECD, 2020), www.oecd.org/tax/forum-on-tax-administration/events/report-fta-workshop-tax-debt-management-network.pdf

Study into the Role of Tax Intermediaries (Paris: OECD, 2008), www.oecd.org/tax/administration/39882938.pdf

Tax Administration in OECD and Selected Non-OECD Countries, Comparative Information Series (Paris: OECD, 2011), www.oecd.org/tax/forum-on-tax-administration/publications-and-products/comparative/CIS-2010.pdf,

OECD/G20 Inclusive Framework on BEPS, *Statement on a Two-Pillar Solution to Address the Tax Challenges Arising from the Digitalisation of the Economy* (8 October 2021), www.oecd.org/tax/beps/statement-on-a-two-pillar-solution-to-address-the-tax-challenges-arising-from-the-digitalisation-of-the-economy-october-2021.htm

Working Party of Senior Budget Officials, '*Draft Principles for Independent Fiscal Institutions: Background Document No 3*' (Paper presented at the Parliamentary Budget Officials and Independent Fiscal Institutions 4th Annual Meeting, Paris, 23–24 February 2012)

Oei, Shu-Yi, and Ring, Diane, 'Can Sharing Be Taxed?' (2016) 93 *Washington University Law Review* 989–1069

Office of the US Trade Representative, 'USTR Announces, and Immediately Suspends, Tariffs in Section 301 Digital Services Taxes Investigations' (2 June 2021), https://ustr.gov/about-us/policy-offices/press-office/press-releases/2021/june/ustr-announces-and-immediately-suspends-tariffs-section-301-digital-services-taxes-investigations

Ogle, Vanessa, 'Archipelago Capitalism' (2017) 122(5) *American Historical Review* 1431–58

Oguttu, Annet Wanyana, and Ann Kayis-Kumar, 'Curtailing Aggressive Tax Planning: The Case for Introducing Mandatory Disclosure Rules in Australia' (2019) 17(1) *eJournal of Tax Research* 83–104 (part 1); and (2020) 17(2) *eJournal of Tax Research* 233–57 (part 2)

Ooi, Vincent, and Glendon Goh, *Taxation of Automation and Artificial Intelligence as a Tool of Labour Policy*, SMU Centre for AI & Data Governance Research Paper No 2019/01 (1 November 2018), https://ssrn.com/abstract=3322306

Ortiz-Ospina, Esteban, and Max Roser, 'Taxation', Our World in Data (2016), https://ourworldindata.org/taxation

Owen, David, *English Philanthropy 1660–1960* (Cambridge, MA: Harvard University Press, 1964)

Oxman, Bernard H, 'Jurisdiction of States' in *Max Planck Encyclopedias of International Law* (Oxford: Oxford University Press, 2007)

Pagone, G Tony, *Tax Disputes* (Annandale, NSW: Federation Press, 2018)

Painter, Antony, and Chris Thoung, *Creative Citizen, Creative State: the Principled and Pragmatic Case for a Universal Basic Income* (London: Royal Society for the Encouragement of Arts, Manufactures and Commerce, 2015), www.thersa.org/discover/publications-and-articles/reports/basic-income

Palan, Ronen, 'Trying to Have Your Cake and Eating It: How and Why the State System Has Created Offshore' (1998) 42 *International Studies Quarterly* 635–44

Paris, Roland, 'The Globalization of Taxation? Electronic Commerce and the Transformation of the State' (2003) 47(2) *International Studies Quarterly* 153–82

Parker, Louise, 'Mutual Assistance in the Collection of Taxes' (2017) 71(9) *Bulletin for International Taxation* 1

Parliament of the Commonwealth of Australia, Senate, 'Revised Explanatory Memorandum, Taxation Laws Amendment Bill (No. 2) 2003 (Cth)', 2003, http://www5.austlii.edu.au/au/legis/cth/bill_em/tlab22003285/memo1.html

Parliament of the Commonwealth of Australia, Senate Economic References Committee, 'An Inquiry into Tax Avoidance and Aggressive Minimization by Corporations Registered in Australia and Multinational Corporations Operating in Australia', www.aph.gov.au/Parliamentary_Business/Committees/Senate/Economics/Corporatetax45th, accessed 24 March 2022

Parliament of the Commonwealth of Australia, Senate Inquiry, 'Centrelink's Compliance Program', www.aph.gov.au/Parliamentary_Business/Committees/Senate/Community_Affairs/Centrelinkcompliance, accessed 24 March 2022

Parliament of the United Kingdom, Public Accounts Committee, 'Tax Avoidance: The Role of Large Accountancy Firms: Follow-up' (6 February 2015), https://publications.parliament.uk/pa/cm201415/cmselect/cmpubacc/1057/105706.htm

Patriquin, Larry, *Inventing Tax Rage: Misinformation in the National Post* (Halifax: Fernwood Publishing, 2004)

Pawson, Ray, Lesley Owen and Geoff Wong, 'Known Knowns, Known Unknowns, Unknown Unknowns: The Predicament of Evidence-Based Policy' (2011) 32(4) *American Journal of Evaluation* 518–46

Pechman, Joseph, *What Should Be Taxed: Income or Expenditure?* (Washington, DC: Brookings Institution, 1980)

Peloza, John, and Piers Steel, 'The Price Elasticities of Charitable Contributions: A Meta-Analysis' (2005) 24 *Journal of Public Policy and Marketing* 260–72

Peltzman, Sam, 'The Growth of Government' (1980) 23(2) *Journal of Law & Economics* 209–87

Perry, J Harvey, *Taxes, Tariffs and Subsidies. A History of Canadian Fiscal Development: Vol 1* (Toronto: University of Toronto Press, 1955)

Peters, B Guy, *The Politics of Taxation: A Comparative Perspective* (Cambridge, MA: Blackwell, 1991)

Pfanner, Eric, 'Starbucks Offers to Pay More British Tax Than Required', *New York Times*, 6 December 2012, www.nytimes.com/2012/12/07/business/global/07iht-uktax07.html?_r=0

Philipps, Lisa, 'Discursive Deficits: A Feminist Perspective on the Power of Technical Knowledge in Fiscal Law and Policy' (1996) 11(1) *Canadian Journal of Law and Society* 141–76

'The Rise of Balanced Budget Laws in Canada: Legislating Fiscal (Ir)responsibility' (1996) 34 *Osgoode Hall Law Journal* 681–740

'Tax Law and Social Reproduction: The Gender of Fiscal Policy in an Age of Privatization' in Brenda Cossman and Judy Fudge (eds.), *Privatization, Law and the Challenge to Feminism* (Toronto: University of Toronto Press, 2002), 41–85

Philipps, Lisa, Neil Brooks and Jinyan Li (eds.), *Tax Expenditures: State of the Art* (Toronto: Canadian Tax Foundation, 2011)

Philipps, Lisa, and Miranda Stewart, 'Fiscal Transparency: Global Norms, Domestic Laws, and the Politics of Budgets' (2009) 34(3) *Brooklyn Journal of International Law* 797–860

Picciotto, Sol, *International Business Taxation: A Study in the Internationalization of Business Regulation* (London: Weidenfeld & Nicolson, 1992)

Piketty, Thomas, *Capital in the Twenty-First Century*, trans. Arthur Goldhammer (Cambridge, MA: Harvard University Press, 2014)

Piketty, Thomas, and Emmanuel Saez, 'Income Inequality in the United States, 1913-1998' (2003) 118 *Quarterly Journal of Economics* 1–39

Piper, Anne-Marie (ed.), *Charity Law: Jurisdictional Comparisons* (London: Thomson Reuters, 2012)

Pistone, Pasquale, 'Coordinating the Action of Regional and Global Players during the Shift from Bilateralism to Multilateralism in International Tax Law' (2014) 6 *World Tax Journal* 1–9

(ed.), *Tax Procedures* (Amsterdam: IBFD, 2020)

Pistone, Pasquale, and Philip Baker (eds.), *IBFD Yearbook on Taxpayers' Rights* (Amsterdam: IBFD, 2020)

Pistone, Pasquale, and Jan JP de Goede (eds.), *Flexible Multi-tier Dispute Resolution in International Tax Disputes* (Amsterdam: IBFD, 2020)

Pistor, Katharina, *The Code of Capital: How the Law Creates Wealth and Inequality* (Princeton, NJ: Princeton University Press, 2019)

Pitrone, Federica, 'Tax Residence of Individuals within the European Union: Finding New Solutions to Old Problems' (2016) 8(3) *World Tax Journal* 357–77

Polanyi, Karl, *The Great Transformation: The Political and Economic Origins of Our Time*, 2nd ed (Boston, MA: Beacon Press, 2001)

Posner, Paul, and Chung-Keun Park, 'Role of the Legislature in the Budget Process: Recent Trends and Innovations' (2007) 7(3) *OECD Journal on Budgeting* 83 www.oecd.org/gov/budgeting/43411793.pdf

Poterba, James, and Todd Sinai, 'Tax Expenditures for Owner-Occupied Housing: Deductions for Property Taxes and Mortgage Interest and the Exclusion of Imputed Rental Income' (2008) 98(2) *American Economic Review* 84–9

Prebble, John, 'Ectopia, Tax Law and International Taxation' (1997) 5 *British Tax Review* 383–403

'Why Is Tax Law Incomprehensible?' (1994) 4 *British Tax Review* 380–93

Prebble, Rebecca, and John Prebble, 'Does the Use of General Anti-avoidance Rules to Combat Tax Avoidance Breach Principles of the Rule of Law? A Comparative Study' (2010) 55 *Saint Louis University Law Journal* 21–45

President Biden (US), Office of Management and Budget, *Budget of the US Government* (Washington, DC: Office of Management and Budget, 2022), www.whitehouse.gov/omb/budget/

President's Advisory Panel on Federal Tax Reform (US), *Simple, Fair and Pro-growth: Proposals to Fix America's Tax System* (2005), https://home.treasury.gov/system/files/131/Report-Fix-Tax-System-2005.pdf

PWC, 'Global Top 100 Companies by Market Capitalisation' (March 2021), www.pwc.com/gx/en/services/audit-assurance/publications/global-top-100-companies.html

van Raad, Kees, and Frank Pötgens, 'The Netherlands' in Hugh J Ault, Brian J Arnold and Graeme Cooper, *Comparative Income Taxation*, 4th ed (Alphen aan den Rijn, Netherlands: Wolters Kluwer, 2020)

Radulescu, Doina, and Michael Stimmelmayr, *ACE vs CBIT: Which Is Better for Investment and Welfare?*, CESifo Working Paper No 1850 (Munich: CESifo Group, 2006)

Ratha, Dilip, 'What Are Remittances?' *Finance & Development*, www.imf.org/external/Pubs/FT/fandd/basics/pdf/ratha-remittances.pdf, accessed 24 March 2022

Ratha, Dilip, Supriyo De and Kirsten Schuettler, 'Why Taxing Remittances Is a Bad Idea', World Bank Blogs, 24 March 2017, https://blogs.worldbank.org/peoplemove/why-taxing-remittances-bad-idea

Reich, Robert, Chiara Cordelli and Lucy Bernholz (eds.), *Philanthropy in Democratic Societies: History, Institutions, Values* (Chicago: University of Chicago Press, 2016)

Reid, Richard, and Linda Botterill, 'The Multiple Meanings of "Resilience": An Overview of the Literature' (2013) 72(1) *Australian Journal of Public Administration* 31–40

Reimer, Ekkehart, and Alexander Rust (eds.), *Klaus Vogel on Double Taxation Conventions*, 4th rev ed (Alphen aan den Rijn, Netherlands: Kluwer Law International, 2015)

Rembar, Charles, 'The Practice of Taxes' (1954) 54 *Columbia Law Review* 338–58

Rhys-Williams, Juliet, *Taxation and Incentive* (London: William Hodge and Co, 1953)

Richman, Peggy, *Taxation of Foreign Income: An Economic Analysis* (Baltimore, MD: Johns Hopkins Press, 1963)

Rider, Cameron, Lillian Hong, Ann O'Connell, Miranda Stewart and Michelle Herring, *Taxation Problems in the Commercialisation of Intellectual Property*, IPRIA Report 2006/01 (Parkville: Intellectual Property Research Institute of Australia, 2006)

Ring, Diane, 'Who Is Making International Tax Policy? International Organizations as Power Players in a High Stakes World' (2009–10) 33 *Fordham International Law Journal* 649–722

Rixen, Thomas, *The Political Economy of International Tax Governance* (New York: Palgrave Macmillan, 2008)

Rixen, Thomas, and Ingo Rohlfing, 'The Institutional Choice of Bilateralism and Multilateralism in International Trade and Taxation' (2007) 12 *International Negotiation* 389–414

Roberts, Alasdair, *The Logic of Discipline: Global Capitalism and the Architecture of Government* (Oxford: Oxford University Press, 2010)

Roeleveld, Jennifer, 'Article 27: Assistance in the Collection of Taxes' in Pasquale Pistone (ed.), *Global Tax Treaty Commentaries* (Amsterdam: IBFD Tax Research Platform, 2019)

Roin, Julie, 'Taxation without Coordination' (2002) 31 *Journal of Legal Studies* S61–S94

Rose-Ackermann, Susan, 'Unfair Competition and Corporate Income Taxation' (1982) 34 *Stanford Law Review* 1017–39

Rosen, Harvey S, 'Entrepreneurship and Taxation: Empirical Evidence' in Vesa Kanniainen and Christian Keuschnigg (eds.), *Venture Capital, Entrepreneurship and Public Policy*, CESifo Seminar Series (Cambridge, MA: MIT Press, 2005)

Rosenbloom, H David, 'International Tax Arbitrage and the International Tax System' (1998) 53 *Tax Law Review* 137–66

  'What's Trade Got to Do with It' (1994) 49 *Tax Law Review* 593–8

  'Where's the Pony? Reflections on the Making of International Tax Policy' (2009) 57 (3) *Canadian Tax Journal* 489–503

Rosenbloom, H David, and Stanley Langbein, 'United States Tax Treaty Policy: An Overview' (1981) 19 *Columbia Journal of Transnational Law* 359–406

Ruding, Onno, *Report of the Committee of Independent Experts on Company Taxation* (Luxembourg: Office for Official Publications of the European Communities, 1992)

  'Tax Harmonization in Europe: The Pros and Cons, The David R. Tillinghast Lecture' (2000) 54 *Tax Law Review* 101–10

Rudnick, Rebecca S, and Richard K Gordon, 'Taxation of Wealth' in Victor Thuronyi (ed.), *Tax Law Design and Drafting: Vol 1* (Washington, DC: International Monetary Fund, 1996), www.imf.org/external/pubs/nft/1998/tlaw/eng/ch10.pdf

Sadiq, Kerrie, and Catherine Richardson, 'Tax Concessions for Charities: Competitive Neutrality, the Tax Base and "Public Goods" Choice' (2010) 25(4) *Australian Tax Forum* 401–16

Saez, Emmanuel, Joel Slemrod and Seth H Giertz, 'The Elasticity of Taxable Income with Respect to Marginal Tax Rates: A Critical Review' (2012) 50(1) *Journal of Economic Literature* 3–50

Saez, Emmanuel, and Gabriel Zucman, *Progressive Wealth Taxation*, Brookings Papers on Economic Activity (Washington, DC: Brookings Institution, Fall 2019), 437–533

Sahm, Claudia, *Direct Stimulus Payments to Individuals* (Washington, DC: Brookings Institution and Hamilton Project, 2019), www.hamiltonproject.org/papers/direct_stimulus_payments_to_individuals

Sainsbury, Tristram, and Robert Breunig, *The Australian Tax Planning Playbook: Vol 1*, TTPI Working Paper 1/2020 (Canberra: Tax and Transfer Policy Institute, Australian National University, 2020), https://taxpolicy.crawford.anu.edu.au/publication/ttpi-working-papers/16280/australian-tax-planning-playbook-volume-1

Salamon, Lester M, Helmut K Anheier, Regina List, Stefan Toepler, S Wojciech Sokolowski (eds.), *Global Civil Society: Dimensions of the Nonprofit Sector* (Baltimore, MD: Johns Hopkins Center for Civil Society Studies, 1999)

Samuelson, Paul A, 'Diagrammatic Exposition of a Theory of Public Expenditure' (1955) 37(4) *The Review of Economics and Statistics* 350–6

'The Pure Theory of Public Economics' (1954) 36(4) *The Review of Economics and Statistics and Statistics* 387–9

Sanchirico, Chris, 'As American as Apple Inc: International Tax and Ownership Nationality' (2015) 68 *Tax Law Review* 207–74

Sandford, Cedric, *Successful Tax Reform: Lessons from an Analysis of Tax Reform in Six Countries* (Bath: Fiscal Publications, 1993)

Why Tax Systems Differ: A Comparative Study of the Political Economy of Taxation (Bath: Fiscal Publications, 2000)

Sarin, Natasha, Lawrence Summers and Joe Kupferberg, *Tax Reform for Progressivity: A Pragmatic Approach*, Hamilton Project/Brookings Institution Working Paper 2020/1 (Washington, DC: Brookings Institution, 2020)

Sassen, Saskia, *Globalization and Its Discontents* (New York: New Press, 1998)

Territory, Authority, Rights: From Medieval to Global Assemblages (Princeton, NJ: Princeton University Press, 2006)

Saturno, James V, *A Brief Overview of the Congressional Budget Process*, Report No R46468 (Washington, DC: Congressional Research Service, 29 July 2020)

Sawer, Marian, and Miranda Stewart, 'Gender Budgeting' in Marian Sawer, Fiona Jenkins and Karen Downing (eds.), *How Gender Can Transform the Social Sciences: Innovation and Impact* (Cham: Palgrave Macmillan, 2021), 117–26

Say, Jean Baptiste, *A Treatise on Political Economy; or the Production, Distribution, and Consumption of Wealth*, 4th ed (Kitchener, Ontario: Batoche Books, 2010)

Schellekens, Marnix, Government Changes Course on Box 3 Reform', June 2020), https://research.ibfd.org, accessed 4 October 2020

Netherlands – Individual Taxation – Country Tax Guides (Amsterdam: IBFD Tax Research Platform), https://research.ibfd.org, accessed 4 October 2020

Schenk, Deborah J, 'An Efficiency Approach to Reforming a Realisation-based Tax' (2004) 57 *Tax Law Review* 503–48

Schenk-Geers, Tonny, *International Exchange of Information and the Protection of Taxpayers* (Alphen aan den Rijn, Netherlands: Kluwer Law International, 2009)

Scherf, Robert, and Matthew Weinzierl, *Understanding Different Approaches to Benefit-Based Taxation*, NBER Working Paper 26276 (Cambridge, MA: National Bureau of Economic Research, 2019)

Schick, Allen, 'The Role of Fiscal Rules in Budgeting' (2003) 3(3) *OECD Journal on Budgeting* 7–34

Scholes, Myron S, Mark A Wolfson, Merle M Erickson, Michelle L Hanlon and Edward L Maydew, *Taxes & Business Strategy, Global Edition*, 5th ed (Harlow: Pearson Education, 2015)

Schön, Lennart, 'The Rise of the Fiscal State in Sweden, 1800–1914' in José Luis Cardoso and Pedro Lains (eds.), *Paying for the Liberal State: the Rise of Public Finance in Nineteenth-Century Europe* (New York: Cambridge University Press, 2010), 162–85

Schön, Wolfgang, 'International Tax Coordination for a Second Best World (Part I)' (2009) 1 *World Tax Journal* 67–70

'National Sovereignty and Taxation' in Thomas Cottier and Krista N Schefer (eds.), *Elgar Encyclopedia of International Economic Law* (Cheltenham: Edward Elgar, 2017)

Schoneville, Holger, 'Poverty and the Transformation of the Welfare (State) Arrangement. Food Banks and the Charity Economy in Germany' (2018) 16(2) *Social Work and Society* https://ejournals.bib.uni-wuppertal.de/index.php/sws/article/view/570

Schui, Florian, *Austerity: The Great Failure* (New Haven, CT: Yale University Press, 2014)

Schumpeter, Joseph A, *Capitalism, Socialism and Democracy* (London: Routledge, 1994)

'The Crisis of the Tax State' [1918] (1954) 4 *International Economic Papers* 5–38, trans. Wolfgang Stolper and Richard A Musgrave

Schwarz, Jonathan, *Schwarz on Tax Treaties* (Alphen aan den Rijn, Netherlands: Kluwer Law International, 2018)

Scutella, Rosanna, *Moves to a BI-Flat Tax System in Australia: Implications for the Distribution of Income and Supply of Labour*, University of Melbourne Working Paper No 5/04 (Melbourne: Melbourne Institute of Applied Economic and Social Research, 2004)

Seer, Roman, and Isabel Gabert (eds.), *Mutual Assistance and Information Exchange* (Amsterdam: IBFD, 2010)

Sekerka, June, *The Public Economy in Crisis: A Call for a New Public Economics* (Cham: Springer, 2016)

Seligman, Edwin RA, *Double Taxation and International Fiscal Cooperation* (New York: Macmillan, 1928)

Essays in Taxation, 7th ed (London: Macmillan, 1915), www.google.com/books/edition/Essays_in_Taxation/JGAtAAAAIAAJ?hl=en&gbpv=1

'Progressive Taxation in Theory and Practice' (1908) 9(4) *American Economic Association Quarterly*, 3rd Series

Sen, Amartya, *Development as Freedom* (Oxford: Oxford University Press, 1999)

Sharman, Jason C, *Havens in a Storm: The Struggle for Global Tax Regulation* (Ithaca, NY: Cornell University Press, 2006)

Shaviro, Daniel, 'Mobile Intellectual Property and the Shift in International Tax Policy from Determining the Source of Income to Taxing Location-Specific Rents: Part One' (2020) *Singapore Journal of Legal Studies* 681–701

'Simplifying Assumptions: How Might the Politics of Consumption Tax Reform Affect (Impair) the End Product?' in John W Diamond and George R Zodrow (eds.), *Fundamental Tax Reform: Issues, Choices, and Implications* (Cambridge, MA: MIT Press, 2008), 75–124

'Why Worldwide Welfare as a Normative Standard in US Tax Policy?' (2006–07) 60 *Tax Law Review* 155–78

Sherlock, Molly F, and Jane G Gravelle, *An Overview of the Nonprofit and Charitable Sector* (Washington, DC: Congressional Research Service, 2009), http://digitalcommons.ilr.cornell.edu/key_workplace/685

Shoyer, Andrew W 'Tax Treatment of Interest Paid to Foreign Investors – Policy and Practice Concerns' (1985) 11 *International Tax Journal* 283

Silver, Benjamin, and Michael Slomovics, 'Retiring the 401(k): A New Framework for Retirement Savings' (2021) 39 *Yale Law and Policy Review Inter Alia* 1–26

Simons, Henry C, *Personal Income Taxation: The Definition of Income as a Problem of Fiscal Policy* (Chicago: University of Chicago Press, 1938)

Simpson, Edward, and Miranda Stewart (eds.), *Sham Transactions* (Oxford: Oxford University Press, 2013)

Singh, Supriya, and Jo Lindsay, 'Money in Heterosexual Relationships' (1996) 32(3) *Journal of Sociology* 57–69

Sinn, Hans-Werner, *The New Systems Competition* (Malden, MA: Blackwell Publishing, 2003)

'Tax Harmonization and Tax Competition in Europe' (1990) 34 *European Economic Review* 489–504

Slack, Paul, *The English Poor Law 1531–1782* (Cambridge, UK: Cambridge University Press, 1995)

Slaughter, Anne-Marie, *A New World Order* (Princeton, NJ: Princeton University Press, 2004)

Slemrod, Joel, 'Tax Principles in an International Economy' in Michael J Boskin and Charles E McLure Jr (eds.), *World Tax Reform: Case Studies of Developed and Developing Countries* (San Francisco, CA: ICS Press, 1990), 11–24

Slemrod, Joel, and Jon Bakija, *Taxing Ourselves: A Citizens' Guide to the Debate over Taxes*, 5th ed (Cambridge, MA: MIT Press, 2017)

Slemrod, Joel, and Christian Gillitzer, *Tax Systems* (Cambridge, MA: MIT Press, 2013)

Slemrod, Joel, and Michael Keen, *Rebellion, Rascals and Revenue: Tax Follies and Wisdom through the Ages* (Princeton, NJ: Princeton University Press, 2021)

Sloman, Peter, 'Beveridge's Rival: Juliet Rhys-Williams and the Campaign for BI, 1942–55' (2015), www.repository.cam.ac.uk/bitstream/handle/1810/251445/Sloman%202015%20Contemporary%20British%20History.pdf

Smith, Adam, *An Inquiry into the Nature and Causes of Wealth of Nations* (London: Methuan, first published 1776, compilation by Edward Cannan, 1904, of 5th ed, 1789), www.econlib.org/library/Smith/smWN.html

Smith, Daniel A, *Tax Crusaders and the Politics of Direct Democracy* (New York: Routledge, 1998)

Smith, Julie P, *Taxing Popularity: The Story of Taxation in Australia*, 2nd ed (Sydney: Australian Tax Research Foundation, 2004)

Sobeck, Kristen, Robert Breunig and Alex Evans, *Corporate Income Taxation in Australia: Theory, Current Practice and Future Policy Directions*, Tax and Transfer Policy Institute (TTPI) Policy Report No. 01-2022 (Canberra: TTPI, Australian National University, 2022), https://taxpolicy.crawford.anu.edu.au/sites/default/files/uploads/taxstudies_crawford_anu_edu_au/2022-03/ttpi_corporate_income_tax_report.pdf

Soler Roch, Maria Teresa (ed.), *Family Taxation in Europe* (Boston: Kluwer Law International, 1999)

Sorenson, Peter Birch, 'From the Global Income Tax to the Dual Income Tax: Recent Tax Reforms in the Nordic Countries' (1994) 1 *International Tax and Public Finance* 57–79

Sorkin, Andrew R, Jason Karaian, Sarah Kessler, Michael J de la Merced, Lauren Hirsch and Ephrat Livni, 'Private Equity's Favorite Tax Break May Be in Danger', *New York Times*, 12 June 2021, www.nytimes.com/2021/04/23/business/dealbook/carried-interest-biden.html

Special Issue on Global Philanthropy (2011) 13(1–2) *The International Journal of Not-for-Profit Law*

Spoerer, Mark, 'The Evolution of Public Finances in Nineteenth-Century Germany' in José Luis Cardoso and Pedro Lains (eds.), *Paying for the Liberal State: the Rise of Public Finance in Nineteenth-Century Europe* (New York: Cambridge University Press, 2010), 103–31, https://doi.org/10.1017/CBO9780511845109.006

Standing, Guy, *Basic Income: And How We Can Make It Happen* (UK: Pelican, 2017)

Staudt, Nancy, 'Taxing Housework' (1995) 84 *Georgetown Law Journal* 1571–647

Steinberg, Richard, '"Unfair" Competition by Nonprofits and Tax Policy' (1991) 44 *National Tax Journal* 351–64

Steinlin, Simon, and Christine Trampusch, 'Institutional Shrinkage: The Deviant Case of Swiss Banking Secrecy' (2012) 6 *Regulation & Governance* 242–59 https://doi.org/10.1111/j.1748-5991.2012.01128.x.

Steinmo, Sven, 'The Evolution of Policy Ideas: Tax Policy in the 20th Century' (2003) 5 (2) *British Journal of Politics and International Relations* 206–36

Taxation and Democracy: Swedish, British and American Approaches to Financing the Modern State (New Haven, CT: Yale University Press, 1993)

Stephens, Robert, 'Radical Tax Reform in New Zealand' (1993) 14(3) *Fiscal Studies* 45–63

Stevenson, Ariel, 'Recovering Lost Revenue through Taxation of Transnational Households' (2016) 34(1) *Berkeley Journal of International Law* 100–56

Stewart, Miranda, 'Australia's Hybrid International Tax System: A Limited Focus on Tax and Development', in Karen B Brown (ed.), *Taxation and Development – A Comparative Study* (New York: Springer, 2017), 17–42

'The David R Tillinghast Lecture: Commentary' (2000) 54 *Tax Law Review* 111–30

'Gender Equity in Australia's Tax System: A Capabilities Approach' in Kim Brooks, Åsa Gunnarson, Lisa Philipps and Maria Wersig (eds.), *Challenging Gender*

Inequality in Tax Policy Making: Comparative Perspectives (London: Hart Publishing, 2011), 53–74

'Gender Inequality in Australia's Tax-transfer System' in Miranda Stewart (ed.), Tax, Social Policy and Gender: Rethinking Equality and Efficiency (Canberra: ANU Press, 2017), 1–32

'Global Trajectories of Tax Reform: The Discourse of Tax Reform in Developing and Transition Countries' (2003) 44(1) Harvard International Law Journal 139–90

(ed.), Housing and Tax Policy (Sydney: Australian Tax Research Foundation, 2010)

'Redistribution between Rich and Poor Countries' (2018) 72(4–5) Bulletin of International Taxation 297–309

'Sham Transactions and Tax Avoidance' in Nigar Hashimzade and Yuliya Epifantseva (eds.), The Routledge Companion to Tax Avoidance Research (London: Routledge, 2017), 48–57

(ed.), Tax, Social Policy and Gender (Canberra: ANU Press, 2017)

'The Tax State, Benefit and Legitimacy' in Paul Harris and Dominic de Cogan (eds.), Studies in the History of Tax Law: Vol 7 (London: Hart Publishing, 2015), 483–515

'Taxation Policy and Housing' in Susan J Smith et al (eds.), International Encyclopedia of Housing and Home (Amsterdam: Elsevier, 2012), 152–66

'Transnational Tax Information Exchange Networks: Steps Towards a Globalized, Legitimate Tax Administration' (2012) 4(2) World Tax Journal 152–79

'Venture Capital Taxation in Australia and New Zealand' (2005) 11 New Zealand Journal of Taxation Law and Policy 216–49

Stewart, Miranda, and Holly Jager, 'The Australian Parliamentary Budget Office: Shedding Light on the Dark Arts of Budgeting' (2013) 24(4) Public Law Review 267–88

Stewart, Miranda, Sarah Voitchovsky and Roger Wilkins, 'Women and Top Incomes in Australia' in Miranda Stewart (ed.), Tax, Social Policy and Gender (Canberra: ANU Press, 2017), 257–91

Stiglitz, Joseph E, Amartya Sen and Jean-Paul Fitoussi, The Measurement of Economic Performance and Social Progress Revisited: Reflections and Overview (Paris: French Observatory of Economic Conditions, Economics Research Center, 2009), http://spire.sciencespo.fr/hdl:/2441/5l6uh8ogmqildh09h4687h53k/resources/wp2009-33.pdf

Stone, Ethan G, 'Adhering to the Old Line: Uncovering the History and Political Function of the Unrelated Business Income Tax' (2005) 54 Emory Law Journal 1475–556

Stone, Lawrence M, 'Federal Tax Support of Charities and Other Exempt Organizations: The Need for a National Policy' (1968) 20 University of Southern California School of Law Tax Institute 27

Stout, Lynn, 'The Economic Nature of the Corporation' in Francesco Parisi (ed.), Oxford Handbook of Law and Economics. Private and Commercial Law: Vol 2 (Oxford: Oxford University Press, 2017), 343–8

Stromberg, Dorothea, 'Successes and Failures in Recent Swedish Tax Policy' in Karl W Roskamp and Francesco Forte (eds.), Reforms of Tax Systems (Detroit, MI: Wayne State University Press, 1981), 121–34

Surrey, Stanley, and Paul McDaniel, *Tax Expenditures* (Cambridge, MA: Harvard University Press, 1985)

Swank, Duane, and Sven Steinmo, 'The New Political Economy of Taxation in Advanced Capitalist Economies' (2002) 46 *American Journal of Political Science* 642–55

Szreter, Simon, Ann Louise Kinouth, Natasha M Kriznik and Michael P Kelly, 'Health, Welfare, and the State – The Dangers of Forgetting History' (3 December 2016) 388 *The Lancet*, 2734–5

Tadmore, Niv, 'Source Taxation of Cross-border Intellectual Supplies – Concepts, History and Evolution into the Digital Age' (2007) 61(1) *Bulletin for International Taxation*

Tanzi, Vito, and Ludger Schuknecht, *Public Spending in the Twentieth Century* (Cambridge, UK: Cambridge University Press, 2000)

Tax Administration Research Centre, University of Exeter, 'About TARC', https://tarc.exeter.ac.uk/thecentre/abouttarc/, accessed 1 April 2022

Tax Policy Center, 'Racial Disparities and the Income Tax System' (30 January 2020), https://apps.urban.org/features/race-and-taxes/

'What Is the Difference between Carryover Basis and Step Up Basis?' in *Key Elements of the U.S. Tax System, Briefing Book* (Washington, DC: Tax Policy Center, 2021), www.taxpolicycenter.org/briefing-book/what-difference-between-carryover-basis-and-step-basis

'What Is the Earned Income Tax Credit?' in *Key Elements of the U.S. Tax System, Briefing Book* (Washington, DC: Tax Policy Center, 2021), www.taxpolicycenter.org/briefing-book/what-earned-income-tax-credit

Taxpayer Advocate Service (US), 'Reports to Congress', https://taxpayeradvocate.irs.gov/reports, accessed 16 March 2022

Thaler, Richard, and Cass Sunstein, *Nudge* (New Haven, CT: Yale University Press, 2008)

Thevenon, Olivier, *Drivers of Female Labour Force Participation in the OECD*, OECD Social, Employment and Migration Working Papers No 145 (Paris: OECD, 2013)

Thuronyi, Victor, 'Adjusting Taxes for Inflation' in Victor Thuronyi (ed.), *Tax Law Design and Drafting: Vol 1* (Washington, DC: International Monetary Fund, 1996, revised 2012), chapter 13, www.imf.org/external/pubs/nft/1998/tlaw/eng/ch13.pdf

'International Tax Cooperation and a Multilateral Tax Treaty' (2001) 26(4) *Brooklyn Journal of International Law* 1641–81

Thuronyi, Victor, Kim Brooks and Borbála Kolozs, *Comparative Tax Law*, 2nd ed (Alphen aan den Rijn, Netherlands: Kluwer, 2016)

Tiebout, Charles M, 'A Pure Theory of Local Expenditures' (1956) 64 *Journal of Political Economy* 416–24

Torgler, Benno, 'Speaking to Theorists and Searching for Facts: Tax Morale and Tax Compliance in Experiments' (2002) 16(5) *Journal of Economic Surveys* 657–83

Tax Morale and Compliance: Review of Evidence and Case Studies for Europe, World Bank Policy Research Working Paper 5922 (Washington, DC: World Bank, 2010)

Torgler, Benno, and Neven Valev, 'Gender and Public Attitudes towards Corruption and Tax Evasion' (2010) 28(4) *Contemporary Economic Policy* 554–68

Transparency International US Office, https://us.transparency.org/news/beneficial-ownership-registry-considerations/, accessed 1 April 2022

Traversa, Edoardo (ed.), *Corporate Residence and Mobility*, EATLP International Tax Series No 16 (Amsterdam: IBFD, 2017)

Traversa, Edoardo, and Alessandra Flamini, 'Chapter 6: Patent Boxes Before and After BEPS Action 5' in Pasquale Pistone and Dennis Weber (eds.), *The Implementation of Anti-BEPS Rules in the EU: A Comprehensive Study* (Amsterdam IBFD, 2018)

Treanor, Jill, 'Avaaz Bank Tax Transparency Petition Attracts More than 200,000 Signatures', *The Guardian* online, 27 February 2013, www.theguardian.com/business/2013/feb/27/eu-tax-transparency-avaaz-petition

Trivedi, Chitvan, 'A Social Entrepreneurship Bibliography' (2010) 19 *Journal of Entrepreneurship* 81–5

Twining, William, *Globalisation and Legal Theory* (Cambridge, UK: Cambridge University Press, 2000)

United Nations, 'Charter of the United Nations' 1 UNTS XVI (26 June 1945), www.un.org/en/about-us/un-charter

United Nations Economic and Social Council, 'ECOSOC Resolution 2004/69 on "Committee of Experts on International Cooperation in Tax Matters" (E/2004/INF/2/Add.3, page 14)' (11 November 2004), www.un.org/development/desa/financing/document/ecosoc-resolution-200469-committee-experts-international-cooperation-tax-matters

'Model Double Taxation Convention between Developed and Developing Countries' (2017), with Commentary, www.un.org/esa/ffd/wp-content/uploads/2018/05/MDT_2017.pdf

'UN Tax Committee', www.un.org/development/desa/financing/what-we-do/ECOSOC/tax-committee/tax-committee-home, accessed 29 March 2021

University of Melbourne, Melbourne School of Government, 'International Tax Design for the 21st Century', https://government.unimelb.edu.au/research/regulation-and-design/research-outputs/research-papers/international-tax-design-for-the-21st-century, accessed 24 March 2022

US Treasury, *Analytical Perspectives on the Budget* (Washington, DC: Department of the Treasury, 2020)

Blueprints for Tax Reform (Washington, DC: US Government Printing Office, 1977)

'Foreign Account Tax Compliance Act', https://home.treasury.gov/policy-issues/tax-policy/foreign-account-tax-compliance-act, accessed 23 March 2022

Integration of the Individual and Corporate Tax Systems: Taxing Business Income Once (Washington, DC: US Government Printing Office, 1992)

The Problem of Corporate Tax Shelters – Discussion, Analysis and Legislative Proposals (Washington, DC: Department of the Treasury, 1999)

'Treasury Secretary Paul H O'Neill, Statement at the Pre-G-7 Press Conference' (Press Release PO-464, 5 July 2001)

'Treasury Secretary O'Neill, Statement on OECD Tax Havens' (Press Release PO-366, 10 May 2001)

Vanistendael, Frans, Democracy, Revolution and Taxation' 71(8) (2017) *Bulletin for International Taxation*

Vann, Richard J, 'General Report' in *Trends in Company/Shareholder Taxation: Single or Double Taxation? Cahiers de Droit Fiscal International: Vol 88a* (Rotterdam: International Fiscal Association, 2003), 21–70

Varela, Peter, *What Are Progressive and Regressive Taxes?*, TTPI Policy Brief 3/2016 (Canberra: TTPI, Australian National University, 2016)

Varela, Peter, Robert Breunig and Kristen Sobeck, *The Taxation of Savings in Australia: Theory, Current Practice and Future Policy Directions*, TTPI Policy Report No 01-2020 (Canberra: Tax and Transfer Policy Institute, Australian National University, 2020), https://taxpolicy.crawford.anu.edu.au/sites/default/files/uploads/taxstudies_crawford_anu_edu_au/2020-07/20271_anu_-_ttpi_policy_report-ff2.pdf

Vording, Henk, 'Talents, Types, and Tags: What Is the Relevance of the Endowment Tax Debate?' in Monica Bhandari (ed.), *Philosophical Foundations of Tax Law* (Oxford: Oxford University Press, 2017), https://doi.org/10.1093/acprof:oso/9780198798439.003.0011

Vording, Henk, and Koon Caminada, 'Tax Co-ordination: Crossing the Rubicon?' in Dirk A Albregtse, Arij Lans Bovenberg and LGM Stevens (eds.), *Er zal geheven worden!, Opstellen aangeboden aan Prof. Dr S. Cnossen* (Deventer: Kluwer, 2001), 335–45

Wagner, Adolph, 'Three Extracts on Public Finance' in Richard A Musgrave and Alan T Peacock (eds.), *Classics in the Theory of Public Finance* (New York: Palgrave Macmillan, 1958), 2–5

Walby, Sylvia, *Globalization and Inequalities: Complexity and Contested Modernities* (London: Sage Publications, 2009)

Walker, Brian, and David Salt, *Resilience Practice: Building Capacity to Absorb Disturbance and Maintain Function* (Washington, DC: Island Press, 2012)

Wang, Hanna, 'Fertility and Family Leave Policies in Germany: Optimal Policy Design in a Dynamic Framework' (2019), https://sistemas.colmex.mx/Reportes/LACEALAMES/LACEA-LAMES2019_paper_320.pdf

Waris, Attiya, *Financing Africa* (Bamenda, Cameroon: Langaa Rpcig, 2019)

Warren, Neil, and Richard Highfield, *Mind the (Tax) Gap! It Is Bigger and More Complex than You Think*, UNSW Business School Research Paper (Sydney: University of New South Wales, 2020)

Watson, Don, *Recollections of a Bleeding Heart: A Portrait of Paul Keating* (Sydney: Random House, 2002)

Wattel, Peter J, 'Progressive Taxation of Non-Residents and Intra-EC Allocation of Personal Tax Allowances: Why Schumacker, Gilly and Gschwind Do Not Suffice' (2000) 40(6) *European Taxation* 210–23

Weigel, Russell H, Dick J Hessing and Henk Elffers, 'Tax Evasion Research: A Critical Appraisal and Theoretical Model' (1987) 8 *Journal of Economic Psychology* 215–35

Weisbrod, Burton A, 'The Nonprofit Mission and Its Financing: Growing Links between Nonprofits and the Rest of the Economy' in Burton A Weisbrod (ed.), *To Profit or Not to Profit: The Commercial Transformation of the Nonprofit Sector* (Cambridge, UK: Cambridge University Press, 2000), 1–22

Weiss, Linda, 'The State-augmenting Effects of Globalization' (2005) 10(3) *New Political Economy* 345–53

Wersig, Maria, 'Overcoming the Gender Inequalities of Joint Taxation and Income Splitting: The Case of Germany' in Kim Brooks, Åsa Gunnarson, Lisa Philipps and Maria Wersig (eds.), *Challenging Gender Inequality in Tax Policy Making* (London: Hart Publishing, 2011), 213–32

White, David, 'The Impact of Economic Theory on Capital Gains Tax Reform Proposals' in Michael Littlewood and Craig Elliffe (eds.), *Capital Gains Taxation: A Comparative Analysis of Key Issues* (New York: Elgar Publishing, 2017), 30–80

Wildavsky, Aaron, 'A Budget for All Seasons? Why the Traditional Budget Lasts' (1978) 38(6) *Public Administration Review* 501–9

The Politics of the Budgetary Process, 4th ed (New York: Little, Brown, 1984)

Wilkie, Scott, 'New Rules of Engagement? Corporate Personality and the Allocation of "International Income" and Taxing Rights' in Brian J Arnold (ed.), *Tax Treaties after the BEPS Project: A Tribute to Jacques Sasseville* (Toronto: Canadian Tax Foundation, 2017), 349–72

Wilkinson, Margaret, 'Paying for Public Spending: Is There a Role for Earmarked Taxes?' (1994) 15(4) *Fiscal Studies* 119–35

Willcocks, Leslie P, Mary C Lacity and Chris Sauer (eds.), *Outsourcing and Offshoring Business Services* (Cham: Springer, 2017)

Williamson, Oliver E, and Sidney G Winter (eds.), *The Nature of the Firm: Origins, Evolution, and Development* (New York: Oxford University Press, 1993), 18–33

Wilson, Peter, *An Analysis of a Cash Flow Tax for Small Business*, New Zealand Treasury Working Paper 02/27 (Wellington: New Zealand Treasury, 2002)

van Winden, Frans AAM, 'The Economic Theory of Political Decision-Making: A Survey and Perspective' in Julien Van Den Broeck (ed.), *Public Choice* (Dordrecht: Springer, 1988), 9–42

Wolfson, Michael, Mike Veall, Neil Brooks and Brian Murphy, 'Piercing the Veil: Private Corporations and the Income of the Affluent' (2016) 64(1) *Canadian Tax Journal* 1–30

Women's Budget Group (UK), https://wbg.org.uk, accessed 19 March 2022

World Inequality Database, https://wid.world, accessed 16 March 2022

Wurth, Elea, and Valerie Braithwaite, 'Tax Practitioners and Tax Avoidance: Gaming through Authorities, Cultures and Markets' in Nigar Hashimzade and Yuliya Epifantseva (eds), *Routledge Companion on Tax Avoidance Research* (Abingdon: Routledge, 2017), 320–39

Wyplosz, Charles, 'Fiscal Discipline in the Eurozone: Don't Fix It, Change It' in *Forum: Fiscal Rules for Europe. CESifoDICE Report* (Munich: ifo Institute–Leibniz-Institut für Wirtschaftsforschung an der Universität München, 2019)

'Fiscal Policy: Institutions versus Rules' (2005) 191 *National Institute Economic Review* 64–78

Young, Claire, 'Taxing Times for Women: Feminism Confronts Tax Policy,' in Richard Krever (ed.), *Tax Conversations* (Amsterdam: Kluwer Law International, 1997), 261–92

Young, Garry, Carl Emmerson, Jagjit Chadha and Paul Johnson, 'Debt Interest as a Share of Revenues at a 320 Year Low' in *COVID-19: Deficits, Debt and Fiscal Strategy* (London National Institute of Economic and Social Research and Institute of Fiscal Studies, 2020), https://ifs.org.uk/uploads/Presentations/Covid-19-Deficits-debt-and-fiscal-strategy.pdf, slide 22

Yun-Casalilla, Bartolome, Patrick O'Brien and Francisco Comín (eds.), *The Rise of Fiscal States: A Global History* (Cambridge, UK: Cambridge University Press, 2012)

Zeballos-Roig, Joseph, 'Finland's Basic-Income Trial Found People Were Happier, But Weren't More Likely to Get Jobs', World Economic Forum (8 May 2020), www.weforum.org/agenda/2020/05/finlands-basic-income-trial-found-people-were-happier-but-werent-more-likely-to-get-jobs/

Zimmerman, Brenda, and Raymond Dart, *Charities Doing Commercial Ventures: Societal and Organizational Implications* (Toronto: Trillium Foundation, 1998), http://epe.lac-bac.gc.ca/100/200/300/cprn/english/cdc_e.pdf

Zodrow, George, 'International Taxation and Company Tax Policy in Small Open Economies' in Iris Claus, Norman Gemmell, Michelle Harding and David White (eds.), *Tax Reform in Open Economies: International and Country Perspectives* (Cheltenham: Edward Elgar, 2010), 109–34

Zumbansen, Peer, 'Defining the Space of Transnational Law: Legal Theory, Global Governance, and Legal Pluralism' (2012) 21 *Transnational Law & Contemporary Problems* 305–36

Legislation

Charter of Budget Honesty Act 1998 (Cth) (Austl)
Congressional Budget and Impoundment Control Act 1974 (US)
European Parliament, Resolution on Gender Equality and Taxation Policies in the EU, 2018/20195 (INI), No 5, 6, 10
Finance Act 2013 (UK)
Federal Accountability Act (2006) (Canada)
Internal Revenue Code (IRC) Title 26 (US)
Income Tax Act 1915 (Cth) (Austl)
Income Tax Assessment Act 1936 (Cth) (Austl)
Income Tax Assessment Act 1997 (Cth) (Austl)
Inspector-General of Taxation Act 2003 (Cth) (Austl)
Land and Income Assessment Act 1891 (New Zealand)
Parliament of Canada Act 1985 (Canada)
President Biden (US), Executive Order on Advancing Racial Equity and Support for Underserved Communities Through the Federal Government (20 January 2021), www.whitehouse.gov/briefing-room/presidential-actions/2021/01/20/executive-order-advancing-racial-equity-and-support-for-underserved-communities-through-the-federal-government/
Prime Minister Hughes (Cth), Second Reading Speech, Income Tax Assessment Bill 1915, House of Representatives, Australian Parliament (18 August 1915), Hansard, 5843
Tax Cuts and Jobs Act 2017 (US)

Cases

Addy v Commissioner of Taxation [2021] HCA 34 (High Court of Australia)
Antle v *R* (2010) 2010 DTC 7304 (Canada)
ASA Investerings Partnership v *Commissioner* 201 F.3d 505 (DC Cir. 2000) (US)
BVerfG of 17 January 1957, BVerfGE 6, 55 (Germany)
BVerfG of 3 November 1982, BVerfGE 61, 319, 347 (Germany)

Cam & Sons Pty Ltd v *Sargent* (1940) 14 ALJ 162 (High Court of Australia)
Case C-10/10, *European Commission* v *Austria* [2011] ECR I-5389
Case C-25/10, *Missionswerk Werner Heukelbach eV* v *Belgium* (C-25/10) ECR [2011] ECR I-00497, ECLI:EU:C:2011:65
Case C-279/93, *Schumacker* ECLI:EU:C:1995:31 (CJEU)
Case C-283/15, *X* v *Staatssecretaris van Financiën* ECLI:EU:C:2017:102 (CJEU)
Case C-318/07, *Persche* v *Finanzamt Lüdenscheid* (C-318/07) [2009] ECR 2009 I-00359, ECLI:EU:C:2009:33
Case C-386/04, *Centro di Musicologia Walter Stauffer* (C-386/04) [2006] ECR I-8203 ECLI:EU:C:2006:568 (CJEU)
Case C-513/03, *Heirs of MEA van Hilten*, 45–52 (2006), ECR 2006 I-01957, ECLI:EU:C:2006:131 (CJEU)
CF Mueller Co v *Commissioner*, 190 F 2d 120 (3rd Cir, 1951) (US)
CIR v *Brown* (1965) 380 US 563 (US)
Commissioners for Special Purposes of the Income Tax v *Pemsel* [1891] AC 531 (House of Lords) (UK)
Compañia General de Tabacos de Filipinas v *Collector of Internal Revenue* (1927) 275 US 87 (Supreme Court) (US)
Cook v *Tait* 265 US 47 (1924) (Supreme Court) (US)
Dynamex Operations W v *Superior Court - 4 Cal. 5th 903, 232 Cal Rptr 3d 1, 416 P.3d 1* (2018) (US)
Federal Commissioner of Taxation v *Everett* (1980) 143 CLR 440 (Australia)
Federal Commissioner of Taxation v *Newton* [1958] AC 450; (1958) 32 ALJR 187 (Privy Council) (Australia)
Federal Commissioner of Taxation v *Spotless Services Ltd* (1996) 186 CLR 404 (High Court of Australia)
Federal Commissioner of Taxation v *Word Investments Ltd* (2006) 64 ATR 482 (Federal Court of Australia)
Federal Commissioner of Taxation v *Word Investments Ltd* (2008) 236 CLR 204 (High Court of Australia)
Re Lowin; Perpetual Trustee Co Ltd v *Robins* [1967] 2 NSWR 140 (Supreme Court of New South Wales, Australia)
Roher v *Canada* (2019) 2019 FCA 313; 2019 TCC 17 (Tax Court of Canada)
Uber BV, Uber London LTD, Uber, Britannia Britannia LTD v *Aslam, Farrar, Dawson and Others* (2017) Appeal No UKEAT/0056/17/DA, Employment Appeal Tribunal (UK)

Treaties

European Commission, Directive 2003/48/EC of 3 June 2003
European Union Maastricht Treaty, 7 February 1992, O.J. 1992 C191/6
OECD, Draft Double Taxation Convention on Income and on Capital (1963)
OECD, Multilateral Convention to Implement Tax Treaty Related Measures to Prevent Base Erosion and Profit Shifting (2016), www.oecd.org/tax/treaties/explanatory-statement-multilateral-convention-to-implement-tax-treaty-related-measures-to-prevent-BEPS.pdf

OECD and Council of Europe, The Multilateral Convention on Administrative Mutual Assistance in Tax Matters (1988)

OECD and Council of Europe, The Multilateral Convention on Mutual Administrative in Tax Matters Amended by the 2010 Protocol (2011), www.oecd.org/ctp/exchange-of-tax-information/convention-on-mutual-administrative-assistance-in-tax-matters.htm

Resolution of the European Council on the Stability and Growth Pact, 1997 O.J. (C 236)

Index

ability to pay
  in equity principle, 78–81
    Carter Commission on, 82–4
    concept of income and, 81–4
    declining marginal utility of income and, 80–1
    distributive justice, 78–9
    endowment, 81–2, 96–7
    faculty and, 81
    Mill, John Stuart, on, 79–80
    Murphy, Liam, on, 84
    myth of ownership, 84–5
    Nagel, Thomas, on, 84
    progressive tax rates, 79–81
    Saladin Tithe of 1188, 79
    Smith, Adam, on, 75–7
    vertical equality, 73, 84, 101
  government funding and expenditures, 43–4
  tax residence and, 260
accident insurance, in Germany, 34
accounting
  creative accounting by governments, 56
  discipline, 11
accrual taxation, 157–9
ACE. *See* allowance for corporate equity
administrative approaches to taxation. *See* tax administration
Administrative Convention. *See* Convention on Mutual Administrative Assistance in Tax Matters
Allocation branch, in fiscal model of government, 44–5
allowance for corporate equity (ACE), 200–1
  in Belgium, 200
anti-avoidance. *See* General Anti-Avoidance Rule; tax avoidance
arbitrage. *See* tax arbitrage
Arnold, Brian, 260

Asian Financial Crisis of 1997, 54
Atkinson, Antony, 96
Australia
  capital income in, jurisdiction exemptions for, 273–4
  charities in, taxation on, 211, 218
  Charter of Budget Honesty, 59
  corporate taxes in, 180, 189–90
  FCT v. Word Investments Ltd, 211
  fiscal transparency in, 59
  hybrid income-consumption tax in, 152–3
  income splitting in, 134
  income taxes in, 37–8, 125
    tax rates for, 120–1
  Parliamentary Budget Office, 61–2
  tax evasion in, 241
  tax reform in, 105
  tax-transfer system in, 86–107
  wealth inequality in, 150
  wealth taxes in, 168–9
Australian Taxation Office, A-Life longitudinal database, 13
automation, progressive income taxes on, 138–9
average tax rate, 119
Avi-Yonah, Reuven, 177, 254, 276

back-end incentive, 196
balanced budgets, 51–2
bank secrecy era, offshore capital during, 285–7
  under Convention on Mutual Administrative Assistance in Tax Matters, 285–6
Banks, James, 152
Base Erosion and Profit Shifting project (BEPS project), 245, 311–22
  Action Plan, 314
  anti-abuse approaches in, 319–20

goals of, 311–14
harmful tax practices and, 320–2
 Action 5 report on, 321–2
Multilateral Instrument (Multilateral Convention to Implement Tax Treaty Related Measures to Prevent Bse Erosion and Profit Shifting), 315–16
multinational enterprises and, 312–13
origins of, 311–14
tax arbitrage and, 313
transnational corporate tax administration, 317–19
 country-by-country reports, 317–18
 Mutual Agreement Procedure, 319
Belgium
 allowance for corporate equity in, 200
 tax unit in, 127
benefit theory of taxation, 43–5, 260, 337
 public benefit and, 50
 public goods, 49–50
Bentham, Jeremy, 35, 80
BEPS project. *See* Base Erosion and Profit Shifting project
Bezos, Jeff, 167–8, 305–7
'big philanthropy,' 214–16
Bird, Richard, 179–87
Bismarck, Otto von, 34
Blueprints for Tax Reform, 103
bracket creep, 123
Bradford, David, 169
brain drain tax, 267–9
Braithwaite, Valerie, 230
Brauner, Yariv, 268
Brennan, Geoffrey, 40, 101
broad-based consumption tax benchmark, 69
Brody, Evelyn, 204
Brooks, Kim, 179
Buchanan, James, 40, 101
budgets. *See also* fiscal institutions
 balanced, 51–2
 constraints on, 51–4
 distributional impact of, 72–3
 gender, 71–2 (*See also* gender budgeting)
  for gender equality, 57–71
  impact analysis for, 72
  as process, 71
 government debt levels and, 53–4
  COVID-19 pandemic and, 54
  in selected OECD countries, 53
 green, 73–4
 before Keynesian economics, 52

line-item, 51
in modern monetary theory, 52–3
as political documents, 70–1
spending influenced by, 65–70
 discretionary, 65
 mandatory, 65–6
 in US, 65
tax expenditures in, 67–70
 benchmarking of, 69–70
 examples of, 94–5
 McDaniel, Paul, on, 67, 224
 measurement of, 67
 social policy and, 68–9
taxes and, 65–70
 earmarking of, 65–6
 taxpayer-voters and, 66
 well-being, New Zealand, 73
Wildavsky, Aaron, on, 51
Buffett, Warren, 167–8
business bail-outs, 64
business cash flow tax, 199–200
 in US, 200
business income, of charities, 211
business taxation. *See* income tax

Canada
 Carter Tax Commission in, 82–4
 fiscal institutions in, budgets for, Parliamentary Budget Office, 61
 income taxes in, 125
  pay-as-you-go withholding, 117–18
  progressive tax rates, 135
 tax avoidance and evasion in, through philanthropy, 217
capabilities approach, to equity principle, 90–1
 Nussbaum, Martha, on, 91
 Sen, Amartya, on, 90
capital. *See also* offshore capital
 complex role of, 144–5
 democratisation of wealth and, 145
 dual income tax and, 152
 economic rent and, 154–5
  Mill on, 154
  in normative theory, 154–5
  Smith on, 154
 hybrid income-consumption tax, 152–4
  in Australia, 152–3
  marginal effective tax rates, 153
  in UK, 152
 as income, 146
 mobility of, 274–7

390   Index

capital. (cont.)
  Smith on, 144–5, 154
    mobility of capital, 274–7
    in theory of taxing savings, 146–52
      in comprehensive income approach, 148
      in consumption tax approach, 148
      over lifecourse, 148–9
      Mill, John, Stuart, on, 148–9
      national transfer accounts, 149–50
    wealth inequality and, 146
      in Australia, 150
      by country, 147
      in Germany, 151
capital export neutrality (CEN), 302
capital gains tax, 155–60. *See also* home ownership; household savings; offshore capital; retirement savings; venture capital; wealth taxes
  accrual taxation of, 157–9
  base-broadening reforms in, 156
  comprehensive income tax, approach to, 157–8, 160
  direct yield of revenues, 156
  dual income tax, 158–60
  income compared to, 155–7
    in civil law jurisdictions, 155–6
  legislative reform for, 156
  mark-to-market approach, 158
  Netherlands 'Box' System, 159
  in New Zealand, 157
  realisation basis for, 156–8
  Simons, Henry, on, 157
  in US, 157–8
capital import neutrality (CIN), 302
capital income, tax jurisdiction over, 274–83
  decolonisation as influence on, 279
  Eurobonds, 279–81
  exit taxes, 275–6
  mobility of capital, 274–7
  offshore capital, 277–9
capitalism, regulation of, through corporate taxes, 179
carried interest rule, 197
Carter Tax Commission, in Canada, 82–4, 125
cash transfers, 64
  universal basic income and, 114–39
CBIT. *See* comprehensive business income tax
CCCTB. *See* Common Consolidated Corporate Tax Base
CEN. *See* capital export neutrality

certainty, for taxation, 77
  Smith, Adam, on, 76–7
  tax administration and, 222–3
CFC rules. *See* controlled foreign corporations rules
charitable exemptions, 207–9
charitable giving deduction, 213–14
  justification of, 214
charities, taxation, 204–13
  in Australia, 211, 218
  boundaries of, 204–5
  under British law, 218
  of business income, 211
  in EU, 218–20
    in CJEU case law, 219–20
  globalisation of, 217–21
    global associational revolution, 217–18
    across national borders, 217–18
    public benefits of, 220–1
  governments compared to, 205
  not-for-profit sector and, 205–7
    commercial activities of, 209–12
    revenue structure for, 206
    in US, 206
  origins and history of, 207–8
  private goods and, 205
  public goods and, 205
  on social enterprises, 212–13
  tax expenditures, 209
  tax privileges for, 207–9
    charitable exemption as, 207–9
    for public welfare role, 208
  in US, 206, 211
Charter of Budget Honesty, in Australia, 59
childcare costs, 127–9
  in Germany, 128
China
  taxation system in, reform of, 8–9
  welfare state in, 8–9
CIN. *See* capital import neutrality
citizen-lenders, in tax state, 31
citizen-taxpayer
  tax residence for, 262–3
  in tax state, 30–3
    in Medieval city-states, 30–1
city-states. *See* Medieval city-states
civil law systems
  capital gains tax in, 155–6
  tax units in, 124–5
CJEU. *See* Court of Justice of the European Union

classical economic model, for tax evasion, 231–2
classical theory, for corporate taxes, 185
Cnossen, Sijbren, 177–8, 202
Colm, Gerhard, 43–4
Common Consolidated Corporate Tax Base (CCCTB), 328–9
common law systems
  tax authorities in, 229
  tax avoidance in, 247
compliance, in tax administration, 230–9
  classical economic model of, 231–2
  Pay-As-You-Go systems, 232
  policy gaps and, 250
  quasi-voluntary compliance, 230–3
  self-assessment and, 233–6
  tax regulation and, 233–6
  taxpayer rights, 236
  in UK, 235
comprehensive business income tax (CBIT), 201–2
comprehensive income, 100
  broad-based tax reform, 41, 96–7
  on business and investment income, 191
  capital gains tax and, 157–8, 160
  income tax on, 21–3
    benchmarks for, 69
  Simons, Henry, on, 116–17, 148
concessions, for research and development, 198
  tax expenditures, 161, 209
Congressional Budget and Impoundment Control Act, US (1974), 61
Constitutional Court, in Germany, 124–5
constitutionalism
  fiscal
    Brennan, Geoffrey, on, 10
    Buchanan, James, on, 10
  of taxation, 4
consumption behaviour
  elasticity of, 92–4
  taxation and, 103–4
consumption taxes, 24–5, 103–4
  Goods and Services Tax, 20, 24–5
  hybrid income-consumption tax, 152–4
    in Australia, 152–3
    in UK, 152
  in theory of taxing savings, 148
  Value Added Tax, 20, 24–5, 103–4
  wealth taxes and, 169
controlled foreign corporations rules (CFC rules), 282

convenience principle, for taxation, 77
Convention on Mutual Administrative Assistance in Tax Matters (Administrative Convention), 285–6
Cooper, Graeme, 50
Corporate Income Tax Act, Germany (1920), 178–9
corporate income taxes, 20
corporate tax reform, 199–203
  allowance for corporate equity, 200–1
  in Belgium, 200
  business cash flow tax, 199–200
    in US, 200
  comprehensive business income tax, 201–2
  through hybrid tax system, 202–3
  taxation of business assets under, 191–2
  in US
    business cash flow tax, 200
    comprehensive business income tax, 201–2
    Growth and Investment Tax, 200
    Tax Cuts and Jobs Act 2017, 183
corporate taxes. See also Base Erosion and Profit Shifting project
  agency theory and, 177
  in Australia, 180, 189–90
  classical theory for, 185
  complexity of, 180–2
  double tax on corporate profit, 187–8
  on economic rents, 190–1
  economic rents on, 190–1
  in Finland, 186
  on foreign investment, 281–3
  in Germany, 178–9
  in global economy, 300–11
    capital export neutrality, 302
    capital import neutrality, 302
    corporate residence issues, 304–7
    Double Irish Dutch Sandwich structure, 309–11
    for multinational enterprises, 305–7
    neutrality models, 308–11
    permanent establishment of, 307–8
    source jurisdiction of, 307–8
    stateless income of corporations, 308–11
    tax jurisdictions, 300–1
  Harberger, Arnold, on, 185, 190
  history of, 178–9
  imputation system, in Australia and New Zealand, 189–90
  incidence of, 184–6
  in New Zealand, 189–90

corporate taxes. (cont.)
    in OECD countries, 182–4
    in open economies, 185–7
    personal tax systems compared to, 186
    purpose of, 177–80
        for regulation of capitalism, 179
    rejection of, 179–87
    on revenues, 182–4
        Gross Domestic Product, share of, 182
    shareholder taxes and, integration with, 187–90
        dividend imputation system, 188–90
        dividends from, 188–9
        Vann, Richard, on, 188
    in Sweden, 178–9
    tax havens and, 311
    tax rates for, 182–4
        trends in, 183
        in US, 186
    in US, 178–9, 183
        tax rates in, 186
Corporate Transparency Act, US (2021), 293
cosmopolitanism, 336–7
Court of Justice of the European Union (CJEU), 219–20
    taxation of labour income, 264–7
COVID-19 pandemic,
    fiscal policy during, 62–4
    post-modern tax state and, 338
    progressive income taxes during, on labour, 136–7
    tax states during, 5, 43
Crawford, Claire, 194
creative accounting budgets, 56
critical race scholarship, tax law and, 89–90
cross-border retirement savings, 273–4
cross-border tax collection, 287–8
Cui, Wei, 256
Current Tax Payment Act, US (1945), 117–18

Dagan, Tsilly, 298
data, tax, 224, 237–9
    administrative, in Denmark, 13
    disaggregated by sex, gender, race, 72, 132–3
    income inequality, measurement of, 86, 132
    longitudinal, in Australia, 13
Daunton, Martin, 32
deadweight loss, 93–4. *See also* efficiency principle; neutrality
debt. *See also* government debt levels
    in tax state, 30–3
        in Great Britain, 31–2
declining marginal utility of income, 80–1

democracy, in tax states, development of, 8–9
Denmark, welfare state in, 42
Desai, Mihir, 306
destination-based cash flow tax, 325–6
Diamond, Peter, 152
digital economies, globalisation of, 322–9
    Common Consolidated Corporate Tax Base, 328–9
    destination-based cash flow tax, 325–6
    digital service tax, 324–5
    electronic fund transfers, 322–3
    Inclusive Framework consensus, 326–9
        Global anti-Base Erosion Rule, 327–8
        implementation of, 328–9
        multinational enterprises under, 327–8
        Pillar One, 327
        Pillar Two, 326–8
    market jurisdictions, 323–4
    tax consequences of, 322–4
    transfer pricing rules, 323
digital service tax (DSTs), 324–5
digitalisation
    post-modern tax state and, 334–5
    tax states influenced by, 5
direct taxes, 19–25
    in Great Britain, 32–3
    in tax state, 28–9
direct yield of revenues, capital gains tax and, 156
discretionary budgets, 65
discrimination, in tax law, 88–90
disposable income, in tax-transfer system, 86
Distribution branch, in fiscal model of government, 44–5
distributive justice
    Duff, David, on, 78
    equity principle and, 78–9
    Murphy, Liam, on, 84–5
    Musgrave, Richard, on, 78
    Nagel, Thomas, on, 84–5
dividends
    imputation system for, 188–90
    shareholder taxes and, 188–9
Double Irish Dutch Sandwich structure, for corporate taxes, in global economy, 309–11
double taxation, through corporate taxes, 187–8
Douglas, Roger, 41
Dourado, Ana Paula, 337
DSTs. *See* digital service tax
dual income tax, 152
    capital gains tax and, 158–60

Index

Duff, David, 49–50, 78
Dworkin, Ronald, 78

earmarked taxes, in budgets, 65–6
Earned Income Tax Credit, in US tax law, 68–9, 139
e-commerce, tax jurisdictions for, 290–4
economic crises
  Asian Financial Crisis of 1997, 54
  tax state influenced by, 39–43
    during COVID-19 pandemic, 43
    economic globalisation, 40–3
    Global Financial Crisis of 2008-2009, 43
    tax reform and, 40–3
economic rents, 154–5
  corporate taxes on, 190–1
  Harberger, Arnold, on, 311
  Mill, John Stuart, on, 154
  in normative theory, 154–5
  Smith, Adam, on, 154
EEC. See European Economic Community
efficiency principle, for taxation, 77, 91–100. See also neutrality; optimal tax theory
  challenges with, 98–100
  incentives in, 91–4
    elasticity of consumer demand, 92–4
    elasticity of labour supply, 120
  limits of, 98–100
  market failure and, 97–8, 192–3
  tax units and, 126–7
EFTs. See electronic fund transfers
elasticity
  of consumer demand, 92–4
  of labour supply, 120
    female, compared to male, 127
  of taxable income, 146–7
electronic fund transfers (EFTs), 322–3
endowment, taxes on, 81–2
entrepreneurship
  income tax, 192–4
  Say, Jean-Baptiste, on, 192
  Schumpeter, Joseph, on, 192
  tax concessions for, 193–5
equality, equity as distinct from, 78–9
equity principle, for taxation, 78–91
  ability to pay in, 78–81
    concept of income and, 81–4
    Mill, John Stuart, on, 79–80
    myth of ownership, 84–5
    Saladin Tithe of 1188, 79
    tax faculty and, 81
  capabilities approach to, 90–1
  distributive justice and, 78–9
  dynamic approaches to, 90
  equality as distinct from equity, 78–9
  gender inequality and, 89
  horizontal equity, 78–101
    progressive income taxes and, 137–8
    tax policy and, 101
  intergenerational equity, 90–1
  lifecourse in, 90–1
  progressive tax rates and, 79–81
    declining marginal utility of income, 80–1
  proportional tax rates and, 80
  substantive equity in, 88–90
  in tax law
    critical race scholarship and, 89–90
    discrimination in, 88–90
    rights in, 88–90
  tax on endowments, 81–2
  tax units and, 126–7
  tax-transfer system, 86–8
    in Australia, 86–107
    disposable income in, 86
    Gini coefficient in, 86–8, 90
    in optimal tax theory, 86
  trade-offs and, between efficiency and equity, 97
  vertical equity, 78
estate taxes, 172–4
EU. See European Union
Eurobonds, 279–81
European Economic Community (EEC), Value Added Tax in, 103–4
European Union (EU)
  charities in, tax law for, 218–20
    in CJEU case law, 219–20
eurozone
  fiscal policy in, 62
  fiscal rules, 62
  Maastricht Stability and Growth Pact, 62
excess burden of tax, 93–4. See also efficiency principle; neutrality
exit tax, 275–6
expenditure levels, in taxation systems, 15

Farrelly, Colin, 84
FCT v. Word Investments Ltd, 211
feminist tax scholarship, 89
  tax unit, 122–5
  Young, Claire, 89
Finanzwissenschaft (financial science of state), 35
Finland
  corporate tax in, 186
  welfare state in, 42

fiscal constitutionalism, tax law and, 10
fiscal discipline, renewal of, 54-5
  Asian Financial Crisis of 1997, 54
  Global Financial Crisis of 2008-2009, 54
  in New Zealand, 55
fiscal institutions, budgets for, 54-63
  in Australia
    fiscal transparency in, 59
    Parliamentary Budget Office, 61-2
  in Canada, Parliamentary Budget Office, 61
  fiscal discipline, renewal of, 54-5
    Asian Financial Crisis of 1997, 54
    austerity and, 54
    Global Financial Crisis of 2008-2009, 54
    in New Zealand, 55
  fiscal policy, 63
    business bail-outs, 64
    cash transfers, 64
    during COVID-19 pandemic, 62-4
    in eurozone, 62
    for healthcare, 64
    under Maastricht Stability and Growth Pact, 62
    tax and expenditure reforms, 64
    tax measures, 64
  fiscal rules, 55-6
    with creative accounting, 56
    in eurozone, 62
    for global investment, 56
    in OECD countries, 58
    in UK, 57
  fiscal transparency, 57-9
    in Australia, 59
    in New Zealand, 57-8
    open budget index ranking, 60
    independent, 59
  in New Zealand
    fiscal transparency in, 57-8
    renewal of fiscal discipline, 55
  in UK
    fiscal rules in, 57
    Office of Budget Responsibility, 61-2
  in US
    Congressional Budget and Impoundment Control Act, 61
    Congressional Budget Office, 60-1
fiscal model of government, 44-5
  Allocation branch, 44-5
  Distribution branch, 44-5
  government functions in, 44-5

market weaknesses in, 44
Musgrave, Richard, on, 44-5
Stabilisation branch, 44-5
Fiscal Responsibility Act, New Zealand (1994), 57-8
fiscal rules, for institutional budgets, 55-6
  with creative accounting, 56
  in Eurozone, 62
  for global investment, 56
  in OECD countries, 58
  in UK, 57
fiscal transparency, 57-9
  in Australia, 59
  in New Zealand, 57-8
  open budget index ranking, 60
flat tax rates
  progressive income taxes compared to, 134
  for universal basic income, 142
Fleischer, Victor, 197
Foreign Account Tax Compliance Act, US (2010), 263, 286
Freedman, Judith, 194
Friedman, Milton, on universal basic income, 141
front-end incentives, 195-6

GAAR. *See* General Anti-Avoidance Rule
Gates, Bill, 167-8, 215, 305-7
Gates, Melinda, 215
GDP. *See* Gross Domestic Product
gender budgeting, 71-2
  for gender equality, 57-71
  impact analysis for, 72
  Korea, 71
  OECD countries, 71
  as process, 71
  Spain, 71
  Womens Budget Group (UK), 71
gender equality, budgets for, 57-71
General Anti-Avoidance Rule (GAAR), 245-9
George, Henry, 174-5
Germany
  accident insurance in, 34
  Constitutional Court in, 124-5
  Corporate Income Tax Act, 178-9
  corporate taxes in, 178-9
  health insurance in, 34
  income taxes in, tax rates for, 120-1
  old age insurance in, 34
  property taxation in, 175-6

Socialstaat in, 33–5
tax rates in, 42
as tax state, *Finanzwissenschaft*, 35
tax unit in, 124–5, 127
   childcare costs in, 128
as welfare state, 33–5
gig economy, progressive income taxes for, 135–8
Gini coefficient, in tax-transfer system, 86–8, 90
Gladstone, William, 214
Global anti-Base Erosion Rule (GloBE), 327–8
global associational revolution, for charity, 217–18
Global Financial Crisis of 2008-2009
   renewal of fiscal discipline policies after, 54
   tax state during, 43
global investment strategies, fiscal rules for, 56
global remittance economy, 270–1
globalisation. *See also* corporate taxes; digital economies
   of charities, tax laws on, 217–21
      global associational revolution, 217–18
      across national borders, 217–18
      public benefits of, 220–1
   tax competition and, 296–7
   tax states influenced by, 5
GloBE. *See* Global anti-Base Erosion Rule
goods. *See* merit goods; private goods; public goods
Goods and Services Tax (GST), 20, 24–5. *See also* Value Added Tax
   tax jurisdiction for, 290–4
Gove, Michael, 332
government debt levels, budgets and, 53–4
   COVID-19 pandemic and, 54
   in selected OECD countries, 53
government funding and expenditures, in tax state, 35–50
   ability to pay in, 43–4
   benefit theory of taxation, 43–5
   merit goods and, 47–8
   public goods and, 45–8
   structure of, by function, 47
government theory. *See also* fiscal model of government; tax state
   taxation in, 9
Gravelle, Jane, 152
Great Britain
   charities in, taxation on, 218
   Poll Tax Riots in, 115
   poll taxes in, public response to, 115

Poor Law in, 33–4
as tax state, 28–9
   annual income in, 31–2
   debt in, 31–2
   direct taxes in, 32–3
   income tax in, 32
as welfare state, 33–4
green budgets, 73–4
Gross Domestic Product (GDP)
   corporate taxes, share of, 182
   indicators in, 14
   measurement of, 14
   tax level, share of selected countries, 9–14
   tax mix, share of selected countries, 17
   taxation systems and, 9–14
Growth and Investment Tax, in US, 200
GST. *See* Goods and Services Tax

Harberger, Arnold, 185, 190–1
Harding, Matthew, 205
harmful tax competition, 298–300
   Harmful Tax Competition project, 299–300
   OECD campaigns against, 298–9
Harmful Tax Competition project, 299–300
Harris, Peter, 79, 178
Hayek, Friedrich, 39
Head, John G., 4
health insurance, in Germany, 34
healthcare, in fiscal policy, 64
Holmes, Oliver Wendell (Justice), 43–4
home ownership, savings through, 163–5
   capital gains tax, exemption, 165–6
   imputed rent, 165–6
   in Netherlands, 166
   in optimal tax theory, 164–5
   pre-paid consumption tax and, 166
   in US, 166
   window tax, 164
Hood, Christopher, 224
horizontal equity, 78–101
   progressive income taxes and, 137–8
   tax policy and, 101
household savings, 163–6
   through home ownership, 163–5
   imputed rent, 165–6
   in Netherlands, 166
   in optimal tax theory, 164–5
   pre-paid consumption tax and, 166
   in US, 166
   window tax, 164

hybrid income-consumption tax, 152–4
    in Australia, 152–3
    in UK, 152

imputed rent, 165–6
    abolishment of tax on, 165
    home ownership and, 165–6
incentives, in efficiency principle, 91–4. *See also* elasticity; neutrality
Inclusive Framework consensus, 326–9
    Global anti-Base Erosion Rule, 327–8
    implementation of 328–9
    multinational enterprises under, 327–8
    Pillar One, 327
    Pillar Two, 326–8
income. *See also* income tax
    capital gains tax compared to tax on, 155–7
        in civil law jurisdictions, 155–6
    comprehensive, 100
    declining marginal utility of, 80–1
    disposable, 86
    as economic concept, 21–2
    as flow, 155–6
    in Great Britain, establishment as annual income tax, 31–2
income effect
    in optimal tax theory, 94–5
    substitution effect, opposite of, 118–39, 142
    universal basic income and, 142
income inequality
    Piketty, Thomas, on, 132
    progressive income taxes and, 130–2
    top 1 percent, 132
income splitting, 133–5
    Australia, 134
    Canada, 135
    labour income, 135
    Murphy, Justice, Lionel, High Court of Australia, 134
    tax unit, individual, 135–8
income tax, 191–7. *See also* progressive income tax; universal basic income; *specific countries*
    on business and investment, 68, 177
    on capital, 88, 103, 105–6, 114, 139, 144
    comprehensive, 21–3
    corporate, 20
    dual, 152
        capital gains tax and, 158–60
    economic origins of, 21

in Great Britain, 32
    progressive, 37
hard left wage tax, 114–17
    tax equality maxim, 116
on labour, 113–14, 122
    income effect and, 118–39
    in New Zealand, 116–17
    substitution effect and, 118–39
    tax burden on, 121–2
    tax wedge, 121–32
marginal effective tax rate for, 192
margins for, in tax rates
    extensive margin, 119
    intensive margin, 119
negative, 140
pay-as-you-go withholding, 117–18
    in Canada, 117–18
    in UK, 118
    in US, 117–18
poll taxes and, 114–17
    colonisation, 116
    equivalent to slavery, 114
    in Great Britain, 115
    as instrument of social control, 116
    in Prussian Empire, 115–16
    as regressive tax, 114–15
    in Russia, 115–16
    social control through, 116
purpose of, 113–14
'real', 22–3
tax rates for, 118–23
    in Australia, 120–1
    average, 119
    design of, 120–3
    in Germany, 120–1
    marginal, 119
    participation, 119
in tax state, during twentieth century
    in Australia, 37–8
    in Great Britain, 32
    progressive income taxes, 37
    trends in, by country, 38
in taxation systems, 21–3, 103–4
    comprehensive income tax, 21–3
for universal basic income, 139–43
    cash transfers, 114–39
    conceptual development of, 139–41
    justification of, 139–41
    negative income tax, 140
    in UK, 139–40

in *Wealth of Nations*, 31–2
work incentives and, 118–23
independent fiscal institutions, budgets for, 59
indirect holdings, in offshore capital, 280–3
indirect taxes, 19–25
  consumption taxes as, 24–5
    Goods and Services Tax, 20, 24–5
    Value Added Tax, 20, 24–5
  in tax state, 28–9
inequality. *See* gender equality; income inequality; wealth inequality
inflation, progressive income tax and, 123
inheritance taxes, 172–4
  design of, 172–3
  Mill, John Stuart, on, 172
  reform of, 173–4
  in UK, 173
innovation, 192–4
  research and development, 193
insurance. *See* accident insurance; health insurance; old age insurance
intangible assets, income taxation, 191–2
intergenerational equity, 90–1
intermediaries, in taxation systems, 18–19
international law, tax jurisdiction under
  for residence and source, 255
  for tax state, 253–4
internationalism, 336–7
"invisible hand" of economic markets, 29

Jessup, Philip, 255–6
jurisdiction, tax. *See also* offshore capital
  Arnold, Brian, on, 260
  for capital gains tax, in civil law systems, 155–6
  over capital income, 274–83
    decolonisation as influence on, 279
    Eurobonds, 279–81
    exit taxes, 275–6
    mobility of capital, 274–7
    offshore capital, 277–9
  in digital economy, 323–4
  for global corporations, 300–1
  international law as factor for residence and source, 255
  tax state under, 253–4
  over labour income, 263–74
    in Australia, exemptions for, 273–4
    brain drain tax, 267–9
    in CJEU case law, 264–7
    conceptual approach to, 263–4
    for cross-border retirement savings, 273–4
    in global remittance economy, 270–1
    mobility of skilled labour and, 271–3
    for transnational workers, 264–7
  League of Nations and, 257
  for residence and source, 254–7
    economic allegiance, 255–6
    under international law, 255
    Seligman, Edwin, on, 256–7
    Smith, Adam, on, 253
  of tax residence, 259–63
    ability to pay and, 260
    benefit theory of taxation and, 260
    citizen-taxpayers, 262–3
    conceptual approach to, 259–60
    definition of, 259–60
    justification of, 260–1
    for new or departing residents, 261–2
    in US, 262–3
  of tax state, 253–9
    boundaries of, 253–4
    under international law, 253–4
    Smith, Adam, on, 253
    under Treaty of Westphalia, 253
  of tax treaties, 257–9
    for bilateral tax treaties, 259
    under OECD Model Convention, 257–60
    under UN Model Convention, 258
  of taxation systems, 18–19
  for US
    controlled foreign corporation rules, 282
    Foreign Account Tax Compliance Act, 263, 286
    for offshore capital, 281–3
    Personal Foreign Investment Company rules, 282–3
    tax residence and, 262–3

Kay, John, 104–5
Keynes, John, 39
  on budgeting, in Keynesian economics, 52
King, Mervyn, 104–5
Kleinbard, Edward, 202, 310

labour, income tax on, 113–14, 122. *See also* jurisdiction
  in New Zealand, 116–17
  progressive tax rates and, 114–17

labour, income tax on, (cont.)
   substitution effect and, 118–39
   tax burden on, 121–2
   tax unit, 122–8
   tax wedge, 121–32
   women's work, 122–5, 129–30
land taxation, 174–6
land taxes, 26
law. See international law; tax law; *specific legislation*
League of Nations, 257, 284
Levi, Margaret, 30, 230
Li, Jinyan, 271
lifecourse
   in equity principle, 90–1
   theory of tax savings over, 148–9
line-items, in budgets, 51
lump sum taxes, 49

Maastricht Stability and Growth Pact, 62
Madagascar, poll taxes in, 116
Magna Carta, 3
mandatory spending, 65–6
MAP. See Mutual Agreement Procedure
marginal effective tax rates (METR), 153
   for income tax on business and investment, 192
   for labour income in tax-transfer system, 153, 192
marginal tax rates, 27, 119. See also progressive tax rates
   for top per cent of earners, 124–33
market failures, in optimal tax theory, 97–8
mark-to-market approach, to capital gains tax, 158
Marriot, Lisa, 162
McDaniel, Paul, 18–19, 224
Meade Report, 103
Medieval city-states, citizen-taxpayers in, 30–1
Mehotra, Ajay, 37
merit goods, 47–8
METR. See marginal effective tax rates
Mill, John Stuart, 35, 51–2
   on ability to pay, 79–80
   on economic rents, 156
   on inheritance taxes, 172
   on proportional tax rates, 80
   on theory of taxing savings, 148–9
Mirrlees, James, 92
Mirrlees Review, 92, 152, 155, 162, 173, 201

MLI. See Multilateral Instrument
MNEs. See multinational enterprises
modern monetary theory, budgets in, 52–3
Modigliani, Franco, 148–9
monetary theory. See modern monetary theory
money laundering, through philanthropy, 216–17
Moran, Beverley, 50
Multilateral Instrument (MLI), 315–16
multinational enterprises (MNEs)
   Base Erosion and Profit Shifting project and, 312–13
   corporate taxes for, in global economy, 305–7
   Desai, Mihir, on denationalisation of, 306
   under Inclusive Framework consensus, 327–8
Murphy, Justice Lionel, 84–5, 134
Murphy, Liam, 84–5
Musgrave, Peggy, 9, 260–1
Musgrave, Richard, 39, 43–4
   on distributive justice, 78
   fiscal model of government, 44–5
      Allocation branch, 44–5
      Distribution branch, 44–5
      government functions in, 44–5
      market weaknesses in, 44
      Stabilisation branch, 44–5
   on Schumpeter, Joseph, 3, 339
   on tax state, 9
   on taxpayer-voters, 48–9
Musk, Elon, 305–7
Mutual Agreement Procedure (MAP), 319
myth of ownership, 84–5
The Myth of Ownership (Murphy, Liam, and Nagel, Thomas), 84

Nagel, Thomas, 84–5
national transfer accounts, 149–50
negative externalities, in optimal tax theory, 97–8
negative income tax, 140
net wealth tax, 171–2
Netherlands, home ownership in, 166
Netherlands 'Box' System, 159
neutral land tax benchmark, 69
neutrality, principle of, 96–7
   broad-based taxes, 96–7
   supply-side tax policy, 97
   trade-offs in, between efficiency and equity of taxation, 97

New Zealand
    capital gains tax in, 157
    corporate taxes in, 189–90
    fiscal institutions in, budgets for
        fiscal transparency in, 57–8
        renewal of fiscal discipline, 55
    Fiscal Responsibility Act, 57–8
    income taxes in, 125
        on labour, 116–17
    Reserve Bank of New Zealand Act, 55, 57–8
    Rogernomics in, 41
    tax reform in, 41, 105
nonexcludable public goods, 45–6
nonrival public goods, 45–6
normative theory, economic rents in, 154–5
Norway, welfare state in, 42
not-for-profit sector, taxation on, 205–7
    commercial activities of, 209–12
    revenue structure for, 206
    in US, 206
Nussbaum, Martha, 91

OECD countries. *See* Organisation for Economic Cooperation and Development
offshore capital, tax jurisdictions for, 277–94
    during bank secrecy era, 285–7
        under Convention on Mutual Administrative Assistance in Tax Matters, 285–6
    cross-border tax collection, 287–8
    for e-commerce, 290–4
    Eurobonds, 279–81
    Goods and Services Tax, 290–4
    for indirect holdings, extension of jurisdiction, 280–3
    League of Nations and, 284
    non-cooperative sovereigns and, 284–5
    OECD responses to, 284–5
    tax havens, 278–9
    taxpayer rights, global context for, 289
    UK responses to, 283
    US tax policy responses to, 281–3
        controlled foreign corporations rules, 282
        under Corporate Transparency Act, 293
        under Financial Account Tax Compliance Act, 286
        Personal Foreign Investment Company rules, 282–3
    Value Added Tax, 290–4
Of Rule and Revenue (Levi, Margaret), 230
old age insurance, in Germany, 34

O'Neill, Paul, 299
open budget index ranking, 60
open economies, corporate taxes in, 185–7
optimal tax theory, 86, 91–4. *See also* efficiency principle; neutrality
    challenges to, 98–100
    deadweight loss in, 93–4
    development of, 92
    differences in tax treatment in, 97–8
    economic model for, 93
    excess burden of tax, 93–4
    home ownership and, 164–5
    income effect in, 94–5
    limits of, 98–100
    market failures in, 97–8
    negative externalities in, 97–8
    Pigouvian taxes in, 98
    principle of neutrality and, 96–7
        broad-based taxes, 96–7
        supply-side tax policy, 97
        trade-offs in, between efficiency and equity of taxation, 97
    substitution effect in, 94–106
    tax policy and, 100, 102–3
    window tax in, 94–5
Organisation for Economic Cooperation and Development countries (OECD countries). *See also* tax state; welfare state
    corporate taxes in, 182–4
    fiscal rules in, for institutional budgets, 58
    government debt levels in, 53
    harmful tax competition and, campaigns against, 298–9
    Model Convention, for tax treaties, 257–60
    offshore capital and, 284–5
    successful tax states, 3
    tax levels in, 43
    tax states and, 3
    tax statistics collected by, 13
    wealth taxes in, 171

participation tax rate, 119
passive investment losses, 241
Pay As You Earn system, in UK, 118
pay-as-you-go withholding, in income taxes, 117–18
    in Canada, 117–18
    in UK, 118
    in US, 117–18
Personal Foreign Investment Company rules (PFIC rules), 282–3

philanthropy, taxation of, 213–17
  'big philanthropy,' 214–16
  charitable giving deduction, 213–14
    justification of, 214
  money laundering through, 216–17
  by private foundations, 214–16
    in US, 215–16
  tax avoidance and evasion through, 216–17
    in Canada, 217
Philipps, Lisa, 54, 56–8, 67, 88–90, 124
Picciotto, Sol, 284
Pigouvian taxes, 98
Polanyi, Karl, 33–4
Poll Tax Riots, 115
poll taxes, 114–17
  in Great Britain, 115
  in Madagascar, 116
  in Prussian Empire, 115–16
  as regressive tax, 114–15
  in Russia, 115–16
  social control through, 116
Poor Law, Great Britain (1834), 33–4
post-modern tax state, in twenty-first century, 330–9
  benefit theory of taxation for, 337
  boundaries of, 332–8
  as community, 332–3
  cosmopolitanism and, 336–7
  COVID-19 pandemic and, 338
  digitalisation and, 334–5
  global cooperation of, 334–5
    tax competition and, 335
  legitimacy of, 336–7
    for tax law, 336
  reassembling of, 332–9
  sovereignty of, 334–5
    administrative, 334–5
    legal, 334–5
    revenue, 334–5
  successful tax state, 330–2
  tax administration in, 335–6
  tax justice and, 336–7
  tax law in, 335–6
    fairness of, 336
    legitimacy of, 336
Prebble, John, 304–5
pre-paid consumption tax, 166
principle of neutrality. See neutrality
private foundations, philanthropy by, taxation of, 214–16
  in US, 215–16
private goods, 205
progressive income taxes, 116, 123
  bracket creep and, 123
  in Canada, 135
  design of, 120–3
  income inequality and, 130–2
  inflation and, 123
  on labour, 133–9
    automation and, 138–9
    capitalisation of, 135
    COVID-19 pandemic and, 136–7
    flat tax rate compared to, 134
    in gig economy, 135–8
    horizontal equity for, 137–8
    income splitting, 133–5
    robots, 138–9
  tax unit and, 123–6
  for top percent of earners, 131–2
    marginal tax rates, 124–33
    tax thresholds for, 132
    women as, 132–3
  wealth inequality and, 130–2
progressive tax rates, 26–7
  equity principle and, 79–81
    declining marginal utility of income, 80–1
  for income, 116, 123
    bracket creep and, 123
    design of, 120–3
    inflation and, 123
  proportional tax rates and, 26–7
  regressive tax rates and, 26–7
  in tax states, 37, 114–17
    tax equality maxim, 116
property rights, tax unit and, 124–5
property taxation, 174–6
  administration of, 175
  in Germany, 175–6
  under Proposition 13, in US, 175
property taxes, 26
proportional tax rates, 26–7
  Mill, John Stuart, on, 80
Proposition 13, 175
public choice theory, 40
public goods, 45–8
  charities and, 205
  definitions of, 45–6
  nonexcludable, 45–6
  nonrival, 45–6
  pure, 46, 49

taxpayer-voter and, 48–9
pure public goods, 46, 49

Ramsey, Frank, 92
Rawls, John, 78
R&D. *See* research and development
Reagan, Ronald, 41
"real" income taxes, 22–3
reform processes, for taxation systems, 19
regressive tax rates, 26–7
  poll taxes and, 114–15
reinforcement, through tax administration, 224
remittance economies. *See* global remittance economy
research and development (R&D), income tax and, 196–7
  innovation and, 193
  tax concessions for, 198
Reserve Bank of New Zealand Act (1989), 55, 57–8
resilience
  in systems theory, 106
  of tax state, 43, 106–8
  of taxation systems, 9, 43, 106–8
    through adaptation, 106–8
    income tax systems, 106
    redundancies in, 106–8
    of tax reform approaches, 105
    threats to, 108
resilience theory, 9
retirement savings, 161–3
  consumption approach to, 161–2
  cross-border, 273–4
  Exempt-Exempt-Tax system, 161–2
  hybrid systems, 162–3
    in Australia, 163
    Individual Retirement Accounts, 162–3
    private savings systems, 163
    public savings systems, 163
    in US, 162–3
  incomes approach, 161–2
  retirement incomes policy for, 161
  Tax-Exempt-Exempt system, 161–2
rights, in tax law
  Charter of Taxpayer Rights
    in EU, 236
    in US, Taxpayer Advocate, 236
  race, gender discrimination, 88–90
  substantive rights, 88–90
robotics, taxation of progressive income tax, 138–9

Rogernomics, in New Zealand, 41
Roman Empire, 30
Russia
  poll taxes in, 115–16
  taxation systems in, 9

Saez, Emmanuel, 170
Saladin Tithe of 1188, 79
Samuelson, Paul, on public goods, 45–6
Say, Jean-Baptiste, 192
Schumpeter, Joseph, 339
  on entrepreneurship, 192
  on fiscal sociology, 8
  on tax state, 24
seigniorage, 29
Seligman, Edwin, 36, 49
Sen, Amartya, 90
shareholder taxes, corporate taxes and, integration with, 187–90
  dividend exemption, 188–9
  dividends imputation system, 188–90
  dual income tax, 158–60
  flat tax, 134
  Vann, Richard, on, 188
Simons, Henry, 49, 81, 100
  on capital gains tax, 157
  on comprehensive income, 116–17, 148
  on progressive income tax, income inequality, 81
  rejection of corporate taxes, 179–87
small or medium-sized enterprises (SMEs), 194–5
  compliance costs of taxation, 237–8
  heterogeneity of, 194
  tax concessions for, 194
  tax gap for, 249–50
Smith, Adam, 29–30, 75, 94
  on capital, 144–5, 154
    mobility of, 274–7
  on debt and taxes, 31–2
    income taxes, 31–2
  on economic rents, 154
  on house-rents, 144
  on "invisible hand" of market, 29
  Maxims of, 75–7
  Mill, John Stuart, on, 75
  on political economy, 29
  on progressive taxes, 145
  on public goods, 45–6
  on revenue for the state, 253
  on state bureaucracy, growth of, 223–6

Smith, Adam, (cont.)
  on tax administration, 222–3, 238
  on tax equality, 116
  on tax equity, 50
  on window tax, 154
social enterprises, taxation of, 212–13
social security taxes, 23–4
  tax burden on labour, 121–2
Socialstaat, in Germany, 33–5
sovereignty, of post-modern tax state, 334–5
  administrative sovereignty, 334–5
  legal sovereignty, 334–5
  revenue sovereignty, 334–5
  tax competition and, 295, 299–300, 319
spending, by governments, budgets as influence on, 55–70
  discretionary, 65
  mandatory, 65–6
  tax expenditures, 67–70
  in US, 65
Stabilisation branch, in fiscal model of government, 44–5
start-ups, 195–7
  back-end incentives for, 196
  front-end incentives for, 195–6
statisics. *See* tax statistics
Steinmo, Sven, 41, 297
Stiglitz, J., 96
substantive equity, 88–90
substitution effects
  income taxes on labour and, 118–39
  in optimal tax theory, 94–106
  universal basic income and, 142
supply-side tax policy, 57, 102–3
Sweden
  corporate taxes in, 178–9
  welfare state in, 42
system adaptability theory, 9
systems theory, resilience in, 106
tangible assets, income taxes and, 191–2
tax administration, 222–9. *See also* compliance; tax avoidance; tax evasion; tax unit; taxation systems
  certainty principle and, 222–3
  convenience principle and, 222–3, 238
  elements of, 223–5
    tax base valuation, 224
    tax channels, 224
    tax data, 224, 237–9
    tax enforcement, 224
    tax reinforcement, 224

Hood, Christopher, on, 224
institutions' role in, 225
in post-modern tax state, 335–6
Smith, Adam, on, 222–3, 238
through state bureaucracy, 223–6
tax authorities, 225–8
  in common law jurisdictions, 229
  functions of, 227
for tax collection, 237–8
tax data and, 224
  automation and, 237–9
  in EU, 237
for tax planning, 239–44
  elasticity of, 242–3
  through tax arbitrage, 242–3
  ubiquity of, 239–43
for transnational corporations, in BEPS project, 317–19
  country-by-country reports, 317–18
  under Mutual Agreement Procedure, 319

tax arbitrage, 242–3
  Base Erosion and Profit Shifting project and, 313
tax authorities, 225–8
  in common law jurisdictions, 229
  functions of, 227
  oversight of, 228–9
tax avoidance, 239–44. *See also* Base Erosion and Profit Shifting project
  in common law systems, 247
  General Anti-Avoidance Rules, 245–9
  judicial anti-abuse doctrines for, 246–7
  legal definitions of, 244–6
  strategies, 244–9
  through tax shelters, 243–4
  in US, 247
tax avoidance and evasion, through philanthropy, 216–17
  in Canada, 217
tax base, 19–25
tax base valuation, 224
tax burden. *See* tax incidence
tax channels, administrative, 224
tax collection mechanisms, cross-border, 287–8
tax competition, 295–300
  economic globalisation and, 296–7
  harmful, 298–300
    Harmful Tax Competition project, 299–300
    OECD campaigns against, 298–9

for post-modern tax state, 335
sovereignty and, 295–8
   average statutory corporate tax rates by region, 297
   Tiebout Hypothesis for, 295–7
tax concessions. *See* concessions
Tax Cuts and Jobs Act, US (2017), 183
tax equality, Maxim, 116
tax equity, Smith, Adam, on, 50
tax evasion, 230–9
   in Australia, 241
   behavioral problems and, 232
   classical economic model of, 231–2
   definition of, 230
   indicators for, 233
   passive investment losses and, 241
   tax gap, 249–50
   in UK, 250
   in US, 241
tax expenditures
   benchmarks for, 69–70
   broad-based consumption, 69
   comprehensive income, 69
   neutral land taxes, 69
   reporting of, 67–70
   social policy, 68–9
tax faculty, 81
tax farming, Roman Empire, 30
tax gap, 249–50
   in UK, 249–50
tax havens, 278–9, 311
tax incidence, 19–25
   corporate income taxes, 20
   direct taxes, 20
   tax unit, 19–20
tax jurisdictions. *See* jurisdiction
tax justice, 336–7
   principles for, 101
tax law. *See also* international law
   accounting and, 10–12
      growth of, 12
   disciplinary approaches to, 7–12
      comparative approach, 7–9
      for public finance, 9–10
      sociological approach, 7–9
      welfare economics approach, 10
   equity principle in
      critical race scholarship and, 89–90
      discrimination in, 88–90
      rights in, 88–90

fiscal constitution and, 10
in post-modern tax state, 335–6
   fairness of, 336
   legitimacy of, 336
scope of, 10–12
tax level
   in OECD countries, 43
   in taxation systems, 9–15
tax mix, 13–18
   in selected countries, 17
tax planning, administrative approaches to, 239–44
   elasticity of, 242–3
   through income splitting, 135
   through tax arbitrage, 242–3
   tax shelters, 243–4
   ubiquity of, 239–43
tax policy. *See also specific fiscal topics*
   in global economy, 100–1
      comprehensive income, 100
      horizontal equity, 101
      optimal tax theory and, 100, 102–3
      supply-side, 97, 102–3
      tax justice principles, 101
      for taxation systems, 19
      vertical equity, 101
tax principles. *See also* convenience principle; efficiency principle; equity principle
   origins of, 75–7
   Smith's Maxims for, 75–7, 79–80
      for certainty, 77
      of convenience, 77
      of efficiency, 77
      for equity, 77
tax privileges, for charities, 207–9
   charitable exemption as, 207–9
   for public welfare role, 208
   Statute of Elizabeth, 207
tax rates, 19–27. *See also* income tax; progressive tax rates
   for corporate taxes, 182–4
      trends in, 183
      in US, 186
   flat, 134
   marginal, 27
   proportional, 26–7, 80
   regressive, 26–7
      poll taxes and, 114–15
tax reform. *See also* corporate tax reform
   in Australia, 105
   Blueprints for Tax Reform, 103

tax reform. (cont.)
  broad-based, low-rate, 168
  Carter Commission and, 82–4
  during economic crises, 40–3
  of inheritance tax systems, 173–4
  in New Zealand, 41, 105
  in UK, 105
    Meade Report, 103
    Mirrlees Review, 92, 152, 155, 162, 173, 201
tax residence. *See* jurisdiction
tax shelters, 243–4
tax state, 3–6. *See also* post-modern tax state; taxation systems; *specific topics*
  benefit theory for, public good result in, 49–50
  challenges for, 4–6
    COVID-19 pandemic as, 5
    digitalisation as, 5
    globalisation as, 5
  citizen-lenders in, 31
  citizen-taxpayer in, 30–3
    in Medieval city-states, 30–1
  debt in, 30–3
    in Great Britain, 31–2
  democracy in, 8–9
  direct taxes in, 28–9
  economic crises and, 39–43
    COVID-19 pandemic as element of, 43
    economic globalisation, 40–3
    Global Financial Crisis of 2008-2009, 43
    tax reform as, 40–3
  as economic term, creation of, 3
  evolution of, 3
    sovereign roles in, 28, 30
  expansion of, in 20th century, 36–9
    through income taxes, 37
  Germany as
    Finanzwissenschaft, 35
    Socialstaat, 33–5
    as welfare state, 33–5
  goals of, 29–30
  government funding and expenditures in, 35–50
    ability to pay for, 43–4
    benefit theory of taxation, 43–5
    merit goods and, 47–8
    public goods and, 45–8
    structure of, by function, 47
  Great Britain as, 28–9
    annual income in, 31–2
    debt in, 31–2
    direct taxes in, 32–3
    income tax in, 32
    welfare state in, 33–4
  history of, 28–30
  income taxes in
    in Australia, 37–8
    in Great Britain, 32
    progressive, 37
    trends in, by country, 38
  indirect taxes in, 28–9
  under international law, tax jurisdiction for, 253–4
  limitations of, 39–40
  in Organisation for Economic Cooperation and Development countries, 3
  origins of, 28–30
  political context for, 3
  public choice theory and, 40
  resilience of, 43, 106–8
  Schumpeter, Joseph, on, 28–9
  seigniorage and, 29
  Seligman, Edwin, on, 36
  sovereignty of, for tax competition, 295–8
    average statutory corporate tax rates by region, 297
    Tiebout Hypothesis for, 295–7
  supply-side tax reform, 41
  as theoretical concept, 28–30
    "invisible hand" of economic markets in, 29
  welfare state and, 33–6
    competitive labour markets and, 33
    as "double movement," 34
    in Germany, as *Socialstaat*, 33–5
    in Great Britain, 33–4
    welfare economics, 40
tax statistics, 12–13
  function of, 13
  Organisation for Economic Cooperation and Development collection of, 13
  publication of, 13
  quality of, 13
  from tax records, 12
tax treaties, 257–9
  bilateral, 259
  multilateral, 259, 327
  under OECD Model Convention, 257–60
  under UN Model Convention, 258

tax unit, 19–25, 122–8, 224
  in Belgium, 127
  in civil law systems, 124–5
  economic independence of women and, 122–5
    childcare costs and, 127–9
    efficiency and, 126–7
    equity and, 126–7
    high effective tax rates for female labour, 129–30
    in UK, 124
  efficiency in, 126–7
  equity in, 126–7
  gender equality and, 57–71
  in Germany, 124–5, 127
    childcare costs in, 128
  history of, 122–5
  labour supply and, 95–6
  progressive income taxes and, 123–6
  property rights and, 124–5
  structure of, 124
  tax-transfer unit, 127–8
tax wedge, 121–32
taxation systems. *See also* efficiency principle; equity principle; *specific topics*
  in China, reform of, 8–9
  consumption behaviours and, 103–4
  consumption taxes, 24–5
    Goods and Services Tax, 20, 24–5
    Value Added Tax, 20, 24–5
  direct taxes, 19–25
  economic purpose of, 4
  elements of, 18–21
    intermediaries, 18–19
    tax base, 19–25
    tax unit, 19–25
    timing as, 18–19
  in government theory, 9
  Gross Domestic Product in, 9–14
    indicators in, 14
    measurement of, 14
    tax mix in, of selected countries, 17
  indirect taxes in, 19–25
    consumption taxes as, 20, 24–5
  jurisdiction, 253–61, 263–94
  land taxes, 26
  liberal approaches to, 35–6
  policy making for, 19
  property taxes, 26
  quasi-constitutional status of, 4
  reform processes for, 19
  resilience of, 43, 106–8

  through adaptation, 106–8
    income tax systems, 106
    redundancies in, 106–8
    of tax reform approaches, 105
    threats to, 108
  resilience theory and, 9
  in Russia, 9
  social approaches to, 35–6
  social security taxes, 23–4
  as sociopolitical process, 8
  structure of, 13–18
    expenditure levels, 15
    tax levels, 9–15
    tax mix, 16–18
  in systems theory, 9
  tax incidence, 19–25
    corporate income taxes, 20
    direct taxes, 20
    tax unit, 19–20
  tax policy for, 19
  tax rates, 19–27
    marginal, 27
    progressive, 26–7
    proportional, 26–7
    regressive, 26–7
  Wagner, Adolphe, on, 35
  wealth taxes, 26
taxes. *See also* direct taxes; indirect taxes; *specific topics*
  budgets and, 65–70
    benchmarked expenditures, 69–70
    earmarked taxes, 65–6
    from estimated revenues, 67
    expenditure reporting, 67–70
    taxpayer-voters and, 66
  definition of, 13–14
  lump sum, 49
  Pigouvian, 98
  in principle of neutrality, 96–7
taxpayer rights, with offshore capital, 289
taxpayer-voters
  budgets and, 66
  public goods and, 48–9
tax-transfer system, 86–8
  in Australia, 86–107
  cash transfers, 88
  disposable income in, 86
  distributive justice, 84
  Gini coefficient in, 86–8, 90
  income inequality and, 86
  in optimal tax theory, 86

tax-transfer system, (cont.)
  tax unit and, 127–8
  universal basic income, 140
Thatcher, Margaret, 41, 115, 231
theory of tax savings, 146–52
  in comprehensive income approach, 148
  consumption taxes, 148
  over lifecourse, 148–9
  Mill, John Stuart, on, 148–9
  national transfer accounts, 149–50
Thuronyi, Victor, 259
Tiebout Hypothesis, 295–7
top one-percent of earners, progressive income
    taxes for, 131, 133
  marginal tax rates, 124–33
  tax thresholds for, 132
  women as, 132–3
transfer pricing rules, 323
transnational corporate tax administration,
    BEPS project, 317–19
  country-by-country reports, 317–18
  Mutual Agreement Procedure, 319
transnational workers, labour income for, 264–7
transparency. *See* fiscal transparency
Treaty of Westphalia, 253

UBI. *See* universal basic income
UK. *See* United Kingdom
ultra-high net worth individuals, 167. *See also*
    top one-percent of earners
United Kingdom (UK). *See also* Great Britain
  economic independence of women in, 124
  fiscal institutions in, budgets for
    fiscal rules for, 57
    Office of Budget Responsibility, 61–2
  hybrid income-consumption tax in, 152
  income taxes in, pay-as-you-go withholding,
    118
  Meade Report, 103
  Mirrlees Review, 92, 152, 155, 162, 173, 201
  offshore capital and, policy responses to, 283
  Pay As You Earn system in, 118
  tax evasion in, 250
  tax reform in, 105
    Meade Report, 103
  universal basic income concept in, 139–40
  wealth taxes in, 168–9
    inheritance taxes, 173
United Nations, Model Convention, for tax
    treaties, 258
United States (US)

Blueprints for Basic Tax Reform, 103
budget, 157
  capital gains tax in, 157–8
  charities in, taxation of, 206, 211
  Congressional Budget and Impoundment
    Control Act, 61
  corporate tax reform in
    comprehensive business income tax,
      201–2
    Growth and Investment Tax, 200
  corporate taxes in, 178–9, 183
    tax rates in, 186
  Corporate Transparency Act, 293
  Current Tax Payment Act, 117–18
  debt, 54
  fiscal institutions in, budgets for
    Congressional Budget and Impoundment
      Control Act, 61
    Congressional Budget Office, 60–1
  government spending in, 65
  home ownership in, 166
  income taxes in, 125
    pay-as-you-go withholding, 117–18
  offshore capital and, tax policy responses to,
    281–3
    controlled foreign corporation rules, 282
    under Corporate Transparency Act, 293
    under Foreign Account Tax Compliance
      Act, 263, 286
    Personal Foreign Investment Company
      rules, 282–3
    for tax residence, 262–3
  private foundations in, philanthropy by,
    taxation of, 215–16
  property taxation in, under Proposition 13,
    175
  supply-side tax reform in, 41
  tax avoidance in, 247
  Tax Cuts and Jobs Act, 183
  tax evasion in, 241
  tax residence policies, 262–3
  wealth taxes in, 168–9
universal basic income (UBI), 139–43
  cash transfers, 114–39
  conceptual development of, 139–41
  definition of, 140
  design of, 141–3
  flat tax rates, 142
  Friedman, Milton, on, 141
  income effects and, 142
  justification of, 139–41

Index

negative income tax, 140
   substitution effects and, 142
   in UK, 139–40
US. *See* United States

Value Added Tax (VAT), 20, 24–5, 103–4
   offshore capital and, 290–4
Vanistendael, Frans, 160
VAT. *See* Value Added Tax
venture capital, income tax and, 195–7
   back-end incentives for, 196
   carried interest rule for, 197
   front-end incentives for, 195–6
vertical equity,78. *See also* ability to pay; horizontal equity
   tax policy and, 101
voters. *See* taxpayer-voters

Wagner, Adolphe, 34–5
   on tax equity, 35
   on taxation systems, 35
wealth inequality,166–8. *See also* top one-percent of earners
   capital and, 146
   in Australia, 150
   by country, 147
   in France, 171
   in Germany, 151
   progressive income taxes and, 130–2
   ultra-high net worth individuals and, 167
Wealth of Nations (Smith, Adam), 29–30, 75, 94
   income tax in, 31–2
wealth taxes, 26, 170–6
   in Australia, 168–9
   consumption tax and, 169
   estate taxes, 172–4
   inheritance taxes, 172–4
      design of, 172–3
      Mill, John Stuart, on, 172
      reform of, 173–4
      in UK, 173
   justification for, 168–70
   land taxation, 174–6
   net wealth tax, 171–2

in OECD countries, 171
property taxation, 174–6
   administration of, 175
   in Germany, 175–6
   under Proposition 13, in US, 175
   as regulatory function, 169–70
   in UK, 168–9
   inheritance taxes in, 173
   in US, 168–9
welfare economics,40. *See also* optimal tax theory
welfare state
   in China, 8–9
   Germany as, 33–5
   Great Britain as, 33–4
   in Nordic countries, 42
   tax state and, 33–6
      competitive labour markets and, 33
      as "double movement," 34
      in Germany, as *Socialstaat*, 33–5
      in Great Britain, 33–4
   welfare economics, 40
White, David, 154–5
Wildavsky, Aaron, 51
Wilson, Harold, 279
window tax, 94–5
   home ownership and, 164
women
   economic independence of, tax units and, 122–5
   childcare costs and, 127–9
   efficiency and, 126–7
   equity and, 126–7
   high effective tax rates for female labour, 129–30
   in UK, 124
   as top 1% of earners, 132–3
Womens Budget Group (UK), 71
work incentives, income taxes and,118–23. *See also* efficiency principle

Yellen, Janet, 327
Young, Claire, 89

Zucman, Gabriel, 170

Made in the USA
Middletown, DE
11 November 2023